LITERATURE AN

IN CROMWELLIAN ENGLAND

LITERATURE AND POLITICS IN CROMWELLIAN ENGLAND

JOHN MILTON, ANDREW MARVELL, MARCHAMONT NEDHAM

BLAIR WORDEN

OXFORD
UNIVERSITY PRESS

OXFORD
UNIVERSITY PRESS

Great Clarendon Street, Oxford OX2 6DP

Oxford University Press is a department of the University of Oxford.
It furthers the University's objective of excellence in research, scholarship,
and education by publishing worldwide in

Oxford New York

Auckland Cape Town Dar es Salaam Hong Kong Karachi
Kuala Lumpur Madrid Melbourne Mexico City Nairobi
New Delhi Shanghai Taipei Toronto

With offices in

Argentina Austria Brazil Chile Czech Republic France Greece
Guatemala Hungary Italy Japan Poland Portugal Singapore
South Korea Switzerland Thailand Turkey Ukraine Vietnam

Published in the United States
by Oxford University Press Inc., New York

First published 2007
First published in paperback 2009

British Library Cataloguing in Publication Data

Data available

Library of Congress Cataloging in Publication Data

Data available

Typeset by Laserwords Private Limited, Chennai, India
Printed in Great Britain
on acid-free paper by
CPI Antony Rowe, Chippenham, Wiltshire

ISBN 978–0–19–923081–5 (Hbk.); 978–0–19–923082–2 (Pbk.)

For Vicki, Edwin, Angus, Lorna, and Shona

Preface To Second Impression

Where it has been practicable to do so, I have corrected slips and infelicities in the first impression. Since its publication three books have appeared which, while they differ in approach both from my book and from each other, share some of my preoccupations and I hope complement my arguments: Paul Rahe, *Against Throne and Altar. Machiavelli and Political Theory under the English Republic* (New York, 2008); Edward Holberton, *Poetry and the Cromwellian Protectorate* (Oxford, 2008); and Nicholas McDowell, *Poetry and Allegiance in the English Civil Wars. Marvell and the Cause of Wit* (Oxford, 2008).

Forthcoming work by Dr Holberton also has a bearing on my text. Drawing on material in the Swedish National Archives, he proposes a re-dating of Andrew Marvell's poem 'In eandem Reginae Sueciae transmissam', which is addressed, on behalf of Oliver Cromwell, to Queen Christina of Sweden. Holberton's evidence indicates that the poem was written not, as has hitherto been supposed, in 1654, when Cromwell had become lord protector, but around September 1653. If so, a dimension is added to our knowledge of the relations of Marvell and Cromwell. Before Cromwell's elevation at the end of 1653, sovereignty was held by Barebone's Parliament, albeit under his mighty shadow. His relations with Queen Christina were as yet unofficial, a fruit of his semi-clandestine pursuit of a semi-independent foreign policy. Holberton's dating invites us to consider the poem as an endorsement of that conduct, and thus as evidence that the political alignment of the two men, which my book explores in 1654–8, had been established before Cromwell's elevation. Marvell's appointment as tutor to Cromwell's protégé William Dutton earlier in 1653 may reflect the same development.

A belated discovery of my own has consequences for one passage of my book. In Chapter 9 I give an account of Milton's involvement in the composition of the weekly newsbook edited by Nedham, *Mercurius Politicus*.

During that discussion I consider (on pp. 205–6) a passage of an editorial of *Politicus* on 4 March 1652, which vindicates the trial and execution of King Charles I by drawing a series of biblical and historical parallels to it. The writer of the editorial explains that he is repeating 'what I once published upon another occasion'. One of the parallels, that with the punishment by death of King Amaziah, reproduces material which is distinctively close to a passage of Milton's work of 1651, *Defensio*. I inferred that, 'at least in the absence of any alternative candidate', the allusion to 'another occasion' seems 'inexplicable other than as a reference' to Milton's treatise. In fact there is another candidate, with unanswerable claims. The words refer to an anonymous tract of October 1651, *Anglia Liberata*, printed by the printer of *Politicus*, Thomas Newcomb. Published in support of the foreign policy of the republic for which Nedham and Milton worked, *Anglia Liberata* proves to be an addition to the long list of anonymous compositions that were written partly or wholly by Nedham and were re-used in later writings of his. It has a section (on pp. 59–61) from which the relevant portion of the editorial in *Politicus* is taken. So there is now no need of my suggestion that the 'I' points us to Milton. None the less Nedham's indebtedness to Milton on the subject of Amaziah, and its significance for our understanding of the proximity of the two writers, remain. They are underlined by a comparison of the passage of the newsbook with the corresponding one in *Anglia Liberata* the previous year, for in *Politicus* Nedham adjusts his wording so as to bring it closer to Milton's.[i]

I shall explore some aspects of Nedham's thought in another light in my forthcoming edition of his *The Excellencie of a Free State*, to be published by Liberty Fund.

[i] Whereas *Politicus* repeats, in parallel wording, the contentious view expressed in *Defensio* that Amaziah was punished by a judicial process, *Anglia Liberata* leaves that question open. The background to the publication of *Anglia Liberata* can be inferred from the text itself and from *Mercurius Politicus* 10 July 1651, p. 915; 24 July 1651, p. 939; 7 August 1651, p. 972; 9 October 1651, p. 1124. The title of the tract complements that of the poem *Anglia Victrix*, which appeared in *Politicus* in 1653 and which is discussed below, p. 132.

Preface

This is an exercise in literary biography, but with a difference. Lifetimes of exact investigation have been devoted to the recovery of John Milton's career. Though less can be learned about Andrew Marvell's, it too has attracted rigorous attention. My book could not have been so much as conceived without those labours, and could not hope to emulate their scale or distinction. Yet something has been missing, at least since the heroic biography of Milton by the Victorian author David Masson, the pioneer of the documentary approach, who wrote before the academic pursuits of literature and history were divided. Literary scholars have begun with what in Milton's case have been called 'life records' – the documents that mention the name of an author, or fix him in time and place, or illustrate his social or professional relationships – and have worked outwards to the evidence around them. The further they have travelled from them, the less comfortable they have been. If the relationship of writers to their times is to be more amply illuminated, an alternative method is needed. We need to reconstruct the wider life of politics or society or ideas: the life to which literature has belonged, and which it can illuminate, but which in main measure can be examined independently of it. That principle is increasingly understood in the scholarly branch of literary studies, where much historically sophisticated work is now done. Yet habits of mind have a way of surviving the undermining of their foundations. Besides, biographical stories can sometimes be reconstructed or deduced from sources outside the biographical records. The prominence of my third writer, Marchamont Nedham, in Marvell's career has gone unnoticed, while his friendship with Milton has rarely seemed more than a curiosity. His significance in their lives and writings becomes apparent only when we reconstruct the political context within which the three men wrote, and when we thus move beyond biography to history.

I ask the forbearance of experts when, for the sake of non-specialist readers, or of readers on one or other side of the academic frontier between history and literature, I provide background information that for some scholars will be superfluous. Some details of presentation should be explained. I have converted quotations (though not the titles of books) into modern spelling and punctuation, except when the sense would suffer. Where I do not indicate otherwise, Marvell's poems are quoted and cited from Nigel Smith's edition; Milton's verse from that by John Carey and Alastair Fowler; Milton's English prose from the Yale edition; Ben Jonson's writings from the edition by Herford and Simpson; James Harrington's from that by J. G. A. Pocock. For texts of classical Latin I have used the Loeb editions. Milton's Latin prose is normally quoted from the Columbia edition, where the original text and a modern translation conveniently face each other, as they do in the Loeb volumes. The discussion of Latin texts in a post-Latinate age poses problems. John Aubrey called Marvell 'a great master of the Latin tongue', and declared that 'for Latin verses there was no man could come into competition with him'. Milton's Latin prose dazzled his contemporaries. Languages differ from each other not only in their rules and vocabularies but in their contours of thought. It is not the fault of the translators if, in English equivalents of Marvell and Milton, the stature of the original has largely to be taken on trust. My own struggles with Marvell's Latin have been valiantly and expertly helped by Rodney Allan, David Hopkins, David Levene, and Tony Woodman, though they must not be implicated in my decisions.

I am lucky to have written after the appearance in recent years of Smith's edition of Marvell's verse; of Nicholas von Maltzahn's *An Andrew Marvell Chronology*, which now complements Gordon Campbell's volume on Milton in the same series; and of David Norbrook's *Writing the English Republic.* My points both of concurrence and of respectful disagreement with Norbrook's volume, a magisterial work that has transformed its field, are too many to be particularized more than occasionally in my own text. Other debts are hard to state succinctly, for I have been sustained by that blessed form of comradeship where friendship and scholarly enquiry merge. I have in mind the encouragement and advice of Martin Dzelzainis, Paulina Kewes, Timothy Raylor, Susan Wormell, and especially of Professor von Maltzahn, whose vigilant and magnanimous guidance has kept me in heart. I am also grateful for the help of Rosanna Cox,

Frances Henderson, Edward Holberton, Mark Knights, Joyce Macadam, and Nicholas McDowell.

I am indebted to the Duke of Northumberland and the Marquess of Bath for permission to make use of manuscripts in their ownership. Although most of the book is freshly written, it makes some use of articles published elsewhere. I am grateful for permission to reproduce material from the following essays: 'John Milton and Oliver Cromwell'; 'Milton and Marchamont Nedham'; 'Milton, *Samson Agonistes*, and the Restoration'; 'The Politics of Marvell's Horatian Ode' (all Cambridge University Press); ' "Wit in a Roundhead": The Dilemma of Marchamont Nedham' (Manchester University Press); 'Harrington's "Oceana": Origins and Aftermath' (Stanford University Press). Sometimes, too, I have made use (though I plan to make more elsewhere) of material from the Carlyle Lectures which I was privileged to give at Oxford in 2002.

I owe more than he knows to the support and encouragement of Andrew McNeillie at Oxford University Press.

Contents

List of illustrations

Abbreviations

AMC	Nicholas von Maltzahn, *An Andrew Marvell Chronology* (Basingstoke, 2005)
BL, Add.	British Library, Additional [manuscript]
Bodl.	Bodleian Library
Cal. SP Dom.	*Calendar of State Papers Domestic*
Case	Marchamont Nedham, *The Case of the Commonwealth of England, State* ed. Philip A. Knachel (Charlottesville, Va., 1969)
CP	D. M. Wolfe *et al.*, eds, *Complete Prose Works of John Milton*, 8 vols. (New Haven and London, 1953–82: the 'Yale edition')
CW	F. A. Patterson, ed., *The Works of John Milton*, 18 vols. (New York, 1931–8: the 'Columbia edition')
Darbishire	Helen Darbishire, ed., *The Early Lives of Milton* (London, 1932)
Excellencie	Marchamont Nedham, *The Excellencie of a Free State* (1767 edn.)
French	J. Milton French, *The Life Records of John Milton*, 5 vols. (New Brunswick, NJ, 1949–58)
Lewalski	Barbara Lewalski, *The Life of John Milton: A Critical Biography* (Oxford 2000)
Ludlow, 'Voyce'	Edmund Ludlow, 'A Voyce from the Watch Tower', Bodl., MS Eng hist. c. 487.
Ludlow, *Voyce*	Edmund Ludlow, *A Voyce from the Watch Tower 1660–1662*, ed. Blair Worden (Camden Society, 1978)
Margoliouth	H. M. Margoliouth, ed., *The Poems and Letters of Andrew Marvell*, revised by Pierre Legouis with E. E. Duncan-Jones, 2 vols. (Oxford, 1971)
Masson	David Masson, *Life of John Milton*, 7 vols. (1859–94)
MC	Gordon Campbell, *A Milton Chronology* (Basingstoke, 1997)
MP	*Mercurius Politicus*
NA	National Archives
Nickolls	J. Nickolls, ed., *Original Letters and Papers of State … addressed to Oliver Cromwell* (1743)

ODNB	*Oxford Dictionary of National Biography*
Parker	William Riley Parker, *Milton: A Biography*, 2 vols., continuous pagination, revised by Gordon Campbell (Oxford, 1996)
PWAM	Annabel Patterson *et al.*, eds., *Prose Works of Andrew Marvell*, 2 vols. (New Haven, 2003)
Smith	Nigel Smith, ed., *The Poems of Andrew Marvell* (London, 2003)
TSP	Thomas Birch, ed., *A Collection of the State Papers of John Thurloe*, 7 vols. (1742)

Introduction

John Milton and Andrew Marvell are immortal writers, read and loved by people who know little if anything of the background of civil war and political strife against which they wrote. We can choose, if we wish, to be indifferent to that background. But if we are interested in the relationship of their writing to it, we must recover, even as we respect the enduring properties of their work, the pressures, the opportunities, the calculations, and the uncertainties of their mortal lives. The embalming of their works in modern editions, often volumes of high and invaluable scholarship, distances them, through no fault of the editors, from the ephemeral context of debate and publication to which much of their writing originally belonged.

This book places Milton and Marvell beside a writer for whom no one would claim the same kind of immortality, and to whom the tactics and techniques of instant print were second nature. The writing of Marchamont Nedham, which may at first seem infinitely remote from theirs, was intimately bound to it. He occupied a unique place in the lives of both men during the Interregnum of 1649–60. As far as we can tell, no other contemporary was so close to the composition of Milton's political writing or, before the Restoration, of Marvell's. His relations with the two men will not circumscribe our investigation of their politics. Often our argument will move away from him. Yet he will repeatedly work his way back.

Like Milton and Marvell, Nedham was a poet. Most of his verses were satires, which at their best have earned comparison with Dryden's[1] (though it was from an elegy that Dryden took one of Nedham's couplets). Yet his name was not made by his poetry. He earned fame, or notoriety, in the capacity in which we shall mainly observe him: as a journalist, the most successful practitioner of the first age of political journalism. In

1. Joseph Frank, *The Beginnings of the English Newspaper 1620–1660* (Cambridge, Mass., 1961), 344–6; *idem*, *Cromwell's Press Agent: A Critical Biography of Marchamont Nedham* (Lanham, Md., 1980), 60–3, 171.

1640–1 the breakdown of Charles I's government, and of the machinery by which the press had been restricted under it, brought novel opportunities for controversial publication, for which the intense public interest in the political upheaval created a large and lively market. Nedham's prose, witty, cheerful, spirited, direct, lucid, and combative, cornered a sizeable portion of it, and did much to shape the genre. It was a genre to which the writings of Milton and Marvell could come nearer than the familiar categorizations of literary purpose allow us to expect.

Even to glance at Milton's career is to see the central place of the Puritan Revolution in it. Three times it transformed his life. The first transformation came in 1641, when he was aged 32. Before then he was knowable only as a scholar and poet, who had been prepared for a life of learning by the encouragement of his father, a well-to-do London scrivener, and by his education at St Paul's School in London and at Cambridge University. Having left Cambridge, he lived privately, studying and writing, in the family's homes in Hammersmith and Buckinghamshire, until his visit to Italy in 1638–9 to explore its culture and literature. He intended to become a clergyman, but abandoned that plan, apparently in revulsion at the ceremonialism and the pastoral deficiencies of the Church under Archbishop Laud. In 1641, when the Long Parliament was breaking the machinery of Charles I's rule, it seemed that a Puritan overhaul of the Church might be achieved. With that prospect before him Milton entered the world of polemic and public controversy. His tracts of the 1640s demanded the reform not only of the Church but of education, of the divorce laws, and of the regulations that restricted the press. The second transformation came in 1649, when King Charles I was tried and executed and the monarchy was abolished. Now Milton became an employee of the state, as Latin Secretary or Secretary for Foreign Tongues. Hitherto his tracts had been written on his own initiative, or anyway without official sanction. Now he wrote on behalf of his new employer, the republic, in defence and celebration of the deed, the regicide, that had brought it to power. For the remainder of the Interregnum, that turbulent era, his works responded to the rapid fluctuations of its politics. The third transformation was the Restoration in 1660, when the religious and political causes he had served were shattered. In the last fourteen years of his life he had to live with that calamity, which, no less than the earlier course of events, is reflected in his writing.

Milton's entry into polemical debate in 1641 occurred around the time of Marvell's twentieth birthday. Marvell, the son of a clergyman in Hull, was likewise educated at Cambridge. He played no part in the civil wars of the 1640s, and instead spent some years on the Continent, though he was back in England by late 1647. Soon thereafter he was writing political poetry. Whereas Milton rejoiced in the regicide, Marvell's sympathies were royalist. Yet by the winter of 1654–5 they had become Cromwellian. By 1657 he, too, was an employee of the Puritan state, where he worked, as Milton did and as Nedham also did, in the office of Cromwell's secretary of state John Thurloe. He had been launched on a political career which would survive the Restoration and last for the remainder of his life.

Posterity has divided Milton and Marvell from the politics with which their lives and writings were intertwined. In Milton's case it happened from the start. The generations after the Puritan Revolution learned to love his verse, but were appalled by, or else ignored, most of his polemical prose. His vindications of the execution of King Charles I dismayed a society which had been torn apart by civil war and Puritan rule, and which – at least as far as we can tell from the commentary that got into print – dreaded their return. His radicalism did have its champions. In the wake of the Revolution of 1688, extreme Whigs republished and silently copied material from his pamphlets in order to aid the revival of the 'good old cause' of bringing kings to account. But mainstream opinion mostly kept its distance from his prose (though his arguments for liberty of expression and of conscience fared better than his attacks on tyrants and bishops and the divorce laws). His poetry, which was deemed 'sublime', was widely held to have transcended its political context. Thus it was that the writer who had escaped, perhaps narrowly, a hideous execution at the hands of the restored government in 1660 was given, in 1737, an imposing monument in Westminster Abbey. Dr Johnson thought Milton's politics those of a scoundrel, but knew most of *Paradise Lost* by heart.

In the later eighteenth century and during the nineteenth, new forces of political radicalism gave those politics a fresh appeal in some quarters.[2] Thomas Hollis and Catharine Macaulay celebrated Milton as a fellow republican. Wordsworth and other Romantic poets were drawn to him in the era of the French Revolution and of Napoleon. Victorian Liberals and Nonconformists, conscious of a debt to the Puritan past, found an ancestor in him. To John Bright, *Paradise Lost* was 'the greatest name in English

2. This paragraph draws on my *Roundhead Reputations: The English Civil Wars and the Passions of Posterity* (London, 2001), q.v. 'Milton, John'.

political history'. The Nonconformist George Dawson, turning traditional judgement on its head, praised Milton for having 'left his poetry' during the Puritan Revolution and having 'plunged into the mud, the mire, the dirt, the storm, of politics'.[3] (Readers of this book may think that he spoke truer than he knew.) Even so, the Victorian admiration for Milton's political stances was hazy. Not much historical information or biographical exploration informed it, at least until late in the century, when assertions about his career could be tested against the scholarship of David Masson and S. R. Gardiner. In the twentieth century, literary criticism revived earlier preferences. In fact, it extended them, for Milton's political opinions became, what even the Tory Dr Johnson had not found them, an impediment to the admiration of his verse. Disparagers of them took strength from his demotion from the elite of English poets by T. S. Eliot and F. R. Leavis.

If Milton's verse has been preferred to his views, Andrew Marvell's views, for more than two centuries after his death, were preferred to his verse. In 1659, the year before the Restoration, he became a member of parliament for his native Hull, a post he would fill assiduously until his death in 1678. During the last six years of his life, when fears rose of a return to civil war, he did what the young Milton had done when civil war approached in 1641–2. He wrote political prose. The consequences for posthumous opinion were very different from those of Milton's choice. In 1844 the *Cyclopaedia of English Literature* uncontentiously remarked that Marvell 'is better known as a prose writer than a poet, and is still more celebrated as a patriotic member of parliament'.[4] The judgement would have been equally uncontroversial at any earlier time since his death. Marvell's poems often conflicted with later tastes: his satires in their impoliteness, his lyric verse in its metaphysical properties. His prose, on the other hand, had a broad appeal. Whereas Milton had rejoiced in the overthrow of kingship, Marvell had had a more respectable theme. He attacked the restored Stuart monarchy, which was toppled by the Revolution of 1688, and which thereafter found ever fewer defenders. His earlier involvement in Cromwellian rule, had it been generally known about, would have dented the esteem in which he was held, but his poems on Cromwell were withheld from publication until 1776. What the eighteenth century admired was Marvell's stand

3. George Dawson, *Biographical Lectures* (1888), 87.
4. Elizabeth Story Donno, ed., *Andrew Marvell: The Critical Heritage* (London, 1978), 166. Donno's valuable collection of documents bears out the point. On Marvell's posthumous reputation see too *AMC*, and the articles by Nicholas von Maltzahn listed there on p. 296.

against the tyranny and corruption of the reign of Charles II. It had been the stand, as posterity preferred not to know, of a hot-blooded partisan. Eighteenth-century interpreters cooled Marvell's blood and obscured his partisanship. He was made to conform, in temper and opinion, to the 'patriot' or country-party ideal, which disliked the cut and thrust of politics and which elevated virtue above them. His exertions on liberty's behalf were prized as evidence, less of his political commitment, than of his Stoic immunity to corruption, the evil that obsessed the age of the Hanoverian oligarchy. Throughout the eighteenth century – and for much of the nineteenth – phrases in his favour occur with numbing regularity. He was 'an incorruptible patriot', 'the inflexible patriot', 'the British Aristides', 'of Roman virtue'.[5]

It was only in the 1890s, in perhaps the most rapid and striking transformation of a literary reputation in English history, that the Marvell of public life yielded to Marvell the poet. Though his lyric verse had been known since the seventeenth century, it had generally been considered at best a sideline from his political activity – and who is to say that Marvell himself had thought otherwise? Now, in the era of late Victorian aestheticism, of Oscar Wilde and Henry James and the early Proust, writers who put private before public experience, the drawing-room before the council-board, Marvell's parliamentary and polemical deeds were held to have polluted the exquisite sensibility of the lyric verse. The new mood was announced in an essay of 1892 by A. C. Benson. 'Few poets', he warned, 'are of sufficiently tough and impenetrable fibre as to be able with impunity to mix with public affairs', for the 'stream' of 'inspiration … is apt to become sullied at the very source by the envious contact of the world'. Marvell's public involvement after the Restoration was judged by Benson a disaster: 'the singer of an April mood, who might have bloomed year after year in young and ardent hearts, is buried in the dust of politics, in the valley of dead bones.' Benson found Marvell's Restoration satires 'filthy' and 'revolting', and his most eloquent prose work, *The Rehearsal Transpros'd*, 'peculiarly distasteful'.[6] Marvell's new poetic standing was swiftly established. In 1901 H. C. Beeching invoked 'the recent rise into fame of the lyrical verse of Marvell' to confirm his judgement that 'our own generation … is markedly' the 'superior' of its predecessors in 'poetical

5. Donno, ed., *Andrew Marvell*; Worden, *Roundhead Reputations*, q.v. 'Marvell, Andrew'.
6. Donno, ed., *Andrew Marvell*, 248–62.

taste'.[7] What Benson had begun, T. S. Eliot and then the New Criticism would develop.

By the late twentieth century another transformation, this one more gradual, had occurred. Politics, which earlier ages had kept out of literary criticism, had come to permeate it. The political Marvell was back – though not, this time, at the expense of the lyric poetry, in which many critics, rather than shielding it from politics, now identified allusions to them.[8] Indeed his politics had assumed a bolder form. The eighteenth-century Marvell stood in the tradition of broad, reputable Whiggism, which opposed the tyranny of kings but declined or hesitated to endorse radical steps against it. Recent authorities present a Marvell not in the moderate but in the extreme Whig tradition, as the friend, with Milton, of regicide and republicanism.[9] That hypothesis, as we shall see, leaves too much out. Yet its premiss, that Marvell's verse engaged with the most pressing issues of Cromwellian politics, is unanswerable. Ever fewer critics try to answer it.

Critical inheritances none the less run deep. They may run deeper than those who react against them realize. The depth and the rounded perfection of Marvell's finest political poetry, and the inspiration of its voice, may even now induce a reluctance to think of him writing it in proximity to Marchamont Nedham, a propagandist with a calculating eye to political and pecuniary advantage and a readiness to swap political sides when it suited him. Marvell's most influential modern biographer was troubled to notice connections between him and Nedham, whom he described feelingly as a 'contemptible person'.[10] Yet Marvell the satirist and polemicist – the author of the verses on Richard Flecknoe and Tom May, and then of the political verse and tracts of the Restoration – is a kindred spirit of Nedham. So, perhaps more unexpectedly, is the Marvell we meet in other writing. The relationship between the two men, as distinct from that between their writings, has to be a matter of speculation. Yet it will come to seem barely

7. Donno, ed., *Andrew Marvell*, 284.
8. Illuminating as that approach has sometimes been, I have not adopted it here. The allusions may well be present, but it is difficult either to establish their presence or, even if we can, to draw biographical inferences from them that add to the evidence of his explicitly political poetry.
9. Christopher Hill, 'Society and Andrew Marvell', in *idem*, *Puritanism and Revolution* (London, 1986 edn.), 324–50; David Norbrook, *Writing the English Republic: Poetry, Rhetoric and Politics 1627–1660* (Cambridge, 1999).
10. Pierre Legouis, *André Marvell: Poète, Puritain, Patriote 1621–1678* (New York, 1965 edn.), 192–3; the point is made more briefly in the abridged English version, *Andrew Marvell: Poet, Puritan, Patriot* (Oxford, 1968 edn.), 101–2.

conceivable that Marvell's poems on Oliver Cromwell, however privately they may have been composed, were not subjects of intense conversation between him and Nedham.

Milton's part in the Puritan Revolution, like Marvell's, receives ever more attention. Yet, at least beyond the confines of specialized enquiry, his verse and prose remain hard to view together. No writer has known more about the separate properties of poetry and prose than Milton, and no reader of him can be heedless of the differences. Three centuries have honoured the superiority of his poetry. What the demarcation of verse from prose can obscure is their common purpose in his mind: his aim of instructing readers in truth, equipping them for tests of virtue, persuading them to right thoughts and choices. The pen, writers of the Renaissance knew, was for public use. In his case the need for it was always urgent. If the poet's gifts are, as he says, 'of power, beside the office of a pulpit, to imbreed and cherish in a great people the seeds of virtue',[11] a writer of prose has the same mission. During the two decades of the Puritan Revolution, from his early thirties to his early fifties, he wrote most of his prose, and mostly wrote in prose. His early verse, and then the achievements of 'On the Morning of Christ's Nativity', of 'L'Allegro' and 'Il Penseroso', of 'Arcades' and 'Comus' and 'Lycidas', belong to the peaceful if inharmonious rule of the early Stuarts. The great late poems, *Paradise Lost*, *Samson Agonistes*, and *Paradise Regained*, appeared in the Restoration.

His choices of genre were ones of means, not of ends. In prose, he knew 'myself inferior to myself'[12] – or anyway at first believed that to be so. His calculated act of self-diminution was measured to accomplish his didactic aims, which lost none of their earnestness. Milton, who knew that poetry can impart virtue 'through the charm and smoothness of the sounds',[13] likewise drew in his prose tracts on 'true eloquence the daughter of virtue' to 'charm the multitude into that which is really good'.[14] If the opening of *Paradise Lost* announces his resolve, through 'things unattempted yet in prose or rhyme', to 'justify the ways of God to men', then in the opening words of the first tract that he committed to print, *Of Reformation* in 1641, he speaks from his 'deep and retired thoughts, which with every man Christianly instructed ought to be most frequent, of God and of his miraculous ways and works amongst men'.[15] The 'great argument' – the

11. *CP* i. 816. 12. Ibid. 808. 13. Ibid. 382. 14. Ibid. 746.
15. Ibid. 519.

thesis or story of free will – that justifies God's ways in the epic is intrinsic to the claims of his prose work *Areopagitica*,[16] and is spelled out in the private prose manual of theology that is the handmaid of the epic poem, *de Doctrina Christiana*, 'my best and richest possession'.[17] Behind his prose as behind his poetry, there lay, he tells us, divine inspiration and a divinely appointed mission. In 1642 he registered the 'inward prompting' that had informed him of his immortal gifts, as a poet, for the service of God and country.[18] He ascribed the composition of the prose *Defensio* in 1651, which he likewise wrote for God and country, to the same impulse, 'a divine monitor within'.[19] In beginning *Paradise Lost* he asks the assistance of his 'heavenly muse': in his prose *History of Britain*, to which he devoted so much labour in the years around the regicide, 'imploring divine assistance ... I now begin'.[20] One of the poet's tasks, he observed in 1642, is 'to deplore the general relapses of kingdoms and states from justice and God's true worship'.[21] His *History* deplored the relapses of ancient Britain, and by explicit analogy that of modern England, from those observances. We catch contemporaries grasping the corrective function of both his poetry and his prose. An early reader of *Paradise Lost* saw the poem as a bulwark against the 'wickedness' of the court and nation. The same observer, it is true, judged Milton's tracts 'criminal', and remarked that 'he writes so good verse that 'tis pity he ever wrote prose'.[22] Yet on the publication of the prose *History*, three years after that of *Paradise Lost*, another reader reflected that 'we needed all ... his sharp checks and sour instructions. For we must be a lost people if we are not speedily reclaimed.'[23]

★★

Milton wrote much more than Marvell in Cromwellian England, which is one reason why there is much more of him in this book. The other is that in the same period Milton's life is much the more fully documented. Yet even at their amplest the sources rarely explain themselves straightforwardly. Much of the evidence for the relations of both Marvell and Milton with

16. Compare *Paradise Lost* III. 80–104 with *CP* ii. 514–15, 527–8; cf. ii. 293.
17. *CW* xiv. 9.
18. *CP.* i. 810.
19. *CW* viii. 69.
20. *CP* v. 4; cf. *CW* viii. 19.
21. *CP* i. 817.
22. Nicholas von Maltzahn, 'The First Reception of *Paradise Lost* (1667)', *Review of English Studies*, 47 (1996), 490–3.
23. Nicholas von Maltzahn, 'Laureate, Republican, Calvinist: An Early Response to Milton and *Paradise Lost*', *Milton Studies*, 29 (1992), 191.

Nedham lies where the animating force of political writing in and after the Renaissance is so largely to be detected: between the lines, or below the surface. There are obvious difficulties, and familiar temptations, in the detection of interlinear or sub-textual evidence, a process that can be neither assisted nor tested by scientific measurement. All we can attempt is to attune ourselves to the facts and moods and conventions of politics, where, in any age, people do not say everything that they think or feel, and need to say things that they do not. The Puritan Revolution immeasurably enlarged the scope of printed expression, and thus of an audience distant from the centre of authority. But among those who wrote for power, or within reach of its displeasure, there persisted the conventions of praise and dispraise, and of politeness and discretion, which literary critics bear in mind when they study the era before the civil wars, but which are sometimes overlooked in accounts of the 1640s and 1650s. A second necessary interpretative process is no less charged with difficulty and temptation: that of deciding whether a parallel between one writing and another is strong enough to constitute evidence of conscious imitation by one author of another, or at least of close affinities of outlook or intent. Here, too, there are no objective tests. We can only try to read ourselves into the mental habits, not only of our authors, but of writers around them, until we think we can tell a distinctive remark from an everyday one.

The examiner of allusions and parallels must sometimes crave the reader's patience while the evidence is mapped. The necessary instrument of analysis is quotation, which, being the separation of words from their contexts, can be a diminishing device. Yet if we examine the common ground between Nedham on the one hand and Marvell and Milton on the other, we discover, in the writings of the two great poets, preoccupations and viewpoints that have escaped notice. We find new things about the circumstances and the chronology of the composition of their writing, and thus about its intentions, and thus about its meaning. And when the similarities between a Nedham and a Milton or a Marvell have been registered, and their significance absorbed, we are also left with a sense of the differences. To view the parallels between Marvell's 'First Anniversary' of Oliver Cromwell's elevation to the protectorate and Nedham's writing for that regime is not merely to notice the closeness and conformity of the poem to government propaganda, but to wonder at the distance that it simultaneously preserves from it. In the same way the stature and distinctiveness of Milton's *Samson Agonistes* stand in sharper relief when we have grasped the concerns that it shares, not, in this case, with writing by Nedham, but with other polemical works of its moment. But if there are differences between Milton or Marvell and Nedham, there are also contrasts, and varieties, within Milton and Marvell themselves. When the two writers depart from Nedham it is because they choose to use or explore sides of themselves that they do not hold in common with him. Wherever the poetry of Milton or Marvell came from, it was not from a unified personality. Their characters seem more complicated and variegated the more we learn of them. So does Nedham's.

Anyone who worked on the same side as Nedham, that agile reverser of his allegiances, was bound to spend time on the opposite one. Here as elsewhere in the milieu of the writers and wits of the revolution, we often have to guess how allies coped with the memory of past differences, or how former collaborators dealt with present ones. There is a larger field for guesswork. It is generally easier to trace connections of Marvell's and Milton's careers and writings to Nedham's than to each other. This may seem surprising, for the relationship of Milton to Marvell has left familiar documentary witnesses, as their associations with Nedham have not. To take only the firmest material, we have Milton's letter of recommendation on Marvell's behalf in February 1653, when the younger man was seeking employment under the Commonwealth; we have Marvell's letter to Milton the following year, on receipt of copies of *Defensio Secunda*; we have Marvell's poem on *Paradise Lost*; we have moments in Marvell's other poems that are manifestly indebted to Milton's verse. Even so, those testimonies of friendship and esteem, fitting as they seem, scarcely take us inside the regular contacts, social and political, between the two.

Early biographers of Milton say that the two men became 'very intimate and conversant' when, from 1657, Marvell assisted Milton in the office of Cromwell's secretary of state John Thurloe,[24] and – though we cannot be sure of the truth of this – that during the time that Milton lived in Petty France, from 1651 to 1660, Marvell 'used to frequent him the oftenest of anybody'.[25] The move to Petty France took place only at the end of 1651, but Milton's association with Marvell is likely to have formed, as the

24. Anthony Wood, quoted by Lewalski, 344.

25. Darbishire, 175. The author of the statement, John Toland, an inventive writer who sought to create a pedigree of seventeenth-century ideas and conduct in which republican and country-party outlooks would merge, had good cause to associate those two targets of Stuart tyranny; see my *Roundhead Reputations*, ch. 4.

partnership of Milton and Nedham did, before then. We can see enough of the dealings of Milton and Marvell, of Milton and Nedham, and of Marvell and Nedham, to be able to assume the existence of a triangular relationship. The evidence of the written word on which we depend enables us only to imagine, but leaves us unable to doubt, the excitement of the talk among our three authors about the relationship of literature to politics, and of books to life. Even so, the friendship of the two more famous writers cannot have been politically straightforward. Like their relations with Nedham, it had to accommodate differences. During the Interregnum Milton and Marvell moved on almost opposite trajectories. The summer of 1648 produced Milton's sonnet 'On the Lord General Fairfax at the Siege of Colchester', which looks to the leader of the new model army to cure England's ills, and Marvell's 'An Elegy upon the Death of My Lord Francis Villiers', which hopes for Fairfax's death at the hands of royalist soldiers. In the 1650s Marvell travelled from royalism, first to an ambivalent Cromwellianism, then to an unambivalent one, Milton from an intense but ambivalent admiration of Cromwell to an unambivalent and no less intense rejection of him. In February 1659, when Richard Cromwell's parliament had met, we find Milton appealing to it on behalf of the ideals of his hero Sir Henry Vane, who had broken with Richard's father, against the power and policies of the protectoral regime. We simultaneously see Marvell working in the Commons on behalf of that regime, which had nominated him for the Hull constituency, where he had defeated Vane in the election.[26]

The figure of Oliver Cromwell, Lord General of the army from 1650 and Lord Protector from 1653 until his death in 1658, presides over the writings of Milton and Marvell in that decade. It is he, too, who at least as much as any other subject brings both writers together with Nedham. The responses of our authors to him are themselves a historical source, for, if a knowledge of political history can illuminate literature, the reverse is also true. All three writers convey, albeit from varied angles, the wonder commanded by the leader who conquered the three kingdoms of England, Ireland, and Scotland; who destroyed both sides, first the king and then the parliament, of the civil war; who from obscure origins became king in all but name; and whose army and navy awed and frightened the great powers of Europe. They also register the conflicts of emotion that he aroused. Everyone

26. *AMC* 56. I am grateful to David Scott for a discussion of the election.

Figure 1. Oliver Cromwell, *c.* 1650

knew that the fate of England and its people would be determined by his character and decisions. Everyone mistrusted him, even his devotees. His former Roundhead allies detested him still more than his Cavalier victims did. There were three conflicts in English politics that principally exercised our writers. There was the struggle of Roundhead and Cavalier. There was the contest, on the Roundhead side, between radicalism in religion and politics and the reactionary or restraining impulses of the Presbyterians. Literary criticism has been less aware of the third conflict. It was conducted between Cromwell and the supporters of the parliament which ruled England, on the principle of the sovereignty of the people's representatives, from 1649 to 1653. Cromwell's stature first threatened that principle and then shattered it. In 1650 Marvell's 'An Horatian Ode' explicitly set a royalist past against a Cromwellian future. But it also set, implicitly, a Cromwellian future against a parliamentary present. It thus announced, with the obliqueness that was as characteristic of literary treatments of sensitive high politics during the Puritan Revolution as before it, the theme which would shape the course of events in the ensuing decade. It was a theme to which Milton and Nedham, in their different ways but with like obliqueness, would bring an intensity and resourcefulness akin to Marvell's.

I

Nedham

Marchamont Nedham is the serial turncoat of the Puritan Revolution. The civil wars, which shaped his life, broke out in the month, August 1642, of his twenty-second birthday. Nedham – or often Needham: his surname should be pronounced, I think, so as virtually to rhyme with 'freedom' – came from a family of moderate substance in Burford in Oxfordshire.[1] After a period at All Souls College, Oxford, he was appointed usher or assistant teacher at Merchant Taylors' School, an experience that would leave him with a long-standing interest in education and a long-lasting awareness of its low levels of pay. In 1641 he found other employment, as a clerk at Gray's Inn. Then, in 1643, the growth of civil war journalism gave him his chance. He wrote for parliament in the first civil war; for the king in the second; for the successive Puritan regimes, each of them antagonistic to the memory of its predecessor, of 1649–60; and for the restored monarchy thereafter. To all appearances he took his transitions in his stride. 'I confess', he remarked airily when embarking on his career as a republican writer in 1650, 'that for a time I was of an opinion contrary to what is here written, till some causes made me reflect with an impartial eye upon the affairs of this new government.' He repeated the statement, almost verbatim, eleven years later, in writing for the restored

1. For fuller documentation of Nedham's career than this chapter supplies, see my '"Wit in a Roundhead": The Dilemma of Marchamont Nedham', in Susan D. Amussen and Mark A. Kishlansky, eds., *Political Culture and Cultural Politics in Early Modern England* (Manchester, 1995), 301–37. Frank, *Cromwell's Press Agent*, is a valuable aid, even where it invites dissent. Nedham is well served in *ODNB* by Joad Raymond, who also discusses him in his *Making the News: An Anthology of the Newsbooks of Revolutionary England 1641–1660* (Moreton-in-Marsh, 1993), esp. 332–79, and in his *The Invention of the Newspaper: English Newsbooks 1641–1649* (Oxford, 1996). Norbrook, *Writing the English Republic*, has many insights into Nedham's writing, of which there are also helpful discussions in Jason Peacey, *Politicians and Pamphleteers: Propaganda during the English Civil Wars and Interregnum* (Aldershot, 2004), and Nigel Smith, *Literature and Revolution in England, 1640–1660* (New Haven and London, 1994. See too below, p. 27, n. 55.).

monarchy.[2] Arguments advanced by him in the Roundhead cause were spurned by him in the Cavalier one. Roundhead statesmen or soldiers whom he lauded as heroes in the first civil war became targets of merciless satire by him in the second. The examples which he drew from his wide historical reading to support his theses proved one thing in his Cavalier prose, the opposite in his Roundhead writing.

During the Puritan Revolution he wrote for Roundhead regimes for around fourteen years, for the royalist cause for less than two. Yet after 'our late blessed and wonderful Restoration' the revolutionary transformations which he had saluted as glorious and heroic exploits became 'our late villainous changes', the work of 'a few fanatic ill-principled spirits'.[3] In the first civil war he accused Charles I of 'triumphing in the spoils of your subjects', and derided the application to him of the term 'his sacred majesty'.[4] After the Restoration he portrayed him as the 'saint' and 'martyr Charles the First of blessed memory'.[5] Having, during the revolutionary period, represented the conjunction of the English and Scottish crowns in 1603 as the disaster of modern English politics, he now rejoiced in that 'happy union'.[6] Having tirelessly remonstrated, in the Puritan era, against the 'twisting' of ecclesiastical with civil power, he asserted under restored Anglicanism that 'there is so strict a connection between them that if you part with one, the other lies open to the next assault'.[7] In the Roundhead cause he had made war on the politically and morally debilitating force of 'custom': now he enjoined his readers to have 'regard' to, and be 'very tender' of, 'antiquity and the custom of former times'.[8] Similar stark contrasts could be drawn between his two newsbooks of the 1640s, the parliamentarian *Mercurius Britanicus* and the royalist *Mercurius Pragmaticus*.[9]

We cannot tell on what terms he lived with his shifts of adherence. At one level he plainly enjoyed them. Opposites seem to have had an inherent attraction to him. The reversal not only of his arguments but of his wording is performed with style and relish. But what did he make of the accusations of unprincipled and mercenary betrayal that were heaped on

2. *Case*, 3; Nedham, *The True Character of a Rigid Presbyter* (1661), preface.
3. Nedham, *A Discourse concerning Schools* (1663), 2.
4. Worden, '"Wit in a Roundhead"', 315.
5. Nedham, *True Character*, 4.
6. Nedham, *Christianissimus Christianandus* (1678), 53.
7. Nedham, *A Pacquet of Advices* (1676), 73. (I have used the edition of this tract in Bodl., Ashm. 1108.)
8. Nedham, *Discourse concerning Schools*, 5.
9. Worden, '"Wit in a Roundhead"', 323.

him? Perhaps he was suspicious of all unbending commitment. Perhaps he concurred with his learned friend and drinking companion, the gentleman-poet Henry Oxinden of Kent, who thought that a man should not 'be startled nor troubled chameleon-like, as the necessity of occasion serves, to turn into all shapes. For the most constant men must be content to change their resolutions according to the alterations of time. Paul himself became all things to all men.'[10] Perhaps, like Oxinden, he saw the contemporary world in terms of Machiavellian duplicity and, amid the rapid changes of power in the 1640s and 1650s, regarded 'the art of dissimulation' as essential to survival in it.[11] Perhaps he adapted to politics the premisses that Oxinden applied to religion. Oxinden reasoned that, since 'the major part of men by far take up their religion upon trust', the rest of us should prudently conform to ecclesiastical trends.[12] He hated Puritanism, and his verse of the late 1640s declared support for the king. He was shocked by the revolution of 1648–9 that produced the regicide, and was scornful of Milton, its advocate.[13] Yet he tried to avoid more than the most temporary commitment to any party. In 1659 he ran, with Anabaptist support, in the election to Richard Cromwell's parliament, and was said during the campaign to be 'against tithing self-seeking ministers' and to stand for 'the pulling down of the ministry'[14] – a posture that would have earned the approval of Milton, whose treatise *Of Civil Power* was prepared for the same parliament. Yet after the Restoration, at which he offered verses of extravagant flattery to Charles II,[15] Oxinden was ordained in the Anglican church and became an absentee clergyman, eager for the collection of his tithes.[16] The surprise for us is to discover, amid both his merriment and his reversals, a serious

10. BL, Add. MS 28001 (Oxinden papers), fos. 117, 118^{v}.
11. For the relationship of the two men, and their social circle, see Dorothy Gardiner, ed., *The Oxinden and Peyton Letters 1642–1670* (London, 1937), 143, 149–50, 160–1, 168, 199–202, 222–3; BL, Add. MS 28002, fos. 141, 328^{v}; Add. MS 28012, fo. 775^{v}; Canterbury Cathedral Library, Elham Pamphlets, no. 1245. Oxinden apparently possessed a manuscript copy of Nedham's pamphlet of 1660, *Newes from Brussels*: Sheila Hingley, 'The Oxindens, Warlys and Elham Public Library' (University of Kent Ph.D. thesis, 2004), 131.
12. BL, Add. MS 28002, fos. 116^{v}–7.
13. It is Oxinden who tells us, on the flyleaf of his copy of *Eikonoklastes*, that in July 1652 Milton 'is now grown blind and has to be led up and down': Canterbury Cathedral Library, Elham Pamphlets, no. 178. Oxinden's views on the events of 1648–9 are evident from his other annotations on pamphlets in that collection. For a guide to them see Hingley, 'Oxindens'.
14. D. Gardiner, ed., *Oxinden and Peyton Letters*, 227–9.
15. Oxinden, *Charles Triumphant* (1660).
16. D. Gardiner, ed., *Oxinden and Peyton Letters*, 313–14. Oxinden addressed a Latin poem to Nedham: Folger MS V. a. 300.

intellect exercised by devotional issues. Who knows what issues privately exercised Nedham?

One of his conceptual innovations was to apply to English politics the idea that men's public behaviour is governed by their competing interests, and that the political health of a community rests on its identification and management of the interests contained within it. Those arguments can be hard to square with his appeals, on other occasions and even on the same ones, to rules of virtuous constancy. His political thought was a jostle of competing premisses, each eloquently sustained as occasion called. But in the principle of interest he found an abiding preoccupation. 'Interest', he declared, 'is the true zenith of every state and person, according to which they may certainly be understood.... All actions are the effects of interests.' Our interests are not amoral. They include an adherence to 'right' and the eschewal of 'wrong'.[17] But we should shed the 'specious' and 'frivolous pretences' of 'religion, justice and necessity' in which we disguise them.[18]

Though he wrote many influential pamphlets, Nedham made his greatest impact in a form of propaganda to which the Puritan Revolution gave birth: the weekly printed newsbook. He rose to prominence in the first civil war as the editor – that is, the compiler of news reports but also the writer of commentary – of a newsbook that was designed to answer that triumph of royalist propaganda, the weekly *Mercurius Aulicus*, edited by John Berkenhead.[19] *Mercurius Britanicus* was founded in 1643, though only gradually was Nedham's editorial partner, Thomas Audley, marginalized.[20] In 1646, when the war was virtually won, parliament closed *Britanicus* down. Over the next year, during which he practised medicine, Nedham collaborated with the Levellers, with whom he had established contact the previous year, and also with the leaders of the Cromwellian army. When that army, in defiance of its masters at Westminster, opened negotiations

17. *MP*, 15 July 1652, 1731–2.
18. Nedham, *The Case Stated between England and the United Provinces* (1652), 23; *idem*, *Interest Will not Lie* (1659), 10.
19. Peter W. Thomas, *Sir John Berkenhead 1617–1679: A Royalist Career in Politics and Polemics* (Oxford, 1969), remains an invaluable introduction to the genre and to the literary milieu in which it thrived.
20. Though Nedham is sometimes supposed not to have been involved in the writing of the early issues, they are full of his traits. The spelling 'Britanicus', with its single 'n', began as a mistake which is unlikely to have been of his making, and for which the newsbook, embarrassed by the charge levelled in *Aulicus* that the error illustrated the illiteracy of the Roundheads, found a spurious pretext.

with the king, Nedham argued for a settlement between them that would bypass the parliamentary majority. Then, when the talks stalled, he went over to the king. In September 1647, soon after his twenty-seventh birthday, he was made editor of one of four new royalist newsbooks. To parliament's exasperation they were produced under its nose in London, the city which was its wartime capital but of whose loyalty it could never be sure. Nedham's new newsbook, *Mercurius Pragmaticus*, greeted Westminster's efforts to suppress it with gleeful taunts about his 'printing-press upon wheels'.[21]

The avowed aim of *Pragmaticus* was to 'write his majesty back into his throne'.[22] It was the most effective of the new newsbooks, partly because Nedham had, as his fellow editors did not, a mole in parliament who enabled him to print informed accounts of parliamentary debates and intrigues,[23] but also because of its literary virtuosity. Satire, lampoon, mockery, and burlesque were its heady methods. Verse joined forces with prose. Lines of ballad, which distilled the developments of the past week, opened each issue. If the ballad material that appeared in the prints in the late 1640s was sung by its readers, then song must have been a main vehicle of royalist sentiment. Nedham edited *Pragmaticus* until just before the execution of the king in January 1649, when, his freedom and safety in mounting peril, he had to abandon the journal. Yet from April to June 1649, to the exasperation of the Commonwealth's new rulers, he was able to resume production. Perhaps it was during that time that he wrote his copy at Minster Lovell, close to his native Burford, where he was 'sheltered' in a 'high room' in the house of the royalist divine and writer Peter Heylyn,[24] who had written the early numbers of *Mercurius Aulicus*, the antagonist of *Britanicus*, until Berkenhead took over. But in June there began what Nedham called his 'scene of calamity'. Having been betrayed, as he believed, by his friend James Thompson, an attorney and fellow wit, he was arrested and sent to Newgate. Acording to Anthony Wood he was 'brought into danger of his life'.[25] The Treason Act of May 1649, like the older treason legislation that

21. *Mercurius Pragmaticus*, 21 Dec. 1647, 2. A number of newsbooks carried the title *Mercurius Pragmaticus*. Those edited by Nedham are identified by Jason Peacey, '"The Counterfeit Silly Curr": Money, Politics and the Forging of Royalist Newspapers in the English Civil War', *Huntington Library Quarterly*, 67 (2004), 27–57.
22. *Mercurius Pragmaticus* 11 Jan. 1648, 8; 12 Sept. 1648, 1.
23. David Underdown, *Pride's Purge* (Oxford, 1971), 138, 165–6, 168, 170 (though also p. 196).
24. Peter Heylyn, *The Historical and Miscellaneous Tracts* (1681), p. xix.
25. Anthony Wood, *Athenae Oxonienses*, 4 vols. (1813–20), iii. 1181.

would be restored in 1660, carried the death penalty for seditious words, of which he had delivered a plentiful and ferocious supply. It was apparently from gaol that he published, in August, a pamphlet urging parliament to do what, in the periods when he wrote for the Roundhead cause, he persistently advised it not to do: show leniency to its enemies.[26] In the same month he escaped. Until November he was 'a pilgrim about the country'.

Then he detected, in the government's decision to impose on the nation an 'engagement' of loyalty to 'the Commonwealth of England, as it is now established without a king or House of Lords' – a pledge which he quickly took – a chance 'to preserve my peace upon rational terms'. He returned to London to put out feelers to the government. While waiting for a response he wrote to his friend Henry Oxinden, begging the loan of £5 and portraying his straitened circumstances in his indomitably sprightly prose.

> I dare not so much as peep abroad to converse with any, but am constrained to associate with rats, old books and cobwebs. ... Nay, did you but see my clothes you would suppose them plundered from half a dozen factions, or begged for God's sake in as many several nations; and this habit I rant in, partly out of necessity, partly on purpose to obscure myself; whereto my periwig likewise very much contributes, being red, and so looks like a cap-case dropped from some well-complexioned sinner that had been executed at Tyburn, begged by the College for an anatomy, and after converted at the 'pothecary's into mummy. The truth in good earnest is, I am much distressed every way.[27]

Yet he got out of trouble. He earned his release, and what was more a handsome salary, by turning his pen to the Commonwealth's cause. Peter Heylyn's early biographer would recall that Nedham, 'like Balaam the son of Beor, hired with the wages of unrighteousness, corrupted with mercenary gifts and bribes, became the only apostate of the nation, and writ for the pretended Commonwealth'; for which Heylin 'could never after endure the mention of his name, who had so disobliged his country, and the royal party, by his shameful tergiversation'.[28]

By the summer of 1650 the tergiversation had produced some imposing literary results. In May he produced a powerful apologia for the new regime, *The Case of the Commonwealth of England, Stated*. In June the former editor

26. Nedham, *Certain Considerations Tendered in all Humility to an Honourable Member of the Council of State* (1649).
27. D. Gardiner, ed., *Oxinden and Peyton Letters*, 160–1.
28. Heylyn, *Historical ... Tracts*, p. xix.

of *Mercurius Britanicus* and *Mercurius Pragmaticus* founded another weekly newsbook, *Mercurius Politicus*. Anthony Wood, in an early biographical account of Nedham, remarked that *Politicus* was 'so extreme different to' *Pragmaticus* 'that the generality for a long time, especially the most generous royalists, could not believe that that intelligence could possibly be written by the same hand'.[29] Like *Pragmaticus* before it, it was the leading newsbook of its time. Except for a brief gap in 1659, Nedham would remain its editor for nearly ten years. He produced it for the Rump – the remnant of the Long Parliament left behind by Pride's Purge in December 1648, when the army removed from the Commons the majority opposed to the trial of the king. He gave support to Cromwell's forcible expulsion of the Rump in April 1653; to his summoning of the nominated assembly, 'Barebone's Parliament', in July; and to the further military coup of December, which put an end to Barebone's and raised Cromwell to the new office of Lord Protector. In each case he looked back in denigration on the regime which the present one had supplanted. He did the same, brutally, in May 1659, when the protectorate, the government he had served for five and a half years, was replaced by the restored Rump. Thereafter he manœuvered his way through the ensuing succession of coups and reversals to retain his post until a month or two before the Restoration.

In 1652 Nedham observed that 'in our late wars ... the pen militant hath had as sharp encounters as the sword, and borne away as many trophies'. For while the sword may subdue men 'by force', 'the pen it is' which prevails by 'reason' and which 'manifests the right of things; and when it is once cleared, it gives spurs to resolution, because men are never raised to so high a pitch of action as when they are persuaded that they engage in a righteous cause'.[30] If so, his pen merits a large place in histories of the period. Other political writers of the time made spectacular impacts, but none sustained so broad an appeal for so long. 'There is not now so much as a young apprentice that keeps shop', proclaimed *Britanicus* in 1644, 'or a labourer that holds the plough, not one from the city to the country', whom the newsbook has not taught to see through the 'lying' and 'juggling' of royalist polemic. 'I have got the success I aimed at, the un-cheating, the un-deluding, the un-masquing, the un-covering, the un-Oxfording, the un-bishoping, and I hope the un-Common Prayering, of the kingdom

29. Wood, *Athenae Oxonienses*, iii. 1181–2.
30. John Selden, *Of the Dominion of the Seas*, ed. and trans. Nedham (London, 1652), ep. ded.

too.'[31] Those were rhetorical and exaggerated claims, but pardonably so. Even its enemies allowed that *Britanicus* had had 'reasonable success among the empty vulgar'.[32]

They also acknowledged the impact of *Mercurius Politicus*. Printed on sixteen small pages, it ran to about 5,000 words a week. It was, conceded its adversaries, 'the Goliah of the Philistines ... whose pen was in comparison with others a weaver's beam. 'Tis incredible what influence' it 'had upon numbers of inconsiderable persons', 'such who have a strange presumption that all must be true that is in print.'[33] Nedham, it was allowed, was 'transcendently gifted in opprobrious and treasonable droll'. 'Droll' had hitherto been the method of Cavalier newsbooks. The newsbooks that had operated under the control of the Commonwealth were concerned, not to amuse their readership, but to anaesthetize it. 'To have no news is good news', declared an early issue of one of them; 'it is a symptom of a placid and quiet state of affairs.'[34] Five months before the founding of *Politicus*, a correspondent remarked that the government newsbooks had 'grown so dull of late', and that they dealt so 'timorously' with 'public concernments ... that they hardly deserve the expense of so much time as to read them'.[35] The Commonwealth, faced with an overwhelmingly hostile public, was fearful of provoking it. Yet Nedham was sure that the battle of the pen, no less than that of the sword, must be fought and won. To win it, he told his new employers, they must cater to public taste. If it is to be 'cried up', *Politicus* must be 'written in a jocular way', because 'fancy ... ever sways the sceptre in vulgar judgement, much more than reason', and because 'truths which the multitude regard not in a serious dress' will only 'undeceive the people' if they are 'represented in pleasing popular airs' and so 'make music to the common sense'.[36] Normally he used the word 'fancy', or 'fantasy', as a term of reproach. His Roundhead writing often employed it to indicate the escapism and self-delusion of royalism.[37] Yet in *Politicus* he adopted royalist methods.

For the 'extreme' difference that Wood noticed between *Politicus* and *Pragmaticus* was one of political doctrine, not of literary technique.

31. *Mercurius Britanicus*, 30 Sept. 1644, 399.
32. *The Spie*, 20 Feb. 1644, 32.
33. Wood, *Athenae Oxonienses*, iii. 1182.
34. *A Briefe Relation*, 9 Oct. 1649, p. 9.
35. BL, Loan 331 (Northumberland MS 552, Firtzjames letter book), fo. 23^{v}: newsletter, 12 Jan. 1650.
36. French, ii. 311.
37. On that literary theme see Timothy Raylor, *Cavaliers, Clubs, and Literary Culture: Sir John Mennes, James Smith, and the Order of the Fancy* (Newark, NJ, 1977).

(1)

Numb. 1.

Mercurius Politicus.

Compriſing the Summ of all Intelligence, with the Affairs, and Deſigns now on foot, in the three Nations of *England Ireland*, and *Scotland*.

In defence of the Common-wealth, and for Information of the People.

——— *Ita vertere Seria Ludo.* {Hor. de Ar. Poet.

From *Thurſday*, June 6. to *Thurſday*, June 13. 1650.

HY Should not the *Common-wealth* have a *Fool*, as well as the *King* had? 'Tis a point of *State*, and if the old *Court*-humors ſhould return in this new Form, 'twere the ready Road to Preferment, and a *Ladies* Chamber. But you'll ſay, I am out of faſhion, becauſe I make neither *Rimes* nor *Faces*, for *Fidlers* pay, like the *Royal Mercuries*; Yet you ſhall know I have authority enough to create a faſhion of my own., and make all the world to follow the humor. Beſides, any faſhion will fit, being now bound beyond *Berwick*, to ſtrike in with *Bread and Cheeſe*, and the *Clouted Commiſſioners*, that are to welcome his *Scottiſh* Majeſty home to the *Stool of Repentance*. For, the truth is, they ſay, he is coming (with better luck than his *Father*;) only, he lingers a little to learn to catch *Mackerel*, or ſome other *odd fiſh* which he hath to *frie* upon his Landing.

A In

Figure 2. *Mercurius Politicus*: the first page of the opening issue

'Why should not the Commonwealth', asked *Politicus* in the first words of its opening issue, 'have a fool, as well as the king had?' The pages that launched the royalist *Pragmaticus* in 1647 had announced its commitment to 'wit' and had scorned the Roundheads' incapacity for it. Nedham's earlier deployment of the same commodity, in the Roundhead *Britanicus*, had earned the scorn of Cavaliers, who declared 'wit in a Roundhead' to be a contradiction in terms.[38] Yet as a tool of propaganda it worked then, and in *Politicus* it worked again in the more extravagant and confident form that he had now developed while editing *Pragmaticus*. Admittedly Nedham did not write ballads or popular satirical rhyme for *Politicus*, but its early prose was, in essence and despite some superficial differences, the prose of *Pragmaticus* revived. His method is the more surprising in that, in the months when *Politicus* was conceived and founded, the official Puritanism of the revolution was at its most severe. Fierce measures were passed against sexual misconduct, and steps were taken against frivolity and ostentation of dress.[39] What he called the 'satires' of the early issues of the newsbook seem to have caused offence within the new Puritan establishment.[40] They were soon modified and were eventually eliminated. Yet through the years 1650–2, the time when the newsbook plays its main part in our story, its wit and sparkle were essential instruments of persuasion.

Non-Puritan in its literary properties, *Politicus* advanced non-Puritan arguments. In revolutions, especially in their desperate moments, the claims of necessity can take precedence over those of ideological consistency. The MPs who governed England in 1650 were desperate men. They had been left in power by the military revolution of 1648–9 that had brought the execution of the king and the abolition of monarchy and the House of Lords. But on what grounds could they demand the obedience of the nation? They, or rather the more committed of them, believed themselves to have liberated England from political and spiritual tyranny. Yet the persuasive power of that claim seemed narrow if not exhausted. In May 1650 Nedham's *The Case of the Commonwealth*, which would soon be serialized in *Politicus*, adopted a different approach. His principal argument was not the

38. *Britanicus Vapulans* (1643), 3.
39. Keith Thomas, 'The Puritans and Adultery', in Donald Pennington and Keith Thomas, eds., *Puritans and Revolutionaries* (Oxford, 1978), 257–82; Blair Worden, *The Rump Parliament 1648–1653* (Cambridge, 1977 edn.), 233–4; *idem*, 'Cromwellian Oxford', in Nicholas Tyacke, ed., *The History of the University of Oxford*, iv: *Seventeenth-Century Oxford* (Oxford, 1997), 756.
40. *MP* 5 Sept. 1650, 193; 12 Sept. 1650, 209; cf. 11 July 1650, 69.

integrity or the godliness of the new order, or the merits of republican rule, but a premiss which had been worked out by Thomas Hobbes: that subjects are obliged to obey any rulers, virtuous or vicious, who command the use of force. 'The power of the sword', explained Nedham, 'is, and ever hath been, the foundation of all titles to government.'[41] What counts – at least after a civil war, when the old constitution has broken down and victory has given rights to the conqueror – is not lawful or *de iure* authority but sovereignty *de facto*. Nedham was not the first writer to deploy that thesis for the Commonwealth,[42] but he brought a new vigour and incisiveness to it.

Yet even as he spelled it out, he had other arguments in hand. His final chapter, 'A discourse of the excellency of a free state', moved beyond Hobbesian arguments to republican ones. So long as the defeat of the royalists remained uncertain, Nedham did not develop the reasoning of that chapter in his newsbook. He did so immediately after the crushing of the king's cause at the Battle of Worcester in September 1651. Now he argued, not for subordination to whatever government was in power, but for the principles which lay, or ought to lie, behind the particular form of government in power now: principles which, once identified and wholeheartedly pursued, could give the republic the ideological confidence it lacked. From September 1651 to August 1652 *Politicus* ran a series of editorials to teach the English, who had been kept 'ignorant of true liberty', to 'understand what true commonweal-principles' – republican principles – 'are'.[43]

Like his arguments from the rights of conquest, Nedham's republican editorials departed from the preoccupations of Puritanism, which looked to godliness to stabilize the land. They broke, too, with the native traditions of English political thought, which had debated the location of powers within the ancient constitution of King, Lords, and Commons. Nedham cast the ancient constitution aside and urged his countrymen to look abroad for instruction in political architecture and to build afresh. His editorials followed the methods, and repeated or adapted many of the arguments, of the *Discourses* of Niccolò Machiavelli. Each editorial announced, as

41. *Case*, pt. i, ch. 2.
42. John M. Wallace, *Destiny his Choice: The Loyalism of Andrew Marvell* (Cambridge, 1968), ch. 1; Quentin Skinner, 'Conquest and Consent: Thomas Hobbes and the Engagement Controversy', in G. E. Aylmer, ed., *The Interregnum: The Quest for Settlement, 1646–1660* (Basingstoke, 1972), 99–120.
43. *MP* 11 Mar. 1652, 1457; 15 July 1652, 1721.

had each chapter of the *Discourses*, a general historical law, deduced from 'reason' and illustrated by an impressive range of historical 'example', which Nedham applied, with brisk intellectual opportunism, to England's present conditions.[44] Like Machiavelli, Nedham found his leading evidence in the history of ancient Rome. But his mind travelled well beyond it, to traverse a wide range of classical, medieval, and recent history. From his historical surveys he drew a radical conclusion. In 1649 England had been declared 'a Commonwealth and free state'. That change, he warned, had been dangerously superficial and incomplete. The monarchical interest, or what he liked to call 'grandee-government', was not confined to the institution of monarchy. The 'poor people' of Rome, he reminded the English, 'were told that they had a free state. And why? Because (forsooth) they had no king.'[45] It was not enough. He wanted England to be a 'state really free', to be a truly 'free republic', to have 'the form of a real republic'.[46] To that end it must acquire the republican values, and learn from the forms of republican rule, that history displayed. If only it did so, its citizens would find that freedom 'edges men's spirits with an active emulation, and raiseth them to a lofty pitch of design and action'; that their minds 'are more inflamed with the love of glory and virtue'.[47] That Italianate vision of republican health and vitality runs through his editorials of 1651–2.

★★

Publication was not Nedham's only source of income. He wrote private newsletters to politicians, Cavalier and Roundhead, and thus had access to the cyphers of his correspondents, a useful bargaining weapon, it was alleged, during his changes of side.[48] Under the protectorate he performed miscellaneous functions for Cromwell's secretary of state, John Thurloe. He acted as a government informer. He wrote or translated, as Milton and, from 1657, Marvell did, documents for the conduct of foreign policy. He orchestrated the submission of petitions from the regions in support

44. The editorials, which were in effect brief essays, can be seen as a pioneering instance of a genre of political commentary that would provide other examples in the chapters of Algernon Sidney's *Discourses concerning Government* and, in the eighteenth century, in *Cato's Letters*.
45. *MP* 30 Oct. 1651, 1158.
46. Ibid. 19 Feb. 1652, 1412; 25 Mar. 1652, 1475; 24 June 1652, 1677.
47. Ibid. 1 Jan. 1652, 1303–4; *Case*, 117; cf. *MP* 25 Sept. 1651, 1079.
48. John Cleveland, *The Character of Mercurius Politicus* (1650), 5.

of the regime.[49] But print was his principal medium. In the 1650s it would bring him something like wealth. Yet Nedham, the most successful of journalists, longed to be more than a journalist. He yearned for the intellectual recognition that, as he acknowledged, will never be granted to the ephemeral writer, for 'serious truth' is 'not regarded in a pamphlet', 'the very name whereof is enough to raise a prejudice upon any other notions, how reasonable soever they be'.[50] No one made better-judged use of the discipline and constraints of the word limit. Yet he baulked at them. Repeatedly his writings proclaim how large is the 'store of observations' with which he could confirm his arguments, how great a 'cloud of witnesses' he could summon, 'how many' or 'innumerable' are 'the instances I could collect elsewhere', how readily and fittingly they might 'swell into a volume', how many 'pains' he has taken to accumulate his material, how much has had to be omitted 'for brevity sake'.[51] While one side of him vaunted the width of his audience, another disdained his obligation to 'tickle and charm the more vulgar fancies, who little regard truth in a grave and serious garb'.[52] In 1656 the republican editorials of *Politicus* were republished as a treatise, *The Excellencie of a Free State*, that would be influentially reprinted in the eighteenth century. *The Case of the Commonwealth* has had a later readership too. In the versions of those works that appeared in editorials of *Politicus*, Nedham omitted most of the learned allusions. Yet the arguments, and most of the text, were essentially the same. His newsbooks addressed a sophisticated as well as a wide audience. He exploited the convention that allowed writers to make, in a single breath, both an esoteric point, which a minority of readers would grasp, and an exoteric one, which would have a common appeal. Though a less profound or original figure than the two best-known political analysts of the period, Hobbes and James Harrington, he merits a high place in the second rank. His gifts were those of a swift and penetrating synthesizer, who spots the inchoate trends and unarticulated possibilities of current debate and gives them shape and direction.

49. *A True Catalogue, or, an Account of the Several Places … where … Richard Cromwell was Proclaimed* (1659), 53–4, 75–6; BL, Loan 331: Northumberland MS 552, Fitjames to Nedham, 23 Sept. 1657, 16 Oct. 1658; Nedham, *Interest will not Lie*, 15. Cf. (e.g.) *MP* 22 Aug. 1650, 175, and the addresses published in *Politicus* in the autumn of 1658.

50. *Mercurius Britanicus*, 1 Dec. 1645, 952.

51. Worden, '"Wit in a Roundhead"', 303, and the sources cited there; and, for the 'cloud of witnesses' (with which compare below, p. 207), Nedham, *Certain Considerations Tendered*, 11.

52. *Mercurius Pragmaticus*, 4 Apr. 1648, 1.

To rivals and enemies he was 'that speckled chameleon', 'that state porter, that *venalis anima*, that mercenary soul'.[53] Yet there were limits to his pliability. Within the constraints of his employment he found scope for a degree of independence of expression, and for the daring exercise of it, that are easily missed. Towards the end of the first civil war, *Britanicus*, with scathing merriment, depicted Charles I as a tyrant stained by the blood of his subjects. That tactic outraged the more moderate parliamentarians, who saw themselves as friends to the ancient constitution and told themselves that they were fighting to rescue the king from the influence of his evil advisers. He even committed what were at that stage the political blasphemies of indicating the need to depose him and of hinting, albeit faintly, at the desirability of republican rule. The results were the suspension and then the closure of the newsbook, and the imprisonment of its printer and licenser and then of Nedham himself. 'I confess I have overshot myself,' he lightly acknowledged in a public apology for an infamous attack on the king in August 1645.[54] The apology apologized for remarkably little, and he was soon back on the attack. In the 1650s he made brinkmanship a literary art. *Mercurius Politicus*, which for the benefit of its exoteric audience proclaimed the superiority of republican over Stuart rule, informed its esoteric one of the threats to republican virtue from within the government that Nedham served. Under the protectorate, when *Politicus* lost some of its sense of adventure, he would find an alternative outlet for criticism of the regime that employed him.

His political masters were never united. Most of his departures from party lines can be surmised to have had highly placed supporters and protectors.[55] Yet that is an insufficient explanation of his deviations from orthodoxy. Sometimes he wrote things that few powerful men can have wished to hear, and that risked offending men whose power was greater. Nedham was a congenital risk-taker. The risks were enhanced by his liking for attention and publicity. Even his boldest pamphlets, though published anonymously, were strewn with indications of his authorship. In March

53. *The Spie*, 20 Feb. 1644, 32; *A Letter of Addresses to the Protector occasioned by Mr. Needhams reply to Mr. Goodwins Book* (n.d. [1657]), 2.

54. *Mercurius Britanicus his Apologie* (1645), 2.

55. That aspect of his career in the 1640s is explored by Jason Peacey, 'The Struggle for *Mercurius Britanicus*: Factional Politics and the Parliamentarian Press', *Huntington Library Quarterly*, 68 (2005), 517–43 (and see *idem*, 'The Management of Civil War Newspapers', *The Seventeenth Century* 21 (2006), 99–127); and by Joyce Macadam, '"Mercurius Britanicus": Journalism and Politics in the English Civil War' (Sussex University D. Phil. thesis, 2005).

1660, when he wrote a clever anonymous pamphlet certain to provoke royalists who were on the verge of reclaiming power and who were ready to call for the death sentence on him, he apparently could not refrain from boasting of his authorship.[56] He survived in his various guises of the Puritan Revolution because his employers needed him, and because they were obliged to grant him leeway in order to keep him on their side. When, in 1647, he worked his way across to the king's party, the motto – taken from the royal house of Scotland – of his new royalist newsbook proclaimed a truth which the parliamentarians who had dismissed and imprisoned him the previous year were now taught with a vengeance: 'Nemo me impune lacessit ('no one attacks me with impunity'). In 1659 he was sacked again, the victim now of the wave of resentment with which the restored Rump purged supporters of the protectorate. Yet three months later he was back at the desk of *Politicus*, even though his reappointment 'stinks in the nostrils of God and his faithful people'.[57]

From time to time Nedham's employers indicated to him their dissatisfaction with his reporting or his commentaries. By giving his audience jocular intimations of that displeasure, he contrived to hint at the curbs on his freedom and to invite his more discerning readers to bear them in mind. It was one of the devices by which, amid all his betrayals, he preserved an individuality, even a consistency, of voice: a quality for which, as his writings prove, sincerity is no indispensable qualification, and of which, in his case, insincerity was an innate component. Nedham is the first of a series of seventeenth-century writers – Henry Stubbe in the Restoration and John Toland after the Revolution of 1688 are his obvious successors – who, amid the spread of mass print and the simultaneous endurance of political instability, find a sustained identity in the adoption of varying postures. Amid the polarizations of the Puritan Revolution, and the conflicting claims of oath and allegiance that were made by the groups that successively dominated it, Nedham discovered that a writer on temporary and provisional terms with the beliefs he professes may be a more intelligent and persuasive commentator than the inflexible partisan. The ideals and hatreds of the revolution created some rigid postures and numb slogans. Like other writers of the time he toyed with them, found room between or around them, and thought beyond them. Born too late

56. John Evelyn ['N.P.'], *A Reply to that Malicious Letter* (1660).
57. *True Catalogue*, p. 14.

to share the political emotions of the 1620s, that scarring and polarizing decade,[58] he discovered, as did others of his age-group, that the party lines of the 1640s did not yield any single perception of the world to which he could be faithful.

Did he have consistent convictions of any kind? If so he was untrue to them. Yet there are suggestive patterns. His works of political theory were all produced on the Roundhead side. When he addressed constitutional issues in his royalist – or, late in life, his proto-Tory – publications, he argued for limited, regulated monarchy, never for absolute or divine-right kingship. When he took risks in the Roundhead cause, it was always for the radical cause: for the war party in the first civil war, then for the regicides and for the uncompromising republicans of the 1650s. The radicalism was social as well as political. His alignment with the Levellers in the mid-1640s was followed, in his writing for the Commonwealth in the early 1650s, by appeals to the rights and interests of 'the people' against aristocratic power. His editorials of that time clothed Leveller thinking in arguments drawn from the history of classical antiquity. While as scornful as anyone of 'the rabble', he argued for fundamental constitutional changes that would advance popular rights against 'grandee-government', whether by kings or by nobles. If there was a single political perspective to which he was drawn above others, perhaps it was close to one developed by the republican thinker James Harrington, to whose arguments his own had near parallels. Harrington saw men's pursuit of their interests as the motor of politics, and reasoned that popular government is the form of rule that benefits the interests of the community. Yet the populist dimension of Nedham's thought, under-explored as it has been, has to be another story, for it was not what brought him together with Milton or Marvell.

The party for which he never wrote were the Presbyterians, who wished to crush the Cromwellian army and the liberty of conscience which it sheltered. For Presbyterianism, that 'malign ulcer',[59] that 'monstrous babe',[60] he reserved a venom that even his most savage attacks on royalism in his Roundhead prose, and on Independents and sectaries and regicides in his Cavalier writing, never quite match.[61] When he wrote for the king in 1647, he looked for the monarch's restoration at the hands, not of the

58. Hugh Trevor-Roper, *Religion, The Reformation and Social Change* (Basingstoke, 1967), 228–9.
59. Nedham, *Pacquet of Advices*, 71.
60. Nedham, *True Character*, 1–2.
61. Worden, '"Wit in a Roundhead"', 311, and the sources there cited.

parliament which the Presbyterians dominated, but of the new model army, which, he knew, would make liberty of conscience, and the thwarting of Presbyterianism, preconditions of Charles's return. If there is a thread of consistency in Nedham's political behaviour from the end of the civil war to the Restoration, it lies in his fear of a Presbyterian ascendancy and his willingness to give support to the Presbyterians' enemies.

★★

Milton and Marvell, too, detested Presbyterian intolerance, and their political conduct was swayed by their hatred of it. All three men were enemies of clerical and doctrinal bigotry. Yet so were many others. To discover the distinctive place of Nedham in the lives of the other two writers, we shall have to look for further common ground. In the case of Nedham and Milton, we shall mostly be setting the prose of the one writer against that of the other. In the case of Nedham and Marvell, we shall mostly compare prose written by the first with verse by the second, for the prose that Marvell is known to have composed lies beyond our guiding chronological range. There is another contrast, which explains the sequence of the chapters immediately ahead. Apart from the testimony to his friendship with Milton, Marvell's companionship before and during the Interregnum has left virtually no documentary witness. The interaction of Marvell and Nedham has left no evidence outside their writings, and has to be inferred from inside them. For the relationship of Milton and Nedham there is evidence of other kinds. It is by seeing something of their partnership that we can best enter the literary and political worlds which they, and Marvell, shared.

2

Milton and Nedham

Milton's friendships can be hard to imagine. In his own accounts of himself he yearned for friendship and treasured it when he found it. True friendship, he maintained, survives when tested. It extends beyond conventional courtesies to Platonic unions of souls. His early biographers tell us of the closeness or 'greatness' or 'intimacy' of his friendships with Charles Diodati, with the wits of the Florentine academies, with Cyriack Skinner and Andrew Marvell and Edward Lawrence in England. Yet the Milton we meet in his writing seems a proudly solitary figure, whose sense both of tragedy and of triumph merges with the pride and the solitude. The writer who acknowledges that 'poets generally put something like their own opinions into the mouths of their best characters'[1] has heroes – Abdiel, Samson, Christ – whose strength seems inseparable from their loneliness. When, in *Areopagitica*, he commends the debate of religious truth among his fellow Londoners, he gives a visual image, not to collective discussion in congregations or homes or taverns, but to solitary readers, 'sitting by their studious lamps, musing, searching'.[2] He cannot bring his own friendships to life on the page, where they remain imprisoned within the conventions he wants them to transcend. His words seem witnesses less to intimacy than to the poet's sense of himself. 'Lycidas', which is ostensibly about the death of Edward King, is famously more about its author than its subject. When, in 'Mansus', Milton sighs for a friendship akin to that which had bound his friend John Baptisto Manso to the poet Torquato Tasso, it is in the hope that Milton himself, like Tasso, will become, in an old age ripe with poetic achievement, the centre of a friend's attention. In his prose, acting within a literary convention, Milton addresses *Of Reformation* 'to a friend' in 1641, and writes the political tract *A Letter to a Friend* in 1659. The

1. *CW* vii. 327. 2. *CP* ii. 554.

Gul. Faithorne ad Vivum Delin. et Sculpsit.
Ioannis Miltoni Effigies Ætat: 62.
1670.

Figure 3. John Milton late in life

friends, though unidentifiable, apparently existed,[3] but they take on no personality.

So when, late in the seventeenth century, Anthony Wood tells us that Marchamont Nedham was 'a great crony of Milton', we may at first be sceptical.[4] Yet we have it on the authority of Milton's nephew Edward Phillips that Nedham, together with Marvell, Lawrence, and Skinner, was among the 'particular friends' who, 'all the time' of Milton's 'abode' in Petty France – that is, from the end of 1651 to the Restoration – 'frequently visited' the poet.[5] Nedham himself lived nearby, in Westminster Churchyard. Like the others in Phillips's list, he was younger than Milton, who had been born twelve years before him, in 1608. As the merest glance at their careers in the 1650s will suggest, their contact was not merely social. In 1650–1 they wrote the principal apologias for the Commonwealth: Nedham's *The Case of the Commonwealth*, which was addressed to an English-speaking audience, and Milton's Latin work *Pro Populo Anglicano Defensio*, which reached beyond it to a Continental one. Just before the publication of *Defensio*, Milton was appointed licenser of *Politicus*, which trumpeted the Continental reception of the tract. Both men responded malleably to the coups of the Interregnum, and served, as few other men of letters and ideas did, the successive regimes of the decade: the Rump, Barebone's, the protectorate, the restored Rump. Under the protectorate they both worked in Thurloe's office – as, from 1657, did Marvell.[6] They wrote the most widely noticed political works of 1654: Milton's *Defensio Secunda* and Nedham's apologia for the protectorate *A True State of the Case of the Commonwealth*. Milton and Nedham were repeatedly linked by their royalist enemies, who in 1660 longed to see them hang together. Two years earlier, on Cromwell's death, they, and Marvell, walked in the protector's funeral procession. So did John Dryden, another member of Thurloe's team, which accommodated – not through any literary inclinations of the regime or of the secretary of state himself – so formidable an array of poetic talent.[7]

Friendships can be attractions of opposites, and in Milton and Nedham there were doubtless many opposites to attract. Nedham's unblushing

3. *CW* viii. 129; *CP* vii. 324.
4. Darbishire, 44.
5. Ibid. 74.
6. That Nedham worked in 'Mr Secretary's office' is confirmed by his letters in BL, Loan 331: Northumberland MS 552. See too NA, SP25/78: 22 June 1658, item 21.
7. At some point before 1662 Dryden came to know Marvell's unpublished 'An Horatian Ode': *AMC* 68.

acknowledgements of his 'tergiversations' contrast with Milton's massive and irreducible sense of his own constancy. Milton's philosophy calls on men to strive towards truth through inevitable error. Yet he never wants us to glimpse his own changes of mind. Sincerity, the last characteristic we would associate with Nedham, was a basic claim of Milton's voice. We cannot imagine Milton invoking, with Nedham, the principles of Hobbes, or recommending the identification of men's interests as the road to political health. We cannot see him dismissing the claims of the individual conscience, which Nedham is capable of calling either a 'pretence'[8] or 'nothing else but a man's settled judgement and resolution';[9] or imagine him candidly acknowledging, with Nedham, the Commonwealth's need to win over 'the worldling', who represents 'the greater part of the world' and is 'led more by appetites of convenience and commodity than the dictates of conscience'.[10] Nedham's writing, for its part, has none of the spiritual dimension of Milton's, none of his Olympian claim to a divinely appointed mission, none of his insistence on inner ethical striving. Though Nedham, a supreme imitator, could put on a Puritan face, more sense of personality is carried by his jaunty satirical ballads. If he ever craved, with Milton, a Platonic union of souls, or if he ever supposed, with Milton, that a poet 'ought himself to be a true poem',[11] then there is nothing in his own writing to hint at those aspirations. Milton, and his early biographers, stress his chastity and abstinence, his temperance and frugality. The surviving correspondence of and about Nedham testifies to a bibulous lifestyle and to some epic nights on the town.[12] The two writers are divided, too, in their conceptions of their audiences. Nedham addressed 'the common people of this kingdom', whom the truth he tells 'most concerns'. Because they 'cannot attend to read chronicles', they should be given courses in popularized political wisdom, and be provided with translations of works 'long locked up' in Latin.[13] Milton hoped that an edition of one of his divorce tracts that was to be published in the Netherlands would appear in Latin rather than English, 'because I know by experience with these books how the common herd is wont to receive uncommon opinions'.[14]

8. *Case*, 28; *MP*, 26 June 1651, 881. 9. *MP*, 26 Oct. 1650, p. 263. 10. *Case*, 4.
11. *CP* i. 890.
12. See, as well as the correspondence in D. Gardiner, ed., *Oxinden and Peyton Letters*, BL, Add. MS 28001, fo. 141.
13. *A Cat May Look upon a King* (1652), 32–3; Selden, *Of the Dominion of the Seas*, ep. ded.
14. *CP* iv. 871–2; cf. *CW* viii. 115.

How then were they friends? We must allow something, perhaps much, for Nedham's gifts of society. Anthony Wood, who called him 'a poet', 'humanitarian' – that is, a devotee of classical languages and literature – 'and born droll', thought of him and Milton alike as men of culture and civility, whom only perverted principles kept from the natural place of cultivated men, on the king's side. Milton's own capacity for both 'courteous' and 'courtly' demeanour is well attested.[15] We need not concur with Wood's political inference to sense the tone of Milton's and Nedham's conversation. The measured verve of Nedham's prose and verse, and the light management of his learning, combine to suggest an urbanity of mind, and a composure of temperament, that he somehow squared with his leaps of allegiance. He sounds a companionable and convivial man.

Milton was a more companionable and convivial figure than we might sometimes guess from his prose. John Aubrey describes him as 'of a very cheerful humour', and adds that he was 'extreme pleasant in his conversation, and at dinner, supper, etc.: but satirical'; 'he would be cheerful even in his gout-fits, and sing'. His disciple Cyriack Skinner records that he had 'naturally a sharp wit', while Anthony Wood calls him 'of a very sharp, biting and satirical wit'.[16] Milton himself remembers that as a young man he hoped to find companionship in one of the Inns of Court. But he does not disclose what we learn from his nephew Edward Phillips, that in or around 1641, the time when he wrote his anti-episcopal tracts, his course of 'hard study and spare diet' was interrupted 'once in three weeks or a month', when 'he would drop into the society of some young sparks of his acquaintance, the chief whereof were Mr. Alphry and Mr. Miller, two gentlemen of Gray's Inn, the beaus of those times', with whom he liked 'now and then to keep a gaudy-day'. In or after middle age, Milton would reflect that 'jollity of mind' is 'excusable in a youth'.[17] Yet at the time of the gaudy-days (regular festivals of the inns) he was already aged around 32, and so was no young spark himself. His prose at that time had higher things than gaudy-days in view. It was then that he anticipated the destruction of 'the great whore' of Antichrist; then that he prepared, 'amidst

15. Leo Miller, *John Milton and the Oldenburg Safeguard* (New York, 1985), 128; French, iii. 59; *CP* iv. 283.

16. Darbishire, 5–6, 29, 39. For Skinner's authorship of the anonymous life quoted here see Peter Beal, *Index of English Literary Manuscripts*, 2 vols. (London and New York, 1987–93), ii. 85–6.

17. Darbishire, 62; *CP* v. 290. On Milton's sociability see also Stephen B. Dobranski, *Milton, Authorship, and the Book Trade* (Cambridge, 1999), 62–81.

the hymns and Hallelujahs of saints', to be 'heard offering at high strains in new and lofty measures to sing and celebrate' God's 'divine mercies and marvellous judgements on this land'; then that he waited for the Second Coming of 'the eternal and shortly expected king'.[18] Phillips's brief and dissonant juxtaposition of Milton's solitary and frugal habits with a search for young, light-hearted company suggests a dimension of the poet's life that his reverential biographer cannot square with Milton's austere image of himself, and to which a more candid recorder would perhaps have given more space. We are left to guess whether the young sparks at Gray's Inn included Nedham, whose employment there began in 1641. We can only guess, too, whether at that time either writer came across Andrew Marvell, who may have had connections at Gray's Inn in the early 1640s.[19]

There was a colourfully unconventional streak to Nedham, the sporter of a striking periwig and, reportedly, of ear-rings.[20] It may be that his own high merriment offered him, among other uses, ways of coping with the extremities of events, with his sharp turns on fortune's wheel, even perhaps with the solemnities and absurdities of the clashes of ideology which he was hired to enter. It is in his royalist stage, in the late 1640s, when laughter and drink were the defiant responses of Cavaliers to the disasters of their cause, that we see most of his taste for them. Yet in his writings, as he insisted, it was to 'a purpose' that he was 'pleasant' and liked to 'jest'.[21] He claimed for the 'satire' and 'wit' of his Roundhead prose the same high moral purpose that Milton asserted for the satire of his own pamphlets. The anti-episcopal tracts which Milton wrote around the time when he kept his gaudy-days at Gray's Inn insist on the 'force of teaching there is sometimes in laughter', in 'grim laughter'. There is an irony in watching the young Milton gunning for that leading defender of episcopacy, the aged bishop Joseph Hall, who in his own youth, in the service of 'truth and holy rage', had helped to lead the innovative satirical movement of late Elizabethan England.[22] For Milton himself, as his anti-episcopal tracts explain, had turned to satire's historic function of correction. Thus 'a satire, as it was born out of a tragedy, so ought to resemble his parentage, to strike

18. *CP* i. 615–16.
19. *AMC* 29. Marvell certainly acquired, at some point, a skill in legal matters: ibid. 132, 177–83.
20. The periwig: Cleveland, *Character of Mercurius Politicus* (1650), 2; *idem*, *The Second Character of Mercurius Politicus* (1650), 2 (cf. D. Gardiner, ed., *Oxinden and Peyton Letters*, 160); the ear-rings: *ODNB*.
21. Worden, '"Wit in a Roundhead"', 307.
22. Richard A. McCabe, *Joseph Hall: A Study in Satire and Meditation* (Oxford, 1982).

high, and adventure dangerously at the most eminent vices among the greatest person'. Milton therefore 'cannot be taxed of levity or insolence: for even this vein of laughing (as I could produce out of grave authors) hath oft-times a strong and sinewy force in teaching and confuting'.[23] 'Eliah mocked the false prophets', adds Milton, 'to teach and instruct the poor misled people.'[24]

Milton's 'grave authors' were Nedham's warrant too. Evidently following Milton's lead, he invoked the model of Eliah (or Elijah) to warrant his own forays into satire in *Britanicus*, which were likewise conducted for the benefit of the poor misled people. He 'bait[ed' the news reports of *Britanicus* 'with some sport', for 'when all the serious treatises would not draw people off from their good liking of the king's ways, I thought it the best to jeer them out of it, not wanting a warrant from the Word itself, as in the case both of Eliah and others'. Both writers appealed to the Lucianic tradition of *joco-serio*, which stands or moves 'between jest and earnest', and where, as Nedham explains, 'in the midst of jest' an author can be 'much in earnest'.[25] Milton's principal authority for the earnest function of laughter was Horace, who, in the words of the translations from his *Satires* which Milton made in justifying his own attacks on prelacy, had laughed 'to teach the truth', for 'Jesting decides great things | Stronglier, and better oft than earnest can.'[26] *Politicus* carried in its regular heading Horace's words in *de Ars Poetica*: 'ita vertere seria ludo' ('thus to turn seriousness into play'). The same newsbook used satire to 'make bold with one of the prophets to jerk the Pharisees of our times', and defended Milton's *Defensio* from readers who 'may find fault with the personal jerks therein';[27] in 1642 Milton himself had commended his own use of 'contempt and jerk' to the end of 'laughter and reproof'.[28] 'A cleanly sharp satire', declared *Politicus*, is the least the Commonwealth's enemies deserve, 'for even the Prophets themselves wrote more bitterly against the hypocrites of their times than ever I did against the present.'[29]

23. *CP* i. 663–4, 903, 916. See also John K. Hale, 'Milton and the Rationale of Insulting', in Stephen Dobranski and John P. Rumrich, eds., *Milton and Heresy* (Cambridge, 1998), 159–75.
24. Ibid. 903.
25. *Mercurius Pragmaticus*, 4 Apr. 1648, 1–2; *CP* i. 907. Cf. Milton's adaptation of his source in *CP* v. 250 and n. Milton's and Nedham's stance was not novel: see Andrew McRae, *Literature, Satire and the Early Stuart State* (Cambridge, 2004), 193.
26. *CP* i. 903–4.
27. *MP*, 5 Sept. 1650, 193; 17 Apr. 1651, 719.
28. *CP* i. 905.
29. *MP*, 29 Aug. 1650, 192.

In *Defensio Secunda* in 1654, as in his anti-episcopal writing earlier, Milton felt his own need to anticipate the charge of frivolity in his methods of controversy. Next year, in *Pro Se Defensio*, he again had recourse to 'the practice of gravest authors' to justify his satirical 'vehemence' in using words 'naked and plain, indignantly uttered'. He vindicated the relentless 'raillery' of his abusive epithets, to which his Latin has given, for modern readers, a decent obscurity, by appeals to a range of biblical, classical, patristic, and Renaissance precedents.[30] He did not go as far as his nephew John Phillips, Edward's brother, who, in a contribution, which was supervised by Milton, to the controversy to which *Pro Se Defensio* belonged, relished exchanges about bottoms and shitting and farting and pissing. But penises Milton treats as fair literary game.[31] The dextrous wit of his personal attacks could indeed claim distinguished literary precedents, but their bawdry assorts ill with the run of Puritan publication. They are closer in spirit (however distant from it in their targets) to royalist burlesque. They resemble, too, the long poem in which, nine days after the publication of Milton's *Pro Se Defensio*, John Phillips would issue what has been called a 'blanket condemnation of Puritanism ... in the vein of royalist satire'.[32] Milton, however, acknowledged no contradiction. He wrote, he was certain, nothing contrary to what 'was right, and true, and pleasing to God'.[33] Alexander More, the victim of the 'defences' of 1654 and 1655, whom Milton mistakenly took to have been the author of a virulent attack on him in 1652, was not his most incisive opponent, but he made some shrewd hits, among them the point that in *Defensio Secunda*, 'which abounds in the pleasantries of dissolute prodigals and in jests from brothels and cookshops, you ... dare to censure the morals of other men and to preach gravely about liberty, about the state, and about the duty of your citizens, as if you were a third Cato who had suddenly dropped from heaven'.[34] A modern editor of *Defensio Secunda* has noticed Milton's taste, in his caricatures of his enemies, for 'sheer fun', his capacity

30. *CW* ix. 109–13. 31. Ibid. 109–11.

32. Lewalski, 333–4. The main target of Phillips's book, *A Satyr against Hypocrites* (1655), was Presbyterianism. The work would be republished in 1661 as *The Religion of the Hypocritical Presbyterians in Meter*, which complemented Nedham's poem of the same year, *The True Character of a Rigid Presbyter*. The purpose and character of *A Satyr against Hypocrites* are interestingly discussed by Nicholas McDowell, 'Family Politics; or How John Phillips Read his Uncle's Satirical Sonnets', forthcoming in *Milton Quarterly*. Phillips's work of 1656, *Sportive Wit*, got him into trouble with the Cromwellian government, which rarely intervened in such cases, but which condemned it as lascivious and profane.

33. *CW* viii. 67. 34. *CP* iv. 1108.

for 'having a very good time' – and his simultaneous, impregnable 'air of moral self-assurance'.[35]

Milton, the reverer of lonely heroes, made a lonely hero of himself, as the 'single-handed' defender, by his 'single efforts' in 'single combat', of English liberty: as the Abdiel of the Puritan Revolution, defiantly and incorruptibly alone.[36] It was a majestic feat of self-representation. As he would have us think, inner divinity and integrity proved fitting vessels for his heavenly muse and were reflected straightforwardly in its productions, nothing impeding the movement of truth or inspiration from his heart or soul to his pen. Yet in his self-praise, no less than in his praise of others, he followed the rules of literature in and after the Renaissance, which idealized those whom it commended. The resulting portrait has proved triumphantly enduring. No major writer has been taken so largely at his own and his disciples' estimation. His tributes to his character are, however, misleadingly selective and uncomplicated. When he entered the world of propaganda in 1649, he accepted the rules of the genre as completely as Nedham did. The stakes were high. His first 'defence' was commissioned after the Commonwealth's agent in the Netherlands, Walter Strickland, had voiced alarm at the Continental impact of the work to which it responds, *Defensio Regia*, the attack on the regicide by Claude de Saumaise, or Salmasius as he was known in international debate.[37] If the Commonwealth were to survive, not only must it equip and deploy a formidable army and navy. The battle of the pen must be waged too, both to persuade the domestic audience which was Nedham's target, and to convert antagonists abroad, where Milton fought it and where an array of kings and princes, to whom the exiled royalists looked for support, had been shocked by the regicide. Readers of Milton's 'defences' are struck by his giant egocentricity. The cause of the English people, which the 'defences' are supposed to defend, becomes subsumed in the battle for his own stature. Yet it was his achievement to merge the personal with the national cause. He dramatized himself as a literary Samson, or a David against Goliath,[38] on whose exploits the fate of God's cause might depend.

35. Ibid. 581–2.
36. *CW* vii. 9, 557; viii. 15 (cf. 111, 255, ix. 3–5, 87; *CP* vii. 420–1). For Abdiel see *Paradise Lost* V. 803 ff., 849–52; VI. 129 ff., 145–7. Other solitary heroes are commended in *Paradise Lost* XI. 700–5, 876; *CP* v. 397–8.
37. NA, SP25/63, pp. 215–6; cf. *CP* v. 586.
38. Cf. *MP*, 20 Feb. 1651, 604; Darbishire, 70.

Even John Thurloe, who as we shall see had every reason to dislike the political message of the 'defences', judged it necessary to stand by Milton's efforts to prove that his anonymous assailant was indeed Alexander More.[39]

The success of propaganda is to be measured by its effect, not by its truth. What kind of 'true poem' was Milton's life in 1649–51, when – albeit with classical practices of oratorical misrepresentation to sanction him – he published miserable libels against the recently executed Charles I, whom he charged, in slippery fashion, with having poisoned his own father[40] (an accusation also brought by Nedham in his Roundhead guise, but repudiated by him in his Cavalier one as a 'slanderous and most shameful insinuation against his majesty'[41]), and with such voluptuous proclivities as fondling the breasts of virgins during theatrical performances?[42] Later, no less preposterously, and amid a barrage of other wilful misrepresentations, he contrived – in the space 'betwixt jest and earnest' which allows an author to take advantage of an imputation without committing himself to its truth – to intimate that Salmasius was a pimp, and that More had begotten bastards and had concealed the offence by infanticide.[43] We shall encounter the doubtless mirthful inventiveness with which Milton worked with Nedham to concoct such charges. But mendaciousness is only part of the story. Propaganda involves choices of material, of angle, of target. Milton was no poodle of the government. Like Nedham he asserted a significant measure of independence of voice. But he embarked without reticence on the game of persuasion. He was, again like Nedham, an able and agile debater,[44] and was never more so than with weak cards in his hand. One of the most perceptive critics of Milton's prose has remarked on 'his tendency, even in writing undertaken on his own behalf, to write with an ear attuned to immediate tactical necessities'.[45] It is a facet of his polemic to which other interpreters have become alert,[46] but which invites wider attention.

39. *CP* iv. 276.

40. Ibid. iii. 438 (cf. ibid. iv. 945–6); *CW* vii. 141, 341–3. For the background to the claim see Hugh Trevor-Roper, *Europe's Physician: The Various Life of Sir Theodore de Mayerne* (London and New Haven, 2006), 279–82.

41. *Mercurius Pragmaticus*, 22 Feb. 1648, 4; *MP*, 12 Sept. 1650, 211 (cf. 22 Aug. 1650, 162; 22 May 1651, 800); *Cat May Look upon a King*, 90.

42. *CW* vii. 237; cf. *CP* iii. 358, 569–70. 43. *CP* iv. 810 n. 44. Ibid. 303 n.

45. Michael Fixler, *Milton and the Kingdoms of God* (London, 1964), 76.

46. The pioneer of this approach was Ernest Sirluck in his Introduction to *CP*, ii. It informs Austin Woolrych's Introduction to *CP* vii. Adroit uses of it also include Thomas N. Corns, 'Milton's *Observations upon the Articles of Peace*: Ireland under English Eyes', in David Loewenstein and James Grantham Turner, eds, *Politics, Poets, and Hermeneutics in*

The same critic observes that the apocalyptic passage at the end of Milton's *Eikonoklastes* in 1649 'has the air of being written after a comparison of Daniel and the Book of Revelation with the latest domestic and foreign news-letters'.[47] In seventeenth-century minds the Bible was the first guide to the understanding of current events. It offered not merely typologies for their interpretation but divinely ordained parallels which pointed observers of them to God's purposes. Would the Puritan Revolution, as Milton initially hoped, prepare the way for the 'shortly expected' Second Coming? Were the English to have the role in the second dispensation, the Gospel, that had been allotted to the Israelites under the first, the Law? Those were questions of everyday impact. So was a great deal more of the apparatus of learning and philosophy which posterity has tugged apart from politics, but which in Milton's mind was inseparable from them. A study of his relations with Nedham, that prominent figure of the world of newsletters, may help us perceive the interaction, in his thinking, of the eternal and the here and now.

If the thought of Milton stooping to collaboration with Nedham requires mental adjustment, an acclimatizing example of it may help us. In his tract of 1659 *Considerations touching the Likeliest Means to Remove Hirelings out of the Church*, which was published in August but seems to have been at least partly written by or in June,[48] Milton welcomed the nation's deliverance from the bondage of the Cromwellian protectorate, and congratulated the Rump on its return to power 'after a short but scandalous night of interruption', which had now yielded to a 'new dawning'.[49] 'Interruption' was the word commonly used by critics of the protectorate to signify the illegality of Cromwell's claim to have dissolved in 1653 an assembly which, by legislation of 1641, could not be disbanded without its own consent.[50] The restoration of the Rump in May 1659 had thus been a return, after the

Milton's Prose (Cambridge, 1990), 123–34; the account of Milton's tract *Of True Religion* by Keith Staveley (*CP* viii. 408–13); and Martin Dzelzainis's Introduction to John Milton, *Political Writings* (Cambridge, 1991).

47. Fixler, *Milton and the Kingdoms of God*, 167. 48. *CP* vii. 84–5. 49. Ibid. 274.

50. See (e.g.) John Streater, *The Continuation of this Session of Parliament Justified* (1659), 12 (cf. its title-page); *idem*, *Secret Reasons of State*, title-page and pp. 2, 3, 20; John Eliot, *The Christian Commonwealth* (1659), title-page; *Cal. SP Dom. 1659–60*, 12, 28, 34, 297, 335, 356; *MP*, 5 Jan. 1660, 996; [Nedham], *The Publick Intelligencer*, 30 Jan. 1660, 1308–9; Norbrook, *Writing the English Republic*, 401, 402; and see S. R. Gardiner, ed., *Constitutional Documents of the Puritan Revolution 1625–1660* (Oxford, repr. 1958), 449; *CP* vii. 86–7. Even Henry Cromwell (*TSP* vii. 784), and even a defender of the coup of April 1653 (*Considerations upon the Late Transactions and Proceedings of the Army* (1659)), were reduced to adopting the term. There have been

interruption, to legality. The point was spelled out by Nedham – his own allegiance to the protectorate now having been ruthlessly disavowed – in August, the month when Milton's tract was published. The coup, Nedham now wrote, had been not a 'dissolution' of the parliament, 'which it could not be', but, 'as now it is called' and 'rightly termed', 'only an interruption of its sitting'.[51]

Critics have been puzzled by Milton's adjective 'short'. Was an interruption of more than six years really a 'short … night'? Yet the distinctiveness of the term proves to be a literary clue. On or about 18 May 1659 a brief and anonymous pamphlet, entitled *A Publick Plea Opposed to a Private Proposal*, was published. It was addressed to the army and the Rump, the assembly which, as the tract observed, had been so 'lawlessly expelled', but which had just been restored in what the title-page calls 'this morning of freedom, after a short, but a sharp night of tyranny and oppression'. The pamphlet urges the punishment of the newly overthrown relations and supporters of Oliver Cromwell, the 'grand backslider'. The Rump should learn from the examples of states which have acted firmly against traitors to liberty, however meritorious their previous conduct might have been. Instances are cited from a range of periods and places, republican Rome at their head.[52] The passage is recycled, with adjustments to meet present circumstances, from writings by Nedham in earlier years, where he had likewise called for the punishment of enemies of the nation's liberty. A habitual reproducer and re-worker of his material, Nedham now drew on passages of prose which he had written for the Levellers in 1646; for the Rump in *The Case of the Commonwealth*; and again for the Rump in 1651–2, in material that would itself be reproduced in Nedham's tract of 1656 *The Excellencie of a Free State, or The Right Constitution of a Commonwealth*.[53]

strained attempts to show that Milton must have been referring to a different episode, but the context of his remark disproves them.

51. Nedham, *Interest Will Not Lie*, 39 (cf. p. 41).

52. *Publick Plea*, 4–5.

53. *Vox Plebis, or The People's Outcry against Oppression, Injustice and Tyranny* (1646), 60–1; *Case*, 107–8 (where Nedham characteristically puts the material to an opposite use, as he does in his *A Plea for the King and Kingdom* (1648), 20); *MP*, 10 July 1651, 901–2; 16 Oct. 1651, 1126–7; 13 May 1652, 1586–7; 24 June 1652, 1673–4; cf. *CP* iii. 565. Some of the passages in *Politicus* had been aimed at royalist and Presbyterian conspirators against the Commonwealth, but others, as will become evident, had Oliver Cromwell as their target. The warning in *A Publick Plea* (p. 5) against 'rapes' on liberty by 'aspirers' to single rule echoes frequent statements by *Politicus*: *MP*, 16 Oct. 1651, 1126; 4 Dec. 1651, 1238; 11 Dec. 1651, 1266; 8 Jan. 1652, 1320; 12 Feb. 1652, 1396; 13 May 1652, 1586; 3 June 1652, 1629.

A Publick Plea was published by Livewell Chapman. In August 1659 Chapman would publish Milton's *Considerations touching the Likeliest Means*, in which the charge about the 'short but scandalous night of interruption' is made; and in February 1660 he would incur the risk of publishing Milton's defiant protest against the advancing Restoration, *The Readie and Easie Way to Establish a Free Commonwealth, and The Excellence Thereof*,[54] a title that would itself have recalled Nedham's *The Excellencie of a Free State, or The Right Constitution of a Commonwealth*. Milton's *The Readie and Easie Way*, like *A Publick Plea*, spoke for what both works call 'the good old cause', which had resisted the Stuarts and Cromwell alike.[55] Never does Milton sound more magnificently alone than in the profound emotion and timeless eloquence of that bravely defiant tract. A prophet crying in a wilderness, he speaks what 'I should perhaps have said though I were sure I should have spoken to trees and stones ... to tell the very soil itself what her perverse inhabitants are deaf to.'[56] As often before, he watches the English repeating the folly of the Israelites, who voluntarily exchanged their republican liberty for monarchical rule. But if the Israelites erred, rules Milton, the present adherents of Christ must not, for Christ 'forbids his disciples to admit of any such heathenish government'. The evidence, says Milton, lies in Luke 22, in an observation by our Saviour at the Last Supper, a text Milton had already used to support a similar argument in his *Defensio* of 1651.[57] Luke, recalls *The Readie and Easie Way*, shows Christ countering 'the ambitious desire of Zebedee's two sons to be exalted above their brethren in his kingdom, which' – unaware that Christ's kingdom is not of this world – 'they thought was to be ere long upon earth'. Christ, in the words of Luke that Milton quotes, contrasts the 'lordship' of the kings of the Gentiles, rulers who are misguidedly 'called benefactors', with his own followers, among whom 'he that is greatest' is to 'be as the younger; and he that is chief, as he that serveth'. Milton, sure as always that the Bible supports the political views that he brings to his reading of it, decides that Christ was speaking 'of civil government'. No form of government, infers Milton, 'comes nearer to this precept of Christ than a free commonwealth', wherein the greatest men

54. David Armitage, 'John Milton: Poet against Empire', in *idem*, Armand Himy, and Quentin Skinner, eds., *Milton and Republicanism* (Cambridge, 1995), 212. In March 1659 Chapman published *An Oration of Agrippa to Octavius Caesar Augustus against Monarchy*. A translation from Dio Cassius, it contrived, by clever adjustments of Cassius's words, to use classical parallels to attack the protectorate: see the italicized passages on pp. 8–10. The analogies recall Nedham's writing.

55. *CP* vii. 462; *Publick Plea*, 2, 3.

56. *CP* vii. 462–3.

57. *CW* vii. 155–7.

'are not elevated above their brethren', whereas 'a king must be adored like a demigod, with a dissolute and haughty court about him'.[58]

That inference is not as freshly conceived as the might of its rhetoric invites us to expect. *A Publick Plea* urges the members of the restored Rump 'to have ever in their minds that precept of our Saviour given expressly to such as should be Christian magistrates in future ages, whereby he plainly pleads against all courtly pride and pomp in Christian governments, as heathenish and unholy'. The pamphlet then quotes the passage of Luke 22 that Milton would use in *The Readie and Easie Way* – and enjoys itself, at the expense of Cromwell's memory, by adding to it. Brazenly it credits Christ with the prediction not only that the kings of the Gentiles will be 'called benefactors', as the biblical text reveals, but that they will be termed 'protectors, or... any such like proud, vainglorious titles'.[59] We can only speculate about the process by which material in *A Publick Plea* came to be reused by Milton. In *Areopagitica* he had professed himself an opponent of anonymous publication,[60] which was Nedham's usual genre. If the explanation none the less includes joint composition by Milton and Nedham of *A Publick Plea*, then that, as we shall find, was not the only occasion of their partnership in writings that were not signed. Indeed it may not be the only moment in *The Readie and Easie Way* when the co-operation of the two men can be glimpsed.

No feature of the literary activity of the period of and after the Renaissance is harder for us to re-enter than the practice of collaborative authorship. It can take many forms. Sometimes the material comes from more than one pen, but alternatively a single hand may write what has been conceived or planned or re-thought in consultation with another or other authors. Critics of the Elizabethan and early Stuart drama accept the fact of collaboration, though even they sometimes struggle to absorb its implications. Few studies of mid-seventeenth-century literature are alive to it. The very thought of it can discomfort us. The contemporary who claimed that Marvell had helped Milton to complete one of his polemical works for the Commonwealth has been viewed with automatic disbelief. When an early biographer of Milton tells us that the poet supervised and vetted the tract of 1652 by his nephew John Phillips that contributed to Milton's own literary campaign on behalf of the regicide, we may struggle

58. *CP* vii. 424–5. (I quote the second ed., which here repeats the first: ibid. 359–60.)
59. *Publick Plea*, 2. 60. *CP* ii. 569.

to imagine the process of co-operation.[61] Our inhibitions hide from us a significant feature of even the most eminent literary careers.

★★

Friends to each other, Milton and Nedham had a powerful friend in common. This was the lawyer John Bradshaw of Gray's Inn. Bradshaw presided over the court that tried and condemned Charles I. He then became president, from February 1649 to December 1651, of the Commonwealth's council of state. In a codicil added to his will in 1655, he remembered the two writers together and left both of them £10.[62] His life had long been involved with theirs. Bradshaw, who may have been related to Milton on Milton's mother's side, acted as the poet's attorney in 1647 during his troubles with the Powell family.[63] Milton's *The Tenure of Kings and Magistrates* (a copy of which he is known to have given to Bradshaw's brother Henry[64]) has been agreed to have 'clear parallels' with the speech of Bradshaw that preceded the sentencing of the king.[65] In or before 1657 Milton used Bradshaw's manuscript copy of the medieval treatise the *Modus Tenendi Parliamentum*,[66] a work that had had a keen pertinence to the defences of the regicide by the two men.[67] It was to Bradshaw that Milton wrote in February 1653 to recommend the appointment of Andrew Marvell as assistant to the blind poet.

Milton's *Defensio Secunda* of 1654 contains a grand eulogy of Bradshaw, that 'friend of my own, of all others the most deserving of my reverence', that 'most faithful of friends, and in every change of fortune the most to be relied upon'. Milton, who was infuriated by a royalist attack on his hero and wrote the eulogy in response to it,[68] begins by describing him as 'a name which liberty herself, wherever she is respected, has commended for celebration to everlasting memory'. He ends with the assurance that Bradshaw will 'spread the renown of his country's noble deeds among all foreign nations, and with posterity to the end of time'.[69] Nedham, before

61. Below, pp. 83, 215-6. 62. Parker, 540. 63. Ibid. 307.
64. See too Nedham's mention of John's and Henry's brother Richard in *MP*, 24 Nov. 1659, 907; cf. *CP* v. 586.
65. *CP* iii. 103–4. 66. Ibid. vii. 497.
67. *CW* vii. 425; Nicholas von Maltzahn, *Milton's 'History of Britain': Republican Historiography in the English Revolution* (Oxford, 1991), 212–13; see too Thomas N. Corns, *Uncloistered Virtue: English Political Literature 1640–1660* (Oxford, 1992), 204.
68. *CP* iv. 637 n.; cf. Miller, *John Milton and the Oldenburg Safeguard*, 157.
69. *CW* viii. 157–61.

his conversion to the Commonwealth, had supplied a less flattering portrait. In a royalist tract of April 1649 he described Bradshaw as 'that monster' who had recently presided not only over the regicide court but, two months afterwards, over the tribunal which produced the execution of the royalist Duke of Hamilton, and which Nedham called 'the most absolute stage of tyranny and injustice that ever was in the world'.[70] In June, in the final issue of his royalist newsbook *Mercurius Pragmaticus*, Nedham assailed 'that bloody Jack Bradshaw, President of Hell'.[71] Yet Nedham's vilifications of individuals were always strategic and always reversible. Politicians were moved back and forth between his *livre d'or* and his *livre noir*. With Nedham's transfer of allegiance to the Commonwealth, Bradshaw's became the most golden name in all his writings.

In November 1649, when Nedham saved himself by agreeing to write for the Commonwealth, he told a friend that Bradshaw's 'favour hath once more turned the wheel of my fortune; who upon my single letter hath been pleased to indulge me my liberty'.[72] '[O]nce more' is frustratingly ambiguous. Is it once more Bradshaw's favour that has turned the wheel, or does Nedham mean merely that the wheel of his fortune has once more turned and that on this occasion Bradshaw has been its turner? It is likely enough that Nedham and Bradshaw had known each other at least since 1646. In that year Bradshaw acted as attorney to John Lilburne, when Lilburne's writings got him into trouble with the House of Lords. In the previous year Nedham's printer and licenser had been imprisoned by the Lords, and Nedham had written a preface to a pamphlet written by Lilburne or anyway in his support, *An Answer to Nine Arguments*. On the other hand Nedham wrote in October 1659 that he had had 'ten years' observation' of Bradshaw's virtues.[73] At all events, by 1650 Nedham had cause to appreciate merits in him to which Milton's tribute drew attention. 'Among his political enemies', observed Milton, 'if any man has happened to return to his right senses ... no man has been more ready to forgive.' Milton also discloses that 'at home' Bradshaw 'is, according to his means,

70. Nedham, *Digitus Dei* (1649), 26. Cf. Bodl., Clarendon MS 34, fo. 86 (Nedham's newsletter of 26 Jan. 1649).

71. *Mercurius Pragmaticus (for King Charles II)*, 19 June 1649, 67.

72. D. Gardiner, ed., *Oxinden and Peyton Letters*, 161. See too NA, SP46/95, fos. 151, 190. The Speaker of the Commons, William Lenthall, who had an estate in Nedham's native Burford, may also have aided Nedham at this time.

73. *MP* 3 Nov. 1659, 842. In the 1650s, of course, Nedham had reason not to draw attention to the course of his career before 1649.

hospitable and splendid'.[74] In August 1650 the poet John Cleveland reported that Nedham was taking meals at Bradshaw's table.[75] In the previous and the following month Nedham worked tributes to Bradshaw into his new newsbook *Mercurius Politicus*. In words that look forward to Milton's tribute he portrayed him as 'a name that shall live with honour in our English histories', 'to whose especial vigilance, indefatigable industry and care we owe much of our present peace and safety'.[76]

In 1659, when Bradshaw died, Nedham published an obituary which, in its length and fulsomeness, is unique among his voluminous publications.[77] Like Milton's eulogy it has a personal touch: 'I cannot but sprinkle a few tears upon the corpse of my noblest friend, and leave the Commonwealth to put on mourning for so great a loss.' Milton's Bradshaw is 'indefatigable ... in exertions for the public': in Nedham's obituary Bradshaw has 'indefatigable affection toward the public affairs'. 'At one time', explains Milton, Bradshaw 'aids the pious, at another the learned': in the obituary he is 'a great patron of ministers, in his own house and abroad', 'a true lover of learned men', and a bestower of 'bounty' on the clergy and scholars whom he has befriended. Milton remembers Bradshaw's courage in presiding over the regicide court, 'marked out as he was by the daggers and threats of so many ruffians': the obituary remembers that Bradshaw 'durst judge the king to ... death' and that he subsequently survived 'notwithstanding all the threats and attempts of adversaries'.

★★

When did Milton and Nedham get to know each other? It cannot have been later than January 1651, when Milton began to act as the government's licenser of Nedham's newsbook *Mercurius Politicus*. From that month the content of *Politicus* entitles us to speak decisively, not merely of an official relationship between author and licenser, but of a literary partnership. It seems unlikely that it was established overnight. From the previous year, if not from late 1649, Nedham and Milton had been fellow employees at

74. Milton's eulogy may itself be a return for favours: *CW* ix. 85.
75. Cleveland, *Character of Mercurius Politicus*, 8. Cleveland adds that 'The lean cannibal has all that while my lord president in his teeth, and gnaws upon him in his mind'. For Nedham and Bradshaw see also D. Gardiner, ed., *Oxinden and Peyton Letters*, 168–9; BL, Add. MS 28002, fo. 331^{v}.
76. *MP*, 25 July 1650, 101; 26 Sept. 1650, 276; cf. 6 Jan. 1653, 2131–2.
77. Ibid. 3 Nov. 1659, 842–3; *Publick Intelligencer*, 7 Nov. 1659, 833–4.

Whitehall. They were fellow propagandists for the Commonwealth, and fellow promoters, as we shall find, of a contentious political programme. In due course we shall encounter intimations that they were already collaborating by 1650. But were they friends earlier?

The signs that they may have been are too suggestive too ignore, yet not quite firm enough to rely on. In an undated document, which has been tentatively assigned to 1647, the social reformer Samuel Hartlib, to whom Milton had dedicated his tract *Of Education* in 1644, drew up a list of possible 'commissioners' for his proposed 'council for schooling', and named Nedham and Milton together. Is that conjunction a mere coincidence, or does it indicate that the two men had pooled their enthusiasm for educational reform?[78] Then there are resemblances between the writings of Nedham and Milton in the 1640s. We have noticed the echoes, in *Britanicus*, of Milton's anti-episcopal tracts when Nedham invoked the prophet Elijah to warrant the satirical methods with

78. French, ii. 169. (Much later, in a plea for educational reform, Nedham, echoing *Eikonoklastes* (*CP* iii. 380–1: 'the ragged infantry of stews and brothels'), would write of 'the little dirty infantry which swarms up and down in alleys and lanes': Nedham, *Discourse concerning Schools*, 2.) There is also the question why Milton was selected by the council of state, not only to license *Politicus* in 1651, but also to act on the other occasion when the government needed an agent to deal with Nedham. That was in June 1649, when Milton, four days after the final issue of *Pragmaticus* and its attack on 'that bloody Jack Bradshaw', was instructed to examine papers of Nedham, who had been arrested and confined to Newgate prison (Parker, 355). The likely instrument, or anyway a likely one, of the appointment of 1651 was Bradshaw, the president of the council of state, whose contentious policies we shall watch *Politicus* promoting. He is also likely to have been involved in the earlier appointment. In May 1649, as part of the government's initiative to which the arrest of Nedham in June belonged, he had undertaken to draw up legislation to crack down on royalist publication (a measure which was enacted in September, and of which Milton, whose pleas for liberty of expression had never extended to royalism, voiced approval). Did Bradshaw, perhaps already hoping for Nedham's conversion to the Commonwealth, engineer the appointment of a man who already knew him? If Milton did know Nedham by June 1649, when Nedham had been writing for the king for nearly two years, we may guess that the acquaintance had formed earlier, before Nedham's transition to the royalist cause in 1647. On the other hand the council, which customarily allocated miscellaneous tasks to writers in its employment or favour, did sometimes order Milton to inspect papers of other royalists, of whom he was no friend. One other possibility merits brief attention. While writing *Eikonoklastes* in 1649, Milton took temporary accommodation with 'one Thomson' in Charing Cross (Parker, 359, 367, 952, 961). Thomson, or Thompson, was hardly a rare name. Might this one none the less have been the attorney and wit, and writer of Latin poetry, Nedham's friend James Thompson (on whom see D. Gardiner, ed., *Oxinden and Peyton Letters*, 135, 145, 147, etc.; BL, Add. MS 28012, fo. 775^{v})? In the summer of 1648 Thompson wrote letters from lodgings elsewhere in London, in Pump Court. But in 1649 he gave his whereabouts only as 'London': BL, Add. MS 28002, fos. 39 ff. A Latin poem to Thompson, 'generoso', by his and Nedham's friend Henry Oxinden is in Folger Library, Washington, MS 4018, p. 117.

which they strove to awaken their audiences. Perhaps he remembers them too in his explanation, in the same newsbook, of the difficulties that thwart the parliamentary armies. The cause, he writes, is the provocation of God by the sinful practices of worship that survive in Roundhead communities: by 'the rubbish in his own house, by the stains in the linen ephod, by one counterfeit jewel in the breastplace of Aaron'.[79] The complaint takes us back to Milton's description of the accoutrements of the Laudian Church, with its 'pure linen ... and gewgaws fetched from Aaron's old wardrobe'.[80] And was Nedham inspired by Milton's tracts in buoyant passages elsewhere in *Britanicus*, close in satirical spirit to Milton if only occasionally in language, which mock the ceremonial practices of the Church of England? In them he demands the removal from the churches of 'idolized stuff';[81] he derides the 'flatuous and windy religion' of the king,[82] with its 'abundance of trumpery, as the cathedral dressings, paintings and carvings';[83] he complains that the Book of Common Prayer 'rob[s] God of the purity of worship due unto him', by 'tickling men's ears, and puffing up their devotions with anthems, and responds blown out of organ pipes';[84] and he celebrates its abolition with a 'farewell' to 'all superstitious First and Second Service, Te Deums, Litany, and the whole bundle of Collects, praying over the dead, enormities of baptism, and Ashwednesday cursings', together with 'the heathenish obscene ceremony of the ring'.[85] Yet such resemblances, when or if they are conscious, might be explained simply as imitations by one author of conveniently available material by another, whom he did not necessarily know. Perhaps, it might be thought, Nedham shared the reverence for Milton, and the impulse to imitate him, that we find in another young journalist, Nedham's literary associate John Hall. In *Areopagitica*, on the other hand, we have what may be a debt in the other direction. In that work Milton spoke against the imposition of as 'cold' and 'frozen' a unanimity in religion 'as any January could freeze together'.[86] Eight months earlier, in *Britanicus*, Nedham had written of

79. *Mercurius Britanicus*, 30 Sept. 1644, 403. 80. *CP* i. 521 (cf. ii. 564).
81. *Mercurius Britanicus*, 8 July 1644, 334. 82. Ibid. 28 Dec. 1643, 141.
83. Ibid. [14] Oct. 1644, 407. 84. Ibid. 13 Jan. 1645, 517.
85. Ibid. 9 Dec. 1644, 475-6. Perhaps Nedham's reference to the 'half-Reformation' of Edward VI (ibid. 1 Sept. 1645, 854–5) is indebted to Milton (*CP* i. 536, 539, 614, 973).
86. *CP* ii. 545, 551, 564 (though also i. 785). The only current publication that Milton mentions in the tract (ii. 558) is that 'continued court libel', the newsbook *Mercurius Aulicus*, Nedham's antagonist – though he does salute works published by John Selden in 1640 and Lord Brooke in 1642.

the 'cold' religion of the bishops and royalist clergy, whose 'souls ... are congealed and frozen' and 'have as much snow' on them 'as any mountain of Wales the last February'.[87]

There is a more substantial possibility: that Milton was influenced in the 1640s not only by Nedham's language but by his ideas, and that Milton's literary development was affected by that contact. We think of Milton first as a poet, Nedham first as a prose-writer. Yet by the late 1640s, when he wrote the bulk of his *History of Britain* and the tracts that followed the regicide, Milton's poetry had almost dried up. Apart from a small number of lines of translation in *The Tenure of Kings and Magistrates* and the *History of Britain*, and the Latin epigraph of *Defensio*, there survive, from between early 1647 and early 1652, only the sonnet to Sir Thomas Fairfax in 1648 and the translations of Psalms in the same year. His autobiographical account in *Defensio Secunda* in 1654 gives no indication that he has ever written poetry or ever will.[88] Elsewhere in that work he does compare the writing of it to the activity of poets, but again says nothing to suggest that he is or might be of their number. Milton's own retrospective pronouncements on his life have encouraged his biographers and admirers to think of it as a long process of self-preparation for the writing of a verse epic, from which the prose was an extended aside. Yet by the late 1640s he had travelled far from that ambition.

Of his writings of that time, the *History of Britain*, which was eventually published four years before his death – and which, alone of his as yet unpublished works, the autobiographical account in *Defensio Secunda* does mention – was the most ambitious.[89] It took the story from the earliest times to the Norman Conquest. In conception it had been much more ambitious, for he wanted to bring the narrative down to his own times. Of the six books that were eventually published, he had evidently written most of the first four by 1649, though he then set the project aside for some years. As a guide to his thinking of the late 1640s the *History* is a very

87. *Mercurius Britanicus*, 18 Mar. 1644, 209. Perhaps the preacher John Saltmarsh also borrowed from Nedham's passage in words that have been seen as an echo of *Areopagitica*: *CP* ii. 545 n. The knockabout attack on Scottish Presbyterian ministers in Milton's poems of the mid-1640s ('Scotch Whatd'ye-call', and so on) is in the spirit of Nedham's customary enjoyment at the expense of both Presbyterians and Scots.
88. *CP* viii. 119 ff.
89. Von Maltzahn's *Milton's 'History of Britain'*, is the essential introduction to the work. Though I disagree with some of his judgements about the composition of the *History* (on which see Appendix C below), his book is of fundamental importance in establishing the place and significance of the project in Milton's life and thinking.

difficult text, for there are strong indications that he revised and added to it after the Restoration, in ways that are hard where not impossible to pin down. It may be that the passages of the work that have commanded most modern attention, in which Milton draws parallels between the history of the ancient Britons and the course of events in the 1640s, were drawn up not, as has been supposed, within the Puritan Revolution but well after it. Yet the heart of the book, which we can safely take him to have composed during the revolution, is permeated by the experience of it and by his reflections on it, even if at that time he did not make the contemporary application of the project explicit. For like most historical writing of the period, the *History* has an eye to the present. It is a melancholy work, which ponders the failings of the nation's character. Its composition marked a sharp break with his earlier literary premisses. In 1641–2 he had supposed it to be the work of other genres to educate his countrymen: poetry, drama, oratory. If history had a role, it was as the ally of those forms, whose literary properties he expected it to share.[90] Now he fashioned a new, abstemious prose that shunned the inspiration of poetry and rhetoric. In *The Reason of Church Government* in 1642 he had taken 'the general relapses of kingdoms and states from justice and true worship' to be the province of poetry.[91] In the *History*, which traces such relapses of his own kingdom, he found that the theme required simple language, devoid of the Ciceronian magniloquence of his early pamphlets. He eschewed the classical and humanist device – a poetic device – of inventing speeches for historical characters, that 'abuse of posterity, raising, in them that read, other conceptions of those times and places than were true'.[92] He told 'the truth naked, though as lean as a plain journal', even though the result 'may seem a calendar rather than a history'.[93]

In his polemical tracts of 1649 as in the *History*, he shed the density and luxuriance that had sustained the poetic component of the prose he had published earlier.[94] If the *History of Britain* took Milton away from poetry, *Eikonoklastes*, in 1649, is almost an attack on it. He always knew that if good poetry can inspire virtue, degenerate poetry has a corresponding power to inspire vice. But *Eikonoklastes* goes further. Were it not for its fleeting invocation of the authority of Spenser,[95] we might take it for a repudiation of the literary imagination. He associates it with the king's

90. Below, pp. 389–90. 91. *CP* i. 817. 92. Ibid. v. 79–80. 93. Ibid. 229–30.
94. Corns, *Uncloistered Virtue*, 217; Lewalski, 155. 95. *CP* iii. 390.

cause and with his religion. Having heard that Charles was 'a more diligent reader of poets than of politicians', and noting the 'poetical ... strains', the 'masquing scene', the 'painted feathers', of *Eikon Basilike* and its debt to the chivalric tradition of 'Amadis and Palmerin', 'I began to think that the whole book might be intended for a piece of poetry.' Milton hits not only at the 'licentious remissness' of the king's 'Sunday's theatre'; not only at 'the old pageantry of some twelfth-night's entertainment'; but even at 'the polluted orts and refuse' and 'heathen orisons' of that 'vain amatorious poem', Sidney's *Arcadia*, a work whose improving power he had earlier saluted but which he now deemed contrary to 'religious thoughts'. Shakespeare's 'stuff' is presented in no reverential spirit, for his writings were 'the closet companion' of the king's 'solitudes'.[96]

By the late 1640s, political poetry had become almost the preserve of royalism. When, in *Absalom and Achitophel*, Dryden sang that 'Never rebel was to arts a friend', he drew on an established practice of deriding the philistine illiteracy of the Roundheads, and of claiming 'wit' and 'learning', the two essential ingredients of poetic inspiration, for the king's side. Recent writing has protested at that equation, which slides over Dryden's own place in Cromwell's funeral procession and his own tribute to the protector, in whose 'praise no arts can liberal be'.[97] We have been taught just how much verse was written in the Roundhead cause.[98] Yet there was also an anti-poetic strain to the parliamentarian endeavour. We find it in the remark by John Cook, solicitor-general at Charles's trial, that the disasters of his reign might have been averted had he 'studied Scripture half so much as Ben Jonson or Shakespeare'.[99]

Where Milton and Cook travelled in 1649, Nedham had been before them. When, in the *History of Britain*, Milton undertook to speak 'the truth naked, though as lean as a plain journal', he was adopting a stance that Nedham had taken in the first civil war. In what he called the 'sincere' and 'plain English' of *Britanicus*, 'as plain as a pikestaff', Nedham spoke, as he explained, 'naked truth'.[100] Other writers, of course, also

96. Ibid. 342, 358, 361–7, 406.
97. Paul Hammond, *The Making of Restoration Poetry* (Woodbridge, Suffolk, 2006), 3.
98. See esp. Nigel Smith, *Literature and Revolution in England 1640–1660* (London and New Haven, 1994); Norbrook, *Writing the English Republic*.
99. John Cook, *King Charls his Case* (1649), 13.
100. *Mercurius Britanicus*, 5 Aug. 1644, 361, 365; 19 Aug. 1644, 368; 30 Sept. 1644, 399–400, 403; 14 Oct. 1644, 415; 28 Oct. 1644, 435; 3 Mar. 1645, 576; 17 Mar. 1645, 598; *Anti-Aulicus* ([Feb.] 1644), 8.

advocated and wrote plain prose. Yet Nedham comes distinctively close to Milton in contrasting that virtue with the 'soft and silken language' of royalist publication,[101] which protected the 'delusions' of the king's cause. Like Milton after him he equated royalist literature with dishonesty and escapism. In *Britanicus* he compared credulous royalists to 'a love-sick novice' reading 'the famous histories of Don Quixote and Amadis de Gaule'.[102] He represented the court's taste for masques as a symptom of its falsity, which he would 'unmasque' and 'unhood' and 'undisguise'.[103] He had higher literary targets too. Behind royalist propaganda, he maintained, there stood the influence of Shakespeare and Jonson, of Beaumont and Fletcher, of Shirley and Davenant.[104] As Milton would do in *Eikonoklastes*, Nedham connects the court's literary tastes to its idolatrous worship of God. Where Milton would refer to Shakespeare's 'stuff', Nedham contrives to place 'Shakespeare's works' in a list of high Anglican devotional publications and of 'such prelatical trash as your clergymen spend their canonical hours on'.[105] The king's party, he predicts, 'will go near to put down all preaching and praying, and have some religious masque or play instead of Morning and Evening Prayer; it hath been an old fashion at court ... to shut up the Sabbath with some wholesome piece of Ben Jonson or Davenant, a kind of comical divinity'.[106] In the second civil war in 1648, Nedham, now wearing a royalist hat, became a friend to literature. But his earlier approach was adopted in the same war by a young journalist who was very close to Nedham and who now took up Nedham's Roundhead mantle:[107] John Hall, a devotee of Milton. Hall portrayed the royalist appetite for chivalry and romance – for Amadis de Gaule, Palmerin, Don Quixote – as a symptom of irresponsible escapism.[108] He repeated the point on the republic's behalf in 1649.[109]

Did Milton consciously follow Nedham's, and Hall's, lead? Did Nedham steer him, in the Roundhead cause, away from poetry? It is impossible to be sure. Only in 1651 does the collaboration of Milton and Nedham become unmistakable. By then, as we shall now find, Nedham had become the collaborator of another of the men who would soon be visiting Milton in Petty France: Andrew Marvell.

101. *Mercurius Britanicus*, 30 Sept. 1644, 400.
102. Ibid. 22 Dec. 1645, 569.
103. Ibid. 19 Aug. 1644, 368; 30 Sept. 1644, 399; 28 Oct. 1644, 431.
104. Ibid. 11 Jan. 1644, 153.
105. Ibid. 2 Sept. 1644, 386.
106. Ibid. 16 Nov. 1643, 89.
107. Below, Ch. 3.
108. Ibid. 23 May–11 July 1648, 16, 30, 37, 54, 66, 68; 1 Aug. 1648, 90.
109. John Hall, *An Humble Motion to the Parliament concerning the Advancement of Learning* (1649), 37; cf. *MP*, 30 Oct. 1651, 1166.

3
Marvell and Nedham

Like Milton, Andrew Marvell can seem a spokesman for solitariness. He 'had not a general acquaintance', liked to 'enjoy ... my privacy', and was 'naturally ... inclined to keep my thoughts private'. Though he 'would drink liberally by himself', to 'refresh his spirits and exalt his muse', he would – unlike Marchamont Nedham – 'never drink hard in company' or 'play the good-fellow in any man's company'.[1] Marvell's writing, like Milton's, makes a virtue of single-handedness. Where Milton's defiant angel Abdiel remains, in the war in heaven, 'single' in his fidelity, Marvell's poem 'Tom May's Death' commends the ideal of the defiant poet who 'single fights forsaken virtue's cause' (66). Like Milton's solitary heroes, Marvell's Oliver Cromwell, who in the poem on 'The First Anniversary' of the protectorate moves 'in dark nights, and in cold days alone' (127), never seems to need a friend or counsellor, and would be a less imposing force beside one. Marvell himself can be vividly alone in his verse. Whereas Ben Jonson, in the great country-house poem of the early seventeenth century, delights in the social world he joins at Penshurst, Marvell, in the great country-house poem of the mid-century, communes with himself in the grounds of Appleton House. In 'The Garden' he finds 'fair quiet' and 'innocence' in 'delicious solitude', to which 'Society is all but rude' (9-16).

Before he found them, however, he 'sought' them 'long | In busy companies of men' (11-12). Marvell's surviving letters, most of them written during the last two decades of his life when he was an industrious member of parliament for Hull, show him, not seeking solitude, but taking refuge from its burdens in 'diversion, business, and activity'.[2] His Restoration writings likewise involved social business, placing him as they

1. *AMC* 144, 218; Margoliouth, ii. 166.   2. Margoliouth, ii. 313.

Figure 4. Andrew Marvell, perhaps in the late 1650s

frequently did in collaboration with publishers and printers and perhaps with other writers. The assaults on misgovernment in his verse in the 1660s, and in his prose of the 1670s, belonged to concerted literary campaigns, even though Marvell himself, secretive as always, covered the tracks of his dealings with their co-ordinators.[3] What then of the earlier Marvell, the Marvell of the Puritan Revolution? Posterity has rarely placed him in busy companies of men. A line has been conventionally imagined between Marvell the writer of private poetry in the 1640s and 1650s and Marvell the political activist, and author of satires and tracts, in the Restoration. That division of his literary career has had difficulty in accommodating his early political verse, which will be our subject. But until recently it could at least be broadly sustained by an assumption of chronology. It was supposed that his lyric and pastoral verse, so little of which indicates the time of its composition, was written before his entry into politics in the late 1650s. Now that he seems to have been found writing pastoral poetry – indeed, writing 'The Garden' – in the reign of Charles II,[4] the circular reasoning behind the assumption dissolves. If the later Marvell is a lyric as well as a political writer, the earlier one proves to be as much a political animal, and as close to the world of public satire and polemic, as his successor.

He too had tracks to cover. Most of the story is lost, and we have largely to guess at its shape and content. But if we turn to his relations with Nedham, we find unmistakable evidence of its existence. In this and the next three chapters we shall trace the association of the two writers from the late 1640s to the mid-1650s, and the transitions which those years wrought in them. At the beginning of that period they are royalist writers. At the end of it they are Cromwellian ones.

★★

In the late 1640s the king's cause suffered military and political destruction. Yet it was buoyant in literature. Poetry, alongside a commitment to the Book of Common Prayer, sustained and developed the identity of royalism.[5]

3. Martin Dzelzainis, 'Andrew Marvell and the Restoration Literary Underground: Printing the Painter Poems' (forthcoming).

4. Allan Prichard, 'Marvell's "The Garden"', *Studies in English Literature*, 23 (1980), 371–88; Paul Hammond, 'The Date of Marvell's "The Mower against Gardens"', *Notes and Queries*, 53 (2006), 178–81.

5. In recent years there have been many illuminating studies of royalist literature, of which the most comprehensive is Robert Wilcher, *The Writing of Royalism 1628–1660* (Cambridge, 2001).

Like the parliamentarian cause, the royalist one had always been a broad coalition. The range of judgement and feeling provoked by the conflict of Cavalier and Roundhead, and the vacillations of sentiment produced by its unforeseen events, could not be accommodated within fixed and starkly opposed viewpoints. In 1647–9, perhaps the years of its greatest literary energy, royalism had many faces. In religion and ethics it ranged from piety to hedonism, from Calvinism to paganism. In politics it extended from, on the one hand, zeal for the military restoration of the king to, on the other, Stoic resignation to defeat and nostalgic recollection of the 'halcyon days' of the pre-war world. Though it was united by loyalty to Charles I, not all royalists of the second civil war in 1648 had supported him in the first, and not all admired him now. Much of his backing derived less from enthusiasm for his person or policies than from the sentiment which the bitterness and defeats of warfare had made into a cohesive force: hatred of parliament and Puritanism and of their agencies and allies. In 1640 the Long Parliament had seemed to speak for a unified nation. Now public opinion, in so far as such a thing can be identified and measured, ran strongly in the king's favour. The parliament's war machine had acquired powers, at the centre and in the localities, that dwarfed those of the pre-war monarchy. In the provinces the old patterns of regional community and autonomy had been broken by intrusive county committees which were staffed by upstarts and closely monitored from Westminster. In place of the Church of England of bishops and the Prayer Book had come the parliamentary Church of zealous and intolerant Presbyterianism. Outside it there stood the anarchic proliferation of sects and the provocative and alarming principle of liberty of conscience.

Collections of royalist verse in the 1640s, which published the diverse voices of royalism, strove to give them coherence. Political and religious differences were subsumed in the assertion of a shared cultural identity. Royalism was projected as a creed – an anti-Puritan creed – of sociability and civility and conviviality, and as a commitment to honour and loyalty. Poets commended the presence of those virtues in politics but also away from them, in love, in song, in wine, in rural retreat. Some royalist writing was produced for a cultivated elite, some for a popular audience. The first kind looked askance at the popular press, as a cause and symptom of the collapse of old values and deference. The second made use of it, as a means to rally popular opinion. Through it the pen could be the partner of the sword; or, if the sword failed, writing might achieve what fighting could not, by exposing the pretences of the Roundhead and Puritan cause and demoralizing its adherents. Well might Milton describe *Eikon Basilike* as an attempt 'to bring about that by fair and plausible words, which the force of arms' had 'denied' the king.[6]

**

From 1643 to 1646 Marchamont Nedham had written for parliament. In those years Marvell had been on the Continent, apparently serving as a tutor for a noble family or families. He returned to England by or in November 1647. We have no idea what he had thought, at the time, about the first civil war. But in 1648–9, the time of the second war and of the regicide and the inauguration of the republic, he wrote three royalist poems.[7] None of them mentions the king, or advocates any exact political principles. What they share is disdain for, where not anger at, the royalists' enemies. The first, the 'Elegy upon the Death of my Lord Francis Villiers', was published on its own.[8] The others, 'To his Noble Friend Mr Richard Lovelace, upon his Poems' and 'Upon the Death of the Lord Hastings', appeared in royalist collections of verse in 1649.

The death of Villiers in a skirmish at Kingston-on-Thames in July 1648 prompted a number of poems in memory of that flower of chivalrous youth, the son of Charles I's principal minister of the 1620s, the Duke of Buckingham. The second civil war was a still more acrimonious conflict than the first, and its verse was more acrimonious too. Marvell's poem has an intensity that suggests, though it does not prove, personal acquaintance with Villiers, perhaps as his tutor on the Continent during the first war, when Buckingham's sons were exiled. The poem is more than an elegy. It sees in Villiers's death not only an occasion for praise and meditative lament but an affront and provocation. It enjoins the royalists who have survived Villiers to kill his enemies, Cromwell and Lord General Sir Thomas Fairfax at their head: 'revenge, if often quenched in tears, | Hardens like steel, and daily keener wears' (23–4). Villiers himself 'died not ... revengeless', for 'A whole pyramid | Of vulgar bodies he erected high' (115–17).

6. *CP* iii. 343; cf. 340–1.
7. Though I hesitate to disagree with James Loxley, who has written so instructively on royalist poetry, his argument that royalism is peripheral to Marvell's verse of 1649 seems to me to rest on too narrow a definition of royalism: Loxley, '"Prepar'd at last to Stricke in with the Tyde"? Andrew Marvell and Royalist Verse', *The Seventeenth Century*, 10 (1995), 39–62; *idem*, 'Marvell, Villiers, and Royalist Verse', *Notes and Queries*, 239 (1994), 170–2. Other critics have made cases similar to Loxley's.
8. I hope that it is by now more or less uncontroversial to attribute the poem to him: Smith, 11.

And we hereafter to his honour will
Not write so many [obsequies], but so many [soldiers] kill.
Till the whole [Roundhead] army by just vengeance come
To be at once his trophy and his tomb.

(125–8)

The poem has no parallels in writing by Nedham that are distinctive enough to prove a literary relationship between him and Marvell. Those come later in Marvell's verse. Even so, there is a suggestive correspondence. In the poem, Villiers's former companions embark on a 'just' mission of revenge. Nedham's *Mercurius Pragmaticus*, which gives an account of the 'unfortunate loss of the truly valiant Lord Francis',[9] likewise reports on the subsequent activities of those companions, who are 'daring to suffer anything for the justice of their righteous cause'. There is a further pointer. Another writer to dwell on Villiers's death was the clever poet and polemicist John Hall, another product of Gray's Inn, who was six years younger than Marvell and seven years younger than Nedham, and who would still be in his twenties when he died in 1656. There are notable resemblances between Marvell's poem 'To his Coy Mistress' and a poem published by Hall in the winter of 1646–7, whose lines Marvell seems consciously to rework.[10] Hall's writings resemble Nedham's so often and so much, and reproduce or anticipate the idiosyncrasies of his prose so frequently, that the two authors can be indistinguishable. There must have been intimate friendship and co-operation between them. By 1650 they would be fellow apologists for the Commonwealth, and Hall would be writing for Nedham's *Mercurius Politicus*.[11] In 1648 he wrote on the Roundhead side. Yet he had royalist literary friends. He was accused by them of being, what Nedham so often got called by both sides, a turncoat. He was charged, as Nedham would be after converting to the Commonwealth in 1650, with having been bribed out of his principles,[12] though, like Nedham, he wrote with a keener argumentative edge on the Roundhead than on the Cavalier side and produced spirited prose for its radical wing. In 1648 Hall edited a vigorous Roundhead newsbook with arguments and in language familiar

9. *Mercurius Pragmaticus*, 18 July 1648, 6.
10. Smith, 76, 84. Forthcoming work by Nicholas McDowell places the Marvell of the late 1640s alongside Hall in the literary circle of the royalist Thomas Stanley.
11. Compare too Hall's tracts of 1651 on the Presbyterian conspiracy of Christopher Love (*A Gagg to Love's Advocate*) and the Amboyna massacre (*A True Relation of the ... Proceedings ... at Amboyna*) with *MP*, 10 July 1651, 916; 1 Jan. 1652, 1316.
12. *Mercurius Bellicus*, 6 June 1648, 7; *Mercurius Elencticus*, 14 June 1648, 224; 21 June 1648, 233.

from Nedham's own. It had the title – and its egregious spelling – of the newsbook edited by Nedham in the first civil war, *Mercurius Britanicus.* Hall's *Britanicus* and Nedham's *Pragmaticus* appeared on the same day of the week, and its editors evidently colluded – in what must have been entertaining conversations – to present diametrically opposing viewpoints.[13] So it is suggestive to find Hall's *Britanicus* departing from its normal contempt for royalists to signal respect for Villiers, who 'expiated part of the folly of his companions, and died by many a wound, which had been brave enough had they been received in another cause'.[14]

When his elegy for Villiers was composed Marvell may already have written his poem for Lovelace. But it appeared in print only in June 1649, five months after the regicide, as one of the tributary poems in Lovelace's collection of his own verse, *Lucasta.* Lovelace had fought for the king and had composed the poems as a prisoner in his cause. We do not know of any direct relations between Lovelace and Nedham, but Lovelace's arrest by the parliamentarians in the autumn of 1648 was an episode of concern to men who were drinking companions and close friends of Nedham, and who were themselves evidently close to Lovelace's family.[15] Lovelace was still in goal at the time in 1649 when *Lucasta* came into print. Shortly before the publication of the volume, Nedham's friend John Hall was given an annual salary of £100 to answer pamphlets written against the Commonwealth. Yet he contributed to the collection a poem in which 'many points of contact' with Marvell's have been noticed.[16] One of them is between Marvell's lament that 'Our civil wars have lost the civic crown' (12) and Hall's declaration, which in its context appears to carry little force unless as a wink to a fellow contributor,[17] of Lovelace's entitlement to 'the civic coronet'.

Marvell's 'civic crown' adorns the literary culture of 'That candid age' (5), the pre-war world, that has yielded to the proliferation of ephemeral authors, 'Of wit corrupted, the unfashioned sons' (20).

> He highest builds, who with most art destroys,
> And against others' fame his own employs.

13. Below, p. 76.
14. *Mercurius Britanicus,* 11 July 1648, 70.
15. See James Thompson's letter to Henry Oxinden in D. Gardiner, ed., *Oxinden and Peyton Correspondence,* 145.
16. Norbrook, *Writing the English Republic,* 172–3; and see Smith, 19, 20. Norbrook has illuminating material on Hall.
17. Cf. Norbrook, *Writing the English Republic,* 173.

I see the envious caterpillar sit
On the fair blossom of each growing wit.
   The air's already tainted with the swarms
Of insects which against you rise in arms.
Word-peckers, paper-rats, book-scorpions....
(13–19)

Nedham was among the scribblers. Yet here his journalism may be, not a target, but a source. In 1646 he had enjoyed himself, in *Britanicus*, at the expense of a new royalist newsbook, *Mercurius Academicus*, which had supplanted the rival of *Britanicus*, Sir John Berkenhead's *Mercurius Aulicus*. Nedham sighed at the change, and asserted for his own prose a cultural superiority that would likewise be claimed by Marvell's poem. Whatever the differences between *Britanicus* and *Aulicus*, he proclaimed, together they had at least kept up literary standards: 'we are both Athenians'.[18] Of *Academicus*, by contrast, he wrote: 'a mere paper-worm it is, a caterpillar that devours many a good leaf which might be better employed; and leaves neither fruit nor pleasure behind: sure this is some *Witty-would-be* in print'.[19] Nedham was fond of the image. In a less respectful mood he had called Berkenhead himself and his Oxford associates 'viperous silk-worms... those gaudy caterpillars which lie so thick about the royal branches, and have almost consumed all the tender buddings and leaves of the Protestant religion which throve in them'.[20] There is nothing improbable in the thought of Nedham, who coveted immortality for his journalism and kept it for reuse, showing off such passages to Marvell, a fellow writer, or else sharing with him some form of unpublished writing that had been related to them. Nedham, himself a derider of the Roundhead scribblers when it suited him, was addicted to such terms as 'paper-worm' and 'paper-brat' and 'paper-kite' as images of ephemeral publication, including his own.[21] Marvell's poem associates the 'paper-rats' with the Presbyterians (19–22): Nedham aimed the term 'paper-worm' at Presbyterian writers. In attacking one of them he remarks, 'I must needs throw away some ink upon this paper-worm,

18. *Mercurius Britanicus*, 5 Jan. 1646, 985–6.
19. Ibid. 19 Jan. 1646, 1001.
20. Ibid. 18 Mar. 1644, 209. Here too Nedham uses the term 'Athenian', though this time less flatteringly to Berkenhead. Cf. *MP*, 23 Jan. 1651, 545.
21. *Mercurius Britanicus*, 5 Jan. 1646, 987 (where *Mercurius Academicus* is a 'paper-kite'); *Mercurius Pragmaticus*, 11 July 1648, 7; 28 Nov. 1648, 8; 24 Apr. 1649, 2; *Cat May Look upon a King* (1652), preface; *MP*, 25 June 1650, 100, and 15 Apr. 1652, 1525–6; *Observator*, 31 Oct. 1654, 3, 4, 11; cf. Milton's fondness for 'paper-galls': *CP* iv. 580; vii. 503.

this great benefactor to the magazine of waste-paper.'[22] Shortly after the licensing of *Lucasta* we find him juxtaposing the terms 'paper-pellet' and 'water-rat'.[23]

Henry Lord Hastings, the subject of the third of Marvell's royalist poems of the late 1640s, died in the month of the publication of *Lucasta* and was given a lavish funeral accompanied by a public procession. Son and heir of the royalist Earl of Huntingdon, Hastings died of smallpox at the age of 19, the day before he was due to marry. The volume in tribute to him, *Lachrymae Musarum*, subtly demonstrated its royalist credentials by the insignia of its publication. After the volume had been prepared for the press, a number of belated contributions were added. At the head of them was Marvell's poem. It was followed by one by 'M. N.', Nedham. On the day before Hastings's death the republic's council of state had ordered Milton to examine Nedham's papers. A few days later Nedham was sent to Newgate 'in danger of his life'. The risk-taker was irrepressible. Marvell's poem for Hastings, like those for Villiers and Lovelace, parades social scorn. As in the Lovelace poem he observes the banishment of merit, which this time is identified with noble blood, by the civil wars. In the same breath he glances at the political destruction wrought by the abolition of monarchy and the House of Lords and by the assumption of sovereignty by the self-styled representative of the people, the militarily purged House of Commons: 'Therefore the democratic stars did rise, | And all that worth from hence did ostracise.' Nedham's poem echoed the thought: 'It is decreed, we must be drained (I see) | Down to the dregs of a democracy.' (These were the lines of Nedham on which Dryden – himself a contributor to the volume for Hastings[24] – would draw in *Absalom and Achitophel*: 'That kingly power, thus ebbing out, might be | Drawn to the dregs of a democracy.'[25]) The advance of 'democracy' had been a recurrent theme of Nedham's *Pragmaticus*, in which he wrote of the 'democratic' Levellers being 'left in the suds'.[26] In the second edition of *Lachrymae Musarum*, which may have been timed to coincide with the first anniversary of the regicide, the order of the poems was changed. Marvell's 'Upon the Death of the Lord

22. Nedham, *Independencie no Schisme* (1646), preface.
23. Smith, 21. Marvell's 'envious caterpillar' likewise seems to be linked in his mind with Presbyterianism: elsewhere Nedham wrote of 'envious Presbytery' (*Cat May Look upon a King*, 102).
24. Smith, 24. 25. ll. 226–7.
26. *Mercurius Pragmaticus (for King Charles II)*, 29 May 1649, 2; cf. Nedham, *Pacquet of Advices*, 8 ('the very bottom of democracy').

Hastings' now appeared next to John Hall's poem 'On the Untimely Death of the Lord Hastings'.[27]

★★

When we move from 1649 to 1650, the proximity of Marvell to Nedham becomes pronounced. At the end of May 1650, Oliver Cromwell returned to England from the triumphant campaign that had broken the back of the military resistance in Ireland. His person and impact would be the dominant preoccupation of Marvell's public poetry until Cromwell's death in 1658. In 'An Horatian Ode' his destiny swiftly unfolds. He rises by 'industrious valour' on the battlefield and proceeds to 'ruin the great work of time, | And cast the kingdoms old | Into another mould' (33–6).[28] In May 1650 Cromwell had been, for the sixteen months since the regicide, much the most imposing and influential public figure in England. To the surprise of his contemporaries his pre-eminence was accorded no formal recognition. In constitutional terms he was but one of the 200 or so MPs who sat in the purged House of Commons and of the forty-one members of its executive arm, the council of state. He was not yet head of the army. The lord general was Fairfax, who had been the supreme commander of the new model army since its inception in 1645, with Cromwell as his second-in-command. But Fairfax's tenure of his post was made increasingly uncomfortable by his doubts about the legitimacy of the republic. In August 1649 it was left to Cromwell to lead the army to Ireland, of which parliament made him lord lieutenant.

For in executing Charles I the regicides had destroyed the king not only of England but of Ireland and Scotland, the countries to which the exiled Charles II now looked for military support. Only by subduing those lands could the Commonwealth hope to be secure in England. Although Cromwell soon won his cruel and emphatic victories at Drogheda and Wexford, there remained stubborn Irish resistance that would occupy him through the winter and spring. Meanwhile Charles's hopes turned to Scotland. In January 1651 he would be crowned king there after disowning his father's loyal followers and making humiliating concessions to the

27. Smith, 25.
28. In another seventeenth-century version of the poem, 'kingdoms' reads 'kingdom' (Smith, pp. xiv, 275). With Smith I prefer 'kingdoms'.

Scottish Presbyterians, to whom he now looked for restoration to his English throne. It was to confront the Scottish threat that Cromwell returned from Ireland. He landed at Bristol on 28 May 1650.[29] Volleys of gunfire saluted him, as they were often to do in the days that followed. He received a stately welcome at Windsor on 31 May, and on the next day proceeded to a heroic reception in London, the largest public event in England at least since his return to London after suppressing the Leveller mutiny a year earlier, and perhaps since the execution of the king. After a large gathering of MPs and officers had greeted him on Hounslow Heath, he passed through Hyde Park to arrive at Westminster, 'accompanied by many more lords, and most of the members of parliament, and the council of state, the officers of the army, and many hundred well-affected gentlemen and citizens'. On 4 June he listened to the thanks of the Commons and to an 'eloquent oration' by the Speaker. Amid the celebrations the menace from Scotland persisted. Cromwell, and parliament, favoured a pre-emptive invasion. Fairfax, no admirer of the republic that he served, was unwilling to lead one. On 2 June Cromwell and Fairfax had a private meeting that was distinguished, as the first issue of Nedham's *Mercurius Politicus* reported, by 'remarkable expressions of mutual love and courtesy', 'sufficient to check the false tongues'.[30] Yet by the end of the month, as *Politicus* revealed in gingerly fashion,[31] Fairfax had resigned his command and been succeeded by Cromwell, who in July led north the army that would destroy the royalist cause, principally through its great victories at Dunbar in September 1650 and Worcester a year later.

Unlike Marvell's royalist poems of the previous two years, his 'An Horatian Ode upon Cromwell's Return from Ireland' was not published at the time. There is an element of supposition in assuming, as I shall, that it was written, in the form in which we have it, at or around the time of the event it describes. There is the same degree of supposition in making the parallel assumption, as I shall, about another of Marvell's unpublished poems, on the death of the writer Tom May, which occurred five months later, in November 1650. But occasional poems – that is, poems to mark occasions – were conventionally written while the mood created by them

29. *A Perfect Diurnall*, 3 June 1650, 278. For the narrative that follows, see W. C. Abbott, ed., *Writings and Speeches of Oliver Cromwell*, 4 vols. (Cambridge, Mass., 1937–47), ii. 261–2.
30. *MP*, 13 June 1650, 3–4; cf. ibid. 16.
31. Ibid. 27 June 1650, 47, 48.

persisted, and tended not to be rewritten thereafter. Sometimes, if the reader is to be spared endless qualification, we must settle for the probable. In this case the probability seems strong.[32]

While Cromwell was being feted in London, Nedham was preparing for the launch of *Mercurius Politicus*. Normally the material in the weekly newsbooks was set up in print day by day, events being described under the heading of the date on which news of them – which, in the case of the journals friendly to the regime, was supplied largely by the government – came through. *Politicus* normally followed that practice. Yet its first issue, which ran from 6 to 13 June, began with an exception to it. Since Cromwell had entered London on 1 June, his reception had no proper place in Nedham's opening number. But so important an event 'cannot here be omitted', and it is duly described.[33] Until now Cromwell, who had been extravagantly vilified and caricatured in royalist publications (not least Nedham's *Pragmaticus*), had been accorded only limited praise in pro-government ones,[34] whose sponsors at Westminster, while utterly dependent on his army and victories, were suspicious of his political intentions. Might he not use his military power against parliament, as he had done in 1647–9, and indeed would do again in 1653 and then as protector? There had, too, been little serious poetry in Cromwell's praise.

Together, Nedham and Marvell transformed his literary standing. Nedham added Cromwell's heroism to the reasons why his readers should commit themselves to the republic. In May 1650, shortly before Cromwell's return, his *The Case of the Commonwealth* observed that in fighting the Irish 'the lord lieutenant hath swept away those adversaries with the besom [broom] of vengeance, and made way by a continued chain of miraculous successes to shackle that rebellious nation .... Every month brings in fresh laurels of victory to their terror and amazement.'[35] *Politicus* develops the theme. Its opening issue declares that if 'reason' and 'interest' are not enough to bring the English to rally round the regime against the threat from Scotland, 'yet let them stoop with reverence at the name of that victorious commander, Cromwell', whose 'most famous services in

32. A third supposition, which again has strong probability but not certainty behind it, is that Marvell was indeed the author of the poems which we know only from the edition of his poems published posthumously in 1681. They include 'Tom May's Death' and the poem on the embassy of Oliver St John in 1651, though the relationship of the first of those poems to 'An Horatian Ode' surely dispels any doubts about Marvell's authorship.

33. Ibid. 13 June 1650, 3–4.

34. Cf. Norbrook, *Writing the English Republic*, 251.

35. *Case*, 57–8.

Ireland', 'being added to the garland of his English victories, have crowned him, in the opinion of all the world, for one of the wisest and most accomplished leaders among the present and past generations'. Even now that he has left Ireland, he conquers there by his 'bare reputation', which is 'strong enough against the stoutest hearts, and most impregnable castles', so that his army 'cannot forget to conquer wherever it comes'. When, on 11 June, Cromwell gave parliament an account of the situation in Ireland, Nedham observed that it is

> the wonder of our neighbour nations, that so much should be done in so little time, notwithstanding so many disadvantages; and for my part, if we take a view of his actions from first to last, I may (without flattery) proclaim him to be the only [that is, the exemplary] *novus princeps* that ever I met with in all the confines of history.[36]

'[S]o much' is likewise done in so little time in 'An Horatian Ode', where the Irish see themselves 'in one year tamed' and ashamedly acknowledge that 'So much one man can do' (73–5). In October *Politicus* published a letter, written or ostensibly written by an Irishman, decrying the failings of the nation's leadership, which have led a hitherto puissant land to yield all to Cromwell 'in one winter's season; such a winter's success in war, by so inconsiderable a party, against so considerable a kingdom, was never read or heard of: Alexander the Great, or Julius Caesar, or William the Conqueror never had the like success.'[37] Ruthless as Cromwell's victories were, Marvell's poem has the Irish confessing 'how good he is, how just' (79): Nedham invites his readers to 'take notice of the noble temper of the Lord General, all whose conquests are ever sweetened with acts of mercy'.[38]

Marvell's 'restless Cromwell ... urgèd his active star' (9–12): in *Politicus*, in July, Cromwell is 'as restless in his own sphere as the great intelligencers' – the stars – 'are in theirs'.[39] In the last section of the ode, Cromwell will carry his conquests from Scotland to France, to Italy, and to 'all states not free' (102). Nedham, whose *The Case of the Commonwealth* sets out 'the excellency of a free state', aims in *Politicus* to instruct 'all the states of Europe' in republican principles. He looks to Cromwell to lead a European

36. *MP*, 13 June 1650, 3–4, 5, 13.

37. Ibid. 31 Oct. 1650, 346.

38. Ibid. 12 Sept. 1650, 219.

39. Ibid. 25 July 1650, 109. Nedham was fond of astral political imagery at this time. In the opening issue of *Politicus*, which relates Cromwell's return to London, the general is a 'great star'. Ibid. 13 June 1650, 16. Cf. ibid. 27 June 1650, 46; 23 Jan. 1651, 545; John Hall's *Mercurius Britanicus*, 21 June 1648, 42–3.

war of liberation: 'this brave Scipio, after he hath wholly subdued Ireland and Scotland to the Commonwealth of England, ought to do the like elsewhere, that so our domineering and insolent neighbours may be brought under'.[40] The early issues of *Politicus* predict that in Scotland Cromwell will free 'the poor peasants and clients' from 'the great lords', who 'ride them *à la mode*, after the French fashion'; the oppressed commonalty there will 'learn which is the way to true liberty'; they would 'make a long leg now to the gallant Cromwell, if he should come and help them to their liberty'; Cromwell is advancing to Scotland 'for the freedom of the people there', who 'begin now to know themselves men, and to breathe after liberty'.[41] In the same issues Nedham portrays the current rebellion against the French monarchy, the Frondes, in the same light. 'The people of France', explains *Politicus*, 'have a mind to free themselves.' Nedham is especially interested in the struggle in Bordeaux, where the 'brave Bordelois', those 'French Roundheads', inspired by a radical programme learned from England, carry the torch. Nedham wishes himself among them 'for one twelvemonth, to teach them to spell the meaning of liberty'.[42] Like Marvell, Nedham looks beyond France to Italy. 'If things thus go on as they begin in Great Britain, Ireland and France', foretells the second issue of *Politicus*, 'the pope himself may in a short time be put to live upon shifts, as well as his faction'.[43]

In *The Case of the Commonwealth*, too, Nedham envisaged a European scenario in words that touch Marvell's ode. ''Tis madness to resist or blame', writes Marvell, 'The force of angry heaven's flame' (25–6). 'If it be considered', reflects Nedham,

> how the worm works in many parts of Europe to cast off the regal yoke, especially in France, Scotland, Ireland and other places, it must needs be as much madness to strive against the stream for the upholding of a power cast down by the Almighty as it was for the old sons of earth to heap up mountains against heaven.[44]

Nedham, like Marvell, represents Cromwell as a divinely appointed instrument: 'it is a privilege of this general, being consigned to him by heaven, to conquer wheresoever he comes; for evidence whereof, collect the many miraculous and signal successes bestowed upon him by God, in England

40. *MP*, 19 Sept. 1650, 255; 3 Oct. 1650, 281–2; cf. ibid. 27 June 1650, 47.
41. Ibid. 20 June 1650, 21–2, 32; 4 July 1650, 55.
42. Ibid. 13 June 1650, 11; 20 June 1650, 22; 27 June 1650, 36; 4 July 1650, 61. Cf. ibid. 27 May 1652, 1613–14; 12 May 1653, 2438.
43. Ibid. 20 June 1650, 26.
44. *Case*, 13; cf. *MP*, 22 Aug. 1650, 174.

and Ireland'.[45] Marvell, in writing of the anger of heaven, rehearsed the contemporary assumption that the civil wars had been the punishment of the nation's sins by a wrathful deity.[46] In Nedham's *The Case* it is 'the weight of sin' that causes the 'fatal circumvolutions' which overthrow and replace governments.[47]

For fate, to Nedham and Marvell alike, is the motor of history, the irresistible force that, with Cromwell as its medium, has destroyed the monarchy and established the military republic. In 'An Horatian Ode', fate is allied to 'Nature that hateth emptiness' (41). *The Case* tells us at its outset that the 'fate' of commonwealths is determined by 'a certain destiny or decree of nature', and later adds that 'after the miserable confusions of a civil war' men may 'use such means as nature instructs them' to erect a form of government that will preserve them.[48] When, in the ode, 'fate' killed the king, 'the state' foresaw its own 'fate' (37, 72). The argument of the opening chapter of *The Case* is 'that governments have their revolutions and fatal periods'. To help its readers 'understand what fate is', it quotes Seneca's definition of it as 'that providence which pulls down one kingdom or government and sets up another', and which 'hurls the powers of the world'. Again Nedham's words recall Marvell's lines on the insanity of resistance to heaven's instrument. Those who commit the 'madness' of opposing 'fate' merely 'fortif[y] castles in the air against fatal necessity to maintain a fantasy of pretended loyalty'.[49] When the royalist cause was finally destroyed at Worcester, Nedham observed 'how fatal it is for men to fight against [God's] decrees, who hath made so many declarations from heaven of his resolution to establish' the republic.[50] Fate has dissolved the ties of subjects to their monarch. 'The old allegiance', argues *The Case*, 'is extinct' and 'must give place to a new':[51] in the ode, nature 'must make room' (43) for the world which 'fate' has decreed.

To Marvell and Nedham alike, fate has laid bare the facts of political might. It was in *The Case* that Nedham declared that 'the power of the

45. *MP*, 25 July 1650, 109.

46. Even in his 'A Poem upon the Death of his Highness the Lord Protector' in 1658, where Cromwell, who in the ode – 'burning through the air' (21) – was a purely or almost purely elemental force, now assumes a human face, he remains the force of 'angry heaven' (16) (even though he is also 'Heaven's favourite', 157). See too *PWAM* i. 167.

47. *Case*, 9.

48. Ibid. 7, 36.

49. Ibid. 9, 14. 'Fate', and 'fatal periods' and fatal individuals and fatal 'blows' and 'interests', run through Nedham's writings.

50. *MP*, 18 Sept. 1651, 1063.

51. *Case*, 4.

sword is, and ever hath been, the foundation of all titles to government'.[52] In the ode, the 'justice' that 'complains' against fate has been separated from power (37), but at the end of the poem justice and power are apparently reunited, in the 'erect' sword that has destroyed the past and will sustain the future (116). *The Case* castigates royalists who explain their refusal of allegiance to the republic on the ground that 'it is by the sword unlawfully erected'.[53] For as Hobbes, explains Nedham, has shown, 'the sword of war' and 'the sword of justice' 'are but one' and 'are in the same hands'.[54] In the ode the 'fate' of the 'state' will be 'happy' (72, 103). The rhetorical and poetically charged conclusion of *The Case* observes that the English will lay 'the foundations of future happiness' by securing their 'free state'.[55] In early July 1650 *Politicus* remarks on the chance which the arrival of Cromwell's army now gives to the Scots to become 'as free as the English', and thus to 'receive their happiness' from him. In January 1651 the newsbook declares that the free state of the Netherlands, if only its people will seize their opportunity of liberty, can be 'happy forever hereafter'.[56]

★★

But will a free state really bring happiness? The Marvell of 'Tom May's Death' does not think so. May, an established poet and playwright before the civil wars, had supported parliament during them. In 1647 he published an approving *History* of the Long Parliament. An abbreviated edition appeared in Latin in March 1650 and in an English translation in June. May died on 13 November of that year and was buried, at the behest of the 'free state', in Westminster Abbey. In 'Tom May's Death', which mocks and scourges May's memory, Marvell resumes his royalist stance of 1648–9. It is the poet's task, he now writes, to 'Sing', amid the destruction of the civil wars, 'of better times' (69). His poem to Richard Lovelace had done so. It mourned, in 'times ... much degenerate from those | Which your sweet muse with your fair fortune chose', the 'candid age' of the pre-war literary world (1–5). 'Tom May's Death' summons, from that world, the memory of Ben Jonson. When Marvell's May arrives, with a hangover, on 'the Elysian side', Jonson's shade castigates that 'Most servile

52. Ibid. 5.
53. That and other parallels between *The Case* and the ode were noticed by E. E. Duncan-Jones, 'The Erect Sword in Marvell's Horatian Ode', *Etudes Anglaises*, 15 (1962), 172–4.
54. *Case*, 136.
55. Ibid. 127–8.
56. *MP*, 4 July 1650, 55; 9 Jan. 1651, 512.

wit and mercenary pen', 'Malignant poet and historian both' (40–2). The 'historian' is the composer of the narrative of the Long Parliament: the 'malignant poet' is the author of the translation, published in 1627, of Lucan's poem *Pharsalia*, a work of republican sympathies. If May had lived, implies Marvell, he would have 'obtruded' on 'the novice statesmen' of the republic 'some Roman-cast similitude' that equated them with heroes of classical antiquity.[57] May's *History* had compared the parliamentary forces of the civil war with 'the armies of Brutus and Cassius, that stood for liberty'.[58] In Marvell's poem, 'Brutus and Cassius' are 'the people's cheats'. There had in fact been nothing crude or polemical in May's analogy. His partisanship was altogether gentler and subtler than Marvell's poem invites us to expect.[59] In updating his *History* in the abbreviated version of 1650 he avoided passing judgement on the regicide. Even so, May was implicated in the rule of the republic, as a colleague of Nedham and Milton (who had himself made extensive use of May's *History* in *Eikonoklastes*) for the new regime. The end of 'An Horatian Ode' looks forward to Cromwell's invasion of Scotland. The incursion was justified by an official declaration in late June which emphatically insisted on its 'justice and necessity'.[60] May was instructed to translate the declaration into Latin for a Continental audience (a task that had initially been entrusted to Milton).[61] This was the time at which the English version of the abbreviated *History* appeared. It is harsher than the longer one in its hostility to the Scots and to Presbyterianism,[62] an attitude which May shared with Marvell and Milton and Nedham, and which is further voiced in a pamphlet of September 1650, in support of the Cromwellian invasion of Scotland, that was reportedly written by May, *The Changeable Covenant*. In anti-Scottish sentiment, many Cromwellians and many royalists could come together. But in other matters the two sides were deadly enemies.

'An Horatian Ode' and 'Tom May's Death' say exactly opposite things. They might have been written to honour the principle, so favoured in

57. Lucan's place in seventeenth-century political literature and thought is a large theme of Norbrook, *Writing the English Republic.*

58. Quoted by Gerard Reedy, ' "An Horatian Ode" and "Tom May's Death" ', *Studies in English Literature*, 20 (1980), 146.

59. J. G. A. Pocock, 'Thomas May and the Narrative of Civil War', in Derek Hirst and Richard Strier, eds., *Writing and Political Engagement in Seventeenth-Century England* (Cambridge, 1999), 112–44.

60. *A Declaration of the Parlement of England, upon the Marching of the Armie into Scotland* (1650).

61. *Cal. SP Dom. 1650*, 228.

62. *ODNB*, 'Thomas May'.

Renaissance intellectual training, of entering into both sides of a question. A theme of Marvell's writing of 1648–50 is the rival claims of writing and fighting. In the poem on the death of Lord Francis Villiers, the men who 'honour' his memory will 'not write so many' poems but 'kill' so many soldiers. In 'An Horatian Ode' the 'forward youth' is likewise enjoined to stop writing and to fight instead. Yet in 'Tom May's Death' the man of the hour is not the soldier. It is the poet who remains loyal to the cause that May has betrayed, and whose writing is itself described in the vocabulary of warfare, for he 'draws, | And single fights'. The satirical thrust of the poem yields to a gravity that we recognize from the lines where the ode itself is gravest, on the subject of the regicide. 'When the sword glitters o'er the judge's head, | And fear has coward churchmen silencéd' (63–4) – the Anglican clergy, almost all of whom kept quiet at and after the time of the regicide[63] –

> Then is the poet's time, 'tis then he draws,
> And single fights forsaken virtue's cause
> He, when the wheel of empire whirleth back,
> And though the world's disjointed axle crack,
> Sings still of ancient rights and better times,
> Seeks wretched good, arraigns successful times.
>
> (65–70)

In 'An Horatian Ode' the 'time' is not 'the poet's' but the soldier's (''Tis time to leave the books in dust'). The 'ancient rights' of which it was May's duty to 'sing still' are pleaded, in the ode, 'in vain', and the forward youth is to 'cease' to 'sing | His numbers languishing'. Instead of espousing 'forsaken virtue's cause', he is to 'forsake' the muses who speak for it (1–8). The 'successful crimes' of the May poem are (apparently anyway) endorsed in the ode, and 'wretched good' (70) – which in the ode is represented by Charles I's 'helpless right' (62) – is (or anyway seems to be) abandoned. If, in 'Tom May's Death', Brutus and Cassius are 'the people's cheats', in the ode the death of 'Caesar' (23), Charles I, has (or seems to have) history on its side. In the ode's concluding lines, the symbol of the erect sword unites (or seems to do) war with justice: in the May poem the sword, glittering o'er the judge's head, is justice's enemy.[64]

63. Wilcher, *Writing of Royalism*, 272.
64. The use of the noun 'architect' in the two poems provides another contrast: Corns, *Uncloistered Virtue*, 234.

On the face of it, the exchange of the pen for the sword in the opening lines of the ode stands for a commitment to the new political order, whose success depends on the disarming of royalism. Poetry is identified with royalism, albeit by a poem – a poem, moreover, which ostensibly renounces the royalist cause. Those opening lines, and others in the poem, are close in spirit and language to words written later in the same year by Nedham's literary partner John Hall. Arguing for submission to the republic, Hall denounces inert royalists who 'sit still' and are 'lulled asleep with some small continuance of peace ... as if the body politic could not languish of an internal disease'. It associates them with 'speculative men', 'men merely contemplative', who follow 'those notions which they find in books' and 'fight only with pen, ink, and paper'. 'The people', he adds, 'languish when their princes' are most powerful, but are 'upon the removal of a prince cheerful and relieved'. Under monarchy they 'languish in a brutish servitude', and 'wax old', unless or until 'better stars and prosperity awaken them out of that lethargy, and restore them to their pristine liberty, and its daughter happiness.'[65] A month after Cromwell's return from Ireland, Nedham wrote in a similar spirit. In the first civil war he had identified royalist writing with a weakness for 'ale'[66] and with 'melancholy'.[67] Now he exclaimed: 'How sweet the air of a commonwealth is beyond that of a monarchy! Is it not much better then to breathe freely, and be lively, upon a new score of allegiance, than pine, and fret, and fume, in behalf of the old non-entity, till wit, soul, and all be drowned in ale and melancholy?'[68] Was the 'wit' of royalist poets being 'drowned' in 1650? Is it, in Marvell's ode, a fault of royalist verse to look, not 'forward' with

65. John Hall, 'The Grounds and Reasons of Monarchy', in John Toland (ed.), *The Oceana of James Harrington and his Other Works* (1700), 4–5, 11, 14. (Toland's edition slightly alters the text of 1650, but not at these points.) Cf. *Mercurius Britanicus*, 25 Nov. 1644, 470; 10 Feb. 1645, 548. Hall's text was completed at some point after the attempted Orange coup in Amsterdam in July 1650 ('Grounds and Reasons', 10).

66. *Mercurius Britanicus*, 11 Jan. 1644, 153.

67. See e.g. *Mercurius Britanicus*, 28 Oct. 1644, 435; 7 July 1645, 802; cf. *The Recantation of Mercurius Aulicus* (1644), 3. (The making of those associations was not, in itself, a distinctively Roundhead impulse. Nedham himself, in his Roundhead phase, got accused of propensities to ale and melancholy, and in his Cavalier one he could level similar charges at parliamentarians. It is as a Roundhead writer, of course, that the poet Tom May carries his hangover in Marvell's poem. Cf. *Mercurius Pragmaticus*, 7 Mar. 1648, 1–2.)

68. *MP*, 11 July 1650, 65. Cf. ibid. 13 June–18 July 1650, 4, 50, 63, 81. In another mood Nedham did write, two months later, that 'the wits of the time are otherwise taken up than with meditations and studies of learning', preoccupied as they are with 'private luxury or public conspiracy'; but in those practices he merely saw alternative outlets for that favourite target of his, 'fancies': ibid. 22 Aug. 1650, 163.

the 'youth' of 'An Horatian Ode', but backward? The second line of his poem to Lovelace addressed his subject's 'sweet muse', which is the victim of present times. His royalist poem on the death of Lord Hastings in 1649 appeared in a volume entitled (conventionally enough) *Lachrymae Musarum* ('The Tears of the Muses'). In the second line of 'An Horatian Ode', where the forward youth is to forsake his muses, it seems that Marvell has cleared and dried his eyes.

Yet in the May poem he reverts to the claims of royalism and of poetry. So close to Nedham in the ode, Marvell now directly opposes him. Nedham composed the inscription on May's tomb in Westminster Abbey. A year later *Politicus* would give high prominence to a long quotation from Lucan's *Pharsalia* in the translation, 'more excellent', declared the newsbook, than the Latin, 'by the best of poets, Thomas May our English Lucan'.[69] Upon May's death the council of state promptly asked his friends the MPs Thomas Chaloner and Henry Marten to make the arrangements for May's burial and to commission a continuation of his *History*, to reach the Commonwealth period.[70] Nedham was those men's friend, too. He had long voiced admiration for Marten. In the winter of 1650–1 *Politicus* recommended policies which Chaloner and his allies were advancing in parliament. Nedham shared their enthusiasm for the building up of commercial and naval strength. ''Tis trade', he maintained, 'must make this nation rich and secure.'[71] Chaloner longed for Cromwell to defeat the Scots and to look 'towards the sea, which [is] our main business now'. Nedham concurred: God, he declared in 1652, had made the English republic great 'by land and will by sea; for without this the land is nothing'.[72] The colourful private lives and irreverent wit of May and his friends in the Commons stood in marked contrast to the Puritan mainstream. Wood wrote that May 'became a *debauchee ad omnia*, entertained very ill principles as to religion', and 'kept very beastly and atheistical company, of whom Tho. Chaloner was one'; and that Chaloner himself was 'as far from being a Puritan or a

69. *MP*, 20 Nov. 1651, 1206; cf. ibid. 15 Jan. 1652, 1335–6.
70. *Cal. SP Dom. 1650*, 432; see too *Cal. SP Dom. 1651*, 1.
71. Worden, '"Wit in a Roundhead"', 326–7.
72. Nickolls, 43; Selden, *Of the Dominion of the Seas*, 483; cf. *Mercurius Pragmaticus*, 15 Feb. 1648, 8. Would that we knew something of Milton's feelings about Chaloner and his friend Henry Neville, who were involved with Milton in the srate's negotiations with the envoy from Oldenburg, Hermann Mylius, in 1651–2 (see the references to them in Miller, *John Milton and the Oldenburg Safeguard)*. When Milton complained at that time that only three or four members of the council of state had ever been abroad (ibid. 172), the men he had in mind must have included the well-travelled and cosmopolitan Neville and Chaloner.

Presbyterian as the east is from the west; for he was a boon companion, of Henry Marten's gang' and 'was of the natural religion, and loved to enjoy the comfortable importances of this life, without any thought of laying up for a wet day'.[73] Marten was a freethinker with a reputation for alcoholic and sexual excess, whom Cromwell, in his apoplectic speech at the expulsion of the Rump, would call a 'whoremaster'.[74] He was a close friend not only of Chaloner but of the equally irreverent MP Henry Neville. During the winter of 1650–1 the reputations of 'Tom Chaloner, Harry Neville and those wits', or 'Tom Chaloner, Tom May (when living) and that gang', affronted the religious sensibilities of the Cromwellians.[75]

Accusations and imputations that are levelled at May in the poem would have been more fairly aimed at Nedham. Nedham, the king's propagandist of 1647–9, had employed more obviously than May a 'mercenary pen' to betray 'great Charles' (76). He had bestowed, in Marvell's term, 'Roman-cast similitude[s]' on the regicides in *The Case of the Commonwealth*, by proclaiming the 'ancient virtue' and 'ancient courage and love of liberty' among the assassins of Julius Caesar; and he was ready to bestow many more. Marvell's May, who drinks with other republicans, stumbles into the afterlife after a spree in the London taverns. There is every chance that in Marvell's imagination Nedham, who left jocular testimony of his own drunken escapades in the early phase of the republic, was on the same jaunt. Two months before May's death the royalist poet John Cleveland asserted that Nedham 'lives as in the days of Pantagruel, and drinks as though it were to quench damnation'.[76] Though the poem alludes to May's poetry and *History*, it is in 'talk', not in writing, that it envisages the portentous drawing of Roman parallels: the talk of 'you all', in 'your wine', as the drunkards transfer 'old Rome hither' (46–9). Who, other than May, is present at the 'talk'? There are 'novice statesmen' present (46), among them no doubt Chaloner, whose pamphlet of 1657, *A True and Exact Relation of the Strange Finding out of Moses his Tombe*, a hoax designed to discredit doctrinal orthodoxy and religious solemnity, was 'invented in

73. Worden, *Rump Parliament*, 260.

74. Abbott, ed., *Writings and Speeches*, ii. 642.

75. Nickolls, 43.

76. *Character of Mercurius Politicus*, 3. For the place of taverns in literary activity (including John Hall's) around this time, see Nicholas McDowell, 'Urquhart's Rabelais: Translation, Patronage, and Cultural Politics', *English Literary Renaissance*, 36 (2005), 273–303. Hall is alleged to have planned the weekly content of his *Mercurius Britanicus* in a tavern: Peacey, *Politicians and Pamphleteers*, 230.

a tavern'.[77] It sounds as if there is larger company too (44–9). Is Nedham there? And may it be that in 1650 he and May not only talked and drank together, but wrote together too? In the first civil war May had reportedly helped Nedham with the composition of *Britanicus*.[78] When Nedham, who liked to publicize the writings of his associates, lauded May in *Politicus*, was he remembering not only a debt in *Britanicus* but a more recent one? Did May earn the otherwise puzzling accusation about 'Roman-cast' parallels by helping Nedham in his writings of 1650? And are Marvell's charges aimed not only at the dead May but at the living Nedham?

That, of course, is but a guess. But even if it is wrong, Marvell's poem attacked everything that, in the year of its composition, Nedham represented. If it was aimed at him as well as May, then Nedham, who was used to making heroes of men in one cause and insulting them in another, could hardly have complained. Would he even have minded? His changes of allegiance, those outwardly zestful adjustments to altered facts of power, conceal whatever lay within him. Yet it is hard to suppose that in writing for the Commonwealth he ceased to understand the royalist sentiments which he had voiced so eloquently in *Pragmaticus*, and equally difficult to imagine him not enjoying a poem whose wit and satire were close in spirit to his own. Could it – to guess again – have been written within and for a coterie of wits, to which Marvell and Nedham belonged, and where the most profound conflicts of political allegiance and perspective were debated in the vein of *joco-serio*: the vein in which Nedham himself liked to proclaim that 'in the midst of jest I am much in earnest'?[79] In the May poem Marvell himself moves, on the most momentous of political subjects,

77. Anthony Wood, quoted in a forthcoming article by Martin Dzelzainis on the 'religious fictions' of Chaloner and Neville.

78. Smith, 117; *Mercurius Aquaticus, or, The Water-Poets Answer* (1643), 1; *Mercurius Aquaticus his Answer to Britanicus* [1643], 1. Royalist critics of *Britanicus* had aimed taunts at Nedham similar to those visited on May in the poem. One such writer, in verses published in 1646, described, in terms reminiscent of Marvell's poem, *Mercurius Britanicus his Welcome to Hell.* (Shortly before May's death, John Cleveland called Nedham 'the Cerberus of Hell': *Second Character of Mercurius Politicus*, 1; cf. *CP* iv. 1049, 1052.) In Marvell's poem, Ben Jonson complains that May 'first prostituted hast | Our spotless knowledge and the studies chaste, | Apostatising from our arts and us' (71–3). A royalist critic of *Britanicus* had remarked that even if its author could claim to have a 'good wit', 'yet to prostitute it to the recreation of a herd of readers', in a scurrilous weekly publication written to 'a poor vulgar ignoble end', 'is to defile and strumpet one of the greatest ornaments God and nature have bestowed upon us; and to make wit, which was born to rule, the fool and jester of the people': *Mercurius Anti-Britanicus, or, The Second Part of the King's Cabinet Vindicated* (1645), 25.

79. Above, Ch. 2.

between jest and gravity. Aubrey may be right to say that Marvell 'would never drink hard in company'. Yet he also tells us that he 'loved wine',[80] and we know him to have drunk it, later in life, with his good friend the bibulous John Rushworth.[81]

There had been at least one previous occasion when Nedham's writing had stood directly opposite a friend's. This was in June 1648, when his antagonist – or apparent antagonist – was his close friend John Hall. The subject of their confrontation was Henry Marten, who more than any other MP had embodied the courageous radicalism for which Nedham's *Britanicus* had spoken, and who in 1643 had been expelled from the Commons, and committed to the Tower, for suggesting that kingly rule was unnecessary. He was soon released, but only in 1646 was he at last readmitted to the House. 'I am glad of it,' remarked *Britanicus* pointedly of his return.[82] As editor of the royalist *Pragmaticus*, it is true, Nedham often mocked Marten, but he did so with hints, even amid the obligatory political antagonism, of affection. On 13 June 1648 Nedham and John Hall, the one as editor of the royalist *Pragmaticus*, the other as editor of the parliamentarian *Britanicus*, turned to standard set-pieces of Roman history to supply, in their descriptions of Marten, a contrast of treatment that was surely prearranged. Thus Hall's *Britanicus*, in the spirit of Nedham's earlier newsbook of the same name, makes Marten a Roman hero. He is 'our English Brutus, that durst in the beginning of these times speak more than others could, and whose continued endeavours ever since hath made the noble love he bore his country sufficiently appear'. On the same day *Pragmaticus* aligns him with a Roman villain. Marten 'having played Catiline in the senate, he means to trace him in his tragedy'.[83]

We cannot know whether Marvell's confrontation with Nedham over Tom May in 1650 was likewise prearranged. Was Marvell himself inspired by, and did he seek to give voice to, the opposition of the political perspectives that his poetry of 1650 encapsulates? At all events there is no sign that the conflicting positions of Marvell and Nedham upon May's

80. *AMC* 218. 81. Margoliouth, ii. 35, 337, 340.

82. *Mercurius Britanicus*, 12 Jan. 1646, 1000.

83. Ibid. 13 June 1648, 35; *Mercurius Pragmaticus*, 13 June 1648, 7. *Pragmaticus*, reporting an attack by Marten on the Scots – on whose faults, if on little else, it and radical Roundheads could agree – had observed that Marten had spoken on the subject 'in such plain language, after his old manner'. See too *Pragmaticus* on the anti-Scottish sentiments of Marten's fellow wit Thomas Chaloner: 28 Sept. 1647, 4.

death caused any difficulty between the two men. Nedham's own career had conditioned him to confrontations of this kind. He was also used to forgetting them and to being allowed to forget them. Time and again his 'tergiversations' led him to vilify politicians who, when they later employed him, would overlook that denigration. Even when his reversals created hostility, it did not last. In his personal dealings we watch him and his friend James Thompson turning on each other in venomous fury when Thompson allegedly betrayed Nedham to the Commonwealth in 1649. Then we find the two men resuming their mirthful comradeship soon afterwards.[84] Among writers, even as they abused each other and highlighted each others' deeds of apostasy, a corporate respect or identity could cross even the fiercest of party divisions and survive the starkest of treachery. Marvell's May, with his 'little mind', suffers hurt feelings upon learning, in the afterlife, that he has been survived by Sir William Davenant, who, as Charles's Poet Laureate, got the job May wanted, and who, in Marvell's lines, 'laughs' at May's death (77–9). The names of Davenant and Jonson, linked in an admiring spirit in the poem, had been joined by Nedham's *Britanicus* in a hostile one.[85] In 1650 Davenant was in the Tower, and in July a vote in parliament named him as one of six royalists to be tried for treason and thus to face the death penalty. Milton laboured to save his life.[86] So – in co-operation with him? – did Nedham, who risked offending his parliamentary masters by voicing in *Politicus* (albeit in the jesting language that was his familiar protective cover) the hope that Davenant might be spared his 'misfortune' and be allowed to live to complete his poem *Gondibert* – as he was.[87] If it is true that Davenant interceded (perhaps with Marvell) to save Milton's life at the Restoration, the solidarity of writers prevailed again. Maybe Nedham, who in 1660 was expected, with as much confidence and reason as Milton, to face the gallows, owed his survival to some similar intervention.

Marvell's poem assigns to Jonson the role that Jonson had given to himself and to poetry, as the arbiter and instructor and reformer of the world. No

84. D. Gardiner, ed., *Oxinden and Peyton Letters*, q.v. 'Thompson'. There is fuller material on this subject in BL, Add. MS 28002.

85. Above, Ch. 2.

86. Darbishire, 30; Lewalski, 288, 667–8.

87. *MP*, 11 July 1650, 70; 18 July 1650, 84–5. Milton is first recorded as performing his duties (which had begun two months earlier) as licenser of *Politicus* on the day, 17 March 1651, on which *Gondibert* was assigned for publication by the printer of the newsbook, Thomas Newcomb (French, iii. 256). Bulstrode Whitelocke, a figure who will recur in this book, may have aided Davenant too: Longleat House, Whitelocke MS X, fo. 20. (John Hall dedicated his translation of Longinus to Whitelocke in 1649.)

writer had been so widely claimed for civil war royalism. We repeatedly come across him in the prefatory poems of that ambitious statement of literary royalism, the edition of the works of Beaumont and Fletcher that was published by Humphrey Moseley in 1647. James Howell's contribution (which, like Marvell's May poem, introduces Jonson familiarly, as 'Ben', without the surname) reproaches the present times as Marvell's Jonson does May: 'Had now grim Ben been breathing', writes Howell, 'with what rage, | And high-swollen fury had he lashed this age.' Likewise the reminder by Marvell's Jonson that the true poet 'arraigns successful crimes' points back to lines, in the Beaumont and Fletcher publication, of Sir John Berkenhead, who in the first civil war had been Nedham's adversary in the conflict of the pen but who in 1647–9 was his ally in it. His poem turns to Jonson in looking back to a pre-war world which was free of the present literary degeneracy, and where 'high crimes were still arraigned'.[88]

Marvell's use of Jonson also recalls the royalist Nedham of the late 1640s. When Marvell's Jonson is found 'Sounding of ancient heroes, such as were | The subject's safety and the rebel's fear' (15–16), Marvell presumably has in mind Jonson's play *Catiline his Conspiracy*, which, despite its failure on the English stage in 1611, had become, in print, a powerful influence on English perceptions of rebellion.[89] The 'ancient heroes' of the play are Cicero and Cato, whom Marvell introduces later in his poem as the kinds of classical hero whose names May had misused, or anyway would like to misuse, in rebellion's cause (48). Nedham's *Pragmaticus*, the newsbook that in June 1648 declared that Henry Marten meant to 'trace' Catiline 'in his tragedy', had eight months earlier described the leaders of the new model army as being 'resolved to follow the example of Catiline in Ben Jonson', and had imagined them saying, as Catiline does (in the first person singular) at the start of Jonson's play, 'The ills which we have done cannot be safe, | But by attempting greater'.[90] Nedham repeated the quotation in November 1648, to characterize the army leaders who had just drawn up the *Remonstrance* that announced their resolve to bring the king to justice.[91] The lines assert something close to what, from a

88. Arnold Glover and A. R. Waller, eds., *The Works of Francis Beaumont and John Fletcher*, 10 vols. (Cambridge, 1905–12), i. pp. xxvi, xliii.
89. Its impact is explored in Barbara de Luna, *Jonson's Romish Plot: 'Catiline' and its Historical Context* (Oxford, 1967), ch. 10.
90. *Mercurius Pragmaticus*, 9 Nov. 1647, 63; Jonson, *Catiline his Conspiracy*, I. 79–80.
91. Nedham, *Plea for the King and Kingdom*, 10; cf. *Mercurius Pragmaticus*, 28 Nov. 1648, 8.

royalist perspective – from the perspective of the Marvell of 'Tom May's Death' – the concluding couplet of 'An Horatian Ode' states: 'The same arts that did gain a power | Must it maintain.' From the same viewpoint the 'restless Cromwell' of Marvell's ode answers to another soliloquy of Jonson's Catiline, who is addicted to

> that restless ill, that still doth build
> Upon success; and ends not in aspiring;
> But there begins. And ne'er is filled,
> While aught remains that seems but worthy desiring.[92]

Yet in their uses of Jonson, too, Marvell and Nedham would again be diametrically opposed. It happened at a much later time, indeed in the last year of both their lives, in a confrontation which would look back at verse written over half a century. In 1627 Jonson had contributed a prefatory poem to May's translation of Lucan's *Pharsalia*. It begins with unease on Jonson's part, which better acquaintance with the work has overcome. When, viewing ancient Rome, Jonson reads

> Of fortune's wheel by Lucan driv'n about,
> And the world in it, I begin to doubt,
> At every line some pin thereof should slack
> At least, if not the general engine crack.

Those lines themselves draw on words of Jonson's *Catiline*. 'Repulse upon repulse?', Catiline there rages. How he wishes

> That I could reach the axle, where the pins are
> Which bolt this frame, that I might pull them out
> And pluck all into chaos with myself![93]

Marvell, in having Jonson say 'And though the world's disjointed axle crack', draws the two passages together. In doing so he points us towards the opening pages of Lucan's *Pharsalia*, a passage which Jonson himself had surely had in mind, and which, as we shall find, is a powerful presence in 'An Horatian Ode'. When, in May's translation of the passage, Caesar breaks the republic, 'the knot of nature is dissolved, | And the world's

92. Jonson, *Catiline his Conspiracy*, III. 864–7.
93. Ibid. III. 174–7; Norbrook, *Writing the English Republic*, 279. In his other Roman tragedy, *Sejanus his Fall* (II. 178–87), Jonson used his own translation of a passage from *Pharsalia* to portray the evils of Machiavellian statecraft.

chaos in one hour dissolved | .... The falling world's now jarring frame no peace | No league shall hold'.[94]

Twenty-eight years later, the invocation of Jonson's texts in 1650 would have a sequel in the episode that brought Marvell and Nedham into opposition again. In 1678 Nedham turned Jonson's play, and perhaps Marvell's poem on May too, against Marvell. In his recently published *An Account of the Growth of Popery and Arbitrary Government*, Marvell had attacked (without naming) Nedham, and had represented the party for which Nedham now wrote as conspirators from the pages of Sallust, the principal source of *Catiline his Conspiracy*.[95] Nedham replied in his pamphlet of March, *Honesty's Best Policy*, for which he was handsomely rewarded by the ministry. In answering (but not naming) the 'virulent scribe' who has written *An Account*, that 'treasonous libellous pamphlet', Nedham maintains that the true Catiline is the hero of Marvell's pamphlet, the Earl of Shaftesbury, whose supporters maintained that the government had never recovered from the dismissal of that indispensable figure from the Lord Chancellorship in 1673. In the passage that then follows, Nedham ventures an allusion to Jonson in which Marvell at least, and perhaps Marvell alone, would have grasped a reference to his and Nedham's earlier joint lives. 'A poet of our own', recalls Nedham of Ben Jonson, 'fancies the frame of the world to be bolted together with a small pin or two; if that be put out, all falls to pieces: therefore when he brings in Catiline in the third act, in a great chafe, because himself was rejected and Cicero chosen consul, he makes him thus vent himself in a lofty rant.' Nedham then quotes the lines from the play that are reproduced above ('Repulse upon repulse ...'). He follows them with a passage in which Shaftesbury becomes, in his own deluded estimate, the 'pin'. Nedham's words also appear to indicate that Marvell's description of May as 'malignant poet and historian both' ought now to be applied to Marvell himself:

> So that you see, if but a pin or so be out, all falls into confusion, if there is truth in poetry. And it may be this was our case, who can tell? For poets have unlucky hits many times, as well as politicians. So have historians too: for the card-keeper (or recorder) of the faction, I mean the author of the new directory for petty statesmen, that is to say *The Account of the Growth of Popery and Arbitrary Government*, etc. reporteth to us that the present Lord

94. Lucan, *Pharsalia*, I. 73–80. In the Loeb translation, 'the whole distracted fabric of the shattered firmament will overthrow its laws'.

95. *PWAM* ii. 193–4.

> Chancellor, another Cicero, came into [Shaftesbury's] place before the end of 1673, as the former Cicero came into that which was aimed at by Catiline.[96]

If Nedham's treatment of *An Account* is severe, it is no more so than the exchanges of insult familiar among writers who endured each other's crossfire in the party struggles of seventeenth-century England. But is the passage not also a piece of knowing playfulness, a private joke for the sole understanding of a fellow author whom events had often brought together with Nedham but had sometimes, as now and as in November 1650, placed opposite him? At the time of Nedham's riposte, the crisis of the Popish Plot was fast approaching. As we shall find when we trace Nedham's relations with Milton, even the most urgent political prospects did not deter the mischievous exchange of private allusions among literary friends. They may even have encouraged it.

At the end of their lives, then, Nedham and Marvell were bound together, albeit as adversaries. But why, at the time of 'Tom May's Death', did the two men, whose writings had been closely aligned in the summer of 1650 and would often be aligned again later in the Interregnum, stand at opposite poles? How was it that Marvell, having apparently forsaken the royalist muses in the ode, returned to royalist poetic duty five months later? To those questions we now turn.

96. Nedham, *Honesty's Best Policy* (1678), 7–8; for Nedham and Marvell in 1678 see too *AMC* 19. The Chancellor was Heneage Finch, Earl of Nottingham.

4

Marvell in 1650

If the occasions that prompted Marvell's two political poems of 1650 had happened in the reverse order – if Tom May had died before Cromwell's return from Ireland – the opposition between 'An Horatian Ode' and 'Tom May's Death' could be given a simple explanation. The May poem would be the last of Marvell's royalist poems, and the ode the first of his Cromwellian ones. We could read the ode as a testament to a conversion from one position to an exactly contrary one. That change was duly followed, we could then say, by the poem, in 1651, in support – or apparently in support – of the republic's embassy, led by Cromwell's cousin and intimate ally Oliver St John, which went to The Hague in March of that year with the purpose of undermining the Stuart cause. Instead, the May poem comes between the occasions that produced the ode and the poem on the embassy. Marvell's courage in the political adversity of Charles II's reign would persuade posterity of his consistency. He himself valued the integrity of his conscience, and his loyalty to it. Yet there was more than one part of him. Nedham had long been termed a 'chameleon'. In the Restoration a satirical critic decided that Marvell was 'begot by some Proteus of a chameleon ... he fights forward and backward' and 'slashes with a two-edged sword and fights both ways'.[1] Marvell was also called, as Nedham had long been,[2] a 'jester',[3] a noun that was not associated with solidity of viewpoint. In both writers contemporaries found an indefinable unstable quality, which in Marvell's case was called 'amphibious',[4] in Nedham's 'double-sexed'.[5] In 1656 Marvell was thought 'a notable English Italo-Machavillian' (perhaps a pun to mean 'Machiavillain').[6] None of

1. Edmund Hickeringhill, in comments reproduced in Donno, *Andrew Marvell*, 40–1.
2. *Mercurius Anti-Britanicus*, 25.
3. *AMC* 142.
4. Ibid. 156.
5. *Mercurius Anti-Britanicus*, 26.
6. *AMC* 44.

those characterizations conforms to the image of him favoured by his memorialists.

Then there is the testimony of an undated letter, apparently written in 1653 or possibly 1654, by Anne Sadleir, who had been a friend and 'constant benefactress' of Marvell's father. She was aunt to Cyriack Skinner, that admiring biographer of Milton who, with Marvell and Nedham, was among the 'particular friends' that, on Skinner's own account, frequented his house in that decade.[7] Sadleir claimed that Milton, because of the state of his eyes, was only able to complete *Eikonoklastes* thanks to the 'help' of Marvell.[8] If that were true, then we would find Marvell doing in 1649 what, in the May poem and the ode, we have seen him doing in 1650: presenting both a royalist and a counter-royalist face. Marvell's principal modern biographer judged Sadleir's claim 'utterly incredible', the worthless testimony of 'a credulous old lady'.[9] We should certainly question it. It is one thing to envisage the author of Marvell's royalist verse of 1648–9 and of 'Tom May's Death' writing 'An Horatian Ode', where the royalism identifiable in the poem is only half the story, another to envisage the same writer voicing the unambiguously aggressive anti-royalism of *Eikonoklastes*. Perhaps the likeliest explanation of her statement is that she misunderstood or misremembered some now irrecoverable literary and political contact, perhaps at some point between 1650 and 1652, between Marvell and Milton, for which, as will become apparent, there would have been ample scope under the Commonwealth. Even so, her testimony is not laughable. It becomes so only if we scorn the possibility in 1649 of a double-sidedness in Marvell's writing that in the following year would make him first the literary partner and then the literary adversary of Nedham.

The Interregnum presented its inhabitants with a series of choices of a hitherto unknown kind, each of them with unpredictable consequences. When Cromwell returned from Ireland, the military defeat of royalism was far from certain. Three months later, on the eve of the Battle of Dunbar in September 1650, the Puritan cause stood on the brink of extinction. The ode, which assigns the royalist cause to the past and the Cromwellian one to the future, is not, in that respect, a statement of the obvious. It is a prophecy. 'Tom May's Death' does not revoke the prophecy. In the poem, after all, the 'cause' of 'virtue' has been 'forsaken'. Though May ought to have stood true to it, Marvell offers no indication that he could have rescued it. May, it is

7. Darbishire, 74. 8. *AMC* 44. 9. Legouis, *Andrew Marvell*, 93.

true, died after Cromwell's victory at Dunbar, whereas the ode had been written before it. Yet that battle, while it severely damaged the royalists' prospects, by no means extinguished them. It was the seriousness of the surviving royalist threat that took Oliver St John to The Hague in March 1651. Only with Cromwell's victory at Worcester the following September would Puritan supremacy be assured. Even then, no one could know what forms the supremacy would take, or foresee the succession of constitutional convulsions that would mark the rest of the decade.

In a setting so fluid, before a future so uncertain, and amid the competing claims and arguments for allegiance, consistency might be an honourable virtue. But it might also be the temptation of stubbornness – a quality that Nedham liked to attribute to those who adhered to whatever party he had most recently deserted – and of simple-mindedness. In 1650 the pressures of polarization had taken a new and intense form. During the previous decade, constitutional debate had mostly been accommodated within old parameters. Which side, king or parliament, was faithful to the ancient constitution? Which of them stood for legality and liberty? The destruction of the constitution in 1649 transformed the vocabulary of debate. In the winter of 1649–50 the republic imposed the engagement of loyalty to kingless rule, to be taken by the population at large: 'I do declare and promise that I will be true and faithful to the Commonwealth of England, as the same is now established, without a king or House of Lords.'[10] There was particular pressure on holders of 'any place or trust of office or profit', and on anyone wanting to go to law, to subscribe. The country was split by the engagement, both at a local level – nowhere more than in Marvell's beloved Hull, which the wars had turned into a garrison town and where, as Nedham reported in a partisan spirit on behalf of the republic, rival preachers extolled and vilified the regime[11] – and at a national one. A long and bitter controversy, which dominated the prints, and to which Nedham's *The Case of the Commonwealth* was (among other things) an intervention on the government's behalf, debated the duty, or legitimacy, or illegitimacy, or sinfulness, of allegiance to the new regime.[12] Could royalists abandon the cause for which so many had fought and died? Could they swallow their resentments? Could the crushing of the ancient

10. S. R. Gardiner, ed., *Constitutional Documents*, 391.
11. *MP*, 24 Oct. 1650, 326–8, 333–5; Worden, *Rump Parliament*, 83.
12. Wallace, *Destiny his Choice*, ch. 1; Skinner, 'Conquest and Consent'.

constitution be conscionably endorsed? Was the engagement compatible with previous pledges: with the oaths of allegiance and supremacy to the Crown, or with the Solemn League and Covenant which the Long Parliament had imposed in 1643 and which committed its subscribers to the preservation of the king and monarchy? Or had military conquest terminated such obligations and imposed alternative ones? Did not power, which alone protects its subjects, demand a requiting obedience? Had not that most omnipotent of sanctions, divine providence – the 'angry heaven' of 'An Horatian Ode' – endorsed the new authority? In Marvell's 'The First Anniversary', in 1654, his 'muse' (125), like the writer's pen in the May poem four years earlier, identifies itself with the sword. This time it does so, not in the royalist cause, but in Cromwell's. It supports 'heaven's choice', for which 'he ... | Who in his age has always forward pressed | ... | Girds yet his sword, and ready stands to fight' (146–8). The armed 'forward youth' of 'An Horatian Ode' likewise annexes his cause to that of heaven's instrument.

And what of the same youth's aspiration to 'appear'? Did loyalty to king and law require the sacrifice of achievement or reward or of scope for public service? Had Nedham's thesis, that the world is governed by men's interests and that it falls to us to identify and serve our own, got through to Marvell, and asserted itself against more conventional ethical assumptions in his mind? When civil war broke out, he and Nedham were in their early twenties. The conflict was not their generation's responsibility, merely its affliction. Like the 'forward youth', its members had to make choices dictated by older men. Until the civil wars had 'lost the civic crown', writers had written, and competed, within a multifarious but unified system of power and patronage. Now they found the landscape partitioned. Nedham took the engagement at once. Milton apparently took it too.[13] We do not know whether Marvell did. We cannot even be sure – for the test was unevenly enforced – whether he was made to choose. Yet anyone hoping for favour from the regime or employment by it, as it looks as if he did by 1651, would have been most imprudent not to have subscribed. To judge by his poems of 1650 he would have faced the choice with a keenly divided mind. To some critics 'An Horatian Ode' is without ambivalence. Others, admiring Marvell but disliking the literary expression of political passion, have acknowledged the ambivalence but have interpreted it as the

13. *CP* vii. 411.

even-handed detachment of a 'balanced' sensitivity. Yet the ode, rather than taking neither side, takes both.

One premiss it shares with 'Tom May's Death'. The regicide, which in the May poem has cracked 'the world's disjointed axle', is no less elemental a force in the ode, where 'that memorable hour | Which first assured the forced power' (65–6) occupies the pivotal lines. The king, absent from Marvell's royalist poems of 1647–9, is present in the poems of 1650, in the ode centrally so. If there are such things as seismic shifts of political consciousness, the regicide brought one. Nedham's argument that 'the old allegiance' has been extinguished by the sword is compressed into four lines of the ode:

> Though justice against fate complain
> And plead the ancient rights in vain,
> But those do hold or break,
> As men are strong or weak.
>
> (37–40)

Yet if the poem recommends that logic, it simultaneously rages, or agonizes, at its cost. Marvell's representation of the martyred king, that point of stillness at the centre of the poem which sets off the movement and animation around it, has been often discussed. Yet critics miss the contrast between Charles's own conduct and that of his killers. In a poem of such metrical perfection, the italicized breach of it – '*He* nothing common did or mean | Upon that memorable scene' (57–8) – speaks loudly. Cromwell may be the scourge of 'angry heaven', but his own rise has been won by the sham providentialism of himself and his fellow regicides, who in bringing the king to execution did 'call the gods with vulgar spite | To vindicate' their deed (61–2). Their 'common and mean' behaviour, 'while round the armèd bands | Did clap their bloody hands' (55–6), is viewed through royalist outrage.

Not for the only time, Nedham, whose republican writing we have found casting light on the ode, proves also to illuminate it by his earlier, royalist prose. There Cromwell is not conquering hero but villain. In the ode, the necessary preliminary to regicide is the episode of November 1647 when Charles escaped from Hampton Court, thereafter to be imprisoned at Carisbrooke castle on the Isle of Wight. Marvell's inclusion of the event is by itself enough to dispose of the notion that the poem is a panegyric – or at least that it is one within the usual conventions of praise and morality.

His lines take up the common royalist accusation that Cromwell, by mixing hints of impending assassination with professions of friendship, had lured the king into fleeing from the captivity of the army's opponents in parliament, so that the army itself could control his fate.[14]

And Hampton shows what part
He had of wiser art.
Where, twining subtle fears with hope,
He wove a net of such a scope
That Charles himself might chase
To Caresbrook's narrow case ...

(47–52)

Nedham often dwelled on that episode, and was the journalist and newswriter who made most of it.[15] In his account of it in *Pragmaticus*, 'fears' and 'hope' are likewise subtly twined: Cromwell and his friends, 'according to Machiavel's gospel', 'went a subtle way' in 'pretending friendship to him by high praises and frighting him with intended attempts upon his person', and thus 'wrought in him a willingness to remove from Hampton'.[16] A year later the newsbook added, in words that again call the ode to mind, that the same men, in inveigling the king to Carisbrooke with the purpose of deposing him, had followed 'that common maxim of all tyrants ... that all equity and right may be dispensed with to attain rule.'[17] It is to Nedham, too, that we owe the report that in January 1649 Cromwell, in explaining to the Commons the need to bring Charles to trial, resorted to sham providentialism. He

> played his cards very cunningly, saying, "Mr Speaker, if any man whatsoever had carried on this design of deposing the king and disinheriting his posterity, or if any man had such a design, he should be the greatest traitor and robber in the world. But since the providence of God hath cast us upon this, I cannot but submit to providence ...." By which speech you may see, they entitle God's providence to all their villainies.[18]

14. James Loxley, *Royalism and Poetry in the English Civil Wars* (Basingstoke, 1997), 147 ff., reveals the substantial place of the episode in royalist verse.
15. Bodl., Clarendon MS 34, fo. 17^{v}; Nedham, *Digitus Dei*, 22; *idem*, *True Character*, 61.
16. *Mercurius Pragmaticus*, 14 Dec. 1647, 6.
17. Ibid. 21 Nov. 1648, 8.
18. Bodl., Clarendon MS 34, fo. 72, newsletter of 11 Jan. 1649; for Nedham's authorship see Peacey, 'Marchamont Nedham and the Lawrans Letters'. The regicides are 'fright[ened] architects' in the ode (70), 'the frighted junto' in Nedham's *Mercurius Pragmaticus*, 26 Dec. 1648, 3.

Because Cromwell would go on to dominate the England of the 1650s, we easily miss how much is stated by Marvell's choice of subject. The authority which claimed sovereign power in 1650, and which might thus have expected to have first call on a poet's gift, was not Cromwell but parliament. Marvell's choice of subject, like the ode itself, lays bare the facts of power. The republic was an improvised regime, with no principle of constitutional design behind it and no roots in English political thought or custom. The purged House of Commons, the remnant of the ancient constitution, would rule only as long as the army, which had placed it in power, kept it there. Contemporaries found it much easier to imagine the replacement of an old king by a new one than the survival of kingless rule. They expected Cromwell, whose 'ambition' was (fairly or not) generally taken for granted, to usurp. That is the prospect summoned by the opening lines of the ode. They draw on the opening of another poem, Lucan's *Pharsalia*, and on the account there of the crossing of the Rubicon by Julius Caesar and his legions,[19] that decisive moment, which in Lucan's account is chill with dread and omen, in the breaking of the Roman republic. Marvell's readers must expect it to be paralleled by the return of the conquering Cromwell to England. The analogy was no remote or merely decorative allusion. At the time of Cromwell's subsequent re-entry into England, in August 1651, when he allowed the Scots to invade and followed them with the army, members of the republic's council of state 'raged and uttered sad discontents against Cromwell, and suspicions of his fidelity'.[20]

The opening pages of Lucan's *Pharsalia*, and their representation of Julius Caesar, who is about to break the republic, echo through the ode. In May's translation, Caesar has

> restless valour, and in war a shame
> Not to be conqueror; fierce, not curbed at all,
> Ready to fight, where hope, or anger call,
> His forward sword; confident of success,
> And bold the favour of the gods to press:
> Overthrowing all that his ambition stay,
> And loves that ruin should enforce his way;
> As lightning by the wind forced from a cloud

19. Smith, 268–9.
20. Lucy Hutchinson, *Memoirs of the Life of Colonel Hutchinson*, ed. N. H. Keeble (London, 2000 edn.), 248–9.

Breaks through the wounded air with thunder loud,
Disturbs the day, the people terrifies,
And by a light oblique dazzles our eyes,
Not Jove's own temple spares it; when no force,
No bar can hinder his prevailing course....[21]

'Farewell all leagues,' says May's Caesar: 'fortune I'll follow thee. | No more we'll trust: war shall determine all.'[22]

Of course, the ode also represents Cromwell as the servant of the republic, who 'can so well obey' it (84). He lays his Irish conquest 'to the Commons' feet', 'And, what he may, forbears | His fame to make it theirs' (87–8). He is a 'falcon', which parliament, the 'falc'ner', 'has ... sure' (91–6).[23] But why then does Marvell tell us 'How fit he is to sway', 'how ... fit for highest trust', and how 'much one man can do' (79–83)? Cromwell's fitness for highest trust was a matter of immediate import. In May 1650 a royalist predicted that Cromwell would be made 'Lord Protector'. On 21 June the poet Abraham Cowley reported that Cromwell, on his return from Ireland, had been received 'with great triumph and magnificence at London; and it is believed, will have some new great title conferred upon him'.[24] To first appearances, the Cromwell of the ode, who before his rise 'lived reservèd and austere' in his 'private gardens', 'As if his highest-plot' was to 'plant the Bergamot' (29–32) – a pear-tree – has had a reluctant rise. But the picture changes when we grasp Marvell's esoteric allusion. The bergamot is the tree of kings.[25] Cromwell's ostensible self-effacement conceals self-advancement and is an instrument of it.

The submissiveness of Cromwell to parliament in the poem conforms, it is true, to the emphases of government publications, which stressed Cromwell's 'modesty' on his return from Ireland. They needed to, for the public perception of him was different. Royalists, and a large proportion of the Roundheads, were accustomed to taking Cromwell's professions of self-abasement for hypocrisy. The question whether he was ready to

21. The resemblance of this and other passages to the ode are noticed by Margoliouth (i. 295–6), who observes that Marvell drew on the Latin original as well as on May's version. I cannot agree with Reedy ('"An Horatian Ode"', 143) that Lucan does not provide 'the right context' for the interpretation of Marvell's political poems of 1650.
22. See too I. 262: 'when light had banished the cold shade of night' (Loeb).
23. Cf. the metaphor from hawking bestowed on Cromwell by Nedham's *Mercurius Pragmaticus* (9 Nov. 1647, 58) during the crisis that provoked the king's flight from Hampton Court.
24. The two statements are quoted by Jeffrey R. Collins, *The Allegiance of Thomas Hobbes* (Oxford, 2005), 150–1.
25. Smith, 372.

'obey' parliament was keenly scrutinized in the months before his return. In January the Commons 'desired' him – that is, in parliamentary language, ordered him – 'to come over' from Ireland 'and give his attendance here in parliament'. State palaces and gardens were awarded him in February, in anticipation of his arrival. But the MP Lord Lisle, who would be a councillor of Cromwell under the protectorate, 'had some doubts of his coming, his interest, I believe, being in many respects to stay there'.[26] In mid-March, still without an answer to its earlier requests, the Commons asked 'to know your resolution, and when we may expect you'. A more urgent message followed a week later; there were two further letters in April, when a ship was sent to collect him; an 'express' followed on 4 May; and on 10 May the Commons resolved to inform him 'that the House still continues in its resolution of having him over; that he is therefore to have his affairs in order that he may repair hither'. It was in response to this last instruction that he finally returned at the end of May.[27] Well might parallels with the crossing of the Rubicon have been nurtured during that ominous delay.

Suspicions of his intentions had been heightened by the printing of a slippery letter of 2 April in which he explained his continued absence to the Speaker. It turned on the words 'obey' and 'obedience'. At first, wrote Cromwell, he had received parliament's resolutions only through 'private intimations'. He had awaited a formal letter, 'which was to be the rule of my obedience ... it being not fit for me to prophesy whether the letter would be an absolute command, or having limitations with a liberty left by the parliament to me, to consider in what way to yield my obedience'. Thinking that the Commons might have changed its mind now that the spring campaign in Ireland was under way,

> I did humbly conceive it much consisting with my duty, humbly to beg a signification what your will is; professing (as before the Lord) that I am most ready to obey your commands herein with all alacrity; rejoicing only to be about that work which I am called to by those God hath set over me, which I acknowledge you to be; and fearing only, in obeying you, to disobey you.

How 'well', then, 'can' Marvell's Cromwell 'obey'?

There are question-marks against Nedham's praise of Cromwell too. Though we know, at any one time, whether Nedham's allegiance is Roundhead or Cavalier, he is capable, within those commitments, of

26. *Historical Manuscripts Commission Reports: De Lsle and Dudley*, vi. (1966), 472.
27. Abbott, ed., *Writings and Speeches*, ii. 193, 221, 237, 253–5; and the sources there cited.

complexity, ambivalence, and contradiction. Under the Commonwealth he, like Marvell, portrays not only a conflict between republic and kingship but one between republic and Cromwell. He was paid to influence the first conflict. As a writer for the government he could not explicitly mention the second. But the oblique hint, which qualifies or even counters the official message, was his *forte*. His readers, he indicates, should be alert to 'the simper or the frown'.[28] Within the high praise that *Politicus* bestows on Cromwell in 1650 there is a darker, less transparent image of him. It is taken from Machiavelli's *The Prince*. When the opening issue of *Politicus* reports Cromwell's return from Ireland, its plaudits take an unexpected twist, for it is then that Cromwell is said ('without flattery', in Nedham's perhaps double-edged phrase) to be 'the only *Novus Princeps* that ever I met with in all the confines of history'. Machiavelli's *The Prince* – 'that unworthy book' as it is called in *Politicus*,[29] a disclaimer customary in publications which made extensive use of the work, as Nedham's newsbook did – was a handbook for the 'new prince', who has acquired a state by a coup or conquest and who must understand how to 'maintain' his power.[30] Nearly half a century ago, the critic J. A. Mazzeo proposed that the Cromwell of 'An Horatian Ode' is a representation of Machiavelli's new prince.[31] In that era, when the New Criticism prospered, Mazzeo's claim, which admittedly was thinly documented, was sniffily received by critics anxious to guard the purity of literature from the intrusion of political theory. Since Mazzeo wrote, the impact of Machiavelli in the minds of seventeenth-century English writers, both of prose and of poetry, has become increasingly evident, not least with respect to Cromwell, whose rise was widely interpreted by his enemies as a Machiavellian achievement. The literary scholar Timothy Raylor has shown from the working notes of Edmund Waller how Waller wrote his panegyric to Cromwell as protector with Machiavelli's writings at his side.[32]

28. *MP*, 11 July 1650, 69.
29. Ibid. 5 Aug. 1652, 1769. Cf. ibid. 6 Mar. 1651, 625; 25 Sept. 1651, 1077; 11 Dec. 1651, 1265; 3 June 1652, 1656; 29 July 1652, 1753–4; Nedham, *Certain Considerations*, 2.
30. Cf. John Hall's tribute to Cromwell in *Mercurius Britanicus*, 8 June 1648, 28.
31. J. A. Mazzeo, *Renaissance and Seventeenth-Century Studies* (New York, 1964), 166–82 (which reproduces an essay of 1960).
32. Timothy Raylor, 'Reading Machiavelli, Writing Cromwell: Edmund Waller's Copy of *The Prince* and his Draft Verses towards *A Panegyrick on my Lord Protector*', *Turnbull Library Review*, 35 (2002), 9–32; *idem*, 'Waller's Machiavellian Cromwell: The Imperial Argument of *A Panegyrick to my Lord Protector*', *Review of English Studies*, 56 (2005), 386–411. Machiavellian properties of the ode are explored in Brian Vickers, 'Machiavelli and Marvell's *Horatian*

Nedham, for his part, had long seen Cromwell as a Machiavellian prince. In his royalist writing, when warning that Cromwell would 'usurp the government to himself', he had explicitly compared him to one of the arch-tyrants of Machiavelli's pages, Dionysius of Syracuse.[33] At that time Nedham represented Cromwell as the principal threat to the royalist cause. Under the republic he saw him as the principal threat to the republican one. To indicate it, he returned to Dionysius's conduct. This time, naturally, he omitted Cromwell's name, but he allowed it to be visible, at least to the esoteric reader, between the lines.[34] Nedham's republican prose intimates that Cromwell is what Machiavelli requires the new prince to be: at once a 'lion' and a 'fox',[35] that is, a master at once of bravery and of cunning – as is the Cromwell of 'An Horatian Ode', who adds to his 'courage high' (17) the 'wiser art' (48) that lures the king to Carisbrooke and thence to the scaffold. Alert to 'designs ... laid in the dark for the converting of liberty into tyranny',[36] Nedham enjoins his readers to be vigilant against 'kingly aspirers' and 'the subtle mining of kingly humours and usurpations', and to beware lest 'at any time it happens that any great man or men whatsoever arrive to so much power and confidence as to think of usurping or to be in a condition to be tempted thereto'.[37] He underlines what Marvell's opening lines recall: the consequences for Roman liberty of Caesar's own moment of opportunity, the crossing of the Rubicon, that 'plain usurpation' as Nedham calls it, which set the Roman leader irretrievably on the path to tyranny.[38] Caesar, remembers Nedham, had acted in the belief that 'all laws may be violated to make way to a domination'; that 'a man may be wicked to obtain or maintain an absolute sovereignty'; that 'a prince ought to account nothing unjust which is profitable'.[39] In August 1652, when the newsbook's implicit criticism of Cromwell assumed a particularly daring form, *Politicus* directed against Cromwell a passage of *The Prince*

Ode', *Notes and Queries* 36 (1989), 32–8, and in my 'The Politics of Marvell's Horatian Ode', *Historical Journal*, 27 (1984), 535–9.

33. Nedham, *Plea for the King*, 25.

34. *MP*, 1 Apr. 1652, 1490–1.

35. Ibid. 5 Aug. 1652, 1770, 1773. *Politicus* characterizes the Prince of Orange in the same way during the prince's assault on republican liberty in Holland (8 Aug. 1650, 137).

36. Ibid. 1 Apr. 1652, 1491.

37. Ibid. 27 Nov. 1651, 1221; 4 Dec. 1651, 1238; 19 Feb. 1652, 1409.

38. Ibid. 27 May 1652, 1611–12; 10 June 1652, 1644. Cf. 20 May 1652, 1596; 17 June 1652, 1661. See too Norbrook, *Writing the English Republic*, 299–300.

39. *Case*, 64. Like the ode, where Julius Caesar is both Charles I (23) and Cromwell, Nedham's *Politicus* has a Stuart Caesar too: in this case Charles II, who, however, is more often 'young Tarquin'.

that is recalled by the concluding couplet of the ode. In it Machiavelli explains that 'a prince, and especially a new prince', is often 'forced, for the maintenance of his state, to do contrary to his faith, charity, humanity and religion. ... Let a prince therefore take the surest courses he can to maintain his life and his state: the means shall always be thought honourable.' Nedham then enjoys himself by quoting, 'without adding or diminishing a syllable', Machiavelli's reference to 'a prince ... in these days' who proves the point and 'whom I shall do well not to name'.[40] Nedham's editorials were terminated a fortnight later.

As in Caesar's Rome, the prospect of a return to single rule under a dynamic military leader had a wide appeal. There were radicals who, impatient with the Rump's failure to reform, looked to Cromwell to replace its rule and 'save the city'.[41] The commonwealthman John Streater, who had come to detest him, would remember in 1659 that 'many thousands of this nation, besides the army, were of opinion' 'that if any man under heaven might be trusted, Gen. Cromwell might be trusted with absolute power'.[42] The prospect of his enthronement had grown since his return to Westminster in September 1651. At the end of that month the government adviser John Dury told a foreign envoy that 'great changes' were impending, for 'General Cromwell's prudence, gallantry, and good fortune prevail. He is the exemplar of heroic virtues.' Perhaps, suggested the envoy in reply, he would be made hereditary ruler. Dury answered that on that point he himself 'cannot verify anything definite. [Cromwell] alone holds the direction of political and military affairs in his hands. He is ... in effect king.'[43] The same envoy reported that a fortnight earlier, on the first Sunday after Cromwell's arrival, the lord general sat with his family in the royal pew in the chapel of Whitehall at a service of thanksgiving for the victory.[44] If so, it is surprising that no other source recorded so symbolic a moment; but if nothing else the envoy's report testifies to the tenor of public expectation. Nedham, between his lines, charged Cromwell with fostering such sentiment by forging and exploiting a reputation as the friend of the people's liberties, on which,

40. *MP*, 5 Aug. 1652, 1771–2. (For Nedham's device of 'not naming', see also ibid. 6 Nov. 1651, 1174.)
41. Nickolls, 36. For hopes or intimations that Cromwell might become king, see too John Blackleach, *Endeavours Aiming at the Glory of God* (1650), 45, 128–9, 163; Walter Scott, ed., *Somers Tracts*, 13 vols. (1809–15), vi. 154–6, 174–6.
42. Streater, *Continuation*, 13.
43. Miller, *John Milton and the Oldenburg Safeguard*, 49.
44. Ibid. 41.

once secured in power, he would turn, and which would be sacrificed to his elevation. Even before Cromwell had returned from Ireland, Nedham's *The Case of the Commonwealth* had remembered the 'arts' of aspiring tyrants of antiquity who secured their bases of power 'by soothing and carrying the people' 'upon high and glorious pretences of liberty'. Thus Julius Caesar, that master of 'the sword',[45] and Dionysius of Syracuse 'pretend[ed] themselves great patrons of liberty' and 'stirred the people up against the senate and counsellors of state' – in English terms, the parliament and its council of state – 'as enemies to that liberty whereof they were indeed the only keepers'.[46]

In the months after Worcester a press campaign developed which gave plausibility to Nedham's thesis. Cromwell was portrayed as the champion of reform and as the supporter of the people against oppression. From late 1651 until mid–1652 the newsbook *The Faithfull Scout*, which had connections with army headquarters, kept readers informed of Cromwell's desire to help the poor and relieve the burden of taxation on 'the meaner sort'. 'The people' were Nedham's constituency, but in 1651–2 he watched Cromwell, or Cromwell's agents, seeking to annexe it. According to *The Faithfull Scout*, Cromwell, 'to whom, next the Almighty, this nation remains indebted for the preservation of their freedom and liberties', was 'meditating of a way for the ease and freedom of the people from the heavy burden of taxes, excise etc. An acceptable piece of service, and worthy to eternize his name to all posterity.' He 'hath declared for liberty and freedom, and is resolved to ease the people of their heavy burdens, and to use means for the increase of trading etc.'. Populist proposals for law reform having been 'seriously weighed and considered by the general, his excellency declared that it was his ardent affection and desire that the law might be so regulated, wherein true and impartial justice may be freely administered, and that he was resolved to the utmost of his power to promote and propagate the same'. Cromwell 'hath visited several committees; and a speedy course will be taken for reducing of the supernumeraries, officers and courts, both

45. *Case*, 17, 25.
46. Ibid. 102. The rulers of the Commonwealth called themselves 'Keepers' of England's liberty (a term mocked with relish by royalists, who compared them to the 'keepers' of prisons). Nedham's perspective (here as elsewhere) may have been influenced by his relations with the Levellers, who had emphasized the hypocrisy of Cromwell's bids for popular support. In 1649 John Lilburne remarked on Cromwell's 'quarrels for the liberty of the commonwealth (as he pretended)': William Haller and Godfrey Davies, eds., *The Leveller Tracts 1647–1653* (New York, 1944), 411.

in city and country; a fair riddance'.[47] *Politicus* indicated what was afoot. Again using the parallel with Caesar, it described how the Roman leader had 'insinuated himself into the people's favour'; how, with 'ambitious thoughts', he 'first took arms upon the public score, and became the people's leader'; and how, 'letting in ambitious thoughts to his unbounded power', he 'soon shook hands with his first friends and principles, and became another man: so that upon the first fair opportunity he turned his arms on the public liberty'.[48]

Cromwell's ruthlessness and ambition lie beneath the surface of Marvell's poem as of Nedham's prose. They are established by allusion, whether to Caesar's crossing of the Rubicon or to the royal pear-tree. On the surface, Cromwell effaces himself 'in his private gardens' (29). He thus resembles three Romans described in *Politicus*, 'the noble Camillus, Fabius and Curius', who, says Nedham, 'were with much ado drawn from the recreation of gardening to the trouble of governing'.[49] Yet in Nedham's Cromwell, as in Marvell's, the self-effacement is seen by the alert reader to be illusory. It was in November 1651, when Cromwell's authority (to the cost of the political standing of Milton's and Nedham's friend Bradshaw)[50] was at its highest point under the Commonwealth, and when his political exertions were making all the running at Westminster, that Nedham ventured his allusion to the Roman heroes who were drawn from the recreation of gardening. In the previous week Nedham had published the editorial that gave high prominence to May's translation of Lucan, and had quoted from it the description of the virtue of Pompey which Lucan put into the mouth of Cato. Again there is a resemblance to the Cromwell on Marvell's surface: Pompey's 'house' was 'chaste [and] unrioted', and he was

powerful grown
Not wronging liberty; the people prone
To serve, he only privat still remain'd;
He sway'd the Senate, but the Senate reigned;
Naught claim'd he by the sword, but wish't what he
Wish't most, the people's peace and liberty . . . .[51]

47. Worden, *Rump Parliament*, 274–5.
48. *MP*, 17 June 1652, 1661.
49. Ibid. 27 Nov. 1651, 1222.
50. Below, pp. 196–9.
51. It is from *Politicus* that I quote the lines: 20 Nov. 1651, 1206. In the last of them, with a characteristic touch, Nedham changes May's text, which set Caesar against, not 'the people', but 'the senate'.

To Lucan, hostile as he is to the glorification of individual leaders,[52] Pompey is not only Caesar's antagonist but, in the virtue of his self-denial, an anti-Caesar. The Pompey whom Nedham takes from May is an anti-Cromwell. Nedham's Julius Caesar 'pretends' to be the 'patron' of popular 'liberty'. By contrast, as Nedham announces in the opening words of the editorial which includes the long quotation from Lucan, 'it was the glory of Pompey (that great Roman general) that both in peace and war he approved himself the grand patron of public liberty'.[53] It was because of Caesar's 'plain usurpation' in crossing the Rubicon that 'the senate and people' had no choice but to 'arm for their liberty' under Pompey. Pompey's death, recalls *Politicus*, was 'a catastrophe' of the 'bloody tragedy' that produced 'the domination of Caesar'.[54] Marvell, using the same passage of Lucan, makes Pompey an anti-Cromwell too. He does so by adjusting the line 'He sway'd the senate, but the senate reigned', so that Cromwell's obedience demonstrates his fitness to supersede the authority to which it is professedly subordinate. Nedham's use of another line of May's representation of Pompey again shows the Roman hero to be the opposite of both Nedham's and Marvell's Cromwell. In the ode, Cromwell is not 'yet grown stiffer with command | But still in the republic's hand' (81–2). Readers of Machiavelli's *Discourses* (Book III, chapter 24) knew that 'the prolongation of commands' had been fatal to the Roman republic.[55] The point that supreme commands should be 'limit[ed] ... in point of time'[56] was repeatedly made, on Machiavelli's authority, by Nedham, who had also long advertised arguments for the termination of Cromwell's military office.[57] By contrast there is the self-denial, quoted by Nedham, of May's Pompey: 'The sword | He took, but knew the time to lay it down.'[58] There was no time limit on Cromwell's authority. If, being 'still' in the

52. Cf. Norbrook, *Writing the English Republic*, 229.
53. MP, 20 Nov. 1651, 1205; 27 Nov. 1651, 1222.
54. Ibid. 10 June 1652, 1644; 15 July 1652, 1723. Sometimes, when Nedham's argumentative purposes were different, he presented Pompey in a less creditable light.
55. I am grateful to Timothy Raylor for alerting me to this point.
56. *MP*, 13 June 1652, 1588.
57. *Vox Plebis*, 66; *Mercurius Pragmaticus*, 18 Apr. 1648, 2; *MP*, 5 Feb. 1652, 1382; 13–27 May 1652, 1572, 1588, 1610–12; Nedham, *Pacquet of Advices*, 51–2, with which compare *idem, The Levellers Levell'd* (1647), 4. The attacks by *Politicus* on 'standing' powers are by no means always aimed at Cromwell (or anyway at Cromwell alone). They are often directed at the Rump, which clings to power, and perhaps against the old House of Lords too. Nedham, maybe self-protectively, sometimes obscures his targets by his nimble shifts from one of them to another. But Cromwell is unmistakably prominent among them.
58. *MP*, 20 Nov. 1651, 1206.

(1206)

beſt of Poets, *Thomas May* our *Engliſh Lucan*, more excellent then the *Roman*, as it is in the ninth Book of his *Tranſlation*; where, upon the ſad news of *Pompey*'s miſerable death, the people were brought in lamenting, and *Cato* ſpeaking (as it were) his *Funeral Oration*.

NOW o're the ſhore when *Pompey*'s death was known,
The Skie was pierc'd with the lamentation;
A grief not ſeen, nor parellel'd at all,
That common people mourn a great man's fall.
But not more pleaſing 'twas to *Pompey*'s ſpirit,
That all the people rail at Heav'n, and twit
The Gods with *Pompey*, then what *Cato* ſpoke;
Few words, but from a faithful breaſt they broke.

A *Roman*'s dead, not like our Anceſtrie
Knowing the Rule of right, but good (quoth he)
In this truth-ſcorning age; one powerful grown
Not wronging *liberty*; The people prone
To *ſerve*, he onely *private* ſtill remain'd;
He ſway'd the *Senate*, but the *Senate* raign'd;
Naught claim'd he by the *ſword*, but wiſh't what he
Wiſh't moſt, the people's Peace and *Liberty*;
Great wealth he had, but to ſee the publick hoard
He brought far more then he retain'd; The *Sword*
He took, but knew the time to lay it down;
Arm'd he lov'd Peace, though *Arms* before the *Gown*
He ſtill prefer'd; and ever pleas'd was he
Entring, or leaving his Authority;
A chaſt unrioted houſe, and never ſtain'd
With her Lord's fortune; To all lands remain'd
His name renown'd, which much availed *Rome*.
True *Liberty* long ſince was gone, when home
Sylla and *Maria* came; but *Pompey* dead,
Ev'n *Freedom's ſhadow* then quite vaniſhed.

Figure 5. Nedham's tribute to Pompey

republic's hand, he is not 'yet' grown stiffer with command, how long will it take? Nedham remembers how Cinna, Marius, Sylla, 'and the rest of that succeeding gang down to Caesar' contrived to 'obtain a continuation of power in their own hands', and how Augustus got his throne by 'many delays and shifts for the continuation of power in his own hand'. Having found means to strip the people, the cultivation of whose favour had won them power, of their liberty, they 'maintained by the same arts' the positions they had acquired.[59]

In the ode, Cromwell will 'climacteric be' – that is, will bring a critical change or epoch – to 'all states not free' (103–4). The obvious meaning is that he will liberate them. Yet it is contradicted by the statement that Cromwell – in Marvell's own 'Roman-cast similitude' – will be a 'Caesar ... to Gaul' (101). All advocates of 'free states' agreed that republics alone export liberty to the lands they annexe. New princes who acquire fresh territories do what Cromwell does at the end of the ode: they maintain power by the arts that have gained it. 'New acquisitions', explains Nedham's *The Case of the Commonwealth*, 'are appropriated to the prince's peculiar, and in no wise conduce to the ease and benefit of the public.'[60] The legislation of Cromwell's protectorate that granted Scotland and Ireland incorporation into England was attacked by republicans on the very ground that it promoted Cromwell's own tyranny at the expense of the freedom of those lands. The measures repeated the programme of the Rump, when, as republicans proudly recalled, it had been 'calculated for a commonwealth, not for a monarchy'.[61] The contradiction in the ode is paralleled in the early issues of Nedham's *Politicus*, where Cromwell is at once the imminent freer of Scotland and a 'novus princeps'. In *The Case of the Commonwealth* Nedham reminds us that 'the sword of Caesar triumphed over the liberties of the poor Britons' – a point to which he returned in an editorial upon Cromwell's return from the Battle of Worcester, when, among other glances at the lord general, Nedham remembered that 'in our own country here, before that Caesar's tyranny took place, there was no such thing as monarchy'.[62] In any case, how sure are Cromwell's

59. *MP*, 11 Dec. 1651, 1156; 15 Jan. 1652, 1335; 15 Apr. 1652, 1522; 6 May 1652, 1572; 17 June 1652, 1661.
60. *Case*, 117.
61. See my 'Harrington's "Oceana": Origins and Aftermath', in David Wootton, ed., *Republicanism, Liberty, and Commercial Society 1649–1776* (Stanford, Calif., 1994), 129–30.
62. *Case*, 25; cf. *MP*, 25 Sept. 1651, 1077–8.

military prospects in the ode? If he will be a Caesar to Gaul, he is also to be 'to Italy an Hannibal'. As Nedham remarked in *The Case*, 'the hand of heaven will assuredly be against' nations led by princes such as Hannibal, who instigated 'an ambitious war against' the Roman republic and lost it.[63] In 1649 the royalist writer John Cleveland had envisaged the overthrow of Cromwell (after he had 'grazed in the bogs of Ireland') in Scotland, and had compared that prospect to the defeat of Hannibal by Scipio.[64]

Marvell identifies France and Italy as the foreign 'states' that Cromwell will set 'free'.[65] The surprising omission is Spain. Spain did rule much of Italy, but it was the Iberian land itself that in England had long been primarily associated with tyrannical rule, and it was Spain that would be the target of Cromwell's foreign policy as protector. The surprise diminishes when we find Nedham indicating, both in *The Case* and in *Politicus*, the need to reverse the anti-Spanish sentiment ingrained in English Puritanism. Nedham, in line with the reasoning of a powerful party in parliament, maintains that it is in England's interest to preserve the balance of power on the Continent, and therefore to support Spain against the stronger power of France,[66] whose monarchy he in any case attacks as the ally both of the Stuarts and of their own ally in the Netherlands, the House of Orange.[67] *Politicus* cries out for the end of tyranny, and the creation of a free state, in France, but, like Marvell's poem, says nothing about such a process in Spain, even though the Spanish monarchy, like the French, had recently been convulsed by revolts. Should we take Marvell to be concurring with Nedham's stand, and thus to be commending, with him, 'the excellency of a free state'? Perhaps. Yet in his royalist guise Nedham had written, with the Dutch republic in mind, of 'the arbitrary vassalage of a free state'.[68] Royalists treated the claim of the military republic to be a 'free state' as a symptom of the debasement of language by the Roundheads, and of their capacity to make words say the opposite of what they mean. A royalist tract

63. *Case*, 77; and compare l. 98 of the ode with *Mercurius Pragmaticus*, 28 Sept. 1647, 13.
64. *Mercurius Pragmaticus (for King Charles II)*, 15 May 1649, 1–2. For Cleveland's authorship see Frank, *Beginnings of the English Newspaper*, 194. Cf. Nedham's *Mercurius Pragmaticus*, 14 Mar. 1648, 3, where Cromwell 'must encounter Antichrist in a [Scottish] blue bonnet'.
65. A long tradition lay behind Marvell's prediction: see my 'Friend to Sir Philip Sidney', *London Review of Books*, 3 July 1986.
66. *Case*, 54; *MP*, 10 Oct. 1650, 307. See too *MP*, 15 Aug. 1650, 170; 22 Aug. 1650, 170; 29 Aug. 1650, 190; 14 Nov. 1650, 379–80; 2 Jan. 1651, 501, 502 .
67. Below, p. 128.
68. *Mercurius Pragmaticus*, 11 Jan. 1648, 2.

of 31 May, the day before Cromwell's entry into London, condemned the use of the term 'free state' by the rulers of a self-evidently 'unfree state'.[69] Can Marvell, who in his poem to Lovelace had made his own observations on literary degeneration, have taken up the phrase 'free state' in the ode with uncomplicated admiration for it? Or does he sharpen it with a satirical edge, and mock a slogan? Are we not again among the 'democratic stars' of the poem to Hastings – or alongside Marvell's Tom May, who 'turn[s] the chronicler to Spartacus' (74)?[70]

The poem is packed with such difficulties. Cromwell is so 'good' and 'just', and bears the sword of 'justice'; yet it is he whose deeds have enforced the surrender of 'justice' to fate. In 'Tom May's Death', words that were put to one use in the ode are deployed to an exactly opposite one. Nedham, in his changes of side, was a habitual practitioner of that device (as in his readiness first to condemn the 'arbitrary vassalage' of a 'free state' and then to commend its 'excellency'). The response of both writers to polarization was to occupy both poles. The difference is that Marvell, in the ode, occupies the two at once. For the poem carries opposition not only to the May poem but within itself. It looks towards the royalism of the May poem and away from it. Its endorsement of Cromwell cannot be satisfactorily taken to be either without irony or only ironical. If 'we would speak true, | Much to the man is due' (27–8). Who would confidently place the tone of that statement on one side or the other of the divide between royalism and Cromwellianism? A purely royalist reading of the poem is unequal to its power and gravity. Irony becomes mere sarcasm, and nothing reverberates. A purely Cromwellian reading, which anyway has to be oblivious to the royalist allusions, misses the poet's struggle of allegiance and emotion. It is a miracle of the ode to create, in a polarized world, a bi-polar language, at once direct and deceptive. In its very syntax the poem makes a principle of fluid meaning. When we reach line 4 we do not know whether 'languishing' belongs to the 'forward youth' or to his 'numbers'. Seven 'grammatical uncertainties' have been noticed in lines 15–24 alone, each carrying an uncertainty of sense.[71] Around the poem

69. *Traytors Deciphered* (1650).

70. See too Nedham's account in *Mercurius Pragmaticus* (26 Sept. 1648, 8), of which he would supply something close to an exactly opposite image in 1650, of the spread of rebellion from the kingdoms of Britain to those of the Continent.

71. Barbara Everett, 'The Shooting of the Bears', in R. L. Brett, ed., *Andrew Marvell: Essays on the Tercentenary of his Death* (Hull and Oxford, 1979), 76.

there are shadows: the shadows of song three lines from the beginning, the shadows of night three lines from the end. They are deepened by Marvell's metrical arrangement, where shorter couplets soften and question the longer ones with which they alternate, so that the reader moves back and forth between a clear centre and a dim or hazy periphery.[72] It is a poem designed for ambiguity and, through it, for ambivalence.[73]

Perhaps no two readers of it will weigh its sympathies identically. That may not matter overmuch. It may be not only easier, but more useful or anyway less contentious, to identify the place of contemporary issues or anxieties within a work of literature than to pinpoint its author's position towards them, which, even if we can be sure of its existence, may have a complicated relationship to the work itself. A poem, after all, is not a vote. Yet how would we read the account of Cromwell in Marvell's ode if we did not know that Marvell would subsequently write, without ambivalence, on his behalf? Perhaps the Cromwell of the ode, the new prince, is at once his nation's necessary saviour and its necessary tyrant. Perhaps the mental worlds of Machiavelli and Hobbes and Christian providentialism merge in Marvell's mind. Perhaps he shares the sentiment voiced in a royalist newsletter of March 1650s which reported Cromwell's Irish exploits: 'Noll yet goes on without fear of the strength or combination of enemies about him. Brave desperate rebel! And in an ill cause too! Were his cause just or honest, I profess I should love him.'[74] Perhaps Marvell's Cromwell accords with Clarendon's later phrase for him – which has Jonson's *Catiline his Conspiracy* behind it – 'a brave, bad man',[75] or with Abraham Cowley's recollection of him: 'sometimes I was filled with horror and detestations of his actions, and sometimes I inclined a little to reverence and admiration of his courage, conduct and success'.[76] Perhaps Marvell can only come to terms with Cromwell, and voice awe at his deeds, by simultaneously

72. Ibid. 74–5, 82.
73. One ambiguity has, I think, gone unremarked. In l. 113, 'thou the war's and fortune's son' is usually taken to be Cromwell. May it not, alternatively, be the 'forward youth'?
74. *The Royall Diurnall*, 4 Mar. 1650.
75. Edward Hyde, Earl of Clarendon, *History of the Rebellion*, ed. W. D. Macray, 6 vols. (Oxford, repr. 1958), vi. 97; Jonson, *Catiline his Conspiracy*, v. 688–90. Possibly the author of the newsbook quoted in my previous sentence had in mind the same passage of Jonson's play, where Cato, responding to testimony to the 'rebellious parts' of the now slain Catiline, says 'A brave bad death. | Had this been honest now, and for his country, | As 'twas against it, who had fallen greater?'
76. Quoted from Abraham Cowley's *A Discourse by Way of Vision, concerning* ... *Oliver Cromwell* (1659), 343, in Nicholas Jose, *Ideas of Restoration in English Literature 1660–1671* (Basingstoke, 1984), 83.

discharging the detestation of him that he had expressed in the Villiers poem in 1648, and which the regicide is unlikely to have softened. But whatever he thinks or feels, there is nothing about Cromwell in the poem that, by the light of Marvell's other public poetry, cannot be condemned for ruthlessness, violence, destruction, hypocrisy, fraud, and self-seeking.

Yet four and a half years later he would publish a poem about Cromwell as Lord Protector, 'The First Anniversary', which recruited phrases and images from the ode,[77] and which says, without irony, everything about him that the protector would have liked to hear said. Marvell's royalism was now distantly past. In 1651 or 1652, in 'Upon Appleton House', he retained his sense of the loss and destruction wrought by the wars, and recalled the Eden of pre-war England, 'that dear and happy isle | The garden of the world' (321–2). That 'happy' condition sounds a long way from the 'happy fate' ostensibly announced for the 'free' 'state' by the ode. Before the ode, however, Marvell had addressed royalist readers on royalist subjects. Now he wrote for and about the parliamentarian general Fairfax, whom his verse had assailed in 1648. 'An Horatian Ode' looks ahead, with the 'forward youth'. Charles I, 'Great Charles' in the May poem (76), belongs to the defeated past in the ode, which makes no mention of his son, Charles II, whose forces Cromwell will confront in Scotland. Cromwell, the force of animation, holds the future: the future that, in the years ahead, Marvell will serve.

★★

Why did Marvell embrace the new, post-royalist world? Why, in it, did he not 'single fight forsaken virtue's cause'? In the milieu of writing and publication he was far from alone in coming round. Thomas Newcomb, Nedham's (and Milton's) printer and the printer of 'The First Anniversary', had transferred his allegiance from the king to the republic, as had Milton's publisher William Dugard.[78] The royalist poet Cowley was reconciled under the protectorate, as was Edmund Waller. Cromwell's panegyrist Payne Fisher had fought for the king and condemned the regicide.[79] It was a writer's instinct to move towards power, in the hope of counselling it,

77. Norbrook, *Writing the English Republic*, 340–1.

78. Peacey, *Politicians and Pamphleteers*, 282. Tradition would ascribe Dugard's conversion to the joint cunning of Milton and John Bradshaw, and have them laughing at their exploit (Masson, iv. 249–50). Though the story was erroneous in substance, it may have had some misremembered joint enterprise by the two men behind it.

79. Norbrook, *Writing the English Republic*, 231.

reforming it, winning reward from it. Cromwell knew the use of poets. If Marvell celebrated the 'First Anniversary' of the protectorate, subsequent ones were applauded in verse by Fisher,[80] whom Cromwell awarded a sinecure in the lifeguard of the occupying forces in Scotland – to the annoyance (or so it looks) of George Monck, the protector's commander there, whose budget had to meet the stipend of the absentee poet.[81] Cromwell put Edward Waller on his council of trade, and took a personal interest in securing the discharge of Waller's estate from the punitive taxation laid on former royalists in 1655–6.[82] Marvell's rise was neither swift nor high. Even so, by 1657 he was working in Thurloe's office. In that year, too, he was commissioned to write songs for the marriage of Cromwell's daughter Mary.

Yet 'An Horatian Ode', after all, is about more than Marvell's own career. It captures both a historic moment and a historical movement. Cromwell's mission, as the instrument of the 'fate' of the 'state', is to 'ruin the great work of time, | And cast the kingdoms old | Into another mould' (34–6). Nedham's *The Case* represents the revolution of the winter of 1648–9 – the performance of Cromwell that occupies the centre of the ode – in the same light. 'Sooner or later', it explains, 'kingdoms all have their fatal periods', and 'their crowns are laid in the dust, and their glories buried in the grave of oblivion. No wonder then if our English monarchy, having arrived to almost six hundred years since the Conquest', should now succumb 'according to the common fate of all other governments.'[83] The 'late commotions between king and parliament' were

80. BL, Thomason Tracts, E. 498[2] (MS); Bodl., Carte MS 73, fo. 61^{v}.
81. NA, SP28/106, fo. 225 (29 June 1655); SP28/108, fo. 442 (30 Nov. 1655). See too NA, SP28/75 (15 Nov. 1654, item 8); *Cal. SP Dom. 1657–8*, 11; *Calendar of State Papers Venetian 1655–6*, 283, 289–90. See also Peacey, *Politicians and Pamphleteers*, 109, 129, 197–8, 282, 290.
82. NA, SP25/76 (6 Mar. 1656, item 37); see too *A Letter from a True and Lawfull Member of Parliament* (1656), 54. There were two kinds of meetings of councillors: official ones, where the proceedings were minuted, and informal ones, where they were not (see my 'Oliver Cromwell and the Council', in Patrick Little, ed., *The Cromwellian Protectorate* (Woodbridge, Suffolk, 2007), 82–104). Decisions taken at informal meetings had to be submitted for approval to official ones. There is, I think, only one recorded exception to this rule: the appointment of Waller. The decision was taken at an informal meeting in Cromwell's lodgings in Whitehall, and accepted by the council at an official meeting later the same day as a *fait accompli*. The procedure would have been unimaginable without, at the least, Cromwell's firm support.
83. John Hall, 'Grounds and Reasons', 14, in explaining that the subjects of monarchy 'languish' and 'wax old', predicts that their servitude will not last beyond 'that period which God prescribes to all people and governments'.

> as so many sharp fits and feverish distempers which, by a kind of antiperistasis [a reaction against action],[84] are ever most violent in old age upon the approaching instants of dissolution. The corruption of the old form hath proved the generation of another....[85]

The new form will in turn have its 'proportion of time allotted by divine providence', which has confirmed its validity 'by a continued series of many signal victories and successes to the envy of all opposers and amazement of the world'. It is at this point that Nedham, considering 'how the worm works in many parts of Europe to cast off the regal yoke, especially in France, Scotland, Ireland, and other places' – Marvell's 'kingdoms old' – declares it to be 'madness to strive against the stream for the upholding of a power cast down by the Almighty'. Marvell's Cromwell, before casting the kingdoms old 'Into another mould', breaks through clouds like three-forked lightning: Nedham says that old governments succumb to 'rapid hurricanes of fatal necessity'.[86]

Nedham's historical perspective is opportunist. His arguments, for all the learning that informs them and the mercurial ingenuity of their presentation, have little depth of investigation beneath them. They do not match the sense of the movement of history that Marvell conveys in the different medium of the poetic imagination. But there were political theorists of the time who did match it. The customary divisions of the modern academic world, which have placed Nedham's journalism in a category distant from Marvell's poetry, have likewise positioned poetry far from political thought. The one has been taken to be the province of feeling and of literary form, the other of ideas and theoretical analysis. Recent critical writing has begun to undermine that anachronistic perception. Yet its obstructive power remains. 'Political thought' is a modern conception, which can obscure the engagement of the practitioners who are claimed for it with the practical dilemmas of choice and emotion that confronted them. The aftermath of the regicide produced 'An Horatian Ode' and, in the following year, Hobbes's *Leviathan*. The two works share a political context and a political vision. *Leviathan* describes the time of its publication as one when, in a 'clean swept house', 'the interests of men are changed (seeing much of that doctrine which serveth to the establishing of a new government must needs be contrary to that which conduced to the dissolution of the old)'.[87]

84. Hall shared Nedham's taste for this word (Hall, *Humble Motion*, 3).
85. *Case*, 12–13. 86. Ibid. 8.
87. Quoted by Collins, *Allegiance of Thomas Hobbes*, 147–8.

'An Horatian Ode' and *Leviathan*, works written by royalists or ex-royalists after the fall of kingship, vindicate, or half-vindicate, that new order, but in terms which carry profound disapproval of the deeds that were its origins, Hobbes in his condemnation of the Puritan rebellion, Marvell in his account of the regicide.

If Hobbes – a profound influence on Nedham, who borrowed extensively from him, as also on John Hall – can help us understand the ode, there is another political thinker who can aid us more. James Harrington earned his fame as the author of *The Commonwealth of Oceana* (1656) – 'Oceana' being a fictionally dressed England. Ten years Marvell's senior, he was himself a poet, who injected his theory of politics into translations of Virgil. Like Marvell, like Hobbes, like Nedham, he moved from loyalty to the king to an acceptance of his overthrow. Harrington can give us a sense not only, as Nedham does, of the logic and spirit behind Marvell's adjustment to the transformed political landscape, but of its pain and cost, as Nedham does not. John Aubrey, who was himself 'an old friend' of Harrington and is generally reliable about people he knew, tells us that Marvell was an 'intimate friend' of Harrington. As it is Aubrey who also discloses that Marvell 'had not a general acquaintance', the exception is impressive.[88] In his list of Harrington's friends Aubrey places Marvell, who was a close neighbour of Harrington in Westminster in the 1670's, towards the end of the two men's lives, second. Before him comes Thomas May's friend and Nedham's old associate Henry Neville,[89] a political disciple of Harrington who devotedly cared for him in those years, when Harrington's mind and body had been damaged by his political imprisonment, on groundless suspicion of conspiracy, during the previous decade. We also learn from Aubrey that on Harrington's death Marvell wrote an epitaph for him, which was not used on his tomb as 'it would have given offence'[90] – that is, offence to the government. We cannot tell when the friendship between Marvell and Harrington was formed.[91] What we can say is that if they were not friends by the time Marvell wrote the ode, they were missing something.

Like Marvell, Harrington was a traveller and a linguist. Both, as young men, travelled in the Netherlands, France, and Italy. Like Marvell,

88. Aubrey's remarks on Harrington are in his *Brief Lives*, ed. Andrew Clark, 2 vols. (Oxford, 1898), i. 288–95; ii. 54, 185.

89. *AMC* 192. 90. Ibid. 191–2, 225.

91. A connection between Marvell and Neville in the early Restoration is suggested, but by no means established, by *Journal of the House of Commons*, 27 June 1662 (cited *AMC* 66).

Harrington kept out of the first civil war. In 1647 parliament appointed him one of three gentlemen of the imprisoned king's bedchamber, a post he held until Charles's death, when reportedly he was present on the scaffold and was given tokens by the condemned monarch. Aubrey tells us that Charles, though dismayed by Harrington's interest in republican constitutions, 'loved' Harrington's 'company'; that Harrington 'passionately loved his majesty'; and that at the meetings of the Rota Club in the last stages of the Interregnum, where Harrington's political theory was debated – and where, according to Samuel Butler, Marvell was among the participants[92] – Aubrey 'often heard' Harrington 'speak of King Charles I with the greatest zeal and passion imaginable, and [say] that his death gave him so great a disease by it, that never anything did go so near to him'.

Oceana argues for a republic, but not for the kind of republic left behind by Pride's Purge and the regicide. Harrington despises the 'base itch' of that 'oligarchy' and the 'venom' at its 'root', and compares its executive council to the thirty tyrants of Athens.[93] He is repelled by the plunder by the Rump of 'our cathedrals, ornaments in which this country excels all others' (295). Where Marvell writes of the 'vulgar spite' that brings in the new order, Harrington despises the fanaticism and unforgiving partisanship of its champions. Their misrule stands in contrast to the monarchy under Charles I, which was 'the most indulgent to, and least invasive of for so many ages upon, the liberty of a people that the world hath known' (535). There is no more taint of evil in Harrington's Charles I than in Marvell's in the ode. In both works the king is a victim of history. In the ode, force and fraud overcome ancient rights and justice, for 'Those do hold or break | As men are strong or weak'. 'A good cause', Marvell would write later, 'signifies little, unless it is well defended. A man may starve at the feast of good conscience.'[94] In *Oceana*, 'a man (you know) though he be virtuous, yet, if he do not understand his [political] estate, may be run out or be cheated of it' (286). The regicide and the end of monarchy are the fulcrum of Harrington's argument, as they are of the ode and of 'Tom May's Death'. In the May poem the world's disjointed axle cracks: in *Oceana* the king's execution is accompanied by 'such horror

92. *AMC* 59.
93. J. G. A. Pocock, ed., *The Political Works of James Harrington* (Cambridge 1977), 205–6, 269, 647, 736–7, 744–5. I have described Harrington's political thought, and its context, in chs. 2 and 3 of Wootton, *Republicanism, Liberty, and Commercial Society*.
94. Margoliouth, ii. 324.

as hath been a spectacle of astonishment unto the whole earth' (235). 'In this age', Harrington adds, 'governments are universally broken or swerved from their foundations' (312). To demonstrate the irreparable destruction of the English constitution, he draws on the text of which 'An Horatian Ode' had made so much, the opening of Lucan's *Pharsalia*. 'Crassus', remarks Harrington, 'was dead and Isthmus broken' (198). In Lucan, Crassus is the link that temporarily prevents war between Caesar and Pompey, and is thus likened to the Isthmus of Corinth, 'that small neck of land' which alone withstands the clash of the two great seas, the Ionian and the Aegean.[95]

Though *Oceana* was not published until 1656, there are indications in its text that it was drafted earlier, at some point under the Commonwealth of 1649–53; and that it was then revised, perhaps in haste and anyway with insufficient care to disguise its earlier genesis, under the protectorate, the regime to which it offers advice. There are great differences between the political stance of *Oceana* and Marchamont Nedham's polemical and partisan endorsement of the regicide and Commonwealth. Yet there are also close resemblances between some of Harrington's arguments and ones advanced in Nedham's republican editorials of 1651–2,[96] not least on subjects where Nedham contrives to indicate that he, too, wishes for a different kind of republic than the Rump. That *Oceana* is in essence a product of the early 1650s is confirmed by the account of the genesis of the work given by John Toland, Harrington's late seventeenth-century editor, who had seen papers of the family that have subsequently disappeared. Toland was not an instinctively truthful writer, but his detectable inventions have identifiable motives behind them. Here he had none. 'After the king's death', he writes, Harrington 'was observed to keep very much his library, and more retired than usually, which was by his friends' – which friends? – 'a long time attributed to melancholy or discontent'.[97] When 'wearied' by their 'importunities to change this sort of life', he 'thought fit to show 'em ... a copy of his *Oceana*, which he was privately writing all that while'. It

95. I. 98–106. 96. See my 'Harrington's 'Oceana': Origins and Aftermath', 111–12.

97. Writing for the protectorate in February 1654, Nedham remarked that 'the way of government in free nations is not to be accommodated unto schemes of freedom which lie in melancholy contemplation, but must be suited to that form which lies fairest for practical convenience and avoiding inconveniences' (*A True State of the Case of the Commonwealth* (1654), 37). Do the words possibly glance at the utopian scheme that Harrington would publish in *Oceana*? At all events they indicate one of the points where Nedham, an anti-utopian if ever there was one, would have parted company with Harrington.

sounds as if the 'disease' which Aubrey says Harrington contracted after the regicide may have been a mental one, akin to his troubles of mind in the Restoration.' If so it was an intellectually fruitful affliction.[98]

Oceana argues, what 'An Horatian Ode' affirms, that in the civil wars there were momentous forces of history at work, which men were powerless to control or withstand. It was to make the same point in 1650 that Nedham portrayed the wars as the expiring 'sharp fits and feverish distempers' of a government that went back to the Conquest. Yet no historical analysis supported Nedham's metaphorical claim. Harrington supplied one, by tracing back to the Conquest a process of economic and social change that over time, he argued, had removed the feudal base of monarchy and of the House of Lords. Toland, fairly summarizing Harrington's argument, explains that the fall of kingship derived from 'natural causes', which 'produce their necessary effects' in politics 'as much as in the earth or air'.[99] 'An Horatian Ode' is hardly a place for economic analysis. Yet in it 'Nature', hating 'emptiness', is likewise the basic fact of power (40–1).[100] In *Oceana*, the point that the end of kingship was 'as natural as the death of a man' is used to show 'that the oath of allegiance, as all other monarchical laws, imply an impossibility, and are therefore void' (203): Marvell's 'nature' overrules allegiances to principles that 'are strong or weak | As men do hold or break' (40).

Oceana was printed by John Streater, to whose role in the opposition to the protectorate we shall come. It is an exceptionally difficult work to interpret, partly because of the evasive playfulness of its fictional setting, partly because of its now unfathomable in-jokes, partly because of its sometimes impenetrable syntax, and partly because of the uncertain relationship of some of its sentences and paragraphs to their predecessors. But the fog need not hide the aspect of the work that has been missed, its suspicion of Cromwell and its resentment at the consequences of his ambition. Like Marvell in 1650, Harrington conveys those sentiments between the lines. In both works, consequently, Cromwell is not what he may at first appear. Nedham had used his own interlinear tactics in depicting Cromwell in the editorials of *Politicus* in 1651–2, which he would publish in book form, with an eye to current events, in the year of the publication of *Oceana*, 1656. Harrington, the translator of Virgil and, like Marvell and Nedham, a

98. Toland, ed., *'Oceana' of James Harrington*, p. xvii.
99. Ibid.
100. Cf. *PWAM* i. 192.

devotee of Horace and admirer of Ben Jonson,[101] has a poet's taste for the interlinear classical allusion. His representation of Cromwell is not without magnanimity. Usurpation, he intimates, has its own tragic logic, for usurpers are impelled to be tyrants 'be it never so contrary unto their own nature or consciences'. Caesar, 'the Roman tyrant' whom Harrington, like Marvell and Nedham, aligns with Cromwell, had a 'great soul', yet 'could not rule but by that part of man which is the beast' (338). None the less, *Oceana* directs us to flaws at the heart of Cromwell's character and rule.[102]

In 1650 Marvell's dilemma was that the instrument of the necessary new order was a leader hateful by the ethical light of the old one. Harrington's dilemma in *Oceana* is that only Cromwell, the man whom the book is ostensibly written to persuade, has the power to cure England's ills; and that Cromwell's character and record point to an opposite outcome. The book confronts a paradox which Machiavelli, the presiding genius of the work, had explained thus:

> because the restoring of a city to a politic and a civil government presupposes a good man; and [because] by violence to become prince of a commonwealth presupposes an evil man; it shall very seldom come to pass that a good man will ever strive to make himself prince by mischievous ways, although his ends therein be all good; nor will a wicked man by wicked means attaining to a peace do good; nor ever comes it into his heart to use that authority well which by evil means he came to.[103]

The only possible remedy held out by Machiavelli is to persuade the usurper that he can achieve greater glory as the founder of a commonwealth, which would replace his own power, than as a tyrant. But how likely, asks Machiavelli, is a man who has seized power to renounce it? Harrington urges Cromwell to renounce his protectoral power for the greater glory of founding a republic. It is the unreality of that prospect that inspires the playfulness of the book, a mood akin to the satire of one of Harrington's models, Traiano Boccalini,[104] who half a century earlier had made despairing sport of the tyrannical propensities of his age.[105]

101. Harrington, Marvell, and Nedham all enjoyed the character of Sir Politic Would-Be in Jonson's *Volpone*: Pocock, ed., *Political Works*, 242; *PWAM* i. 161; *Mercurius Britanicus*, 19 Jan. 1646, 1001; *Observator*, 31 Oct. 1654, 2.

102. The context for what follows is set out in my 'Harrington's "Oceana"'.

103. Machiavelli, *Discourses*, I. 18.

104. Pocock, ed., *Political Works*, 74–5.

105. Boccalini appealed to Nedham and John Hall too: *MP*, 20 Feb. 1651, 602; Hall, *Gagg to Love's Advocate*, 13.

Here, as often, Harrington and Nedham tread the same path. 'Machiavel saith', recalled Nedham in *The Case of the Commonwealth* in May 1650, that 'not he that placeth a virtuous government in his own hands or family and governs well during his natural life, but he that establisheth a lasting form' – a republican form – 'for the people's benefit is most to be commended'.[106] Nedham reprinted the passage in September 1651, in opening the first of his republican editorials in *Politicus*. It appeared eleven days after Cromwell, on the first Sunday after his return from Worcester, had reportedly sat with his family in the royal pew in Whitehall chapel, and two days before John Dury's conversation with a foreign envoy about the prospect of Cromwell's elevation. All eyes were on the general's intentions. To the passage as it had appeared in *The Case*, Nedham now added the observation that 'whoever hath this opportunity may improve his actions to a greater height of glory than ever followed any ambitious idol that hath grasped a monarchy: for, as Cato saith in Plutarch, even the greatest kings or tyrants are far inferior to those that are eminent in free states and commonwealths'.[107] In *Oceana* the same 'opportunity' is given to the Lord Archon, the idealized Cromwell of Harrington's narrative, the man Cromwell ought to be and, it becomes clear, is not. The 'greater height of glory' held out by Nedham is now bestowed on the Archon, whose 'immense glory' (346) derives from his decision to renounce his power and become 'the founder of the commonwealth' (358).

Alas, Cromwell, the vehicle by which republican rule is established in Harrington's fiction, is in the real world the impediment to it. The Archon is repeatedly praised for having done and said precisely the opposite of what Cromwell has done. Repeatedly, too, Harrington reports – often throwing Cromwell's own words back at him in the process – that the Archon has 'not' committed the misdeeds, or revealed the moral failings, that men who were dismayed by Cromwell's elevation agreed to have disfigured his rise and rule. Harrington's purpose is signalled by the dedication of the book, which is addressed to the protector. Offered in the barest terms and without any of the customary courtesies of praise and adornment, it is in effect an anti-dedication, just as the Archon is an anti-Cromwell. Only after Cromwell's death, under his weak successor, did Harrington cast fiction aside and straightforwardly recommend his proposals as practical

106. *Case*, 118; see too Nedham, *A Parallel of Governments* (1648), 2–3.
107. *MP*, 25 Sept. 1651, 1077–8.

solutions to England's plight. Only then, too, did he explicitly voice his view of the rule of Cromwell, 'the late tyrant' (742) and 'late usurper' (750). *Oceana* is close in spirit to the literary pranks and spoofs and satires of those eccentric figures on the Puritan side, the 'wits' who had been among Nedham's parliamentary allies of 1650–1, and whose scepticism, and relish for frivolity, had offended earnest Puritans close to Cromwell at that time:[108] Harrington's intimate friend, and fellow-writer of verses, Henry Neville, who – despite his recent election to the Rump – was allegedly the author of a pamphlet of January 1650 which mocked the new 'free state' and made fun of Cromwell and its other leaders;[109] Neville's intimate friend Thomas Chaloner; and their common friend the MP Henry Marten – whose own verse about Cromwell has the ironic quality we have found in Marvell's ode and Nedham's prose.[110] Though Harrington's own logic drove him to reject monarchy, he was temperamentally never a Roundhead. He looked forward, under a republic free of partisanship, to the revival of 'wit and gallantry' (253).[111] Even his admiring modern editor remarks on his capacity for 'intolerable facetiousness',[112] though the levity becomes altogether more bearable once we recognize its principal target. Like Harrington's poetry, the fictional dress of *Oceana* is closer to royalist than to parliamentarian literature. By 1656 countless writers had reproduced the image of Cromwell as a self-seeking hypocrite, whose usurpation had sacrificed his nation's liberty to his own ambition. By his creation of the Archon, the anti-Cromwell, Harrington brings a novel angle to the theme. He presents Cromwell's failings, tongue in cheek, as virtues.

Thus the Archon, 'whose meekness resembled that of Moses' (291), is 'impatient of his own glory, lest it should stand between' his countrymen and their 'liberty' (346). Though he 'had it in his power to have done us the greatest mischief that befell a poor nation' (349), fortunately he 'conceived... a loathing of their ambition and tyranny who, usurping the liberty of their native countries, become slaves to them selves' (338). Such statements, if written by an apologist for Cromwell, would have prompted hoots of derision. At the least, running as they did so contrary to public

108. Nickolls, 43.
109. Verses by Neville are in the Beinecke Library, Yale University, Joseph Spence papers, MS 4, box 4, folder 107. I owe my knowledge of them to the kindness of Mark Knights. The pamphlet is *Newes from the New Exchange, or The Commonwealth of Ladies*.
110. Norbrook, *Writing the English Republic*, 317–19, 496.
111. Cf. Pocock, ed., *Political Works*, 337–8; *MP*, 25 Sept. 1651, 1079.
112. Pocock, ed., *Political Works*, 105.

perception, their truth would have had to be supported by illustration, as in *Oceana* they are not. Harrington states with equal baldness that the Archon's actions have made his countrymen 'firm in the opinion that he could be no seeker of himself' (350). Cromwell's enemies and critics had the opposite 'opinion'. In a speech to parliament of 1654 which had been widely printed and quoted, and which Harrington himself would remember after the Restoration when recalling the writing of *Oceana* (859), Cromwell had to insist, at defensive length, that he had 'called not myself to this place. I say again, I called not myself to this place.'[113] The Archon, Harrington assures us, did 'not' have 'any private interest or ambition' in framing the new constitution of Oceana (339). While Harrington had no love of the Rump, Cromwell's expulsion of it in April 1653 was a bitter memory for him, as it was for his fellow republicans. John Streater, the printer of *Oceana*, was cashiered from the army and imprisoned for his opposition to the coup, when, as he would recall, 'the good old cause was eclipsed'.[114] Harrington's text alludes to the 'file of musketeers' (419) who executed the coup – those 'violent' soldiers, as they are called in a document of protest which was written immediately afterwards and which survives in the papers of Henry Neville.[115] Reports of the dissolution describe how Cromwell, having called the soldiers into the chamber, had them 'pull' the Speaker down from his chair and 'put their hands upon' the MP Algernon Sidney, who sat next to the Speaker, 'as if they would force him to go out'.[116] The remaining members were escorted from the House.

In the senate of Oceana the exact opposite happens. The Archon, instead of seizing power, is eager to surrender it, while the senate, instead of suspecting, as the Rump fiercely did, the lord general's intentions, is eager to retain his services. In a deliciously ingenious passage Harrington mocks Cromwell's conduct by, as it were, running the film of history backwards. 'The Archon withdrawing and being almost at the door, divers of the knights flew from their places, offering as it were to lay violent hands upon him' (342).[117] There follow, in the same sentence, two further

113. Abbott, ed., *Writings and Speeches*, iii. 452. 114. Streater, *Continuation*, 12.

115. Berkshire Record Office, D/EN/F8/1. The document is discussed in my 'Harrington's "Oceana"', 116 ff.

116. Abbott, ed., *Writings and Speeches*, ii. 642.

117. Harrington heightens the irony by placing, just before that passage, the statement that Christianity 'forbid[s] violent hands'.

reversals of the coup, and thus two further contrasts between Cromwell's profession and his practice. Shortly before the dissolution, the famously lachrymose Cromwell had 'protested to the House, with weeping eyes', that he would defend the Rump from those who wished to destroy it.[118] When the Archon escapes the senators' clutches, his departure leaves them with 'tears in their eyes'. The second reversal alludes to Cromwell's defence of himself, before parliament in September 1654, from the charge of self-seeking. He then claimed that prior to the dissolution of the Rump he had longed and begged 'to have had leave to retire to a private life'.[119] The Archon, having made his escape, 'retired into a country house of his, being remote and very private'.

Oceana alludes again to the dissolution of the Rump in a passage of which the purpose and the edge become evident only when its local reference is understood. The citizens of Oceana are warned that 'mercenary soldiers' may thwart their aspirations to 'liberty' by saying to them, 'Gentlemen, parliaments are exceeding good, but you are to have a little patience, these times are not so fit for them' (228). In the printed version of his speech at the opening of Barebone's Parliament, Cromwell, whose coup had thwarted the Rump's plans to hold parliamentary elections, conceded that such elections were none the less desirable in principle. Indeed 'Who can tell how soon God may fit the people for such a thing, and none can desire it more than I!' But the nation, he ruled, was not yet 'fit' to be trusted with them.[120] Six years later John Streater remembered that on the day of the coup Cromwell had declared that 'the people' were 'not fit to be trusted with their own liberty' to hold elections.[121] A document in the papers of Henry Marten reports Cromwell as saying, on the day of the dissolution, that 'the people shall not have their liberty, I say the people shall not have their liberty', to choose a parliament.[122]

Harrington, like Marvell in the ode and like Nedham in *Politicus*, links Cromwell's aspirations with those of Julius Caesar, whose 'prodigious ambition', recalls *Oceana*, reduced Rome to 'havoc' (338). Other parallels, classical and biblical, assist Harrington's characterization of Cromwell. In describing the 'ambition' and 'tyranny' of those who 'usurp the liberty of their native countries', he brings us back to the concluding lines of the

118. Worden, *Rump Parliament*, 357. 119. Abbott, ed., *Writings and Speeches*, iii. 453.
120. Ibid. 364. 121. Streater, *Secret Reasons of State*, 3.
122. The document is reproduced as an appendix to C. M. Williams, 'The Political Career of Henry Marten' (Oxford University D. Phil. thesis, 1954).

ode by citing an episode in Tacitus when the conspirator Piso moves against the Emperor Nero. In urging his soldiers to rise, recalls Harrington, Piso observed that 'imperial power gained by wicked means no man has ever used with good arts' ('bonis artibus').[123] Later in Harrington's treatise we are again reminded of the lines of the ode where the 'erect' sword is the instrument, certainly of war, but doubtfully of justice. If 'the sword of war', Harrington explains, is 'any otherwise used than as the sword of magistracy for the fear and punishment of those that do evil', it 'is as guilty in the sight of God as the sword of a murderer'. On what grounds, asks Harrington, can we revere Alexander the Great, since his conquests were 'but a great robbery' (345)?[124] If Alexander had instead 'restored the liberty of Greece, and propagated it unto mankind, he had done like the Lord Archon, and might truly have been called Great'. Yet whose 'liberty', the reader is left to ask, has Cromwell himself restored, and what 'justice' has he brought?

In *Oceana* Cromwell's sword has conquered the Scots, as, in Marvell's ode, it soon will. It has 'nailed them with his victorious sword to the Caucasus' (345). Did Harrington here add to the allusions that were drawn within the literature of the revolution to Jonson's play *Catiline his Conspiracy*, which we have seen Marvell and Nedham invoking? For Jonson's Catiline remarks how 'fire' might 'rivet' his fellow conspirator Cethegus 'to Caucasus' (III. 198–9)?[125] Harrington's next sentence cites Machiavelli's warning against those who take their estimate of Julius Caesar from the tributes paid to him when the Romans had 'changed their freedom for flattery'; for 'if a man would know truly what the Romans thought of Caesar, let him observe what they said of Catiline' (345–6).[126] At all events, Harrington makes it clear that no tyrant ever freed a foreign land. Like Nedham he looks to an English republic to inspire, by leadership and example, a sequence of revolutions abroad that, as he puts it, will free the 'oppressed' and 'afflict[ed]' peoples of the Continent (322, 329–30), who

123. Tacitus, *Histories*, I. 30; Pocock, ed., *Political Works*, 338.
124. Harrington calls Alexander a 'mighty hunter', the Bible's term for the archetypal tyrant Nimrod. In the ode, 'the English hunter' Cromwell (110) may be Nimrod too. Nedham had written in *Pragmaticus* that Cromwell 'plays Nimrod' (26 Oct. 1647, 42). 'Proud Nimrod in Ireland', a royalist writer called him in January 1650 (*The Man in the Moon*, 2 Jan. 285–6). For Nedham on Cromwell and Alexander see above, Ch. 3.
125. Catiline's allusion to the fate of Prometheus appears to be Jonson's invention.
126. Cf. Nedham's observation that the means taken by a prince to maintain his power 'shall always be thought honourable': above, p. 93.) For *Politicus* (in a letter from Leiden: cf. below, p. 210) on Cethegus, see *MP*, 6 Feb. 1651, 1579; cf. Nedham, *Levellers Levell'd*, 5.

'groan under tyranny' (312). Yet so long as Cromwell retains power, that scenario has no prospect.[127]

Marvell's 'The First Anniversary' also compares Cromwell to Alexander the Great. There, however, the parallel is a tribute, one not alloyed with the irony that aligns 'An Horatian Ode' with *Oceana*. The contrast indicates the political distance which Marvell had travelled since 1650.[128] But his journey, as we shall now see, was not uncomplicated.

127. Like Nedham, Harrington knows the danger of a 'standing general' (Pocock, ed., *Political Works*, 316; cf. 350).

128. Other resemblances between *Oceana* and 'The First Anniversary' may point to contact between the two writers. Norbrook, *Writing the English Republic*, 367, notes the similarity between Harrington's description of the workmen who 'squared every stone unto this structure in the quarries of ancient prudence' (210) and ll. 51–2 of 'The First Anniversary'. There is also the statement at the beginning of the 'Corollary' of Oceana, which recalls not only Marvell's poem but words of Nedham that the poem itself resembles (below, p. 147), that 'there is nothing so like the first call of beautiful order out of chaos and confusion as the architecture of a well-ordered commonwealth' (341). Another similarity lies in the apocalyptic, yet not quite Puritan, hopes of the liberation of Continental peoples from tyranny – the difference being that in Harrington it is a republic ('the minister of God upon earth', 321), not Cromwell, that carries freedom abroad. Another, perhaps, lies in Harrington's remark that 'there are kings in Europe to whom a king of Oceana would be but a petty companion. But the prince of this commonwealth is the terror and the judge of them all' (352).

5

Marvell and the Ambassadors

After 1650 Marvell forwarded himself on two fronts. He was a poet; and he aspired to a post in diplomacy or foreign affairs. In February 1653, Milton, the now blind Latin Secretary, wrote to his and Nedham's friend the Commonwealth's statesman John Bradshaw to ask, in vain as it turned out, for Marvell to be offered a job as his own assistant. It was particularly 'in point of attendance at conference with ambassadors' that Milton looked for help from the younger writer, who, he tells Bradshaw, 'offers himself' to 'the state to make use of... if there be any employment for him'. Milton pointed to Marvell's experience, put 'to very good purpose as I believe', of foreign travel, and his knowledge of the Dutch, French, Italian, and Spanish languages. On that basis he made the audacious claim that 'in a short time' Marvell would be able to do 'as good service' for the republic as that performed by Anthony Ascham, its ambassador to Madrid until his murder by royalist refugees in June 1650, just after Cromwell's return from Ireland.[1] Perhaps Marvell's upbringing at the great port of Hull, which traded with northern Europe, helps to explain why he cultivated a particular interest in the affairs of those rivals for mastery of the Baltic, the Netherlands and Sweden, the subjects of his political poetry from early 1651 to early 1654. When, finally, he gained an appointment in Thurloe's office in 1657, most of his recorded work was concerned with Swedish or Dutch affairs.[2] After the Restoration, in 1663–5, he would belong to the Earl of Carlisle's embassy to Russia, Sweden, and Denmark.

In January 1651, Oliver St John, who had come to prominence in conducting the legal case against ship-money in 1637, and who had become a leading figure of the Long Parliament in the 1640s, was appointed, together with his fellow MP Walter Strickland, to an embassy to the Netherlands. It is

1. *AMC* 38. 2. Ibid. 47 ff.

Figure 6. The ambassador: Oliver St John in 1651

a measure of the stature of Cromwell, who though absent on campaign in Scotland kept himself closely informed of developments at Westminster, not least through letters from St John and Strickland,[3] that those two men, both close friends of his though not of each other, were chosen.[4] The mission, which was aimed to secure an alliance between the two republics, was the occasion of Marvell's short Latin poem 'In Legationem Domini Oliveri St John ad Provincias Foederatas': on St John's embassy to the seven United Provinces which made up the Netherlands. Most literary critics have passed the poem by.[5] Yet it is a significant document in Marvell's life. It is also an ambivalent one. Written as it was only months after 'Tom May's Death', it indicates, at least on its surface, a defining reversal of political attachment on Marvell's part, from the royalism of that poem to its opposite. Yet the indication is surrounded by doubt and complexity. The text, of only sixteen lines, is full of difficulty, and the occasion and purpose of its composition are full of uncertainties (some of which will be treated separately, in Appendix A). They are ones of mood as well as of content. The poem, like so much of Marvell's Latin verse, is sportive in its puns and its allusiveness and its elusive nuances. Yet it has a darker side. It portrays diplomacy as an enclosed and secretive and duplicitous environment, a Tacitean world where language is slippery and where the most important things may be left unsaid. Marvell's lines convey those features by mirroring them.

There is an ambiguity in the very presentation of the poem. Its lines address St John, a 'great man'. They seem to be written for his eyes, to please him, to counsel him. They are meant, it seems reasonable to infer, to recommend the poet himself to him. Yet in its title the poem is 'on' the embassy (the Latin 'In'), not 'to' it or to its leader or in his praise. 'In' can be hostile. Thus Cicero's invectives are 'In', or against, Catiline or Piso or Verres, whereas his speeches of defence or advocacy are 'Pro' – for, or on behalf of – Flaccus or Ligarius or Marcellus. Marvell's other poem to a member of an embassy, written in 1654, is addressed 'to' Dr Nathaniel Ingelo – though we cannot know whether the title, which was evidently added well after the event, was Marvell's. The lines of the poem on St John's embassy can themselves be read, without strain, at both St John's

3. They are printed in Nickolls.
4. The proposal to send St John and Strickland was submitted by the council to the Commons through Cromwell's and Strickland's intimate friend Sir Gilbert Pickering: *Journal of the House of Commons*, 23 Jan. 1651.
5. Norbrook, *Writing the English Republic*, 280–7, is an exception.

and the republic's expense. Like 'An Horatian Ode', the poem points in opposing directions. There is what seems to be an antagonistic or satirical undercurrent, perhaps one to be privately understood, in the way that the esoteric allusions to Cromwell's ruthless ambition in the ode may have been, by the author and his friends. St John's stature is stated rather than illustrated. We learn much, from Marvell's puns and allusions, about the significance of the envoy's name, but nothing about his past, or about his exploits, that would explain his stature or show why the name befits him. He lives in the poem only in relation to the embassy and its purpose. The sole characteristic that we discover him to have – or anyway to need to have if the mission is to achieve its ends – is what in the ode is the 'wiser art', the political calculation, of Marvell's Cromwell. St John is told, mysteriously, that he does not need 'to hide allowed deceptions with shifting guile' ('varia licitos condere fraude dolos'), because he can achieve the same ends – the same permissibly duplicitous ends, Marvell seems to mean – by holding his tongue. This is the kind of language which the enemies of monarchical tyranny, Nedham and Milton among them, associated with the sealed and faithless world of courts and cabinets. It is surprising to find it endorsed, or anyway ostensibly endorsed, in a tribute to an ambassador for the Commonwealth. St John's mission was designed to fortify the regime which the regicide – the occasion when, in Marvell's poem of November 1650, 'the sword glitter[ed] o'er the judge's head' – had brought to power. If the embassy succeeded, the Stuarts' hopes of restoration would be gravely damaged. Taken by themselves, Marvell's injunctions to the ambassador endorse that purpose as emphatically and decisively as, taken by itself, the advice to the forward youth in 'An Horatian Ode' enjoins him to forsake his muses and embrace the Cromwellian future. Yet, here as there, it seems that Marvell can recommend the future only by adhering within himself, or within part of himself, to the loyalties or resentments of the past.

Oliver St John bears 'Foedera seu Belgis seu nova bella': either new treaties (or leagues) with the Dutch, or new wars with them. We know from his name, explains Marvell, that he commands 'the iron locks of Janus' (10). For the name, like the poem, faces two ways. One half of it makes St John, in line 9, the 'messenger' of 'war', the other of 'peace' ('Scilicet hoc Martis, sed pacis nuntius illo'). But which half stands for which? Translators and editors identify 'Oliver' with the olive-branch of peace, which, at first sight anyway, is indeed the obvious equation. With more difficulty they equate St John with war, remembering that St John the Apostle is a 'son of thunder', or suggesting that Marvell has in mind St John of the Book of Revelation, a prophet of wars.[6] Is that a sufficiently firm analogy – especially given that the word 'Scilicet' ('certainly') seems to bestow sureness on the warlike property of that half of the name? Deliberately or not, the correspondences are ambivalent. For Marvell's wording allows the opposite interpretation to the one adopted by modern authorities. The Gospel of St John is one of peace, while Oliver is the name the ambassador shares with his cousin and friend, who in 'An Horatian Ode' pursues 'adventrous war' because he cannot 'cease | In the inglorious arts of peace'. According to the prominent MP Bulstrode Whitelocke, St John was appointed to the embassy as 'Cromwell's creature'.[7] Marvell would refer to Cromwell's own 'olive' in 'The First Anniversary' ('Didst, like thine olive, still refuse to reign', 258). If the poem of 1651 does allude to him, it not only resembles the ode but is connected to it. So perhaps there is another dimension to the ambiguity of the ambassador's name.[8]

Whether there is or not, the Dutch must choose between the envoy's two halves. Marvell's poem concludes with a threat: 'Dutchmen, do you wish Oliver or Saint John? Antiochus stood not in a tighter circle.' The allusion is to an episode in AD 168 when Antiochus IV, King of Syria, besieged Rome's ally the royal house of Egypt. The Roman senate sent envoys to get him to withdraw. One of them, the grandee Gaius Popilius, drew a circle round the king with his staff, and told him that he would keep him within it until he had promised not to attack Rome's allies. The ploy worked, and Antiochus pledged himself accordingly.[9] The story survives in two forms, the first in Book XLV of Livy's history of the Roman republic, the second, written a little later, in Book VI of the account of the remarkable deeds of Roman history drawn up by Valerius Maximus. In both narratives, Popilius scored a triumph, which asserted the majesty and potency of the republic over the kings with which it dealt. In Valerius's account, Antiochus greeted Popilius with the hand and countenance of 'friendship', only for Popilius to interpret his amicability as a delaying tactic. Angered by it, he answered with such

6. For the latter suggestion see William A. McQueen and Kiffin A. Rockwell, eds., *The Latin Poetry of Andrew Marvell* (Chapel Hill, NC, 1964), 50; Norbrook, *Writing the English Republic*, 286.
7. Bulstrode Whitelocke, *Memorials of the English Affairs*, 4 vols. (1853), iii. 28.
8. Thus where, in l. 9, one of the two sides of the name is 'hoc' ('this'), and the other 'illo' ('that'), either word could refer to either the peaceful or the warlike connotation. I am grateful to David Hopkins for discussion of this point.
9. Marvell reverted to the story in *Mr. Smirke*: *CPAM* ii. 68–9.

authority that 'one might have thought that it was not an envoy speaking, but the senate house itself set before one's eyes'. 'How effective', Valerius is moved to observe, 'is a curt, impressive attitude and speech', which in this case transformed the diplomatic landscape of the eastern Mediterranean. Livy highlights the effectiveness of the tactic too. 'This embassy', he notes, 'gained a great reputation among the nations.' Yet there is unease behind his tribute. Livy cannot warm to Popilius or unambiguously admire him. The envoy got his way 'asperitate animi', 'by harshness of spirit'. Elsewhere in Livy's narrative, that harsh man, 'vir asper', speaks with a 'grim face and prosecutor's tone' ('voltu truci et accusatoria voce'). His bluntness and severity do not seem unmixed blessings to the state.

Marvell's analogy, whatever understanding of it he invites, is uncommonly bold. St John's own embassy, though it would break down in high acrimony, went to The Hague with amicable intentions and (unlike Popilius's mission) exchanged professions of amity on its arrival. Though he set out for Holland with firm resolves, he would not have threatened, or proclaimed England's superior might over, a nation whose amity the republic badly needed. Why did Marvell place the example of Popilius before him? There is another puzzle. St John, Marvell tells us, has been entrusted with 'compellatio fallax'. The phrase has a number of possible meanings and shades of meaning, as Marvell must have known, and as he perhaps intended. Translators into modern English have had to plump for a single meaning. Evidently assuming the poem to be an untroubled tribute to St John, they have decided on tame renderings of the phrase, which has been given in one case as 'this elusive encounter', in another as 'the captious meeting'.[10] The first version removes from the adjective ('fallax') any imputation of deliberate deception. In the second, 'captious' perhaps carries that connotation, but is a mild equivalent of a Latin word that could be more obviously translated as 'false' or 'deceitful' or 'treacherous'. And what of the noun, 'compellatio'? If it simply means an encounter or meeting – that is, the negotiation with the Dutch – then any captiousness or treachery can perhaps be attributed to them rather than to St John. Yet in its most common meanings 'compellatio' conveys

10. The first translation is by Estelle Haan, which appeared in her *Andrew Marvell's Latin Poetry: From Text to Context* (Brussels, 2003). The second, by McQueen and Rockwell, appeared in Andrew Marvell, *The Complete Poems*, ed. Elizabeth Story Donno (Harmondsworth, 1972). McQueen and Rockwell's is reproduced in the first edition of Nigel Smith's edition of Marvell's poems, Haan's in the revised one of 2006.

something more. It implies that the Dutch are either 'accosted' by St John or 'reproached' by him – in which case 'fallax' seems to be a quality that he brings or at least helps to bring to the encounter.[11]

★★

In so far as we can make the poem intelligible, it is by moving beyond those uncertainties of meaning to the poem's context, which Marvell's lines take for granted, and in which they intervene. We need to turn, that is, to the political and diplomatic background to the embassy. St John's mission was a critical moment in the life of the new republic. Like the embassy of Popilius, it asserted the prowess of a republic against monarchical interests. The English struggle between king and parliament had always interacted with, and to an extent had corresponded to, one in the Netherlands. The Dutch conflict was between the monarchical aspirations of the House of Orange, whose leader of the 1640s, the young William II, was son-in-law to Charles I, and the republican sentiment whose chief strength lay within the most powerful and prosperous of the seven United Provinces of the Dutch confederation, Holland. It was in Holland, especially at Amsterdam and The Hague, that the chief battles for control were fought. If the Orange interest prevailed, the English Commonwealth might expect Holland to be the base of a Stuart invasion to reclaim the throne. That prospect had been remote before 1648, but the international standing of the United Provinces rose in that year with the Treaty of Munster, which ended the long war between the United Provinces and Spain and at last brought the Dutch their independence from Madrid. Thus in 1648–9 two new republics had been created. But in both countries, too, there was formidable anti-republican sentiment. In the English case it looked to an exiled king, in the Dutch one to a crypto-king within the existing polity. The Netherlands themselves came close to civil war in the summer of 1650, when William attempted a military coup in Amsterdam. The Dutch struggle, like the English one, had international dimensions. Orange and Stuart alike had close links with the French monarchy, which now gave shelter to Charles II. William pressed

11. A distinguished Latinist has suggested to me that 'compellatio' could simply mean 'name'. If so, the play on the name's ambiguity could give 'fallax' a good-humoured and innocuous meaning, such as 'innocently deceptive' or 'misleading'. But it could also – particularly if 'Oliver' points to Cromwell – have a nocuous meaning: more nocuous than the word 'captious' conveys.

for an alliance of three rulers that would restore Charles to the English throne and secure the supremacy of the Orange house in the Netherlands. He also did what he could to aid Charles's struggle against Cromwell in Scotland.

Then, in October, William unexpectedly died, to be succeeded by an infant son. The event transformed Dutch politics. It dramatically reversed the trend towards monarchy, gravely weakened Orange power, and paved the way for a republican oligarchy that would rule for two decades. That outcome, however, took time to become clear. During the embassy the support for the Orange cause in Holland proved surprisingly, and stridently, resilient. Like all domestic upheavals of the era, William's death had international ramifications. Though the Thirty Years War had ended in 1648, the war between France and Spain would persist until 1659. It was fought largely in Flanders, the neighbouring territory with which the United Provinces had been affiliated until the late sixteenth century. The pacific policies of Charles I, and then the civil wars, had kept England out of the European conflict, but that immunity was unlikely to survive the abolition of monarchy for long.

Marvell's expectation that there would be either new treaties ('foedera') or new wars ('bella') would not in itself have been controversial. Alliance and war between the two republics were indeed seen as alternatives, and other powers could be expected to be drawn into the one or the other. At the end of December 1650 the leading MP Sir Henry Vane predicted to his colleagues that soon the French and the Dutch would either 'fall out with us downright', 'and turn downright enemies', or seek an alliance with England.[12] That was not how the ambassadors would have put it to the Dutch, but the official instructions to the envoys did require them to impress upon their hosts 'how great an influence for good or for evil the union or disunion' of the two powers must have upon their common interests.[13] The poem also conveys, albeit in strikingly undiplomatic terms, the growing mood of international self-confidence within the government. For although the royalist threat persisted, it had been reduced by the victory at Dunbar and by the exploits of the navy under Robert Blake. Among Europe's monarchies the republic had been, at first, an outcast,

12. Nickolls, 41.
13. Bodl., Dep. C171N, Nalson MS XVIII, fo. 192; Steven A. Pincus, *Protestantism and Patriotism: Ideologies and the Making of English Foreign Policy, 1650–1668* (Cambridge, 1996), 26.

but now those crowns had to take account of a power to which the revolution had brought military and naval resources infinitely greater than the ones the Stuarts had commanded. In the winter of 1650–1 foreign powers sent embassies to London and jostled for the good affections of the regime. Within the government there was a determination to stand on its diplomatic dignity and, in negotiations with foreign powers, to insist on stiff terms in negotiations.

Yet a rift over the conduct of foreign policy had opened at Westminster and Whitehall. Marvell's poem takes sides in it: Nedham's side. As Nedham's and Milton's friend John Bradshaw, the president of the council of state, complained, many MPs shirked the hazard of confrontation and showed an unseemly 'haste to ingratiate' the republic with foreign powers.[14] *Politicus*, which we find supporting Bradshaw in domestic policy at this time, backed him in foreign policy too. Its stance is that of Popilius as Marvell represents it, and of the senate for which the Roman envoy spoke. Livy records that only when Antiochus had pledged himself, under the duress that Popilius had imposed on him, to obey the senate's decrees did Popilius extend the hand of 'friendship' to him. Nedham's newsbook wants to see Continental nations 'scrape for acquaintance and friendship' with the English republic, which should not 'stoop to any, for the reputation of every state is its chiefest strength'.[15]

The government should also, in Nedham's view, make maximum use of the Commonwealth's naval power.[16] It was against the Dutch that, in 1652, the might of that power would be directed. Yet among the rulers of the Commonwealth the Anglo-Dutch war of 1652–4 was divisive. In the winter of 1650–1 the handling of the Dutch divided them too. The hard-line view within the government was that the Netherlanders, who had failed to accord diplomatic recognition to the republic, should do so by sending their own legation to England before the English sent one to The Hague. They should also make amends for the murder in May 1649, by royalist exiles who had found shelter among them, of the English envoy there, Isaac Dorislaus, the man who had prepared the charge of treason against Charles I. Walter Strickland, who had been parliament's agent at The Hague since 1642, had been recalled in July 1650 in protest

14. Nickolls, 40; Worden, *Rump Parliament*, 255–6.

15. *MP*, 5 Dec. 1650, 433; 6 Mar. 1651, 623–4.

16. Ibid. 13 Mar. 1651, 650; 26 June 1651, 886. Cf. ibid. 7 Oct. 1652, 1928; 16 Mar. 1653, '2507'; *Cat May Look upon a King*, 99–101.

against Dutch intransigence, and diplomatic relations had been broken off.

Strickland, whose appointment as St John's fellow ambassador Marvell's poem ignores, had his own perspective. He had a Dutch wife and perhaps a Dutch pension, and was suspected of both partiality and weakness towards the Netherlands. He favoured a strategy of accommodation towards the province of Holland, on whose decisions and loyalties the likely diplomatic posture of the Netherlands as a whole depended. If England and Holland could be brought to stand together, he reasoned, the House of Orange could be isolated and the menace to the Commonwealth from the Continent greatly reduced. That would not be easy, not only because of the extent of Orange influence in Holland, but because many Hollanders who wanted a republic in their own land had none the less been shocked by the regicide. They were also horrified by the religious radicalism of the new regime. In religion, as in politics, their sympathies were with the English Presbyterians. But their objections, Strickland judged, could be overcome. To that end it was worth making minor diplomatic concessions to Holland, in order to give encouragement to those friends whom the English republic did have there and to show other Netherlanders that amity would pay.[17] In December 1650 parliament agreed to send Strickland back to The Hague. Bradshaw's ally George Bishop bemoaned the 'carnal fears' behind that decision. 'It doth not become those whom God hath owned in such a manner' as the rulers of the republic, he protested, 'unworthily to fall at the feet of those that have spurned and abused us.'[18]

In January parliament rescinded its resolution and decided on an alternative diplomatic strategy. Strickland would still return, but not as a resident envoy. He would go to The Hague as a special ambassador, with St John, to secure a treaty of alliance with the Dutch. For that change of strategy there were arguments which hard-liners could recognize. However reluctantly they concurred in the Commonwealth's readiness to talk to a power that had declined to honour it, they saw in the embassy a means to their own assertive ends. The death of the Prince of Orange, the consequent marked shift of power towards the province of Holland, and the meeting in January of a Grand Assembly of the Netherlands, gave the English a chance to tilt the balance of Dutch politics to their own advantage. They sought to take it by sending St John's and Strickland's grand and numerous legation,

17. For Strickland's views see *TSP* i. 115–31; Nickolls, 51.

18. Nickolls, 55.

which conveyed an image not of weakness but of strength. *Politicus*, in the spirit of Bradshaw's party, voiced mixed feelings about the embassy. It regretted the English readiness to 'creep to Holland', a province which 'cannot subsist without' English friendship, by sending an embassy before the United Provinces had recognized the English republic.[19] Marvell's parallel with Popilius warns against any comparable derogation of power. Nedham knew of the antagonism to England in the States-General, whose members were anxious, he reported, 'to show their teeth at England'.[20] He distrusted the appearance of friendship which welcomed St John – as Popilius had distrusted the welcome of Antiochus. Yet *Politicus*, like Bradshaw, accepted the case for St John's legation – provided it imposed the Commonwealth's will on the Dutch.

The embassy carried with it the most ambitious proposal in English diplomatic history, the extent of which was to be revealed to the Dutch only if or when a basis for diplomatic progress had been established (as it never was) and the prospects of success been assessed. The English proposed not only a treaty of alliance but the integration of the two nations. The province of Holland would either carry the rest of the confederation with it into the union with England, or detach itself from the weaker provinces around it, to which Orange power would henceforth be confined. The idea seems fanciful in retrospect, and may have been doomed at the time. Yet the newly independent Dutch Commonwealth, for all its standing abroad, looked an improbable coalition of states, one by no means sure to last. A revision of international frontiers was far from impossible. Uncertainty has always surrounded the English proposal. Though there was much talk before and during the negotiations of a 'more strict' or 'more intrinsical' union or alliance or 'conjunction' between the two countries, those phrases were, intentionally, of uncertain and flexible meaning. But in its most audacious form the proposal would have created a single republic, with resources of might and wealth and population that any monarchy would have hesitated to confront. It was an idea worthy of a power with international ambition on a Roman scale.

The scheme seems the likely explanation of what is otherwise an impenetrably obscure statement in Marvell's poem. The ambassador is told that it is not 'necessary to entrust secret meanings to paper' ('Non opus arcanos chartis committere sensus') or 'to hide allowed deceptions with

19. *MP*, 17 Apr. 1651, 724. 20. Ibid. 17 Nov. 1650, 371.

shifting guile'. The proposal for a full union was never committed to paper, and it required diplomatic deception of the normal, or 'allowed', kind. Its particulars were never revealed. The silence was tantalizing. When the ambassadors had returned to England empty-handed, *Politicus* carried a letter, written from Leiden in Holland but bearing the mark of the editor's intervening hand, which referred to the plan as one for a 'marriage' of the two republics that 'would make us one'. The Spanish ambassador in London, adds the letter, 'longs ... to know' what the English envoys had in mind in making a proposition of such 'noble and heroic importance, worthy the actings of free Christian states'. But 'his golden key will not fit the lock of your cabinet to find those secrets, which it seems the world is not worthy to know. I can assure you some else are as inquisitive as he about it, but they seem to weary themselves at your door, as the blind men did at Lot's door, and could not find entrance.'[21]

If that interpretation of the lines is correct, then Marvell commends the proposal for union.[22] Strickland, the advocate of a mollifying stand towards the Dutch, viewed the scheme with scepticism.[23] It was *Politicus* that gave it public advocacy. During the embassy Nedham voiced, as no one else did publicly, the wish that 'England and Holland may become as one entire body'.[24] Other comments of the newsbook, while not referring to the proposal explicitly, indicate his enthusiasm for it. *Politicus* called for the 'conjunction of those two great republics' of England and Holland, which were 'equally hated by all monarchies in Europe', for they were 'formidable to kings', who not only feared them but saw in them 'bad precedents for others to follow'.[25] Through that 'union' the two states would 'embrace and twist interests against the common enemies of our liberty so dearly purchased'.[26]

For in Nedham's mind the proposal for union belonged to a programme of international republicanism, to be pursued in what an early issue of the new newsbook had called 'an age for kings to run the wild-goose-chase':[27] the programme to which 'An Horatian Ode' had (in whatever tone) alluded

21. Ibid. 10 July 1651, 913; 24 July 1651, 946.
22. Perhaps Marvell's choice of the word 'foedera', which can merely mean treaties but can also mean more than that, is meant to allude to the scheme. The title of his poem, '.... Ad Provincias Foederatas', refers to an existing amalgam of states, which the new 'foedera' envisaged by the scheme would transform or terminate. Yet 'foedera' may simultaneously have the intentional ambiguity characteristic of official pronouncements about the proposed treaty.
23. At least, he had done so when it was first floated in 1649: *TSP* i. 130.
24. *MP*, 3 Apr. 1651, 696–7.
25. Ibid. 20 Feb. 1651, 600; 20 Nov. 1651, 1211.
26. Ibid. 6 Feb. 1651, 579. Cf. ibid. 19 Sept. 1650, 253; 9 Jan. 1651, 512; 1 May 1651, 760.
27. Ibid. 4 July 1650, 54.

in claiming that Cromwell 'to all states not free | Shall climacteric be'. In Nedham's accounts of them, the political conflicts in the Netherlands were linked to and paralleled with the struggles to replace tyranny by free states in Scotland and France. The Dutch revolt against Spain in the sixteenth century, he insisted, had been a war not merely against tyranny but against kingship itself, and the same struggle had been fought there ever since between Orange and republic. Nedham had long been interested in it. In 1644 he had remarked that the 'free states' of the United Provinces 'know the miseries of tyranny and slavery'.[28] Now he looked for an end to those afflictions. 'The storm that began in England', declared the opening issue of *Politicus*, 'having taken its course by France, is like to end in the Low Countries', and William II should 'look for the same fate that attends the English monarchy'.[29] In the winter of 1650–1 Robert Blake, the commander of the Commonwealth's fleet, was reported to have declared in the public square of Cadiz 'that with the example followed by London all kingdoms will annihilate tyranny and become republics. England had done so already; France was following in her wake; and as the natural gravity of the Spaniards rendered them somewhat slower in their operations, he gave them ten years for the revolution in this country.'[30] The story was surely indebted to a lively imagination, but its circulation indicates the mood in England that Nedham was seeking to exploit. Marvell's poem reflects that mood too. If the embassy was to be the prelude to the overthrow of continental kingship, new 'wars' or 'treaties' would indeed follow. The diplomatic map of Europe would be redrawn, and there would surely be a resumption of international conflict on the scale which had been reduced only by the Peace of Westphalia in 1648.[31]

In Marvell's 'An Horatian Ode', it is the sword of justice that carries the wars of liberation into 'all states not free'. In *Politicus* in December 1650, 'as justice holds the balance over the world, so dost' the English republic 'in Europe'.[32] To fulfil that destiny it must master its foreign enemies. In January 1651 the newsbook announced that Scotland – a foreign country

28. *Mercurius Britanicus*, 5 Feb. 1644, 165. Cf. ibid. 25 Mar. 1644, 216; 24 June 1644, 312; Nedham's preface to *An Answer to Nine Arguments* (1645); Hall, *Humble Motion*, 23–4, 31.
29. *MP*, 13 June 1650, 16.
30. *Calendar of State Papers Venetian 1647–52*, 169–70.
31. McQueen and Rockwell, perhaps because they have only the relations between England and the Netherlands in view, translate 'bella' and 'foedera' in the singular, as 'war' and 'treaty'. They may be right, for Marvell's plurals could reflect the demands of metre. But the literal interpretation seems the likelier one.
32. *MP*, 5 Dec. 1650, 433; cf. 6 Mar. 1651, 623–4.

again since the decapitation of its king had ended the union of the two crowns – must be made 'a province to England' once Cromwell has conquered it.[33] Nedham is equally firm in relation to the Netherlands, for there the 'fatal house' of Orange succours the 'fatal house' of Stuart.[34] In the Netherlands as in Scotland, *Politicus* saw at work the evils not merely of royalism but of Presbyterianism, many of whose English devotees had been driven by the regicide into making common cause with royalists. Presbyterianism was numerously represented in the exiled community in Holland. The 'religion' of the Orange party, reported *Politicus*, 'which is near of kin in practice to that of Scotland', 'is nought else but a mere formality' – that is, a mere shell of outward observation, which lacks an inner substance.[35] A radical revolution is needed that will destroy the 'design of tyranny'[36] which the Orange house – 'the Orange tree', as Nedham likes to call it – pursues. Like the Scots, like the French, like the Romans from whom modern nations should take their lessons, the Dutch have an 'opportunity' – one of those rare historical moments that Machiavelli called an *occasione* – to seize a lasting 'liberty': a 'fit opportunity', which they must not 'let ... slip', 'for the redeeming of their former liberties, which the Prince of Orange had so engrossed to himself'.[37] Nedham uses the same language of the parallel struggle in France, where 'now is the time they must win their liberty or never'.[38]

In January 1651, the month of the appointment of the embassy and of Nedham's injunction to the Dutch to seize their 'opportunity', John Milton became the official licenser of *Politicus*, which in the first issue that he supervised proclaimed the imminent appearance of his *Defensio*. Milton's treatise was written with a Dutch audience prominently in mind. Its early pages remember how, in the attempted Orange coup of 1650, 'slavery and a new master' were 'made ready for' the Dutch, and how close their 'liberty' had come to extinction. The reasoning of Salmasius in *Defensio Regia*, maintains Milton's reply to it, assails the 'foundations and causes' of the Dutch republic 'precisely as he attacks ours; by one and the same effort, in fact, he strives to undermine them both, and to make

33. Ibid. 9 Jan. 1651, 508; cf. *Cat May Look upon a King*, 35, 102.
34. *MP*, 23 Jan. 1651, 545; 19 June 1651, 871; cf. ibid. 26 June 1651, '882'.
35. Ibid. 19 Sep. 1650, 254–5.
36. Ibid. 16 Jan. 1651, 529.
37. Ibid. 9 Jan. 1651, 512; cf. 30 Oct. 1651, 1158.
38. Ibid. 27 June 1650, 42; 1 Aug. 1650, 122 (cf. *Mercurius Britanicus*, 18 May 1646, 1118). Nedham's recurrent insistence on the seizing of moments, and his ubiquitous usage of the phrase ''tis time' – or, more commonly, ''tis high time' – recall the opening of 'An Horatian Ode', where 'now' ''tis time' for the forward youth to act.

them totter to their fall; and under our names foully maligns the most eminent champions of liberty there'. Salmasius, whom Milton represents as an instrument of the Orange party, had a chair at Leiden, though he was currently in Sweden. 'Every free state' ('omnis libera civitas'), asserts Milton, should exclude him from its borders.[39] (Elsewhere, albeit in words of which – or so it looks – he altered and softened the import before their publication in 1654, when peace with the Dutch had been restored,[40] Milton recalled evidence that they were 'desirous neither of a treaty nor of a war with us' ('nobiscum nec foedus nec bellum velle') – the alternatives before them in Marvell's poem.[41]) The militancy of Marvell's poem, and its message to the Netherlanders that the English will beat them if they cannot join them, breathe the spirit of Nedham and of Milton. Yet there is another spirit too, hard as it is to assess its prominence. In 'An Horatian Ode', Marvell moved from royalism, not to the position of balance or detachment which some critics have found there, but to an advocacy of boldness and ruthlessness in the revolutionary cause. The advocacy was combined with its opposite, to which it brought an equal intensity. The St John poem has the same pattern. Radicalism and royalism again confront each other. Who that reads it, and ponders its ambiguities and allusions, can be any surer than a reader of the ode that England's 'free state' will be an instrument of liberation rather than, as Nedham predicted in his royalist phase, an 'arbitrary vassalage'?

★★

Two years after the poem for the embassy, and following his sojourn at Appleton House and his return south in or before late 1652, Marvell reverted to the subject of the Dutch in 'The Character of Holland'. There was no ambivalence now, no ironic undercurrent. In Marvell's political verse for the reminder of the Interregum there never would be. The satire of 'The Character of Holland' is overt. It is directed outwards, at England's foreign enemy. The occasion which it celebrates is the great English naval victory of February 1653, when the Anglo–Dutch war was in its eighth month. It was on 21 February, just after the battle, that Milton sent his testimonial for Marvell to Bradshaw, who was expected to interview him the following day. The poem may – but may not – have been written in

39. *CW* vii. 19. 40. Below, Ch. 12. 41. *CW* viii. 195; *CP* iv. 1074.

two stages. Only in its last third (from line 101) does Marvell refer to the war. The rest could perhaps have been written as early as the breakdown of the English embassy of 1651.

In this poem the proximity of Nedham, hard to pin down in the poem on the embassy, was more obvious, as it would be in Marvell's other political verse over the next two years. During the war Nedham had a prominent role in the English propaganda effort, not only in *Politicus* but in more substantial writings. Late in 1652 he published, at the government's behest, a handsomely produced translation, with supplementary material angled towards current events, of a book he had long admired, John Selden's *Mare Clausum*, the work of 1635 which, in response to Hugh Grotius's *Mare Liberum*, had championed England's sovereignty of its neighbouring seas. That was the issue that had sparked the war, when Dutch ships refused to strike sail to English ones in the Channel.

'The Character of Holland' adopts the satirical mode that characterized Nedham's treatment of the foreign enemies of the English republic. Did Marvell, in writing the opening couplet that describes Holland 'As but th'off-scouring of the British sand', recall Nedham's description in 1650 of Scotland, a 'country which sticks like a scab upon the fair body of this unfortunate island'?[42] At all events 'The Character of Holland' makes contact with more recent publications of Nedham. When, during the Anglo-Dutch war of 1672–4, the Earl of Shaftesbury used the phrase 'Carthago delenda est', the equation between the rivalry of the two modern nations and that of the ancient republics of Rome and Carthage had almost become a commonplace. But it was Nedham and Marvell who established it, under the Commonwealth. In Marvell's poem 'their Carthage overcome | Would render fain unto our better Rome' (141–2). In July 1651 *Politicus* conveyed, in the letter from Leiden that told of the proposed 'marriage' of England and Holland, the resistance to the scheme by Dutchmen who reasoned 'that Rome and Carthage are too stout to allow either to be the sole mistress'.[43] In December 1652 the newsbook meditated, this time in a document published as a letter from Oxford, on 'the old game betwixt

42. *Case*, 59. See too *MP*, 18 July 1650, 95, on 'the petty toes of the French monarchy'. Milton's *Defensio* speaks of the Irish as 'offscourings' (*colluviem*): *CW* vii. 39; cf. p. 35.

43. *MP*, 10 July 1651, 913. In its account of the Dutch nation, 'that very pay-bas' whose 'spirits and principles' have sunk, the letter recalls the opening of 'An Horatian Ode': the country 'now begins to blunt and rust with our swords'. For Carthage see too ibid. 20 Feb. 1651, 604.

Rome and Carthage (the two great Commonwealths of the elder time)', and invited its readers to 'apply' the contrasts between them to 'the present complexion of affairs'. In the poem, treacherous Dutch diplomacy ignores the obligations imposed by existing 'leagues' of amity (107), and negotiates 'feigned treaties' (117) with its ostensible allies. The passage in *Politicus* recalls that, whereas the Romans were 'punctual observers of leagues', the Carthaginians were 'of crafty and over-reaching wits, infamous for their breaches of faith and promises'. Elsewhere in 1652 Nedham warned the English to 'take heed how they make leagues and union with such a people' as the Dutch, who 'can as easily swallow down leagues contrary to one another as earth is to heaven', and 'to discern those serpents under all green and smooth expressions of friendship'. Marvell sets the 'infant Hercules' of the English republic beside 'their Hydra of seven provinces' (137–8): in *Politicus* the Romans were 'the younger state, but better-limbed', whereas the Carthaginians are so 'ill-jointed' as to have 'no coherence'. Marvell's jibe at 'pickled heeren' (34), and his scorn of the village princes who pass for rulers, have a parallel in Nedham's contempt elsewhere for the Dutch 'herren' who 'have no presence or awful authority'.[44]

In March 1653 *Politicus* printed an anonymous Latin poem, with a liberal English translation alongside it, entitled 'Anglia Victrix',[45] of which Nedham is likely to have been the author or an author. Like Marvell's poem it celebrates the naval triumph of the previous month. In July 1651, in the letter from Leiden that referred to the 'secrets' of the proposed Anglo–Dutch merger, *Politicus* had reported the Dutch feeling in favour of their principle of 'mare liberum'.[46] Now 'Anglia Victrix' alluded to Nedham's translation of Selden, and spurned the Dutch claim to 'mare clausum', which violated England's 'sacred rights'. Marvell's poem turns the phrase 'mare liberum' against the Dutch (26), pokes fun at another work by Grotius (113), and observes that the Dutch refusal to strike sail affronts England's 'ancient rights' (107). Other parallels between the two poems, both of literary manner and of allusive detail, are shrewdly observed by Marvell's recent editor.[47]

★★

44. *MP*, 2 Dec. 1652, 2053–5; *Case Stated between England and the United Provinces*, 5, 46, 53 (cf. pp. 1, 15).
45. *MP*, 17 Mar. 1653, 2296–7; and see Norbrook, *Writing the English Republic*, 294.
46. *MP*, 24 July 1651, 945.
47. Smith, 248 (and see p. 256).

Milton's testimonial did not produce official employment for Marvell. In the summer of 1653 Marvell did earn the post of tutor at Eton to Cromwell's protégé William Dutton, whom he would later take to the Continent, where Marvell did intelligence work for John Thurloe. Not until 1657, however, would he gain employment at Whitehall. Whatever held him back, it was not any want of loyalty in the poetry he wrote for the protectorate.

By the end of 1653 the focus of both his and Nedham's attention to English diplomacy had moved from Holland to Sweden. The Anglo–Dutch war of 1652–4 was the Commonwealth's war. Cromwell viewed it with unease. Though he never warmed to the Dutch, and as protector was unyieldingly tough in negotiating with them, he did not want conflict with a fellow Protestant power. He looked for an alliance of Protestant states against the great Catholic Habsburg ones: against the Spanish empire and the Holy Roman Empire of and around Austria and Germany. Towards the end of 1653, shortly before he became protector, he took two initiatives to that end. First, he privately discussed peace terms with Dutch representatives. The negotiations would move swiftly after his installation as protector, when the war was quickly ended. Secondly, he persuaded Barebone's Parliament to send an ambassador, Bulstrode Whitelocke, to secure a treaty with Europe's other main Protestant power, the Sweden of Queen Christina. Marvell, having in 1651 addressed a poem to an English ambassador in Holland, now turned to the embassy to Sweden. The embassy left in November 1653, and returned in June 1654. In February 1654 Marvell's Latin poem 'A Letter to Dr Ingelo' was sent to Sweden in the diplomatic mail. Ingelo, a friend of Marvell, was a chaplain on the mission. The poem was written for the eyes of the Swedish queen, and was presented to her by Whitelocke, who described its author to her as a 'friend' of his.[48] Two other Latin poems by Marvell on Christina, both of them brief, 'In Effigiem Oliveri Cromwell' and 'In eandem Reginae Sueciae transmissam', were evidently written to accompany a portrait of the protector thought to have been sent to her after the conclusion of the treaty won by Whitelocke's embassy. It was the first mark of official favour, at least as a poet, that Marvell had achieved.

48. Edward Holberton, 'The Textual Transmission of Marvell's "A Letter to Doctor Ingelo": The Longleat Manuscript', *English Manuscript Studies*, 12 (2005), 234. Holberton's article throws fresh light on the poem.

The longer poem, 'A Letter to Doctor Ingelo', is a eulogy of the queen, which urges the treaty of alliance with Cromwell for which the protector longs. He wishes her to fulfil a Continental role worthy of her father, King Gustavus Adolphus, whose victories in the Thirty Years War made him the hero of European Protestantism. Cromwell's Protestant diplomacy was the revival of the ideal of his generation of 'the godly', which had yearned for the liquidation of the Habsburg empire and had seen Gustavus as its instrument.[49] In 1653–4 Cromwell looked to Christina as an ally in the cause of international Protestantism. Marvell's poem tells of Cromwell's desire 'to drive the [Austrian] eagle from its German nest, and to rout the she-wolf [the Catholic Church and whore] from the Palatine mount'.[50] The Palatinate, which before the Thirty Years War had been the focus of international Protestantism, was lost to the Habsburgs under James I's son-in-law the Elector Palatine, whose throne the Stuarts, to the despair of their subjects, had shamefully failed to rescue. Cromwell and Christina, urges Marvell, should reverse that disaster and jointly 'fall on the Austrians and Spanish'.

If Marvell was a 'friend' of Whitelocke, Marchamont Nedham, who as early as 1644 had puffed him as 'that godly patriot',[51] had connections with him too. After the Restoration he would act as Whitelocke's doctor. Before and during the embassy he supplied him with private newsletters; and he tried to see him before the ambassador's departure for Sweden.[52] Nedham

49. In 1645, during the first civil war, Nedham's *Mercurius Britanicus* gave voice to the Protestant international outlook, in language that looks forward both to Cromwell's foreign policy and to Marvell's poetry for him. It printed a letter to parliament from Christina, 'so heroic a queen', whose 'zeal', Nedham observed, 'sparkles out of that cold region'. *Britanicus* remembers the exploits of Gustavus in Germany, 'where (like another Samson) he burnt up the Philistines' corn, the harvest (I mean) of superstitions, which was ready ripe for destruction by fire and sword. I am persuaded that this valiant and warlike nation will be a main wheel in the work of providence, to bring about the approaching ruin of the great whore [Antichrist]: to help once again to pull down that proud, tyrannous and incestuous house of Austria, the only grand pillar of the Roman fabric; which being once shaken, Italy must soon tumble to the depth of infamy and vengeance' (*Mercurius Britanicus*, 13 Jan. 1645, 516). The language is repeated at ibid. 10 Feb. 1645, 548. In *Defensio Secunda* Milton wonders at the virtues of Christina that shine in the 'freezing cold': *CW* viii. 107.

50. Smith, 265–6.

51. *Mercurius Britanicus*, 25 Mar. 1644, 218.

52. Ruth Spalding, *Contemporaries of Bulstrode Whitelocke* (Oxford, 1990), 216–81. Whitelocke took medical advice from Nedham, in 1664 (Ruth Spalding, ed., *The Diary of Bulstrode Whitelocke* (Oxford, 1990), 691). Resemblances have been noted between Marvell's poem to Dr Ingelo and another, written by another 'friend' of Whitelocke, that was also presented to the queen (Haan, *Andrew Marvell's Latin Poetry*, 150–1). It seems likely to have been by Cromwell's councillor Sir Charles Wolesley; but perhaps Nedham too is a candidate. See too Holberton, 'Textual Transmission'.

had a 'dear friend' on the expedition in Cromwell's former chaplain Robert Stapleton (or Stapylton), and had other contacts on it too.[53] *Politicus* supplied colourful reports of Whitelocke's mission. Since its vigorous republican editorials of 1651–2, the newsbook had become less sprightly. It now sought, as its political masters wished, to lower the political temperature. But it brought life to the subject of the embassy. Much of the space of *Politicus* was habitually occupied by newsletters from foreign parts (such as those from Leiden), which by the time they got into print had acquired Nedham's distinctive language and mannerisms. The newsbook, which had published a series of anonymous letters from a member of the embassy to The Hague in 1651, did the same for the Swedish mission. The letters are notable both for some knowing observations and phrases, reminiscent of Nedham's own prose, about the principles of statecraft, and for their poetic flourishes. Their extravagant tributes to the queen answer to the extended conceits of Marvell's poem, and indicate that the message which it sent to her was one which the English government wanted its own subjects to hear.

The poem, which declares that 'since a better world began, no age has borne the equal of Christina', makes much of the maidenhead of the queen, that 'ornament of perpetual virginity', 'a royal virgin capable of giving laws to men' – in other words, a Baltic Queen Elizabeth. Her virginity, though a not infrequent theme of the panegyrics of Christina that were written throughout Europe, was no obligatory subject of commendation.[54] Milton's paean to her in *Defensio Secunda* says nothing of it. But Marvell, and Nedham, made much of the attribute. Marvell emphasized it again in his brief Latin poem to her, ''In eandem Reginae ...'. In a letter to Whitelocke in January 1654, Nedham described Cromwell's 'great good fortune' in having 'so admirable a tongue' as Whitelocke 'to conquer the affections of that royal virgin' on England's behalf.[55] In March and April *Politicus*, on behalf of Nedham's correspondent on the embassy, echoed that thought. It reported that the French nation, whose law forbids female occupancy of the throne, would remove that prohibition if they were so fortunate as to have 'this virgin lady', 'such a virgin', who was 'as accomplished a princess as ever had the honour of swaying a sceptre', 'to rule amongst them'.[56] Another conceit of the poem is reminiscent of Nedham. Marvell

53. For Stapleton and Whitelocke see too Spalding, *Contemporaries*, 216–18.
54. Iiro Kajanto, *Christina Heroina: Mythological and Historical Exemplification in the Latin Panegyrics on Christina Queen of Sweden* (Helsinki, 1993).
55. Spalding, *Contemporaries*, 217.
56. *MP*, 2 Mar. 1654, 3309; 27 Apr. 1654, 3443.

commends Christina's palace as 'a home of the muses'[57] (much as one of the letters from Leiden which were published by *Politicus* in 1651, and which bear the marks of Nedham's embellishment, had called that city 'the seat of the muses').[58] Whitelocke's mission, which was bathed in poetic tributes and descriptions, seems to have held the literary hopes of Christina's court which Marvell's description announces.[59] If so, it was disappointed. When, near the end of the embassy, the court left its base at Uppsala, the departure of the royal entourage, according to a document published in *Politicus* as a letter from Nedham's correspondent on the embassy, 'left the muses very desolate in this academy, which at best is no paradise'.

★★

Northern Europe was but one theatre of Cromwellian diplomacy. Once the Dutch war had ended, the main focus of foreign policy was the war of the two great Continental powers France and Spain, and the relations with them of England, a minor power before the civil wars but now equipped by its army and navy to be a major one. In 'The First Anniversary of the Government under His Highness the Lord Protector', the first political poem of his to be published since 1649, Marvell adjusts to that change. There too he turns to the subject he has previously avoided, the protector's occupancy of power at home.

57. *MP*, 18 May 1654, 3489. 58. Ibid. 23 Jan. 1651, 545.
59. Christina's patronage of writers was lauded by Milton: *CW* viii. 17; ix. 171.

6

Marvell and the First Anniversary

In March 1649, two months after the execution of the king, Oliver Cromwell permitted himself what he admitted might be a 'carnal', as opposed to a godly, political thought. He suggested, as an incentive for the British wars that he was about to fight, that Englishmen who were opposed to the Commonwealth might prefer its rule to conquest by the Scots or the Irish.[1] If there is one means by which a regime that has been brought to power by revolution can broaden its appeal, it is through conflict with external enemies. From 1649 the English looked outwards from the internal convulsions that had absorbed them: first to the conquest of Ireland and Scotland, and then to the assertion of the nation's might against the Continental powers. Marvell's poems take the same course. Was he won to non-Stuart rule by the foreign exploits of the rulers, and by the long-lost esteem that was thus won for his native country? In the poem on the first anniversary, which fell on 16 December 1654, of Cromwell's elevation to the protectorate, Europe's inert kings wonder to observe that Cromwell 'rig[s] a navy while we dress us late' (351): in Marvell's 'Last Instructions to a Painter' in 1667, humiliatingly, 'our ships' are 'unrigged' (433, 573) when Dutch ships sail unopposed up the Medway. Before 'The First Anniversary' Marvell wrote next to nothing about the internal politics of the Puritan regimes whose external policies he favoured. He was virtually silent about the political tensions and convulsions of the two years and more following the victory at Worcester. The protector's standing abroad is a main theme of 'The First Anniversary'. In celebrating it, Marvell projected the images of the protectorate that Marchamont Nedham's writings of 1654

1. Abbott, ed., *Writings and Speeches*, ii. 38–9.

had already fostered. Under the protectorate, *Politicus* with rare exceptions eschewed the irony that had made it so incisive a publication under the Commonwealth. The contrast parallels that between 'An Horatian Ode' and 'The First Anniversary', for in the second poem Marvell sheds the tension of competing meanings that marks the first. In the ode, Cromwell, in his ostensible self-effacement in his 'private gardens', plots his rise to kingship: in 'The First Anniversary' he 'resign[s] up' his 'privacy so dear' (223) solely for the public benefit. In the ode he 'could not cease | In the inglorious arts of peace': in the second poem he has stayed in public life only because 'heaven would not that his pow'r should cease' (243). So doubtful a friend to 'justice' in the ode, he is now its unambiguous instrument (153, 207). *Politicus* had come to confine itself to unambiguous propaganda. 'The First Anniversary' supports its teaching.

In 1655 Cromwell made war on Spain and allied with France. But at the time of the anniversary, that alignment lay in the future. In 1654 Cromwell obliged the two monarchies to compete for his favour. The poem presents them as at once the friends of popery and the enemies of England. Marvell shows the English navy striking 'dread' and 'terror' into Europe's kings, who 'Captives are on land' (370–83). In the summer of 1654 *Politicus* kept its readers informed of the 'fears' and 'very great fright' that the movements of Blake's navy had brought to France; of the 'great storm' and 'black cloud' that had consequently hung over that land;[2] and of Blake's success in forcing the French to embark on a programme of coastal fortification that diverted resources from the theatre of war against Spain in Flanders. Marvell links the 'slow and brittle' military campaigns that the kings fight in pursuit of worldly acquisition to the hereditary principle that has enthroned them: 'Well may they strive to leave them to their son, | For one thing never was by one king done.' 'Some', admittedly, are 'more active', but only for 'a frontier town' (20–4). As the campaigning season neared its end in 1654, Nedham reflected on the '*petits*... successes' of the French forces; on their readiness to 'employ their time' in minor disruptive manoeuvres or in the garrisoning of 'little' places 'of no consideration', 'upon the frontiers', which 'were but slightly guarded' and which 'will hardly quit cost'; on their willingness to settle for 'keep[ing] what they have

2. *MP*, 11 May–1 June 1654, 3468, 3485, 3494, 3516–17; 24 Aug. 1654, 3714; cf. 11 Jan. 1655, 5047.

got... upon their own frontiers'.[3] In Nedham's writing as in Marvell's poem, the hereditary kings 'tell' a 'useless time' (41). 'It may be said of those monarchies' of France and Spain, declared a report in *Politicus* in January 1654, 'which is spoken of the sea, that what it gains in one place it loseth in another, and so *e contra*: just so is Fortune ever ebbing and flowing between these two mighty monarchs; what they gain in one year they lose the next, and what in one place they lose in another, and that is the issue of their wars, to vex themselves and all Europe to no purpose.'[4] Again, Marvell writes that one of Europe's kings 'triumphs at the public cost, | And will have won, if he no more has lost'. That monarch and his regal colleagues are strong 'only... against their subjects': 'Their other wars seem but a feigned contest, | This common enemy is still oppressed' (25–30). *Politicus*, reviving (in a less excited form) the theme of international social oppression that it had proclaimed in the early 1650s, notes how the subjects of Spain's territories in Flanders and Italy 'have long groaned' under the regal 'yoke' and are 'treated like slaves', while the French 'people', who have 'little' to 'gain' from the war, 'are squeezed at home'.[5]

In 'The First Anniversary', as in Marvell's earlier poem to Dr Ingelo, Cromwell's foreign policy challenges Antichrist. He 'Pursues the monster thorough every throne: | Which shrinking to her Roman den impure, | Gnashes her gory teeth; nor there secure' (128–30). In February 1654 Nedham wrote, and published in *Politicus*, a brief Latin poem to mark the protector's inaugural entry into the city of London.[6] There, too, Cromwell has Antichrist in his sights. Nedham prophesies that Cromwell will 'attack' the 'gods' of 'profane Rome' and 'tame the triple-headed tyrant', the papacy.[7] In Marvell's poem, Cromwell is let down by Europe's kings, who 'adore' the Roman 'whore' whom rightly 'they should massacre'. If only they would be 'won' by his 'pattern' they would join him in

3. Ibid. 7 Sept. 1654, 3740; 5 Oct. 1654, 3802; 12 Oct. 1654, 3818, 3821, 3826, 3828–9; cf. 22 June 1654, 3568, on the 'slow' Spanish advance.
4. Ibid. 19 Jan. 1654, 3198.
5. Ibid. 26 Oct. 1654, 3851; 2 Nov. 1654, 3867; 18 Jan. 1655, 5060, 5064. The 'regal sloth' and 'long slumbers' of Marvell's Continental kings (322) perhaps have their counterpart in Nedham's incessant presentation of them as men sunk in the pleasures of balls, ballets, masques, feasts, and other 'jollities' – though on that point, it should be said, news reports in other sources were likewise insistent.
6. *MP*, 16 Feb. 1654, 3270; Norbrook, *Writing the English Republic*, 328–30.
7. Derek Hirst, '"That Sober Liberty": Marvell's Cromwell in 1654', in John M. Wallace, ed., *The Golden and the Brazen World: Papers in Literature and History, 1650–1800* (Berkeley and Los Angeles, 1985), 39.

'the great designs kept for the latter days'. Instead they follow the blind worldly principle of 'reason, so miscalled, of state' (105–14). So Cromwell has to confront Antichrist 'alone' (127). In November 1654, the month before the anniversary, *Politicus* published a letter written, according to the newsbook, in Transylvania, the beleaguered condition of whose Protestants was a source of anxiety to the Cromwellian regime. The writer, we read, has recently visited England and been impressed by the protector's labours on behalf of God's people, exertions which, the letter predicts, will win eternal reward. 'And if [only] there were but one more to be found among the potentates and governors of Christendom, of the like mind and disposition! But alas there is none, they all seek their own, and that but temporals, being little acquainted with, and therefore not regarding nor hoping for, other.'[8] Nedham, much of whose own more innovative thinking might be taken to support the principle of reason of state, had attacked it at length in *Politicus* in 1651–2, when he described it as not 'the equitable result of prudence and right reason' but 'a corrupt principle'.[9]

★★

By the time of 'The First Anniversary', Marvell is ready to praise Cromwell's deeds not only abroad but at home. Marvell's poem was acquired by the bookseller George Thomason, normally a prompt collector of new publications, on 17 January 1655, 32 days after the anniversary of Cromwell's accession. The issue of *Politicus* that appeared on the 18th announced that the poem was 'newly printed and published'. So either the poem was written (or revised or completed) after the anniversary, or the decision to publish it took place some time after its composition. Nedham's advertisement does not prove that 'The First Anniversary' had the government's blessing or encouragement, for he was capable of promoting works by his friends on his own initiative, just as Thomas Newcomb, the printer both of the poem and of the newsbook, was adept at publicizing work by his own clients. None the less, subsequent anniversaries of the protectorate would be celebrated with the government's connivance. Marvell, who for a year

8. *MP*, 9 Nov. 1654, 3893–4.
9. Ibid. 31 July 1651, 959 (cf. 21 Aug. 1651, 997); 1 July 1652, 1690. Nedham liked to attack 'politicos': ibid. 2 Oct. 1651, 1100; *Observator*, 7 Nov. 1654, 31. The messianic aspirations which Marvell opposes to 'reason of state' have a counterpart in a tract by Nedham two years earlier, which unexpectedly breaks with the cool secularism of most of his prose: *Case Stated*, 19–21, 54.

and a half had been tutor to a *protégé* of Cromwell, and who during that time had been commissioned to write poems for Queen Christina on Cromwell's behalf, is unlikely to have published 'The First Anniversary' without, at the least, covert approval in Whitehall. The poem certainly says about Cromwell's government of England what the protector would like to hear. In February 1654, the month of Nedham's poem to mark Cromwell's entry into London,[10] the journalist also published the principal work of propaganda written for the protectorate during its history, *A True State of the Case of the Commonwealth.* In dissolving parliament on 22 January 1655, virtually the only occasion in his long parliamentary speeches when he cited a government publication, the protector invoked and followed *A True State* in explaining the rationale of his government. Had he wanted to cite a poem for the same purpose it would surely have been 'The First Anniversary', which had appeared a few days before his speech.

At the time of its publication the government needed all the help, political or literary, that it could get. Marvell shows the protector in supreme control. In fact the regime was in dire straits. The Instrument of Government, the constitution by which Cromwell became protector, had been a hastily improvised solution – for all the political innovations of the Interregnum were improvised – to the public emergency of December 1653, when Barebone's Parliament was evicted in the second military coup of the year. In trying to win support for his government, Cromwell could play on the fear of anarchy, and on the concern for the rights of property, that had been aroused by the measures planned by a majority in Barebone's Parliament for overhauling the Church and the legal system. He could also exploit the hostility to unicameral republican rule which the years 1649–53 had engendered. Yet the military origin of his regime, and its dependence on military enforcement, were huge obstacles to its public acceptance. The coups of December 1648 and April 1653 had, between them, antagonized the majority of the members of the Long Parliament, the body that had challenged and fought Charles I. Only a handful of them accepted posts under the protectorate. The ruling group was mostly confined to Cromwell's own friends and relations.

10. Norbrook, who recovers this poem and offers an astute analysis of it, perhaps underemphasizes its conformity to the perception of the regime favoured by Cromwell (*Writing the English Republic*, 328–30).

There was but one way out of the government's impasse. The Instrument required the protector to summon a parliament for September 1654. Though royalists were to be forbidden, for a period of years, to vote or stand, the elections at least allowed for the return to political life of that broad parliamentarian opinion which had been excluded from it since Pride's Purge and the regicide. If the assembly could be persuaded to give statutory sanction to the Instrument, then the regime might claim a basis of legitimacy on which it could build. Instead the Commons assailed both the illegality and the content of the Instrument. Cromwell responded, nine days into the parliament, with yet another military purge. To the MPs who remained, however, he offered to yield some of the powers which the Instrument had given him. His concessions were insufficient. By the time of the first anniversary of the protectorate in December the disagreements looked superable scarcely if at all. The Instrument required Cromwell to allow the parliament to sit for at least five months. To end it at the earliest moment he was reduced to taking 'months' to mean lunar months, so that the period expired, not in early February, but on 22 January, when he duly dissolved the assembly. The failure of the parliament was the heaviest of blows. Cromwell was henceforth dependent on the naked military rule that was institutionalized later in 1655 in the rule of the Major-Generals. The awkward, fundamental reality of Cromwellian rule, the supremacy of the army, is absent from Marvell's poem.

For 'The First Anniversary' attunes itself with singular delicacy to Cromwell's predicament and dilemmas. The poem's very title announces its conformity to the protector's thinking. The political 'anniversaries' marked by previous poetry of the Interregnum had been those of the regicide. The Commonwealth had dated the years of its rule as the 'first', 'second', and so on years of 'England's freedom, by God's blessing restored'. In 'The First Anniversary', Year One, as it were, starts not in 1649 but in 1653. Cromwell did not want to have the regicide remembered, or the abolition of the monarchy that had followed it. Not one signatory of Charles I's death-warrant was to be found among the twenty men who during the course of the protectorate sat on its executive council.[11] Cromwell aimed to reconstruct the broad parliamentarian consensus of 1640; to reconcile

11. In one of the poems for Queen Christina that were apparently intended to accompany the portrait of Cromwell which was sent to her, 'In eandem Reginae Sueciae transmissam', Marvell has Cromwell assure the queen that his features are not 'always hostile to kings' ('Nec sunt hi vultus regibus usque truces').

men alienated by the revolution of 1648–9; and, if only they would recognize his rule, to bring royalists back into the political community. One of the first acts of the protectorate was to repeal the engagement of allegiance to the kingless regime that had divided the land at the time of his return from Ireland. Marvell, who placed the regicide at the centre of 'An Horatian Ode', says nothing about it in 'The First Anniversary'. Though he reprimands the obstinate critics of Cromwell within the Roundhead cause, and reproaches the Rump's 'tedious statesmen' (69), he says nothing that is unmistakably about the royalist opposition to his rule. It is the nation's indifference to Cromwell's godly mission, not the persistence of loyalty to the Stuarts, that impedes the protector (134 ff.).

When he assumed power in December 1653, Cromwell declined the title of king, which the Instrument of Government had contained in its draft form. He wanted the advantages of kingship but not the odium of having usurped the title. His elevation to monarchy would have given powerful ammunition to the large section of Roundhead opinion which resented his accession to single rule and which attributed it to personal ambition. From 1649 until he became protector, England had officially been a 'Commonwealth', a term that thrived on its useful ambiguity. It could mean a republic – that is, a 'free state', the unambiguous phrase which the Rump also adopted but which the protectorate dropped. Alternatively it could mean a political community under any form of government, or else the common good or 'common weal' of that community. The protector appropriated the word for his government, and made use of its non-monarchical associations. England, though it now had a protector, officially remained a Commonwealth, which a monarchy could not be. A member of the parliament called by Richard Cromwell in 1659 observed that under the protectorate the government 'was still asserted to be a Commonwealth .... Formerly a king and his realm: here a protector and Commonwealth.' Only the fact that 'the single person was here more conspicuous', maintained the speaker, distinguished the regime from the Commonwealth of 1649–53.[12]

So there was significance in the title of Nedham's *A True State of the Case of the Commonwealth.* He would make comparable use of the term in *Politicus* in September 1654, just after the meeting of the first parliament of the protectorate, where Cromwell's elevation was coming under heavy

12. J. T. Rutt, ed., *Diary of Thomas Burton*, 4 vols. (1828), iv. 267.

fire. The newsbook's sentiments look forward to Marvell's poem: 'With the blessing of God, by a prudent parliament, a powerful army, and terrible navy, under the command of his highness, who hath given large testimonies of his abilities to govern, great things may be erected over and above. ['Tis] needful for our commonwealth.'[13] Marvell, too, turns the term 'commonwealth' to Cromwell's advantage. In 'The Character of Holland', written under the Rump, the word had been divided into two, so as to signify the common prosperity of the nation: 'The Common wealth doth by its losses grow, | And, like its own seas, only ebbs to flow' (130–1). But a couplet of the same poem contrived also to identify the term with the rule of the republic, 'our sore new circumcised Commonwealth' (118), 'our state' (145), 'our infant Hercules' (138). In the couplets of 'The First Anniversary', by contrast, the word, though again given a double meaning, is annexed to the rule of the protector, for only with the introduction of the Instrument of Government was the common good served: 'The Commonwealth then first together came, | And each one entered in the willing frame' (75–6); 'The Common-wealth does through their centres all | Draw the circumf'rence of the public wall' (87–8).[14]

Marvell's Cromwell 'doth scorn to be a king'. 'Thou rather didst', Marvell reminds him, 'yourself depress | Yielding to rule because it made thee less' (227–8). Here as elsewhere the poem accords with Cromwell's own representation of his rule. The protector explained to parliament in 1654 that he, whose power as lord general had been unacceptably 'arbitrary', had agreed to the office of protector because it 'limited and bound me'.[15] But Marvell also says what Cromwell could not decently say: that to be Cromwell 'is a greater thing | Than ought below or yet above a king' (225–6).[16] Nedham's writings of early 1654 are likewise coloured by Cromwell's decision not to take the crown. In his poem of February 1654 on the protector's entry into London, Cromwell is 'a greater Caesar because he did not want to be one. Let others seize the crown; it was

13. *MP*, 14 Sept. 1654, 3750. Only in its inclusion of the army does Nedham's portrait differ from Marvell's in 'The First Anniversary'.

14. Here I follow Margoliouth's edition, which exactly reproduces the spelling and punctuation of the original publication; but we cannot assume that seventeenth-century printers were faithful to their manuscripts in these matters.

15. Abbott, ed., *Writings and Speeches*, iii. 456.

16. On this subject Marvell is at one with Milton, whose *Defensio Secunda*, published in May 1654, has Cromwell 'despising the name of king for majesty far more majestic': *CW* viii. 225. Yet their descriptions were penned, as we shall see, from contrasting perspectives.

enough for him to have been able to do so.'[17] Marvell makes nothing, and Nedham little, of Cromwell's new title, Lord Protector, which fails to suggest the dynamism that they seek to convey. They prefer to portray him as a 'captain'. Both in Marvell's poem (119), and in the letter that Nedham had sent to Whitelocke in Sweden in January 1654 to report and praise the introduction of the protectorate, Cromwell is 'such a captain'. Whereas Marvell sets the exploits of Cromwell, who 'cuts his way still nearer to the skies' (46), beside the 'regal sloth' (122) and petty aims of the hereditary kings who 'contribute' so little 'to the state of things' (43), Nedham's letter appends to his praise of 'such a captain' the reflection that it is

> the glory of our nation to have such a governor, whose high achievements have given him a right beyond all the tituladoes of hereditary princes, and made him to be indeed what most of them are but in name; so that for my own part I must profess I would much rather serve him upon any terms than be a favourite to any of those golden things that are dropped in adventure into the world, with crowns upon their heads.[18]

The Continental kings 'confes[s]' (394) that Cromwell, who scorns the title of king, has supreme kingly worth. 'Even the enemies will confess', proclaims Nedham's *A True State*, 'that he is every way worthy to rule'.[19]

Cromwell's government was divided from the start between statesmen who hoped, and those who feared, that the inauguration of the protectorate would be the first step in a return to hereditary – though now Cromwellian – monarchy. The protector held the regime together with a purposive ambivalence. Both in his politics and in his iconography, he represented himself as half a king.[20] Marvell's poem answers to that policy. But always the protector had to look over his shoulder at those of his followers, well represented both in the army leadership and on the civilian council, who had accepted his elevation only as a necessity, and who expected, as a condition of it, that he would eschew the aggrandizement of himself and his family. He needed to persuade other groups, too, that his new office was not the fruit of ambition: that, as he vigorously protested to

17. Norbrook, *Writing the English Republic*, 329.
18. Longleat House, Whitelocke MS XV, fos. 1–4, partially reproduced by Spalding, *Contemporaries*, 217–18. Nedham's liking for the noun 'tituladoes' (cf. *MP*, 19 Feb. 1652, 1411; 25 Nov. 1652, 2027) was shared, with so many of his literary characteristics, by John Hall.
19. Nedham, *True State*, 47.
20. For the iconography see Laura Knoppers, *Constructing Cromwell: Ceremony, Portrait, and Print 1645–1661* (Cambridge, 2000).

parliament in the speech parodied by Harrington, he had 'called not myself to this place'.[21]

Marvell's poem offers him help. In Puritan politics, intentions and images were conveyed by biblical allusions and analogies. To assuage his critics, Cromwell adopted the analogy that Marvell himself uses when he compares Cromwell to Gideon, the military deliverer of Israel:

> No king might ever such a force have done,
> Yet would he not be Lord, nor yet his son.
>   Thou with the same strength, and an heart as plain
> Doth (like thine olive) still refuse to reign....
>
> (255–8)

Behind those lines there lie chapter 9 of the Book of Judges and, with it, Isaiah 1:26, which reveals God's ideal of a purged and purified commonwealth that will have 'judges as at the first, and... counsellors as at the beginning'. Though there was uncertainty among biblical expositors about the form which that pristine rule had taken, the protectoral regime was able to portray Cromwell as England's equivalent of a judge of Israel, and in particular of Gideon, a judge but not a king, 'who would not rule over them, neither should his son rule over them'. At the outset of the protectorate, as the government cast around for support and arguments, its newsbook *Severall Proceedings of State Affairs*, which carried a more devout face than its companion *Politicus*, announced that the protector, after 'some days' of pressure on him to accept the new title, had agreed to do so

> as the only means to rescue the people from the danger of ruin; which was made so clear and plain to him, and from God's holy words such satisfactory scriptures were brought to his mind that he might comfortably expect a blessing in, from some promises, which hath of old been his excellency's recourse unto, who in this had much sought the Lord day and night.[22]

The identity of the 'promises' emerged in Cromwell's own speech to parliament on 22 January, so soon after the publication of Marvell's poem. The protector recalled that he had taken the title after 'considering that promise in Isaiah, that God would give rulers as at the first, and counsellors as at the beginning'. For 'I did not know but that God might begin, and

21. Abbott, ed., *Writings and Speeches*, iii. 452 ff; above, p. 122.
22. *Severall Proceedings of State Affairs in Parliament*, 28 Dec. 1654, 3892.

though at present with a most unworthy person, yet as to the future it might be after this manner, and I thought this might usher it in'. He had liked the analogy, he added, because it confirmed his 'judgement against having [the government] hereditary'.[23]

The poem conforms to other stances of the protectorate too. Along with Nedham, indeed with the incessant claims of government propaganda in 1654, Marvell shows the protector creating order out of the impending anarchy of 1653. In 'The First Anniversary' Cromwell is at once the architect who builds from raw materials and the 'tune[r]' of the 'ruling Instrument', the figure whose 'sacred lute creates | Th'harmonious city of the seven gates' (65–8). Nedham's letter of January 1654 to Whitelocke (himself a man of poetic impulses, if lumbering ones) rejoices to report that under the Instrument 'we have a new world formed (like the old) out of chaos, by the prudence and industry of that excellent person', Cromwell.[24] The thought reappears in *A True State*: 'we were in the beginning of a new government necessitated to bring a little world out of chaos, and bring form out of confusion' (46). The tract presents the protectorate as a middle way between, 'on the one side', parliamentary sovereignty, with its attendant 'division, faction and confusion', and 'the inconveniences of absolute lordly power on the other', so that 'the frame of government appears so well bounded on both sides against anarchy and tyranny that we hope it may now... prove a seasonable mean... of peace and settlement to this distracted nation' (51–2). Marvell's poem likewise commends Cromwell's middle way: ' 'Tis not a freedom, that where all command: | Nor tyranny, where one does them withstand' (279–80). Cromwell, who has to build with the recalcitrant material of 'stubborn men' (78), sets 'bounders' to their liberty (281): *A True State* has the Instrument setting 'bounds' to 'the wavering humours of the people'. In the poem, the captain Cromwell

23. Abbott, ed., *Writings and Speeches*, iii. 589. Parallels and contrasts between Cromwell and Gideon were a recurrent feature of the political literature of the protectorate. See *Strena Vavasoriensis* (1654), 16; Johannes Cornubiensis [pseud.], *The Grand Catastophe* (1654); Hirst, ' "That Sober Liberty" ', 29–31, 48.

24. Spalding, *Contemporaries*, 217. The Leveller John Wildman's anti-Cromwellian tract *The Lawes Subversion* (1648), 2, observes that 'every nation is but a rude undigested chaos, a deformed lump until laws or rules of government be established'. The opening section of Wildman's tract lists examples from classical history in a manner that recalls Nedham and is out of character with the rest of the pamphlet. It is not unimaginable that Nedham, an ally of the Levellers a little earlier and an admirer of them even when attacking them on behalf of his political masters, co-operated with them during his royalist phase. We saw that he crossed party lines to work with John Hall in the same period.

avoids 'shipwreck' by thwarting the suicidal instincts of the 'giddy' and discontented passengers: Nedham's Cromwell saves 'a sinking nation out of the gulf of misery and confusion caused by the changeable counsels and corrupt interests of other men' (28). The parliamentary sovereignty repudiated by *A True State* is rejected in the poem too, where it seems as much a recipe for inertia as the hereditary kingship which it replaced in 1649. Marvell welcomes the political demise of the 'tedious statesmen' of the Rump, who, in contrast to Cromwell's swift decisiveness, 'many years did hack | Framing a liberty that still went back' (69–70). 'Those great moliminous bodies of parliament', reflects *A True State*, 'are but slow in motion' (24). During the embassy to Holland in 1651 *Politicus* had published complaints, by, or ostensibly by, a member of the English negotiating party, about the cumbersome constitutional machinery of the Netherlands with which the English negotiators had to deal: 'Great states (like all great bodies) move very slowly'; 'you may see what a tedious work they make of it, and how slowly they move with that great body.'[25] In May 1653 a tract of which Nedham's and Marvell's literary associate John Hall was the author, or one author, attacked the 'Spanish slowness' of the recently dissolved Rump, its 'laziness' and 'lethargy'.[26]

Had Marvell ever warmed to the republic? In 'An Horatian Ode' – if we take it at face value – he wants, with Nedham, to see free states established in Europe. That a side of him was drawn to the principle of republican government at that time is suggested too by the resemblance of mood and language between the opening lines of the ode and John Hall's anti-monarchical tract of the same year.[27] Then, in 1651, there comes the poem to St John, which, on the interpretation offered above, subscribes with one part of itself to Nedham's, and Milton's, international republicanism of that year. Yet outside the years 1650–1 his writings give no sign of such attraction. Even within them, his ardour, if such it is, is at least largely directed outwards, towards English achievement abroad. He shows less enthusiasm, if any, for the experience of republican rule in England. In 'An Horatian Ode' the 'emptiness' that is left by the regicide is filled, not by the civilian leaders of the Rump, but by the single 'greater spirit' (44), Cromwell, that threatens to usurp them. Marvell gives no sense that anything would be lost by that prospective alteration.

25. *MP*, 24 Apr. 1651, 749.
26. John Hall, *A Letter Written to a Gentleman in the Country* (1653), 9, 13–14.
27. Above, p. 72.

The ode gives to England's rulers at Westminster a transitory air, and says nothing to regret their insecurity. All that we learn about them, apart from Cromwell's threat to them, is that they are 'fright[ed]' (70), an apt verb for the nervous constitutional improvisation which created the republic in 1649, and also for the mood of alarm and despair that, in Cromwell's absence in Ireland, settled on the regime in the first half of 1650. In 1653 Marvell's 'The Character of Holland' mocks the kingless polity of the Netherlands, that 'wat'ry Babel' (21). Again, though this time in different imagery, we are among the 'democratic stars' whose ascent Marvell regretted on the death of Lord Hastings in 1649. In 'The Character of Holland', admittedly, 'our state', the Commonwealth, has become 'Darling of heaven, and of men the care'. Yet even in a poem written with its author's career prospects evidently in mind, a political warning undermines the tribute and is more revealing than the praise: 'Provided that they be what they have been, | Watchful abroad, and honest still within' (147–8). It was largely on the ground that they were not 'honest still within' – that they had been morally and financially corrupted by power – that Cromwell and the army stirred up opposition to the Rump in its later stages and that his musketeers expelled it two months after the poem. In 'The First Anniversary', when they are no longer his potential patrons, he assails the corruption of the 'tedious statesmen', 'Whose num'rous gorge could swallow in an hour | That island which the sea cannot devour' (71–2). It is true that the 'ruling instrument' (68), the Instrument of Government, provides for a 'senate free' (97), but only within a framework established by the rule of a single person. In any case Marvell's interest is less in the constitutional provisions of the regime than in the dynamism of Cromwell, their tuner. Of course, one might be a republican without approving of the Rump. Marvell could have thought, with Nedham and Harrington and indeed Milton too, that the Rump's trouble was not that it was a republic but that it was not a proper one. Yet nothing he ever wrote suggests that he shared that perspective.

At all events he did not lament the Rump's demise. Even after the Restoration, when he would contend to the hilt against 'arbitrary government', he had little faith in parliaments, where, to his eyes, only a minority contended for truth and liberty. The majority was unfriendly not only to civil but to religious freedom. Marvell's own defence of religious freedom in 'The First Anniversary' is circumscribed. He commends the 'sober liberty' (289) of conscience that the protectorate provides. But he also denounces the frantic sects who threaten civil order and civil life: the Quakers and, more emphatically, the 'Chammish issue' (293) of the Fifth Monarchists, whose leaders Christopher Feake and John Simpson, those vitriolic critics of the protectorate, the poem unexpectedly stoops to name (305). Marvell is once more at one with Nedham, whose *A True State* commends the liberty allowed by the Instrument to 'those who profess truth in sobriety' (43), but rounds on sects which do not, chief among them 'the hot men at Blackfriars', where the Fifth Monarchists gathered. Likewise Nedham's and Marvell's associate John Hall, in a work of propaganda for the protectorate published a month after its inauguration, contrasted the 'odd and fanatic notions' and 'chimerical discourses of the fifth monarchy', which had infiltrated and convulsed Barebone's, with the 'sober' principles of the 'sober party' which had resisted them.[28] Nedham was the Fifth Monarchists' scourge. In the early stages of the protectorate he spied on their meetings for the government, and reported contemptuously and at length on the vituperative onslaughts on the regime by Feake and Simpson.[29] He returned to the attack in print in the autumn.[30] For Nedham as for Marvell, Quakers are normally a subsidiary target, but a fortnight before Marvell's poem appeared *Politicus* paused to assail the 'hare-brained ... frenzy called Quakerism'.[31]

On religious as on constitutional matters 'The First Anniversary' follows Cromwell's lead. His opening speech to parliament in 1654 commended the 'glorious thing' of 'liberty of conscience' – that 'fundamental' principle of his government, as he would insist to the Commons eight days later – but also rounded on 'the prodigious blasphemies' of those who 'abused' them or aided 'the mistaken notion of the fifth monarchy'.[32] *Politicus* gave extensive coverage to that passage of the speech.[33] The government and its agents regularly distinguished between the noisy sects and the 'sober' godly. In March 1654 Cromwell's son Henry, who had been sent by his father to investigate the opposition to the protectorate among the English governors of Ireland, reported that 'sober men (not Anabaptists) are overjoyed with hopes' of the new government.[34] An official declaration of February 1655, the month after Marvell's poem, emphasized the protectorate's commitment

28. John Hall, *Confusion Confounded* (1654), 3, 5, 7, 16.
29. *Cal. SP Dom. 1653–4*, 304–8, 393.
30. *Observator*, 31 Oct. 1654, 4–11; 7 Nov. 1654, 30; Hirst, '"That Sober Liberty"', 45.
31. *MP*, 4 Jan. 1655, 5033–4.
32. Abbott, ed., *Writings and Speeches*, iii. 436–8, 459.
33. *MP*, 7 Sept. 1654, 3744–6.
34. *TSP* ii. 14.

to 'liberty for all to hold forth and profess' their beliefs 'with sobriety', and to the protection of all God-fearing people 'in the sober and quiet exercise of religion', but disowned the bitterness and contentiousness of those who 'abuse this liberty'.[35]

Whenever we can trace Marvell's thoughts about religion, he is a friend to the 'sober liberty' commended in 'The First Anniversary'. In the Restoration it was the self-restraint of the Dissenters, the 'sober principles' of 'sober and intelligent citizens', that won his admiration for them.[36] He was always sympathetic to the moderate and more tolerant Puritans, though he was never one of them. How were they to be aided? His experience, first of the Long Parliament, then of the Cavalier Parliament, taught him what *The Rehearsal Transpros'd* would make clear: that there was less hope of religious freedom from parliaments than from a single ruler. That, at least, was true under Cromwell, for whom – albeit within limits that were unacceptable to John Milton – it was the dearest of principles, and who, in the parliament of 1654–5, risked his own rule to secure it; and then under Charles II, whose position Marvell knew to be more pragmatic but no less indispensable to the provision of freedom of conscience. In *Mr. Smirke*, in 1676, Marvell offered, as evidence of the persistence of persecuting tendencies, the fact that the medieval statute *de heretico comburendo*, for the burning of heretics, remained on the statute-book.[37] We can imagine his feelings when, twenty years earlier, MPs invoked it in clamouring for the death sentence, against Cromwell's opposition, to be passed on the Quaker James Nayler.[38] Nayler indeed offended against Cromwell's, and Marvell's, ideal of religious sobriety, but the ruler who resisted bigotry against him had more to recommend him to Marvell than the parliament that voiced it.

★★

'The First Anniversary' is what 'An Horatian Ode' is not: a panegyric. The Cromwell of the ode is a troubling figure, a force of war and destruction. In the anniversary poem he becomes a source not of discord but of harmony. Though he 'troubl[es] the waters' he 'yearly makes them heal' (401–2). We cannot say how far the messages of 'The First

35. Abbott, ed., *Writings and Speeches*, iii. 626–7; cf. George Wither's poem on Cromwell's recently deceased friend Thomas Westrow, *Westrow Revived* (1654), 8–9.

36. *PWAM* i. 104 (cf. pp. 128, 136–7).

37. Ibid. 72.

38. Rutt, ed., *Diary of Thomas Burton*, i. 118.

Anniversary' are to be explained by the demands of panegyric, how far by the convergence of Cromwell's policies with Marvell's sympathies. Either way, it is an unquestioning poem. Poetry of idealization gave scope for the communication of corrective advice, but 'The First Anniversary' is devoid of it. In the new Cromwellian order, it seems, Marvell found hope of patronage; of national achievement abroad;[39] and of a liberty of conscience that would thwart the persecuting instincts of the Presbyterians. Perhaps he also found hope of the stability for which his dislocated generation craved. At all events he moved smoothly with Cromwell from the Instrument of Government to the new, parliamentary constitution of 1657, the Humble Petition and Advice, which brought the regime much closer to the traditions of monarchy. Cromwell's new son-in-law Lord Fauconberg, for whose marriage to Cromwell's daughter Mary in November of that year Marvell wrote songs, was the most forthright advocate in the protector's entourage of a full return to kingship.[40] The wedding was a landmark in the return to the norms of courtly and monarchical rule.

On his deathbed in 1658 the protector named, or reportedly named, his elder son Richard as his successor. Marvell, who in 'The First Anniversary' had joined Cromwell in turning the example of Gideon, the Old Testament judge, against the hereditary principle, took Richard's succession for granted in 'A Poem upon the Death of his Late Highness the Lord Protector'. Those who had wanted to enthrone Oliver had aimed, in doing so, to tranquillize him: to tame the danger in him and, by confining him within the rules of constitutional forms and conduct, to end his unpredictable violence and make him a stabilizing figure. Something of that aspiration may inform Marvell's poem on his death. In the ode we saw Cromwell, alarmingly, 'burning through the air'. In 'The First Anniversary' alarm yields to beneficence, but he remains an elemental force, whom we are shown 'cut[ting] his way still nearer to the skies'. In the elegy he becomes, in the repose of death, a knowable mortal, and the recipient of the poet's personal affection. There has been another change, which again enhances Cromwell's beneficence. In the ode, because he 'could not cease | In the inglorious arts of peace', he took the path of 'advent'rous war' (9–11). In

39. That story would be easier to tell if Marvell could still confidently be regarded as the author of the poem 'On the Victory over the Spaniards' in 1657, but the attribution increasingly seems unlikely: Smith, 423.

40. Fauconberg's political outlook and allegiances are well displayed in the letters to and from him in vols. vi and vii of *TSP*.

'The First Anniversary' the claims of the two activities on his personality become equal: he 'Here shines in peace, and thither shoots in war' (102), and his power 'walk[s] still middle betwixt war and peace' (244). By the time of the elegy the balance has swung to the pacific: 'nature' had 'made' him 'all for peace', even though 'angry heaven unto war had swayed' him (15–16).[41]

The poem confirms the story, which has been the subject of these chapters, of Marvell's transition from royalist to Cromwellian. Yet there is a difference in kind between it and his earlier political poems. Now that Marvell's position has stabilized, and that the conflicts of loyalty within him are of the past, the elegy does without the polemical force of the previous poetry. Cromwell's death was a fraught moment, which threw the future character of the regime, and its very survival, into doubt. Yet the poem, unlike Marvell's elegies of 1648–9 – indeed unlike all his public verse over the past ten years – does not engage with the immediate demands and choices of public life. Though his loyalty to Richard is clear, he eschews contention on his or anyone's behalf.

In Richard's parliament in 1659, having been elected as a court candidate, Marvell joined the court party which held out against the advocates of parliamentary sovereignty.[42] One of them, inside parliament, was his former patron Sir Thomas Fairfax.[43] Another, outside it, was Marvell's friend Milton. For while the protectorate had turned Marvell into a Cromwellian monarchist, it had moved Milton in an opposite direction. It is to Milton's political journey during the Puritan Revolution that we now turn.

41. In 'In eandem Reginae Sueciae transmissam', Marvell represents Cromwell as an old and sluggish man, a very different figure from the 'restless Cromwell' of the ode (Haan, *Andrew Marvell's Latin Poetry*, 184) – but almost equally distant too from the Cromwell of 'The First Anniversary'. His 'In Effigiem Oliver Cromwell' remarks on the 'quiet leisure' which Cromwell has given the English.

42. *AMC* 56, 57.

43. *TSP* vi. 706; vii. 615–16; Rutt, ed., *Diary of Thomas Burton*, iii. 48.

7
Milton and the Civil Wars

If Milton had happened to die in January 1649, the month of the regicide, how would he be remembered? We would still think of him, of course, as a poet, albeit not as the author of the great late poems of the Restoration. We would think of him too – though, without those late poems to bring him to our minds, we would do so less often – as a prose-writer. His longer poems were all written either by 1639, the year of 'Damon's Epitaph', or after about 1658, when he apparently began to write *Paradise Lost*. In the intervening two decades he wrote mainly 'of my left hand', 'in the cool element of prose'.[1]

On one front, however, we would remember him scarcely at all. We would not think of him as a political writer – at least if we mean by that a writer on forms of government, or on the powers or rights of king or parliament or subjects. The prose that he published before the regicide had two phases. There are the anti-episcopal or anti-prelatical tracts (the pamphlets against bishops) of 1641–2; and there are the pamphlets of 1643–5 which argued against the divorce laws, against the licensing of the press, and for the reform of education. His political polemic likewise had two phases, but both of them came after the regicide. The first belonged to 1649–54, when he wrote mainly to justify the king's punishment; the second to 1659–60, when he sought to avert the Restoration. There are, as he observed in the Latin of his *Defensio Secunda* in 1654, 'three species of liberty ... namely ecclesiastical, domestic or private, and civil'. He had written, he then recalled, on the first two species in 1641–5, but had remained silent on civil – or political – liberty until 1649. He had held his peace because he 'saw the magistrate diligently employed about' it and 'perceived it drew sufficient attention from the

1. *CP* i. 808.

magistrate'.[2] Milton encourages us to understand that in his two periods of political publication he broke, for special reasons, with a habitual readiness to 'resig[n] myself to the wisdom and care of those who had the government'.[3] Thus his silence ended first in 1649, and then in 1659. In 1649 he was commissioned to write his *Observations*, published in May, upon the Commonwealth's enemies in Ireland; and then *Eikonoklastes*, which appeared in October. When he re-entered the political fray ten years later, following the military coup of October 1659, he invoked a different sanction. This time there was, he explained, no magistrate to entrust, for the nation had been left 'in anarchy without a counselling and governing power'.[4] Except in those two periods, it seems, he had never found 'that either God or the public required more of me than my prayers for them that govern'.[5] Even if we leave aside the question of the authorship of *A Publick Plea*, the work of May 1659 that protested against the 'short, but a sharp night' of protectoral tyranny, his protestations of deferential reticence sound surprising, even improbable. He was free with his advice to rulers on other subjects.[6] He seems to have shared the conventional supposition that, when parliaments are in session, citizens are entitled to bring proposals for the public benefit to public view.[7] Besides, his explanation slides uneasily over his entry into the political fray, which on his own account was self-prompted, in *The Tenure of Kings and Magistrates* in February 1649, before he was commissioned to write his later tracts of 1649.[8]

However we explain his move to political writing in that year, it transformed his literary career. From his own perspective it surely rescued it. By January 1649 he had, to appearances anyway, lost his way as a writer. He had printed his single collection of poems in the mid-winter of 1645–6, but had added very little to them since. It is possible that in the later 1640s he experimented with his plans for a verse epic, but if so they were not completed. His prose pamphlets of the earlier 1640s had won some attentive readers,[9] but their influence had not been remotely commensurate with their ambition to instruct and reform the nation in its momentous conflict. Only his campaign against the divorce laws had made a conspicuous impact, and that of a highly unwelcoming kind. Now he had abandoned the writing

2. *CW* viii. 131, 135. Cf. ibid. vii. 127–9, 149–51; *CP* i. 878; iii. 197.
3. *CP* vii. 324.
4. Ibid. 329.
5. Ibid. vii. 324.
6. Cf. ibid. vii. 274.
7. Ibid. i. 669; vii. 408.
8. *CW* viii. 135–7.
9. David Loewenstein, *Milton and the Drama of History* (Cambridge, 1990), 1–34.

of pamphlets, and was trying to write instead an entire history of Britain, a project which not surprisingly came nowhere near to completion. In the parts of the history that he did write, he eschewed his literary gifts in favour of an unremarkable plain style which aimed at, but only intermittently achieved, a 'lightsome brevity'.[10]

Then, in 1649, he found a role. It was in the wake of the regicide that he became not only a political writer, as the champion of that deed, but an employee of the state, with the post, which he would hold for ten years, of Latin Secretary (or Secretary for Foreign Tongues). The Commonwealth's decision to use his pen in and after 1649 was a brave one for a regime that had come to power by a deed of such evil repute. For if Milton himself had a reputation in 1649 it was as the advocate of his shocking views on divorce. His appointment enabled him to serve and teach the public, not as the mere petitioner of power, but as its literary representative. What writer of the epoch, which gave such seriousness of mind and such esteem to the literary representation of power, could have asked for more?

Milton may not have warmed to his first polemical duties for the Commonwealth. The autobiographical account in *Defensio Secunda* does not mention the first of them, his *Observations*. It tells us that the second, *Eikonoklastes*, was 'a work assigned rather than by me chosen or affected'.[11] It was only in 1650, with the invitation to reply to Salmasius, in Latin and before an international audience, that he found a literary task equal to his sense of his powers. In *Defensio Secunda* he would glory in the tribute that had been accorded him when he, and he alone, was selected by the state to answer Salmasius.[12] For at least until the composition of *Paradise Lost*, the writing of *Defensio* was in his own mind the central event of his life. If we instinctively think of Milton as a poet, to whom prose came second, then his pronouncements on the loss of his sight, which he attributed to the writing of the prose *Defensio* against medical advice, come as a surprise. He had decided, he explained, 'that, as the use of light would be allowed me for so short a time, it ought to be enjoyed with the greatest possible utility to

10. *CP* v. 4.
11. Ibid. iii. 339. Cf. ibid. vii. 244; *CW* viii. 5. There was also the work that Milton was asked, at the very outset of his official duties in March 1649, to write against the Levellers. Its failure to appear cannot be taken to indicate, as has sometimes been supposed, that Milton had sympathy with the Levellers: see Martin Dzelzainis, 'History and Ideology: Milton, the Levellers, and the Council of State in 1649', in Paulina Kewes, ed., *The Uses of History in Early Modern England, Huntington Library Quarterly*, special issue, 2005, 269–87.
12. *CW* viii. 5, 15, 111.

the public'.[13] The sonnet he addressed to Cyriack Skinner – a brief poetic aside from his undertakings in prose – dwells on the same achievement. 'What supports' him in the blindness of his eyes is 'The conscience, friend, to have lost them overplied | In liberty's defence, my noble task | Of which all Europe talk from side to side.'[14] To posterity, which has long outlived the events of Puritan England, and which struggles to empathize with the invective and vituperation of his 'defences', his brief poems on the loss of his sight may seem worth more than his thousands upon thousands of words against Salmasius and his followers. The virtuosity of the Latin of his 'defences', which in the seventeenth century struck even readers who were appalled by their arguments,[15] is almost lost to us. Milton's priorities of the Interregnum have been lost with it.

There remains the puzzle of the writing of *The Tenure*, the work in which he rejoined the arena of polemic after so long a silence. He wrote it in the weeks around the regicide, and published it two weeks after it. In the autobiographical account in *Defensio Secunda*, which explains that he kept his silence on politics until 'the magistrate' asked him to break it, he simultaneously represents the writing of *The Tenure* as the work of a private citizen, privately conceived. After writing it, he insists, he returned to his private studies, until his unexpected call, in mid-March, to serve the council of state. Apparently alive to the inconsistency, he points out, as if this would resolve it, that in *The Tenure* he 'neither wrote nor advised anything concerning Charles', but dealt only with the general principle of the right to depose tyrants.[16] He had drawn the same distinction in *The Tenure* itself.[17] Yet in the autobiographical passage the term 'civil liberty' covers the subject-matter of *The Tenure*. His remarks on the composition of the pamphlet are implausible, or anyway incomplete.[18] They are coloured, as is his description in the same account of his literary activities immediately after the publication of *The Tenure*,[19] by his eagerness to present himself as a man immune to the temptations of office and reward. And what of the

13. Ibid. 71. 14. 'To Mr Cyriack Skinner upon his Blindness'.

15. For views on its language in that era see *CP* iv. 970; Parker, 980; Nicholas von Maltzahn, 'The Whig Milton 1667–1700', in Armitage *et al.*, eds., *Milton and Republicanism*, 237; Lewalski, 402; Darbishire, 152–3.

16. *CW* viii. 135–7. 17. *CP* iii. 197.

18. He could instead have chosen to say of *The Tenure*, as he would of his political writing of 1659, that he had composed it at a time of 'anarchy' (written as it was between Pride's Purge and the establishment of the Commonwealth). Was there more obviously an anarchy in 1659 than in 1642–9?

19. Below, Appendix C.

'clear parallels' between *The Tenure* and the speech with which his friend John Bradshaw, the president of the regicide court, passed sentence on the king?[20] By the time the book was published, Bradshaw was president of the new government's council of state. Would Milton have written and printed it without, at the least, Bradshaw's approval? If we ask, too, how Milton came to to be appointed Latin Secretary during the month after *The Tenure*, his friendship with Bradshaw is the obvious clue. Though *The Tenure* was not officially commissioned, it is easy to envision Bradshaw sanctioning it privately. If he did, the question why in early 1649 Milton was no longer ready to tarry for the magistrate disappears, and *The Tenure* can be seen as inaugurating, rather than preceding, his career as a writer for government.

Whether or not we accept that hypothesis, there is another question to be addressed. For all the attractions of official employment, accomplished writers did not queue to write for a regime that had been brought to power by regicide and military force. The government's decision to employ a writer of Milton's reputation may have been a mark as much of its desperation as of its recognition of his talents (vindicated though its decision would eventually be by the success of *Defensio*). But why, in turn, was he willing to write for so detested an administration? For there is nothing in his publications before 1649 to prepare us for this step. We can only guess whether he would have written for the Long Parliament before 1649 if he had been invited to do so. It may be, for all we know, that his early prose publications were written with the hope of attracting commissions from it. Yet if so, his masters would have required of him works altogether less radical and explosive than his tracts from 1649. The regicide, and the purge of parliament that made it possible, transformed the character of the revolution. Milton's outlook was transformed with them.

**

Milton's early political views are a difficult and divisive issue.[21] His seemingly lifelong aversion to royal courts[22] is already evident in 'A Masque

20. Above, Ch. 2.
21. The extent to which the evidence can be intelligently marshalled to support opposing conclusions on this subject is illustrated by the contrasting approaches of Barbara Lewalski (*Life of John Milton*, 13 ff.) and Thomas N. Corns, 'Milton before *Lycidas*', in Graham Parry and Joad Raymond, eds., *Milton and the Terms of Liberty* (Cambridge, 2002), 23–36.
22. See e.g. *CP* iii. 217, 333, 347, 370, 569; vi. 796–7; vii. 360; viii. 429; *Paradise Lost* IV. 767–8; XI. 750–1.

Presented at Ludlow Castle' ('Comus') in 1634,[23] though it did not there have the sting that it would acquire. As a young poet he spurned or missed opportunities to write congratulatory verses to royalty and to its intimate associates.[24] By the early 1640s (if the pertinent entries in his surviving commonplace-book have been correctly dated) he had read Machiavelli's *The Art of War*, had been impressed to discover the Florentine's view that 'a commonwealth is preferable to monarchy',[25] and had recorded the observation of the Church Father Sulpicius Severus, which Milton would use in *Defensio* in 1651, that 'the name of kings has always been hateful to free peoples'.[26] Yet those private reflections may indicate no more than the humanist distaste for kingly and courtly power which was common among widely read men in pre-civil war England, but which in that time was compatible with approval or at least acceptance of the demands of loyalty to the Crown.[27]

At all events, when in 1641–2 he began to write about current developments it was the fate of religion, not of the constitution, that preoccupied him. It was the liberation (as far as it went) of the Church, not the relief of the state, that in those years gladdened his heart and inspired his hopes of the 'shortly-expected' Second Coming.[28] Often enough within the same period, it is true, he voiced – though always passingly – a wish for the reform of 'the state', whose 'very jubilee and resurrection' at parliament's hands he hailed.[29] Yet even in those passages it is the religious content of 'the new Jerusalem'[30] that dominates his thinking.[31] It was to the 'full and perfect reformation' of 'the Church' that he urged parliament to 'go on'.[32] Not only was religious reform more important than its constitutional counterpart. It was its necessary precondition. If spiritual and ecclesiastical health could be restored, he reasoned, political health would return almost as a matter of course. Once the 'minds and spirit of a nation' are freed from 'sin and superstition', 'all honest and legal freedom of civil life cannot long be absent'.[33] If only the government of the Church can be settled according to

23. ll. 321–5. 24. Lewalski, 17. 25. *CP* i. 421. 26. Ibid. 440; *CW* vii. 291.
27. See my 'Republicanism, Regicide and Republic: The English Experience', in Martin van Gelderen and Quentin Skinner, eds., *Republicanism: A Shared European Heritage*, 2 vols. (Cambridge, 2002), i. 307–27.
28. *CP* i. 616. 29. Ibid. 669. 30. Ibid. 703.
31. In *Areopagitica*, admittedly, he would speak of the need for 'great' 'things ... in the rule of life both economical and political'. Yet rather than saying what he has in mind he proceeds to write on the needs of 'the Church' (*CP* ii. 550–1).
32. *CP* i. 928. 33. Ibid. 853.

the word of God, 'what nourishing and cordial restorements to the state will follow'.[34] By the same token it is pointless to look for political achievement until religion is corrected. In 1642 he argued that, 'be our captains and commanders never so expert', it would be 'as great an error in the art of war as any novice in soldiership ever committed' to seek the reconquest of Ireland, which had flared into rebellion, 'by other method' than 'beginning at the reformation of our Church'. If, on the other hand, that 'right course' were taken, the opposition would collapse.[35] Even after he had turned to political writing, he affirmed that 'no model whatsoever of a commonwealth will prove successful or undisturbed' until the Church is reformed.[36]

In the 1640s God's cause was annexed to a political programme for which Milton showed little enthusiasm. It is not that he ignored the constitutional and legal struggles of Crown and parliament, though only fleetingly did he descend to the specific. What he did say on the subject was mostly said in 1641–2, before war had broken out. He portrayed the act for triennial parliaments in 1641, and the execution of the king's leading minister the Earl of Strafford in the same year, as deliverances from 'tyranny'.[37] He wrote of the 'temporal' as well as the 'spiritual tyrannies' which had been wrought by episcopacy, that 'agent and minister of tyranny', and of the resolve of the bishops and their instruments to 'reduc[e] monarchy to tyranny' and 'enthral our civil liberty'.[38] Yet when war came he took a low view of men who fought for secular motives. He thought little of those who supported parliament for reasons of 'the purse': in order, that is, to end illegal taxation, or because their rights of property had been invaded. The war, he thought, would not have been worth fighting solely to secure the 'public immunities' of civil life.[39] It was apparently at some point in the early 1640s that he observed that 'to those who on account of their religion defend themselves with arms, many persons slyly attach themselves for other reasons, not the best'.[40] In any case, he evidently judged the legitimate aims of such people to have been largely met by the legislation of 1641. For nothing had been added to those measures when he told parliament in 1644 that 'we are already in good part arrived' at 'civil liberty', of which 'the utmost bound... that wise men look for' is the operation of a machinery for the rectification

34. Ibid. 598 (cf. p. 797). 35. Ibid. 800. 36. Ibid. vii. 275.
37. Ibid. i. 924, 926.
38. Ibid. 725, 732, 851, 913, 923–4, 946 (cf. pp. 439, 572, 614, 615).
39. Ibid. ii. 438, 559–60; iii. 191. 40. Ibid. i. 501.

of grievances.[41] Both at the time and in retrospect, he saw an infinitely more profound and exalted purpose in the conflict. It was a war of religion, fought – or fought by the minority who saw the light – for the emancipation of God's truth and his followers from worldly power. If the struggle was their burden, its outcome was their triumph. It was, he claimed, the persecuted friends of divine truth who overcame Charles I, first in standing up to him before the war, then in beating him in battle, then in bringing him, as God's enemy, to justice. 'A small handful of men', he explained, though 'defamed and sp[a]t at with all the odious names of schism and sectarism', had rescued both state and Church by 'those actions before men by which their faith assures them they … are had in remembrance before the throne of God.'[42] It 'pleased God to choose such men as he chooses to be made partakers of the light of the Gospel' for 'the execution of his decrees upon the most potent kings of this world'.[43] Milton's priorities are reflected in the pattern of his own writing. In the year in which the first civil war ended, 1646, when his 'right hand' returned (briefly) from a period of poetic silence, it was for religious, not for political, liberty that his verse called. Another long period of poetic silence ended in 1652 with poems on the subject of liberty of conscience. From 1655 to 1659 he published almost nothing new, in either prose of poetry. The ending of that silence in 1659 was followed by two tracts which voiced religious, not political, grievances. Of his private writings it was his theological manual, *de Doctrina Christiana*, that was his 'best and richest possession'.[44] 'The whole freedom of man', observed Milton in 1660, 'consists either in spiritual or civil liberty'. Of the two, religion was 'the best part'.[45]

To detach Milton's religious from his political concerns, admittedly, can be misleading. Indeed it can lead to a fundamental misunderstanding of his thought. If he had only a limited interest in the organization and workings of politics, no one had more ardent convictions about the values that should inform them. The separation of the Church from political power became for him the most fundamental aim of public life. Yet he never divided religious virtue and obligation from their civic, or 'civil', counterparts. The pairing of 'religious and civil life', of 'virtue with true religion', of 'religion with civil prudence', of the health of 'civil life' with that of

41. Ibid. ii. 487. 42. Ibid. iii. 348, 577. 43. *CW* vii. 67. Cf. viii. 153; *CP* ii. 567.
44. *CW* xiv. 9. 45. *CP* vii. 420, 456.

'divine worship', is an instinctive feature of his writing.[46] Puritan merits of frugality and self-denial blended easily in his mind with classical and pagan conceptions of austere public spirit and of civic aptitude. In 1642 he looked for the education of the nation in 'wisdom and virtue' through two complementary media: preaching from 'the pulpit' (the 'office' alongside which he places that of the poet); and devices and fora of civic instruction that he borrowed, at least in spirit, from the classical world: 'theatres', 'porches', 'wise and artful recitations sweetened with eloquent and graceful incitements to the love and practice of justice, temperance and fortitude'.[47] What other Puritan of his time would thus have brought the two together? Who else would have merged, with no sense of strain, the Aristotelian and the Old Testament conceptions of 'justice' that inspire his hymns to the regicide? Who else, as the Puritan cause collapsed, would in a single breath have appealed to the political injunctions of 'our Saviour' and lamented the failure of the revolution to make the English Commonwealth 'another Rome in the West'?[48] Who else would have combined, with no appearance of difficulty, the components of biblical inspiration and Greek tragedy that come together in *Samson Agonistes*?

For if religion comes before politics, civic virtue is none the less the partner of the life of the spirit. When, in *Eikonoklastes*, Milton notes that the virtuous minority of the Puritan Revolution, God's 'sole remainder', get called 'sectaries' and promoters of 'schism', his protest praises, not their distinctive saintliness, but their civic merits: their 'wisdom ..., valour, justice, constancy, prudence'.[49] His writings time and again associate 'piety' with the public expression of virtue and justice.[50] 'Sanctity of life', and 'the heavenly grace of faith', are the properties not of a Calvinist elect but of the possessors of 'true virtue' and 'manhood', qualities which he invokes in the spirit as much of the Renaissance as of the Reformation, and which to him are the friends, not the rivals, of 'civil happiness', 'civil virtue', 'civil glory'.[51] Their possessors are present-day Scipios, modern equivalents to the heroes of republican Rome.[52] For models of instruction, Milton looks not only to 'the holiest nations' but to 'the civilest, the wisest'.[53]

46. *CP* ii. 578; vii. 243, 359; *CW* viii. 7. 47. *CP* i. 816–19. 48. Ibid. vii. 357.
49. Ibid. iii. 348. 50. Ibid. i. 571, 597, 795, 817; iii. 542; v. 449; *CW* vii. 245.
51. *CP* i. 836; iii. 237–8; v. 40.
52. *Ibid.* i. 588; ii. 366–7; *CW* viii. 217. Cf. *CP* ii. 557; vii. 216 (where Woolrych's argument is surely right).
53. *CP* ii. 355.

His own writing aspires to emulate both the seers among 'the Hebrews of old' and 'the greatest and choicest wits of Athens, Rome, or modern Italy'.[54] Despite the blessings of Christian revelation, 'ancient and famous commonwealths'[55] are ever present in his mind as the yardsticks with which the aspirations and character of his countrymen are to be measured.[56]

★★

Continuous as that theme is in his writing, the tracts of 1649 mark an abrupt change of direction. They do so not only by their political subject-matter but in their political radicalism. In 1641–2 he had adopted, in the service of religious radicalism, a conventional political stance. He portrayed the bishops as 'clippers of regal power' and 'the greatest underminers and betrayers of the monarch', who had undermined the king's strength and authority.[57] He remembered the 'insolences and affronts to regal majesty' by Thomas Becket.[58] Charles I he represented as a sleeping prince, a Samson whose 'laws and just prerogatives which were his ornament and strength', 'those bright and weighty tresses', had been 'wickedly shav[ed] off' by the prelates, and who could reclaim his might with 'the jawbone of an ass'.[59] It would take but 'one puff of the king's' to 'blow them down like a paste-board house'.[60] The nation, once freed from the prelates, would return to its 'divinely and harmoniously tuned' constitution, in which 'a free and untutored monarch' would collaborate smoothly with parliament.[61] There is a transparent disingenuousness in those assurances, as there is in many parliamentary professions of loyalty to the monarch in the 1640s. In practice it is entirely to the Lords and the Commons that he gives the credit for the reforms of 1641 and that he looks for further reformation. In effect they exercise by themselves 'the indiminishable majesty', in which the king should properly share, 'of the law-giving and sacred parliament'.[62] None the less Milton, so *avant-garde* in his religious positions of 1641–2, played no part in the evolution of the novel constitutional reasoning with which parliament justified its intransigence in those years and its readiness to fight.

54. Ibid. i. 812 (cf. *CW* viii. 13, 193).
55. *CP* ii. 493.
56. Ibid. i. 719, 925; ii. 557; v. 449–51; *CW* vii. 451; viii. 7.
57. *CP* i. 858–60.
58. Ibid. 580–1.
59. Ibid. 858–9.
60. Ibid. 583.
61. Ibid. 599.
62. Ibid. 593.

In Milton's injunctions on political life there is a paradox. The design of constitutions, he knew, is at once a crucial and an exacting science.[63] As he noted in 1641, 'in the guidance of a civil state to worldly happiness, it is not for every learned or every wise man... to invent or frame a commonwealth': to be a Lycurgus or a Numa.[64] He was distressed by the incapacity of England's 'narrow politicians' to devise the forms of 'a well-amended commonwealth'.[65] In the Puritan Revolution, he observes, there was set before the nation 'civil government in all her forms', among which his countrymen had their free choice. Yet, 'trusting only on their mother-wit', they had failed to read the works of ancient and foreign political thought that would have equipped them for that task.[66] In 1660, in *The Readie and Easie Way*, he blamed the failure of his cause on its deficiencies of constitutional design. 'When monarchy was dissolved' in 1649, he then lamented,

> the form of a commonwealth should have forthwith been framed, and the practice thereof immediately begun, that the people might have soon been satisfied and delighted with the decent order, ease and benefit thereof; we had been by this time firmly rooted past fear of commotion or mutations, and now flourishing. This care of timely settling a new government instead of the old, too much neglected, hath been our mischief.[67]

Yet to read *The Readie and Easie Way* is to encounter in Milton the very shortcoming of which he accused the nation's leaders. What 'form' should have been created in 1649? In that year he shelved the question 'what form of government is best'. Admittedly he had tactical grounds for doing so, for the issue divided and embarrassed his political masters. Yet he betrayed no eagerness to address the problem. When, in *Defensio* in 1651, he acknowledges that the 'constitution' that prevails after the abolition of monarchy 'is not such as were to be desired, but such as the persistent strife of wicked citizens will suffer it to be',[68] we ask in vain what constitution he would judge desirable. As far as we can tell, he contributed nothing to proposals for the constitutional architecture that he deemed essential.

He was in truth never comfortable in the discussion of constitutional arrangements and rights. The instinct of his mind was to turn towards

63. His reformed educational system would accordingly have trained men not only 'for the wise administration of a commonwealth' but for what everyone knew to be the main challenge facing the designer of a state: 'giving it its utmost possible duration' (*CW* viii. 133).
64. *CP* i. 753.
65. Ibid. v. 441, 449–51.
66. Ibid. v. 449–51.
67. *Ibid.* vii. 430.
68. Ibid. iii. 455; *CW* vii. 29.

the inner spirit of government, not to its outward forms. His inmost preoccupation was with the ethical and religious spirit behind them, and the ethical and religious equipment of the men who administered or lived under them. 'Piety and justice', he explained in 1641, 'are our foundresses; they stoop not, neither change colour for aristocracy, democracy or monarchy', for they are 'far above the taking notice of these inferior niceties'.[69] In 1659 he pronounced that the choice between aristocracy and democracy, a decision we might expect to have been confronted by a writer as desperate as Milton was to avoid the return of monarchy, 'is too nice a consideration for the extremities wherein we are'.[70] He lost patience with such problems. In 1659–60 he was exasperated by James Harrington's propositions for the erection of classical models of government. Their 'new or obsolete forms, or terms, or exotic models', he complained, put constitutional formulae before the attainment of virtue, and so threatened to 'manacle the native liberty of mankind'.[71] Harrington in turn despaired at the readiness of writers such as Milton to trust to 'good men' rather than to 'good laws', a delusion which, he maintained, stood between Puritan England and the achievement of stability and civil life.

It is not only in relation to constitutional forms that Milton's political thought avoids the concrete. In all his discussions of political liberty, its practical content is more often than not intangible. His mind is elsewhere, on an underlying principle. It is a classical or Aristotelian one. There was no more devoted a seventeenth-century follower than Milton of the classical premiss (which he, with many others, absorbed into the precepts of Christianity) that the state is an extension of the souls of its citizens. That assumption, so widely held in earlier generations, was under fundamental challenge by the mid-seventeenth century, but in this as in other respects his mind remained within the Renaissance. He set forth his position in 1641 when, citing Aristotle, he explained that 'a commonwealth ought to be but as one huge Christian personage ... for look what the grounds and causes are of single happiness to one man, the same ye shall find them to a whole state'.[72] In that perspective, liberty is the projection of the sovereignty of reason within us, tyranny the triumph of passion. It was within the soul, therefore, that the conflicts of the civil wars must be fought out. In 1654 he insisted that 'real and substantial liberty ... is to be sought not from without, but within, and is to be obtained principally not by fighting, but by the

69. Ibid. i. 605–6. 70. Ibid. vii. 331. 71. Ibid. 445. 72. Ibid. i. 572.

just regulation and by the proper conduct of life'.[73] 'The straight and only way to true liberty' is 'by innocence of life and sanctity of manners.'[74] Thus it is that 'to be free is precisely the same thing as to be pious, wise, just and temperate', and that 'none can love freedom heartily but good men'.[75] The opposite of liberty is 'licence', the self-indulgence of the wicked that enslaves them to passion and lust: 'Licence they mean when they cry liberty.'[76] Milton's conception of liberty explains his choices of subject for his prose during the first civil war. The removal of the divorce and licensing laws, and the reform of education, were to him the keys to liberty of the soul and to the regeneration, civic and spiritual, that would flow from it. The bondage of matrimony made men 'unserviceable and spiritless to the commonwealth' and 'unactive to all public service'.[77] So 'farewell all hope of true reformation in the state' so long as the 'household unhappiness' imposed by the divorce laws persists.[78] It would be 'to little purpose', he wrote in *Defensio Secunda*, for a man who, in a loveless marriage, 'is in bondage to an inferior at home', 'a species of bondage of all others the most degrading to a man', to 'make a noise about liberty in the legislative assemblies'.[79]

The themes of Milton's civil war polemic distanced him from the run of writers on parliament's behalf, who generally approached the issues of the decade in a more direct and practical spirit. So eccentric were his preoccupations, indeed, that if he had died in January 1649 there would be only thin evidence to show that he was interested in the outcome of the wars. In *Defensio Secunda* he explains that, though 'I was neither unskilled in handling my sword, nor unpractised in its daily use', he had chosen to serve parliament with the pen, 'with much greater utility and with no less peril'.[80] Like Marvell and Nedham, he represents his writing as a form of fighting.[81] Yet before 1649 his pen had disclosed no taste for the wars. Never, before the regicide, did he name, let alone commemorate, any of the leaders of the war effort in the House of Commons, even on the deaths of John Hampden and John Pym in 1643.[82] His pen was silent in the same year when the trained

73. *CW* viii. 131 (cf. i. *CP* 925). 74. *CW* viii. 9. 75. Ibid. 249–51; *CP* iii. 190.
76. 'On the Detraction which followed upon my Writing Certain Treatises'.
77. *CP* ii. 347, 632 (cf. p. 247). This aspect of Milton's thought is illuminated by Martin Dzelzainis, 'Milton's Classical Republicanism', in Armitage, *et al.*, eds., *Milton and Republicanism*, 3–24.
78. *CP* ii. 229. 79. *CW* viii. 133. 80. Ibid. 9–11, 61. 81. Ibid. 253.
82. In *Areopagitica* he did pay eloquent tribute to the radical peer Lord Brooke, who had been killed in battle soon after the outbreak of civil war, but it was for his religious, not for his political, beliefs that he praised him: *CP*. ii. 560–1.

bands filled by fellow Londoners of Milton set out on their famous march to relieve the army of the Earl of Essex at Gloucester. Instead, in the previous autumn, at the start of the war, when it seemed that the king's forces would invade the capital, he had written, and (apparently) posted on his door, a sonnet beseeching the invaders to spare his house: 'Lift not thy spear against the muses' bower.'[83] He does seem to have subscribed to the Solemn League and Covenant, that pledge of loyalty to the Roundhead cause in 1643,[84] though he soon turned against the Presbyterians who had imposed it. He did, albeit more in sorrow than in anger, momentarily castigate the MPs who left Westminster to join the king at Oxford, those 'poor, shaken, uncertain reeds'.[85] Otherwise he was silent about the failings of the royalists. He had much more to say about those of the parliamentarians. Only in the winter of 1644–5 did he acknowledge, glancingly, the 'happy successes' of the parliamentary cause and the progress of 'armed justice in defence of beleaguered truth'.[86] His collection of poems in the middle of the decade reveals no Roundhead sympathies. Indeed it would have been compatible with Cavalier ones, as, by itself, it is with Anthony Wood's picture of Milton as a natural royalist. His sonnet in response to the attack on his writings on divorce, apparently written in 1646, lamented 'all this waste of wealth and loss of blood'.[87] In *Eikonoklastes*, admittedly with the polemical purpose of dissuading readers from returning to civil war, he called the conflict through which they had lived a 'horrid wilderness of distraction and civil slaughter'.[88]

The seclusion of Milton's youthful studies had been followed by his Continental journey. 'As I was preparing to pass over into Sicily and Greece,' *Defensio Secunda* tells us, 'I was restrained by the melancholy tidings from England of civil war.' 'For I thought it base that I should be travelling at my ease, even for the improvement of my mind abroad, while my fellow-citizens were fighting for their liberty at home.' In fact, as the same account reveals in one of the autobiographical inconsistencies that somehow did not trouble him, he was back much earlier. He returned, after a long and leisurely journey home, in July 1639, sixteen months before the meeting of the Long Parliament and three years before the outbreak of civil war.[89] Back in London, rather than aiding his fellow citizens, 'I hired, for me and my books, a sufficiently spacious house in the city' – in one of

83. Sonnet VIII; Corns, *Uncloistered Virtue*, 38. 84. *CP* ii. 578. 85. Ibid. 398.
86. Ibid. 440, 489, 554, 557, 585. 87. Sonnet XII. 88. *CP* iii. 580.
89. Conceivably his mind conflated the 'civil war' with the foreign war with the Scots in 1639, but even on that interpretation his account would remain heavily inaccurate. Hugh

the streets of London, adds Edward Phillips, most 'free from noise' – where 'I returned with no little delight to my interrupted studies'.[90] In 1641 the attack on the bishops drew him into the public realm. Yet if the civil war gave him any sense of civic fulfilment, it more conspicuously brought him perturbation of mind, a condition that is always, for him, an enemy both to ethical well-being and to literary achievement.[91] Early in 1642 he reflected 'with what small willingness I endure to interrupt the pursuit of' his poetic vocation – for at that time it would have seemed only a temporary interruption – 'and leave a calm and pleasing solitariness ... to embark in a troubled sea of noises and hoarse disputes, put from beholding the bright countenance of truth in the quiet and still air of delightful studies'.[92] In 1647, in a letter to his Florentine friend Carlo Dati that recalls his plea for the muses' bower five years earlier, he lamented 'the extremely turbulent state of our Britain', which after his return from Italy 'quickly compelled me to turn my mind from my studies to protecting life and property in any way I could. Do you think there can be any safe retreat for literary leisure among so many civil battles, so much slaughter, fight, and pillage of goods?'[93] In the same year his poem to the librarian of the Bodleian, John Rous, hoped for 'an end to this damnable civil war and its skirmishes', which have removed 'our life-giving pursuits', and in which 'the muses' have been made 'homeless', banished as they are 'from almost every corner of England'.[94] He might be Andrew Marvell, lamenting a year or two later to the 'sweet muse' of Richard Lovelace that 'Our civil wars have lost the civic crown'. Later in 1647 Milton moved to a house where, according to his early biographer John Toland, 'in the midst of all the noise and confusion of arms, he led a quiet and private life, wholly delighted with the muses and prosecuting his indefatigable search after useful and solid knowledge'.

Toland also observed that Milton had 'now grown discontented ... with the parliament'.[95] In the first half of the 1640s Milton had exercised the amplitude of his gift of eulogy on its behalf. Before the war began, he saluted the 'glorious and immortal actions', 'the wisdom, the Christian

Trevor-Roper, *Catholics, Anglicans and Puritans in Seventeenth-Century England* (London, 1987), 246 n.

90. *CW* viii. 127; Darbishire, 62.
91. *CP* i. 244, 816; ii. 260, 632; vii. 490; *Samson Agonistes*, prologue, ll. 4–6 and 1758.
92. *CP* i. 821–2.
93. Ibid. ii. 764.
94. 'Ad Joannem Rousium'.
95. Darbishire, 134.

piety', 'the justice and constancy so high, so glorious, so reviving', of the 'worthies' and 'deliverers' and 'benefactors of their country' at Westminster, the 'height' of whose due praises it is 'hopeless' to try to 'reach'. Their achievements, which even by 1642 have surpassed those of parliaments 'through many ages', are what 'few had the courage to hope for'. Indeed it would 'but diminish and impair their worth' to compare their deeds 'with those exploits of highest fame in poems and panegyrics of old'.[96] During the war the temperature of commendation drops, but only a little. We still learn of the parliament's 'laudable deeds' and 'illustrious exploits', its 'prudent spirit' and 'noble and valorous counsels' and 'indefatigable virtues' and 'faithful guidance and undaunted wisdom'. It has acted with 'more prowess and constancy' than any parliament since the Reformation.[97] On his return to England from Italy, as he remembers in *Areopagitica*, 'it was beyond my hope that those worthies were then breathing in her air who should be her leaders to such a deliverance as shall never be forgotten by any revolution of time that this world hath to finish'.[98] Yet his tributes to the parliament were invariably coloured by the strategic purpose of a writer who could look only to that institution to implement his programme, and who to that end adopted the customary methods of laudatory persuasion. They were also tinged with doubt and dissatisfaction. Milton's praise almost always is. He longed to find ideal objects of panegyric, but could only rarely identify them. In any case, his applause of the parliament was conditional. In an era when literary praise characteristically both idealized and cautioned its recipients, his eulogies brought intensity both to the idealization and to the cautioning. To the immortality which he bestows on parliament in *Areopagitica* there is the proviso that runs through the pamphlet. Parliament must rescind the licensing order that is the occasion of Milton's tract. Otherwise the liberation from spiritual thraldom that it has initiated will be reversed. That prospect is unimaginable to the beholder of the parliament as Milton idealized it. The English, he tells its members, 'can grow ignorant again, brutish, formal and slavish, as ye found us; but you then must first become that which ye cannot be, oppressive, arbitrary and tyrannous, as they were from whom ye have freed us'.[99] In the real world the parliament could easily become those things, and in Milton's mind it did.

96. *CP* i. 596, 615, 729, 919, 922, 925; cf. p. 878.

97. Ibid. ii. 440, 448, 487, 578.

98. Ibid. 538–9.

99. *Ibid.* 559. There are comparable warnings in his pamphlets on divorce: ibid. 439 (near the top of the page), 583 (near the bottom), 585 (the concluding words).

It was not merely that the licensing order and the divorce laws survived, or that in December 1644 he was summoned to appear before judges appointed by the House of Lords to answer complaints about the unlicensed printing of his pamphlets (a challenge by which, characteristically, he refused to be silenced). Parliament stalled over the abolition of episcopacy and eventually agreed to it only as the price of bringing the Presbyterian Scots into the war. It failed to curb, and in large measure encouraged, the Presbyterian intolerance which Milton impugned in his civil war pamphlets and in his poems of around 1646. If, as he concluded in one of those poems, 'new presbyter' was 'but old priest write large',[100] then what, from his perspective, had been gained by parliament's victory? With the failings of policy there were those of character. The public spirit for which he had commended the parliament yielded, in his perspective, to self-interest and moral degeneration. Between March 1645 and the regicide he had nothing to say to the parliament or in its favour. In 1648 he looked for reform, not to parliament, but to Sir Thomas Fairfax, the leader of the new model army which, in the previous year, had forcibly (though temporarily) driven away the Presbyterian majority from the Commons. Milton urged Fairfax to rescue the land from the spirit of persecution, and the corruption, for which the formerly heroic parliament was to blame:

> For what can war but endless war still breed,
> Till truth and right from violence be freed,
> And public faith cleared from the shameful brand
> Of public fraud. In vain doth valour breed
> While avarice and rapine share the land.[101]

More than twenty years later Milton published his *History of Britain*. It was to have contained a 'Digression', which in the event was omitted. The 'Digression', a parallel between early British history and the present plight of the English, recounted in despairing terms the betrayal of the revolution by the Long Parliament and its followers. The date of the 'Digression' is a problematical subject. I shall propose later that it was written, at least in the form in which we have it, well after the Restoration.[102] Yet everything suggests that the view of the parliament which the 'Digression' expresses was also the one he had held at the time, and to which the

100. 'On the New Forcers of Conscience under the Long Parliament'.
101. 'On the Lord General Fairfax at the Siege of Colchester'.
102. See Appendix C.

sonnet to Fairfax gives voice. The 'Digression' lamented the sickness of the land in the 1640s, when 'justice' was 'delayed and soon after denied', and when, as in the Fairfax poem, the 'public faith' – that is, the provision for repayment of those who had lent money to aid the war effort – was violated. England succumbed to 'faction', 'wrong and oppression', 'bribery', 'foul and dishonest things', 'the ravening seizure of innumerable thieves in office'. MPs 'fell to huckster the commonwealth', while loyal supporters of the parliament who petitioned it for payment of their debts 'were tossed up and down after miserable attendance from one committee to another'. 'And if the state were in this plight, religion was not in much better', for parliament, as the secular power, had abetted the Presbyterian goal of a 'spiritual tyranny' by summoning the Westminster Assembly of Divines, whose members were chosen, Milton alleged, for neither piety nor knowledge but 'as each member of parliament in his private fancy thought fit'.[103]

The end of civil war in 1646 had brought little rejoicing. The victorious but bitterly divided parliament presided over an exhausted nation which had learned to detest the victors and resented their accumulation of power and money. Post-war settlement or reconciliation was a distant if not impossible prospect. How had the parliamentary hopes and reforms of the early 1640s, and the achievements of 'armed justice', left so barren and despondent a legacy? In his pamphlets of 1641–4, Milton had famously remarked on God's special relationship with the English. 'This island', which 'he hath yet ever had ... under the special indulgent eye of his providence',[104] was 'chosen before any other' to receive the light brought by Wycliffe. So now, 'decreeing to begin some new and great period in his Church, ... what does he then but reveal himself to his servants and, as his manner is, first to his Englishmen?' Yet even at that stage there had been anxieties behind Milton's assumption. Why had Wycliffe's message been refused? Why, after its God-given 'precedency', had England subsequently been the last reformed nation to overthrow the popish structure of its Church? And why, even when parliament has voted down the bishops, who were Wycliffe's antagonists, do 'we mark not the method of his counsels, and are unworthy'?[105] By the time he begins to write the *History of Britain* he no longer thinks of England as enjoying special favour or protection. Now,

103. *CP* v. 443–7. 104. Ibid. i. 704. 105. Ibid. 525–6, 704; ii. 553.

like other nations, it gets what it deserves.[106] In the 1640s it deserved ill, and got it.

The pessimistic analysis in the *History* is paralleled not only in the poem to Fairfax but in *The Tenure of Kings and Magistrates* in 1649. There he lamented, in words which the 'Digression' from the *History* echoes, the inconstancy of those of his countrymen who in the civil wars 'would seem good patriots', but who fell away when their virtue was tested. Ancient Britain, the 'Digression' tells us, witnessed 'the apparent subversion of all truth, and justice in the minds of most men', while in the 1640s 'the people... after a false heat became more cold and obdurate than before'.[107] 'Most men', explains *The Tenure*, 'are apt enough to civil wars and commotions as a novelty, and for a flash hot and active', but they draw back when 'the roots and causes' of their grievances are addressed.[108] In both *The Tenure* and the 'Digression', the virtues of 'good men' are thwarted by the vices of the 'bad'.[109] Parallels with *The Tenure* surface not only in the 'Digression' but in passages of the *History* which we can ascribe, albeit with varying degress of confidence, to the later 1640s. The ancient Britons had been 'servile in mind, slothful of body':[110] Milton's contemporaries, he ruled in *The Tenure* as elsewhere, were 'servile',[111] and had shrunk from the challenge of virtue through 'sloth or inconstancy'.[112] The Britons had had a taste for 'civil and unjust war'.[113] Had the conflict of the 1640s merited any more pleasing an epithet? Milton pondered the 'useless' triumph of the Britons at Mons Badonicus, 'so fair a victory' which had 'come to nothing' – indeed worse than nothing, for after it 'the peace they enjoyed, by ill using it, proved more destructive to them than war'.[114] What, then, of the victories of the English civil war and of the peace that followed it?

In 1643 he reminded parliament that it faced a massive task – the one that he would later wish on Cromwell – of reforming a nation 'from what corruption, what blindness in religion', 'in what a degenerate and fallen spirit from the apprehension of native liberty and true manliness', 'with what unbounded licence rushing to whoredoms and adulteries'.[115] Milton had his moments of optimism about the condition of the people, or anyway gave the appearance of having them. In *Areopagitica* – where his argument rested

106. Fixler, *Milton and the Kingdoms of God*, 138. 107. *CP* v. 174 (cf. i. 746; iii. 344).
108. Ibid. iii. 191–2 (cf. v. 443, 449). 109. Ibid. iii. 190; v. 449. 110. Ibid. v. 130.
111. Ibid. i. 522, 594, 851; iii. 190. 112. Ibid. iii. 192. 113. Ibid. v. 174.
114. Ibid. 174–5, 178. 115. *CP* ii. 226–7.

on the capacity of a nation freed from censorship to sustain virtue – he sounded a celebrated upbeat note, and transferred on to the nation the image of a waking Samson that he had earlier bestowed on the king. The response of the English to the lifting of the Caroline tyranny has shown them to be 'in what good plight',

> not degenerated, nor drooping to a fatal decay, but casting off the old and wrinkled skin of corruption to outlive those pangs and wax young again, entering the glorious ways of truth and prosperous virtue destined to become great and honourable in these latter ages. Methinks I see in my mind a noble and puissant nation rousing herself like a strong man after sleep, and shaking her invincible locks....[116]

Other statements of optimism owe something, though it is hard to say how much, to the requirements of the government propaganda in which they can be found. There is, for example, the claim in his *Defensio* of 1651 that although the English, having 'learned' their vices 'under their Pharoahs', the Stuarts, perhaps could not be expected to 'unlearn them at once', there was none the less 'good hope' of their recovery.[117] In moving between optimism and its more frequent opposite, Milton faced a recurrent question. Were the nation's failings ingrained, the inescapable product of 'nature'? Or might they have resulted from defects of 'industry or custom'?[118] If the latter, might they be cured, or have been cured, by the programme of reform – the reform of religion, of the household, of education – which he pressed in the earlier 1640s?[119] *Eikonoklastes*, though it offers a gloomy account of the nation's ethical state, attributes it to man-made forces. Contemplating the 'low dejection and debasement of mind in the people', 'I must confess I cannot willingly ascribe [it] to the natural disposition of an Englishman, but rather to two other causes.' First – much as, in the *History*, the early Britons had become 'servile' through 'long subjection' to the Romans[120] – there had been a 'perpetual infusion of servility'. It had come from a source that had likewise debilitated the Britons in the post-Roman period: the clergy, 'whose lives' before the civil wars were 'without the least pattern of virtue'.[121] That was why, as he acknowledged even amid the optimism of *Areopagitica*, 'this iron yoke of outward conformity' which the bishops imposed, and which the Presbyterians, in their own manner, seek to perpetuate, 'hath

116. Ibid. 557–8. 117. *CW* vii. 177–9. 118. *CP* v. 130 (cf. iii. 581).
119. Cf. ibid. vii. 437. 120. Ibid. v. 130 121. Ibid. iii. 344.

left a slavish print upon our necks'.[122] Alas, nothing that happened in the remainder of the revolution suggested to him that the print had faded. The second 'cause', explains *Eikonoklastes*, was 'the factious inclinations of most men divided from the public by several ends and humours of their own'.[123] But Milton could not say in that treatise, a work of polemic for the new government, what the 'Digression' from the *History* reveals: that, just as the struggle for liberty by the early Britons had been betrayed by the concealed ambition of their leaders, so the present 'factious inclinations' were rooted in the conduct of the very parliament whose task was to reform the nation.[124]

★★

Yet from the bleak background of 1648 there sprang, against all expectation, the 'deliverance', as he loved to call it,[125] of the regicide: that 'heroic', 'glorious', 'matchless' deed,[126] carried out, to 'the renown and everlasting glory of the English nation, ... with such a resolution as we hardly found the like recorded in any history'.[127] It came at the gravest hour, 'when the commonwealth nigh perishes'.[128] Milton sometimes found it hard to decide which was the greater enemy to liberty: royalism (the political partner of the episcopal Church) or Presbyterianism (the political partner of the intolerant majority in the Westminster Assembly). In the autumn of 1648 the two, which had already had their moments of alliance, seemed about to coalesce, with the aims of restoring the king and isolating the Cromwellian army. In the negotiations with Charles on the Isle of Wight the Presbyterian representatives from Westminster hammered out the basis of a settlement. To withstand that threat the new model army marched into London at the beginning of December. It forcibly purged the Commons and left the minority of MPs who remained to arrange the trial and execution of the king, and to announce that the sovereign power of the people's representatives lay in the Lower House.

It is after that deliverance that Milton is a changed writer. Not only does he embark on his career of political polemic. The challenges of current politics themselves become an essential component of his thought. Though

122. Ibid. ii. 563–4. 123. Ibid. iii. 344. 124. Ibid. v. 441 ff.
125. Ibid. iii. 191, 233, 585; *CW* vii. 65; viii. 1, 5, 231, 251.
126. *CP* iii. 194, 237, 344; *CW* vii. 253; viii. 553. 127. *CW* vii. 63–5 (cf. *CP* iii. 194).
128. *CP* iii. 194.

he never faltered in his conviction that the political condition of a nation is the mirror of its spiritual and ethical state, he no longer expected political change to wait upon measures for spiritual and ethical improvement. The fate of religion remained his ultimate priority. But for its supremacy in his mind, the writer who had stood back from the parliamentary politics of the 1640s, and been dismayed by the secular programme of too many of the parliament's supporters, would surely not have entered the political fray in 1649. Equally he would surely not have remained in it through the convulsions of the 1650s had not the succession of regimes, unsatisfactory as all of them were to him in other ways, offered the hope – albeit of varying strength – that episcopalian and Presbyterian intolerance might be kept at bay. What changed was that the cause of religion became indissolubly connected in his thinking to the constitutional arrangements that might protect it. Already in the earlier 1640s, it is true, he had maintained that God had 'inseparably knit together' the causes of 'religion' and 'native liberty', for they had both had to contend against the combination of 'tyranny and superstition'.[129] But at that time he ascribed the tyranny not to the king but to the political influence of the bishops and their instruments of power. Of course, that was then the prudent thing to say. Milton could not call Charles I a tyrant in 1640–2, as he would easily and relentlessly do from 1649, when the king had been decapitated as a warmonger and a traitor to his people. There is indeed, in those earlier years, a restraining prudence in the language of Milton's references to the monarchy.[130] Even so, his allusions at that time to civil oppression and grievances, so subsidiary as they are to his ecclesiastical preoccupations, are readily intelligible not as signals of his own preoccupations but as appeals to the sympathies of readers with secular or constitutionalist perspectives that were foreign to him.

In 1649, by contrast, the alliance of 'public' or 'civil' or 'native' liberty with 'religion' is an insistent theme.[131] From now on the collaboration and interdependence of 'superstition' and 'civil tyranny',[132] apparent when 'a king must be adored like a demigod',[133] are an article of faith for Milton.

129. Ibid. i. 923–4; ii. 227.

130. Not least there is his insinuation, a conventional enough device in covert criticisms of a present tyanny, that what he fears is a future one: ibid. i. 588, 853. Sometimes in the early 1640s Milton, perhaps designedly, leaves us uncertain whether the tyranny to which he refers is ecclesiastical, or political, or both: e.g. ibid. 705.

131. Ibid. iii. 227, 238, 332, 348, 422, 493.

132. Ibid. 511, 577 (cf. p. 511); *CW* vii. 553 (cf. p. 65).

133. *CP* vii. 425.

He explained in that year how Charles I had beset the nation with the twin burdens of 'prelatical superstition' and 'civil tyranny';[134] how 'temporal and spiritual tyranny' had been the 'two twisted scorpions' of his reign;[135] how the 'combination between tyranny and false religion' had 'very dark roots' which 'twine and interweave'.[136] 'Gloriously hath' God 'delivered you', Milton told his countrymen in *Defensio*, 'from what surely are the two greatest mischiefs of this life, and most pernicious to virtue – tyranny and superstition.'[137] Perhaps the surge of Anglican feeling behind the attempt to restore Charles I to the throne in 1648 played its part in Milton's new perspective. Yet it was in the huge public impact of *Eikon Basilike* that he recognized the proneness of the English 'not to a religious only, but to a civil kind of idolatry in idolizing their kings'.[138] Henceforth 'tyranny' and 'slavery', words he had hitherto applied only intermittently to the political sphere, pervaded his accounts of it.

There had been another change. He had found the political heroes he had earlier sought in vain. Occasionally, and tenuously, his writings after the regicide do link the 'deliverance' of Pride's Purge and the regicide to the virtue and courage of the early stages of the Long Parliament, the time of that previous 'deliverance', and congratulate the 'worthies' whose constancy had endured through the 1640s. Yet he knew that the revolution of 1648–9 had little continuity, either of purpose or in the personnel of its leadership, with that of 1640–2. Most of the surviving leaders of the Long Parliament in its initial phase had become Presbyterians. When, from 1649, Milton recalls the events of the previous decade, his choices of subject-matter are largely determined by the emphases of the literary adversaries to whose writings he replies. Yet he chooses his own emphases too. It is only from the summer of 1647, when the army seized the king from his parliamentary captors, marched on London, and put the Presbyterian leaders at Westminster to flight, that the pattern of events in the revolution remains (even if sometimes in a confused form) in his consciousness. His sonnet to Oliver Cromwell remembers the general's great victories of 1648–51, but not those of the first civil war. Likewise his recollection of the failings of parliament and the Presbyterian clergy in the earlier and mid–1640s, keen as it would remain, took no chronological shape in his mind. The events of that time merged into a single, and generally dismal, whole. By contrast the

134. *CP* iii. 446. 135. Ibid. 570. 136. Ibid. 509. 137. *CW* vii. 553. 138. *CP* iii. 343.

decisive episodes of the sixteen months after August 1647 – the king's flight to Hampton Court; the parliamentary vote to offer no more terms to the king; the second civil war, with the invasion, that 'perfidious ... irruption', wrought by 'malignance',[139] of the Scots, the 'false north';[140] the treaty between king and parliament on the Isle of Wight and its termination by Pride's Purge – retained a hold on his memory. To him the purge and the regicide were the miraculous reversal of the Presbyterian-royalist trend. They were the army's triumphant termination of its two-year conflict with the parliamentary leadership, which had treated it, as he would recall, with such provocative ingratitude.[141]

From 1649 Milton maintained that the new model, 'that invincible army', hated by Presbyterians envious of 'its glorious deeds',[142] was distinguished from other armies – not least the parliament's own forces before the military reforms of 1644–5 that had produced the new model[143] – by its valour, its discipline, its moderation, its avoidance of plunder and drunkenness and other vices. He was still more eager to praise its political than its military deeds. He did briefly acknowledge the role of the civilian MPs who survived Pride's Purge and who gave parliamentary sanction to the revolutionary exploits of 1648–9, though he described the purged Commons not, as it thought of itself, as the master of the army but merely as the partner of 'the military council'.[144] But the true representatives of the people were the soldiers. They were a citizen army[145] and – since citizenship and godliness go together in his mind – a godly one. They were 'renowned for the civilest and best ordered in the world, and by us here at home the most conscientious'.[146] It is in their godliness that he most rejoices. They are 'not only the bravest of armies but the most modest and religious', 'the champions of the Church'. They devote the hours of leisure which other soldiers spend on 'drunkenness', and on 'various lusts, for rapine, gaming, swearing and perjury', to 'the search of truth', to 'diligent attention to the holy Scripture; nor is there anyone' among them 'who thinks it more honourable to smite the foe than to instruct himself and others in the knowledge of heavenly things'.[147] The new

139. Ibid. 331 (cf. *CW* viii. 221). 140. 'On the Lord General Fairfax', l. 7.

141. *CP* iii. 233; *CW* viii. 211. In *Eikonoklastes*, where Milton has to cover the whole history of the 1640s, he passes quickly over 'the various events' of the civil war (*CP* iii. 528–33). His narrative acquires more shape and vigour from the time of the army's entrance into politics in 1647.

142. *CW* vii. 491. 143. *CP* ii. 412. 144. *Ibid.* iii. 194, 237 (though also p. 311).

145. *CW* vii. 357, 493. 146. *CP* vii. 329. 147. *CW* viii. 179.

model was the protector, and a principal home, of the Independents and sectaries, the groups which the Presbyterians yearned to extinguish and to whom, amid the national backsliding and corruption of the 1640s, Milton looked as the preservers and discoverers of truth. In his thinking the army, whose 'matchless deeds' had alone brought Charles I down, merged with 'the saints'.[148] The regicide, the army's towering accomplishment, was the saints' hour. For God, as they knew from Psalm 149 and as Milton reminded his readers, gave them 'honour' 'to judge wicked kings', 'to bind them in chains'.[149]

Yet those saints were 'very few'. Though he sometimes claimed that they and the supporters of the regicide were more numerous than they appeared,[150] he was more inclined to make a virtue of their paucity of numbers, since in the sternest of times it is 'the sole remainder' in whose steadfastness God delights. In Milton's thinking the hostility of the great majority of MPs to the purge and the regicide did nothing to invalidate those events. Parliamentary majorities were to be applauded when they were right, as they had been in dismantling the instruments of prerogative power in the early 1640s, but to be removed when they were wrong. For 'there is nothing more agreeable to nature, nothing more just, nothing more useful or more for the interest of man, than that the less should yield to the greater: not number to number, but virtue to virtue'.[151] It did not trouble him that 'the people' opposed the regicide, for 'the true power of the people' lay in 'the sounder part' of their representatives, in those who, in opposition to the 'rabble', favoured their liberty, not their slavery.[152] In every sense that mattered, therefore, 'the people' could be said, not to have opposed the revolution of 1648–9, but to have supported it. Equally it did not trouble him that the regicide broke every constitutional and legal rule. In Marvell's 'An Horatian Ode', 'justice' complains at the regicide and pleads 'the ancient rights' against it. To Milton the king's execution, 'that impartial and noble piece of justice, wherein the hand of God appeared so evidently on our side',[153] is the execution of divine judgement, which will not stay for Marvell's 'ancient rights'. In bringing the king to trial, the parliament and army have followed 'the glorious way wherein justice and victory hath set them: the only warrants under all ages, next under

148. *CP* iii. 560–1. 149. Ibid. vii. 115.
150. Ibid. iii. 197 (cf. ii. 557); *CW* vii. 355; viii. 149–53.
151. *CW* viii. 153–5 (cf. *CP* iii. 197). 152. *CW* vii. 357. 153. *CP* iii. 311.

immediate revelation, to exercise supreme power' in so epic and exalted a circumstance.[154] The 'justice' that destroyed the king was 'the strength, the kingdom, the power and majesty of all ages', and the soldiers who enforced it were 'the guardians of justice in martial uniform'.[155] We might be reading Thomas Carlyle.

In Marvell's poem the sword of justice is held erect, with troublingly ambiguous significance. In Milton's tracts of 1649 the regicide is recurrently the feat, beyond ambiguity or doubt, of the same sword, of 'the unsparing sword of justice', 'the supreme sword of justice'.[156] The justice enacted by the regicide conforms, as God wishes it to do, to that to be dispensed by him on the Day of Judgement.[157] It has nothing to do with man-made laws, which are invalidated when they impede the execution of the divine will.[158] In any case, fidelity to human statutes can lie not in a 'peevish' adherence to their 'letter' but in breaches of it,[159] which serve the larger purpose of law. For 'irregular motions may be necessary on earth sometimes, as well as constantly in heaven. That is not always best which is most regular to written law. Great worthies heretofore by disobeying law oft-times have saved the commonwealth.'[160] Opponents of the regicide might, in their legalistic way, 'disput[e] forms and circumstances when the commonwealth nigh perishes for want of deeds in substance'.[161] But if the king's judges were ready to act 'without precedent, if it appear their duty, it argues the more wisdom, virtue and magnanimity' in them.[162]

Such were the arguments with which Milton vindicated the revolution of 1648–9. Now we shall see how close were his reasoning and his language to those deployed, in the same cause, by Marchamont Nedham.

154. Ibid. 194 (cf. i. 597). 155. Ibid. 585; *CW* viii. 179.
156. *CP* iii. 193, 197, 346, 454, 584, 585.
157. The point is powerfully made in Fixler, *Milton and the Kingdoms of God*, 156–7. Fixler brings out the unique standing of the regicide in Milton's political thinking.
158. *CW* vii. 427. 159. *CP* iii. 588 160. Ibid. 562. 161. Ibid 194.
162. Ibid. 237; cf. John Hall, *A Serious Epistle to Mr William Prynne* (1649), 10–11.

8

Milton and the New Order

Milton and Nedham were fellow writers for the government that came to power in 1649. The treatises that Milton published for it were written in its first two years, when its rule was precarious. Only the presence of the army and its garrisons, paid for by huge and in the long term unsustainable levels of taxation, kept down royalism, which looked for relief to the forces that opposed Cromwell's army in Ireland and Scotland and hoped for an invasion from the Continent in the Stuart cause.[1] The tens of thousands of soldiers in the regions could not prevent royalist conspiracy, let alone win the hearts or minds of the population to republican rule. Clandestine royalist literature, in prose and poetry, taunted the regime. Like Nedham's writing for the Commonwealth, Milton's warned his countrymen against the madness, as both writers presented it, of adherence to royalism. Nedham's polemic, as the standard heading of his newsbook explains, is written 'for information of the people': Milton hopes that, by giving them 'better information', he can dissuade them from reverting to 'war and bloodshed'.[2] If only, he reflected, 'it were my happiness to set free the minds of Englishmen from longing to return poorly under that captivity of kings'![3] 'Again and again' he adjured them to 'consider what kind of king ye are likely to have' if the Stuarts returned.[4] Having, in the civil war, eschewed 'the service of the camp' because his 'services could be of more avail' in the medium of print,[5] Milton now devoted his pen to what we now call propaganda – though to grasp his esteem for that activity we need to set aside the pejorative modern connotations of the word.

1. H. M. Reece, 'The Military Presence in England, 1649–1660' (Oxford University D. Phil. thesis, 1981).
2. *CP* iii. 338–9.
3. Ibid. 585.
4. *CW* vii. 541.
5. Ibid. viii. 11.

Milton's proudest and most ambitious work for the Commonwealth, *Defensio*, was completed by the end of 1650. But his role in the polemic of the regime did not end with it. From January 1651 to January 1652 he and Nedham shared an official role in the government's service. During that time the printer Thomas Newcomb, a frequent printer of Milton's works in the 1650s, registered with the Stationers Company, 'under the hand of Mr Milton', the weekly issues of Nedham's *Mercurius Politicus*. In that capacity Milton would have been responsible to the council of state, his regular employer, for the content of the newsbook.[6] It was in the first issue which he licensed that the newsbook first mentioned Milton's own writing. It gave 'notice that a very victorious reply to Salmasius is now in motion at the press'.[7] *Politicus* would promote *Defensio* no less warmly thereafter, and would give publicity to other writings of Milton for the rest of the decade. There is no indication that Milton's duties as licenser were a curb on Nedham. Rather, they facilitated a creative partnership.

In their vindications of the regicide and of the rule of the republic, Milton's and Nedham's writings developed common arguments and a common vocabulary. The resemblances, at least in their persistence, set their prose apart from the run of polemic in the Puritan cause. Behind its shared features lie premisses and rhetorical methods that derive largely from the classical world, to whose history, and to whose civic values, both writers so often appeal. From that source they acquired a confident intellectual cosmopolitanism that is rarely matched in other defences of the new order of 1649–53, most of which were narrowly biblical or providentialist or legal or prudential in scope.

On no subject are Milton and Nedham closer, in sentiment and vocabulary, than the trial and execution of Charles I. They bring to it a language of civic heroism for which other apologists lack either the inclination or the talent. Both authors found it impossible to over-praise the king's judges, or to exaggerate either the grandeur or the implications of their achievement. The 'proceedings' of those who seized power in 1648–9, asserted Milton in *The Tenure of Kings and Magistrates*, 'appear equal to what hath been

6. The arrangements for the registration of newsbooks were not orderly, and it is conceivable that he also licensed earlier issues of *Politicus*, which began life in June 1650. For the sake of safety and simplicity, however, I shall shun that tempting possibility. We cannot say how much licensing Milton did. We know only by accident that he sanctioned a contentious publication of August 1650: below, pp. 242–3. In October 1651 he acted as a substitute licenser, for one issue, of another government newsbook: Parker, 1000.

7. *MP*, 23 Jan. 1651, 546.

done in any age of nation heretofore'.[8] England's 'high achievements' since 'the extirpation of tyranny' in 1649, maintained *Politicus*, 'may match any of the ancients'.[9] To Milton the deliverers of their country had been 'endued with fortitude and heroic virtue' and had performed 'exemplary and matchless deeds'.[10] The regicide was 'such a solemn and for many ages unexampled act of due punishment',[11] 'that impartial and noble piece of justice',[12] 'an action ... so worthy of heroic ages',[13] performed with 'so great a resolution as we hardly find the like recorded in any history'.[14] It was marked by the 'courage'[15] and 'magnanimity' – 'the 'magnanimity peculiar to heroes' – of the revolutionaries,[16] and was 'to be justly attributed to their immortal praise'.[17] *Politicus* employs the same vocabulary. It, too, rejoiced in the 'courage'[18] and 'magnanimity'[19] of the king's judges. The regicide, 'this famous action', was, it proclaimed, 'a noble act of justice', 'so heroic an act of justice', 'one of the most heroic and exemplary acts of justice that ever was done under the sun'.[20] Milton and the newsbook come even closer. 'The Greeks and Romans', recalls Milton, treated tyrannicide as 'a glorious and heroic deed, rewarded publicly with statues and garlands.'[21] 'In the monuments of the Grecian and Roman freedom', agrees *Politicus*, 'we find those nations were wont to heap all the honours they could invent by public rewards, consecration of statues, and crown of laurel upon such worthy patriots.'[22] Cicero, recalls Milton, recorded that the Greeks 'ascribe divine worship to men who have killed tyrants'.[23] The Greeks and Romans, *Politicus* reminds us, 'enrolled' the slayers of tyrants 'in heaven among their deities'.[24]

To both writers the revolution of 1648–9 had saved the nation and its liberty at a moment of high peril. Before that 'deliverance', Milton remembered, the commonwealth 'was tottering and almost quite reduced to slavery and utter ruin'.[25] *Politicus* regarded as 'almost incredible' the same 'deliverance', 'whereby we have been rescued out of the claws of

8. *CP* iii. 194. 9. *MP*, 22 Jan. 1652, 1552. 10. *CP* iii. 191, 237.
11. Ibid. 596. 12. Ibid. 311. 13. *CW* vii. 51. 14. Ibid. 63–5.
15. Ibid. 51, 451. 16. Ibid. 65, 511; *CP* iii. 194, 237; vii. 355. 17. *CP* iii. 577.
18. *Case*, 37 (cf. p. 113); *MP*, 4 Mar. 1652, 1441. 19. *Case*, 89 (cf. *MP*, 22 Jan. 1652, 1349).
20. *MP*, 2 Feb. 1651, 886; 10 July 1651, 886; 4 Mar. 1652, 1442, 1444. The term 'the sword of justice', which Milton invoked in glorifying the regicide, and which Nedham liked to use on the Commonwealth's behalf, is used by the editorial of the first issue of *Politicus* licensed by Milton (*MP*, 23 Jan. 1651, 535).
21. *CP* iii. 212 (cf. ibid. 589–90; *CW* vii. 329). 22. *MP*, 4 Mar. 1652, 144–3.
23. *CW* vii. 305. 24. *MP*, 4 Mar. 1652, 1442–3.
25. *CW* vii. 511 (cf. p. 451; *CP* iii. 194).

the old tyranny', 'which ... was at the very point of returning in again upon us'.[26] With Milton, Nedham traced what he called the 'malice, falsehood and faction of the late Presbyterian drivers' who strove to betray the cause to the Scots and to the king.[27] With him, too, he recalled the cause's rescue by a heroic minority: first in 1647, when, as *Politicus* remembered, 'the army with extreme hazard' marched on London and put the Presbyterian leaders to flight; and then, decisively, through Pride's Purge, 'this noble act of prevention' by which alone 'the hazard of a new war' was averted.[28] To Nedham as to Milton, it was principally the army, not the civilian MPs whom the purge left behind, which deserved the nation's gratitude. In 1647 Nedham had looked to 'so potent, so religious, so resolute, so well-accomplished, well-disciplined and victorious an army', an army so commendable for the 'justice' of its 'proceedings'.[29] Under the Commonwealth he rejoiced in the army's 'special protection from heaven, God having sealed them for his own by many miraculous victories and successes to the wonder of the whole world'.[30] In the first civil war, as editor of *Mercurius Britanicus*, he had championed the army's material needs and, within the limits of political discretion, had promoted the political demands of its radical component. During that time he formed contacts in the army, which he may have retained even during his royalist period of the late 1640s.[31] In 1647 he went into print to aid the army's efforts to secure a settlement with the king. Perhaps he wrote or helped to write some of the celebrated official publications in which it defined its political position in that year. Such at least is the obvious inference, in the light of his habits of self-promotion, from his knowing tribute to 'those unspotted letters and declarations from the army (no less admirable for style than equity)'.[32] In *Politicus* he resumed the tactics on the new model army's

26. *MP*, 22 July 1652, 1739.
27. *Case*, 69; *MP*, 19 June 1651, 864–5; 15 Apr. 1652, 1523.
28. *MP*, 19 June 1651, 864; 8 Apr. 1652, 1509; 15 Apr. 1652, 1523; 22 July 1652, 1739.
29. Marchamont Nedham, *The Lawyer of Lincolnes Inne Reformed* (1647), 1. Cf. *Case*, 77; John Hall's *Mercurius Britanicus*, 8 June 1648, 27.
30. *Case*, 77.
31. Nedham, *Plea for the King*, 23; *idem*, *Pacquet of Advices*, 22, 51–2. Did Milton acquire such links too? In his paper war on behalf of the English people he was able to learn details of past events from members of the army (*CP* viii. 209). Perhaps we would anyway expect that information to have been made readily available to him. But how did he come to form his close friendship with the army officer Robert Overton? Bradshaw may also have had his own contacts in the army. Milton tells us that Bradshaw 'relieves, from his private fortunes, brave men of the military profession who have been reduced to want' (*CW* viii. 159).
32. Nedham, *Lawyer of Lincolnes Inne*, I.

behalf that he had deployed in *Britanicus*. He supported calls for the prompt and adequate supply of weapons;[33] reminded comfortably housed readers of the hardships of military campaigns;[34] drew attention to the political and social demands which the army pressed upon a reluctant parliament;[35] and reminded his audience how the creation of the new model in 1645, the achievement that thwarted the advocates of a sell-out, had saved the Roundhead cause.[36]

Nedham sought arguments and words that would bring the recalcitrant English to 'understand' that their interest lay, not in the return of the monarchy, but in the liberty that the republic offered them. Milton, in the same cause, strove to awaken readers 'who have not more seriously considered kings other than in the gaudy name of majesty ... as if they breathed not the same breath with other mortal men'.[37] He knew the causes of their ignorance: 'custom, simplicity, or want of better teaching'.[38] Instead of being 'governed by reason', men 'give up their understanding' to 'custom' and 'blind affections'. *Politicus* concurs. It is because of 'our former education under a monarchy',[39] and because 'so strong an impression is made ... by education and custom from the cradle, even upon men that are endued with reasonable souls',[40] that 'most men here in England ... naturally ... are of a supple humour and inclination to bow under the ignoble pressures of an arbitrary tyranny, and utterly unapt to learn what true freedom is'.[41] From 1649 Milton ascribes the hold of monarchy on the popular mind to 'the idolizing' of monarchy. *Politicus* attributes it to 'idolatry', 'kingly idolatry', 'the idol of majesty', the alliance of 'idolatry and tyranny'.[42] Like Milton the newsbook notices the 'superstitious' worship of kingship. Men of virtue, says Nedham, are thwarted because their compatriots are 'more superstitiously inclinable to adore the greatness of a tyrant than really affectionate to the worth of liberty'.[43] 'This doctrine of tyranny', explains *Politicus*, 'hath taken the deeper root in men's minds, because the greatest part was ever inclined to adore the golden idol of tyranny in every form, by reason of its outward splendour and present power; by which means

33. *MP*, 3 Oct. 1650, 289; 29 May 1651, 817; 30 Oct. 1651, 1161.
34. Ibid. 3 July 1651, 887; cf. Worden, '"Wit in a Roundhead"', 110.
35. *MP*, 7 Aug. 1651, 980; 19 Aug. 1652, 1803–6.
36. Ibid. 6 Nov. 1651, 1174.
37. *CP* iii. 338; cf. *CW* viii. 101.
38. *CP* iii. 338.
39. *Case*, p. 114.
40. Ibid. 112.
41. *MP*, 2 Oct. 1651, 1095.
42. *Case*, 15; *MP*, 20 June 1650, 32; 27 June 1650, 46; 8 Aug. 1650, 131; 19 Sept. 1650, 230; 22 May 1651, 813; 3 July 1651, 886; 10 July 1651, 914; 18 Sept. 1651, 1067.
43. *Case*, 114.

[1093]

Numb. 69.

Mercurius Politicus.

Compriſing the ſumme of all Intelligence, with the Affairs and Deſigns now on foot in the three Nations of *England*, *Ireland*, and *Scotland*.

In defence of the Common-wealth, and for Information of the People.

——*Ità vertere Seria.* {Hor. de Ar Poet

From *Thurſday* Septemb: 25. to *Thurſday* Octob. 2. 1651.

EE who have been educated under a *Monarchy*, may very fitly be reſembled to thoſe Beaſts, which have been caged or coop't all their lives in a Den, where they ſeem to live in as much pleaſure as other Beaſts that are abroad; and if they be let looſe, yet they will return in again, becauſe they know not how to value or uſe their Liberty: So ſtrong an impreſſion is made likewiſe by education and cuſtome from the Cradle, even upon men that are endued with reaſonable ſouls, that they chuſe to live in thoſe places and cuſtoms of government, under which they have been bred, rather then ſubmit to better, which might make more for their content and advantage. Hence it is, that thoſe poore ſlaves under the *Turk*, *Tartar*, *Muſcovite*, *Ruſſian*, *French*, and *Spaniard*,

Yyyyyy with

Figure 7. Nedham on the legacy of monarchy

the rabble of mankind', 'having placed their corrupt humour or interest in base fawning', vent their fury on those who call tyrants to account.[44]

The 'adoration' of monarchy would be Milton's theme in 1660, in *The Readie and Easie Way to Establish a Free Commonwealth.* It is in that work that Milton follows the pamphlet of May 1659, *A Publick Plea,* written or partly written by Nedham, in citing the 'precept of Christ', in Luke 22, in favour of republics.[45] 'In a free commonwealth', explains the same passage of *The Readie and Easie Way,* 'they who are greatest are perpetual servants and drudges to the public at their own cost and charges; neglect their own affairs; yet are not elevated above their brethren; live soberly in their families; walk the streets as other men; may be spoken to freely, familiarly, friendly, without adoration; whereas a king must be adored like a demigod, with a dissolute and haughty court about him, of vast expense and luxury.'[46] In January 1652 *Politicus* offered a similar contrast: 'The state of Athens, ... while it remained free in the people's hands, was adorned with such governors as gave themselves up to a serious abstemious severe course of life', where 'temperance and liberty walked hand in hand'; but thereafter it yielded 'to the charms of luxury, and afterwards to all the practices of an absolute tyranny.'[47] The newsbook approvingly recalled the watchfulness against tyrannical aspirations that characterized the people of republican Rome, who 'observed every man's looks, his very nods, his garb and his gait; whether he walked, conversed, and lived as a friend of freedom among his neighbours'.[48] No less approvingly it quoted, at length, the paean to William the Silent in Fulke Greville's life of Sir Philip Sidney – a ruler, as Nedham observed, so unlike 'luxurious grandees and princes', and so different a figure from the debauched and tyrannical leaders, as *Politicus* represents them, of the present-day House of Orange. William, recollected Nedham, wore such a gown as 'a mean student in our inns of court would not have been well pleased to walk the streets in'.[49] Nedham, who repeatedly emphasizes, in a vein at once classical and Miltonic, the connection of 'luxury' with 'tyranny', is equally insistent, in that same vein, on the association of 'liberty and sobriety'; of 'liberty' and 'severity' or 'frugality' or 'plainness'; and of

44. *MP*, 4 Mar. 1652, 1442. 45. Above, p. 43. 46. *CP* vii. 425.

47. *MP*, 15 Jan. 1652, 1334–5 (cf. p. 1336). Further resemblances between *The Readie and Easie Way* and *Politicus* are discussed in Ch. 14 below.

48. *MP*, 6 Oct. 1651, 1126.

49. Ibid. 15 Jan. 1652, 1336–7; cf. my 'Marchamont Nedham and the Beginnings of English Republicanism', in Wootton, ed., *Republicanism, Liberty, and Commercial Society*, 70–1.

'freedom' and what to Milton is the 'axle' on which 'the flourishing and decaying of all civil society are moved to and fro': 'discipline'.[50]

Again on classical principles, but again in a manner distinctively close to Milton, *Politicus* insists on the contrast between 'liberty' and 'licence'. To Nedham, 'liberty', that 'inestimable jewel', 'consists not in a licence to do what ye list'.[51] At the outset of Milton's *The Tenure*, 'none can love freedom heartily but good men; the rest love not liberty but licence'. Licence, he adds, 'never hath more scope or more indulgence than under tyrants'.[52] To Nedham, 'licentiousness' is an 'enem[y] to liberty' and is 'a tyranny itself'.[53] Milton's sonnet of 1646 'On the detraction which followed upon my writing certain treatises' recalls that in his divorce tracts he unwittingly provoked a 'barbarous noise' from his Presbyterian enemies by speaking for 'the known rules of ancient liberty'. 'But this is got by casting pearl to hogs, | That bawl for freedom in their senseless mood | ... | Licence they mean when they cry liberty; | For who loves that must first be wise and good.'[54] 'It is a wonder', observed Nedham in 1650, 'how lightly men prize' the 'invaluable jewel of liberty ... trampling the precious pearl under their feet like swine.'[55]

★★

In celebrating the regicide, and in damning its Presbyterian opponents, Milton and Nedham spoke not, or not only, for the new government, but for a party within it. Only within limits was the Commonwealth a revolutionary regime. A majority of the MPs who now held sovereign power had agreed only with reluctance to the king's execution, or had stayed away from parliament between the purge and the regicide and rejoined it only afterwards. Many of them told themselves that by remaining in power they could restrain the impetus of the revolution or protect their constituents against its impact. They regretted the purge and wanted to bring Presbyterians, with whom they often had more sympathy than with the regicides, back into the political fold. It was hard for them to express their views openly. A regime that owed its existence, and had asserted its right to power, through the purge and the regicide could not disown those

50. *CP* i. 751 (cf. pp. 588, 841; *CW* vii. 511); *Case*, 113, 114; *MP*, 2 Oct. 1652, 1094; 15 Feb. 1652, 1335; 29 Feb. 1652, 1367; 27 May 1652, 1611.
51. *Case*, 111; *MP*, 2 Oct. 1651, 1095.
52. *CP* iii. 190.
53. *Case*, 100 (cf. p. 96); *MP*, 10 June 1652, 1641; ibid. 17 June 1652, 1657.
54. Sonnet XII.
55. *Case*, 111 (cf. *Mercurius Pragmaticus*, 12 Sept. 1648, 2–3).

coups. The momentum lay with the men who had effected the revolution, and who had the army behind them. The radicals demanded that the regime break boldly with the monarchical past; that it refuse all compromise not only with its Cavalier but also with its Roundhead opponents; and that firm measures be taken to assert the Commonwealth's authority and reduce its critics and enemies to obedience. In the years 1649–51 those radicals fought and won a series of battles to bring moderates and waverers, inside parliament and among the wider nation, into line. First there was the imposition of the engagement of loyalty to the kingless regime. But it was after the victory at Dunbar in September 1650, which brought relative (though only relative) security to the government, that the rift between radicals and moderates at Westminster opened, and that the former went on the offensive with a series of new initiatives. There was the demolition of royal statuary and images. There was the Commons' resolution, in December 1650, to enter the proceedings of the king's trial in the parliamentary records 'for the transmitting the memory thereof to posterity', and to congratulate the regicides, as the second anniversary of their exploit approached, on their 'courage and fidelity'. There was the trial for treason in the summer of 1651 of the Presbyterian clergyman Christopher Love, who despite intensive lobbying for mercy was executed in August on the charge of conspiring with royalists.

Politicus consistently took the radical line. Englishmen must choose, it told them, between 'the republic and the late family', for 'there can be no medium of reconcilement betwixt' them,[56] there being 'as vast a contrariety' as between 'God and Belial, light and darkness, liberty and slavery, free state and tyranny'.[57] So men who would not declare themselves friends to the regime must be declared its enemies. In the first civil war *Britanicus* had assailed 'lukewarm wretches', 'Laodiceans', 'secret enemies which lur[k] here under the notion of neuters, or moderate friends'.[58] *Politicus* likewise targets 'that amphibious animal, the neutral of Laodicea', and disparages 'lukewarm' and 'moderate' men, who would bend with the wind if the royalists secured ascendancy.[59] The government must root out 'both the wild geese and the tame, the malignant and the neutral',[60] from central and

56. *Case*, 61; *MP*, 27 Feb. 1651, 607. 57. *MP*, 21 Aug. 1651, 997.
58. *Mercurius Britanicus*, e.g. 25 Mar. 1644, 218; 18 Aug. 1645, 833.
59. *MP*, 22 Aug. 1650, 173; 21 Aug. 1651, 997; 6 Nov. 1651, 1174–5; 5 Feb. 1652, 1385.
60. Ibid. 6 Nov. 1651, 1174.

local government. Nedham's *The Case of the Commonwealth* explained that the Commonwealth had survived until now only because it had 'a party of its own throughout the nation, men of valour and virtue, ... sensible of liberty', who had stood out against 'the general debaucheries of all sorts of people which render them admirers of the pomp of tyranny and enemies to that freedom which hath been so dearly purchased'.[61] It must therefore confine power to 'that party' which stood 'firm to the interest of freedom'. It must take note of the 'jealousies and sorrows of some of the parliament's best friends', who 'think that surely there are some persons in authority that have an evil influence to hinder the much desired reformation'.[62] Even the imposition of the engagement, ruled the newsbook, was an inadequate safeguard, for there were trimmers who took it merely to keep their posts.[63] *Politicus* befriended the cause of beleaguered minorities in local government, the overburdened handful of 'zealous magistrates', those 'worthy instruments' who sought to impose the Commonwealth's authority in the face of 'malignant' or 'timorous' JPs and of 'that general dissatisfaction to the present government' which their obstructive or craven conduct fostered. The very lives of the regime's true friends in the localities would be 'a burden, did not their loves to God and country bear them up'.[64]

In the Old Exchange in London, the great gathering point of the city, there stood, until August 1650, a statue of Charles I. It had been decapitated since the regicide, but not removed. Now, as *Politicus* was delighted to report, parliament 'upon second thoughts' ordered 'that the whole statue should be taken down'. In the niche there was placed a Latin inscription, in gold letters,[65] commemorating the fall of 'the tyrant, the last of the kings', on 30 January 1649, 'the year when England's liberty was restored'. 'These', observed *Politicus*, 'are characters not to be blotted out by all the art under heaven.'[66] The decision to enrol the proceedings of the regicide and to congratulate the king's judges was solemnly recorded by *Politicus*, which commended it as 'well worthy' the parliament's 'best resolutions',[67] and which likewise drew attention to the second anniversary

61. *Case*, 114. The radicals' own sense of their distinctiveness is brought out by David Underdown, '"Honest" Radicals in the Counties', in Donald Pennington and Keith Thomas, eds., *Puritans and Revolutionaries* (Oxford, 1978), 186–205.

62. *MP*, 24 Oct. 1650, 328.

63. Ibid. 8 Aug. 1650, 144; 24 Oct. 1650, 328.

64. Ibid. 24 Oct. 1650, 326–8, 335; 21 Nov. 1650, 391–2.

65. Miller, *John Milton and the Oldenburg Safeguard*, 26–7.

66. *MP*, 22 Oct. 1650, 162 (cf. 5 June 1651, 844; 13 May 1652, 1587).

67. Ibid. 19 Dec. 1650, 464.

of the regicide.[68] Later in 1651 the newsbook sustained a campaign for the execution of Christopher Love, supported those in the army who warned against clemency to him, and aimed weekly tirades at the misdeeds of Love's fellow Presbyterian clergy.[69] In 1645, during the treaty between king and parliament at Uxbridge, Love, as *Politicus* recalled,[70] had preached a fierce sermon against the king's misdeeds. That episode was often recalled to support a case which, under the Commonwealth, Milton like Nedham vigorously expounded: that in the first civil war the Presbyterians had been bent on Charles's destruction, but that through corruption and perversity they had fallen away from that resolve and had then vented spleen on those who stood firm for his punishment.[71]

Milton's partisanship in the radical cause was less dogmatic than Nedham's. It was also less frontal. Addressing a Continental audience that had to be persuaded of the legitimacy and buoyancy of the new regime, he naturally did not dwell on the divisions within it. His views emerge none the less. Like Nedham he wrote for a virtuous minority, heroic in the exploits that had created the Commonwealth but, within it, beleaguered by the forces of compromise. Milton's publications of the 1640s, like Nedham's, had scorned 'lukewarm', 'Laodicean', 'neutral' men, who cloaked their sloth and equivocation 'under the affected name of moderation'.[72] At that time he had religious controversy in mind. Now he transferred the sentiment to politics. Nedham, in vindicating the radicalism of *Britanicus* in the first civil war, had explained that he wrote it for 'the well-affected reader',[73] a term which would normally have included at least a wide range of Roundhead opinion, but which in Nedham's language was confined to the most committed side of it. In *Eikonoklastes* Milton spoke, in the same spirit, for 'the best-affected people'.[74] There too he complained that those Presbyterians who had not deserted to the king had taken refuge in 'neutrality'.[75] In his eyes as in Nedham's, the revolution of 1648–9 divided the nation into two parties, the friends of 'liberty' and those of 'slavery'.[76] If Milton recognizes that the allies of freedom are 'so few', Nedham acknowledges how 'few' are the 'noble souls' or 'heroic minds'

68. *MP*, 20 Feb. 1651, 603.
69. Worden, *Rump Parliament*, 245.
70. *MP*, 10 July 1651, 903.
71. *CP* iii. 193–4, 231; *CW* vii. 59–61.
72. *CP* i. 683, 690, 868; ii. 551 (cf. ibid. vi. 697).
73. *Mercurius Britanicus his Apologie*, 1. He there distinguished them from 'the malignant ignorant rabble': *Eikonoklastes* concludes with a denunciation of 'an inconstant, irrational, and image-doting rabble' (*CP* iii. 601).
74. *CP* iii. 512.
75. Ibid. 349, 600.
76. Ibid. vii. 363; *CW* vii. 511.

who have been faithful to it – and for that reason how easily they might be thwarted.[77] Both writers, to vindicate the occupancy of power by the 'few', re-define 'the people', on whose behalf Milton writes *Defensio* in 1651, and whom the editorials of *Politicus* in 1651–2 present as the proper source of power. 'It was the people' who abolished the House of Lords in 1649, claimed Milton. 'For whatever the better ... part of the legislature did, ... why may not the people be said to have done it?'[78] 'In this case', explained Nedham, 'these only are to be reckoned the people' who have not disqualified themselves by treason or neutrality from the revolutionary cause.[79] Nedham was thus able to declare, in terms close to Milton's, that 'had not the people been more constant, firm and resolute' than the Prebsyterian majority in parliament in the late 1640s, 'we might then have bid farewell to the liberties of England'.[80]

The memory of the regicide dominates the second phase of Milton's polemical prose, that of 1649–54. The execution of the king must be honoured, and its legacy must be protected, by resistance to the conciliatory and temporizing forces within the government. *Politicus* insisted that the regicide, 'that heroic and most noble act of justice', was 'the basis whereon the Commonwealth is founded. And if it ever be completed it must be by honouring and entrusting those noble instruments and hands who laid the foundation, or now help with open hearts to carry on the building.'[81] Another of Nedham's editorials repeated the point and the metaphor: 'phlegmatic souls of the moderate or middle temper' are 'neither good for the foundation, nor fit for the building of a republic'.[82] Milton, with the same perspective, brings the same metaphor to the soaring climax of *Defensio Secunda*. If the achievement of 1649 is lost, posterity will say that in the 'heroic action' and 'transcendent deed' of the regicide, which Milton's own prose, he tells us, has immortally 'embellished', 'the foundation was strongly laid... but it will be enquired, not without a disturbed emotion, who raised the superstructure, who completed the fabric!'[83] In *The Readie and Easie Way*, too, he hears posterity 'say of us, but scoffingly as of that foolish builder mentioned by our Saviour, who began to build a tower and was not able to finish it: where is this goodly tower of a Commonwealth, which the English boasted they would build,

77. *Case*, 113; *MP*, 24 Oct. 1650, 327. 78. *CW* vii. 357.
79. *MP*, 6 Nov. 1651, 1175. 80. Ibid. 15 Apr. 1652, 1523.
81. Ibid. 15 May 1651, 783–4. 82. Ibid. 21 Aug. 1651, 997. 83. *CW* viii. 253–5.

to overshadow kings and be another Rome in the West? The foundations indeed they laid gallantly', but they have 'left no memorial of their work remaining'.[84]

Like Nedham, Milton knows who the builders should be or have been. They are to be found among Nedham's 'party of its own'. Oliver Cromwell, *Defensio Secunda* tells him, must eschew his own accommodating instincts and choose as his principal counsellors the military heroes who achieved 'the deliverance of the commonwealth from tyranny' and 'brought even the king to judgement and refused to spare him when condemned'. 'I see not in what men we can at last confide', adds Milton, 'if we are not to have confidence in these and such as these.' So 'let us not suffer ourselves to think that there are any who can preserve it with greater diligence'. The words 'and such as these' are a necessary qualification, for although the five officers whom he then names had all had distinguished military careers against the royalists, only one of them, Edmund Whalley, had been a signatory of Charles I's death-warrant. Three of the others, John Desborough (or Disbrowe), Robert Overton, and John Lambert, had, admittedly, been on military duty outside London at the time, though Lambert would perhaps in any case have been unlikely to agree to take part in the trial. The fifth, Charles Fleetwood, a man of soldierly valour but political hesitancy, had withdrawn from politics well before the regicide and had returned to them only after it. Under the protectorate, it is true, he, with Desborough and Overton, would oppose the anti-monarchical turn of the regime. Overton would do so with defiance and at a bitter personal cost. Even so, Milton's rhetoric, and the conveniences of eulogy, cover some cracks in his thinking. In early 1652 he told the envoy from the German principality of Oldenburg, Hermann Mylius, that too many members of the council of state were ill-equipped for rule because they were mere 'sons of Mars and Mercury' – soldiers and merchants.[85]

Yet his public face gave away nothing of that sentiment. Outwardly he viewed only with reverence the army which steered through the purge and the regicide and pressed for radical measures thereafter. His praises of it were at odds with the outlook of the moderates who remained in parliament, and who aimed to distance the regime from its revolutionary

84. *CP* vii. 357.

85. Von Maltzahn, *Milton's 'History of Britain'*, 44; Martin Dzelzainis, 'Milton and the Protectorate in 1658', in Armitage *et al.*, eds., *Milton and Republicanism*, 198–9.

origins and to subordinate the soldiery to civilian rule. Their hostility to the army's political pretensions, and the support their stance commanded, were starkly demonstrated in February 1649, when the Rump resolved to omit from the council of state the two army officers who bore most responsibility for Pride's Purge, Henry Ireton and Thomas Harrison.[86] The civilian moderates would not have enjoyed Milton's reminder, in *Defensio*, that in the winter of 1648–9 'our soldiers showed better judgement than our senators, and saved the commonwealth by their arms when the other by their votes had almost ruined it'.[87] With Nedham, too, Milton looked to the beleaguered party of virtue outside parliament, which remained true while the rest fell away. 'They who were ever faithfullest to the cause', he reflected, and who 'freely aided' parliament 'in person or with their substance', were 'slighted' and exploited by the parliamentary leaders.[88]

In the Long Parliament before Pride's Purge, ruled Milton, there were 'some indeed men of wisdom and integrity', but 'the rest, and to be sure the greatest part', had succumbed to ambition or corruption.[89] Nothing he ever wrote about Pride's Purge suggested that it had cured the assembly of those evils. The virtue of the coup was to have 'delivered' the nation from royalism and Presbyterianism and to have paved the way for the regicide. But the army had wanted to go further, and dissolve the parliament entirely.[90] Even between the purge and the regicide there were many sitting MPs of 'neutral' or 'lukewarm' or 'moderate' disposition. There were many more thereafter, when a large number of members who had kept away from Westminster in those weeks returned. There is a mighty contrast between Milton's professions of adulation for the army and the regicide and his representations of the Commonwealth in 1649–53. His pamphlets of the earlier 1640s had been packed with high eulogy of the Long Parliament, even when he doubted the virtue and policies of that assembly. Yet in his propaganda for the Commonwealth, which says so much in celebration of the regicide, there is next to nothing in commendation of the parliament that ruled after it. Nedham's eulogies of the civilian rulers of the republic can seem forced, but at least he supplied them.

Milton does, in *Defensio*, describe the republic as 'more potent' than the monarchy before it,[91] but its might appears to lie in its military prowess

86. Worden, *Rump Parliament*, 74–5, 79. 87. *CW* vii. 55. 88. *CP* v. 445.
89. Ibid. 443. 90. The authoritative account is Underdown, *Pride's Purge*.
91. *CW* vii. 17.

rather than in any civilian political virtue. Just after the regicide he looks forward to 'the flourishing deeds of a reformed Commonwealth'. Even then, however, his injunction to critics of the recent coup to leave the decision to 'the uprighter sort' of the magistrates, 'in whom faction least hath prevailed above the law of nature and right reason',[92] does not suggest unqualified confidence. In May 1649 he wishes that the 'ensuing actions' of the parliament 'may correspond and prove worthy that impartial and noble piece of justice'.[93] Yet those momentarily expressed hopes, which are never particularized, carry little if any conviction, and nothing in his subsequent writing suggests that they were fulfilled. When the military leaders of the Commonwealth were vilified, he responded with celebrations of their matchless heroism. But when the civilian leaders in the Commons were called 'dregs and scum' because of their complicity in the regicide, he supplied a muted refutation which stretched only to the statement that the people esteemed them 'worthy to sit in parliament'.[94] When Cromwell and his soldiers forcibly dissolved the Rump, Milton welcomed its expulsion. It had had an essential use until the victory at Worcester, as the standing authority behind the military campaigns against the Stuart cause. Once the royalists were defeated in 1651 his interest in defending the regime lapsed. It was to the achievement of the regicide, and to it alone, that as a political writer he remained committed. To that cause, as we shall soon see, he devoted not merely his eloquence but the resources and arts of journalism.

92. *CP* iii. 197.　　93. Ibid. 236, 311.

94. Ibid. 311, 315. One of the letters in *Politicus* from Leiden observes that the Commonwealth's enemies in Holland ignorantly ascribe the 'memorable act of justice' of January 1649 to 'the vilest and basest scum of the earth' (*MP*, 2 Oct. 1651, 1100).

9
Milton in Journalism

As writers of propaganda, Milton and Nedham were not immediately answerable to the parliament which had assumed sovereignty in 1649. They wrote at the behest of its executive arm, the council of state, which also employed Milton to write and translate diplomatic correspondence. Most members of the council, an annually elected body of forty-one members, also sat in parliament, but those who were not MPs included the president, Milton's and Nedham's friend John Bradshaw. It may have been partly because he did not have a seat at Westminster that he was made president, for the principle that all MPs were entitled to equal authority was essential to such harmonious relations as were achieved among them. Not everyone admired his chairmanship. The MP and councillor Bulstrode Whitelocke, always ready with disparaging comments on colleagues whose jobs he thought he could do better, remarked that Bradshaw, whose duty as chairman was 'only to gather the sense of the council and to state the question', 'seemed not much versed in such businesses' and 'spent much of their time in urging his own long arguments'.[1] Whitelocke may have had other grounds for discontent. He was a trimmer, no friend to the regicide. When, in December 1650, parliament resolved to enter the proceedings of the regicide court in its records, it also instructed the three Commissioners of the Great Seal, Whitelocke, his temporizing colleague Sir Thomas Widdrington, and the regicide John Lisle (another of Whitelocke's enemies), to register the court's proceedings in the records of Chancery.[2] It is easy to imagine Whitelocke's and Widdrington's discomfort and to envisage the pleasure that radical MPs, who resented their influence, would have taken in it. Bradshaw championed the radical cause that repelled Whitelocke. In going out of their way to laud him – Nedham in *Politicus*

1. Whitelocke, *Memorials*, ii. 552, 558. 2. *MP*, 19 Dec. 1650, 464.

in the summer and autumn of 1650, Milton in *Defensio Secunda* – the two writers were not merely paying tribute to a friend. They were hailing a figure whose name and presence had become a symbol of the achievement of regicide and of adherence to the principles that had warranted it. It is likely (as we shall find in Chapter 12) that the eulogy of Bradshaw in *Defensio Secunda*, though published in 1654, was written under the Rump, when he was in the thick of its political struggles.

In the winter of 1650–1, when Nedham celebrated parliament's decision to replace the statue of Charles I in the Old Exchange, and when Milton glorified the regicide in *Defensio*, Bradshaw's role became contentious. There were moves to unseat him from the presidency.[3] He survived, but only until the annual elections to the council in November 1651, after which a monthly rotation of the chairmanship was introduced. His principal antagonist in the winter of 1650–1 was Cromwell, who, though away fighting in Scotland, kept closely in touch with the proceedings of the government and exercised what influence he could upon it. The conflict of Bradshaw and Cromwell, which opened up in the wake of Dunbar, represented the opposing directions in which the Commonwealth might move. Bradshaw would never have aspired to the single eminence that Cromwell acquired. During the Interregnum, single rule was or became anathema to him. In January 1649, it is true, he and Cromwell had been working allies. Cromwell's political and military authority, and Bradshaw's chairmanship, had forced through the trial and the sentence. Yet Cromwell, though he never regretted the king's death, was dismayed by the purge of the Commons which had been necessary to achieve it, and which gave so much power to the revolutionary minority. Here was Milton's recurrent dilemma. Among the 'deliverers' of 1649 there was none who could begin to rival Cromwell's stature or achievements. Yet the same man was also the supreme opponent of the policies favoured by Milton as by Nedham and by Bradshaw. Cromwell never wanted, what *Politicus* demanded, the restriction of authority to the Commonwealth's 'party of its own'. In the weeks before the king's trial, he tried to reverse Pride's Purge. For the remainder of the Commonwealth period he would strive to persuade MPs who had voluntarily withdrawn from parliament in 1648–9 to return to it. He was mistrustful of the engagement of loyalty imposed by the Rump, and sought to limit its enforcement. He opposed the execution

3. Nickolls, pp. 50–1.

of Christopher Love in 1651.[4] Those courses set him at odds with the bolder opinion in the army which Milton and Nedham supported, and deepened the radicals' mistrust of Cromwell.

In the mid-winter of 1650–1, just before *Politicus* took up Milton's literary cause, a contest between Bradshaw and Cromwell for the chancellorship of Oxford University was resolved in Cromwell's favour.[5] The appointment was no merely ornamental one. Cromwell would make maximum use of the post to try to change the religious and political complexion of the university.[6] If the learned Bradshaw shared Milton's views on educational reform and on the need to reform the universities, no doubt he would have done the same – but with fewer compromises with the forces of conservatism. Before his election at Oxford, Cromwell had already made it clear to the leaders of Cambridge University that he would resist any attempt to use the imposition of the Rump's engagement of loyalty to purge moderates from their posts there.[7] Nedham's *Politicus*, by contrast, complained of the survival at Oxford, despite the engagement, of 'malignant' and 'odd-affected university-governors' and of 'high and insolent' Presbyterian clergy.[8] There were other grounds of difference between Cromwell and the radicals. Not least, he earned their 'censure' by his policy of accommodation with the moderate Presbyterians in Scotland.[9] *Politicus*, where Scottish Presbyterians were an incessant target, favoured the alternative policy of subjugating the Scots to the English republic and imposing radical policies on them. Nedham's campaign for the Commonwealth's 'party of its own' gained impetus from October 1650. Until that month *Politicus* (with whatever interlinear ambiguity) had bestowed the highest praise on Cromwell.[10] Now those tributes stopped. When Cromwell was elected at Oxford early in the new year of 1651, *Politicus*, which a few months earlier would have taken the opportunity for hyperbole on the general's behalf, reported the event in curtly neutral terms.[11]

Among Nedham's fellow admirers of Bradshaw was a former captain in the new model army who was radically opposed to monarchical power. This was George Bishop, the assistant in the intelligence system of Thomas Scot, who had long had contacts with Nedham[12] and was now

4. His political stances of 1648–53 are examined in my *Rump Parliament*.
5. Spalding, ed., *Diary of Bulstrode Whitelocke*, 254.
6. Worden, 'Cromwellian Oxford'.
7. Abbott, ed., *Writings and Speeches*, ii. 281.
8. *MP*, 8 Aug. 1650, 144; 21 Nov. 1650, 391–2.
9. Nickolls, 21, 58. Cf. *MP*, 17 Oct. 1650, 319–20 (a letter probably written to Bradshaw: cf. below, p. 327 n. 6); 13 Mar. 1651, 640.
10. Above, pp. 65–8.
11. *MP*, 16 Jan. 1651, 521.
12. NA, SP46/95, fo. 190.

the supplier of his news. Bishop tried to bring Cromwell round to the president's continuation in his post. He backed Bradshaw's policies too. In December Bradshaw and Bishop both wrote to Cromwell – who had a way of pursuing his own semi-independent foreign policy[13] – to argue for the more robust diplomatic measures that *Politicus* also favoured, and to alert him to the evidence of divine displeasure that the two men attributed to the regime's failure to adopt them. Bishop was also Bradshaw's ally in domestic politics. In December 1650 some royalist conspirators, whose activities Bishop had uncovered, were put to death after a trial in Norwich. The refusal of mercy delighted the Commonwealth's 'party of its own'. Bradshaw tried to persuade Cromwell that 'the terror of the example may happily do good and help to prevent numerous mischiefs still plotting of that kind'.[14] *Politicus* agreed: the plotters had been executed 'to the terror of all evil-doers, but to the rejoicing of them that do well ... the parliament's authority hath not been more publicly manifested in any place, or thing, than in the carriage of this present affair'.[15] Bishop, delighting in the 'zeal' of the judges, inferred from the fate of the conspiracy that 'God hath cursed that kingly race' of the Stuarts 'and whoever hath to do with it'. None the less Bishop was distressed to observe 'the temper' of parliament and the general 'neglect of justice and righteousness'. 'A tender heart', he observed, 'would weep for the day of visitation that is coming,' for there were 'too few honest hearts among us', a defect which he linked to the moves to unseat Bradshaw from the presidency.[16] His gloom was echoed three weeks later in *Politicus*, in one of the newsbook's abrupt shifts into Puritan gear, when Nedham published a letter from a soldier in Scotland who lamented that in England 'too many study faction': 'self-greatness is too much eyed and aimed at' by the enemies of a God who 'will purge out all our ... dross'.[17] In July, Bishop demanded the execution of Christopher Love and warned his colleagues in the army not to 'draw your own blood and others on your heads' by seeking clemency for him. With Bradshaw, Bishop would bitterly resent Cromwell's usurpation of power in 1653. He was sacked from his role in intelligence after it, and thereafter conspired, with Bradshaw, against the protectoral regime.

Even moderates in parliament recognized that the regicide, which had established the new government, had to be vindicated by it. With Nedham,

13. Cf. *MP*, 2 Jan. 1651, 501. 14. Nickolls, 39. 15. *MP*, 2 Jan. 1651, 491.
16. Nickolls, 49–51. 17. *MP*, 6 Feb. 1651, 568–9; cf. Nickolls, 36.

Milton took attack to be the best form of defence. His *Defensio*, published in 1651, does not merely justify the trial and execution of the king. It glorifies it, in language which we have seen to be strikingly close to that of *Politicus*, and which moderates must have found uncomfortable reading. On the council, over which Bradshaw presided, the radicals did not have a built-in majority. But they did have a built-in advantage, in the regime's need, which it fell to the executive arm of government to meet, to establish its authority and, to that end, to create a distinctive and confident image of itself. The council gave a warm reception to Milton's *Defensio* and sought to make maximum use of it in the propaganda war. In June 1651, in an unusual gesture of fulsome congratulation, it thanked him for his 'many good services' to the Commonwealth, 'particularly' in refuting 'the calumnies and invectives' of Salmasius, and declared its 'resentment and good acceptance of the same'.[18] In the same month the council fought and won a battle with parliament to enable Milton to keep his lodgings at Whitehall, for which the Commons sought other uses.[19] But when, in November, the council changed to a rotating presidency, Milton's stock fell. Behind its decline there lay – though not, or anyway not necessarily, through any interposition of Cromwell himself – the lord general's return to Westminster after the Battle of Worcester in September.

For Cromwell, whose political influence was now at its highest point since his departure for Ireland in 1649, had embarked on a series of policies, 'catholic projects' as they got called,[20] to broaden the base of the regime and to reconcile its more malleable critics. At Westminster much less was heard now about the regicide. It is likely to have been at Milton's suggestion that Hermann Mylius, the agent from Oldenburg, chose the third anniversary of the regicide in January 1652 for the occasion of a letter to Bradshaw, whose support in Mylius's own protracted negotiations with the government the agent needed. The letter ingratiatingly recalled that earlier day, 'fatal to monarchs and monarchies' and 'natal day to the Parliament of the Commonwealth'.[21] But this year parliament took no notice of the anniversary, and there would be no more official celebrations of it. References to the regicide in *Politicus* ceased in the summer of 1652. When, in a different publication in November of that year, with which Bradshaw reportedly helped him, Nedham reminded parliament

18. Lewalski, p. 255. 19. *CP* iv. 144–5. 20. Nickolls, 85.
21. Miller, *John Milton and the Oldenburg Safeguard*, 156–7.

of the 'zeal and magnanimity' of the regicide, that 'highest act of justice (when justice sat more gloriously enthroned than ever it did before on any earthly tribunal)', his language already looked dated.[22] So, in another publication a little later, did his praise of *Eikonoklastes*, a work 'fairly written by so white a hand'. There, too, in an implied rebuke to the indifference of moderates within the government, Nedham plaintively wondered at the Commonwealth's failure to track down and punish the author of the work to which *Eikonoklastes* had replied, *Eikon Basilike*, 'so gross an imposture'.[23]

In November 1651 the impact of Cromwell's return to Westminster was reflected in the annual elections by the Commons of the members of the council of state, in which Cromwell himself inevitably topped the poll. The elections produced a strong shift in the political balance of the council's membership, to the loss of the radicals.[24] Bradshaw, no doubt to soften the blow, was allowed to remain president for the first month of the system of rotation that was now introduced, and he remained a councillor for the remainder of the Rump period. Yet his prominence was gone. Under the new council Milton almost immediately lost his lodgings, and had to move to a new home in Petty France. His reappointment as Latin Secretary was held up for four weeks. Then, in January, the council of state seized the published copies, and arrested the publisher, of a heretical tract whose publication he had taken it on himself to license. He would himself be interrogated about the book the following month. Immediately after the council's intervention he ceased to act as licenser of *Politicus*. At this stage, it is true, his remaining sight was vanishing, and some reduction of his workload may have seemed desirable. Yet the council continued to rely on him for less contentious duties. Then, in February 1652, the month of his interrogation over the heretical tract, he told Mylius that he had received 'harsh words', and been 'stamped on', for showing state papers to him, and for corresponding privately with him, without the council's approval.[25] It must have been an uncomfortable period for Milton, whose opinion of his masters would not have been raised by the experience.[26] When Mylius's negotiations ran into difficulty, Milton gave him an explanation that brings out his view of the majority both in parliament and on the new council. The

22. Selden, *Of the Dominion of the Seas*, ep. ded.
23. *Cat May Look upon a King*, 81–4 (cf. Nedham, *Interest will not Lie*, 23).
24. Worden, *Rump Parliament*, 280–2.
25. Lewalski, 263.
26. The episode is recounted in Miller, *John Milton and the Oldenburg Safeguard*, 179–80.

envoy's problems arose, Milton explained to him, from 'the inexperience and wilfulness of those who enjoyed the plurality of votes' on the council. They were 'in public political affairs mostly inexperienced', and of such men 'the more powerful part of the Commonwealth consisted'. So Mylius must not blame 'the sounder men', whose wishes were frustrated.[27] As usual with Milton, virtue lay in the minority.

★★

Allies for radicalism at home, Milton and Nedham also joined to promote it abroad. Milton, who describes the struggle, not of 'one people only', but of 'the universal race of men, against the enemies of man's freedom', tells 'listening Europe' that 'I am bringing back, bringing home to every nation, liberty, so long driven out, so long an exile'.[28] Nedham's aim, in addressing 'all the states of Europe', is that 'the people of every commonweal which mean to preserve their freedom may be informed how to steer their course'.[29] With Nedham – and with the side of Andrew Marvell that looks forward to the emancipation by England of 'all states not free' – Milton hopes in *Defensio* that the regicide, 'that wholesome lesson to the rest of the kings' as he calls it,[30] will start a chain of liberation. Nedham reports on the 'tottering monarchy' of France:[31] *Defensio* asks its readers to 'take my word for it' that 'the right of kings seems to be tottering, and even hastening to its own downfall'.[32] The 'happy fate' of Marvell's free states, and the 'happiness' that Nedham predicts for the English republic and for republics on the Continent,[33] are matched by the 'future happiness' which Milton promises his countrymen when in 1649 they 'reject a king… wherein we have the honour to precede other nations, who are labouring to be our followers'.[34] Near the end of *Eikonoklastes*, in a fleeting revival of his apocalyptic vision of world revolution in 1641–2, Milton proclaimed that 'the earth itself hath too long groaned under the burden of' regal 'injustice, disorder and irreligion', and that it is the appointed task of God's saints 'to overcome those European kings, which receive their power, not from God, but from

27. Ibid. 171–2.
28. *CW* viii. 13, 15, 19.
29. *MP*, 19 Sept. 1650, 255; 13 May 1652, 1586.
30. *CW* vii. 23.
31. *MP*, 4 July 1650, 63; 19 Sept. 1650, 232.
32. *CW* vii. 93 (cf. *CP* iv. 924).
33. Above, p. 69.
34. *CP* iii. 236 (cf. *CW* viii. 185). For Milton's equation of 'happiness' with self-government see too *CP* iii. 236; v. 443; vii. 427 – though the goal of national 'happiness' was a frequent theme of his, not confined to that preoccupation.

the Beast'.[35] Milton's and Nedham's international cause was inadvertently assisted by the arguments of Salmasius, who sought to rally the crowns of Europe against the English republic, and who, by portraying the regicide as an attack on kingship everywhere, enabled his English adversaries to answer on the same ground.

Milton's Latin 'defences' were written with French and Dutch readers especially in mind.[36] In the Netherlands they were intended to sway native opinion against the royalist exiles, 'beggarly refugees' as he called them, who flocked there.[37] According to *Politicus*, the embassy of St John and Strickland, which left for Holland less than three weeks after the publication of *Defensio*, took with it copies for distribution there (or anyway planned to take them).[38] The Dutch representative in London bought twenty-five copies for members of the provincial government of Holland.[39] During the embassy a correspondent in Leiden reported that the book was 'in everybody's hands', and that a Dutch translation was being 'hawked about'.[40] With Nedham, Milton recalls the heroic resistance of the Dutch against Spanish tyranny in the late sixteenth century. With him he draws a contrast between the 'Orange faction',[41] which has betrayed that inheritance, and the party of freedom in Holland, whom he calls 'true offspring of the ancient liberties of their country'.[42] Milton highlights the attempted Orange coup in Amsterdam in the summer of 1650, and the peril to liberty which it posed. Again the wording of the two writers comes close. 'That liberty which had been won by so many years of toil and battle would have perished from your midst', recalls *Defensio*, 'had not the providential death of that headstrong youth', William II of Orange, 'allowed it to breathe again.'[43] The designs on the 'free republic' by 'the House of Orange', concurred *Politicus* with William's death in mind, 'had they not been strangely prevented by a miracle of providence,

35. *CP* iii. 598.
36. Thomas N. Corns, 'Milton and the Characteristics of a Free Commonwealth', in Armitage *et al.*, eds., *Milton and Republicanism*, 32.
37. *CW* viii. 177.
38. *MP*, 6 Mar. 1651, 638.
39. Leo Miller, 'Milton's *Defensio* Ordered Wholesale for the State of Holland', *Notes and Queries*, 231 (1986), 33.
40. French, iii. 24–5.
41. *CW* viii. 37, 141 (cf. pp. 169, 175). (The legitimacy of my use of *Defensio Secunda*, which I quote here, to illustrate Milton's views on this subject in the Rump period will become evident in Ch. 12.)
42. *CW* vii. 19 (cf. ibid. viii. 193–5; *CP* iv. 1072–5); *MP*, 13 May 1652, 1586.
43. *CP* iv. 312.

might in all probability have reduced' the Dutch 'under the yoke of kingly power'.[44]

Milton and Nedham did their best to embroil Milton's contest with Salmasius in the struggle for liberty in the United Provinces. They accused Salmasius – baselessly, though Milton's imagination brought local colour to the story – of having been 'hired' to write the book by the House of Orange.[45] For how was it, Milton asked in *Defensio*, that *Defensio Regia*, the work in which Salmasius attacked the regicide and pleaded for divine-right monarchy, had come to be 'written by a free man in a free state', let alone 'in the most excellent Dutch republic': written, moreover, at the University of Leiden, where Salmasius was professor, and whose foundation in 1575 had commemorated the heroic relief of the Spanish siege of the city in the previous year'?[46] 'Is it not fine then', agreed *Politicus*, 'that Holland, a Commonwealth, should employ Salmasius, the pander of tyranny', 'that dirty and most dissolute parasite of kings'?[47] It was in connection with the newsbook's tactics that Anthony Wood called Nedham a 'great crony' of Milton. Nedham, he accurately recalled, made it his 'usual practice ... to abuse Salmasius ... as Milton had done before in his *Defensio*'.[48] Nedham's invective against Salmasius is in keeping with Milton's. The newsbook followed closely the reception of 'Mr Milton's book' in Holland, remarked on the hostility to it at princely courts, and greeted attempts to suppress it as evidence that its 'doctrine' of freedom had rattled the friends of monarchy and was catching on among 'the ingenuous sort of men'.[49]

Politicus anticipated, and seems to have hoped to provoke, replies to *Defensio* from Salmasius or others, which would heighten the controversy and enable Milton to respond in writings that would raise it further. At last, in late August 1652, there was published at The Hague the anonymous work *Regii Sanguinis Clamor*, almost certainly written by the Anglican clergyman Peter du Moulin. Milton got the authorship wrong. He attributed it to Salmasius's friend Alexander More, a professor at Amsterdam, who had had a small role in the publication but had not written the main text. Thanks to that error, More, like Salmasius before him, would be subjected to page after page of scurrilous invective from Milton's pen. As Wood says, Milton abused More 'not only ... in his Answers, but by his friend Nedham in his

44. *MP*, 13 May 1652, 1587–8 (cf. 16 Jan. 1651, 529); W. McNeill, 'Milton and Salmasius, 1649', *English Historical Review*, 80 (1965), 107–8.
45. *CW* viii. 29, 141; *MP*, 22 July 1652, 1751.
46. *CW* vii. 71–3, viii. 69 (cf. viii. 193–5).
47. *MP*, 22 July 1652, 1751.
48. Darbishire, 44.
49. *MP*, 10 July 1651, 915.

Politicus, whereby the reputation of that learned man [More] was severely touched'.[50] It was in reply to *Clamor* (as for convenience the book may be called) that Milton published *Defensio Secunda* in 1654. Next year, in reply to More's own response to that work, he published *Pro Se Defensio*, his 'defence' of himself. There, as proof of More's authorship of *Clamor*, he quoted a letter sent from Holland in September 1652, where *Clamor* is described as 'that book of More's'. The letter, Milton added, had appeared in 'the public journal published in this country on Thursdays'.[51] It had indeed been printed by *Politicus*, on Thursday 30 September 1652, where it was presented as an epistle from Leiden.[52]

★★

Scholars have noted resemblances of style between editorials in *Politicus* in 1650–1 and Milton's writings for the Commonwealth. 'In serious polemical passages', it has been acknowledged, 'Milton's style resembles that of Nedham more closely than that of any other author.'[53] Those great late Victorian commentators David Masson and S. R. Gardiner were so impressed by the parallels as to wonder whether Milton had written for the newsbook.[54] Their suggestion appeared to be invalidated when it was discovered that editorials in which they had suspected Milton's hand had been lifted from Nedham's tract of May 1650, *The Case of the Commonwealth*, which bears Nedham's name and his alone.[55] There are in fact many parallels or near-parallels of phrasing, which Masson and Gardiner did not record, between Milton's tracts and passages of *Politicus* that had not appeared in *The Case*. In most instances, however, there is, or may be, a simple explanation of them. Milton wrote his tracts of 1649–51, in which most of the moments of his prose that correspond to passages of *Politicus* are to be found, before the analogous material appeared in the newsbook. Nedham, we can or could infer, simply took material from his colleague's work. If so, in using it he adapted it. For even when the resemblances are closest they generally carry inflections of tone or phrasing that characterize Nedham's

50. Darbishire, 45. 51. *CW* ix. 29. 52. *MP*, 30 Sep. 1652, 1910.

53. *CP* iv. 124 (cf. ibid. 49–58). cf. Dobranski, *Milton, Authorship, and the Book Trade*, 46–50.

54. Masson, iv. 334–5; S. R. Gardiner, *History of the Commonwealth and Protectorate*, 4 vols. (New York, 1965 edn.), ii. 17–20.

55. J. Milton French, 'Milton, Needham, and *Mercurius Politicus*', *Studies in Philology*, 33 (1936), 236–52; Elmer A. Beller, 'Milton and *Mercurius Politicus*', *Huntington Library Quarterly*, 5 (1942), 479–87.

prose. His use of Milton's writings in those instances, even if that is all it is, has its own import, for we can be sure that, at least as long as Milton acted as licenser of the newsbook, Nedham's borrowings had, if nothing more, his friend's approval. But borrowings, in those many cases, are the most that we can or need assume them to have been.

Yet there is material in *Politicus* which that explanation cannot accommodate. In an editorial of 4 March 1652 we find a passage that reopens the question which Masson and Gardiner raised. By March 1652, it is true, Milton had ceased to license the newsbook, but he had by no means lost interest in its content. The editorial, which defies the desire within the government to forget about the regicide, defends that 'noble act of justice'. It then asks its readers' 'leave to show (what I once published upon another occasion), that 'tis no new thing for kings to be deprived, or punished with death, for their crimes in government'. No surviving work that is known or suspected to be by Nedham answers to that description. Who then is the 'I'? The use of italic will help us answer. In the usual manner of *Politicus*, the editorial summons historical examples to support its claim. One of them is the demise of Amaziah, King of Judah, who '*was put to death for his idolatry*'. His execution is presented as a warrant not only for the punishment of Charles I but for its manner. The English regicides, as Milton himself remembers in his tribute to Bradshaw,[56] took pride in their courage in bringing the king to trial, rather than in making away with him, as Edward II and Richard II had been removed, by conspiracy or assassination. According to the editorial in *Politicus*, the death sentence on Amaziah '*seems by the words*' – the words, presumably, of 2 Kings 14: 19–21, where the slaying and replacement of Amaziah are recorded – 'to have been done by judicial process, *in a full assembly of the people*, and speaks much to the honour of those' – the judges of Charles I – 'who have had the courage to imitate so heroic an act of justice, by a solemn and serious proceeding'.[57] That seems an effortful if not improbable slant on the biblical text, which is silent on the manner of Amaziah's death.[58] Yet *Politicus* was not alone in offering it. A year earlier *Defensio* had set out to prove the case about the punishment of kings which the 'I' of the editorial remembers making. One of the kings was Amaziah, 'a cowardly *idolatrous king*', who

56. *CW* viii. 159 (cf. vii. 49, 553; *CP* iii. 329).

57. *MP*, 4 Mar. 1652, 1442–4.

58. Cf. James A. Montgomery, *A Critical and Exegetical Commentary on the Books of Kings* (Edinburgh, 1951), 442.

'*was put to death, not by a few conspirators, but rather, it should seem* ['quod verisimilius est'], *by the nobility and people*'.[59] The parallel is a momentary one. Yet – at least in the absence of any alternative candidate – the passage of the editorial seems inexplicable other than as a reference to *Defensio*.[60]

Even without that sentence, the editorial is one that comes particularly close to Milton's writings. It is in it that we learn that 'the greater part' of men 'was ever inclined to adore the golden idol of tyranny', and there too that we are informed, in words so close to those of *Eikonoklastes* and *Defensio*, that 'in the monuments of the Grecian and Roman freedom we find those nations were wont to heap all the honours they could invent, by public rewards, consecration of statues and crown of laurel upon such worthy patriots; and as if all on earth were too little, they enrolled them in heaven among their deities'. This does not mean that the whole editorial was written by Milton. It evidently was not, for there are passages that have Nedham's distinctive touch. There are attacks on the 'lordly' or aristocratic 'interest' that lies behind kingly power, and on the dangers of an oligarchical 'standing senate', which have no parallel in Milton's tracts, but which recur time and again in *Politicus*.[61] The prose of the two writers has, by some process, intertwined.

The same 'I' appears to have spoken in another editorial in *Politicus*, ten months earlier, on 15 May 1651. That editorial, too, vindicates the regicide. Where the later one calls it 'a noble act of justice' and 'so heroic an act of justice', in the earlier one it is 'that heroic and most noble act of justice'. It was also, adds the earlier one, 'an act agreeing with the law of God (which observes no respect of persons), consonant to the laws of men,

59. *CW* vii. 235. But see above, pp. vii–viii.
60. Even if an alternative source were found, we would still have to ask whether *Defensio* itself was indebted to it. That the words were not Nedham's may also be suggested by his omission of them when, in 1656, he republished the passage in *The Excellencie of a Free State* (p. 45). J. Milton French spotted the autobiographical passage in the editorial, but uncharacteristically confused himself in explaining it. He supposed it to refer to *The Tenure of Kings and Magistrates*, but, perhaps aware that no passage of that tract is close enough to it to warrant that inference, changed or half-changed his mind about the authorship even as he wrote. 'To the best of my ability to find out', he declared, 'this is virtually the only sentence' in the editorials of *Politicus* 'which can with any safety be attributed to Milton.' But a few lines later he judged that, 'in short', 'Milton *may* have written it' (French, iii. 205 n.).
61. *MP*, 19 Feb. 1652, 1410–13; Worden, 'Marchamont Nedham and the Beginnings of English Republicanism', 63–4, 68. (The 'lordly states' in Milton's translation of Psalm 82 (l. 2) do not carry the social connotations of Nedham's writing (cf. *CP* i. 420; iii. 202, 237, 458; *Paradise Lost* XII. 93).) The editorial uses the phrase 'the cockatrice in the egg', a favourite image of Nedham.

and the practices of all well-ordered states and kingdoms (not excepting even France and Spain), as I shall make it evident ere long (among many other particulars) in a set treatise, by a cloud of instances derived from the scope of holy writ, the principles of right reason, law and example'.[62] No such work seems to have appeared. It looks, however, as if the editorial of March 1652 was based on a plan or draft for the treatise promised in the earlier one. For the later one accomplishes, in a compressed form, what the 'set treatise' was intended to achieve. 'We can collect precedents out of all nations', it announces, to prove the accountability of kings. The claim is supported by examples from biblical, classical, and European history, instances involving the French and Spanish monarchies among them.[63] Again, however, the editorial is unlikely to be Milton's alone. The promise to prove the argument 'in a set treatise, by a cloud of instances' echoes the distinctive language of Nedham, whose yearning to demonstrate the full range of his learning in a treatise is a *motif* of his prose.[64]

We have to guess how writing by Milton got into *Politicus*, and how it got stitched together with writing by Nedham. How deliberate was the presence of Milton's 'I'? Did Nedham borrow material from work that Milton was drafting for other purposes, and merge it with his own prose, perhaps with the haste of an editor with deadlines to meet?[65] Milton does seem, in 1651–2, to have been writing prose that he expected to use against Salmasius in due course.[66] Whatever explanation we envisage, it must involve a close working partnership between Milton and Nedham, one geared to the immediate needs of propaganda.

62. *MP*, 15 May 1651, 784. (Like the editorial of March 1652, the passage had not appeared in Nedham's *The Case of the Commonwealth*.)

63. *MP*, 4 Mar. 1652, 1443–4.

64. Above, Ch. 1.

65. One detail may suggest that Nedham exercised a revising hand over Milton's material. We have seen that, in *Defensio*, Amaziah is put to death 'by the nobility and the people', whereas in *Politicus* he is sentenced by 'a full assembly of the people'. The newsbook, with the vein of social radicalism that is foreign to Milton, developed a sustained attack on 'the power and ambition', throughout history, of the 'nobility', and argued on behalf of 'the people's assemblies' against it. On the other hand the change in *Politicus* could merely be a tactical adjustment, made to meet the difficulty that the regicide court had not had the sanction of the House of Lords. Elsewhere in *Defensio* Milton, apparently for that reason, mounts his own brief defence of autonomous 'assemblies of the people' (*CW* vii. 229; cf. *CP* iv. 103). Edmund Ludlow (*Voyce*, 137) vindicated the killing of Amaziah as an aristocratic coup.

66. Below, Ch. 12. There we shall find that *Defensio Secunda* was mostly written under the Rump. In it Milton refers to *Defensio* by a phrase, 'libro altero', that can be translated either as 'another book' or as 'the other book' (below, p. 268). Perhaps the words in the editorial 'I once published upon another occasion' are a translation, altered to meet the circumstances of publication in a newsbook, of the same or a similar phrase in a draft of *Defensio Secunda*.

It is not always an easy process to compare the known writings of Milton with the publications of Nedham, which can have such different formal properties. There is particular difficulty in setting the long Latin treatises which Milton wrote in reply to individual adversaries beside the brief editorials which Nedham composed in English against the range of the republic's enemies. None the less the styles and polemical manners of the two authors are more often than not distinguishable. Besides, behind the compositions of the two writers there lay years of at least partly separate reading. For while Milton's tracts, in their use of appeals to historical examples, share an argumentative method with the newsbook, the examples chosen by him and those selected by Nedham overlap only occasionally. So there were limits to the partnership of the two authors. The number of words from Milton's pen in *Politicus* may be small, though if so the number that borrow from it is much larger. Even so, Milton's presence in *Politicus* forbids us to place him where his representations of himself invite us to situate and salute him, in lonely eminence above the collaborative world of civil war polemic. We must wonder whether, even in the 'single-handed' exertions and the oratorical flights of *Defensio*, the conversation of Nedham is ever far away.[67]

★★

There is at least one other moment in *Politicus* when Milton's hand is surely present. It occurs in the letter from Leiden which appeared in *Politicus* in September 1652, and which Milton used in 1655 in ascribing *Clamor* to Alexander More. It is a sportive passage, which demonstrates, alongside the lofty ambition of the Latin 'defences', the joint enjoyment by Milton and Nedham of a heady comic zest. Milton had directed that talent at the bishops in 1641–2. In the 1650s, when he turned it against Alexander More, it was fortified by an indifference to factual accuracy and to scruple – virtues that had not been his priorities in the anti-episcopal tracts themselves – that will surprise anyone accustomed to taking his character at his own valuation. The letter of September 1652, written about three weeks after the publication

67. A tract of 1651, *The Life and Reign of King Charls. Or, The Pseudo-Martyr Discovered*, has been attributed to Milton. It is surely not his (Parker, 1001), but there is material peripheral to the main body of its text that may be by Nedham. Among it is the description (p. 179) of Milton's 'white mittens' in refuting the king's cause, which recalls Nedham's reference, in 1652, to Milton's 'white ... hand' in the same service: *Cat May Look upon a King*, 81–4.

of the offending treatise, tells, passingly and contemptuously, of a book by 'Monsieur Morus, entitled *Clamor Regii Sanguinis ad Coelum*', which 'hath been much cried up and down' in Holland.[68] This was the only document that Milton ever adduced as evidence that, at the time of the publication of the book, More had been taken to be its author. On the same subject Milton did publish, again in *Pro Se Defensio*, what he presented as extracts from three other letters, all undated, of which nothing has survived in any other form, and about the identity of whose authors he is resolutely vague. One of them was 'written to myself... from a person of integrity, who had no ordinary means of searching this affair to the bottom', the second by 'a man of the first honour and understanding' who 'was certainly well-informed'. The third reports a statement by 'a person of consequence'. But even if independent testimony of the existence of those letters could be found, their statements about the authorship of *Clamor* would at most amount to hearsay testimony, written, as far as we can tell, well after the event. Milton is aware of the thinness of his documentary case. He claims to have information which, having promised his sources not to divulge it, he unfortunately cannot reveal, but which would provide 'facts... far clearer than those I now publicly produce'. And there is 'a yet greater accumulation' of evidence which 'may perhaps be forthcoming' later, though neither it nor the material from confidential sources ever materialized.[69]

Much hung on the accuracy of the Leiden letter. If Milton were to be proved wrong about the authorship of *Clamor*, then the credibility of his whole literary campaign, and thus the esteem of the government whose reputation he had contrived to bind to his own, would be damaged. In Milton as in Nedham, high political stakes seem to have stimulated rather than impaired a sense of fun – in Milton's case even amid the desolation and suffering of his new blindness. Milton claims that the Leiden letter 'was sent to a certain friend of mine by a person of learning and prudence, and very well acquainted with affairs – a man sufficiently known to myself, and in Holland very generally known'.[70] For the identity of the 'friend of mine' we need look no further than the editor of *Politicus*, where the letter appeared. But who was the sender? No known acquaintance of Milton in the Netherlands answers to the description of him. It is an odd gap in our knowledge. How should someone 'very generally known' in Holland, and 'sufficiently known to' Milton himself, have left,

68. *MP*, 30 Sept. 1652, 1910. 69. *CW* ix. 37–41; *CP* iv. 716–17. 70. *CW* ix. 27.

even for the vigilant modern investigators of his career, no clue to his identity?[71]

To answer, we must first learn a little more about the series of missives from Leiden to which the letter of September 1652 belongs. Newsletters from foreign parts were a familiar feature of the newsbooks of the Puritan Revolution. Mostly they were flatly factual. But under the Commonwealth a new approach developed. We have noticed the practice by which, before they appeared in *Politicus*, letters were rewritten and parts of them expanded. The revision was done with brio. Thanks to it the letters were peppered with linguistic and stylistic habits and tricks which are familiar from Nedham's own prose. Readers were given a new perspective on English affairs by accounts, transparently altered or inserted by his pen, of foreign perceptions of them, which were made to conform to the lines taken in the newsbook's editorials. Nedham particularly enjoyed himself in letters from various cities in the Netherlands, and most of all in those from Leiden. The Leiden letters were based on genuine documents. In their original forms they were sent by a sprightly writer who had spied on the Stuart court for Thomas Scot's intelligence system, and who, in that capacity, had travelled with the royal entourage in France and Holland until Charles's departure for Scotland in June 1650, when the writer withdrew to Leiden.[72] But Nedham gave his own methods away in an editorial of July 1652. In it he attacked the pernicious principle of 'reason of state'. He had previously included that passage in a letter from Leiden published in *Politicus*, which charged the Dutch with adherence to that evil in their dealings with the English embassy of that year. Now he republished it in the editional, which he conceded to be 'its more proper place'.[73]

71. There were writers and scholars in Holland, indeed in Leiden, who were enemies of Salmasius and who took some pleasure in the discomfort Milton caused him: *CP* iv. 973–4; and the index entries to Nicholas Heinsius in French (*Life Records*); in Masson (*Life of Milton*); in Paul R. Sellin, *Daniel Heinsius and Stuart England* (Leiden, 1968); and in F. E. Bock, *Isaac Vossius and his Circle* (Gronginen, 2000). But none of them has been or can be plausibly identified as the author of the letter.
72. The letters written by the spy before he took up residence in Leiden are mostly published in S. R. Gardiner, ed., *Letters and Papers Illustrating the Relations between Charles the Second and Scotland* (Scottish History Society, xvii (1894)); and see Pieter Geyl, *Orange and Stuart 1641–72* (London, 1939), 53–5, 62–5, 69–71.
73. *MP*, 31 July 1651, 959; 1 July 1652, 1690. The story of Nedham and the Leiden letters may have started earlier, before *Politicus* began its life. In the months before the founding of the newsbook, as well as for a period after it, the correspondent's letters appeared in the weekly government newsbook, controlled by Thomas Scot, which *Politicus* would in effect replace: *A Briefe Relation*, a generally dull publication which the spy's letters enlivened.

It was in the Leiden letters that *Politicus* did much of its reporting, and did its most vivacious reporting, of the reception of Milton's *Defensio* in Holland. One of them appeared in the first issue of the newsbook that Milton licensed. It reports the surprise in Leiden, where Salmasius held his chair, that the English should 'suffer our Salmasius to crow and cry *Victoria* so long without bidding him battle'. That is the statement which gives *Politicus* its opportunity to announce, in response, that 'a very victorious reply to Salmasius is now in motion at the press'.[74] By the following month, the time of the publication of *Defensio*, doubts had arisen about the authenticity of the letters. Nedham, with the drollery typical of the newsbook, responded with a denial which, to readers with the intelligence or inside knowledge to guess at the truth, effectively conceded what it ostensibly refuted. He now published a letter containing 'the very cream of all the Dutch affairs', which readers were invited 'to take nakedly, as

In Nedham's career under the Commonwealth there is a gap. Why is there nothing from his pen between his deal with John Bradshaw in November 1649 and the appearance of *The Case of the Commonwealth* the following May, which was followed by the founding of *Politicus* in June? *The Case* would have required some fresh reading and thinking by Nedham, but it is a short book, which used the kind of historical material that he was used to deploying apace. His standing in the intervening period is, admittedly, uncertain. He was not yet, officially anyway, on the government's payroll. Yet the Commonwealth, which needed all the literary help it could get, gave writers, even those without stipends, a variety of *ad hoc* tasks. Nedham in turn depended wholly on the regime for immunity from prosecution and for the hope of income. In the spy's letters, as published first in *A Briefe Relation* and then in *Politicus*, there is a consistency of tone and manner that invites a suspicion. Did Nedham edit them for the first as well as the second newsbook? There are touches familiar from Nedham's own prose (e.g. 'the thing monarchy', the 'cockatrice egg', the account of England's diplomatic 'opportunity': S. R. Gardiner, ed., *Letters and Papers*, 74, 78, 113). If Nedham was thus employed, his involvement may direct us to another point of contact between him and Milton in 1650. On 8 January 1650 the council of state commissioned Milton to reply to Salmasius's *Defensio Regia*. A month later, on 7 February, *A Briefe Relation* (pp. 299–302) delivered a broadside against Salmasius which anticipates the campaign against him in *Politicus* from January 1651 (see also *MC* 103). The printer of the newsbook was Matthew Simmons, who around 15 February produced a new issue of Milton's *The Tenure of Kings and Magistrates*. On 19 February – just before the publication of *Defensio* – *A Briefe Relation* published (p. 337) an editorial (a device unusual in that newsbook) which repeats, in adapted form, the opening of *The Tenure*. Milton's tract begins: 'If men within themselves would be governed by reason, and not generally give up their understanding to a double tyranny, of custom from without and blind affections within ....' The editorial begins: 'If the minds of men were not forestalled with a prejudice that proceeds more from will and faction than from a clear and calm understanding ....' A close resemblance of typographical layout precludes the possibility that the parallel is accidental. The differences between the two texts, of which the second has a more practical, and less ethically elevated, flavour, recall similar divergences in material in *Politicus* from passages of Milton's known writing on which they appear to be based.

74. *MP*, 23 Jan. 1651, 545–6.

it came contractedly in an express from a gentleman of Leiden, lately at The Hague'. Its author is 'thankfully glad of the promise *Politicus* gives us' of the publication of *Defensio*, 'which we greedily expect; and Salmasius himself seems to desire it, Goliah-like despiting all his adversaries as so many pygmies'. Playfully the letter alludes to another one by the same author, which *Politicus* had published a fortnight earlier. 'I cannot praise your ingenuity' in publishing it, the new letter tells the editor. For royalists in England, in writing to 'their privadoes' at The Hague, have 'so far imposed upon the credulity of their confidants, as to beget a faith in them that this Leiden-letter was penned in England, and by one of all men that is furthest (as I hear) from pretending to Mercurial wit'.[75] On that as on other occasions, Nedham uses jocularity to convey that he writes under restraints, which the reader should keep in mind in interpreting him. It is somehow known to the author, or authors, of the second of the two letters that, before the first one got into print, the editor had had to 'geld it of more masculine passages' concerning the activities of the royalist exiles, who, we are led to infer, have their protectors or sympathizers in Whitehall. But mirth had other political uses for Nedham too.

Milton also knew its political uses. They alone make sense of the passage of *Pro Se Defensio* that cites the Leiden letter of September 1652. For if the passage about More was written, not in Holland, but in England, then there is one man who answers to the description of its author as a man of 'learning and prudence', 'very well known to myself', and – thanks to the impact of *Defensio* there – 'very generally known in Holland': Milton himself.

The joke became a running gag. The same passage of the letter reappeared not only in *Pro Se Defensio* but, the previous year, in *Defensio Secunda*. It contained a punning Latin distich (or epigram), which thus appears in all three documents. The two lines of verse – which are notoriously untranslatable – allege that More has impregnated a servant of Salmasius's wife, a charge which the letter contrives to merge, as it would be merged in gossip on the Continent, with the accusation about the authorship of *Clamor*. The poem spread quickly from *Politicus* to Holland, where it occasioned much merriment. Milton made merry with it too. *Defensio Secunda* introduces the distich by recalling the 'mirth and derision' which the pregnancy has caused 'at almost all convivial meetings and parties. This gave occasion to somebody (and whoever he was, he had no contemptible genius

75. Ibid. 20 Feb. 1651, 602–4.

for wit) to write' the distich.[76] By the time he composed *Pro Se Defensio*, Milton knew perfectly well, as he may have done when he wrote *Defensio Secunda*, that the charge about the maid was untrue.[77] But nothing would stop him. *Pro Se Defensio* quotes 'a Dutch author, and that noted distich', and alludes impishly to a textual variant 'in another manuscript, which I have by me'.[78] It seems superfluous to add that no such manuscript, and no Dutch source for the distich, has been found. Milton's early biographer John Toland, himself a forger of genius, got the point, and printed the distich, in his *Life* of Milton, as an example of 'Milton's wit'.[79]

Thus the crucial document of Milton's relentless effort to identify More as the author of *Clamor* was concocted by Milton, either by himself or in partnership with Nedham, whose newsbook first published the supposedly decisive evidence. If *Eikon Basilike* had been, in Nedham's words, 'so gross an imposture', then he and Milton, on the republic's behalf, took revenge in kind. In his earlier newsbook *Britanicus*, Nedham had confessed that he liked 'to laugh in my sleeve now and again'. It was a taste shared by his correspondent at Leiden, who, as Nedham publishes him, uses the same phrase.[80] It was evidently shared too by Milton, who laughed again in *Pro Se Defensio*, when he cited, as evidence of the authenticity of the letter of September 1652, the fact of its appearance in 'the public journal'. The document's 'claim to credit', he writes, 'is easily proved, by the authority of the writer or publisher; by which authority too my own credit is saved.... I know not what clearer proof could be expected or required.' No proof could have been less clear, as anyone who was aware of his relations with his 'great crony' would have known.[81]

★★

76. *CW* viii. 37. 77. *CP* iv. 275. 78. *CW* ix. 241.

79. Darbishire, 163. Toland had privileged knowledge of Milton's life, but his assertion has been subsequently dismissed (e.g. *CP* iv. 570 n.). The distich is close in spirit to a poem on Salmasius in *Defensio Secunda* (*CW* viii. 57) which Milton included in his collected poems in 1673. He would hardly have owned to his authorship of the distich.

80. *MP*, 24 July 1651, 945.

81. *CW* ix. 29. Milton's hand is unlikely to be at work throughout the letter of September 1652. The passage about More, which is brief and appears near the end, looks like an insertion. There are passages in the Leiden letters earlier in *Politicus* which also bring Milton to mind. There is the correspondent's observation, which recalls Milton's announcements in the earlier 1640s of God's 'choice' of 'this island' and of 'his Englishmen' (*CP* i. 526, 704; ii. 552, 553), that 'God hath seemed to choose your islands for his theatre, wherein above any other place or people to act his chiefest works of wonder' (*MP*, 2 Oct. 1651, 1099; cf. ibid. 12 June 1651, 859, and 11 Sept. 1651, 1056). The same passage refers to 'the memorable acts of justice' that

Politicus made a practice of printing poems ostensibly written in Holland. In November 1650 Nedham included a Latin 'distich sent over in an express out of Holland', which voiced republican antipathy to the House of Orange.[82] In January 1651, in the first issue of *Politicus* licensed by Milton, the one which alerted the public to the imminent appearance of *Defensio*, the newsbook carried a poem celebrating the death of the infant Prince of Orange: *Politicus* has 'received' 'out of Holland' lines of verse 'which we here give you both in Dutch and English, as it came to hand'. ' 'Tis Dutch poetry', adds the newsbook with uncharacteristic superfluity.[83] The addition is puzzling unless there is a chuckle behind it. Perhaps the lines are indeed poetry written in Holland – or perhaps they are made to look like it.[84] It is doubtful whether Milton knew Dutch, or enough Dutch, to have written them, though it is not impossible.[85] But if the poem was manufactured, Milton, as licenser of *Politicus*, would have known what was going on. And if he was ready to write the Latin distich of September 1652, might he not also have written the Latin one on the death of the Prince of Orange two years earlier?

Whether he did or not, his forgery of September 1652 was part of a long-running propaganda war between London and The Hague, in which, as so often in the sixteenth and seventeenth centuries, poets were recruited for the service of the state. That conflict supplies the background to the publication of the Leiden letters in *Politicus* – and is also in the background of Marvell's poem on the English embassy to The Hague. We first

have brought such contumely on the heroes of the regicide: *Eikonoklastes* had portrayed the regicide as a 'memorable act of judicature' (*MP*, 2 Oct. 1651, 1100; *CP* iii. 589). The Leiden correspondent also noticed, in a letter which reports on the Continental impact of *Defensio*, the Dutch instinct for political idolatry that Milton – like Nedham – laments in England: 'such idolators are we that we crouch like asses to a baby' – the infant heir to William II – 'in the cradle and in his clouts' (*MP*, 10 July 1651, 914; cf. *CP* iii. 446).

82. *MP*, 14 Nov. 1650, 387–8.

83. Ibid. 23 Jan. 1651, 542.

84. In March 1653 'These following Latin verses were brought by the last week's post from beyond the sea' (*MP*, 17 Mar., 2295). The poem, which is accompanied by an English translation, is 'Anglia Victrix', the celebration of the recent English naval triumph over the Dutch which we have seen to carry parallels to Marvell's 'The Character of Holland'.

85. His friend Roger Williams remembered that during his own visit to England from (apparently) late 1651 to early 1654, 'It pleased the Lord to call me for some time, and with some persons, to practise' a number of languages. 'The secretary of the council, Mr Milton, for my Dutch I read him, read me many more languages.' Williams appears to mean that Milton, in exchange for teaching or explaining the other languages to Williams, was himself learning – or improving? – his Dutch. Perhaps Williams was helping to equip Milton for his dealings with Dutch ambassadors within the period December 1651–July 1652. Parker, 410, 1008.

encounter the English literary campaign in September 1649, when Walter Strickland, then the Commonwealth's resident envoy at The Hague, wrote to Gualter Frost, the secretary of the English council of state, about the circulation of royalist literature in Holland. 'The verses you sent me', wrote Strickland, 'were printed here, and have been answered as you see: pray set him' – an unidentifiable government author – 'on work to reply, and send me a copy, and I will disperse them, for I can make them multiply.'[86] He also dispatched to his masters new books in the royalist cause. Of one of them, written in Dutch, he wrote that 'you have such as understand it', of another that 'I hope you have men to read and answer such books'.[87] It was Strickland who, around the same time, sent over an advance copy of the preface to Salmasius's *Defensio Regia*. On receiving it, the council instructed him 'earnestly to press', 'as a thing this Commonwealth is much concerned in', for the suppression of the work in Holland, written as it was by 'a servile pen' and 'filled with extreme virulence and bitterness'.[88] We cannot know whether Milton, apart from the writing of *Defensio*, was involved in the battle of Anglo–Dutch literary relations in 1649–50. But the number of writers employed to write propaganda for the Commonwealth during that time was (as far as we can tell) very small, and they must have had dealings with each other. None of them, in 1649, was given a wider range of tasks than Milton. It is artificial to detach him from the world of propaganda of which the tracts written in his own name in 1649–50, and his anonymous contributions to *Politicus* thereafter, were a part.

★★

If Milton and Nedham collaborated in the production of *Mercurius Politicus*, were other writers involved too? Was there a role for Milton's nephew, the aspiring writer John Phillips, who in 1652, at the age of 21, produced *Joannis Philippi Angli Responsio*, a reply to the first substantial attack on *Defensio*? The tract repeatedly echoes Milton's own arguments and language. It seems that Phillips, perhaps in conjunction with his uncle, may have been engaged in intelligence work for the Commonwealth.[89] According to John's brother Edward, Milton committed the writing of the book to John, 'but with

86. *TSP* i. 120. Frost was at that time setting up *A Briefe Relation*: cf. above, p. 210, n. 73.
87. *TSP* i. 127–8.
88. NA, SP25/65, pp. 215–16.
89. McDowell, 'Family Politics'. McDowell offers further insighte into the relations of the two men.

such exact emendations before it went to the press, that it might very well have passed for his, but that he was willing the person that took the pains to prepare it for his examination and polishment should have the name and credit of being the author'.[90] In a conversation in January 1652 with the learned Hermann Mylius, Milton boasted of 'the drubbing of Salmasius'. Then he gave Mylius a copy of *Joannis Philippi Angli Responsio* and, Mylius recorded, 'invited my opinion of it'.[91] Phillips's tract describes the rise and fall of the Roman republic in words that largely encapsulate, in a single sentence, the thesis of Nedham's editorials.[92]

Or what of another younger man, John Hall, whose pen, where Nedham, is to be found, is often close by? He had been on the government's literary staff since 1649; he worked and wrote for *Politicus* in Scotland during Cromwell's campaign there of 1650–1; and in Chapter 12 we shall find him in literary partnership with Milton in 1653. Can he have been far away from the writing of *Politicus* during the time of its republican editorials of 1651-2?

And what, finally, of yet another younger man, and another literary associate of Hall, Andrew Marvell? We do not know when it was that he went to Appleton House to be tutor to Mary Fairfax, or when he returned to London. He may have been there in the summer of 1651[93] or even earlier, and he was evidently back by late 1652.[94] Yet we have observed his literary relations with Nedham. We have seen how Marvell, Nedham, and Milton all gave voice – in various tones – to international republicanism

90. Darbishire, 71.
91. Miller, *John Milton and the Oldenburg Safeguard*, 128.
92. *CP* iv. 945: '... all histories ... without exception attest that the Roman republic rose to its glory under the authority of the consuls and senate, but that it at once declined under the luxury, tyranny and sloth of the emperors ....'
93. Derek Hirst and Steven N. Zwicker, 'High Summer at Nun Appleton, 1651: Andrew Marvell and the Lord Fairfax's Occasions', *Historical Journal*, 36 (1993), 247–69.
94. *AMC* 37. I am not persuaded by the view that Marvell is likely to have been in Yorkshire by November 1650, when, or by when, there was gathered the collection of poems, which includes two by Marvell, for a book by the Hull physician Robert Witty (though it would not be published until May 1651). If he was, then we have to envisage him writing 'Tom May's Death' and the poem on St John's embassy in the north. That is in itself possible, metropolitan though the tone of those poems seems. But Marvell could easily have sent the poems for the Witty volume from London. The source of the supposition that he was in Yorkshire is the tribute in one of the poems for Witty to 'Celia', who is generally taken to be Fairfax's daughter Mary, whom Marvell tutored at Appleton House. But (i) it is not clear that Celia is a pupil; (ii) if she is, she need not be Mary Fairfax: Marvell had evidently tutored before (and would do so again), and if tutoring was a normal source of income for him he could have moved from another female pupil to Mary; (iii) even if she is Mary, Marvell could already have taught her in the south before Fairfax, at a point after his resignation in July 1650 that we cannot pin down, withdrew from the capital to Yorkshire. Marvell's whereabouts in 1651 are also discussed in Appendix A, below.

early in 1651, in relation to the English embassy to the Netherlands.[95] If Marvell was in Yorkshire at the time of Milton's move to Petty France in December 1651, then Edward Phillips's (loose) statement that Marvell was one of those who regularly visited him from that time cannot be exactly right. Yet the likelihood must be that at least some of the friendships which Phillips lists were formed before that month. If and when Marvell was in London during the time of Milton's and Nedham's collaboration on *Politicus*, it seems unlikely that he did not, at the least, discuss it with them.

★★

The editor and the licenser of *Politicus*, then, were literary partners. But literary partners do not always agree with each other. We shall now see how Milton, even as he expounded political views on behalf of the Commonwealth that are so close to Nedham's, preserved his own perspective on it.

95. Above, Ch. 5.

10

Milton and the Commonwealth

Milton and Nedham agreed that Pride's Purge and the regicide, those emergency measures, had delivered England from a return to tyranny. But what should come next? How should liberty be guaranteed, and what political or constitutional forms should it take? So long as the royalist military threat survived – that is, until the Battle of Worcester in September 1651 – Nedham's propaganda was mainly negative. It had more to say about the evils of royalism and Presbyterianism than about the virtues of kingless rule. Yet the concluding chapter of *The Case of the Commonwealth* in May 1650, a work published when the morale of the government was at its lowest point and when the regime was desperate for survival,[1] departed from that policy and supplied his adventurous 'discourse of the excellency of a free state above a kingly government'. By the time of the Battle of Worcester he had, on the same subject, a book or series of essays up his sleeve. After the victory he began to publish that material in the weekly editorials that developed the arguments of the 'discourse' of 1650. They ran until August 1652, and would be published in book form in 1656 as *The Excellencie of a Free State.*

They were a novel departure in English political thought.[2] Before 1649, arguments about the public arena had been conducted predominantly within the language of the ancient constitution, whose rules king and parliament accused each other of breaking. When that constitution collapsed

1. Worden, *Rump Parliament*, ch. 11.
2. Its significance in the long-term development of political thought can be deduced from J. G. A. Pocock, *The Machiavellian Moment* (Princeton, 1975), though Nedham's place in the story is, I believe, larger than Pocock, who first recognized it, allows: see my 'Marchamont Nedham and the Beginnings of English Republicanism'.

in 1649, supporters of the new regime had to look elsewhere to vindicate its occupancy of power. Four ideas were developed. There was the appeal to divine providence: to the verdict of a God to whose judgement both sides of the civil war had ceaselessly appealed, and whose outstretched arm had shattered earthly and customary forms. Secondly there were the rights which the victors of the civil wars had acquired by conquest, and the obligation of subjects to obey a government which, since it held the sword, could alone give them protection. Thirdly there was the claim that the people were the origin of all legitimate authority and that they, or at least the virtuous or the victorious part of them, were entitled to abolish existing forms of rule and to create new ones at their wish. Those three approaches can be found, to varying degrees and with varying emphases, in the prose of Milton and Nedham. But none of them established a claim for the adoption of one particular form of government rather than another. All of them could have been used to vindicate a decision by the new rulers in 1649 to retain or restore the monarchy.

Nedham's editorials developed the fourth approach, the argument for republican rule. At their surface level, the level of straightforward propaganda at which their appeal was meant to be most extensive, his arguments vindicated the transformation of England into a Commonwealth and Free State in 1649. His 'discourse of the excellency of a free state' was written 'to manifest the excellency of the present government'.[3] He had some high praise for England's present rulers, even if he was freer with general commendation than with particularization of their achievements. *The Case of the Commonwealth* hailed 'their great wisdom, courage and care ... in carrying on the work of freedom to this height wherein we now see it'.[4] Being 'grave, serious, abstemious and vigilant', and being 'every way qualified like those Roman spirits of old',[5] they seem to embody the ideal of austere public service which Nedham and Milton alike exalted. By 1652, when the might of the new order had not merely conquered Britain but challenged the maritime and commercial supremacy of the Dutch and awed the great Continental monarchies, Nedham was ready to call England 'the most famous and potent republic this day in the world', 'the greatest and most glorious republic that the sun ever saw, except the Roman'.[6]

3. *Case*, 111. 4. Ibid. 97, 111. 5. Ibid. 114; cf. *CW* vii. 17.
6. Selden, *Of the Dominion of the Seas*, ep. ded. and p. 483.

Yet that qualification – 'except the Roman' – has its own significance. Nedham's editorials cannot openly refer to the shortcomings of the republican government for which he writes, but he can indicate them, in the customary manner of political commentary in the period, through reflections on the lessons of historical examples. His attitude to earlier republics is not uncritical. England is to learn from their errors as well as their merits. Above all it must understand the weaknesses that led to their decline or overthrow, and take steps to guard the survival of its own free state. Yet it must also study and emulate both the ethos of liberty and the kinds of constitutional arrangements which have enabled previous republics to flourish. England's new government was far removed, in Nedham's eyes, from the republican ideal of Machiavelli, that intoxicating model of citizenship which likewise centred on Roman history. Nedham sought to transplant it from the Renaissance city-state of Machiavelli's Florence to a predominantly rural land that, at least since remote antiquity, had known only monarchical rule. *Politicus* indicates that England, though it has ostensibly been liberated, remains half in chains. In 1649 it was 'declared' a free state, but it was not 'free indeed'. Its new governors had abolished 'the name king' but not 'the thing'.

In passing sentence on Charles I, Nedham's and Milton's hero John Bradshaw had made his own departure from native political language. He told Charles that 'what the tribunes of Rome were heretofore in the Roman Commonwealth, and what the Ephori were to the Lacedaemonian state, we know that is the parliament of England to the English state'.[7] Unlike Nedham's, Bradshaw's parallels were not an argument for constitutional change. Rather, they gave decorative endorsement to powers claimed by the purged parliament under the existing constitution. They differed from Nedham's subsequent reasoning in another way too. To portray parliament as England's tribunes might have its uses in justifying the regicide. But in Nedham's republican teaching of 1651–2, which looked to the next stage of revolution, Rome's tribunes acquired a role that cast an altogether less flattering light on the parliament. Implicitly he aligned the Commons not with them but with the senate, the representative body not of the people but of the privileged. England's problem, he implied, is precisely that it has no 'tribunes' – 'that necessary office' – or 'popular assemblies' to balance the senate. The Rump is an oligarchy or 'grandee-government', whose rule

7. *CP* iii. 589 n.

demonstrates that 'the interest of monarchy may reside in the hands of many as well as of a single person'.[8]

Though England was declared a Commonwealth and Free State in 1649, and though the subsequent engagement of loyalty required the submission of the nation to kingless rule, the constitutional future remained an open question. To the majority on the Roundhead side, the abolition of monarchy, which had gone far beyond the original intentions of those who fought the king, and which had broken every law and oath on which political legitimacy and stability depended, had been far disproportionate to the problem it ostensibly addressed. In their eyes the difficulty had lain, not with monarchy, but with a particular monarch; and not with kingship, but with tyranny. Charles I was executed as a tyrant. But how many of those who agreed to his trial and execution were committed to the abolition of monarchy? And what of the large body of MPs who steered clear of the regicide but reclaimed their seats in parliament after it?

Those questions were mostly left aside while the Irish and Scottish threats persisted, but they returned to view after Worcester. At a conference of civilian and military leaders, held at the Speaker's house in December 1651, Cromwell stated the question for debate: 'whether a republic, or a mixed monarchical government, will be best to be settled'. The lawyers, who were well represented in parliament, were 'generally for a mixed monarchical government', and argued that 'the government of this nation, without something of monarchical power, will be very difficult to be settled so as not to shake the foundation of our laws and the liberties of the people'. The army officers 'generally ... were against anything of monarchy', and asked 'why may not this as well as other nations be governed in the way of a republic?' Cromwell concluded that the question 'will be a business of more than ordinary difficulty! But really I think, if it may be done with safety, and preservation of our rights, both as Englishmen and Christians, that a settlement with somewhat of monarchical power in it would be very effectual.' At the conference there was talk, not for the first time, of enthroning Charles I's third son, Henry Duke of Gloucester, who was 'too young to have been in arms against us, or infected with the principles of our enemies'.[9] Yet the Stuarts were unlikely to agree to any such proposal. There was, as everyone knew but as almost everyone hesitated to say, an

8. Worden, 'Marchamont Nedham and the Beginnings of English Republicanism', 65, 68.
9. Abbott, ed., *Writings and Speeches*, ii. 505–7 (from Whitelocke's *Memorials*).

alternative and more realistic possibility: that Cromwell himself be crowned. After the conference the question of kingship was shelved but not forgotten.

Nedham's editorials of 1651–2, which were written against that background, resist all compromise with 'the interest of monarchy'.[10] In *The Case of the Commonwealth* he had declared there to be 'no difference between king and tyrant'.[11] *Politicus* adhered to that premisse.

★★

Nedham's republican editorials breathe a sense of intellectual discovery and excitement akin to that of Harrington's *Oceana*, a work which was conceived if not drafted around the same time, and whose arguments, indeed whose wording, Nedham's often resemble. To Nedham as to Harrington, the collapse and destruction of the ancient constitution, and the necessity of reconstruction, gave a direct pertinence to the experience and examples of other lands, past and present, which had different constitutions and different histories. If the breakdown of the monarchy was one impetus to republican thinking, another was the military and naval achievements of the new regime. Under the monarchy England had been, or anyway become, a minor power, incapable of confronting the mighty monarchies of France and Spain. Whatever the shortcomings of the Commonwealth, its conquests generated a confidence and esteem that encouraged comparisons with the deeds of republican antiquity.

Milton seems to have been excited, or anyway stimulated, too. Here, admittedly, there is another of those problems of dating that bedevil the study of Milton's thinking about politics. From his youth until 1652, he recorded observations on his reading in a commonplace-book.[12] It is hard, where not impossible, to date the entries in it with certainty. But if the conclusions of the handwriting experts are correct – provisional conclusions, but ones which independent evidence of the development of his thinking generally supports – then they add to the picture of Milton's partnership with Nedham. Entries which have been ascribed, largely on palaeographical grounds, to the months between November 1651 and February 1652 reveal preoccupations close to the editorials in *Politicus* in and around those very months. That was also the time when Milton's and Nedham's patron Bradshaw lost the presidency of the council of state;

10. *MP*, 11 Mar. 1652, 1458. 11. *Case*, 127. 12. It is printed in CP i. 362–508.

when Cromwell's own power and policies were threatening the radical political stance that the three men had taken; when Milton's own standing at Whitehall fell; and when he lamented to Hermann Mylius the ignorance and insularity of the councillors of state. Never can he have felt more acutely his dismay at 'the principles' of the 'home-grown' and 'narrow politicians' whom, as he complained, England now as always produced, and few of whom had ever travelled on the Continent. Deficient in civil wisdom and virtue, they could hope to remedy that defect only by an acquaintance with 'foreign writings' and 'examples of best ages'.[13] It is in the entries that have been allocated to that period that Milton explored the teaching of one particular 'foreign writing', whose analysis of 'examples of best ages' was simultaneously being imitated in Nedham's editorials, the *Discourses* of Machiavelli (whose *The Art of War* Milton already knew). Milton recorded Machiavelli's observation that one may learn 'by reading Roman history how a good realm can be ordered' (475). He approvingly noted that Machiavelli 'much prefers a republican form to a monarchy' (477). He endorsed Machiavelli's principle, which is a basic premiss of Nedham, that republics need to be renewed at their source 'by restoring the control of things to the decision of the people' (475–7).[14] He discovered that Machiavelli had justified the slaying of tyrants (456).

He also derived from the *Discourses* two conclusions about the relations of republics with foreign powers. First, it is imprudent of states which lack a healthy republican basis of government to seek to conquer and absorb other nations (499). That view, which was common ground among the English republicans of the Interregnum, was advanced, with the aid of material drawn from Machiavelli, in an editorial in *Politicus* on 26 February 1652 (a week before the editorial that follows Milton's *Defensio* in citing the slaying of Amaziah).[15] The commentary of 26 February deploys the principle to support ambitious proposals, of a kind that, says the editorial, would have been impracticable under a monarchy, for the incorporation of Scotland into the English Commonwealth. Secondly Milton approved Machiavelli's statement that 'a federation or league formed with a republic can be trusted more than one formed by a prince'. That was the view which

13. Miller, *John Milton and the Oldenburg Safeguard*, 172; *CP* v. 451.

14. Cf. *CW* vii. 359.

15. *MP*, 26 Feb. 1652, 1425–9 (cf. *CW* viii. 221, and Nedham's use of Sallust, Milton's favourite historian, on the same theme: *MP*, 25 Sep. 1651, 1079). Material from the editorial of 26 Feb. reappears in the anonymous tract *The Antiquity of England's Superiority over Scotland* (1652), which is evidently by Nedham.

Politicus promoted in urging the government towards a republican foreign policy. Milton also endorsed the republican argument of Machiavelli about domestic politics that was perhaps most provocative to conventional English opinion: that the conflicts or 'tumults' between the Roman nobles and people were not to be condemned for the disorder they caused, but should rather be commended as 'the principal means of keeping Rome free', 'for good laws were derived from those disturbances'.[16] The editorial run by *Politicus* on 1 April 1652, which likewise defended such 'tumults', observed that they invariably gave the Roman people either 'good laws' or 'an augmentation of their immunities and privileges'.[17]

Two further pieces of evidence suggest that the pertinence of Roman history to current events was on Milton's mind in the period of the republican editorials. In January 1652 we find him conversing, on behalf of the council of state, with Hermann Mylius. Once the diplomatic business between them was done, recorded the agent, 'we had many other discussions: we talked particularly of their' – the English republic's – 'constitution, and that of the Roman empire'. (It was after this that the talk turned to Milton's *Defensio*, to 'the drubbing of Salmasius', and to the new publication in the name of Milton's nephew John Phillips.)[18] Secondly, in July 1652 Milton essayed in verse a blunt political analogy of a kind unusual in his poetry. He clad his hero Sir Henry Vane in a toga: 'Than whom a better senator ne'er held | The helm of Rome.' Another line of the sonnet registers Milton's reflection on an observation of Machiavelli's *Discourses* that appears to have been on Milton's mind not long before the composition of the poem, for it is noted at two separate points in the entries in the commonplace-book that have been ascribed to the winter of 1651–2.[19]

John Aubrey wrote that Milton's 'being so conversant in Livy and the Roman authors, and the greatness he saw done by the Roman commonwealth, and the virtue of their great commanders, induced him' to think that 'the liberty of mankind ... would be greater under a free state than under a monarchal government'.[20] Admittedly Aubrey was not one

16. *CP* i. 505. 17. *MP*, 1 Apr. 1652, 1492.
18. Miller, *John Milton and the Oldenburgh Safeguard*, 128.
19. Milton, 'To Sir Henry Vane the Younger'; *CP* i. 414–15, 498. The line, which describes 'gold' as one of the 'two main nerves' of 'war', endorses a view of which, in the commonplace-book, Milton quotes (apparently approvingly) Machiavelli's denial. (Vane is 'that faithful and noble senator', and 'our gallant and worthy senator', in *Mercurius Britanicus*, 5 Feb. 1644, 167; 22 July 1644, 349.)
20. Darbishire, p. 14.

to underestimate the political influence of the reading of Livy. Milton, with the literature of the classical world at his feet and its spirit in his soul, took his political values as much from Greece as from Rome. Even within the realm of Roman politics his mind is closer to that of Sallust, the analyst of the republic's corruption and decline and the 'utter enemy of tyrants',[21] 'whom I prefer ... to any other Latin historian whatsoever',[22] than to Livy, the proud chronicler of its prowess and expansion. Yet when he pondered the failings of his own country and of the Puritan Revolution, he drew a comparison that might have been taken from Machiavelli's commentaries on Livy or from the editorials that Nedham modelled on them. 'Other nations both ancient and modern', he reflected, 'with extreme hazard and danger have strove for liberty as a thing invaluable, and by the purchase thereof have so ennobled their spirits as from obscure and small to grow eminent and glorious commonwealths.'[23] To Milton, as to Nedham, the collapse of the Roman republic was a disaster. It was evidently in the late 1640s, perhaps in 1649, that he seemed to indicate a wish to write of 'Julius Caesar ... and of the Roman free state'.[24] In *Defensio*, in language close to Nedham's, he remembers how Julius Caesar, 'by impiously taking up arms against the Commonwealth', 'got all the power into his hands'. *Defensio* dwells too on the betrayal of Roman liberty by Mark Antony, 'that monstrous tyrant' and 'destroyer of the commonwealth', and Octavius Caesar, the consequences of whose 'fraud and hypocrisy' were so dire. The result was that 'the people of Rome', though they 'preferred that condition of their republic, no matter how much vexed with civil broils', were subjected to 'the unbearable yoke of the Caesars'.[25]

★★

Yet on political subjects Milton often thinks more than one thing. For all the similarities of viewpoint between him and Nedham when they looked back on Rome and other republics, there are differences too. The 'ancient virtue' which Nedham rejoices to find in ancient Rome diverges subtly but distinctively from the classical virtue celebrated by Milton.

21. *CW* vii. 93. 22. *CP* vii. 500. 23. Ibid. v. 441.

24. Ibid. 41; cf. iii. 441. The subject 'more than what appertains' is 'not here to be discoursed'. Here as elsewhere Milton leaves us uncertain whether he is considering the composition of a work that in the event he would not write. For other cases see ibid. i. 922; iii. 516; vii. 272; *CW* vii. 179; viii. 91, 215 (cf. pp. 113, 145).

25. *CW* vii. 107–9, 191, 321. Cf. ibid. 331; viii. 177; *CP* v. 61; *Case*, 17, 80, 101, 131.

Nedham in his republican vein is interested in men only as citizens. Their interior or spiritual worlds, which matter so much to Milton, lie beyond Nedham's gaze – save if they earn his disapproval, as when the republic's domestic enemies appeal to the claims of 'conscience' as a pretext for disobedience. The health of religious beliefs, or 'opinions' as he likes to call them, is to be judged by their consequences for government and citizenship. Milton is alive to those consequences too, but his essential concerns are the truth of a religious belief and the sincerity of its holders. In Nedham's mind, 'discipline' is an aid to measurable political goals, 'licence' an impediment to them. The 'inestimable jewel' of 'liberty' consists in concrete benefits: in 'wholesome laws suited to every man's state and condition'; in the provision of 'cheap and easy' judicial proceedings; in the disposition and control of government by the people; in the free election of members of parliament.[26] To Milton, on the other hand, the public struggle between 'liberty' and 'licence', or between 'discipline' and 'licence', is the extension to the state of the struggle between reason and passions for the sovereignty of the individual soul. Nedham occasionally invokes that classical principle, but without Milton's ardour. Besides, Milton adapts it to, and absorbs it within, a Christian framework, as Nedham does not.

The cast of Milton's mind is always ethical, of Nedham's always practical. Milton enjoins the pursuit of 'virtue, from which springs that true liberty which is felt within'. Political slavery is, to him, the fitting consequence of the sinfulness that is 'the tyrant... within'.[27] For Nedham, virtue is what 'beg[ets] a desire of' outward 'liberty' and inspires the courage and resolution that defend it, while 'corruption and depravation of manners' are what lose it.[28] When men become 'slaves to their own lusts',[29] the consequence which he laments is not for their souls but for their political allegiance. Men who 'deserve to be slaves' earn their plight not by inner depravity but by allowing themselves to be 'deceived' by aspiring tyrants into yielding their liberty.[30] When Milton observes that, under free governments, austere rulers 'walk the streets as other men', the moral elevation that he commends is an end in itself. To Nedham the 'serious, abstemious, severe course of life' of the rulers of Athens is admirable because, thanks to it, the Athenians became 'the only arbitrators of all affairs in Greece'.[31] Their lives are thus a model

26. *MP*, 2 Oct. 1651, 1095. 27. *CW* viii. 133.
28. *Case*, 113; *MP*, 2 Oct. 1651, 1094. 29. *Case*, 112.
30. *MP*, 5 Aug. 1652, 1773. 31. Ibid. 15 Jan. 1652, 1334–5.

for the leaders of the English republic, which he wants to be 'grand arbiter of affairs in Europe'.[32] Both writers, we saw, take 'custom' and bad 'education' to be obstacles to the enlightenment of England. *Politicus* looks to educational reform to break down men's unthinking adherence to customary forms of government and to instil enthusiasm for republican rule.[33] Milton, too, sees education as an instrument of political correction. It can make the people 'fittest to choose' their representatives, 'and the chosen fittest to govern'.[34] But the process will involve a grounding in ethics from which political wisdom, in Milton's mind but not in Nedham's, is inseparable.

⋆⋆

To Nedham in 1651–2, the political health of England rested on the achievement and preservation of republican forms. The republicanism of the Interregnum, novel as it was, had roots in the thinking of earlier English generations, when the ideas and examples of the Italian republics had been closely studied. Before the civil wars it had been common enough, even among writers who were unquestioningly loyal to monarchy, to reflect on the unsatisfactory rule of 'most kings'. Sometimes that perspective extended to an acknowledgement that republican rule was or could be superior to monarchical government. Yet those views were matters for speculation.[35] They were contemplated by thinkers who knew, from Aristotle, that intelligent political analysis requires comparison among the various forms of rule, but they were rarely if ever advanced as reasons or recipes for constitutional change. They were not proposed as challenges to the sanctions of laws and custom, or to the pressures and ties of allegiance, that supported the English monarchy.

From 1649 the characteristics of republics were no longer an abstract question. In Milton's tracts of the ensuing eleven years there are many passages that appear to proclaim the superiority of republican government. Most of them come near the end of the Interregnum, especially in *The Readie and Easie Way to Establish a Free Commonwealth*, but sometimes they, or at any rate their premisses, are to be found in his earlier writings of the Interregnum too. In 1649 he was already willing to argue that God and earthly kings 'for the most part' were 'opposite masters', and that

32. Ibid. 6 Mar. 1651, 623–4.
33. Ibid. 2 Oct. 1651, 1093–4; 3 June 1652, 1629–33.
34. *CP* vii. 443.
35. Worden, 'Republicanism, Regicide and Republic', 307–14.

England's new deliverers had exchanged the second for the first.[36] In 1651 *Defensio* reveals God's judgement that 'under human conditions' – 'ut sunt res humanae'[37] – a republic 'is a more perfect form of government than a monarchy'.[38] In that and other works of the 1650s he protests at the subordination of wise and virtuous men to rulers who are unlikely to match them in worth.[39] In *The Readie and Easie Way* Milton amplifies those points. 'I doubt not', he states, 'but all ingenuous and knowing men will easily agree with me, that a free commonwealth without single person or House of Lords is by far the best government, if it can be had'.[40] Republics are 'fittest and properest for civil, virtuous and industrious nations, abounding with prudent men worthy to govern'.[41] They observe the 'precept of Christ' that forbids lordliness among men, and they befriend liberty of conscience, Milton's supreme goal.[42]

Milton brought to politics the ideal of freedom that he had worked out in religion. In religion God gives his servants the freedom of choice that Calvinist theories of predestination deny them, and wants them to be independent of all man-made ideas and institutions that stand between him and them. They attain their salvation by their own exertions, and their faith by their own enquiries. The growth of their faith takes them from spiritual infancy to adulthood, from credulity to thought, from 'custom' (that rooted antagonist of 'choice'[43]) to truth. God 'uses not to captivate' a man 'under a perpetual childhood of prescription, but trusts him with the gift of reason to be his own chooser'.[44] The service of the Gospel is 'rational, manly, and utterly free'.[45] In politics the same language applies, for there too God casts us on 'our own active virtue and industry'.[46] In *The Tenure of Kings and Magistrates*, his first political tract, Milton observes that dependence on kings leaves us only with 'a ridiculous and painted freedom, fit only to cozen babies'.[47] By 1660 he thinks it 'unmanly' for us to 'hang' our 'felicity' on a king, as if we are 'sluggards and babies', and to 'devolve all on a single person ... more like boys under age than men'. So 'the happiness of a nation must needs be firmest and certaintest in a full and free council of their own electing, where no single person, but reason

36. *CP* iii. 236, 581; cf. *Paradise Regained* III. 441.
37. For the import of the phrase see *CP* ii. 514; cf. below, p. 299.
38. *CW* vii. 77.
39. *CP* iii. 409, 460; vii. 448; *CW* vii. 127, 305.
40. *CP* vii. 364–5.
41. Ibid. 481–2; cf. *Case*, 123.
42. *CP* vii. 359–60, 364, 382; cf. iv. 111.
43. Ibid. i. 746.
44. Ibid. ii. 513–14.
45. *CW* xvi. 181.
46. *CP* vii. 362.
47. Ibid. iii. 236.

only, sways'.[48] We learn from Milton's *History of Britain* how nations which God has made 'masters of their own choice' discover 'the weight of what it [i]s to govern well themselves', and how their fate is decided by the response of their 'virtue and industry' to that opportunity of 'true liberty'.[49] To politics he brings, too, the contempt for 'custom', for 'sloth', and for 'servile and thrall-like fear',[50] which runs through his writings on religion. It is a failing which, in public life, he identifies with subordination to monarchical rule.

All those arguments and sentiments might seem to make a republican of Milton. Yet he is never a doctrinaire one. Even in 1660, when the experience of the protectorate had made the thought of single rule in England repellent to him, he allowed that 'monarchy itself may be convenient to some nations'.[51] He agreed with Nedham that a new form of government should have been designed in 1649, and judged that the nation had paid a heavy price for that omission.[52] Yet his pleas for the superiority of republics, which are scattered through his tracts, sustain no sequences of argument. For the most part they are improvised ripostes to the sneers of the regime's enemies. When he wrote *The Tenure*, the decision to convert England into a Commonwealth and Free State had yet to be taken. The tract, which slides quickly over the question whether 'the people' will exercise its 'right' of 'changing its own government',[53] is finely attuned to the uncertainty of the new rulers, a feature of the work which encourages the supposition that he had guidance from among them in writing it. In May 1649 the inauguration of the Commonwealth and Free State was at last declared. Milton adjusted his case accordingly. Yet his explanations of the change of government are defensive and unambitious. He does not say that the English of earlier generations were mistaken in subjecting themselves to monarchy, or that his compatriots will err if they revert to it at some future point. 'Certain it is', explains *Defensio*, 'that the same form of government is not equally fitting for all nations, or for the same nations at all times.'[54] It is not any inherent superiority of republican rule that has made monarchy wrong for England now, but rather the extremity of Charles's misrule, which drove his opponents to the opposite extreme, 'even', as he explains in *Eikonoklastes*, to 'the taking away of kingship itself'.

48. Ibid. vii. 361–2.
49. Ibid. v. 131, 441, 449.
50. Ibid. i. 522.
51. Ibid. vii. 377–8.
52. Above, p. 164.
53. *CP* iii. 207 (cf. p. 192).
54. *CW* vii. 191–3.

'Wherefore', Milton asks a little earlier in the same tract, 'should we not hope to be governed more happily without a king?'[55] The question, posed almost defensively, is no unambiguous or confident endorsement of the change of government. Likewise in 1660, the reason why, in England, kingship 'cannot but prove pernicious' lies not in its innate failings but in the particular experience of the revolution, after which the returning Stuart house would be bent on tyranny and 'revenges'.[56]

Admittedly we need, when interpreting Milton's statements on the monarchy in the years after the regicide, to allow for the tactical pressures under which he composed them. As the Restoration approached, he wrote to persuade men less radical than he to avert it. Earlier his Latin 'defences' were addressed largely to Continental audiences, whom candid republicanism would readily have offended, and whose monarchs were potentially dangerous enemies. In February 1650, the month after he was commissioned to write *Defensio*, he either composed, or put into Latin, letters of state to the kings of Spain and Portugal. The documents explain how the parliamentarians had been 'forced' to take up arms against their king, and how they had now been 'driven to the point' where, 'if we wished to save the nation, we had to alter its form of government'.[57] Yet even when tactical considerations have been weighed, Milton's thinking is distant from the republicanism of Nedham's polemic in the same year, with its 'discourse of the excellency of a free state above a kingly government'. Milton's private reflections suggest that the constraints of propaganda are an insufficient explanation of his reticence. There, no less than in his public writings, we find a contrast between his most radical statements on religion and his hesitation about constitutional forms. Even the portion of his commonplace-book that has been placed in 1651–2, where he welcomes Machiavelli's reasons for preferring a republic to a monarchy, does not commit Milton to them. In any case the argument of Machiavelli which he picks out suggests that the superiority of republican rule is relative rather than absolute: a republic makes 'fewer mistakes' than a principality in the choice of magistrates and advisers.[58]

Milton's commendations of republican rule jostle with contrary perspectives. Even after the abolition of the monarchy he acknowledges the

55. *CP* iii. 455, 458. 56. Ibid. vii. 377–9. 57. Ibid. v. 505, 507.

58. Ibid. i. 477. Like (perhaps) Andrew Marvell around the same time, Milton seems to have found it easier to savour the prospect of republican rule abroad than at home.

merits of 'regulated', 'mixed', 'limited' kingship.[59] In his private comments on Machiavelli's *Discourses* he condemns hereditary rule but finds beneficial examples of elective monarchy, a system in which he also appears to acknowledge virtues even in *The Readie and Easie Way*.[60] Whereas Nedham argues that 'there is no difference between king and tyrant',[61] Milton goes out of his way to distinguish them. 'Look how great a good and happiness a just king is,' urges *The Tenure*, 'so great a mischief is a tyrant.' 'If I inveigh against tyrants', he says in *Defensio Secunda*, 'what is that to kings, between whom and tyrants I make the widest difference? As much as a good man differs from a bad, so much do I maintain that a king differs from a tyrant.' 'You make a king and tyrant identical,' he charges his adversaries on the Continent who cry up divine-right monarchy, 'inasmuch as you ascribe the same right to both.'[62]

Whereas, in Nedham's reasoning, kings and tyrants are the same, in Milton's they are not merely different: they are opposites. For alongside his condemnation of the world's kings, who 'most commonly' or 'for the most part' rule unworthily if not tyrannically,[63] there runs a commitment to the classical principle on which, as Milton has it, 'every good man is a king'.[64] 'Aristotle and the best of political writers', he remembers in *The Tenure*, 'have defined a king him who governs to the good and profit of his people, and not for his own ends.'[65] There as elsewhere Milton used the ideal of the 'good prince' opportunistically, as a stick with which to beat bad ones.[66] Yet such a ruler has the power for good that the tyrant has for bad. There is a tension in the mind of Milton, as of many who lived under Renaissance and seventeenth-century monarchy, about the character of true kingship. One half of him assumes that good government is 'mild'.[67] The other knows, not only that 'too much gentleness' in a king can be 'disastrous',[68] but that to cleanse his realm he must be stern and uncompromising. Milton welcomed divine punishment on 'potent' harmful kings, yet also knew the power of a 'potent monarchy' for good.[69] The ideal of a ruler of

59. Ibid. iii. 453; *CW* vii. 213–15, 351 (cf. viii. 49), 477.
60. *CP* i. 475; vii. 377.
61. *Case*, 127.
62. *CP* iii. 212 (cf. i. 439, 443, 453; iii. 498); *CW* viii. 25, 27 (cf. vii. 223, 475–7).
63. *CP* iii. 243, 484, 486, 581; *CW* vii. 115, 123, 129.
64. *CW* viii. 27.
65. *CP* iii. 202.
66. Ibid. iii. 460; *CW* vii. 245.
67. *CP* i. 616; ii. 488, 559; *Paradise Regained* IV. 134 (cf. III. 160). Cf. *CP* i. 575; *CW* vii. 45–7; Sonnet XVI, l. 11.
68. *CP* i. 450.
69. *CW* vii. 67; *CP* i. 800.

'extraordinary virtue',[70] whose unitive capacity, and whose single energy, can reform and transform the realm, has its hold on him. There is Agricola in Roman Britain, that 'public father'.[71] There is King Alfred, in Milton's mind 'the mirror of princes', who administered justice 'so severely' and whom Milton wishes were here to reform it now.[72]

Perhaps there lies, behind Milton's representations of ideal kingship, another one: the portrait of King Euarchus in Sidney's *Arcadia,* the stern and implacable king whose brisk methods rescue the kingdom of Macedon from a corrupt oligarchy.[73] Milton – apparently writing well before he turned on Sidney in the anti-poetic mood of *Eikonoklastes* – pronounced that passage of the *Arcadia* 'excellent', and noted that the oligarchy had brought on 'the ruin of royal sovereignty'.[74] Euarchus enters the disintegrating dukedom of Arcadia as a 'stranger'. In *Areopagitica* Milton speculates what might happen 'if some great and worthy stranger should come among us, wise to discern and mould the temper of a people, and how to govern it'. Elsewhere, too, it is to a single political redeemer that his thoughts move. In 1647 he asks, in Latin verse, what 'god-begotten man' might redeem England from its civil chaos.[75] Even in the winter of 1659–60, when his pamphlets urged his countrymen to renounce the principle of single rule, he wrote privately that what his country needed was 'one' man who could save it.[76] However often he praised the 'worthies' who delivered England in 1641–2 and 1649, he could never bring a recognizable or laudable collective image to his accounts of them. He found single rulers – as he did solitary heroes – easier to extol. Even when, in 1642, parliament had virtually taken over the government, his thoughts turned instinctively to the scope which 'one' 'man' or 'lawgiver' might have 'in the guidance of a civil state to worldly happiness'.[77]

Milton's readiness to find merit in kingship, like most of his stances on constitutional arrangements, is not held consistently. Sometimes he contradicts it. His claim, which is made in the passage of *Defensio Secunda* that flatters Queen Christina of Sweden, to have written 'not a syllable' against kings is disingenuous,[78] for often in his treatises of the Interregnum

70. *CP* ii. 578. 71. Ibid. v. 84–5 (cf. iii. 552).
72. Ibid. i. 386–7, 424; v. 289–92. Even in Machiavelli's *Discourses* he found evidence that there could be 'golden times' for liberty of conscience under 'good princes': ibid. i. 476–7.
73. Blair Worden, *The Sound of Virtue: Philip Sidney's 'Arcadia' and Elizabethan Politicus* (London and New Haven, 1996), q.v. 'Euarchus'.
74. *CP* i. 463. 75. Milton, 'Ad Joannem Rousium'. 76. *CP* vii. 515.
77. Ibid. i. 753. 78. *CW* viii. 105.

'king' is a dirty word, almost as dirty as 'tyrant'.[79] When he invokes the Aristotelian ideal of kingship, which in the real world he knows to be a rare exception to the rule, it is normally with the aim not of inspiring its fulfilment but of shaming princes who betray it. In any case his confidence in the regenerative capacity of good rulers seems to waver. There are a number of good kings in the *History of Britain*, but only temporarily do they stem the tide of national wickedness. Even so, Milton, who glories in the destruction of a tyrant, yearns for the ideal on the opposite side of the coin. The regicide, that supreme triumph, for him, of both 'justice' and 'heroic virtue', transposes to the destruction of a king the language in which he earlier saluted 'royal dignity, whose towering and steadfast height rests upon the immovable foundations of justice and heroic virtue'.[80] Milton's capacity to invest intensity of feeling, both positive and negative, into his observations on single government would reach its summit in his depictions of the man who broke the republic in 1653, Oliver Cromwell.

★★

When Milton wrote that 'the same form of government is not equally fitting for all nations, or for the same nations at all times', he added that 'sometimes one, sometimes another' is appropriate 'according as the diligence and valour of the people wax or wane'. The appropriateness of constitutional arrangements is to be measured not by their innate qualities but by the ethical condition, the 'fitness', of the citizens. Like other writers before and after him, he sees republican rule as an aspiration that may lie beyond present attainment. Like them he fears that without a sufficient stock of national virtue a republic will not last. The example of the fall of the Roman republic confirms his point. In a passage of his commonplace-book that appears to have been composed in the early 1640s, he observes that, in the prime of the republic, the Romans were 'ripe for a more free government than monarchy, being in a manner all fit to be kings'. But when they had been corrupted by 'over much prosperity', they became 'fit to be cursed with a lordly and dreadful monarchy; which was the error of the noble Brutus and Cassius, who felt themselves of spirit to free a nation, but considered not that the nation was not fit to be free; while forgetting

79. e.g. ibid. vii. 145; *CP* iii. 243, 409, 457, 509.

80. *CP* i. 582 (cf. p. 584).

their [the Romans'] old justice and fortitude, which was made to rule, they became slaves to their own ambition and luxury'.[81]

That thought hangs like a shadow over Milton's writings during and about the Puritan Revolution. He returns to it in explaining the revolution's failure. For 'stories' – histories – 'teach us that liberty sought out of season in a corrupt and degenerate age brought Rome itself into further slavery'.[82] The *History of Britain* records that after the victory at Mons Badonicus, which gave the natives their opportunity for virtuous freedom, goodness was to be found in 'some so very few as to be hardly visible in a general corruption'.[83] At the conclusion of the *History*, too, he reflected that in 1066, when the wickedness of 'the generality' made the land a prey to the Normans, 'some few' stood out, but could only suffer under 'evil times'.[84] He saw the same problem in the England of 1649. Though 'some few ... yet retain in them the old English fortitude and love of freedom, and have testified it by their matchless deeds', 'the rest', 'with a besotted and degenerate baseness of spirit', remain sunk in civil and religious idolatry.[85] His view of the parties of virtue and vice was not Manichaean. Between them there stood men who were misled but reclaimable.[86] But could they, and could the nation, be made worthy of the task God had chosen for them? The *History*, which asks how Milton's countrymen are 'fitted to undergo matters of ... main consequence',[87] reaches a melancholy answer. He notices 'with what minds and by what course of life' the natives have 'fitted themselves' for their 'servitude'.[88] Likewise the members of the Long Parliament 'unfitted themselves to be dispensers of the liberty they fought for', and 'unfitted the people also'.[89]

What then of Pride's Purge and the regicide? Did not those 'matchless deeds' show the capacity of the virtuous minority to effect radical change? If the minority could be identified with 'the people', as, in Milton's fluctuating use of that term, it sometimes was, then were not the people fit to be free? As in the 1640s, so thereafter, his judgements of the condition of the English have their hopeful moments. In 1660 he allowed himself the thought that the deeds of the Commonwealth of 1649–53 had 'testified a spirit in this nation no less noble and well fitted to the liberty of a commonwealth than in the ancient Greeks or Romans'. Yet 'in this nation'

81. Ibid. 420; cf. *CW* vii. 249. 82. *CP* v. 449 (cf. ii. 487). 83. Ibid. 174.
84. Ibid. 403. 85. Ibid. iii. 344. 86. Ibid. 601. Cf. iii. 585; *CW* vii. 75.
87. *CP* v. 130. 88. Ibid. 402. 89. Ibid. 449.

is likelier to mean 'within' it than 'of' it.[90] Even as he penned that tribute, the evidence of national degeneration pressed upon him. In the years after the regicide as in those before it, pessimism was a more frequent refrain. In 1649, despite the regicide, he feared lest the English would prove 'not fit for that liberty which they cried out and bellowed for', and show themselves 'fitter to be led back again into their old servitude'.[91] *Defensio Secunda*, five years later, inspects the moral condition of Milton's countrymen and leaves it very doubtful whether they are 'fit' for 'liberty'. In 1660, as the Restoration approached, he watched a nation 'fitted and prepared for slavery' returning to its 'befitting thraldom'.[92] The return of the monarchy, which engulfed the virtuous minority, left him to address a 'fit audience ... though few'.[93]

Nedham shared Milton's dismay at the state of the English. Like him he found a parallel in late republican Rome, where both writers traced the softening influence of luxury that had destroyed the Romans' vigilance for liberty and had instilled a taste for tyranny. Nedham, too, pondered the failure of Brutus and Cassius. He reached a similar conclusion. Nedham's *The Case of the Commonwealth* explains that because the 'sparks of ancient courage and love of liberty ... were kindled only in a few of the more noble souls and the generality corrupt and degenerate from their old virtue', 'such heroic minds', even 'when they took off Caesar himself', could not persuade the majority to 'assert their liberty'.[94] Yet Nedham is for the most part without Milton's pessimism. He still thinks it 'probable enough' that, 'after the death of Caesar', the Romans 'might then have recovered their liberty'. What thwarted them was not the degeneracy of the majority but a practical error. They allowed power to remain in the triumvirate of Octavius, Antony, and Lepidus.[95] Political dexterity, which could have saved Rome, can likewise, implies Nedham, meet the challenges of the English republic. If the regime is true to its friends and inflexible to its enemies, if it creates republican forms and instils republican values, the English will come to see that their interests lie in the preservation of the Commonwealth. Milton appeals not to men's interests but to their virtue – and finds it wanting.

★★

90. *CP* vii. 420. 91. Ibid. iii. 581. 92. Ibid. vii. 357, 482.
93. Cf. *Paradise Lost* XII. 480–2; *Paradise Regained* III. 58–9. 94. *Case*, 113.
95. *MP*, 11 Dec. 1651, 1256.

Nedham insists that the people – that is, in the England of the early 1650s, the part of the people which belongs to the Commonwealth's 'party of its own' – have or ought to have two fundamental political powers. There is the 'right inherent in every nation to alter particular governments as often as they judge it necessary for the public weal and safety',[96] and to 'dispose the government in such a form as shall best please themselves'.[97] Secondly there is the 'free election of members to sit in every parliament'.[98] Since 'the life of liberty consists in the succession of powers and persons',[99] elections must be held regularly and frequently.

The principle of freedom of choice is essential to Milton's conception of liberty. In *Areopagitica* he spelled out, as he would again in *Paradise Lost*, its place in the development of the soul. When God gave Adam 'reason, he gave him freedom to choose, for reason is but choosing'.[100] Milton applies the same principle to politics, the arena where virtue is supremely tested. For 'whoso takes from a people their power to choose what government they wish takes that indeed in which all civil liberty is rooted'.[101] A people's 'right', granted by God, 'of choosing, yea of changing their own government'[102] is, to appearances, more important to Milton than the particular choice it makes. John Phillips was right to say, in words of 1652 that Milton endorsed, that Milton 'has always left it to the free choice of every people whether they wanted monarchy or some other form of government; he has only opposed the imposition of monarchy upon people against their will'.[103]

A free nation, Milton tells us, can terminate kingship at any time, even when kingly rule takes neither 'illegal' nor 'intolerable' forms.[104] At other moments, however, he is more tentative. Kingship, he then suggests, may be removed only 'upon urgent causes', 'when it grows too masterful and burdensome',[105] and kings may be deposed only when their rule 'turn[s]

96. *MP*, 5 June 1651, 831; 2 Oct. 1651, 1095.
97. Ibid. 26 Feb. 1651, 567; 30 Oct. 1651, 1157; cf. *Case*, 34.
98. Ibid. 2 Oct. 1651, 1095.
99. Worden, 'Marchamont Nedham and the Beginnings of English Republicanism', 65.
100. *CP* vii. 513–14, 527.
101. *CW* vii. 193. Cf. pp. 169, 191, 479; *CP* iii. 206–7. (He made an exception of the Irish: *CP* iii. 303.)
102. *CP* iii. 207.
103. Ibid. iv. 907.
104. Ibid. iii. 237; cf. *CW* viii. 167. This aspect of Milton's thinking is emphasized by Quentin Skinner, 'John Milton and the Politics of Slavery', in Parry and Raymond, eds., *Milton and the Terms of Liberty*, 1–22.
105. *CP* iii. 236, 458.

to tyranny'.[106] For in practice his commitment to the principle of political choice proves to have limits. Like Nedham's, his invocations of the people's right to change their rulers are deployed to justify the *status quo*: to endorse the rule of the Commonwealth which has been introduced in the people's name. Unlike Nedham, however, he is wary of intimating that the power of altering governments might be rightfully exercised thereafter. In 1660 he asked the champions of monarchy, who had been scandalized by the introduction of the republic, 'how our forefathers' could be supposed to have bound us 'to any certain form of government, more than we can bind our posterity'.[107] Yet at the same time he proposed the perpetuation of the restored Rump 'even to' the Second Coming of Christ.[108] No doubt that choice, in turn, would have been reversible by posterity. Yet Milton's proposal is a world away from the spirit of political accountability to which his own logic pointed, and for which Nedham's proposals provided.

Nedham, even though he thought that 'most men here in England' are 'utterly unapt to learn what true freedom is', insisted on the people's entitlement to exercise their 'native right and liberty', 'however they may abuse it'.[109] The abuse of it stopped Milton in his tracks. For him, too, 'most men' are deficient in the understanding of liberty. 'I confess there are but few', he wrote in *Defensio*, 'and those men of great wisdom and courage, that are either desirous of liberty or capable of using it.'[110] Not merely were the many not equipped for liberty. They were licentious. Their proper lot is repression or subordination. He reflects in 1660 that if 'free commonwealths' have always been judged 'fittest' for virtuous and industrious nations, then 'monarchy' has been found 'fittest to curb degenerate, corrupt, idle, proud, luxurious people'.[111] 'For liberty', as he pronounced in contemplating the wreckage of the Puritan Revolution, 'hath a sharp and double edge fit only to be handled by just and virtuous men; to bad and dissolute it become[s] a mischief unwieldy in their own hands.' England, alas, has lacked men with 'the happy skill to know' how 'good men may enjoy the freedom which they merit, and the bad the curb which they need'.[112]

How then can the licentious majority be entrusted with political choice? For 'what if the majority of the legislature should choose to be slaves?'[113] The very chapter of the Bible which, as Milton insisted, demonstrated

106. Ibid. 198. 107. Ibid. vii. 481. 108. Ibid. 374.
109. *MP*, 6 Nov. 1651, 1175; above, p. 184. 110. *CW* vii. 75.
111. *CP* vii. 481–2. 112. Ibid. v. 449. 113. *CW* vii. 357.

God's gift to men of the right to choose their own government, 2 Samuel 8, was also, as he reflected no less often, the archetypal instance of their abuse of it, for the Israelites in their wickedness chose a king and brought servitude on themselves. Of course, Milton was able, with Nedham, to define 'the people' so as to exclude the wicked. Yet a restriction of political or electoral participation to the virtuous would have posed severe practical problems. How could voting rights be made sufficiently narrow to exclude the enemies of liberty, yet sufficiently broad to give the regime some basis and air of legitimacy? Milton's and Nedham's masters grappled unavailingly with that difficulty. Unlike Nedham, however, Milton showed little interest in the imposition of outward tests of loyalty, which could never have measured the inner virtue that to him was the cardinal qualification for rule.

Occasionally Milton does endorse the principles of the accountability of governments to the people,[114] and of parliaments to the electorate.[115] Yet that premiss yields to alarm when it threatens to be implemented. His dislike and fear of parliamentary elections took acute forms. *Defensio Secunda* tells the English people, in forceful terms, of the dangers attendant on 'the privilege of returning whom you please to parliament'. What hope is there of virtuous rule if 'you may elect the man, however unfit, who should treat you with the most lavish feastings' and 'with the greatest quantity of drink'?[116] In the same work he answered the royalist charge that Pride's Purge and the regicide had had no sanction from the electorate. 'Was the nod of the people to be waited for, on which to hang the issue of counsels so important? ... What would have been the end of this referring forward and backward?' What, indeed, if the people 'had demanded that Charles should be restored to the kingdom?'[117] The attraction of Machiavelli's argument, which Milton approvingly cited in the commonplace-book, in favour of 'tumults' as aids to popular liberty is belied in *The Readie and Easie Way*, where he warns against the 'licentious and unbridled democracy', and 'the noise and shouting of a rude multitude',[118] that elections would bring. Nedham had warned tirelessly against the 'corruption' which the prolongation of the Long Parliament would foster. *The Readie and Easie Way*, shrugging off such objections, asks, 'what can a perpetual senate have wherein to grow corrupt'?[119]

114. *CP* ii. 488–9; vii. 431; *CW* vii. 359. 115. *CP* iii. 399.
116. *CW* viii. 245–7. 117. Ibid. 151–3. 118. *CP* vii. 438, 442.
119. Ibid. 461.

Milton showed no more enthusiasm for elections during the Commonwealth of 1649–53 than after it. Yet what hopes could he have had, at that time, from the avoidance of them: from, that is, the prolongation of the rule of the Rump? In *Defensio Secunda*, addressing Cromwell, Milton castigated the Rump's political and ethical failings.[120] The same tract describes the tyranny, the corruption, the fraud, and the incompetence that, he indicates, are the norm of parliamentary rule. No more than the electors, it transpires, are the elected fit for freedom. His language reveals that the rule of the Rump had if anything deepened his disillusion with the parliament of which it was the survivor. On the subjects of parliamentary government and parliamentary elections, the contrasting positions of Nedham, the friend of accountability, and Milton, in theory also its friend but in practice its enemy, would for a time push the two friends in opposite directions.

★★

Were there achievements of the Rump that gave Milton pleasure? It did agree, under pressure from the army, to two measures of which we might expect him to have approved. It ordained that legal proceedings be held in English rather than in what Milton called the 'Norman gibberish' of tradition.[121] Yet he never mentions the measure. Secondly the Rump revoked the legislation, vexatious to the sects, that enjoined attendance at services of the established Church on Sundays. He is silent here too – unless fleetingly and obliquely, in words published nine years after the event, when he had tactical reasons to find virtues in the Rump's legislative record.[122] He would have known how narrow in scope the new law was, and with what transparent reluctance it had been passed.[123] The only legislation between the founding of the Commonwealth and the expulsion of the Rump of which he voiced approval was its 'prudent and well deliberated act', passed in the same year, against blasphemy.[124] For Milton's tolerance did not extend to the permission of impiety or of affronts to God's honour.[125] There was no conflict, in his mind, between that stance and his unalterable

120. *CW* viii. 221. 121. *CP* i. 424; cf. iii. 193. 122. Ibid. vii. 241; below, p. 302.

123. Worden, *Rump Parliament*, 239. One might expect a side of Milton to have warmed, as Nedham did, to the Commonwealth's performance on another front, the strengthening of English sea power: *CP* v. 321.

124. *CP* vii. 250. See too p. 258; *Case*, 123 (cf. p. 259).

125. David Loewenstein, 'Treason against God and State', in Dobranski and Rumrich, eds., *Milton and Heresy*, 176–98.

commitment to the principle of liberty of conscience. The act against blasphemy, after all, was a 'curb' on the wicked.[126] But in 1652 the Rump, far from aiding liberty of conscience, challenged it. Milton found himself, not the supporter of a legislative proposal by the purged parliament, but – in close alliance with Nedham – its opponent. In his disillusion with parliament in 1648, Milton had turned, with a tributary sonnet, to the then lord general of the army, Sir Thomas Fairfax. Now, with another tributary sonnet, he again turned not to parliament but to the present lord general, Fairfax's successor Cromwell. In doing so he addressed the man who would dominate his thinking about politics in the years ahead.

126. In a forthcoming article ('Milton and Antitrinitarianism', in Sharon Achinstein and Elizabeth Sauer, eds, *Milton and Toleration*, Oxford, 2007), Martin Dzelzainis most interestingly sets Milton's endorsement of the measure against blasphemy in a different perspective, which brings out, not the proscriptions of the act, but the limits to them, which Milton's words indeed intimate. Milton's remarks, delivered six years after the event, are, most uncharacteristically, chronologically specific: '... that prudent and well deliberated act August 9, 1650'. That day, Dzelzainis points out, was the one before Milton wrote a note that would facilitate the publication two years later of the antitrinitarian work *The Racovian Catechism*, whose appearance would get him into hot water with a parliamentary committee, an episode to which we shall come in the next chapter. In Dzelzainis's account it is the mildness of the act that appealed to Milton. Unlike the severe parliamentary ordinance against blasphemy in 1648, it did not include anti-trinitarianism among the offences it sought to suppress. Dzelzainis, whose essay vividly demonstrates the significance of the licensing and publication of the *Catechism* in Milton's life and mind, suggests that he saw the act as 'the green light for licensing' the *Catechism*. Some such explanation is highly probable. Yet there is a perplexity. The legislation of August 1650, whose target was the blasphemous offences associated with the people called Ranters, had no occasion to refer to anti-trinitarianism, and did nothing to revise or repeal the legislation of 1648. Why then should Milton have seen, in the act of 1650, a green light? Perhaps he had feared that the measure, which was passed in an atmosphere of religious and moral alarm, would be more wide-ranging, as – or so the scant evidence hints – it might have been but for exertions by Milton's hero the MP Sir Henry Vane, who will likewise figure in the next chapter: see *Journal of the House of Commons*, 9 Aug. 1650. Perhaps the limits to the measure of August 1650 persuaded Milton that – the Presbyterian element in parliament having been reduced by Pride's Purge – the ordinance of 1648 would not be invoked against the licensing or the content of the *Catechism*. At all events, his remarks on the measure of 1650 make plain his unsympathetic view of the Ranters.

11

Milton and Cromwell

The civil wars, which ended persecution by the bishops, raised, in Milton's perspective, 'new forcers of conscience': 'new presbyter', which is 'but old priest writ large'. At Pride's Purge the programme for a uniform and compulsory Presbyterian Church was seen off, at least for the time being. Yet the Rump did not repeal the post-war legislation which had paved the way for the Presbyterian system; indeed it came within one vote of giving it its official blessing. Presbyterian influence in high places persisted. In 1652 what Milton now called 'new foes' to liberty of conscience rose again, when parliament considered a scheme for the 'propagation of the gospel'. It was submitted to parliament in February, published in March, and debated through the spring. There were two main parts to it. First there was the proposal which would be implemented, in a revised form, during the protectorate, and which became known as the system of 'triers' and 'ejectors'. It took up the long-standing Puritan concern with the quality of the ministry. The terms were given to the bodies appointed by Cromwell to vet candidates for church livings and to remove unsatisfactory ministers from the parishes. The second part, which is the one Milton addresses in 1652, derived from the growing alarm among orthodox Puritans, including many who were committed to the republic, at the rapid proliferation of the sects and of heretical beliefs. The scheme laid down stipulations about liberty of conscience, which it proposed to guarantee within certain limits but to forbid beyond them. It called for the suppression of the preaching or promulgation of doctrines contrary to 'those principles of Christian religion, without the acknowledgement whereof the Scriptures do plainly affirm that salvation is not to be obtained'.[1]

1. Worden, *Rump Parliament*, 296, and sources there cited.

The promoters of the plan had one heresy above all in their sights: the repudiation of the doctrine of the holy Trinity. They particularly drew parliament's attention to a recent Latin publication which would come to be known as *The Racovian Catechism*, and which set out the creed of the anti-trinitarian movement that had flourished in Cracow in Poland. The book would be publicly burnt by parliamentary order in April. Yet it was reprinted, under a false imprint, in June.[2] Anti-trinitarianism was the riskiest heresy of seventeenth-century England. The last people to have been burned for heresy in England, in 1612, denied the doctrine of the Trinity.[3] Alone of non-Roman beliefs, anti-trinitarianism was excluded from the liberty granted by the Toleration Act of 1689. If anything, Puritans were still more alarmed by it than Anglicans were. In 1648 a parliamentary ordinance enjoined the death penalty for it. In January 1649, the month of the regicide, the Rump suspended one of its members, John Fry, for his anti-trinitarian convictions. In 1651 it expelled him, 'chiefly', it was reported, 'upon a Presbyterian interest', and ordered his writings to be publicly burned.[4]

Yet the biblical foundation of trinitarianism was thin. In private, leading thinkers of the century drew back from the doctrine. Newton and John Locke were among them. So was Milton.[5] Milton's private manual of theology, *de Doctrina Christiana*, is almost a compendium of the century's most provocative heresies and doctrinal deviations. It argues, with urgent intensity and a zestful contempt for those of a different mind, against infant baptism; against the doctrine of predestination; for the doctrine (or something like it) that the soul sleeps after death; for polygamy. The treatise spells out his anti-trinitarian position, which is also implicit in *Paradise Lost*. Under the Rump he took a brave chance on its behalf, and in so doing placed himself in the eye of the anti-heretical storm of 1652. For Milton, like his friend Nedham, was a risk-taker. It was he who, in August 1650, had

2. Carolyn Polizotto, 'The Campaign against the Humble Proposals of 1652', *Journal of Ecclesiastical History*, 38 (1987), 577.
3. Ian Atherton and David Como, 'The Burning of Edward Wightman: Puritanism, Prelacy and the Politics of Heresy in Early Modern England', *English Historical Review*, 120 (2005), 1215–50.
4. Worden, *Rump Parliament*, 241.
5. On Milton and the Trinity see John P.Rumrich, Milton's Arianism: Why it Matters', in Dobranski and Rumrich, eds., *Milton and Heresy*, 75–92; Midrael Lieb, *Theological Milton* (Pittsburgh, 2006) 213–78; and, now, Dzelzainis, 'Milton and Antitrinitarianism'.

licensed, or anyway aided, the publication of *The Racovian Catechism*.[6] The printer, William Dugard, registered it for publication in November 1651, and the book was out in the new year, when Milton's relations with the government were already difficult enough. The council of state acted swiftly to order the seizure of the copies and to have Dugard arrested. Under interrogation he revealed that he had produced the work with Milton's blessing. In February Milton was in turn questioned, perhaps by a parliamentary committee, and reportedly replied that he had indeed sanctioned the work; 'that men should refrain from forbidding books; that in approving of that book he had done no more than what his opinion was'.[7] Directly after the council's intervention, Milton's duties as licenser of *Politicus* were brought to an end. As far as we know he never acted as a state licenser again.

It was early in July 1652 that Milton addressed a sonnet to the MP Sir Henry Vane. It would be boldly published, ten years later, in a hagiographical life of Vane that was quickly brought out after his execution for treason. Vane was the only civilian member of the Rump to be named or individually praised by Milton during its tenure of power (indeed, John Selden apart, the only civilian member of the House of Commons to be thus favoured during the whole of the Long Parliament). He was a leading member of the Commonwealth regime and a dominant figure in the formation of its policies at home and abroad. Yet on one subject he was in a minority. Since his contentious tenure, in his youth, of the governorship of Massachusetts, he had been a defender of sectaries and of unorthodox beliefs. He was one of the very few MPs, and much the most influential one, to argue for the separation of Church from state. In 1647 he gave protection to the anti-trinitarian John Biddle (or Bidle), who would later translate *The Racovian Catechism* into English. In 1651 Vane came (unavailingly) to the defence of the anti-trinitarian MP John Fry. William Dugard, the printer of *The Racovian Catechism*, presented an inscribed copy of Milton's *Defensio* to Vane, whose brother Charles also received a copy.[8] Vane shared his views on Church-state relations and on the permission of heresy with his former ally in New England Roger Williams, who was in England in 1652, and with whom, like Milton,

6. Stephen B. Dobranski, 'Licensing Milton's Heresy', in Dobranski and Rumrich, eds., *Milton and Heresy*, 139–58.

7. Lewalski, 284–5.

8. Journal of the House of Commons, 31 Jan. 1651; Lewalski, 624.

he was in touch. In mid-June 1652, around three weeks before Milton's sonnet, there was published an anonymous tract, *Zeal Examined*, which has plausibly been attributed to Vane, and which makes arguments for liberty of conscience akin to those of Williams.[9] Williams himself, in alliance with Vane's brother Charles, protested against the scheme for the propagation of the gospel. He informed parliament that the assumption of 'a judgement in spirituals' by 'the civil power' was 'against the liberties given by Christ Jesus to his people'.[10]

Milton's sonnet, which may be a tribute to *Zeal Examined*, applauds Vane's grasp of the proper relations of Church and state:

> ... to know
> Both spiritual power and civil, what each means,
> What severs each, thou hast learned, which few have done.
> The bounds of either sword to thee we owe;
> Therefore on thy firm hand religion leans
> In peace, and reckons thee her eldest son.[11]

Milton's words are echoed in his tract of February 1659, *Of Civil Power*, which he addressed to Richard Cromwell's parliament. It was the first of two pamphlets of that year in which he argued that Christ's spirit is contaminated, and his truth perverted, at the moment when religion depends on either 'force' – the persecution of the conscience – or 'hire', the compulsory payment of ministers by their parishioners or congregations. Milton must have had Vane near the front of his mind when he wrote in *Of Civil Power*: 'I remember to have heard often for several years', at the Rump's council of state, 'some' of its members 'so well joining religion with civil prudence, and yet so well distinguishing the different power of either, and this not only voting, but frequently reasoning why it should be so, that if any there present had been of an opinion contrary, he might doubtless have' learned the importance of entrusting power to men who 'discern between civil and religious'.[12]

9. The attribution is perceptively made in Polizotto's essay, 'Campaign', 578–9.
10. *CP* iv. 169–76.
11. 'To Sir Henry Vane the Younger'.
12. *CP* vii. 240. It is (like other autobiographical recollections of Milton) a perplexing statement, for the council, at least in its formal deliberations, did not 'often' debate the principle of liberty of conscience. Normally the formulation of religious policy was reserved to parliament, which entrusted the council, the executive arm of its rule, with the practical challenges of administration and finance and warfare and diplomacy. The council did, however, intervene in the religious sphere in January 1652, when, five days after Milton's last recorded act as a

A month or two before his sonnet to Vane, Milton had addressed another sonnet, on the same subject, to Cromwell. It survives with the heading 'To the Lord General Cromwell, May 1652. On the proposals of certain ministers at the Committee for Propagation of the Gospel'. Within the similarity of theme between the two poems there is a contrast of argument. The sonnet to Vane congratulates its recipient. It does not advise him. With John Bradshaw and Robert Overton, Vane is one of the very few men whom Milton ever praises both in the highest and in unqualified terms. Since Vane 'knows' as well as Milton the proper boundaries of Church and state, he has nothing to learn from him. Cromwell has much to learn. Four years earlier, Milton's sonnet to Fairfax, whom Cromwell would succeed as lord general, had moved, in its ninth line, from praise of the recipient's exploits in 'war', which can only 'endless war still breed', to the 'nobler task' of reform in peace.[13] In the poem to Cromwell, where 'peace hath her victories | No less renowned than war', the ninth line brings a comparable transition from past to future, and from accomplishment to challenge.

Cromwell, our chief of men, who through a cloud
  Not of war only, but detractions rude,
  Guided by faith and matchless fortitude
  To peace and truth thy glorious way hast ploughed,
And on the neck of crowned fortune proud
  Hast reared God's trophies and his work pursued,
  While Darwen stream with blood of Scots imbrued,
  And Dunbar field resounds thy praises loud,
And Worcester's laureate wreath; yet much remains
  To conquer still; peace hath her victories
  No less renowned than war, new foes arise
Threatening to bind our souls with secular chains:
  Help us to save free conscience from the paw
  Of hireling wolves whose gospel is their maw.

The earlier part of the poem records Cromwell's three greatest victories, all of them over the Scots: at Preston in 1648, at Dunbar in 1650, at Worcester in 1651. Milton, who made heroes of England's military

licenser, it ordered the seizure of copies of *The Racovian Catechism* and of its printer, William Dugard, also Milton's printer, from whose testimony it was that the council learned that Milton had licensed the publication. Yet Vane was not present.

13. 'On the Lord General Fairfax at the Siege of Colchester'.

deliverers, made his greatest hero of Cromwell, his 'country's deliverer'.[14] Where would Milton's cause have been but for Cromwell's military exploits, in England's two civil wars and then in Ireland and Scotland? What would have become of liberty in 1648–9 but for the political intervention of the army he had moulded? All that is good and great about him is concentrated, in a remarkable feat of balance and economy, into six words: 'faith', 'matchless fortitude', 'peace', 'truth', 'glorious'. Yet there is a silence. The earlier part of the poem to Vane commends his achievements as a 'senator', as a member of parliament. Cromwell was a member of parliament too, by far the most powerful one. Milton, however, dwells only on Cromwell's military exploits, not on his performance in parliament. That performance troubled Milton. Not least, it dissatisfied him on the subject of liberty of conscience. The reticence of the sonnet would be repeated in the tribute to Cromwell in Milton's *Defensio Secunda* in 1654, which barely mentions the general's relations with parliament after Worcester, and which passes over his handling, in those dealings, of the issue of religious liberty.[15]

From viewpoints less radical than Milton's, Cromwell was that principle's greatest friend. Early in 1652 he went so far as to say, in Roger Williams's hearing, that he 'would rather that Mahomedanism were permitted among us than that one of Christ's children should be persecuted'. Liberty of conscience for Christ's children was the abiding preoccupation of his career. In 1654–5, when he might have secured parliamentary approval for his rule by surrendering the guarantees of religious liberty which the Instrument of Government provided, he endangered the survival of the protectorate by clinging to them. Yet Cromwell's reforming ambitions, on this as on other fronts, were limited in scope. Though ready with imperative statements on the claims of freedom of conscience, he was prepared to sanction the imposition of tests of theological orthodoxy that would restrict it. He wanted to preserve the parish system. To Milton, to whom the only proper gatherings of believers were voluntary ones, freed from geographical constraints, and for whom the only proper ministers were those whom congregations chose to appoint and support, the system was at best redundant. Cromwell was reluctant to press for the abolition of tithes, that system of 'hire' whose removal, in Milton's mind, was the necessary partner of the establishment of religious liberty. Milton, with

14. *CW* viii. 225, 245. 15. Ibid. viii. 221.

a little simplification – for he did see a role for the magistracy in the encouragement of faith, and forbade only its enforcement of it[16] – can be called an advocate of the separation of Church from state. To Cromwell, whose position earned profound mistrust among the sects, the structure and government of the Church, and the definition of orthodox doctrine, were matters for the state, which must guard against the usurpation of its functions by an intolerant clergy. To him as to mainstream Puritans, the Church was a national organization, whose boundaries – whatever ties and affinities of sympathy among the godly might transcend them – were those of the nation. Under the protectorate the state-controlled system of 'triers' and 'ejectors' would be the centrepiece of a reform of the ministry in whose achievements Cromwell took pride, but whose premisses affronted Milton's principles.

After Worcester, when Cromwell turned from war to peace, from military campaigning to politics at Westminster, the religious no less than the political future of England rested above all on his policies and resolutions. As a reformer he liked to expound general principles and to give power and influence to subordinates who would work out the details. He left the details of ecclesiastical policy, both before and after he became protector, to a group of Independent or Congregationalist divines, of whom the principal was John Owen. Owen had been his chaplain on his military campaigns in 1649–50. In 1652 Cromwell, as Chancellor of Oxford University, installed him as his vice-chancellor. It was Owen who submitted to parliament the scheme for the 'propagation of the gospel' that dismayed Milton in that year, though there were a number of other signatories who were likewise close to Cromwell. Owen was horrified by the public campaign for the abolition of tithes. He would have been as pleased as Milton must have been appalled by parliament's decision in April 1652, a little before the sonnet to Cromwell, to confirm its commitment to the principle of compulsory maintenance and to order that tithes be duly paid until some alternative system of public maintenance – to which Milton would likewise have been opposed – was found. Another principle scandalized Owen: the conviction, promoted by the sects, that the nation's rulers have 'nothing to do with the interest of Christ and the Church'. By Milton's lights Owen's denunciation was self-condemning, for calls by churchmen for the interposition of civil power in religion were

16. Ibid. 179–81; xvii. 395.

'an argument that all true ministerial and spiritual power is dead within them'.[17]

Owen's views were alarming to Milton in another respect too. With other English Independents, Owen was an eager advocate of liberty of conscience – but within limits. Like Cromwell he was at home with a variety of Puritan beliefs. Yet those beliefs, even at their most fiercely contested, generally lay within recognizable boundaries. They were debated within a familiar range of biblical interpretation and according to familiar premisses of biblical analysis. They were all compatible with the Calvinist scheme of salvation. During the Puritan Revolution the beliefs came under mounting attack, not only from royalists, who habitually equated the Roundhead cause with heresy, but from within that cause itself. In the years afer the regicide, as Owen acknowledged in a vexed and despairing sermon to parliament in October 1652, the assault gained a new impetus and was marked by an ever deeper radicalism.[18] Orthodoxy was impugned by appeals – especially from the emerging Quaker movement – to the inner light of the spirit; by invocations of the efficacy of human reason in those matters of faith which orthodox Puritans believed to lie beyond it; by challenges to the historical existence of Christ; by 'antinomian' assertions of the freedom of God's elect from moral laws; by rejections of all theological learning; by assaults on the Calvinist apparatus of predestination and salvation; and by the spreading of 'Socinianism', as anti-trinitarianism was generally called.[19] Owen had a special horror of the 'cursed Socinians', on whom he blamed the 'flood' of 'scepticism, libertinism and atheism' which had 'broken upon the world', and whose principles he wrote hundreds and hundreds of thousands of words to refute. 'The Trinity', he affirmed, was 'the great fundamental article' of Protestantism, the 'mystery the knowledge whereof is the only means to have a right apprehension of all other sacred truths'. It was he, with other ministers, who drew parliament's attention to the publication of *The Racovian Catechism*. His hostility to heresy, however, was by no means confined to anti-trinitarianism. Owen and his friends, 'in explanation' of their proposal to forbid the expression of opinions incompatible with salvation, listed fifteen 'fundamentals' of belief.

17. *CP* vii. 257.
18. Worden, *Rump Parliament*, 292–4.
19. The term also had broader meanings: see Sarah Mortimer, 'The Challenge of Socinianisim in mid-Seventeenth-Century England' (Oxford University D.Phil. thesis, 2007). H.J. McLachlan, *Socinianism in Seventeenth-Century England* (Oxford, 1951), remains a good introduction to the anti-trinitarian movement.

The 'fundamentals' were the 'proposals of certain ministers' to which the heading of Milton's sonnet refers.[20]

So the 'new foes' who 'arise' derive encouragement from, and bear responsibility for, an initiative for the curtailment of liberty of conscience in which Cromwell is deeply implicated. Of course, Cromwell need not be the prisoner of Owen's scheme. The poem has no purpose unless Milton has some hope that Cromwell will 'Help us'. If any one person has the power 'to save free conscience' from 'hireling wolves', it is Cromwell. Yet 'Help us' is a plea, not an expectation. It quickens the poem with an urgency, and troubles it with an uncertainty, that we miss if, as editors and commentators often do, we take Cromwell's and Milton's minds to be at one. If Cromwell had followed Milton's advice in 1652, the sonnet to Vane that followed it might have been needless. As it was, Milton turned from Cromwell to Vane.

★★

Marchamont Nedham, the ally of the Independents in the 1640s, had long been, with them, a friend to the principle of liberty of conscience. If, for Milton, the conduct of the Westminster Assembly of Divines showed new presbyter to be but old priest writ large, *Politicus* remembered in June 1651 that when 'the sticklers of the Presbyterian clergy began to show their teeth' in the Assembly, they 'made more bold than the bishops to intermeddle with civil affairs'.[21] Readers may wonder at Milton's readiness to accuse the Presbyterians, those devotees of sober devotion and conduct, of a love of 'licence' (for it is they who 'licence ... mean when they cry liberty').[22] Yet, not for the only time, a surprise of Milton's language corresponds to one of Nedham's. For *Politicus* hits at the 'licentious way' of the Presbyterians. It also charges them, as Milton does, with damning the friends of true liberty as 'heretics and schismatics'.[23] In 1646–7, the time of Milton's poems against the Presbyterians, Nedham had confronted the Presbyterians'

20. Blair Worden, 'John Milton and Oliver Cromwell', in Ian Gentles, John Morrill, and Blair Worden, eds., *Soldiers, Writers and Statesmen* (Cambridge, 1998), 266–8; Worden, 'Toleration and the Cromwellian Protectorate', *Studies in Church History*, 21 (1984), 202 ff.
21. *MP*, 19 June 1651, 863–4.
22. Stephen Honeygorsky, 'Licence Reconsidered: Ecclesial Nuances', *Milton Quarterly*, 25 (1991), 59–66, discusses Milton's choice of the noun. See also John Leonard, 'Revolting against Backsliding in Milton's Sonnet XII', *Notes and Queries*, 241 (1996), 269–73; McDowell, 'Family Politics'.
23. *MP* 24 Oct. 1650, 328; 19 June 1651, 865; cf. 21 Oct. 1652, 1946.

'cursed principle of universal compulsion', and their taste for 'worldly pomp and power', with arguments, and sometimes in language, that recall Milton's writings of the same decade. There is no reason, Nedham wrote, why 'a variety of opinions' should impair 'the unity of the spirit'. It is 'madness to persecute men', for, 'since we lost perfection in Adam', there are inevitable limits to our knowledge of God and to the certainty of our doctrines. In our imperfection we must work our own way to truth, by a process of progressive revelation. 'Is there not a passing from grace to grace, from glory to glory, in gospel-knowledge? Does God reveal all at once? Have we attained perfection?' If we persist, we will make 'further discoveries in the hidden things of God.... We should all be seekers in this kind.'[24] There were writers other than Milton who would have endorsed those sentiments. Yet, on this as on other subjects, there are moments when Nedham's prose takes on a Miltonic ring. In *Areopagitica* Milton rejoiced in the religious explorations of his fellow Londoners, whom he portrayed 'searching, revolving new notions and ideas ... reading, trying all things, assenting to the force of reason and convincement'.[25] Nedham observed in 1647 that 'it hath pleased God to stir up men's hearts wonderfully at present, to search the Scriptures themselves, to take upon them to question, reason cases, and try spirits, and not to pin their souls and understandings upon presbyters' sleeves'.[26]

Nedham, like the mainstream Independents, normally advocated neither the separation of Church and state nor unlimited liberty of conscience. Though he time and again charged the Presbyterians with 'twist[ing] the church-discipline with the interest of state' or with 'twist[ing] together civil and spiritual slavery', he usually did so from an Erastian viewpoint. That is, he wanted the Church and the clergy to be controlled by the state, not freed from it. Nedham's discussions of religion, which for the most part adjusted themselves to the language of the Puritan godly, involve sudden departures from his customarily secular tone. His thinking on the subject, rationalist and sceptical, had no discernible doctrinal content. Profoundly anticlerical, it was close to the positions of such Erastian figures as the scholar and MP John Selden and Thomas Hobbes. For all the distance of belief and perspective between them, Erastians often made common cause with

24. Nedham, *Independencie no Schisme*, (1646), 3, 10; *idem*, *The Case of the Kingdom Stated* (1647), 3, 7.

25. *CP* ii. 554.

26. Nedham, *Independencie no Schisme*, 3.

Independents, with whom they shared an antagonism to Presbyterianism and to persecution. Nedham was a bridge between them. In common with both groups he accepted the need, or anyway the inevitability, of limits to the toleration of unorthodox belief.

Yet on three occasions in 1651–2 he strikingly departed from those premisses. In each case he stood by his friend Milton. It was in February 1651, six months after Milton had approved the publication of *The Racovian Catechism*, that the Rump, 'chiefly, as was conceived, upon a Presbyterian interest', expelled John Fry from the Commons as the author of racily written pamphlets which had challenged, in a rational and sceptical spirit, both the doctrine of the Trinity and the tactics of intellectual and clerical mystification that, Fry alleged, lay behind it. *Politicus* reported the episode at length. Normally a government newsbook which paid so much attention to such an event would either have merely recorded the House's decision in official prose or have glossed it to indicate its correctness.[27] *Politicus* took a different course. It reproduced from Fry's books chirpy, colloquial passages which had been read out in the debate – and which blended easily with the perky humour of the newsbook. Nedham's audience read Fry's attacks on 'that chaffy and absurd opinion of three persons or subsistences in the godhead'; on 'that gross and carnal opinion of three distinct persons or subsistences in the godhead'; on trinitarian inferences from the Scripture which are 'fit only to keep ignorant people in carnal and gross thoughts of God'; on clergy who pretend that belief is 'above reason'. *Politicus*, which thus publishes Fry's case, does not present that of the Rump. Instead of explaining parliament's reasons for condemning the tracts, Nedham merely prints, without comment, the resolutions with which the parliament voted the offending passages 'erroneous', 'profane', 'highly scandalous', and so on. The effect is to make the Commons seem an instrument of unthinking and humourless repression, an enemy of rational enquiry, and the ally of the persecuting clergy. The newsbook, in defiance of the official government line, thus gives ostensibly condemnatory but in effect supportive publicity to opinions which conform to Nedham's own rationalism and anticlericalism.[28] They also conform to the convictions of Milton, not only an anti-trinitarian but a detester of clerical presumption, and a spokesman too for 'rational liberty' and for the equation of 'true liberty' with her 'twi[n]',

27. Thus see *Severall Proceedings in Parliament*, 27 Feb. 1652, 1115–16.
28. *MP*, 27 Feb. 1651, 616–18.

'right reason'.[29] Nedham's coverage of the episode was as bold as Milton's support for *The Racovian Catechism* in the following winter would be.

The other two occasions are to be found in 1652, when Owen's proposals for the propagation of the gospel were submitted to the Rump and protractedly debated by it. On both of them it is again hard to imagine that Milton was far from Nedham's desk. The reporting of the issue by *Politicus* differed significantly from that by the other principal government newsbook, *Severall Proceedings in Parliament*. Through the spring and summer *Severall Proceedings* supported a campaign, which had an orchestrated movement of petitioning and pamphleteering behind it, against heresies and sectaries. Matters came to a head at the end of April and the start of May. On 1 May, to indicate its support of Owen's scheme, *Severall Proceedings* urged the 'settl[ing]' of 'government ... in the Church' and called for action against 'the publishing of blasphemies and such things as tend to the beating down of the fundamentals of religion'.[30] Three days earlier, on 28 April, Milton's and Vane's friend Roger Williams published a contribution to the debate which supported those men's position. It was on 29 April that the Rump heartened the orthodox and dismayed the radicals by voting to confirm the retention of the system of tithes. On the same day an editorial of *Politicus* defied the orthodox stance promoted by its fellow newsbook *Severall Proceedings*, and defended the position which Milton would soon advance in his sonnets to Cromwell and Vane. The editorial, which sets Nedham's customary Erastianism aside, repudiates the 'national way of churching'. For 'not all nations in a lump, nor any whole nations or national bodies', are 'to be formed into churches'. God's 'Church or people now under the Gospel are not to be a body political but spiritual and mystical', that is, a voluntary association of 'such as are called and sanctified'. Belief is not to be 'forced' by 'worldly power and prudence'. The binding of consciences under colour of 'discipline', and of 'preventing of heresy and advancing of Christ's kingdom, ... hath been the very right hand of Antichrist, opposing Christ in his way, whose kingdom, being not of this world, depends not upon the helps and devices of worldly wisdom'.

Milton traced the worldly aspirations and persecuting spirit of the clergy back to the Emperor Constantine.[31] Nedham's editorial does the same. To orthodox Christians, Constantine's conversion was a great breakthrough

29. *Paradise Lost* XII. 82–5. 30. Worden, *Rump Parliament*, 296–7.
31. *CP* i. 554–61; vii. 279; cf. *CW* viii. 183.

for Christianity. To radicals it contaminated God's truth and spirit with power and human interests. With Constantine's favour to Christianity, explains *Politicus*, 'Satan had a new game now to play'. The editorial laments that men are 'forced in by the commands and constitutions of worldly power and prudence', and protests against the confusion of 'the spiritual power' with 'the worldly and secular interest of state' that has been wrought by 'the Church-national pretenders'. Nedlam thus matches Milton's tribute to Vane, who understands the relationship between spiritual and civil power, and the poet's warning to Cromwell against 'secular chains'. The editorial also looks forward to the foretelling by the angel Michael in *Paradise Lost* of the corruption of the Church, whose ministers will 'join | Secular power' to their worldly designs, 'though feigning still to act | By spiritual'; 'and from that pretence, | Spiritual laws by carnal power shall force | On every conscience' (XII. 516–22). Never had *Politicus* displayed more passion than in that editorial. 'I fear I have been too large', acknowledges Nedham, 'but could not avoid it, in regard you have not yet half my mind.'[32]

The implications of the editorial of 29 April for Owen's scheme, though obvious, were decently veiled. On 12 August, when *Politicus* returned to the theme, it barely troubled to conceal its target. Again the newbook's editorial is impassioned. Its subject is the principle, promoted 'in all times by the furious drivers of the clergy',

> that there ought to be an establishment of some certain chief heads, articles and principles of faith, as fundamental and orthodox, which all men must be bound to hold or believe, or else incur the censure of heretics, sectarians and schismatics. This position (I say), under what disguise soever it come, with whatever pretences it be clothed, or by what persons soever it be owned, is ... the very spirit and principle of the pope and Antichrist. It hath been the dam of that white devil called ecclesiastical policy, or national uniformity, a device subservient to that inveterate project of national churches, which is in a word the interest not of Christ but the clergy.[33]

'[W]hat persons soever ...': the attack on Owen and his clerical colleagues is unmistakable and frontal. In 1645 Nedham's *Britanicus* had been temporarily suspended after he had, in his own words, 'overshot myself' in a daring attack on the tyranny of Charles I. It looks as if, in his assault on

32. *MP*, 29 Apr. 1652, 1553–6 (cf. 22 Apr. 1652, 1551–2).
33. Ibid. 12 Aug. 1652, 1785–90. See also ibid. 18 Dec. 1651, 1276; 6 May 1652, 1576–8; 19 Aug. 1652, 1803.

Cromwell's *protégé* Owen, he overshot himself again. Cromwell was at this time anxiously seeking to contain the forces of radicalism within the army and to create a united parliamentary and military front for his reforming programme, of which Owen's scheme was a central if not the central element. The observations of *Politicus* attacked that policy.

The editorial was Nedham's last. Henceforth *Politicus* appeared solely as a reporter of news, occasionally peppered with wit and mischief but now shorn of its argumentative vitality. It may be that the material for his series of editorials on the merits of republican rule, in which the contributions of 29 April and of 12 August are somewhat artificially placed, had anyway run its course, though, if so, one would expect him to have been ready with a body of commentary on another theme. It may be, too, that the rising temperature of the conflict between parliament and army, which would peak with the forcible expulsion of the Rump the following April, had made the publication of opinionated editorials in the government press too delicate or divisive a business. It may also be that Nedham had committed an offence at least as provocative in his editorial of the previous week, which had implicitly portrayed Cromwell as a ruthless Machiavellian prince.[34] For in August 1652, when radical feeling in the army acquired a new intensity, Nedham, in its support, went out on a limb in matters political as well as ecclesiastical. None the less, just as the last issue of the newsbook to have been licensed by Milton was the one that appeared immediately before the council of state's investigation into the printing of *The Racovian Catechism*, so its final editorial was written in Milton's religious cause.

★★

The unhappy change in Milton's relationship with the government had occurred after the return of Cromwell to Westminster following the Battle of Worcester, and with the consequent decline of the Commonwealth's 'party of its own'. Nedham's republican editorials, which ran from September 1651, defied that trend for nearly a year, but then succumbed to it. At least, however, there remained the battle of the two writers against Salmasius. That conflict, which had seemed in danger of fading, was obligingly revived at the end of August 1652, around ten days after the last editorial of *Politicus*,

34. Above, pp. 92–3.

by the publication of *Regii Sanguinis Clamor*, the attack on Milton's *Defensio*. It was to the conquest of Alexander More in literary combat that Milton's energies now turned; and when, in the following month, he needed to supply evidence that More was the author of *Clamor*, Nedham's practice of publishing letters from Leiden supplied the vehicle.

In 1655 Milton remembered that *Clamor* 'was scarcely complete in sheets before it was put into my hands in the council', and that soon afterwards another copy was sent to him 'eo ... qui quaestionibus tum praefuit', which means, or approximately means, 'by him who at that time was in charge of interrogations'. Perhaps he was referring to the director of the Commonwealth's intelligence service, Thomas Scot (the supervisor of *Politicus*). The second copy was 'accompanied with the intimation that the Commonwealth expected my services to stop the mouth of' the author.[35] Milton's first 'defence', to his delight, had been officially commissioned by the council, which congratulated him on it. Though the writing of the second 'defence' is indeed likely to have been encouraged by individual councillors, Milton does not quite say that the council – whose minutes contain no reference to *Clamor* – commissioned his reply to it. Given his eagerness to give as strong an impression as possible of the official support for his exertions on the Commonwealth's behalf, the omission is conspicuous. Perhaps someone handed him the book, with an indication that he might or should reply to it, while a council meeting was gathering or dispersing. Or perhaps – for his memory of events at the council board seems to have had a fanciful element[36] – he misremembered the episode or embroidered upon it. At all events, the defenders of the Rump would have no reason to be grateful for *Defensio Secunda*, which, when it eventually appeared in 1654, would attack its memory.

His repudiation of it would divide him from former allies. A few hours after Cromwell's forcible ejection of the Rump on 20 April 1653, there was an attempt by a group of his opponents, John Bradshaw among them, to reassemble the parliament's executive arm, the council of state. According to a source which, though it has come down to us only in a garbled form, is likely to be essentially reliable, Cromwell took other army leaders with him to the council chamber and told the assembled members that the parliament had been dissolved and the council with it; to which Bradshaw answered, 'you are mistaken; for no power under heaven can dissolve them

35. *CW* ix. 13. 36. Above, p. 244 n.12.

but themselves; therefore take you notice of that.'[37] Bradshaw was alluding to the act of 1641 which forbade the dissolution of the parliament without its own consent. The coup of April 1653, which he and many others would never forgive, destroyed such basis of legitimacy, and such continuity with the genesis of the revolution in 1640 when the parliament had assembled, as had endured. In December 1653 there was a further coup. The Rump had been replaced in July by an assembly chosen by the army, Barebone's Parliament as it came to be tauntingly known after the surname of one of its members. When army officers engineered the dissolution of Barebone's in December, Cromwell became Lord Protector under the new constitution, the Instrument of Government. The Rump had abolished rule by a 'single person' and had sought, through its engagement of loyalty, to commit the nation to government without one. Cromwell broke that injunction. Now, by the Instrument of Government, 'the exercise of the chief magistracy' was to reside in 'one person', the protector.[38] Those such as Bradshaw who insisted on the illegality of the Rump's expulsion became known as 'commonwealthmen' or 'commonwealthsmen'. They were dedicated to the restoration of the Rump and to the rule of a sovereign House of Commons. To them Cromwell's 'usurpation' was a profound betrayal, which sacrificed the revolution to the ambition of the self-styled protector.

Milton took a different path. He served the government of the ruler who had earned Bradshaw's undying hostility, and praised Cromwell in *Defensio Secunda*, which appeared at the end of May 1654. On the publication of the book he sent a copy of it, with an accompanying letter, to 'my lord'. The usual supposition that 'my lord' was Bradshaw is not beyond question, but he does seem much the likeliest candidate.[39] The book and letter were delivered to 'my lord' by Andrew Marvell, who then reported the meeting with him to Milton. Marvell's account suggests that Milton was nervous about the lord's reaction; that Marvell's task had been to smooth the path of the book's reception by him; and that the lord himself, who greeted

37. C. H. Firth, ed., *Memoirs of Edmund Ludlow*, 2 vols. (Oxford, 1894), i. 357; see too Austin Woolrych, *Commonwealth to Protectorate* (Oxford, 1982), 104.

38. S. R. Gardiner, ed., *Constitutional Documents*, 405–6.

39. The document reveals that Milton had earlier written a letter to 'my lord' in Marvell's favour (Margoliouth, ii. 305). He had indeed written thus to Bradshaw in 1653. In the usage of the Interregnum, holders of high offices of state, such as those occupied by Bradshaw in 1649–51, retained the title of 'lord' afterwards. The identification with Bradshaw was made by Masson (iv. 620–2), but what seems to be an inadvertent ambiguity of wording by Masson has created the belief, for which there is no evidence, that Bradshaw is known to have been in the vicinity of Eton, as the 'lord' apparently was, at the time.

Marvell evasively, was uneasy about what the documents might contain. Marvell was able to give Milton a qualified assurance: 'my lord ... did then witness all respect to your person, and as much satisfaction concerning your work as could be expected from so cursory a review and so sudden an account as he could then have of it from me'.[40]

If the 'lord' was indeed Bradshaw, Milton had good cause for anxiety. While there was much in the book with which Bradshaw would gladly have concurred, there was also much that risked antagonizing him. *Defensio Secunda* not only lauded Cromwell but vindicated, albeit in the very briefest terms, the two coups of 1653 that had brought him to power. Milton looked now to one man for the nation's salvation. 'Consider often', *Defensio Secunda* urges Cromwell, 'how precious a thing you hold deposited with you': 'liberty, commended and entrusted to your care by your country, who, what she before expected from the choicest men of the whole nation, now expects, and hopes to attain, through you alone. Respect this high expectation of you, this only hope of your country' (225). 'Cromwell, we are deserted; you alone remain; the sovereign authority of the state is returned only into your hands, and subsists only in you. To your invincible virtue we all give place' – all, that is, except those who 'look with envy' on him (223), the motive of opposition that Milton here implicitly ascribes to the commonwealthmen. In vindication of Cromwell's elevation, Milton invokes Aristotle's precept that rule should be bestowed on the worthiest, and that if a single person is superior to the rest he should govern them. The rule of the 'supremely excellent' Cromwell[41] is opposed by men who 'without equal ability are desirous of equal honours', and who 'know not that there is nothing in human society more pleasing to God, or more agreeable to reason; that there is nothing more just in a state, nothing more useful, than that the most worthy should possess the sovereign power' (223). Before and after the protectorate Milton repeatedly made a very different use of Aristotle's argument. What right, he then asked, has a Stuart, or perhaps any ruler, to impose his will on countless subjects at least as worthy as he?[42] Yet in 1654 he avows that Cromwell's unique excellence 'is acknowledged by all', for he is, as he tells him, 'the greatest and most glorious of our citizens, the director of the public counsels, the leader of the bravest of armies, the father of your country' (223–5). His 'exploits have surpassed, not merely those of kings, but even those which have been

40. Margoliouth, ii. 305–6, 378. 41. *CP* iv. 666. 42. Above, Ch. 10.

fabled of our heroes'. He has 'little less than divine virtue', and in him there lives 'an energy whether of spirit and genius, or of discipline, established not by military rule only but by the rule of Christ and of sanctity' (215).

Eulogy could scarcely reach higher. There is awe in it, perhaps even worship, as there was in his sonnet to Cromwell in May 1652. Even so, the eulogy is charged, as the sonnet is and as most of Milton's praises of men are, with doubt and anxiety and warning. The theme of Milton's great late poems – as of 'Comus' earlier – is temptation: the temptation of Adam and Eve, of Samson, of Christ in the wilderness. In *Defensio Secunda* Cromwell, about whose 'temptations' his enemies and even his friends talked insistently, confronts the lure of ambition and aggrandizement. Like our first parents in Paradise, like the fallen men of *Areopagitica*, like the English nation, as Milton represents it, in the Puritan Revolution, Cromwell faces a test of virtue. For only by 'trials' against vice, Milton knew, is virtue formed and proved.[43] The regicides, *Defensio Secunda* reminds us, had passed a 'trial of virtue fair and glorious' (7). The same work discloses that Cromwell's trial is to be conducted, as the joint cause of virtue and liberty always is, within the inner man.

> You have taken upon you the heaviest burden, which will try you thoroughly; it will search you through and through, and lay open your inmost soul; it will show what is the predominant disposition of your nature, what is your strength, what is your weight; whether there is indeed in you that living piety, that faith, justice, and moderation of mind, for which we thought that you above all others deserved, by the will of God, to be elevated to this sovereign dignity. (227–9)

The question what Cromwell 'deserved' had been a tireless theme of *Politicus* in 1651–2. With the lord general in mind, Nedham had warned the English against the rise of self-seeking great men, 'though never so deserving', or even if they 'have deserved never so well by good success or service', or even though 'a man be never so good a patriot'. Some of the greatest heroes of the Roman republic, Nedham recalled, had 'sufficiently deserved what befell them' when, after they had turned their power against the people's interest, the people overthrew them.[44]

43. *CP* i. 975; ii. 515.
44. *MP*, 16 Oct. 1651, 1126; 25 Dec. 1651, 1288; 12 Feb. 1652, 1386; 15 Apr. 1652, 1523–4; 24 June 1652, 1674. One of Nedham's offending Romans is Camillus, a point on which James Harrington agreed with him (Pocock, ed., *Political Works*, 342). In *Defensio Secunda*, Cromwell, with or without irony, is 'our Camillus' (211).

Alexander More, the immediate target of *Defensio Secunda*, was no admirer of Cromwell. Yet in replying to it he was startled by what seemed to him the impertinence of Milton's treatment of the protector: 'you prescribe duties' for him and 'present threats if he should act' contrary to Milton's instructions.[45] Together with his moral injunctions to Cromwell, Milton supplies equally candid practical ones. He has a programme ready for him. The pleas of the sonnet of 1652, where Cromwell is 'our chief of men', reappear in the treatise, where he is 'the greatest and most glorious of our citizens' ('civis maximus et gloriosissimus'). The sonnet, having extolled Cromwell's past, tells him that 'much remains' for him to do: *Defensio Secunda*, having extolled it too, urges him to 'go on' to new great deeds (225). Cromwell has to overcome 'detractions rude' in the sonnet, 'envy' in the prose work (223). In the treatise as in the sonnet, Milton sets the greatness of Cromwell's past against the exacting challenges still before him. In the sonnet, 'Peace hath her victories no less renowned than war': in the treatise the tasks awaiting him are 'arduous things, in comparison of which war is a play-game'. The sonnet alerts Cromwell to the threats of 'secular chains' and 'hireling wolves', while Milton's poem to Sir Henry Vane, which complements it, praises Vane for knowing 'Both spiritual power and civil, what each means, | What severs each': *Defensio Secunda* complains against 'hire for preaching the gospel', and urges Cromwell not to 'suffer the two powers, the ecclesiastical and the civil, which are so totally distinct, to commit whoredom together, and, by their intermingled and false riches, to ... subvert one another' (235).

Further advice follows. Cromwell is to reform the law and to free the press (237–9). He is also urged to choose his principal counsellors from among the military heroes of the civil war, and from the regicides and men like them. He must resist the temptation of supposing that there are better preservers of the cause (231–3). That was not the principle of Cromwell, whose 'catholic projects' of the Commonwealth period had been designed to bring moderates, even some former royalists, back into government, and who pursued the same goal during the protectorate, when he sought to distance the regicide in the nation's memory. Yet *Defensio Secunda* concludes with a paean to Milton's own Homeric achievement in lauding the 'heroic action' of the regicide, and in celebrating, 'in praises destined

45. *CP* iv. 1109.

to endure forever, the transcendent deeds' of England's deliverers of 1649 'and those who performed them' (253–5).

There is other pointed counsel too. In 1651–2 *Politicus* had warned the English to recognize, in displays of personal ostentation among rulers of a republic, the threat of usurpation. The newsbook's language, we saw, anticipated Milton's observation in 1660 that the rulers of free peoples 'walk the streets as other men', whereas a king 'must be adored like a demigod'. In *Defensio Secunda*, the obligation 'to shun the pomp of wealth and of power' is pressed on the protector (229). Other advice offered him by Milton is bolder still, coming as it does from a government employee to the head of state. Again it takes us back to Nedham. We saw that in 1650–2 Nedham hinted at parallels, as did Marvell in 'An Horatian Ode', between Cromwell, whose sword threatens to end the English republic, and Julius Caesar, whose sword killed the Roman one; and that he used the analogy of Caesar to indicate Cromwell's strategy of wooing the people by portraying himself as the friend of their liberty, which in reality he designed to betray.[46] It was with Cromwell in mind that *Politicus* contrasted Caesar, who 'pretends' to be the 'patron' of 'liberty', with the frugal Pompey, that 'true patron of the people's liberty', who 'both in peace and war ... approved himself the grand patron of public liberty'.[47] A parallel point is made in *Defensio Secunda*, which asks whether Cromwell, who has been the champion of liberty in war, will be its friend or enemy in peace. 'Last of all' Cromwell is to 'suffer not that liberty, which you have gained with so many hardships, so many dangers, to be violated by yourself, or in any wise impaired by others'. For 'he who forcibly seizes upon the liberty of others is ... the first to become a slave'; and 'if the patron himself of liberty ... should at last offer violence to her whom he has defended, this must ... be destructive and deadly ... to the very cause of all virtue and piety' (227).

By 1654 that was, in many eyes, precisely what Cromwell had done. The expulsion of the Rump in April 1653, and his own elevation to the protectorate in December of the same year, were viewed as a fundamental violation of liberty not only by Milton's hero John Bradshaw and other commonwealthmen but by the wide range of parliamentarian opinion, so

46. Above, pp. 88–99. 47. *MP*, 20 Nov. 1651, 1205; 17 June 1652, 1661.

few of whose representatives would accept office under the protectorate. Why did Milton publish such advice after the event? Why, in 1654, did he reproduce the warnings and prophecies, which time had vindicated, of Nedham and Marvell in 1650–2? To seek answers we must look more closely at *Defensio Secunda*. For it proves to be a more complicated work, and from a historical perspective a more revealing one, than it appears.

12

Milton's Second Defence

Defensio Secunda is a response to another Latin work, *Regii Sanguinis Clamor*, 'The Cry of the Royal Blood', which was published anonymously in or around late August 1652. *Clamor* took up the cause of Salmasius against the English regicides and against Milton.[1] It savagely attacked the first 'defence' (*Defensio*) and the character of its author. Milton supposed that it had been written, in France or Holland, by the clergyman Alexander More, a friend of Salmasius. Though More contributed prefatory material to *Clamor* and helped it through the press, it was almost certainly composed, in England, by the Anglican clergyman Peter du Moulin. Milton, who had manufactured evidence to support his mistake in 1652, thereafter refused to acknowledge his error, though by the time *Defensio Secunda* appeared (albeit possibly not when it went to press) he must have been fully aware of it. In response to More's own replies to *Defensio Secunda* Milton extended the attack on him in the vituperative tract *Pro Se Defensio* in 1655, where, as in *Defensio Secunda*, the forged distich that had supported his attribution in 1652 reappeared.

However much or little encouragement he received from councillors of state for the writing of *Defensio Secunda*, it was not from them alone that the suggestion of a reply to *Clamor* came. While *Clamor* was in the press, its printer at The Hague, Adrian Vlacq, sent the sheets to Milton's friend Samuel Hartlib in the hope that Milton would write a reply, which Vlacq would also publish. Vlacq, who seems to have believed that his proposition had been well received, was subsequently unable to understand why Milton did not 'reply at once' to *Clamor*, and why his response appeared only

1. Above, pp. 254–5. Pertinent selections of *Clamor* can be read in translation in *CP* iv. 1041–81. Selections from Salmasius's *Defensio Regia*, the target of Milton's first 'defence', are supplied, again in translation, in the same volume, pp. 985–1039.

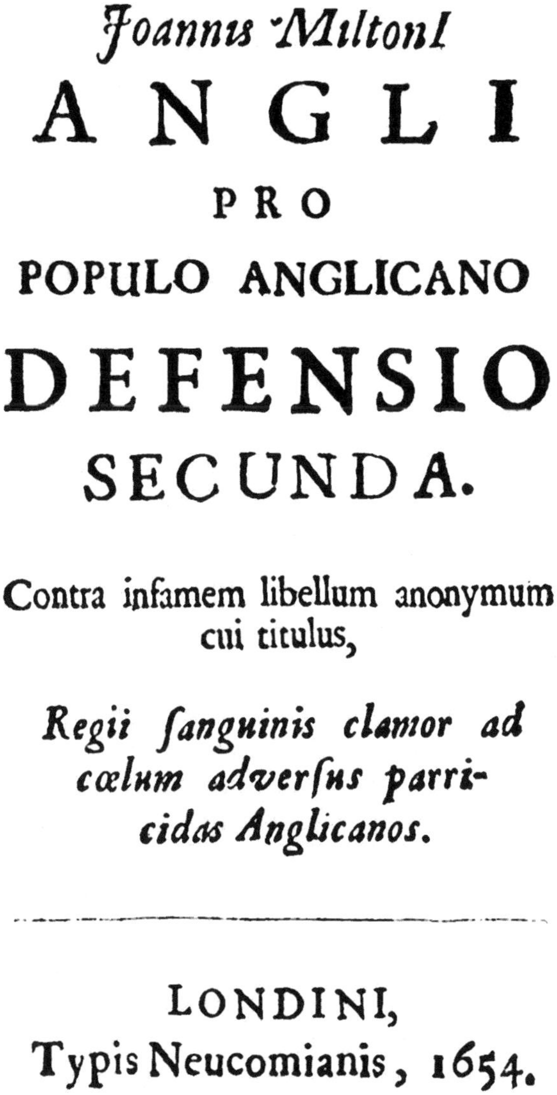

Joannis Miltoni

ANGLI

PRO

POPULO ANGLICANO

DEFENSIO

SECUNDA.

Contra infamem libellum anonymum
cui titulus,

*Regii ſanguinis clamor ad
cœlum adverſus parri-
cidas Anglicanos.*

LONDINI,
Typis Neucomianis, 1654.

Figure 8. Milton's *Defensio Secunda*: title-page

'at last, at long last', 'almost two years' after Vlacq had sent him the sheets.[2] They were good questions. In *Pro Se Defensio*, Milton forcefully refutes the accusation that he 'spent two years' in writing *Defensio Secunda*. Yet the refutation is oddly worded. It seems half to concede what it simultaneously denies: that he indeed took that 'long time in labouring and polishing' the work.[3] Earlier in *Pro Se Defensio* he gives an account of the genesis of *Defensio Secunda*. It raises more questions than it answers. When he received the request to reply to *Clamor*, he recalls, he was 'oppressed' by other concerns: ill health, two family bereavements, and his now complete blindness. Besides, there was, he says, a consideration that led him to decline, or anyway to postpone, the task. For he expected an attack from an 'adversary ... far more desirable'. This was Salmasius himself, the target of *Defensio*, who

> daily threatened to descend upon me with all his force. But considering myself relieved from a certain portion of my task by his sudden death [in late August 1653]; and being somewhat re-established in health, by its being in part restored and in part desperate; that I might not appear as disappointing altogether the expectation of persons of first consequence, and amid so many calamities to have abandoned all regard for reputation; as soon as an opportunity was given me of collecting any certain information concerning this anonymous crier, I attack.[4]

Yet Milton, when he heard of the existence of *Clamor* in September 1652, had immediately used every means to learn about the man he took to be its author. It is only a few pages after his account in 1655 of the writing of *Defensio Secunda*, indeed, that he cheerfully recalls the Leiden letter of September 1652 which both ascribed *Clamor* to More and supplied the spurious information about his private life to which Milton would stubbornly adhere.

Milton's description of the circumstances of his decision to 'attack' is a translator's nightmare. However it is given in English, the passage is slippery and obfuscating. It also carries a puzzle. Critics and editors have taken Milton's words to mean that he did not conceive of the book until late August 1653. The writing itself, they assume, took place entirely or mostly after Cromwell had become protector in December. Thus the most exhaustive biography of Milton decides that the book 'took shape in Milton's mind' 'during the autumn and winter of 1653', and that it was then

2. *CP* iv. 1088. 3. *CW* ix. 95. 4. Ibid. 13–15.

'prepared with all possible speed'.[5] If so, we are left to wonder why, having failed to write it at the behest of the 'persons of first consequence' – a term which Milton presumably wants us to take to mean either the Rump's council of state or prominent figures within it – he composed it after those 'persons' had been evicted from power. Perhaps his words are intended to encourage the assumption about dating which has prevailed. But they do not demand it. 'I attack' ('aggredior') could indicate, not that the work was a response to Salmasius's death, but that that event prompted him to prepare for publication a work already far advanced. Milton's words are compatible with the hypothesis, of which we shall learn the truth, that when he made his attack, the treatise – 'my task' – already existed in some draft form, and had been awaiting its moment.[6]

There are passages near the end of *Defensio Secunda* which, since they trace the steps by which Cromwell became protector and describe challenges that await him in that role, were clearly written (or rewritten) after the inauguration of his regime in December 1653. The treatise also contains references to the death of Salmasius, references which, of course, cannot be dated earlier than August 1653.[7] All those allusions are brief, though Milton does give himself space to boast of the possibility that it was literary defeat at his hands that brought his adversary to the grave. Yet the proportion of the work that can only have been composed after August 1653 is very small. *Defensio Secunda* was not written at a single time. Milton was a practised reviser of his writings, accomplished at the adjusting of an existing text and at the weaving in of new material.[8] Sometimes he revised works already published – *The Doctrine and Discipline of Divorce*; *The Tenure of Kings and Magistrates*; *Eikonoklastes*; *Defensio*; *The Readie and Easie Way* – for new editions. But he also altered and expanded works before publication. We shall meet this process in his *History of Britain*. We find it here too.

As usual we have no manuscript of Milton's text, only the published version. But it will become evident that his manuscript, or manuscripts, must have been frequently amended, as the political background to the writing of the work altered. Some puzzles of the work could even derive from difficulties of the printer, who perhaps worked from a frequently corrected

5. Parker, 423, 434.
6. The translation that I have otherwise followed loads the dice by rendering 'aggredior' as 'I commence my attack'.
7. *CW* ix. 21–3, 39, 57, 95, 103, 141 (and, arguably, p. 99).
8. I am grateful to Martin Dzelzainis for discussion of this point.

and a consequently disordered text.[9] *Defensio Secunda* was essentially written under the Rump. Revision took place, perhaps on more than one occasion, during the aftermath of the dissolution of the parliament. It again occurred, partly or wholly at the same points of the text, under the protectorate, also perhaps more than once. It also seems to have taken place in the Rump period itself, for there are signs that Milton, after the publication of *Clamor*, absorbed or reworked material that he had drafted earlier. Many obstacles impede the recovery of the process of writing and rewriting. Milton's eloquence, which aims to transcend the concrete and the particular, has a way of obscuring them. His meanings are often vague or ambiguous, his tenses sometimes uncertain. If we read the treatise in translation we are in the hands of the translators, whose unenviable decisions sometimes seem to be determined by the assumption that the work was written (or mostly written) in 1654. Within Milton's language there is only the occasional incongruity or wrinkle to indicate the vulnerability of that premiss. But when we relate the language to the facts which it addresses, the premiss crumbles. We shall come later to the question why, in 1654, Milton published prose to which events since its composition had given a new perspective. Here I shall try, within the limits which the evidence imposes, to uncover the successive layers of the composition of *Defensio Secunda*.

Though the force of Milton's eloquence, and the hints of the classical structural divisions of the oration, almost disguise the fact, the treatise is a patchwork of themes and arguments. Until near the end its miscellaneous matter has a common goal. It constitutes a reply to More and an attack on him and Salmasius. Then the character of the work changes. A principal target of *Clamor* was Cromwell, to whose defence Milton comes. 29 pages from the end of the 173 pages of *Defensio Secunda*, More is forgotten. The defence of Cromwell then turns into a eulogy of him, which is combined with an exhortation to him. Eleven pages from the end, Milton moves from Cromwell to an exhortation to the English people, which itself makes way, three pages from the end, for a tribute by the author to himself. Of the material before we reach the praise of Cromwell, there is much that is only intelligible, and much that is most readily intelligible, on the assumption that it was written before the expulsion of the Rump. In the same material there is, with the conspicuous exception of the references

9. Compare the discussion on pp. 420–1, below, of the difficulties in the printing of other manuscripts by the blind Milton.

to the death of Salmasius in August 1653, very little that need have been written, or that gives any indication of having been written, after the coup of April 1653. Two of the references to Salmasius's death end awkwardly, as if the material around them has been disrupted by their insertion.[10] In other passages Milton apparently refers to him as to a man still alive. Thus 'the man who, of yesterday, blossomed in the meridian beams of favour, is today almost withered' (17); 'I would advise Salmasius not to inflate his cheek overmuch; for ... the more it be swollen out, the fairer will he present it for slaps' (53); Salmasius 'is threatening an invasion of our shores' (55).[11] If we leave the passages concerning the death of Salmasius aside, everything suggests that virtually all but the late portions of *Defensio Secunda* was written by April 1653. The late portions are more problematical. In them Milton presents himself as the builder of a 'monument' (253): to Cromwell, to virtuous deeds, to himself. Monuments freeze the passage of time, to which Milton alludes as little as he needs, and of which he gives as little sense as possible. Yet with patience we can learn enough about the composition of the tract's treatment of Cromwell to find a new way into Milton's mind in the Interregnum.

★★

Milton's full title is *Joannis Miltoni Angli Pro Populo Anglicano Defensio Secunda. Contra infamem libellum anonymum cui titulus, Regii Sanguinis Clamor ad coelum adversus parricidas Anglicanos* ('John Milton, Englishman, his Second Defence of the People of England against the infamous anonymous libel entitled *The Cry of the Royal Blood to Heaven against the English Parricides*'). The title accurately describes the main portion of the book, which precedes the tribute to Cromwell. Nowhere within that main portion does Milton indicate that the government of England has changed hands since 1649. He writes as if both the Rump and its executive body of 1649–53, 'the council of state, as it is called', are still in being (139–41, 185). (There was no 'council of state' under the protectorate, which, disliking the republican resonance of the term, dropped it in favour of 'the council'.) Milton gives – in the same portion of the book – no indication that Cromwell has become protector. That omission contrasts with a

10. *CW* viii. 21–3, 39. The reference on p. 103 comes at the end of a paragraph. So do some other passages of the tract that may be insertions.
11. See too ibid. 49, 59.

backward glance early in *Pro Se Defensio* in 1655, when, referring to the time when *Clamor* was published, Milton writes that Cromwell 'was at that time the leader of our armies, but ... is now the first man in the state'.[12] Neither in the celebrated autobiographical passage of *Defensio Secunda*, which ends with an account of the writing of the first 'defence' (139), nor elsewhere in the treatise, does Milton tell us anything of his own conduct after the Rump period or of his response to the events that followed it. His very title places the book within the Commonwealth period. It was in the name of the English people that the regicide had been carried out and the republic established, and that the Rump ruled.

That was why Milton's first 'defence' had carried the title *Joannis Miltoni Angli Pro Populo Anglicano Defensio contra Claudii Anonymi, alias Salmasii Defensionem Regiam* ('John Milton, Englishman, his Defence of the People of England against Claudius Anonymous, alias Salmasius, his *Defence of the King*'). Neither Barebone's nor the protectorate claimed to have been established by the people or to derive legitimacy from the regicide. The second 'defence', which refers to its predecessor as 'the other book' ('libro altero': 154),[13] is a sequel to or partner of it, and in essence belongs to the same political environment, that of the rule of the Rump. In defending Cromwell against More, Milton complains that the Presbyterians 'impute not to the parliament in general, but to Cromwell alone, any measure which they may think harsh towards themselves' (207). Those words must have been written while the Long Parliament remained in being.[14] They conform to the rest of Milton's defence of Cromwell – that is, to the material about him that precedes the transition to eulogy and exhortation. Within that portion of the book Milton refers only to the figure known to us from the period before the coup of April 1653. Contemporary readers of *Defensio Secunda* would have seen it, as modern ones have done, from a perspective shaped by Cromwell's occupation of the protectorate. Yet his prominence in the work did not arise from his elevation to that office. It was a response, a quickly made response, to the severity of the attack which had been made on him in *Clamor* in 1652.[15]

12. See too below, p. 269.
13. *CP* iv. 636 and n.
14. That is surely true even though Milton is writing not of Cromwell's present behaviour but of his conduct in the year before Pride's Purge.
15. Some confusion may be caused by the appearance in translations of *Defensio Secunda* of the word 'protector' to describe Cromwell. The Latin word, 'conservator', does not (or does not necessarily) indicate the headship of state (219, 225).

When we turn to the eulogy itself, we are brought back to the resemblances between it and the representations of Cromwell that are to be found, within the year after the Battle of Worcester, both in Milton's sonnet to Cromwell and in Nedham's *Politicus*. Those similarities, of course, do not by themselves prove that the tribute was originally written under the Rump. Another statement within it, however, points firmly in that direction. Milton warns Cromwell that if 'our republic' ('nostra republica'), 'which has sprung up with so much glory' – that is, with the regicide – 'should vanish as soon as it has arisen, no equal disgrace and shame could fall upon this nation' (227). It is true that under the protectorate (as under Barebone's) England formally remained a 'Commonwealth', a term that may have given reassurance to some men who were uneasy about Cromwell's elevation.[16] In 1655 Milton himself, to whose own unease about the protectorate we shall come, clung to the thought that he was living in a republic.[17] But in 1654 it would have been one thing to argue that the essence of the republic still survived, another to write as if alternative perceptions of the coups of 1653 were not even worth mentioning. The latter course would have courted ridicule. It was the insistent and furious claim of the commonwealthmen that the republic had indeed 'vanished'; that Cromwell had committed treason by terminating it; and that the nation had consequently been visited by the disgrace against which Milton's words warn.[18] There was no more eminent a commonwealthman than John Bradshaw, whose own appearance in *Defensio Secunda* is another clue to the timing of its composition. Milton's tribute to him describes his public exertions in the present tense. It makes more sense as an account composed during Bradshaw's time in power than after his removal from it in April 1653. Again there is a contrast with *Pro Se Defensio*, where Bradshaw is 'the illustrious man who was at that time president of the council of state'.[19]

When, in the main part of *Defensio Secunda*, Milton alludes to recent events, it is always to occurrences well before the end of the Rump.

16. Above, pp. 143–4.
17. *CW* ix. 225.
18. In 1654 Milton's words could only have been written as brutal sarcasm. It is not impossible that they were. In 1656, as we shall find in Chapter 13, Marchamont Nedham would use that weapon against Cromwell in just such a way. Yet nowhere else does the account of Cromwell in *Defensio Secunda* cross the boundary that divides sarcasm from irony.
19. *CW*. ix. 125. In an allusion to Horace (CP iv. 638 n.), *Defensio Secunda* calls Bradshaw 'the consul, as it were, not of a single year' (*CW* viii. 159). The wording suggests that Milton was either writing before late 1651, when Bradshaw, who had three times been appointed to the annual presidency, lost it, or, if he composed the passage later, making a pointed comment on his deposition.

There is a cluster of material that looks back to the high summer of 1652. Milton has been 'lately informed' that Alexander More has been required to resign from his position as pastor of a church at Middelburgh (199). The resignation, of which Milton, who strained to learn everything of More's activities, cannot long have remained ignorant, occurred in July 1652.[20] A few pages earlier, Milton records the approval earned by *Defensio* from Leonard Philaras of Athens (191). In June 1652 Milton wrote to Philaras to acknowledge that endorsement.[21] The letter is close in theme and tone to the corresponding passage of the treatise. That resemblance, while it would be inconclusive in itself, takes on significance when we set it beside the allusions in the surrounding passages of the tract to events of that time. Just after the reference to Philaras, Milton refers affectionately to the 'departed spirit' (193) of the Dutch ambassador Adrian Pauw (or Paul), who had sought friendly contact with Milton on a visit to England in the summer of 1652, when acting as an agent for the United Provinces in a vain attempt to prevent the outbreak of war. It is to his return to the Netherlands at the end of June that Milton refers. By 1653 or 1654 the departure was too long past for the language to be apt.

Milton's representation of the Dutch nation in *Defensio Secunda* reads oddly from the perspective of 1654. Though one of the few passages of the treatise that must have been written under the protectorate refers fleetingly to the Anglo-Dutch peace of that year (195), another passage can only have been written earlier, in the midst of the war (77). In *Pro Se Defensio* in 1655, Milton answered the charge that he was prejudiced against the Dutch. He there assures us that, when war with them broke out in 1652, there was no one to whom it was more 'abhorrent' than he. No one 'prosecuted it, when begun, with less zeal' or 'more sincerely rejoiced' in its conclusion in 1654. No one 'thinks more highly of that republic' or 'prizes more and … oftener applauds their industry, their arts, their ingenuity, their liberty'.[22] Yet – despite the tribute to Pauw himself – there is little of that spirit in *Defensio Secunda*. Rather there is material which explains the charge of anti-Dutch prejudice. The treatise attacks 'the Orange faction' (37, 99, 141); it condemns the conduct of the Dutch both after the execution of Charles I and during St John's and Strickland's embassy of 1651; and it declines the opportunity to present the two nations as natural allies (169, 193–7). We are much closer to the mood of republican belligerence to be

20. *CP* iv. 660 n. 21. Ibid. 852–3. 22. *CW* ix. 103.

found in *Defensio* than to the stance of the protectoral government, which wanted a Protestant alliance with the Dutch. We are closer too to the line in Milton's sonnet to Vane in July 1652, which carries a scornful pun on Holland – 'the drift of hollow [Holl-Low] states, hard to be spelled' (6) – that in turn recalls the satire on the Dutch written by Marvell in or before February 1653.[23]

Published as it was as late as 1654, *Defensio Secunda* fought yesterday's battles. Its reply to More was concerned mainly to justify events of 1647–51, which the political convulsions of 1653–4 had distanced from public debate. We can go further, for some of the battles were yesterday's even when *Clamor* appeared in 1652. For that, there is, on the face of it, an obvious explanation. *Clamor*, which like *Defensio Regia* centres on the evil of the regicide, dwells on the years around it. It focuses on events up to the summer of 1651. To answer More, Milton – whenever it was that he wrote *Defensio Secunda* – had to fight on that earlier territory. But the explanation is insufficient. When Milton addresses the events of 1647–9 on which More concentrated, his prose has, as we would expect of any work written well after them, a retrospective air. Yet when he covers events of 1650–1 there is a change. He writes as if he is addressing, not distant episodes, but live current issues.

Why? To find the answer we must remember that More is only part of Milton's target. Were it not for the subtitle of the tract, we would be well into *Defensio Secunda* before we realized that he has *Clamor* in his sights. In Milton's mind the chief antagonist of 'the English people' is Salmasius.[24] More is 'merely the harbinger of the whale Salmasius' (55). Milton's account of the writing of *Defensio Secunda* has this much truth in it: that from the time of the publication of *Defensio* in February 1651, he expected a reply from that 'adversary ... much more desirable' than

23. Norbrook, *Writing the English Republic*, 283. (It is true that as protector Cromwell was firmly opposed to the Orange interest, but that was not a sentiment he wanted to advertise or to let hinder cordial relations between the two countries.) Another passage of *Defensio Secunda* remarks that the Presbyterian clergy are 'now ... struggling tooth and nail in defence of tithes' (161), words that point to the vigorous controversy, which swelled in 1652 and again in 1653, over the movement for the abolition of tithes. The movement lost its heart with Cromwell's elevation. Like the reference to the Dutch war, that passage could have been written after, rather than before, the dissolution of the Rump, i.e. between April 1653 and the end of Barebone's in December. But in either case we would have to think of it as an interpolation, for which there would have been no discernible motive, into material that all the other evidence suggests was written before April 1653. The passages are thus likelier to belong to the Rump period.

24. See too *CP* iv. 562n.

More. Though Milton, when it suits him, presents More and Salmasius as antagonists to each other, and though he alleges that Salmasius 'held' More 'in abomination' (141), the passage that precedes his first attack on More confusingly seeks to merge the two men and to present them as a single 'adversary'. There Milton allows us to understand that, but for the rumours and warnings that an attack by Salmasius on Milton was impending, he would have published a sequel to *Defensio* sooner – though we cannot tell whether he has in mind *Defensio Secunda* or another text which was not finished and which does not survive. As things were, 'I thought it behoved me to wait, that I might reserve my strength entire against the more potent adversary' (21). Salmasius did indeed work on an answer to *Defensio*, which he did not live to complete. It sounds as if the 'task' from which Salmasius's death relieved Milton of 'a certain portion' had been under way for some time, for *Defensio Secunda* contains a zestful epigram against Salmasius which 'I had in readiness for the long-awaited edition of the famous book'[25] – that is, for the prospective reply to *Defensio*. How much else had Milton 'in readiness', and when had he readied it? He may have had a habit of drafting or planning treatises in advance of any occasion for their publication that might arise.[26] In *Defensio Secunda* he explained how – unlike Salmasius – he had 'learned to be long silent, to be able to forbear writing'. He had 'carried silently in my own breast' writings which, had he 'chosen' to publish them, could 'long since' have brought him fame.[27] We found, in an editorial of *Politicus* in May 1651, an indication that he was then planning a treatise whose subject-matter was, or included, the legitimacy of tyrannicide, the theme of the first 'defence'. Did Milton, having published *Defensio* in February 1651, then begin to write *Defensio Secunda*, albeit in a version that would be transformed after the publication of *Clamor*? Did he even include, in the second 'defence', matter left over from the first, that work in which, he wrote, he was 'overwhelmed with' the 'plenty' of his material?[28]

That the genesis of the treatise well precedes the appearance of *Clamor* is suggested by passages both within the eulogy of Cromwell, to which we shall come, and in the main portion of the tract, which we now take first. Milton proudly mentions, in the tone of one who has only recently learned of it, that tribute to the impact of *Defensio*, the public burning of

25. Ibid. 580 (cf. *CW* viii. 113).
26. Cf. below, pp. 338 n. 40, 406 n. 2, 407–8, 415; Lewalski, 698 n. 84.
27. *CW* viii. 113.
28. Ibid. vii. 307.

the work at Paris and Toulouse in June 1651. Of the event at Toulouse, where 'I find I have been also burnt', Milton wonders to discover that 'the people' there 'should have become so unlike their ancestors ... as now to burn the defence of liberty and religion in the very city in which ... liberty and religion had been before so signally defended' (187–9). News of the burnings reached the English public in July, in a gloating passage of one of the Leiden letters in *Politicus*. The next issue of the newsbook carried, under the heading of a letter from Paris, the remark that the burning of the book there showed how 'great a hatred is borne to any piece that speaks liberty and freedom to this miserable people'.[29]

Then there is Milton's 'digression' in tribute to Queen Christina of Sweden. If the passage was written, as commentators assume, under the protectorate, there is a puzzle. Why does it not mention the embassy which Bulstrode Whitelocke, who is himself praised in *Defensio Secunda*, led to Sweden in November 1653, which was still there when the treatise was published, and which attracted so much attention from Nedham and from Marvell? Why is there no reference to Cromwell's hopes, which the embassy was intended to fulfil and which Marvell and Nedham commended, of a Protestant alliance between England and Sweden? Salmasius had been invited to Christina's court on the strength of his *Defensio Regia*, and had remained there until the late summer of 1651, when he returned to his chair at Leiden. Milton wants us to understand (though, if he ever believed it, he cannot have done so for long) that Christina's attitude to Salmasius had been changed by her reading of Milton's reply to him; and that Salmasius – who in reality returned to Holland for private reasons – had left Sweden because of his loss of favour.[30] 'The report goes', as *Defensio Secunda* tells 'the most serene Queen of the Swedes', that 'your mind underwent so visible a change that from that time it was plain that you neither paid the same attention to him as before, nor made much account of his genius and learning; and what was altogether unexpected, showed an evident inclination to favour his adversary' (103).[31]

29. *MP*, 10 July 1651, 915; 17 July 1651, [932].
30. For Salmasius's relations with the queen see the account by Kathryn A. McEuen in *CP* iv. 962 ff.
31. It could be that the eulogy of Christina (as distinct from the account of her treatment of Salmasius) was written or revised after the rise of tension between England and the Dutch republic in the summer of 1652. See the tribute to Sweden in *MP*, 24 June 1652, 1678–9. Earlier *Politicus* had blown hot and cold on the subject of that nation, in line with the fluctuations of government policy. For Milton and Christina see too *CW* viii. 21; ix. 169–71.

Such a 'report', as by now we should not be surprised to discover, was published in *Politicus* early in September 1651. It appeared in a letter sent or ostensibly sent from Delft in Holland. 'The reason why Salmasius left Sweden', we there learn,

> was because Milton's book having laid him open so notoriously, he became thereby very much neglected, the queen not having sent for him nor seen him for the space of two months; so that perceiving a decay of her favour, he came himself and desired leave of departure, which was very readily granted, the queen having at length understood how impolitic it is for any prince to harbour so pretentious a parasite and promoter of tyranny.[32]

It was just about this time, or a little before it,[33] that John Phillips, in the contribution to the controversy which Milton vetted, concluded a lavatorial sally against Salmasius with the words: 'It is clear now why they say at the court of Sweden that you stink.... It is no wonder if the Queen of Sweden, who was at first deceived by common opinion, detected you by her own sharp qualities... and has now expelled you with disgust.'[34] Only in the late summer of 1651, and only, it seems, within Milton's circle, did the story have currency.[35] Even *Politicus* made no further use of it. Four months later one of its Leiden letters referred to Christina, accurately, as a friend to royalist political thought, and said nothing about the supposed influence of *Defensio* on her.[36] The likely date of Milton's statement about Christina's neglect of Salmasius is around the time of the reports of it in the newsbook and in Phillips's tract. It was just at this time, too, that Christina's desire to abdicate, on which *Defensio Secunda* touches, became public knowledge and occasioned a trial of strength between her and the Swedish senate.

In the treatise, Milton's mind largely stays, not merely within the Commonwealth period, but within the earlier part of it, which concluded with the Battle of Worcester in September 1651: the time which preceded Cromwell's return to Westminster and the consequent diminution of

Eulogies of Christina, which were something of an international sport, were not to be done by halves: see Kajanto, *Christina Heroina*.

32. *MP*, 11 Sept. 1651, 1056.
33. Parker, 990. Compare too the remark on the composition of *Defensio Secunda* in *CW* ix. 21 with the statement in Phillips's 'Response' in *CP* iv. 889–90.
34. *CP* iv. 903.
35. See McEuen's discussion in ibid. 962 ff.
36. *MP*, 1 Jan. 1652, 1316. The same things are true of another Leiden letter, published by *Politicus* on 10 July 1651, 914–15.

the standing of Milton's patron Bradshaw and of Milton himself. That is true even of passages which – at least in the form in which we have them – must have been written after the publication of *Clamor*. Even the friendly but momentary reference, in a passage that bears signs of late and hasty adjustment, to the Anglo-Dutch peace agreed early in 1654 (though not signed until April) cannot disguise the presence of the anti-Dutch spirit familiar from Milton's own first 'defence' and from writings of Marvell and Nedham at the same time.

That Milton's immersion in the period 1650–1 can be only partly explained by the obligation to tread the same ground as *Clamor* is confirmed when we turn to material in the tribute to Cromwell, where *Defensio Secunda* has left *Clamor* behind. Most strikingly there is the praise, unexpectedly inserted into that encomium, of Sir Thomas Fairfax (217–19), the recipient of Milton's sonnet of 1648. Since other leading officers of the army are also lauded in the work, we should not be surprised to be told of Fairfax's heroism in war. Yet Milton's interest lies elsewhere. Having referred in passing to Fairfax's 'highest courage', he moves to the real subject of the tribute, the lord general's resignation in July 1650. In his 'present secession, like that of Scipio Africanus of old at Liternum', Milton tells him, 'you hide yourself, as much as possible, from public view'. Fairfax enjoys – what Marvell's 'Upon Appleton House' described in 1651 or 1652 – 'the most delightful and glorious of retirements'. Possessing 'the greatest modesty' and 'the most exemplary sanctity of life', he has 'conquered', not the enemy alone, but 'ambition' and 'glory' – as, in Marvell's poem, 'he did, with his utmost skill, | Ambition weed, and conscience till' (ll. 353–4). Why did he resign his command? Was it, Milton asks him rhetorically, 'on account of your health, which I am most inclined to think', or 'from any other motive'? In the midsummer of 1650 that was delicate territory: after it, its interest gradually became remote. *Politicus* drew attention to its delicacy in its opening issues.[37] Milton's words, which he would have been unlikely to write long after the event, bring out its delicacy too. Bulstrode Whitelocke, who attended a critical conference on 24 June 1650 at which Fairfax and Cromwell discussed the situation with other grandees, concluded that Cromwell, even as he professed the hope that his superior would retain his command, wanted the opposite outcome. Milton none the less claims to be sure of one thing: nothing would have persuaded Fairfax to resign

37. Above, p. 64.

had he not known that the cause of liberty could be safely entrusted to Cromwell. The statement reads like a companion to the nervous coverage of the episode by *Politicus* in 1650.[38]

In other words we are back in the world of 'An Horatian Ode', even if some of the passages that recall that environment must have been written later in the Rump period, and even if all of them may have been. We are back too – as we are in the warning to Cromwell, the 'patron of liberty', not to 'violate' it – with the question, which animates the ode and which preoccupied *Politicus* in 1650–2, of Cromwell's intentions. Fairfax, says Milton, has conquered ambition and glory by retirement. What then of Cromwell, who, in the representations of him by Marvell and Nedham, has the opportunities and temptations brought by the prolongation of military power, and who threatens to grow 'stiffer with command' and usurp the republic? What is the passage about Fairfax's retirement doing in *Defensio Secunda*, if not to indicate the contrast? And what of the eulogy of Bradshaw, whose relationship with Cromwell was or became hostile in 1650–1, and who, after Cromwell's return to Westminster in 1651, had been dislodged from the presidency of the council of state?[39] The ambiguity about Cromwell, and the combination of the great or heroic with the sinister or the threatening, that colour Marvell's ode also run through the later part of *Defensio Secunda*. In the first 'defence' Milton offered an observation on Julius Caesar which, when we recall Nedham's and Marvell's parallels between Caesar and Cromwell, confirms that ambiguity and offers a clue to Milton's attitudes to the English leader. He replies to Salmasius's reminder that Caesar's murderers, Rome's equivalent of the English regicides, had failed. 'Indeed,' replies Milton, 'if I would have had any tyrant spared, it should have been he. He did, to be sure, though a citizen of the republic, forcibly enter upon the exercise of royal power; yet he perhaps more than anyone else deserved it.'[40] Given Nedham's

38. That the tribute to Fairfax was written before the protectorate is also suggested by the statement that England's prosperity will be assured so long as Cromwell is 'in safety' – rather than, as we might otherwise expect Milton to have written after 1653, so long as he is ruler (219). Milton's comparison with Scipio has its complications, for Scipio was forced into public retreat by a charge of corruption (*CP* iv. 669 n.). No one would have levelled such an accusation at Fairfax, to whom Milton had looked in 1648 to purge 'public fraud'. See too *CW* ix. 5–7; *Case*, 107–8.
39. Above, p. 196.
40. *CW* vii. 337. The statement is the more remarkable in the light of Milton's readiness elsewhere to damn Ceasar as a tyrant and a usurper of liberty: *CP* v. 41, 49, 61; *CW* vii. 321; see too *Paradise Regained* III. 39–42.

indications about what Cromwell 'deserved', we should not overlook the 'perhaps'.

On one reading of 'An Horatian Ode', Milton's sentiment about Caesar might be said to summarize that poem. Milton's Cromwell has other properties of Marvell's. In Milton's sonnet of 1652, Cromwell reaches greatness 'through a cloud'. In the ode we find the rising Cromwell 'Breaking the clouds'. Is the echo a conscious one? Is there even an intentional contrast between the two Cromwells: Milton's, who proceeds through 'war' to the 'glorious way' of 'peace', and Marvell's, who fights 'adventrous war' because – unlike Milton's Fairfax, the conqueror of 'glory' – he 'could not cease | In the inglorious arts of peace'? In Marvell's poem, Cromwell is a 'greater spirit' who emerged from 'his private gardens where | He lived reserved and austere', and whose 'active star' is 'nursed'. In *Defensio Secunda* he 'grew up in the privacy of his own family' – a family, in Milton's flattering account of its social standing, grand enough to have had gardens – and, in adulthood, 'nursed his great spirit' 'in private' (213). Marvell's Cromwell tames the Irish 'in one year': Milton's Cromwell conquers the Scots 'in about one year' (221).[41] That last statement must, of course, have been written after Worcester. But when Milton urges Cromwell to respect 'what foreign nations think of us; what great things they promise themselves from our liberty' (225–7), we are again mentally in the era before that battle. It was in that earlier period that Milton looked forward to the overthrow of 'European kings' and of the 'tottering' monarchies of the Continent, and that he urged 'every free state' to exclude Salmasius from its borders. It was during that time, too, that 'An Horatian Ode' portrayed a Cromwell who 'to all states not free | Shall climacteric be', and that *Politicus* confirmed that image of him.[42] Those aspirations mostly faded after Cromwell, no champion of

41. Sometimes *Defensio Secunda* reads, as does *Politicus* in 1650–1, like a reply to a royalist reading of the ode. That is at least partly because of the proximity of the ode itself to royalist writing. Marvell's account of Charles I's fate is close – strikingly close – to that in *Clamor*, to whose words Milton replies. So when Milton refutes the ascription of Charles I's flight from Hampton Court to 'the wiles and artifices of Cromwell' (207), or answers the imputation 'that the common soldiers did behave with insolence' (169–71) at the king's execution, he need not have Marvell's poem in mind, for *Clamor* amply makes those claims. But in 'making', 'on the scaffold', 'his exit from the stage', and thus contriving to act so as to 'leave behind him in the minds of men a feeling of compassion, or a conviction of his innocence' (175), Milton's Charles comes closer to that of Marvell than to that of *Clamor*. Elsewhere, the 'Response' of John Phillips recalls the ode in answering a royalist claim about the maltreatment of 'temples' by the Roundheads (*CP* iv. 918).

42. Above, pp. 66–7, 98–100.

republicanism either at home or abroad, returned to Westminster after Worcester.

★★

All the signs are, then, that the eulogy and exhortation of Cromwell, like the main part of *Defensio Secunda*, derive from the Rump period. What then of material, in the last part of the book, which (at least in the form in which it was published) demands to be placed, not before the expulsion of the Rump, but after it? One such passage will repay particular attention here. It is to be found within, yet stands out from, the exhortation, near the end of the work, to the English people. The passage is the attack on the election of parliaments by corrupt voters and on the kinds of MP that they return (245–51). Appearing just before the book's final paragraph, which turns to the role of Milton himself, it reads like an insertion, akin to the 'Digression' which Milton wrote for inclusion in his *History of Britain*, and where he attacks the Long Parliament in similar terms. The passage describes in scathing terms how bribed and drunken voters, and the 'faction and cramming' that manipulate them, produce an assembly of 'victuallers and hucksters from the city-shops, and herdsmen and graziers from the villages, for our senators'. The administration of the state succumbs to 'peculation' and is entrusted to men 'who have never learnt what law means, what reason, what is right or wrong'; who suppose that 'all power consists in violence, dignity in pride'; and 'whose first acts in parliament are to confer corrupt favours on their friends'. They appoint to administrative posts 'their friends and relations', who 'defraud the public' by amassing 'huge sums'. Milton's picture of the electoral process, which reasserts familiar themes of his writings, has a practical point. It is deployed to show why, unless the English reform themselves, their present rulers will rightly deny them the privilege of holding elections. For men who are 'unworthy of liberty', 'however they may bawl for it', are slaves within themselves, and 'it does not suit, it does not fall to such men' to be free to choose MPs. Elections would return 'so few' who understood freedom or were worthy of it. So 'who would now fight, or incur the least danger, for the liberty' – the liberty to vote – 'of such men?' Unless the English learn to 'keep aloof from factions, hatreds, superstitions, injuries, lusts and plunders', then 'those who are now your deliverers' will not think them 'fit' persons 'in whose hands to leave liberty'.

The passage makes no sense if we place the writing of it in 1654. The Instrument of Government guaranteed triennial parliamentary elections. It provided for the first of them, which the new government never considered cancelling, to be held in the summer of 1654. The writs went out a few days before *Defensio Secunda* was published.[43] Milton's words, we shall now find, have a different context. They must have been written in the weeks or months following the expulsion of the Rump on 20 April 1653. They could, it is true, have drawn on something drafted earlier. In the later stages of the Rump the army's disillusion with it, which pervades the passage, had been a source of heated discussion between parliament and the soldiery over the military demand for the termination of the assembly. Much of what Milton says would have been pertinent to the debate. But it is the aftermath of the expulsion that gives his diatribe its point.

Earlier in *Defensio Secunda*, Milton, addressing Cromwell, explains the dissolution of the Rump thus: 'perceiving that delays were artfully contrived; that everyone was more attentive to his private interest than to the interest of the public; that the people complained they were disappointed of their expectations, and circumvented by the power of a few, you put an end to their arbitrary authority, which they, though so often advised to it, had refused to do' (221). That was the view of the parliament which had long been reached by the army and by Cromwell himself, who would recall in 1654 that he had 'pressed the parliament... to period themselves, once, and again, and ten and twenty times over'.[44] He and his military colleagues would often remember the 'corrupt' rule,[45] and the 'arbitrary' power and proceedings,[46] that had characterized the Rump. On 4 July 1653, in his address at the opening of Barebone's Parliament, a document to which Milton's passage bears particular resemblances, Cromwell remembered that from around the previous August the army had exerted political pressure on the parliament, 'finding the people dissatisfied in every corner of the nation' with it.[47] Five months before the dissolution he had complained

43. One puzzle about the passage is Milton's remark concerning the consequences of elections 'though the customary number of 500 [MPs] should be returned'. All the electoral proposals of the earlier 1650s envisaged a reduction to 400 members: see my *Rump Parliament*, Ch. 8.

44. e.g. Abbott, ed., *Writings and Speeches*, iii. 453.

45. e.g. S. R. Gardiner, ed., *Constitutional Documents*, 401; Abbott, ed., *Writings and Speeches*, ii. 642.

46. Abbott, ed., *Writings and Speeches*, iii. 453, 454; iv. 487.

47. Ibid. iii. 55. Milton's charge that the MPs awarded posts to their 'friends' supports Cromwell's complaint, in his speech of July 1653, about the factional conflict that arose in parliament 'if anybody were in competition for any place of real and signal trust' (ibid. 57).

to Bulstrode Whitelocke of the 'pride and ambition' of the MPs, of their 'engrossing all places of honour and profit to themselves and their friends', 'their daily breaking forth into new and violent parties and factions'. For they cannot 'be kept within the bounds of justice, law or reason'. 'Little hopes of good settlement' can be held of them. Then there are 'the scandalous lives of some of the chief of them'. Cromwell would return to that theme in his explosion of anger in expelling the parliament, when he declared 'that some of them were whoremasters... that others of them were drunkards, and some corrupt and unjust men and scandalous to the profession of the gospel'.[48]

It was one thing for the army to demand the termination of the parliament, another for it to know how to replace it. The Rump's own conduct threw the military leaders into confusion. Having long resisted the army's demand for parliamentary elections, the parliament resolved in the opening months of 1653 to hold them. It would sooner return power to the electorate, it decided, than continue to live under the army's shadow. Either there would be – as a party within the Commons wanted – elections to fill the seats which had been left vacant since Pride's Purge, or – as the parliament finally decided – a wholly new parliament would be chosen.[49] Faced with those prospects, the army had to confront a basic inconsistency in its position. It favoured the principle of elections, but feared their consequences. It had committed itself to the ideals of popular sovereignty and accountable government, and saw frequent parliaments as the means to their attainment. Yet it knew how narrow was its base in the constituencies. The Rump did plan to exclude royalists and former royalists from voting. But what of the unregenerate mass of the people? What of those 'Presbyterians' and 'neuters' against whom the propaganda of Nedham and Milton on the Commonwealth's behalf had been largely aimed? What would become, at their hands, of the republic's 'party of its own', which had won power at their expense? It was at the very moment that the parliament was about to pass its bill for new elections that Cromwell rose to harangue the House. He called in his musketeers, cleared the chamber, and declared the parliament dissolved. At that time the officers had no plans for a constitutional alternative, but by the end of April they had agreed in principle on the next step. Having thwarted the

48. Ibid. ii. 588–9, 642.

49. Worden, *Rump Parliament*, pt. 5; Woolrych, *Commonwealth to Protectorate*, ch. 3.

Rump's plan for a new parliament elected by the nation, they resolved to call instead an assembly chosen by themselves. The result was Barebone's Parliament, the body of around 140 members which was chosen by the army over the course of May and which met on 4 July.

The passage in *Defensio Secunda* which discusses the consequences of elections, and condemns the kinds of MP that they produce, corresponds to Cromwell's and the army's position. Its picture of an elected assembly simultaneously incorporates the features of the Rump that were attacked by the army, and argues against the Rump's replacement by a parliament still more degenerate and still more dangerous to liberty – the prospect which the Rump's electoral bill had created. Only in its contempt for 'hucksters' from shops and for herdsmen, a distinctively Miltonic touch, do his words depart from the army's line. How, asks Milton, would newly elected MPs treat 'our deliverers'? Echoing an observation he had made in 1649 about the unthankfulness shown by the Long Parliament to its army,[50] he remarks that the sorts of men whom an unreformed electorate will choose 'are commonly the first to show their ingratitude' to their liberators (249). Milton brings together, as if they were one, two distinct objections to the electorate: its aversion or indifference to the cause of virtue, and the itch of Presbyterians to impose their views on others (251). The objections went together in the army's mind too, where denunciations of 'neuters' mingled with antipathy to Presbyterians. Cromwell, in explaining the dissolution of the Rump to Barebone's, remarks that 'the next parliament' would have been 'like to consist of all Presbyterians' and 'neuters', and that the Rump's electoral bill would have resulted in 'the bringing in neuters, or such as should impose upon [the consciences of] their brethren', whom they would have had 'at mercy'. Cromwell adds that the Rump's bill, by 'drawing the concourse of all people' to the polls, would have put power 'into the hands of men that had little affection to this cause', and would have 'thrown away the liberties of the nation into the hands of those who had never fought for it', even of 'such as had given testimony to the king's party'.[51] He would repeat the point in 1657, when again recalling the expulsion of the Rump: the 'throwing of the liberties of the people of God, and of the nation, into a bare representative of the people ... was then the business we opposed'.[52]

50. Above, p. 177
51. Abbott, ed., *Writings and Speeches*, iii. 59–60; and see Worden, *Rump Parliament*, 350–1.
52. Abbott, ed., *Writings and Speeches*, iv. 488.

It was on the day of the coup that Cromwell declared that the people were 'not fit' for the 'liberty' of holding elections.[53]

Defensio Secunda endorses that decision in a passage that reveals the tactical purpose of Milton's attack on parliamentary elections. In words which can only refer to the calling of Barebone's, he approvingly observes that 'the privilege of voting is allowed to those only to whom it was proper to allow it': that is, not to the fickle electorate but to the officers of the army which had brought the king to justice (221). Cromwell did not propose to abolish parliaments, which he acknowledged to be essential to 'the liberties of the people of England', and without which he saw no hope of a lasting settlement. What he insisted on was their 'temporary suspension'. With time, he believed, his programme of reform, which would Puritanize the land, would make the resumption of parliamentary liberty practicable. Barebone's was granted sovereignty on the understanding that there would be a return to parliamentary elections by 1655.[54] Cromwell's attitude to that timetable is likely to have been flexible. Yet his address to Barebone's did look forward to elections – once the nation was worthy of them. This was the occasion of the expostulation of Cromwell to which James Harrington alluded in *Oceana*: 'Who can tell how soon God may fit the people for such a thing, and none can desire it more than I!'[55] *Defensio Secunda*, in the exhortation to the English people that precedes Milton's observations on the electoral process, places the English people on trial. Cromwell places them on trial too. Milton describes the trial in his own language of virtue. Cromwell, lacking the classical equipment and instinct that in Milton's mind are merged with Puritanism, describes it in the exclusive vocabulary of the saints. But in the minds of both men the outcome of the trial will have practical consequences. When Milton warns his countrymen that, unless they conquer their vices, 'those who are now your deliverers' – those who have rid them of the Rump – will not think them 'fit persons in whose hands to leave liberty' (251), he subjects them to the test of electoral worthiness that Cromwell imposes on them too.

Was Milton's passage written as an endorsement of Cromwell's address to Barebone's? At all events it is intelligible only if set within the period between the decision to summon that assembly and some point fairly soon after the speech. That time frame directs our attention to a pamphlet of

53. Above, p. 113.
54. Abbott, ed., *Writings and Speeches*, iii. 67.
55. Above, p. 113.

mid-May 1653 (when the decision to call Barebone's had been taken), which likewise vindicated the army's decision to summon a nominated rather than an elected parliament.[56] Entitled *A Letter written to a Gentleman in the Country*, it justifies, in somewhat shifty terms, Cromwell's expulsion of the Rump. It is signed 'N. ll.', who was properly identified by the historian C. H. Firth as [Joh]n [Ha]ll. The pamphlet, like so much that Hall wrote, carries resemblances to the writings of Nedham, who was also involved in the army's vindications of the coup. But was the pamphlet Hall's, or else Hall's and Nedham's, alone? The politically alert bookseller George Thomason made a different attribution. He ascribed the pamphlet to Milton. He could have been entirely wrong. Yet he ought not to have been. Milton had given copies of several of his treatises to Thomason, inscribed 'ex dono authoris', and in 1646 he wrote a sonnet 'on the religious memory of' Thomason's newly deceased widow Catharine, 'my Christian friend'.[57] It may be that the relationship between the two men faded after Catharine's death. Yet by 1653 Milton, largely through his propaganda of 1649–51, was a famous – or notorious – name. He was not a likely object of careless misattribution by a bibliophile such as Thomason.

The style and tone of the tract – let us for the sake of simplicity call it Hall's – have no parallels in anything known to be from Milton's pen. Like Nedham's writing it has none of Milton's preoccupation with inner virtue. Yet its substance aligns it with *Defensio Secunda*. With Milton, Hall wonders why the glorious liberation of 1649 has proved so fruitless. The two writers make the same complaints against the Rump. In *Defensio Secunda* 'delays were artfully contrived': in the pamphlet the MPs 'spin out the time'. Milton recalls that 'every one was more attentive to his private interest than to the interest of the public', Hall that 'while they seemed to look direct upon the public interest, their business was to look asquint upon their own'.[58] In *Defensio Secunda*, 'the people complained they were disappointed in their expectations': in the pamphlet, 'the parliament have not satisfied the people', who are left 'discontented' by the assembly's refusal to address their grievances. In Milton, the people's wishes were 'circumvented by the power of a few': in Hall, 'so few' sat in parliament – 'and fewer active' – that they were able to gang up in pursuit of their 'private

56. *Pace* Woolrych, *Commonwealth to Protectorate*, 110 n., the tract was in print by 16 May. See the discussion of the document in McDowell, 'Urquhart's Rabelais', 291 ff.

57. Parker, 930.

58. Hall, *Letter*, 4.

interests... while thousands of poor creditors and petitioners starved at the door'.[59] Both works emphasize the financial corruption and fraud of MPs and their friends. Milton claims that corruptly appointed provincial administrators 'amass immense sums of money which they convert to their own use, and thus defraud the public': Hall explains that, through the Rump's machinery of corruption, 'many people of very inconsiderable fortunes have now prodigiously arrived to vast estates'.[60] Milton writes that 'it does not fall to the lot' of evil men 'to be free' to vote (249): Hall endorses the view that the unregenerate electorate 'have forfeited their liberty'.[61]

Hall, in a pose calculated to win a wider appeal than naked propaganda might do, writes with the detachment of a man ostensibly distant from the centre of power. Yet he uses inside information to press the new government's case. He supplies a fuller account than any previous statement had given of the contents of the Rump's electoral bill, which had vanished, and had apparently been destroyed, after Cromwell took it away with him.[62] To those who 'will say' that 'the liberty of the people is stifled' by the coup, Hall tries to explain why the essence of 'liberty' may be dependent on the forms of 'slavery', and vice versa. He has Cromwell's, and Milton's, objections to parliamentary elections. They would give power to 'the Presbyterian party', 'which is merely a Jesuit in a Geneva cloak, but somewhat more insupportable', and to morally unredeemed neutrals, or, as Hall calls them, people who 'never offended the state but in their ale'. In *Defensio Secunda* the army, by preventing elections, has again been what it was for Milton in 1648–9, the nation's 'deliverer' from slavery. It is the nation's deliverer for Hall too. Since parliament has failed in the task of settlement, and since 'the people like troublesome idiots cannot do it', 'the army as wise guardians must do it'. 'The liberty of the people', writes Hall in words that Milton had often anticipated, has been 'recovered by the sword.' There is another suggestive point of similarity. Just before Milton recounts the events that led to the expulsion of the Rump, he remembers that Cromwell, by conquering Scotland 'in about one year', 'added to the dominion of England a kingdom which all our kings, during a period of eight hundred years, had been unable to subdue' (221).[63] The Commonwealth, recalls Hall, had reduced 'those

59. Ibid. 2–3. 60. Ibid. 8; cf. Hall, 'Grounds and Reasons', 3.
61. Hall, *Letter*, 10. 62. Worden, *Rump Parliament*, 353–4, 365.
63. Cf. *CP* vii. 224. For 'guardians' cf. above, p. 179.

dominions which a series of proud and lusty monarchs could not in six centuries do'.[64]

Hall is an elusive figure. Yet what can be pieced together of his political career between the regicide and his early death in 1656 suggests a pattern close, where not identical, to that to be found in Milton: support for the regicide and for the radical party in the Rump; disenchantment with the Rump in its later stages; delight in Cromwell's coup of April 1653; initial support for the protectorate and subsequent disillusion.[65] Even if Thomason was wrong to ascribe the pamphlet of May 1653 to Milton, it does seem as if the two writers worked together in the cause of government propaganda after the dissolution of the Rump much as Milton and Nedham had done under the Commonwealth; and that the passage about elections in *Defensio Secunda* – though written, like Hall's tract, with an air of detachment from power – was drawn up in that cause.[66]

★★

There are very few passages in *Defensio Secunda*, all of them brief, that can only have been written, or written in their final form, after Cromwell's elevation to the protectorate. One of them refers to his assumption of 'something like a title, resembling most that of father of your country' ('assumpto quodam titulo patris patriae simillimo', 225). The wording is strange. Why should the office of lord protector, from which he derived his power, be referred to, and only referred to, as 'something like a title'? Milton may have had some aversion to the title of protector, which at no point in his writings did he bring himself to name (unless he had a hand in the passage that spits at it in the tract of 1659, *A Publick Plea*).[67] But there is another reason. It lies in the preceding passage, which Cromwell's assumption of the protectorate contradicts, and which must have been written before it. There Cromwell is lauded on the very ground that, even though he is 'the greatest and most glorious of our citizens, the director of the public counsels, the leader of the bravest of armies', he refuses a title. 'All

64. Hall, *Letter*, 2 (cf. Hall, *Confusion Confounded*, 11–12). For another suggestive parallel between *Defensio Secunda* and Hall's prose, compare *CW* viii. 177 with Hall, *Serious Epistle*, 14.

65. Peacey, *Politicians and Pamphleteers*, 199–200, 263–4, 268, 279, 289, 290.

66. Whoever wrote the *Letter*, or however many people wrote it, it recalls Nedham in its regretful omission of material 'which I could make good in a whole treatise' (p. 14): above, pp. 26, 207.

67. Above, pp. 42–4.

good men hail' him with the 'title' of 'father of your country', but 'other titles' – that is, formal ones – 'your actions know not, endure not'. His deeds 'surpass every title' and 'rise above the popular atmosphere of titles' (223–5). Cromwell's adoption in December 1653 of what his exhorter is reduced to calling 'something like a title' casts egg on Milton's – or is it Cromwell's? – face.

Then too there is the passage which lays down the policies that Milton wants Cromwell to adopt in the exercise of his 'sovereign dignity': reform of the Church and law, the freeing of the press (235–9). Was it freshly composed under the protectorate, or merely revised from an earlier time, when Milton would have been no less eager for Cromwell to pursue the same policies? We cannot be sure. One phrase, which asserts that the Church 'is one half [of], and at the same time most remote from, your own province', possibly indicates that Cromwell is already head of state. Yet it is on that subject that Milton's advice is so close to that of the sonnet of 1652. As the poem indicates, Cromwell's policies were as keenly scrutinized, and seemed as critical to the fate of God's cause, in 1652 as under the protectorate. His choice of 'new friends'[68] among the moderates and former royalists, and his eagerness (which he would dramatically but only briefly suspend in 1653) to accommodate Presbyterians within both parliament and the Church, caused particular suspicion. Milton could have voiced in 1652 as easily as in 1654 the 'fervent wish' that Cromwell 'should listen the least of all to those who never fancy that themselves are free unless they deprive others of their freedom; who labour at nothing with so much zeal and earnestness as to enchain not the bodies only but the consciences of their brethren; and to introduce into Church and state the worst of all tyrannies – the tyranny of their own misshapen customs and opinions' (239).

The last of the passages of the encomium to Cromwell that invite our attention to their timing is the most tantalizing, for it is the one where Milton's advice is most concrete. It tells Cromwell which men he should choose as his advisers (229–35). It is a remarkable passage, for suppliers of literary counsel customarily wrote in allusive generalities. They did not usually particularize the people to whom a ruler should listen. No one else gave such advice publicly to Cromwell. Milton's list, admittedly, had

68. Firth, *Memoirs of Edmund Ludlow*, i. 282. This is a source to be used with caution (Worden, *Roundhead Reputations*, chs. 1–4) but it is reliable here as a guide to Ludlow's sentiments.

another purpose too, for it gave him scope to praise, and to recommend himself to, leading figures of the time – and in some cases, perhaps, to reciprocate benefits he had received from them.[69] Even so, his counsel to Cromwell on this subject is surprisingly direct. Cromwell's likeliest hope of meeting the challenges before him, Milton tells him, is 'by associating those, as you do, among the first in your counsels whom you had first as companions of your labours and of your dangers': his old military comrades. Milton names and lauds Charles Fleetwood, John Lambert, John Desborough, Edmund Whalley, and Robert Overton. Then he adds 'some whom, as distinguished for the robe and arts of peace, you have nominated as your counsellors, and who are known to me either by friendship or reputation': Bulstrode Whitelocke, Sir Gilbert Pickering, Walter Strickland, William Sydenham, Viscount Lisle, Edward Montagu, Henry Lawrence, 'besides numberless other citizens, distinguished for their rare merits, some for their former senatorial exertions, others for their military services'. 'To these accomplished men and chosen citizens', he adds, 'you doubtless might properly commit the care of our liberty; indeed it is not easy to say to whom it could more safely be committed or confided.'

On this subject, too, rewriting has left its traces. Milton, who praises Cromwell for having declined a title and then recognizes that he has accepted one, does something similar here. He twice says which men Cromwell should choose as his advisers, and twice says, almost simultaneously, that he has already chosen them. Milton's list of names itself points to a process of revision. Some of his recommendations are intelligible only on the assumption that they were committed to paper in the weeks after the dissolution of the Rump, in order to advise the protector whom to summon to the hand-picked assembly, Barebone's, that replaced it. Others of them cannot have been made at that time. The complicated process of the composition and recomposition of the passage is explored in Appendix B. Here the likeliest explanation can be summarized. Milton wrote the words recommending the names of the soldiers to Cromwell in the later part of the Rump period, when he feared that the lord general, in choosing 'new friends', was abandoning the radical cause. He named most of the civilians, by contrast, after the end of the Rump, with an eye to the membership of Barebone's. He returned to the list after the end of Barebone's, either in the four days between that coup and the proclamation of the protectorate

69. *CW* viii. 233; ix. 85.

or in the weeks or months thereafter. Milton, in other words, kept pace with rapid political transitions and, by stitching and rewriting, adjusted his advice accordingly.

Having recovered, as far as we can, the stages by which *Defensio Secunda* was written, we can now assess the implications for an understanding of Milton's political thinking. The treatise, we have seen, is essentially a work of the Rump period. Like *Defensio* before it, it vindicated the regicide and urged the nation and its leaders to adhere to the principles behind it: principles which, when the appearance of *Clamor* in 1652 spurred Milton to revise and complete the work, were losing their hold on the regime, largely through Cromwell's influence. By 1654, when *Defensio Secunda* was published, the political scene had been twice convulsed. In the further revision of *Defensio Secunda* after those events, and in the publication of the treatise, we can find evidence with which to gauge Milton's responses to the dramatic developments that brought Cromwell to power.

13

Milton and the Protectorate

Milton welcomed both the coups of 1653. *Defensio Secunda* supports the attacks of Cromwell and the army officers on the character of the Rump, endorses its expulsion, and approves its replacement by an assembly chosen by Cromwell and the army officers. Those sentiments were not coloured by retrospect. The passage of *Defensio Secunda* that reveals most about Milton's attitude to the Rump was written shortly after its dissolution, with the intention of vindicating Cromwell's action. At that time Milton aimed to please Cromwell. He first proposed, and then approved, the appointment of civilian advisers whom Cromwell chose. The men he named would form the core of the Cromwellian party in Barebone's, and would then sit on the ruling council of the protectorate.

Two pairs of Milton's nominees are particularly suggestive. First, he places together Sir Gilbert Pickering and Walter Strickland. The two, who operated in almost inseparable alliance, were the civilian politicians to whom Cromwell was closest. They worked with him, alongside the army officers, in the days after the dissolution of the Rump and, with another of Milton's names, William Sydenham, sat on the interim council which Cromwell set up at the end of April.[1] The other two, 'both men', says Milton, 'of the first capacity, and polished by liberal studies', were Edward Montagu, a former colonel in the new model army (and the patron of Samuel Pepys), and Henry Lawrence, who would be president of the protectoral council. Lawrence is the 'virtuous father' in Milton's sonnet to his 'virtuous son' Edward, whom Edward Phillips names, with Marvell, Nedham, and others, among the 'particular friends' who regularly called on Milton in the 1650s.[2] Under the Rump, Montagu and Lawrence

1. Woolrych, *Commonwealth to Protectorate*, 106–7.
2. Darbishire, 74; cf. *CP* vii. 496.

had withdrawn from parliament and politics. Cromwell, dismayed by their absence, pressed them to return, as now they did.[3] If there are four men whose prominence in and after the months following the dissolution of the Rump can be safely attributed to Cromwell's own choice, they are Pickering, Strickland, Montagu, and Lawrence. There is here none of the spirit of admonition that accompanies Milton's nomination of military advisers. Milton says that the civilians he names – seven in all – 'are known to me either by friendship or reputation' (235).[4] Alas, it is impossible to tell which of them were the friends.[5] What we can say is that in compiling his list Milton was a man in the know.

His support for the dissolution divided him from that large body of parliamentarians who, from the start, regarded it as a violation of their cause. Most obviously there was Bradshaw, whose policies and perspectives Milton, in the Rump period, had preferred to Cromwell's, even as the poet hailed Cromwell's greatness. But it was Bradshaw's commitment to the regicide, not to the Rump, that Milton shared. Milton's own commitment to republican rule had been uncertain, his view of the parliament of 1649–53 at best unenthusiastic. The violence of the coup of April 1653 echoed that of the revolution of 1648–9, when parliament had been forcibly purged and the king brought to justice. In Milton's celebrations of that earlier deliverance, delight in the enforcement of justice merged with relish for the violence of destruction. It would do so again in the poetry of *Samson Agonistes*, as well as in his search for other literary subjects that involved obliterative punishment by divine vengeance.[6] Milton, it is true, never glorified the Rump's expulsion as he had the revolution of 1648–9. Later, in bitter disillusion at what had followed, he would denounce

3. Abbott, ed., *Writings and Speeches*, ii. 328.
4. That the list was drawn up well before the protectorate is perhaps also suggested by the absence from it of two men who would become prominent councillors under that regime, but who became part of the Cromwellian entourage only during Barebone's: Anthony Ashley Cooper (the future Earl of Shaftesbury) and Sir Charles Wolseley – though, as ex-royalists, they are in any case unlikely to have been viewed warmly by Milton.
5. See too *CW* ix. 85. Lord Lisle, whom Milton also names, was a patron of letters (see e.g. James Winn, *John Dryden and His World* (New Haven and London, 1987), 437, 450). (The character of the surrounding names indicates that Lisle (Philip Sidney) is the person Milton means by the name 'Sidney', but, strictly speaking, he could mean Philip's younger brother Algernon, a bitter opponent of Cromwell's usurpation.) Milton and Pickering (who was Dryden's patron) are glimpsed together in *MC* 148–9.
6. *CP* viii. 555, 559, 592–3. For this aspect of Milton's writing see Loewenstein, *Milton and the Drama of History*, esp. 140–51; Feisal G. Mohamed, 'Confronting Religious Violence: Milton's *Samson Agonistes*', *Publications of the Modern Language Association*, 120 (2005), 327–40.

it. At the time, however, it cleaned the slate. Over the course of the Puritan Revolution he welcomed four feats of destructive deliverance: the overthrow of the Laudian Church in 1641–2, the regicide, the expulsion of the Rump, and the military overthrow of the protectorate in 1659. It was the ensuing attempts at reconstruction that in each case gave him difficulty.

In April 1653 Cromwell's coup led Milton to an encouraging reappraisal of him. Many people who had been dismayed by the lord general's 'catholic projects' after Worcester, and by his choice of 'new friends', for a time had their faith in him restored by the expulsion of the Rump. A body of radical saints in Durham wrote to tell him that, on hearing of the coup, 'we were at first like men in a dream, and could hardly believe for rejoicing, to see the wonderful goodness and kindness of God, in renewing a remembrance of your former engagements for this poor nation'. In their despair prior to the dissolution, 'that which did very much add to our sorrow was the fear of God's presence withdrawing from you, which fear was caused by your long silence; but now to see [how] the Lord hath quickened you, is as life to our dying expectations'.[7] Their kindred of Hereford were equally enthusiastic. 'Oh! my lord, what are you,' they exulted, 'that you should be the instrument to translate the nation from oppression to liberty, from the hands of corrupt persons to the saints?'[8] Milton would not have chosen such sectarian language, but his own sentiment is unlikely to have been far distant. Certainly he was ready, in the wake of Cromwell's coup, to describe it, as he had done his management of the regicide, as the act of a 'deliverer'.[9]

Milton's endorsement of the second coup of 1653 is, on the face of it, more surprising. *Defensio Secunda* passes swiftly and cryptically over Barebone's and its fall. Barebone's had been chosen on principles that Milton explicitly approved, and included the members whose names he had recommended. Yet the treatise remembers only that 'the elected meet; do nothing; and having harassed one another for a while with their dissensions and altercations', come to a proper sense of their own unworthiness and assent to their own downfall. 'Liberty' has thus been let down by 'the choicest men of the whole nation', who, as Milton puts it, have 'deserted' the virtuous among their countrymen – a disingenuous allusion, perhaps, to the skilful manœuvre that enabled Barebone's, even though it was dissolved by naked force, notionally to resign its power of its

7. Nickolls, 90–1. 8. Ibid. 92. 9. *CW* viii. 245, 249.

own volition. The assertion that the members 'do nothing' ('nihil agunt') is perplexing.[10] They had done a great deal, which is why Barebone's was dissolved. If their most adventurous legislation had not been passed, that was only because the coup had prevented its passage. Cromwell had turned against the Rump because it had failed to supply the reforms for which he called. He turned against Barebone's because it reformed all too readily, in ways of which we might expect Milton to have thoroughly approved. Its assault on the legal system, though it accorded with his views, would perhaps have been a secondary consideration.[11] But its readiness to abolish lay impropriations – that is, the rights that entitled owners of church livings to levy tithes – should have rejoiced his heart. One of its legislative initiatives we know to have pleased him. In 1659 he declared that, in its act for civil marriages, it had 'prudently ... recovered the civil liberty of marriage from the encroachment' of 'divines'.[12]

Why was Milton ready to discredit a body that came far closer than any other regime of the Interregnum to adopting his own beliefs, and to turn instead to the man whose opposition to its policies was the main cause of its downfall? His criticisms of it were far milder than those made in government propaganda of the early protectorate, Nedham's included. Milton writes more in sorrow than in accusation. Perhaps, instinctively attracted as we have seen him to have been to the unifying and energizing potential of single rule, he had despaired, for the second time in 1653, of collective government. Perhaps the want of breeding and of civil wisdom that he had long lamented in England's rulers seemed to him a graver defect than ever in Barebone's, whose members, on average, had lower social origins and less political experience than the elected parliaments of the era. If England's problem, in Milton's judgment, was 'narrow politicians', in Barebone's they were narrower still.[13] Perhaps, too, he shuddered at the prospect of the anarchy which the policies and divisions of Barebone's threatened to create, and was prepared to disown the assembly in the cause of averting chaos.

Here indeed may lie the clue to his statement that the members of Barebone's 'do nothing'. Nedham, in the tract of February 1654 in which he vindicated the dissolution of the assembly, explained that the

10. Ibid. 221–3. 11. See *CP* vii. 331–2. 12. Ibid. 300.
13. Woolrych, *Commonwealth to Protectorate*, ch. 6; above, p. 164.

anarchic principles of its radical members 'led them to a pulling down all, and establishing nothing'.[14] The obvious beneficiaries of anarchy would have been the royalists. In 1649–51 Milton had mounted all his polemical skills to thwart the prospect of a Stuart restoration. In 1659–60, when he saw the 'common enemy', the royalists, 'gaping to devour us', he did the same.[15] In late 1653 the threat was less direct or imminent, but it was there. As Edward Hyde, the future Earl of Clarendon, acknowledged at the time, Cromwell's elevation was a serious blow to the royalists, who had hoped to profit from the instability that preceded it.[16] Whatever arguments Milton might find for or against the rule of Cromwell, he had always to remember the alternatives: the rule of the Stuarts, the dominance of the Presbyterians, the joint sway of those forces.[17] None the less the disintegration of Barebone's must have left him much to ponder. He was used to distinguishing the virtuous minority of the nation from the rest, and to claiming the rights of the people for the former. It has been observed that his translations from the Psalms in August 1653, written as Barebone's began to plunge into disarray, 'register his perception of the widening divide between the virtuous lovers of liberty who can be entrusted with government and the disaffected masses'.[18] Yet now even the party of virtue was failing, in a parliament that had been chosen not by the unregenerate electorate but by the party itself. *Defensio Secunda* acknowledges that what 'liberty ... expected from the choicest men of the whole nation', by whom 'we are deserted', it can now look for only from Cromwell, who 'alone remain[s]' and is 'the only hope' of his country (223–5).

Milton himself has hope. But he has, as far as *Defensio Secunda* allows us to see, no optimism. After his unequivocal endorsement of Cromwell in the period following the dissolution of the Rump, his earlier suspicions of him have returned. In the years ahead the hope would dissolve, and the suspicions would turn to anger and revulsion. Cromwell became, not a flawed hero, but a villain. In December 1653 Milton turned to government by a single person as an alternative to the hazards of parliamentary

14. Nedham, *True State*, 13. For Milton's phrase see too *CP* vii. 376–7; *CW* xii. 78–9.
15. *CP* vii. 329, 331.
16. Bodl., Clarendon MS 48, fo. 44.
17. Macaulay observed in his essay on Milton nearly two centuries ago that, for Milton, 'the choice lay, not between Cromwell and liberty, but between Cromwell and the Stuarts'. Thomas Babington Macaulay, *Literary and Historical Essays* (Oxford, 1913 ed.), 38.
18. Lewalski, 297.

sovereignty. He would end the Interregnum as a defender of parliamentary sovereignty against the evils of single rule.

Defensio Secunda appeared nearly two years after the publication of the work it attacked, and five and a half months after the installation of Cromwell as protector. There is no difficulty in understanding why its completion or publication might have been recurrently postponed. The writing of polemic on behalf of the radical element within the Commonwealth regime, which was the initial purpose of *Defensio Secunda*, became increasingly problematical towards the end of the Rump, as Nedham found when, around the time that *Clamor* was published, the editorials of *Politicus* were brought to an end. The coup of April 1653 was followed by eight months of severe fluctuation and uncertainty. After the further coup of December 1653 it took time for the character of the protectorate to become clear. But why, when he did publish the book in May 1654, did Milton bring it before the world in the form that he did? Why did he retain so many passages whose moment, and whose pertinence to the political landscape that he so earnestly strove to influence, had apparently passed? Why did he not remove or alter statements that had become anachronistic? Perhaps he had lived with the book long enough. Yet no student of his career and character would think boredom or carelessness a plausible explanation. He cannot have been unaware of the effect of the anachronisms, which is to give the work the character of dramatic irony. The stark warning of the shame that awaited the nation if the republic 'should vanish as soon as it has arisen'; the still starker recognition that Cromwell, the 'patron of liberty', might 'violate' it; the eulogy of Milton's hero John Bradshaw, who so defiantly accused Cromwell of having done that very thing, and at the expense of whose political vision Cromwell had risen; the contrast between the retirement of the first leader of the new model army, Fairfax, who shunned ambition, and his successor, who after his elevation in December 1653 was so widely charged with it: those passages stand in ominous assessment over the protector.

Other statements carry the same import. The praise of Cromwell for refusing a title is followed a sentence later by the embarrassing information that he has taken one after all, a title moreover that Milton will not name. The description of the calamitous consequences of parliamentary elections, first written as a justification of Cromwell's refusal to call them in the spring of 1653, becomes in the published text a commentary on the electoral process which began just before it got into print. The very act of publishing in defence of 'the people of England' assumes an ironic aspect now that Cromwell has turned his back on the principle of popular sovereignty. Then, too, there is the emphasis on the heroism of the regicide, the deed which the second 'defence', like the first, was intended to vindicate, and which the protectoral regime wanted to relegate to the past. Cromwell had had the same desire in the later Rump period. Towards the end of 1652 Nedham had defied that wish by recalling the glory of the king's execution.[19] Milton, in writing (or rewriting) the bulk of *Defensio Secunda* at or about the same time, had defied it too. Now he did so again by printing it. The Commonwealth government had made a fuss of the first 'defence', but the protectoral regime, not surprisingly, took no public notice of *Defensio Secunda*.[20] Nedham, whose newsbook usually gave publicity to Milton's publications whether or not they conformed to the government line, and who had drawn attention to the first 'defence' so conspicuously, did duly mention the appearance of *Defensio Secunda*, but even he gave it only a muted acknowledgement, beneath a more prominent advertisement of a political treatise by another author.[21]

The final sentences of *Defensio Secunda* confront the prospect that the English will 'basely fall off from your duty', and that their liberty, whose 'foundation' has been laid, will remain unbuilt (253–5). We cannot know when Milton wrote (or rewrote) those words. But they carry a melancholy, almost a valedictory, air. His conclusion, as it envisages the failure of the revolution, consoles him with the reflection that 'there was not wanting one' – Milton himself – 'who could give good counsel, who could exhort, encourage, who could adorn and celebrate' the transcendent deeds of the deliverers (255). We are not far away from the Milton who, in *The Readie and Easie Way* in 1660, would portray himself as a prophet in the wilderness, and would warn lest nothing be 'built' on the excellent 'foundation' of 1648-9;[22] and not far either from Abdiel, who 'single hast maintained | Against revolted multitudes the cause | Of truth'.[23]

If we have not yet quite reached that bleak scenario, then in 1654 only Cromwell, with whatever regenerative capacity he may possess, stands in its way. In looking to the violator of liberty to 'restore' it (229), *Defensio Secunda*

19. Above, pp. 199–200.
20. The point is made by John Creaser, 'Prosody and Liberty in Milton and Marvell', in Parry and Raymond, eds., *Milton and the Terms of Liberty*, 48.
21. *MP*, 8 June 1654, 3540.
22. *CP* vii. 357 (cf. pp. 432, 436).
23. *Paradise Lost* VI. 30–2.

addresses, in Milton's own terms, the dilemma that we saw in the thinking of James Harrington. Harrington, too, knew Cromwell's stature. Yet he recognized an insoluble difficulty, which had been anticipated in almost identical terms by Nedham. Cromwell's power to create public liberty had arisen from the very deeds, and was vested in the same personality, that had destroyed it.[24] Milton's analysis centred on Cromwell's soul, not, as Harrington's – and Nedham's – did, on inferences from Machiavelli. None the less, in essence Milton and Harrington and Nedham tell a single story: of the consequences for England, and for godliness or virtue, of the flawed greatness of 'our chief of men'.

Milton's public silence during the protectorate casts us on speculation. But at least we can suggest the considerations that might have jostled in his thoughts. There were two differences, from his perspective, between the coups of April and December 1653. The dissolution of the Rump removed an obstacle to reform: the dissolution of Barebone's removed an instrument of it. Secondly, the Rump was replaced by another sovereign assembly. Cromwell did not yet rule 'alone'. It was the replacement of Barebone's by his single rule that cast the fate of the revolution on his own struggle with temptation. Perhaps Milton knew by the mid- or late spring of 1654, when *Defensio Secunda* was presumably printed, that the building whose 'foundation' had delighted him was doomed. That suggestion can be only a hypothesis, for we do not know at what point or points he wrote or rewrote the passages which refer to the existence of the protectorate, and which indicate that, however ambiguously and uncertainly, he has his 'hope' of it. But if he wrote them very early in the protectorate, then by the spring there had been developments which we might expect to have removed his hope. In February, Nedham promoted, by his poem on the protector's entry into London, a view of the regime that distinguished it from the pomp and self-advancement of monarchy.[25] Yet the monarchical style of the government, which was not predictable at the time of the modest and low-key ceremony of Cromwell's installation on 16 December 1653 or in the weeks after it, emerged as the creation of Cromwell's court in the royal palace at Whitehall began. The decision to refurbish Hampton Court was taken by mid-March, and Cromwell took up residence in Whitehall Palace in mid-April. In the area of government policy about which Milton would have been most concerned, the Church, there were developments in February and March 1654 which, as we shall

24. Above, p. 110. 25. Norbrook, *Writing the English Republic*, 328–9.

soon see, are likely to have dashed any hopes he may have held at the outset of the regime. If he already despaired of Cromwell's government before the book went to the printer, then the publication of the advice that the book offers him had a different purpose from its composition. Written as counsel, it appeared as a testament to the cause that Cromwell has betrayed. If that was the case, then the anachronisms, which had arisen inadvertently, acquired a political purpose. If, on the other hand, he worked on the book as late as the early spring, then he retained those hopes at that time – qualified by doubt and by warning as they were – and lost them only later.

★★

For lose them he did. Outside the official papers that he drew up for Thurloe, and aside from brief passages he inserted in *Defensio Secunda*, Milton never mentioned the protectorate during Cromwell's tenure of power; and he never mentioned it kindly after it. In *Pro Se Defensio* only the parenthetical information that Cromwell 'is now the first man in the state' intimates that republican rule is over.[26] Milton is silent on the naval victories of the protectorate; silent on Cromwell's initiative for the readmission of the Jews to England; silent on the regime's vigorous initiatives for religious, legal, educational, and moral reform. Only once does he address a subject close to Cromwell's own preoccupations. In 1655 the protector waged a diplomatic campaign (as a bargaining tool in its negotiations with France) to redress the sufferings of the Protestants of Piedmont after the massacre committed by forces of France's subordinate ally, the Duke of Savoy. Here, at least, Milton had cause to welcome the protector's measures. He was himself involved in the preparation of documents to implement them. His sonnet on the massacre, 'Avenge, O Lord, thy slaughtered saints', appears to take details from accounts which reached Thurloe's office, and which were published in Nedham's *Politicus*.[27] Yet the poem offers no praise of, or advice about, Cromwell's response to the massacre, and says nothing of any steps the government has taken or might take to help God 'Avenge' it.

The Victorians, whose cult of Cromwell has had a lasting legacy, read the poem as evidence of collaboration between Milton, the supreme poet of the Puritan Revolution, and Cromwell, its supreme statesman, between

26. *CW* ix. 13.
27. Robert Thomas Fallon, *Milton in Government* (University Park, Pa., 1993), 144–5; *MP*, 31 May 1655, 5365–6; 21 June 1655, 5409–13.

whom they imagined a close and happy relationship. There is no evidence that the two men were ever alone together, and nothing to indicate what, if anything, Cromwell thought of Milton. Yet Thurloe's assistant, in Victorian hands, became Cromwell's 'personal secretary', living 'under his roof' and 'sitting every day at the same table', where the 'poet-statesman' discussed and helped to shape the protector's decisions about foreign policy.[28] The Victorian legacy persists. Modern authorities have argued, not for so close a relationship, but none the less for a comparable alignment of principle and sympathy. Their case has no better evidence. It is true that Milton continued to work for the protectorate, in Thurloe's office, though just how much work he did for it remains a matter of conjecture.[29] But his duties as a composer or translator of diplomatic documents involved him only in the execution, not in the formation, of policy. His activity on behalf of the regime, as we shall see, proves nothing about his opinion of it. There were, in any case, evidently limits to his sense of involvement in it.[30] In December 1657 he was asked by a Continental friend to use

28. Worden, *Roundhead Reputations*, 236–9, 355–6.
29. Hard facts on this subject are elusive. The valuable labours of Fallon (*Milton in Government*) have produced a good case for his view, advanced largely on *a priori* grounds, that as Latin Secretary under the protectorate Milton is likely to have written, or to have translated into Latin (or some combination of the two), more diplomatic documents than has been realized, both among papers that survive and among others that have gone missing. His argument is strengthened by the statement of the Swedish envoy Christer Bonde that 'the blind Miltonius must translate everything they want done from English to Latin' (quoted ibid. 174). Yet there are difficulties. Challenging the supposition that Milton's workload markedly declined under the protectorate, Fallon argues (pp. 6, 124, 130–1) that the paucity of the appearances of his name in the records of the protectoral council from 1653 to 1659 derived from a process of bureaucratic reorganization. As a result of it, he maintains, the Latin Secretaries ceased to be answerable to the council and worked instead in 'an office quite separate from the secretariat of the council', that of the secretary of state John Thurloe. The evidence of the reorganization that he adduces (in NA, SP25/76, 17 Apr. 1655) does not seem to me to require that interpretation – or to explain the paucity of references to Milton in the conciliar records before that date. I tentatively suggest that, both before and after the reorganization, the relationship between Cromwell, Thurloe (who after all held the post of secretary to the council), and the council itself was of a complicated, triangular kind. I am not convinced by Fallon's explanation (p. 136) of the absence of references to Milton's name in the huge collection of Thurloe's own papers in the Rawlinson MSS in the Bodleian; by his claim (pp. 19, 125) that the protectoral council had little to do with foreign policy, to which in fact it devoted a great deal of its time (though it is true that a number of its discussions of it, where Milton's name might have figured, have left no record); or by his suggestion (p. 178) that the shortage of references to Milton's activity under the restored Rump, when on Fallon's account the council had resumed its control of the Latin Secretaries, derived from the fact that 'there was precious little to do'. I have discussed Thurloe's role during the protectorate in my 'Oliver Cromwell and the Council'.
30. A similar point is made by Martin Dzelzainis, 'Juvenal, Charles X Gustavus and Milton's Letter to Richard Jones', *The Seventeenth Century*, 9 (1994), 25–35.

his influence with the president of the privy council, Henry Lawrence, a Baptist and a friend to liberty of conscience, whom Milton had commended to Cromwell in *Defensio Secunda*. Yet that, he replied, 'is not in my power', for 'my influential friends are very few (since I stay nearly always at home – and willingly)'.[31]

We have seen that Milton rewrote pieces of *Defensio Secunda* to take account of Cromwell's new office. He then made (or repeated) suggestions in that treatise about Cromwell's choice of advisers that conformed to the protector's own preferences. There would have been no point in those passages without Milton's initial 'hope'. What might he have hoped for? He seems to have had no expectation from the new form of government itself. Nedham's work of propaganda for the protectorate, *A True State of the Case of the Commonwealth* in February 1654, analyses the virtues of the Instrument of Government, a document which, he argues, combines the merits of the pre-war system with a novel arrangement for the balance of constitutional powers. Milton looks only to the agency and personality of Cromwell himself. If Milton has any form of rule in mind, it is a biblical one. We saw that Cromwell and some of his followers invited the public to compare him to Gideon, a judge rather than a king, a comparison that was floated in the government press six days after Cromwell's installation.[32] In *Defensio* Milton drew an inference from Judges 8 that Marvell would take from the same text in 'The First Anniversary'. 'That heroic Gideon', Milton there writes, is 'greater than a king' and yet not a king, for the Old Testament office of judge was compatible with republican rule and is both different from and preferable to kingship.[33] The thought is amplified in the 'Response' of John Phillips in 1652, which proclaimed that 'no one will be able to find any more excellent form of government, as mortal affairs go' ('ut sunt res mortalium', a phrase that echoes wording of prose in Milton's own name[34]), than the rule of the judges, and which contrasted their government with that of kings.[35]

Did Milton, at the outset of the protectorate, want to see Cromwell, 'this magnanimous deliverer of his country',[36] in the light in which, in *Samson Agonistes*, he would portray the 'matchless Gideon', Israel's 'great

31. *CP* vii. 507. Various developments may lie behind that statement: the reorganization of Thurloe's office in September 1657 which reduced Milton's burden of work (*CP* vii. 2; see too Darbishire, 28–9); his domestic happiness at this time; his embarkation upon *Paradise Lost*. But the remark distances Milton from the regime.

32. Above, p. 146. 33. *CP* vii. 135, 191. 34. Above, p. 228.

35. *CP* iv. 922; *Joannis Philippi Angli Responsio* (1652), 118. 36. *CW* viii. 213.

deliverer' (279–80)? In 1660 he recalled that Gideon 'not only was no king, but refused to be a king or monarch when it was offered him', for 'this worthy heroic deliverer of his country thought it best governed if the Lord governed it in that form of a free commonwealth which they then enjoyed, without a single person'.[37] Cromwell in December 1653 refused the offer of kingship too. Did Milton hope that the protector, in 'restoring' liberty, might become merely the chief office-holder of a republic? In 1641 Milton had remembered that 'Brutus that expelled the kings out of Rome' was 'for the time forced to be as it were a king himself, till matters were set in order, as in a free commonwealth'.[38] Under the protectorate there were those who told themselves that Cromwell's assumption of powers which had hitherto been held by a sovereign parliament might prove temporary, and who 'waited, hoping better things'.[39] John Toland, in his *Life* of Milton in 1698, maintained that Milton 'confidently hoped' that the protector 'would employ his trust and power to extinguish the numerous factions of the state, and to settle such a perfect form of free government wherein no single person should enjoy any power above or beside the laws'.[40] Though Toland's claim is too much coloured by his own republican agenda (and his own hatred of Cromwell's memory) to be relied on, it could be that it drew on knowledge that had come down to him.

But need Cromwell's occupancy of power be merely a holding operation? What if he should embark on the programme of reform that *Defensio Secunda* enjoined on him? Milton, after all, believed that forms of government must vary as the virtue of the citizens waxes and wanes. Cromwell, as Milton presents him, has become protector because it has waned. But what if he introduces measures, as Milton urges him to do, 'to form and increase virtue' (237)? What if he adopts the concrete programme of *Defensio Secunda*: if he takes steps to 'make a better provision for the education and morals of youth'; to free the press – 'for nothing could contribute so much to the growth of truth'; to reform the legal system;[41] above all to 'take away the power of the Church' (235–9), introduce liberty of conscience, and emancipate the Gospel from the corruption of power

37. *CP* vii. 473–4. 38. Ibid. i. 640.
39. *The Cause of God* (1659), 22; cf. *Letter from a True and Lawfull Member*, 58–9.
40. Darbishire, 166.
41. Milton's plea that Cromwell 'introduce fewer laws' (237) matches Nedham's complaint in the same year against 'the multitude of unnecessary laws' (Nedham, *True State*, 11).

and the world? Might not the virtue of the citizens then wax again, and make them once more 'fit' for liberty?

Milton had enough experience of the gap between his own political goals and instincts and those of Cromwell to view such suggestions cautiously at best. Yet – at least outside his apocalyptic phases – he was no political utopian. He knew that virtuous rule requires prudence, management, compromise; he knew the obstacles of public mood and vested interests that Cromwell faced; he knew the wickedness of the nation that Cromwell had to reform. In civil matters he was ready for imperfection. 'This', he had explained in *Areopagitica*, 'is not a liberty which we can hope, that no grievance ever should arise in a commonwealth; that let no man in this world expect.'[42] And might it not seem, when Cromwell took power, that as protector he might have less need to gratify the conservative or moderating interests which, since Worcester, he had been too ready to accommodate? There was a real possibility of reforms, even if of a kind more limited than those sought by Milton. In its early stages the protectorate was eager to carry through a series of practical and substantial changes in the legal system which the Rump had shirked – although also to shun the root-and-branch proposals for law reform that had won a majority in Barebone's. As Chancellor of Oxford University, Cromwell tried strenuously to 'make a better provision for the education and morals of youth' – although from 1652 he had made John Owen, Milton's adversary of that year, the leader of the project.[43]

One subject would have exercised Milton above all others: the Church. Here, too, improvements were imaginable. Shortly after his elevation to the protectorate, Cromwell reportedly promised to remove 'that ugly maintenance by tithes (for those were his very words)' before the first parliament of the protectorate met.[44] The Instrument of Government itself looked forward to the removal of tithes 'as soon as may be', though it envisaged only the provision of a less contentious principle of public maintenance, not the 'removal of the power of the Church' for which *Defensio Secunda* called, and which, as Milton must have known by 1654,

42. *CP* ii. 487.
43. I have described Cromwell's initiatives for the reform of Oxford in my 'Cromwellian Oxford'. In 1656 Milton expressed a dim view of Oxford's intellectual condition (*CP* vii. 492).
44. *True Catalogue*, 7. For other versions of the episode see *The Protector (so called) in part Unvailed* (1655), 51–2; Bodl., Rawlinson MS A21, fos. 324–5; S. R. Gardiner, *History of the Commonwealth and Protectorate*, iii. 20 n.

Cromwell would never have countenanced. Then there were the provisions in the Instrument of Government that promised liberty of conscience to 'such as profess faith in God by Jesus Christ'.[45] The document persuaded many sectaries, including a number who otherwise viewed Cromwell's elevation with dismay or unease, to support the protectorate, even to think of the new constitution as 'the saints' civil Magna Charta'.[46] Cromwell told parliament in 1654 that 'liberty of conscience' was 'a fundamental' on which he would not move.[47] When the Commons none the less assailed the clauses of the Instrument that guaranteed it, he stood defiantly by them.

The Instrument, however, did not allow for the separation of Church and state or anything like it. Would Milton ever have settled, in religion, for reforms short of his revolutionary ideal? In 1659, even when urging that ideal, he acknowledged – not, admittedly, without a tactical eye to his parliamentary readership – that 'the governors of this commonwealth, since the rooting out of prelates, have made least use of force in religion, and most have favoured Christian liberty, of any in this island before them since the first preaching of the gospel; for which we are not to forget our thanks to God, and their due praise'.[48] No one had played as large a part in that achievement as Cromwell, even if in 1659 Milton is unlikely to have counted him among those benefactors. Even so, the protectorate delivered less than it may at first have seemed to promise. The clauses of the Instrument that provided for liberty of conscience were riddled with ambiguities, whose import emerged in the early months of the protectorate.[49] In February 1654 Nedham, who after his support for Milton's religious radicalism in 1651–2 had resumed his normal Erastian stance, pointed out on the government's behalf that the wording of the new constitution could properly be taken to mean that a 'public profession' of doctrine, worship, and discipline would be drawn up. Welcoming that implication, he remarked on 'our want of some settlement in religious matters'. The government should 'lay a healing hand to those mortal wounds and breaches, by holding forth the truths of Christ to the nation in some solid establishment, and not quite ... lay aside or let loose the golden reins of discipline and government in the Church'.[50] In the same month Cromwell initiated a series of meetings in which Presbyterian divines joined

45. S. R. Gardiner, ed., *Constitutional Documents*, 416. 46. Nickolls, 134.
47. Abbott, ed., *Writings and Speeches*, iii. 458–9. 48. *CP* vii. 245.
49. See my 'Toleration and the Cromwellian Protectorate'.
50. Nedham, *True State*, 40–3.

Independent ones with the aim of framing 'a confession of faith' or – an adjective that again recalled John Owen's scheme of 1652 – a 'fundamental confession'.[51]

It was in 1652, too, that Owen had voiced his horror at the notion that 'the magistrate' – the state, as we would say – 'hath nothing to do with the interest of Christ and the Church', and has no authority to suppress the heresies raging through the land.[52] In March 1654 a government declaration, echoing Owen's words, attacked false doctrines that were being 'justified under the notion of liberty, it being too commonly said that the magistrate hath nothing to do either in repressing or remedying these things'.[53] On the same day the regime issued an ordinance, modelled on Owen's scheme of 1652, for the establishment of state-appointed commissioners – the 'triers'– to vet candidates for church livings. In September 1654 a further ordinance, likewise based on Owen's plan, provided for another body of state-appointed commissioners, the 'ejectors', who were to remove ungodly ministers from the parishes. Three years later, in 1657, the Instrument of Government gave way to a new constitution, the Humble Petition and Advice. With Cromwell's candid approval it provided for the drawing up of a national confession of faith, and laid down boundaries to liberty of conscience that excluded a range of heresies, among them the anti-trinitarianism that Milton had riskily promoted under the Rump.[54] Meanwhile the prospect of the removal of tithes had receded from view. On other fronts, too, the forces of reaction prevailed. If Milton retained any hopes for the freeing of the press, they would have been extinguished by the tightening of government controls in September 1655. The programme of law reform which the protectorate initially pursued with energy was effectively abandoned by 1656.[55]

John Owen was a key figure in the formation of the protectorate's ecclesiastical policies. By 1657, however, people whose views were still further removed from Milton's had increased their influence at Owen's expense.[56] At least Owen was an Independent or Congregationalist, and not a Presbyterian. But Cromwell, despite Milton's warning to him to shun their

51. Worden, 'Toleration and the Cromwellian Protectorate', 217.
52. Above, p. 247.
53. *CP* vii. 32.
54. S. R. Gardiner, ed., *Constitutional Documents*, 454–5; Abbott, ed., *Writings and Speeches*, iv. 445, 454.
55. Nancy L. Matthews, *Cromwell's Law Reformer* (Cambridge, 1984), pp. 186–207.
56. Worden, 'Cromwellian Oxford', 745–7.

counsels, was eager to reconcile both political and religious Presbyterians to his regime, provided he could get them to compromise on the issue of liberty of conscience. Milton, like Nedham, would have regarded any concessions from them on that front with immovable suspicion. The repeal of the Commonwealth's engagement of loyalty at the outset of the protectorate belonged to the same strategy of Cromwell. As the years of his government went by, an ever wider range of political opinion was represented in it. Milton's hope that the protector would give primacy to the advice of soldiers and regicides became ever more distant from reality. The judgement that was passed by *Defensio Secunda* on the likely consequences of parliamentary elections was vindicated by the clamorous electoral campaign of 1654. Like the further elections of 1656, it returned a powerful body of Presbyterians, who steered the Commons in the direction of religious reaction.[57]

What, meanwhile, of Cromwell's soul? On no subject was *Defensio Secunda* firmer than in its injunction to Cromwell 'to shun the pomp of wealth and power'. Cromwell showed no personal taste for it, but he knew the political value of ceremony and display. His was a sober court, but a stately and costly one none the less, which became grander with time and which attracted resentments akin to those provoked by the pre-war court.[58] Milton's treatise, edgy as it was over Cromwell's assumption of the title of protector, could at least commend him for 'despising the name of king ... and justly so: for if, after becoming so great, you should be captivated with a name' which, in 1649, he had removed, 'it would be all one as if, after subduing, by the help of the true God, an idolatrous nation, you were to worship as gods those whom you had brought under subjection' (225). Here was the nub, for, as Milton knew from the reign of Charles I, a nation with an idolatrous ruler becomes idolatrous itself. Cromwell carefully considered the offer of the crown by parliament in 1657. Even when he had refused it, he was reinstalled as protector with regal costume and accoutrements that supplied a sharp contrast to his plain dress at his modest ceremony of installation in December 1653. He had

57. Worden, 'Toleration and the Cromwellian Protectorate', 218–27; David L. Smith, 'Oliver Cromwell, the First Protectorate Parliament and Religious Reform', *Parliamentary History*, 19 (2000), 38–48.

58. This and a number of other aspects of the protectoral government are now illuminated in Little, ed., *Cromwellian Protectorate*. Another valuable recent guide to the regime is Barry Coward, *The Cromwellian Protectorate* (Manchester, 2002).

become a king in all but name.[59] His official advisers, whom the Instrument had appointed as 'the council', and who in that capacity imposed formal limits on his authority, gave way in 1657 to Cromwell's 'privy council', a body with a title from the time of royalty and with fewer powers of restraint than its predecessor. Its members, unlike the councillors of the Instrument of Government but in common with those of pre-war kings, were called 'their lordships'. Under the Instrument, the office of protector was elective. Under the Humble Petition the incumbent protector was to name his own successor. That provision was a large step back towards the ancient constitution, as was the simultaneous creation, which infuriated the commonwealthmen, of a second parliamentary chamber. When Richard Cromwell succeeded Oliver, the hereditary system had effectively returned.

**

The protectorate had no wish to antagonize Milton. It employed him for work which hardly needed his special gifts. He is sometimes thought to have written the contentious declaration of October 1655 with which the government justified its decision to go to war with Spain,[60] but the uncertainty about the authorship is itself a mark of the document's want of literary individuality. The translations which he undertook for the government could have been produced more rapidly by other employees. At least one foreign ambassador was given to understand that the regime's slowness in the production of Latin documents was caused by Milton's blindness[61] – though it may be that that resourcefully procrastinative administration found the delays convenient. The government quietly took his side in his controversy with Alexander More. It knew the power and, after the impact of *Defensio*, the esteem in which Milton's pen was held. It would not have wanted to see that power turned against it.

The protectorate knew the power of Marchamont Nedham's pen too. Nedham, Milton's regular visitor in Petty France through the political *bouleversements* of the Interregum, had adjusted with his customary dexterity to the political changes of 1653. He joined Milton and John Hall in vindicating Cromwell after the dissolution of the Rump. If, as seems likely, it was he who wrote the declaration that was put out by the army two

59. Roy Sherwood, *Oliver Cromwell: King in all but Name* (Stroud, 1997); see also *idem*, *The Court of Oliver Cromwell* (Stroud, 1989).
60. *MC* 162.
61. Fallon, *Milton in Government*, 174.

days after the coup, then we find there him venturing, amid the general conformity of the document to the needs of Cromwellian propaganda, a characteristic moment of independence, which took him in an opposite direction to Milton and Hall even as he otherwise concurred with them. The declaration hopes that in time the people will come to 'understan[d] their true interest in the election of successive parliaments'.[62] That had been the refrain of the republican editorials of *Politicus*, which always strove to teach the people to 'understand' their liberty. 'The interest of freedom', the newsbook had emphasized, 'consists in a due and orderly succession of the supreme assemblies.'[63] The expulsion of the Rump, by aborting the parliament's electoral bill, had prevented the exercise of that freedom. Yet Nedham, not for the first or last time, survived his deviation from Cromwellian orthodoxy. Thereafter, indeed, he was Cromwell's principal propagandist. In February 1654 he produced *A True State of the Case of the Commonwealth*, a measured, adroit, and widely read statement of the principles by which the protectorate wished to be recognized. In the autumn, *Politicus* was briefly complemented by another newsbook edited by Nedham, *The Observator*, which gave him scope for the wit and playfulness that had now been largely eliminated from *Politicus*.[64] But in the sober world of protectoral politics the experiment did not last.

Then, in November 1655 – the month after John Bradshaw remembered Milton and Nedham together in his will – there was registered for publication a work that would appear, anonymously, the following June: Nedham's *The Excellencie of a Free State, or The Right Constitution of a Commonwealth*. We have seen that two of the best-known political works of the protectorate, Milton's *Defensio Secunda* (1654) and James Harrington's *Oceana* (1656), had been conceived or written under the Rump. *The Excellencie of a Free State* was a third. It consisted mostly of material reproduced from editorials of *Mercurius Politicus* in 1651–2, though its title also recalls the 'discourse of the excellency of a free state' that Nedham included in *The Case of the Commonwealth* in 1650. The publisher of *The*

62. S. R. Gardiner, ed., *Constitutional Documents*, 402. The prominence given to the declaration by *MP* (28 Apr. 1653, 2386–91) also suggests Nedham's authorship.
63. *MP*, 27 Nov. 1651, 1221.
64. Nedham's choice of title for his new venture recalls his approving reference in *A True State* (p. 36) to a statement made by 'the Observator ... at the beginning of the war'. He refers to the *Observations* of that skilful polemicist Henry Parker in 1642. On this and other grounds, I suspect that the relations of Parker and Nedham would repay inspection (and see Beller, 'Milton and *Mercurius Politicus*', 480).

Excellencie was Thomas Brewster, who produced a number of works critical of the protectorate, prominent among them another work of 1656, *A Healing Question Propounded*, by Milton's hero Sir Henry Vane, who, like his other hero John Bradshaw, had dramatically broken with Cromwell at the dissolution of the Rump.[65] Nedham's tract appeared in time for the parliamentary elections of the summer, and concluded with 'a word of advice, in order to the choosing of the supreme assemblies'.[66] Vane's treatise was likewise written with the parliament of 1656 in mind. So was Harrington's *Oceana*. Everyone knew that the parliament would debate the future of the protectorate, for the regime had reached a constitutional impasse. The failings of the Instrument of Government, which the previous parliament had declined to ratify, were increasingly obvious.

There were two opposite directions in which the government might move. One, the development favoured by John Thurloe, was the return, partial or total, of the ancient constitution and the creation of a Cromwellian monarchy. The other was a revival, in some form, of the principle of parliamentary sovereignty. The choice between monarchical and parliamentary government had been the theme of *Politicus*, where the launching of Nedham's republican editorials upon Cromwell's return from Worcester had been timed to coincide with a heightening of the public expectation that the lord general would be crowned. *The Excellencie of a Free State* addressed the same question. Ostensibly the tract is a reply to recent works of political theory, which he calls 'high and ranting discourses of personal prerogative and unbounded monarchy'. But that target, having been fleetingly identified at the outset, is immediately forgotten. Nedham's concern is a debate within the Roundhead cause.[67] In 1656 Nedham's readers are invited to decide which of two courses 'will best secure the liberties and freedoms of the people from the encroachments and usurpations of tyranny': monarchical – that is, Cromwellian – rule, or the ideal to which Nedham clung in the days after the expulsion of the Rump, and

65. See especially Brewster's production *A Discovery of some Plots of Lucifer* (1656), and the list of books advertised at the back of it. The list includes Vane's treatise of 1655 *The Retired Mans Meditations* as well as Nedham's *The Excellencie*, which Brewster commends as an illustration of the teaching of Machiavelli. It also advertises the abbreviated version of Thomas May's history of the Long Parliament.
66. Nedham, *Excellencie*, 172.
67. *Politicus* had adopted a similar tactic. Attacking 'the royal sticklers' – the supporters of Charles II, who are the ostensible target of the newsbook – it contrived simultaneously to assail the Cromwellian promoters of 'the interest of monarchy' (*MP*, 11 Mar. 1652, 1458).

which he now defines as 'a due and orderly succession of the supreme authority in the hands of the people's representatives'.[68] This was the issue he had implicitly raised after the Battle of Worcester, when the launching of the republican editorials in *Politicus* had coincided with the expectation that Cromwell would be crowned. The answer is never in doubt. As is indicated by its very title, which thrusts the term 'free state' in the face of a government that has dropped it, *The Excellencie* is a daring attack on the protectorate. It flaunts those glories of a 'free state, or government by the people' which Nedham's editorials had proclaimed on behalf of the 'Commonwealth and Free State' of 1649–53.

The publication of Milton's *Defensio Secunda* gave dramatic irony to passages, written earlier, which had warned against the violation of liberty and the termination of the republic. *The Excellencie of a Free State* is rich in the same characteristic. Nedham, like Milton, had warned against Cromwell's usurpation. By 1656 many writers had railed at Cromwell's 'apostasy' and 'usurpation', but none could claim as convincingly as Nedham to have predicted them. It was *Politicus* that had urged in 1652 that the people must not be 'won by specious pretences and deluded by created necessities' to abandon 'the rules of a free state' or succumb to an aspirer to monarchy.[69] Since that time, Cromwell and his supporters – none more than Nedham himself – had repeatedly invoked 'necessity' to vindicate the coups of 1653 and the creation of the protectorate.[70] 'We are ready', Cromwell told parliament on his government's behalf in 1656, 'to excuse most of our actions – aye and to justify them as well as to excuse them – upon the grounds of necessity.'[71] *Politicus* had advised its readers that it 'concerns any people or nation to make a narrow search into' such 'pretences [of] necessities, whether they be feigned or not':[72] Cromwell explained to Barebone's that he had dissolved the Rump on the 'ground of necessity ... which was not a feigned necessity, but real'.[73]

Nedham had no need to alter those passages of *Politicus* when he reproduced them in *The Excellencie*. They had stood still while Cromwell's usurpation had given them an altered context. Events had borne out details too.

68. Nedham, *Excellencie*, p. v.
69. *MP*, 6 May 1652, 1570–1; and see Woolrych *Commonwealth to Protectorate*, 37.
70. See e.g. S. R. Gardiner, ed., *Constitutional Documents*, 403; Samuel Richardson, *Plain Dealing* (1656), 22–3; and the numerous invocations of 'necessity' in Nedham's *A True State*.
71. Abbott, ed., *Writings and Speeches*, iv. 261; cf. iii. 591.
72. *MP*, 5 Aug. 1652, 1772–3.
73. Abbott, ed., *Writings and Speeches*, iii. 60.

How Nedham must have enjoyed reproducing the statement that Julius Caesar, who in *Politicus* had been his recurrent parallel to Cromwell, 'durst not' take the title of king and therefore 'clothed himself with the more plausible title of emperor'.[74] For Cromwell, who decided against the title of king in 1653 and was wary of the dangers of accepting it, contemplated the title 'emperor' in 1655, at a time, five months before the registration of *The Excellencie*, when there was widespread expectation that his rule was about to assume an openly monarchical form.[75] How Nedham must have relished, too, the reproduction of his warning 'not to let two of one family to bear offices of high trust at one time, nor to permit the continuation of great powers in any one family'.[76] For *The Excellencie* was registered just after Cromwell had outraged the commonwealthmen by giving his son Henry command of the forces in Ireland. Time had borne out, too, the observations in *Politicus* that 'all tyrants and usurpers' invariably strive to dress their authority with a 'show of legality', and that it is 'the custom of all usurpers to make their investitures appear as just as they could, by getting the community's consent *ex post facto*'.[77] For that was exactly what Cromwell had done in 1654, in seeking parliamentary ratification of the constitution brought in by the military in December 1653.

Yet Nedham was not content merely to reproduce in 1656 material of 1651–2 to which events had given a new twist. Like Milton in *Defensio Secunda* in 1654, he made slight adjustments to his earlier text. Light of touch as they were, they were potentially incendiary. Whereas Milton's publication of *Defensio Secunda* brings a sense of tragedy to the failings of the protectorate, the revisions of *Mercurius Politicus* carry Nedham's unquenchable sense of mischief to the depiction of them. *Politicus*, in urging the English not to readmit the Stuarts, had advised them 'to keep close to the rules of a free state, for the barring out of monarchy', and had commended those founders of commonwealths, such as England's rulers of 1649, who 'have blocked up the way against monarchal tyranny, by declaring for the liberty of the people'. In 1656, when England had got or was getting, under whatever name, a new monarchy, *The Excellencie* amends that wording so as to cite 'the rules of a free state, for the turning out of monarchy', and to commend founders of commonwealths 'who shall

74. *MP*, 9 Oct. 1651, 1110: Nedham, *Excellencie*, p. xxi.
75. S. R. Gardiner, *Commonwealth and Protectorate*, iii. 304–5.
76. *MP*, 20 May 1652, 1593: Nedham, *Excellencie*, 109.
77. *MP*, 22 Apr. 1652, 1540: Nedham, *Excellencie*, 90.

block up the way against monarchic tyranny, by declaring for the liberty of the people'.[78] Other alterations heighten warnings against 'the rapes of usurpation',[79] and against giving scope to the 'temptations' of 'ambition', so as to bring Cromwell's forcible elevation to mind; others produce echoes of the insistent reminders in the pamphlets of commonwealthmen that in 1649 England had been 'declared' a 'free state', and that Cromwell's usurpation had been a treasonous breach of that commitment;[80] still another indicates that the events of 1653 proved that liberty, while it had been 'procured' in 1649, had not been 'secured' at that time.[81] To the observation in *Politicus* that, in republican Rome, Sulla and Marius 'got power into their hands upon the people's good, as many did before and after', *The Excellencie* – in case the allusion to the Commonwealth of 1649–53 be missed – adds 'not only in Rome, but in other free-states also'.[82] In *Politicus* 'it is good commonwealth language' to maintain that 'a due and orderly succession of power and persons' is the only means to preserve the people's freedom and avoid tyranny: in *The Excellencie* 'it was, and is, good commonwealth language' to do so.[83] Further emendations strike at other targets of the commonwealthmen: the new 'monarchists and royalists' who seek a Cromwellian dynasty as the only alternative to a Stuart one;[84] former commonwealthmen who, in their 'apostasy', have gone over to Cromwell;[85] and – at least on one reading of the text – Cromwell's spuriously 'holy war' with Spain.[86]

When *The Excellencie* was registered for publication in November 1655, the fortunes and morale of the protectorate were at their lowest ebb. The ideal of a harmonious relationship between protector and parliament had been shattered by the parliament of 1654–5 and had subsequently yielded to the rule of the Major-Generals. In the late summer, news had come through of the ignominious rout of the expedition sent by Cromwell,

78. *MP*, 6 May 1652, 1573: Nedham, *Excellencie*, 103.
79. *MP*, 12 Feb. 1652, 1396: Nedham, *Excellencie*, 42 (and see ibid. p. v).
80. *MP*, 22 Jan. 1652, 1352: Nedham, *Excellencie*, 28; *MP*, 11 Mar. 1652, 1457: Nedham, *Excellencie*, 46; *MP*, 13 May 1652, 1586: Nedham, *Excellencie*, 104; *MP*, 17 June 1652, 1661: Nedham, *Excellencie*, p. 135.
81. *MP*, 22 Jan. 1652, 1352: Nedham, *Excellencie*, 28.
82. *MP*, 1 Apr. 1652, 1491: Nedham, *Excellencie*, 67. The addition recalls the adaptation of the Bible by *A Public Plea* (above, p. 44) to make Christ an enemy of 'protectors'.
83. *MP*, 11 Dec. 1651, 1257: Nedham, *Excellencie*, 8.
84. *MP*, 11 Mar. 1652, 1462: Nedham, *Excellencie*, 55.
85. *MP*, 5 May 1652, 1385: Nedham, *Excellencie*, 38 (cf. p. 174).
86. *MP*, 1 July 1652, 1692: Nedham, *Excellencie*, 145.

as a prelude to the 'holy war', to strike at the Spanish empire in the New World. Perhaps Nedham was preparing, as often before, to desert his current masters. Perhaps he believed that an effective coalition of its opponents could topple them.[87] The readiness of commonwealthmen to combine with royalists against Cromwell may be reflected in *The Excellencie*, which takes a much softer line against the Stuart cause than *Politicus* had done. 'The late tyrant' Charles I repeatedly becomes, in 1656, 'the late king'.[88] *Politicus* had attacked 'the odious ... name of Stuart', but in *The Excellencie* that target is changed to the usurper Richard III, whose name came to stand, in anti-protectoral literature, for Cromwell's.[89] In June 1655 we find Nedham's old friend Henry Oxinden sending him a letter which mocks 'the saints' in rollicking anti-Puritan verses that recall the royalist Nedham of *Mercurius Pragmaticus*.[90] In other poems of the same year Sir John Berkenhead, Nedham's literary partner of the late 1640s, derided Cromwell's aspirations to kingship by comparing them, as *Politicus* and *The Excellencie* do, with the ambition of Sulla. Berkenhead writes that Sulla, who had 'a copper face' (the familiar feature of Cromwell), 'taught but two arts, speacking' – speac-king – 'and cutting throats'.[91]

How did Nedham, an employee of the state writing under the nose of John Thurloe, get away with publishing a document which effectively charged Cromwell with treason, and which advocated a political course that Thurloe would have judged catastrophic?[92] Of all the signs of Nedham's indispensability, and of the leeway that his employers were obliged to grant him sooner than face his open desertion, *The Excellencie* is the most remarkable. Thurloe was feared by virtue of his intelligence service, which detected and interrogated conspirators. He must have had some idea what Nedham was up to. Yet he may not have been in a position to enquire too closely. The protectorate, awesome as its power might seem to its

87. It is possible that a cost-cutting exercise by the government in April 1655, which terminated Nedham's salary (and John Hall's), had a bearing on his conduct, but the decision proved to be temporary, and in any case he made alternative arrangements with the regime to secure his financial well-being: *Cal. SP Dom* 1655, 127, 139, 604; Peacey, *Politicians and Pamphleteers*, 195, 292.
88. *MP*, 11 Dec. 1651, 1257; 29 Jan. 1652, 1366; 15 Apr. 1652, 1523; 8 July 1652, 1709; Nedham, *Excellencie*, 8, 30, 80, 153.
89. *MP*, 11 Dec. 1651, 1257: Nedham, *Excellencie*, 8. Cf. William Prynne, *King Richard the Third Revised* (1657).
90. D. Gardiner, e.d., *Oxinden and Peyton Letters*, 200–2.
91. P. W. Thomas, *Sir John Berkenhead*, 188.
92. For Thurloe's control of *Politicus* during the protectorate see Peacey, *Politicians and Pamphleteers*, 228–30.

opponents, was preoccupied with the daily business of management and survival. Thurloe struggled in vain, with a small staff, to keep pace with a huge burden of business and with the daily challenge of the government's endurance. He would undoubtedly have known of the publication of *The Excellencie*, but no one in his office would have had the time to trace Nedham's amendments to the earlier material. In any case Thurloe's power had its limits. The government was beset by internal conflicts, which can only have worked to Nedham's advantage. We saw that the council was divided between those (including Thurloe) who hoped, and those who feared, that protectoral rule would lead to the restoration of kingship. The latter group was prepared to lend help to writers critical of the regime. One of the leading figures in the government, Cromwell's son-in-law the councillor and army officer Charles Fleetwood, who despite his acquiescence in the protectorate retained sympathy with the views of the commonwealthmen, gave encouragement to Sir Henry Vane to publish *A Healing Question Propounded* in 1656 (though his support did not prevent Vane from being brought before the council and imprisoned). Fleetwood gave shelter to other commonwealthmen too.[93] In 1654 another leading councillor, Cromwell's brother-in-law the army officer John Desborough, mediated with Cromwell to protect that eloquent champion of commonwealth principles, John Streater, from pursuit by Thurloe, 'the instrument of his trouble', after Streater had written against Cromwell's usurpation.[94]

Defensio Secunda had recommended Fleetwood and Desborough to Cromwell as counsellors. It had also urged him to choose as an adviser William Sydenham, the councillor who in the protectorate was closest in spirit to the commonwealthmen, and who alone of those members would be welcomed into the leadership of the restored Rump on the overthrow of the protectorate. Nedham's tract, like those of Vane and Streater, had features of which Fleetwood and Desborough and Sydenham would have approved. They had accepted the need for Cromwell's elevation, but wished to restrain or curtail his powers and to prevent its hereditary entrenchment. For all its unmistakably subversive shafts, there are passages of *The Excellencie* which conform to that essentially loyal standpoint. In them Nedham, like that other republican critic of the protectorate James Harrington in *Oceana* a few months later, accepted Cromwell's single rule as the necessary condition

93. Firth, *Memoirs of Edmund Ludlow*, i. 416, 431, 432; *TSP* iii. 246; iv. 100, 107–8.
94. Streater, *Secret Reasons of State*, 18–20.

of constitutional change. Under the Rump, Nedham had been unusual in frequently alluding to the regime not only as a Commonwealth and free state, which it had declared itself to be, but as a 'republic', a term which its more moderate members appear to have disliked and which it had generally eschewed. The term was dropped at those moments in *The Excellencie*.[95]

There was a more significant set of changes. In *Politicus* Nedham had insisted that England's republic be kept from 'mixture' with 'any other form' of government, wording that ruled out the return to the limited or mixed form of government for which Cromwell had argued after his return to Westminster in 1651. That demand was also omitted from *The Excellencie*.[96] In amending another passage of *Politicus*, Nedham inserted words that allowed for the possibility of a king, who would be 'chosen by the people's representatives, and made an officer of trust by them'.[97] The phrasing recalled the thinking of the new model army until, after Pride's Purge, it committed itself to the abolition of monarchy.[98] Nedham's words pointed the way to the rewriting of the protectoral constitution so as to reassert the rights of the people that Cromwell had betrayed, but, at the same time, to accommodate a limited form of monarchy within it. It was a goal conformable to the outlook of Fleetwood and Desborough and Sydenham. It was also closer than the unremitting republicanism of *Politicus* to the general run of Roundhead sentiment. The impression that Nedham was providing a platform for a coalition of interests is heightened by the persistent dilution, in *The Excellencie*, of the social radicalism that had been a marked feature of *Politicus*. In the parliamentary elections of 1656, for which Nedham's tract seeks to prepare the minds of voters, commonwealthmen hid their own more extreme views and played on themes that would appeal across the anti-Cromwellian spectrum.

★★

At the radical end of that spectrum stood the pamphleteer and printer John Streater, who printed Harrington's *Oceana* in 1656. His sentiments, even his words, are sometimes so close to Nedham's that his name must be added to the

95. *MP*, 13 May 1652, 1588: Nedham, *Excellencie*, 107; *MP* 20 May 1652, 1594: Nedham, *Excellencie*, 110. See too *MP*, e.g. 20 Feb. 1651, 600; 25 Nov. 1652, 2028–9.
96. *MP*, 8 Jan. 1652, 1320: Nedham, *Excellencie*, 18–19.
97. *MP*, 5 Feb. 1652, 1384: Nedham, *Excellencie*, 37.
98. Worden, 'Republicanism, Regicide and Republic', 321.

list of his literary collaborators. Like Nedham, Streater roamed history, especially classical history, for examples to support contentious claims of political theory. He had none of Nedham's taste for tactical compromise or adjustment. Unlike him he stuck to the social dimension of his radicalism. In that respect as in others, his writing is closer to *Politicus* than to *The Excellencie*. Yet most of the common programme of the two writers survives in Nedham's tract of 1656.[99] Among its demands were regular parliamentary elections; the rejection of what Streater, like Nedham, called the vesting of 'standing' power in either a single ruler or a parliament (or senate);[100] and, to prevent that evil, the imposition of time limits on the tenure of office-holders.[101] When Streater lists the 'excellencies' for which 'a free state is to be chosen before any other government', he begins with the assertion that 'the benefit of a free state, and welfare of a free people, consists in the due succession of the supreme assembly'.[102] His words are either adapted from *Politicus* or written jointly with its author. Perhaps the same is true when in 1659, echoing the assertion in *Politicus* that 'liberty ... consists not in a licence to do what ye list',[103] Streater declares that 'liberty consisteth not in everyone's doing what he listeth'. His complaint in the same place that, despite the ostensibly republican rule of 1649–53, 'England yet was never a free-state' recalls Nedham's own yearning, under the Commonwealth, for 'the form of a real republic'.[104]

Streater's activities under the protectorate provide an indication that, well before the registration of *The Excellencie*, Nedham at the least connived at anti-protectoral publication, if he did not indeed contribute to it. In 1653, having recently returned from military service in Ireland, Streater was imprisoned after attacking the dissolution of the Rump. The 'excellencies' and 'true excellence of a free state' were a preoccupation of Streater.[105] In the late spring of 1654 he published, as a short-lived weekly newsbook, *Observations, Historical, Political and Philosophical, upon Aristotle's First Book of Politics*. The 'observations' were contained in editorials which Streater planned to publish separately in book form, as Nedham would republish editorials from *Politicus* in 1656. In Streater's editorials, as he would recall in 1659, 'the excellency of a free state was maintained, and the inconveniences

99. The essential introduction to Streater's political thought is Nigel Smith, 'Popular Republicanism in the 1650s: John Streater's "Heroic Mechanics"', in Armitage *et al.*, eds., *Milton and Republicanism*, 137–55.

100. John Streater, *A Shield against the Parthian Dart* (1659), 16.

101. Streater, *Continuation,* 15. 102. Ibid. 103. *MP*, 2 Oct. 1651, 1095.

104. John Streater, *Government Described* (1659), 8; above, p. 25.

105. Ibid.; Sreater, *Continuation*, 15.

of a tyranny or single person were fully demonstrated'.[106] In May 1654 – a week before the appearance of *Defensio Secunda* – Streater published a provocative work, half-tract, half-newsbook, *A Politick Commentary on the Life of Caius Julius Caesar, written by Caius Suetonius Tranquilius.* He was 'prosecuted vigorously' on account of it, and endured months of house arrest thereafter. For related misdemeanours he was seized by soldiers in his own house and brought to Whitehall before obtaining his release.[107]

With a mischief reminiscent of Nedham, *A Politick Commentary* assures Streater's readers, lest they 'wonder that in this discourse I should undertake to prove Caesar a tyrant and usurper', that 'I shall not commit treason against him', for 'I am told he is dead long since'. With Nedham, Streater identifies Cromwell with Sulla as well as with Caesar. The analogies illustrate his claim that 'a people are always deceived by these two vizards, viz. pretence of liberty and religion'. It was common ground among Cromwell's enemies that religion was his main pretence. Sulla, recalls Streater, chastised Caesar 'out of a religious pretence'.[108] But it is Caesar who supplies Streater's main parallels. His 'ambition prompted him forward to his great undertakings'; 'his cloak or vizard for his ambition was public affection to the interest of the commons, whom he made slaves'; his 'design was to pretend the serving of the commonwealth'; he 'made great use of the discontents of the people as a footstool to ascend, together with pretending to ease them from servitude'; 'by fair words and promises he inviteth' the people to expect liberty; he 'intends ... in his rising to make music to their ears'; but 'instead thereof behold slavery'. Streater reflects on the tactics favoured by the kind of usurper who – like Cromwell – has 'the sentence of death' passed on the existing ruler and then 'not only jumpeth into his place, but also clotheth himself with his iniquity also; and ... pretends that the state of the commonwealth necessitates him thereto'; for, 'now being at the top', he 'is the only person to judge of the necessities of the commonwealth'. With Nedham – and Milton – he relates the rise of tyranny to the failings of its victims, for 'it is a time for tyrants and usurpers to thrive, when a commonwealth is degenerated in virtue'.[109]

106. Streater, *Secret Reasons of State*, 18.
107. His travails are recounted in his tract *Secret Reasons of State.*
108. 'The deepest policy of a tyrant', Milton had remarked in 1649, at that time with Charles I in mind, 'hath ever been to counterfeit religious' (*CP* iii. 361).
109. Streater, *A Politick Commentary in the Life of Caius Julius Caesar, written by Caius Suetonius Tranquilius* (23 May 1654), 1–4; *Perfect and Impartial Intelligence*, 26 May 1654, 13–16.

Streater's opposition to the protectorate was unequivocal, and brought him harassment and trouble. Nedham, the practised survivor, overcame any difficulty that the publication of *The Excellencie* may have caused him. In the year after its publication, however, he indicated that he had sailed close to the wind: perhaps very close, and perhaps in Streater's company. For *The Excellencie*, risky as it was, may not have been Nedham's most hazardous venture into anti-Cromwellian literature. We discover the extent of his brinkmanship from material in *Politicus* in March 1657. At that time the newsbook, briefly recovering its earlier merriment of spirit, ran a series of playful letters, tantalizing in their deployment of knowing allusions that are largely irrecoverable by a later age, 'from Utopia'. One of the letters contains a mocking reference to 'that wondrous wise republican called Mercurius Politicus (who served up the Politicks in sippets)'.[110] 'The Politicks in sippets' would be an apt description of Streater's *Observations*, which extracted brief passages from Aristotle's *Politics* and commented on them.[111] The prose of the *Observations* bears no trace of Nedham's style, but his remark in 1657 may indicate that he had collaborated in their publication. At all events the letter alludes to a risk taken by Nedham, whether at that point, or in the publication of *The Excellencie*, or on some other, now vanished, occasion. The fictional correspondent equates Nedham with the author of *Utopia*, Sir Thomas More, who, *Politicus* tells us, lived most of his life by the motto, 'joco-serio, betwixt jest and earnest', the words that Nedham had claimed as his own badge.[112] Only 'once in his days' did More 'leav[e] off' that principle and become 'earnest'. It was that solitary 'error' that brought him to the block. So Nedham's readers are to understand that 'whatever I write is no further in earnest than you please to make it so. Indeed (sir) 'tis but drolling.'[113] We have to guess what, and how much, is being laughed away.

At all events, Nedham had worked his way back. The letters from Utopia are those of a licensed jester. Six days after the appearance of the analogy with More, Nedham encountered Cromwell at Whitehall, who 'asked him the news'. With an eye on the movement to crown the protector, Nedham answered that 'vox populi' was prophesying the appointment of

110. *MP*, 12 Mar. 1657, 7644 . I say 'mocking' because the term 'republican', which no writers of the time claimed for themselves, was pejorative.

111. Milton, too, found political radicalism in Aristotle's *Politics*: *CP* vii. 484–5.

112. Above, p. 37.

113. *MP*, 12 Mar. 1657, 7642.

Puritan Archbishops of Canterbury and York.[114] When the letters from Utopia appeared, parliament was debating the proposal to crown Cromwell. *Politicus* helped to prepare the public for that change and for the 'settlement' it would bring. One of the letters explained that liberty and monarchy are compatible, and renounced the arguments of the commonwealthmen in terms that recall Nedham's writings for the protectorate in 1654.[115] In April, during Cromwell's negotiations with parliament over the Humble Petition and Advice, the protector fell back on arguments and language that derived from Nedham.[116] Nedham displayed unblemished loyalty for the rest of the protectorate. In the summer of 1657 he published a sharp reply to John Goodwin, a former apologist for regicide whose views, in both politics and religion, had parallels with those of Milton, with whose career his own sometimes interacted. Nedham's target was a scathing attack by Goodwin on the ecclesiastical system created by John Owen.[117] In the next year, when Cromwell died, *Politicus* published a laudatory obituary as free from any taint of criticism as is the poem by that now unqualified Cromwellian Andrew Marvell on the same event.[118] There is nothing to prepare us, either towards the end of Cromwell's reign or during the rule of his son, for the savagery of Nedham's attack on the protectorate in *A Publick Plea* in May 1659, where Nedham and Milton come together, and where the views that had been expressed obliquely in *The Excellencie of a Free State* were openly avowed.

★★

In 1652, readers of *Politicus* had been invited to compare Cromwell to a tyrant depicted by Machiavelli, Dionysius of Syracuse, who 'clothed himself with a pretence of the people's liberties'. In *Politicus*, Dionysius is described as the Syracusans' 'leader'. In *The Excellencie*, after another of Nedham's delicate adjustments, he is their 'general',[119] the title by which the commonwealthmen, to indicate their refusal to acknowledge the protectorate, pointedly referred to Cromwell after 1653. Streater, in his anti-Cromwellian literature, likes to call him 'General Cromwell'.[120] In May

114. Abbott, ed., *Writings and Speeches*, iv. 432.
115. *MP*, 26 Mar. 1657, 7673–5.
116. Worden, *Rump Parliament*, 362.
117. Nedham, *The Great Accuser Cast Down* (1657).
118. *MP*, 9 Sept. 1658, 802–3.
119. Ibid. 1 Apr. 1652, 1490; Nedham, *Excellencie*, 66.
120. Streater, *Continuation*, 13; see too *idem*, *Shield*, 22–3, on Dionysius.

1659 – around five days after the publication of *A Publick Plea* – Streater wrote a 'narrative of his ... troubles at the beginning of the late monarchy erected by General Cromwell'.[121]

The protector is 'General Cromwell' too in *Defensio Secunda* (165). It is hard to decide, from the context, whether Milton was using the phrase pointedly. Whether he was or not, there was plenty of other material in his treatise that cast an unfavourable light on events that had occurred since the time of the Rump, when the bulk of it had been written. Like the editorials in *Politicus* that reappeared in *The Excellencie*, the text of *Defensio Secunda* had stayed mainly still while the context had changed. To set *Defensio Secunda* beside *The Excellencie* is to be conscious of marked differences as well as of similarities. For one thing, there is the difference of date. In 1654 Nedham, whose *A True State* of that year was a powerful work of straightforward propaganda for the government, allowed himself, as a newswriter, only the mildest of indications of sympathy for the commonwealthmen.[122] The character of protectoral politics was transformed in late 1654 and early 1655, first by the forcible removal of the commonwealthmen from parliament in September, then by the premature dissolution of the parliament in January, which left the regime devoid of constitutional legitimacy and dependent on naked force. But even in 1656 one could not imagine Milton appealing, with Nedham, to a broad coalition of interests against Cromwell, or wooing royalists or conservative parliamentarians, or calling for frequent parliamentary elections.

Yet the resemblances between *Defensio Secunda* and *The Excellencie* are telling too. Milton, like Nedham, worked for Thurloe and received a government stipend. It is a mistake, however, to project modern notions of civil service responsibility and discretion on to the seventeenth century, when resignations on matters of principle were a rare occurrence. What Milton did at his masters' bidding is not to be confused with his views on them. It may also be mistaken to discount, in an assessment of the motives of a writer who responded as pliably as Milton – and Nedham – to the changes of regime in the 1650s, the financial rewards of office. Milton acknowledged a liking for 'a temperate use of our honest acquisitions in the provision of food and raiment, and of the elegancies of life',[123] earnings which, as he wanted 'listening Europe' to know, had in his case

121. Streater, *Secret Reasons of State*, title-page.

122. Below, p. 332

123. *CW* xvii. 233.

been overtaxed.[124] Who else would have paid him, when his salary was at its highest, nearly £300 a year? Of course the picture of his personality projected by his own writings, an image which appealed to Victorian instincts of propriety and public service, is radically at odds with that suggestion. So are the accounts of him by his early, reverential biographers Cyriack Skinner and Edward Phillips. Writing after the Restoration, they hastened over his work for the regimes of the 1650s and instead, by echoing his own disclaimers, elevated his character above the inducements of financial reward. Even today the suggestion that he might have been glad of a salary is enough to induce indignation. Yet poets, whatever their stature, are human beings. Milton would have needed no scruples in accepting paid work in Thurloe's office, whose main task was to prevent, by both its foreign and its domestic exertions, the return of the Stuarts. His readiness to do so does not betoken approval of it. His public silence about the protectorate tells a different story, as would become clear after Cromwell's death, when the silence was broken. In any case, the silence was not complete. Like Nedham he found, as we shall soon see, indirect ways of indicating his sentiments. In *de Doctrina Christiana*, which he seems to have begun to compile in the mid- or late 1650s, he wrote that he was 'far from denying' that 'it may be the part of prudence to obey the commands even of a tyrant in lawful things, or, more properly, to comply with the necessity of the times for the sake of public peace, as well as of personal safety'.[125] It is hard to think that he wrote that passage without, at the least, pausing for autobiographical reflection.

★★

Milton's view of Cromwell, sharp and severe as it sometimes was, has a largeness of perspective that distinguishes it from Nedham's. There are two reasons for this. The first is the tension or ambiguity in Milton, who, though so alert to the evils that attend power, is simultaneously drawn to great men. We saw it in his statement in *Defensio* that Julius Caesar, who forcibly entered on power, perhaps deserved it. Like Harrington, with whom he disagreed profoundly elsewhere, Milton brings a sense of loss, of the waste of human greatness, to the failure of the protectorate – something Nedham would not have attempted.

124. Ibid. viii. 137. 125. ibid. xvii. 403–5.

Secondly, Cromwell's defects are only a part of the problem facing the England he rules. There are also the failings of the nation itself. 'No man, not Cromwell himself', warns *Defensio Secunda*, could deliver England again if it succumbed to corruption (245). So there is a limit to the scope of virtue even if it is exercised by the 'supremely excellent' ruler whom, with one half of his mind, Milton – at the time he wrote that passage – judged or hoped Cromwell to be. In 'The First Anniversary', Andrew Marvell speculates what 'heroic Cromwell' might achieve if only 'a seasonable people still | Should bend to his, as he to heaven's will' (ll. 133–4). Milton does not imply, as Marvell's panegyric does, that the test of England's virtue is its readiness to obey the protector, who in Milton's work, but not in Marvell's poem, has still to prove his equipment for the challenges of peace. Yet even in 1659, when the damage wrought by the protectorate loomed large in Milton's mind, he remained no less conscious of the nation's own 'retrograde motion of late, in liberty and spiritual truths'.[126]

Almost at the end of *Defensio Secunda* there is an exhortation to the English people (239–45). It mirrors two other passages of exhortation. First there is the advice to them at the end of the first 'defence'.[127] In both 'defences' the people face a trial of virtue, and must choose between internal liberty and internal slavery. In both cases, as Milton explains, the people's tasks of war have yielded to the greater challenge of peace. In *Defensio* the people, having 'subdued your enemies in the field', 'must have highest courage to subdue what conquers the rest of the nations of men – faction, avarice, the temptations of riches, and the corruption that waits upon prosperity'. Otherwise, having been 'valiant in war', they will 'grow debauched in peace'. In *Defensio Secunda*, the banishing of 'avarice, ambition, luxury' from the mind 'is the warfare of peace', and such triumphs within 'are victories ... more glorious than the warlike and the bloody' (241–3). Secondly, the exhortation to the people in *Defensio Secunda* seems intended to complement the injunctions in the same work to Cromwell. Cromwell has the same battle to fight within his soul; he likewise has prevailed in war; he likewise confronts the demands of peace. *Defensio Secunda* tells the people 'to be masters of yourselves' and to reflect on the fate awaiting the man 'who has no command of himself' (251): in the same work it is part of Cromwell's greatness to be 'a commander first over himself' (215). Both

126. *CP* vii. 511. 127. *CW* vii. 551–5.

Cromwell and the people are warned that men who betray virtue become 'slaves' within themselves (227, 251).

Milton's anxieties about the fitness of the English for liberty are as persistent a theme as any in his political writing. Yet he knows that the qualities of the people reflect those of their leaders. In that respect they are like an army. Milton thrilled to the virtues of the new model army. Yet, perhaps writing after losing his faith in it, he noted that soldiers 'most commonly are as their commanders, without much odds of valour in one nation or another, only as they are more or less wisely disciplined and led'.[128] It was, he decided, the parliamentary leaders of the 1640s, and their clerical allies, who 'unfitted ... the people' for the challenge of liberty.[129] Weeks before the Restoration the last words of *The Readie and Easie Way*, scornful as they are of the 'multitude', portray them as victims, for they have been 'misguided and abused'.[130] So whatever the limits which the nation's failings may impose on Cromwell's scope for virtuous achievement, it is on his leadership that its hopes of liberty rest.

**

It seems to have been either around late 1655 – the time when Nedham's *The Excellencie* was registered for publication – or else at some subsequent point of Cromwell's remaining life that Milton returned to his *History of Britain*,[131] the first four books of which he had written in the late 1640s, though the work would be published only in 1670. How much of the remainder he wrote in the 1650s, and how much – if any – of his narrative he composed only after 1660, it is impossible to tell. In the section he began under the protectorate he remained preoccupied with his country's sinfulness and with the servitude it merited. But Cromwell is in his mind too, and with him are the habitual deficiencies of monarchical rule. The analogies with the present are neither exact nor sustained, for they are subordinated to a narrative that has its own requirements of chronology and argument; but they are there. Book v opens with an account of King Egbert which, in outline though not in detail, might be a summary of the condition of protectoral England:

> The sum of things in this island, or the best part thereof, [being] reduced now under the power of one man; and him one of the worthiest, which,

128. *CP* v. 337. 129. Ibid. v. 449. 130. Ibid. vii. 463.
131. Von Maltzahn, *Milton's 'History of Britain'*, 169–70.

> as far as can be found in good authors, was by none attained at any time before unless in fables; men might with some reason have expected, from such union, peace and plenty, greatness, and the flourishing of all estates and degrees.[132]

Egbert 'enjoyed his conquest seven peaceful years' and reached – in the phrase that Nedham had ironically bestowed on Cromwell – 'height of glory'.[133] Yet there are insecurities beneath Egbert's rule. His 'victorious army' was 'long since disbanded', and 'the exercise of arms' was 'perhaps laid aside', a failing which Milton sees as evidence of that national wickedness which Egbert's merits are powerless to allay.[134] Under the protectorate Cromwell's own army was being reduced, and in the eyes of the commonwealthmen its 'military discipline', a virtue on which Milton – like Nedham[135] – set such store, had lost its prowess with Cromwell's usurpation, a development which the humiliating fate of the attack on Spanish territory in the Caribbean in April 1655 appeared to confirm.

Besides, however 'worthy' Egbert may be, his government is a 'yoke'.[136] In the later portion of the *History* – the parts written during or after the protectorate – Milton is exercised by the shortcomings of rule even by excellent, or apparently excellent, men. His earlier ideal of the Aristotelian king had dissolved since Cromwell's accession to the protectorate. In 1641, when in his attack on episcopacy he had to deal with the inconvenient evidence of the 'personal excellence' of a particular bishop, he had argued that such merit, while it may seem 'like an antidote' to overcome 'the disease' of 'corruption', will only help to 'hid[e]' it for a while 'under show of a full and healthy constitution'.[137] The *History* developed a parallel thought with respect to kingship. In his mind the Aristotelian ideal had long coexisted with more sceptical perceptions of single rule. In the early part of the *History*, in a passage we can take to have been written in the late 1640s, the Roman governor Agricola, as a 'public father', does just what Cromwell is urged, as the 'father of his country', to do in *Defensio Secunda*, which invites him 'to form and increase virtue'. Agricola spends his time 'in worthy actions, teaching and promoting… the institutes and customs of civil life'. Yet even beneath that virtuous rule there runs, it

132. *CP* v. 257; Trevor-Roper, *Catholics, Anglicans and Puritans*, 257; von Maltzahn, *Milton's 'History of Britain'*, 172.

133. *CP* v. 259; above, p. 110.

134. *CP* v. 259.

135. *Case*, 60; *MP*, 25 Aug. 1653, 2679; 9 Sept. 1658, 802.

136. *CP* v. 256.

137. Ibid. i. 675–6.

seems, a Tacitean current. Agricola's achievements led to the imitation of Roman fashions, 'which the foolisher sort called civility, but was indeed a secret art to prepare them for bondage'.[138] In the later part of the *History*, the portion written in or after the protectorate, the excellence of virtuous leaders becomes a mirage. There is King Edgar, who at first seems a paragon. While always 'well prepared for war', as a good king must be, he 'governed the kingdom in great honour, peace and prosperity'; he took energetic steps 'to see justice well administered' and to free the poor from oppression; he was 'much extolled for justice, clemency, and all kingly virtues'. Yet his rule was flawed. Opinion betraying its tendency to serve power, his accomplishments are exaggerated by the monks who record them. They were in any case vitiated, for Edgar 'unaware' allowed foreign 'vices' to enter the land, and 'perhaps' earned divine displeasure by 'taking too much honour to himself'.[139]

In the last book of the *History*, other outwardly imposing or meritorious kings are found to have inward flaws. There is Ethelred, 'reported by some fair of visage, comely of person, elegant of behaviour; but the event will show that with ... vices he quickly shamed his outside'.[140] There is Harold, the king defeated at Hastings, who as king 'began to frame himself by all manner of compliances to gain affection'; he 'endeavoured to make good laws', befriended the Church, was 'courteous and affable to all, reputed good, a hater of evil-doers'; he 'charged all his officers' to enforce justice on the wicked, and 'by sea and land laboured in their defence of his country: so good an actor is ambition'.[141] Milton, we shall see, had things to say elsewhere about the acting of ambition by Cromwell.

In 1658, perhaps in May, Milton ventured into print for the first time – unless we include any documents by him among state papers published at Thurloe's bidding – since the publication of *Pro Se Defensio* three years earlier. He published a manuscript which he had had 'many years in my hands', and which he had found 'lately by chance among other books and papers'. He attributed it, wrongly, to Sir Walter Ralegh, and printed it as *The Cabinet-Council: containing the Chief Arts of Empire and Mysteries of State; Discabinated in Political and Polemical Aphorisms*. The work

138. Ibid. v. 85.
139. Ibid. 321–4. Again Philip Sidney's zealously reforming king, Euarchus, that embodiment of 'justice' who 'kept in peacetime a continual discipline of war', comes to mind: Worden, *Sound of Virtue*, 132.
140. *CP* v. 331.
141. Ibid. 394.

is one of those collections of maxims of statecraft, secular and sceptical in spirit, to which the appeal of Tacitus and other terse and epigrammatic writers had given rise in the Renaissance. Milton despised the genre. He hated 'aphorisms' and the language of 'reason of state' which they condensed. He detested arguments that discussed power as if it could be warrantably separated from virtue. He knew the evils of 'cabinet-councils', those small and secret gatherings where tyranny was plotted, and of the 'cabin-counsellors' who plotted it.[142] He loathed to see the writing of Tacitus, whom he saw as 'the greatest possible enemy to tyrants',[143] turned into material for handbooks for them. Why, then, did he publish a work so opposed to his own convictions? In an essay of remarkable scholarship and insight, Martin Dzelzainis has argued that the work is a resourcefully oblique commentary on the Tacitean tyranny of Cromwell: that in the 'chilling' Machiavellian precepts that it publishes there lay ironically 'corrupt advice for a corrupt regime'.[144] Dzelzainis's argument turns on an interpretation, which a summary would oversimplify, of the Latin epigraph, taken from Horace, which appears under Milton's name on the title-page, and which, as Dzelzainis interpets it, conforms to Milton's deployment, on other title-pages of his, of classical epigrams to pointed political purposes. In the last year of his life Milton would turn to the most oblique methods of political commentary to seek to undermine the prospects of succession of the future James II.[145] There is nothing improbable in the thought of his using a similar technique under Cromwell.

On the other hand, as Dzelzainis concedes, the epigraph from Horace has more than one possible meaning. There is also the difficulty of understanding why Milton should have attributed the book to Ralegh, who, whether or not Milton believed him to be the author, had a wide and admiring Puritan following. Nedham, who often cited Ralegh's arguments to support his own, described him in 1647 as a man 'whom the world will witness for, that he was no flatterer to kings or monarchs, much less to tyrants'.[146] *Politicus* presented him as 'that gallant man' who succumbed to the tyranny of James I.[147] Perhaps a book which carried two famous names, those of Ralegh and Milton, on its title-page, and which as an assembly of political maxims belonged to a marketable genre, was

142. Dzelzainis, 'Milton and the Protectorate', 193–5. 143. *CW* vii. 317–19.
144. Dzelzainis, 'Milton and the Protectorate', 193, 201. 145. Below, pp. 385–6.
146. Nedham, *Parallel of Governments*, 3. 147. *MP*, 22 May 1651, 800.

published with a commercial aim.[148] If so, the statement that Milton had long possessed the manuscript, and had recently chanced upon it in his papers, may merely be a conventional ruse of publicity. In 1654, after all, he had implausibly claimed to have acquired manuscript versions of his distich about Alexander More.[149] In the end, Dzelzainis's hypothesis can be neither proved nor disproved.[150] Even so, what we have seen of the literary tactics both of Milton and of Nedham in the 1650s invites us to keep it in mind. So does the view of the protectorate that, as we shall soon see, emerges from Milton's writings after Cromwell's death.

148. Nicholas von Maltzahn, 'Blank Verse and the Nation: Milton and his Imitators', in Paul Stevens and David Loewenstein, eds., *Early Modern Nationalism and Milton's England* (Toronto, forthcoming), finds similarities between *The Cabinet-Council* and the text of another publication by the same bookseller, Thomas Johnson, which was entered for publication by Thomas Newcomb, its printer, in June 1658 and apparently published in 1659: *Aristippus, or Monsieur de Balsac's Masterpiece: Being a Discourse concerning the Court.* Perhaps Newcomb's preface, which explains how the manuscript came into his hands and remarks that 'the author's name who composed this discourse' – that of Jean Louis Guez, Sieur de Balzac – 'cannot but be a sufficient inducement to the reading thereof', is to be read as an echo of the other publication. The tribute to Queen Christina of Sweden in the author's preface is of interest to students of Newcomb's clients Milton and Nedham.

149. Above, p. 213.

150. Dzelzainis's argument has been criticized by Paul Stevens, 'Milton's "Renunciation" of Cromwell: The Problem of Raleigh's *Cabinet-Council*', *Modern Philology*, 98 (2001), 363–92. Stevens maintains that the work is an expression of what he calls 'Protestant nationalism', and was written in support of Cromwell's war with Spain. We are left to wonder why Milton, who, if he had wanted publicly to voice a favourable view of the war, could have done so openly and easily, and would have delighted the government by taking that step, should have resorted to so arcane and obscure a mode of expression. I am not quite persuaded by the argument of David Armitage that *Paradise Lost* contains criticism of the disastrous Cromwellian expedition to the Caribbean in 1654. But there is nothing inherently improbable in the idea, and his essay is full of valuable perception (Armitage, 'John Milton: Poet against Empire'; see too *idem*, 'The Cromwellian Protectorate and the Languages of Empire', *Historical Journal*, 35 (1992), 531–55).

14
Milton and the Good Old Cause

In Milton's praise of the advisers with whom *Defensio Secunda* urges Cromwell to surround himself, one name stands out. The tribute to Colonel Robert Overton is much the longest, and is unique in its personal stamp (233–5). Overton, Milton reminds him, 'has been connected with me for these many years in a more than brotherly union, by similitude of studies, and by the sweetness of your manners'. Naming, for the only time in his writings (other than as a point of chronological reference), a battle of the first civil war, Milton recalls Overton's exploits at Marston Moor in 1644. He follows his citation of them with an allusion to Overton's achievements in the Cromwellian conquest of Scotland. Milton proclaims that Overton – to whose humanity to his enemies there is independent testimony[1] – has been acknowledged by the Scots as 'the humanest of enemies' and as a 'civilizing conqueror'. The other officers proposed by Milton – Fleetwood, Desborough, Lambert, Whalley – were within Cromwell's milieu (even if Lambert had not the intimate bond with the protector that was shared by the others). Overton, as far as we can tell, was never close to Cromwell, with whom he had uneasy relations at least from the early period of the Commonwealth. His inclusion in Milton's list of candidates, whenever it was that Milton compiled it, bore an uncomfortable message for Cromwell.

Milton's tribute is our only source for the 'more than brotherly union' and 'similitude of studies' that he shared with Overton, who was himself

1. Barbara Taft, '"They that pursew perfection on earth": The Political Progress of Robert Overton', in Gentles *et al.*, eds., *Soldiers, Writers and Statesmen*, 287. Taft's essay (hereafter Taft, 'Overton'), and her life of him in *ODNB*, are indispensable guides to him. See too *CP* vii. 139; David Norbrook, '"The blushinge tribute of a borrowed muse": Robert Overton and the Overturning of the Poetic Canon', *English Manuscript Studies*, 4 (1993), 220–66, *see below p. 438*, Norbrook.

a poet and a scholar, though, as a fair-minded contemporary remarked, he was 'a little pedantic'.[2] Overton's political statements combine, as Milton's sometimes can, eloquence of language with a certain fuzziness of thought. A person of earnest religious convictions, and an advocate of liberty of conscience, he was also a wit, with a propensity to 'frivolous discourse'.[3] If Milton's friendship with him had already endured for 'many years' in or around 1652 (when the tribute is likeliest to have been written), perhaps it was Milton who introduced him to Nedham, in the pages of whose *Politicus* Overton had a presence under the Commonwealth. In the summer of 1650 Overton left his post as governor of Hull to join Cromwell's invading force in Scotland, where he acted as a correspondent for the newsbook, and where he urged on Cromwell the confrontational policy against the Presbyterian clergy for which *Politicus* likewise called but which Cromwell himself resisted.[4] The narrative of the victory at Dunbar in September 1650 that appeared in *Politicus* was written by Overton.[5] A week later Nedham published a letter of military news from Overton at Edinburgh, addressed to a 'Dear Friend'.[6] Three weeks after that, in pursuit of its campaign on behalf of the Commonwealth's 'party of its own throughout the nation' and against the Presbyterians and moderates who opposed it, *Politicus* carried a letter from Hull commending the efforts which 'honest Colonel Overton' had made in the party's cause.[7] They were long-standing. Since 1647 his exertions, first as deputy-governor, then as governor, on behalf of the self-styled 'well-affected' citizens and soldiers had provoked among the city's conservative or Presbyterian leaders a fierce antagonism

2. Taft, 'Overton', 287.
3. Bodl., Rawlinson MS A10, 339.
4. Nickolls, 24; above, p. 197. For Overton's radicalism see also Nickolls, 161.
5. *MP*, 19 Sept. 1650, 296–300. Overton's authorship is established by ibid. 26 Sept. 1650, 266–7; see too ibid. 22 Aug. 1650, 164–6.
6. *MP*, 26 Sept. 1650, 266–7. The letter remarked on the lack of heavy ammunition that was impeding the English forces. So perhaps Overton was among the 'greatest and wisest commanders' at Edinburgh who, in the next issue of *Politicus* (3 Oct. 1650, 289), were reported in a letter from the Scottish capital by John Hall to be making the same point (albeit about a different military situation). Hall's letter, and another (anonymous) one from Edinburgh the following week, were addressed to 'my lord', a 'person of honour' or 'honourable person'. The likely 'lord' is John Bradshaw, the lord president of the council of state. So perhaps Overton was already part of a circle that included Bradshaw, Milton, Nedham, and Hall. *Politicus* hailed Overton's standing in Scotland in January 1652, just before the establishment of the garrison in the Orkneys that is mentioned in Milton's *Defensio Secunda* (*MP*, 29 Jan. 1652, 1369; see too ibid. 17 Oct. 1965, 319–20; 25 Dec. 1651, 1290).
7. *MP*, 24 Oct. 1650, 335.

which had reduced the city to a 'much distracted' condition,[8] and which persisted now.

The bond between Milton and Overton either produced or reflected a common political perspective. Milton, in his despair at the nation's condition in 1648, turned to Sir Thomas Fairfax as a deliverer. Soon afterwards Overton did the same. Until the deliverance of the winter of 1648–9, Milton expected parliament to restore the king and crush the cause of liberty. Between the purge and the regicide Overton beseeched Fairfax, 'in the last act of our age', to lead the army with the resolution 'rather to perish with your honest officers and soldiers than otherwise to enjoy the genius of a temporal happiness'.[9] Overton welcomed the execution of the king. Yet throughout the politics of the Interregnum he would retain reservations about the new occupants of power. In June 1649 he went into print to promise obedience to the government, 'yet ever with such due reservations as ten[d] to the keeping inviolable my particular and private trust, which... I purpose never to part withal'. It was not the ringing public endorsement that the army leadership needed and expected. Then, early in July 1650, when at Hull he was supporting the 'party of its own' that Cromwell's own policies were simultaneously undermining, Overton wrote him a cool if not barbed letter. Cromwell had just succeeded Fairfax as lord general, the transition that was handled in a tense manner both by *Politicus* and in *Defensio Secunda*. Overton, on behalf of the Hull garrison and of himself, promised Cromwell obedience 'in all things pertaining to a public improvement', a phrase which indicates that the 'reservations' of 1649 persisted. The same letter offered a grudging endorsement of Cromwell's succession to Fairfax, 'seeing providence hath so disposed it'.[10] Overton was not the only man on Milton's list of military advisers in *Defensio Secunda* to be troubled about Cromwell's ascent. Two months later John Desborough warned the new lord general that 'high places are slippery, except God establisheth our goings'.[11]

8. Bodl., Nalson MS. VII, fos. 90–9; *Historical Manuscripts Commision Reports, xiii, Appendix 1: Portland*, 468, 478; Abbott, ed., *Writings and Speeches*, i. 513–14. A Presbyterian clergyman prominent in the opposition, hoping that the new model army would be reduced to impotence, prayed publicly that it 'might be as flax about the arms of Samson' (cf. Judges 15: 14). Bodl., Nalson MS XV, fo. 336.
9. Taft, 'Overton', 289.
10. Nickolls, 10. In that printed version the letter is wrongly attributed to 'Richard' Overton, the Leveller; see Society of Antiquaries, SAL/MS/138.
11. C. H. Firth and Godfrey Davies, *A Regimental History of Cromwell's Army*, 2 vols. (Oxford, 1940), i. 205.

Overton must have irritated his superiors, not for the first time, in June 1653, by a printed letter to Cromwell which he sent as commander of the Hull garrison, where he had returned to his command. It endorsed the dissolution of the Rump, but again with qualifications. Like Milton both in the sonnet to Cromwell and in *Defensio Secunda*, he places Cromwell under scrutiny. 'This nation for many years patiently expected what the late masters of our vineyard' – the Rump – 'would do, and seeing now the Lord hath put their power upon you' – Cromwell and his fellow-commanders – 'we doubt not' God

> will so wisely and worthily dispose thereof, as it may appear you are the persons appointed to perfect that work, for neglect whereof the late parliament was laid aside. If herein the Lord shall please to honour your excellency, and the army, I doubt not but religion and liberty shall again flourish, while tyranny and oppression, like a desolate woman, shall die childless.

Yet there is an undercurrent of uncertainty, which the double 'doubt not', the second of them qualified by the 'If', strengthens. Are the Cromwellians indeed 'the persons appointed to perfect that work'? Overton adds that should 'our patient abiding bring forth' good fruit, an outcome that 'would' delight God's followers, it 'is undoubtedly neither treason nor tumult to pray for' Cromwell and 'praise' him. But another 'if' supplies a let-out: 'however if the issue of our endeavours here do not justify us, our consciences will'.[12] (The last sentence of *Defensio Secunda* offers its author a let-out too: should the revolution betray its origin, at least 'it will be seen ... that there was not wanting one who could give good counsel'.) After the Rump's expulsion the army leadership had put pressure on the outlying regiments to send declarations of support. In a lukewarm letter which accompanied Overton's, and which was spaciously printed in *Politicus*,[13] his fellow officers acknowledged that they had been slow to respond. They wrote now only lest their continued silence 'might occasion a question to be made of our integrity to the present proceedings'. Army headquarters had at last got what it wanted. Yet 'questions' about Overton's loyalty were bound still to be 'made'.

After Cromwell's assumption of the protectorate they were made in plenty. Again the outlying forces came under pressure. Early in 1654 the

12. *More Hearts and Hands appearing for the Work* (1653), 1–2.
13. *MP*, 16 June 1653, 2502–5.

garrison at Hull was asked to subscribe to an address pledging obedience to Cromwell, 'his highness', in 'the station God hath placed you'. Overton, as a friend of his would recall five years later, found the document 'oppugnant to the designs and ends of the late wars, and contrary to those oaths and engagements he was concerned in'. So 'he opposed and declined it, and immediately came up to London, and declared his dissatisfaction' to the protector, who 'several times debated the case with him', but was 'unable thoroughly to convince him of the reality of the necessities alleged' for the protectorate. Eventually Overton accepted a commission to serve in Scotland, 'upon this consideration, that he was free to engage', if not for protectoral rule, then 'against the common enemy', the royalists.[14] One of the Rump's rulers in Ireland, Edmund Ludlow, who seems to have accepted the dissolution of the Rump with feelings as hesitant as Overton's, but who, like him, was appalled by the coup of December 1653 and gave the protector considerable trouble in consequence, also found an argument for clinging to his military command – in his case the point that the Commonwealth had appointed him to it and that he could continue to serve that regime's ideals.[15]

Overton, according to the same friend of his, told Cromwell that 'if', as protector, 'he prosecuted the public good of these nations, he would serve him with his life and fortune; but in case it should otherwise appear that he had designed propagating of his own interests upon the ruins of the rights and liberties of the people of England, he could not, nor would not set one foot before another to serve him; wherewith the protector' – it sounds an authentic touch – 'seemed so well pleased, that he told him, he was a knave if he did otherwise'.[16] In *Defensio Secunda*, too, Cromwell is on probation. It is 'if' Cromwell succumbs to the temptations of power, and betrays the cause of liberty, that he will fail the trial of virtue and so lose the heroic status that entitles him to rule; and it is thus that we shall learn 'whether there is indeed in you that living piety, that faith, ... for which we have thought that you above all others deserved ... to be elevated to this sovereign dignity'. Much of the early support for the protectorate was conditional. A week after the appearance of *Defensio Secunda*, there was published a pamphlet in commendation of Cromwell by John Price, an ally of the unorthodox minister John Goodwin, whose own path often ran

14. *The Sad Suffering Case of Major-General Robert Overton* (by 'J.R.', 1659), 5.
15. Firth, *Memoirs of Edmund Ludlow*, i. 377–8.
16. *Sad Suffering Case*, 5.

close to Milton's, and whose own decision to endorse Cromwell's new office was a propaganda coup for the new government. Goodwin himself, in a tract that appeared in April 1654, invoked Nedham's *A True State of the Case of the Commonwealth* in arguing that the nation had a duty to obey the new government, and urged the godly to reflect on the benefits of the recent change of government 'if' it 'shall work together for good to those that love God'. Goodwin's was none the less a tepid endorsement, reminding its readers as it did that God never punished men for obedience to a ruler 'how unduly soever advanced to his seat of power'.[17] Price's own tract draws a series of contrasts between a protectorate and a tyranny, in terms that at once vindicate Cromwell and warn him to remember the differences.[18]

In Overton's eyes, Cromwell failed the test. We do not know how long Overton remained in London during his visit of 1654. It was on 2 June that Andrew Marvell (of whose native Hull Overton, who himself came from a family that had long lived close to the city, had just ceased to be governor) wrote to Milton about the newly published *Defensio Secunda* and, perhaps prompted by its tribute to Overton, voiced in the same breath 'an affectionate curiosity to know what becomes of Colonel Overton's business'.[19] How much of that 'business' did Milton know? There was more to it than Overton's discussions with Cromwell. A report in late June that he had been stripped of his commission[20] proved mistaken, but it was understandable. Notes taken by and for Thurloe, in whose office Milton worked, give a series of indications of the colonel's activities during his stay in the south, though we cannot tell how much Thurloe learned or suspected at the time and how much he discovered later. His information, derived from the interrogation of other suspects, was that Overton attended 'many meetings' which were called to organize resistance to the protectorate in England and Ireland, and in which he collaborated closely with the most eloquent and effective mobilizers of discontent, John Wildman, Edward Sexby, Matthew Alured, and John Okey. John Bradshaw, that other hero of *Defensio Secunda*, was involved in the movement, in conjunction with his old ally George Bishop, whose views, in conjunction with Bradshaw's, *Politicus* had championed in 1650–1. The theme of the discussions was

17. John Goodwin, *Peace Protected, and Discontent Disarmed* (1654), 13, 30, 75–6.
18. John Price, *Tyrants and Protectors set forth in their Colours* (1654).
19. Margoliouth, ii. 306.
20. O. Ogle *et al.*, ed., *Calendar of the Clarendon State Papers*, 5 vols. (Oxford, 1869–1970), iii. 380.

that Cromwell had 'invaded all freedom and liberty and that we were the most enslaved people in the world'. With other critics of the protectorate, Overton took his stand on the protector's breach of 'oaths and covenants': that is, of the army's declarations of 1647 and of the Commonwealth's engagement of loyalty. It may be that, like Wildman, he embarked on discussions with royalists, on the principle that, if there were to be a single ruler, ' 'twere better to have one of the right line'.[21]

On his return to Scotland he reportedly sent word back to London 'that there was a party which would stand right for a commonwealth'. Not until the autumn, however, did disaffection within the army take alarming forms. When, in September, the newly called parliament refused to ratify the Instrument of Government, Cromwell resorted to yet another military purge. MPs who wished to remain in the House had to subscribe to a 'recognition' of the legitimacy of the regime. Most of the commonwealthmen in the Commons refused and were accordingly excluded. Next month three colonels, Matthew Alured, John Okey, and Thomas Saunders, members of the group with whom Overton had held meetings earlier in the year, published an explosive broadsheet against Cromwell. Nedham duly denounced it on the government's behalf, but, daring to put a sympathetic slant on it, emphasized that the colonels were 'honest men' whose good intentions had been manipulated by less scrupulous figures.[22] Cromwell took a less charitable view. All three colonels lost their commissions; Okey was tried for treason; Alured was imprisoned for a year. The following February, Wildman, who had apparently drafted the colonels' document, was arrested while penning his call for an uprising, 'The declaration of the free and well-affected people in arms against the tyrant Oliver Cromwell'.

Overton joined the protests. When he learned of the 'recognition' imposed on MPs in September 1654, recalled his friend, 'his dissastifaction was so revived that he [resolved] upon a return to England, to have resigned up his commission'. If so he took his time. In December, officers at his headquarters in Aberdeen drew up, with his 'privity and con[sent]', a circular letter to fellow sympathizers. It called for a meeting to consider whether the army, in endorsing the protectorate, had remained true to 'the freedoms of the people in the privileges of parliament'. Other evidence shows that

21. Bodl., Rawlinson MS A41, pp. 560–1, 576; S. R. Gardiner, *History of the Commounwealth and Protecterate*, iii. 228–9. Cf. Ogle *et al.*, ed., *Calendar*, iii. 344, 361.

22. *Observator*, 31 Oct. 1654, 11–12.

Overton was speaking freely against the protector, and was comparing his own predicament under Cromwellian rule with that of Cremutius Cordus, the historian who had been prosecuted under the Emperor Tiberius and whose name had acquired, during the Renaissance, a symbolic stature among critics of tyranny.[23] George Monck, the commander-in-chief of the forces in Scotland, had Overton and other commanders arrested in January, 'upon which many' officers and soldiers 'seemed to be very much discontented'. Some of them compared Cromwell's conduct with that of Sethos, King of Eyypt, who 'growing mighty grew so proud withal that he made his tributary kings to draw his chariots by turns'.[24] In Overton's papers were found verses mocking Cromwell as 'the ape of a king'. He was sent to London and was imprisoned for more than five years, first in the Tower, then in Jersey.

Though he denied allegations of disloyalty, his disavowals did not impress Thurloe. The protectorate, normally mild in its handling of dissidents, treated Overton with a severity that made a martyr of him. In March 1659, in Richard Cromwell's parliament, the commonwealthmen used his case to launch a fierce attack on protectoral tyranny. He returned to London in triumph to address the Commons and was immediately released. After the fall of the protectorate two months later, he was restored to his commands. He had, in the account of his friend, defied the instinct – of which Milton was so conscious – of 'most' men for 'slavery and servitude'. For 'the Lord hath reserved unto himself some', 'the salt of the earth', who 'retain a public spirit, and have, with noble heathen Cato, ... chosen rather to be their country's sacrifice than any Caesar's slave'.[25] In Overton's eyes the deliverance of 1648-9, which he remembered in terms that recall Milton's – and Nedham's – tributes to it, had been betrayed. After 'the Lord had signally saved us from those inundations which seemed to threaten the ruin of all our rights and liberties', the protectorate had brought 'far worse incursions upon the privileges both of parliament and people'. During the 1660s, when he was again incarcerated in Jersey, he reflected on the betrayal of his cause by 'Cromwell and his creatures', whose 'ambition', and 'religious pretences', had led them 'many times' to 'tear and pull their masters' – parliament – 'in

23. *TSP* iii. 67, 75–6; Blair Worden, 'Ben Jonson among the Historians', in Kevin Sharpe and Peter Lake, eds., *Culture and Politics in Early Stuart England* (Basingstoke, 1994), 78–9; see too *CP* ii. 499 n.
24. *A Declaration of the Army concerning the Apprehending of Major Gen. Overton* (1655), 4–5.
25. *Sad Suffering Case*, 2. For Cato see also Taft, 'Overton', 300.

pieces'.[26] We cannot know, though from his loud silences about the protectorate we can guess, how Milton, during the rule of the Cromwells, regarded Overton's activities and experiences of those years. What we can say is that, by 1659, the two men had the same view of the regime.

★★

'What I have spoken', declared Milton in 1660 after warning his countrymen against the imminent return of the king, 'is the language of that which is not called amiss the good old cause.'[27] The explanation was needed, since his proposed solution, the perpetuation of what remained of the Long Parliament, ran contrary to a fundamental premiss of the commonwealthmen, those spokesmen for the 'good old cause', and of none of them more than Nedham when he took their part: the holding of regular elections and the accountability of MPs to the electorate. In another respect, however, Milton was now wholly with the commonwealthmen. His hopes of single rulers, however 'supremely excellent', had been destroyed by the rule of Cromwell. The ruler who had seemed to him a bulwark against the Stuarts now appeared of a kind with them. Milton may not have wanted a newly elected parliament in 1659–60, but he did want one with undivided and unlimited power. Nedham, as he worked his way back from the protectorate to the Rump, had to overcome venomous resistance to his own re-employment from among the commonwealthmen, who particularly resented his orchestration and publication of addresses in the Cromwellian interest.[28] In *A Publick Plea* we see him angling for the commonwealthmen's approval. Milton, who had had nothing to do with those addresses, encountered (as far as we know) no such hostility. Yet eyebrows may have been raised. Is there a touch of acerbity in the letter to him from his former contemporary at Cambridge, the commonwealthman Moses Wall, in 1659, perhaps in March,[29] which remembered Milton's 'friendliness to truth in your early years and in bad times', but also recorded Wall's uncertainty 'whether your relation to the court (though I think a commonwealth was more friendly to you than a court) had not clouded your former light'?[30] Even if not, Wall's words suggest another reason why Milton needed to inform readers of *The Readie and Easie Way* that he spoke the language of

26. Taft, 'Overton', 300, 303. 27. *CP* vii. 462. 28. *True Catalogue*, 14.
29. Parker, 1251. 30. *CP* vii. 510.

the good old cause. On the title-page of the second edition of that work he placed an epigram from Juvenal: 'We have advised Sulla himself; now we advise the people.' 'Sulla', the Roman dictator, is sometimes taken to stand for George Monck,[31] to whom Milton may, like others, have temporarily looked as a saviour of the cause early in 1660, but who had proved to be its betrayer. Yet will that fleeting aberration by Milton explain so portentous an allusion? The reference is surely to Cromwell, for whom Sulla had almost become a standard analogy, particularly in Nedham's writing.[32]

From Cromwell's death in September 1658 the cracks within the regime became ever wider. On Richard Cromwell's privy council the division sharpened between members sympathetic to the commonwealthmen and those eager to return to kingship. In October Milton republished, with additions and amendments, that apologia for the republic, his *Defensio* of 1651. His textual adjustments subtly reinforced the heroism of the regicide and of his own role in championing it.[33] But the alterations were not extensive, and the republication would have retained its primary significance without them. As in *Defensio Secunda*, and as in the material from *Mercurius Politicus* that Nedham republished in 1656, writing that had been composed before the protectorate had taken on, in an altered context, a meaning critical of it. The point is emphasized by the printing of a dividing line in the text of *Defensio*, where the new conclusion is separated from the earlier material.[34] In February 1659, when Richard Cromwell's parliament had met, Milton took a bolder step. Now, as the protectorate weakened, he returned to pamphleteering. The works of his own that he had published since 1645 had all been written with the endorsement of governments or on behalf of deeds of power. Now he went back to outsider's writing, and to the petitionary prose that he had deployed before and during the first civil war. There was another change too. He returned from the oblique to the explicit – or rather, he moved to the partially explicit. Here too the vulnerability of the regime supplies the clue. It was in the same month, and for the same reason, that James Harrington, who in Cromwell's lifetime had veiled his political proposals and sentiments in fictional analogies, reduced the recommendations

31. Ibid. 205.
32. Here I agree with Dzelzainis, 'Milton and the Protectorate', 199–200, and Armitage, 'John Milton: Poet against Empire', 212.
33. The amendments are traced by Robert W. Ayres in *CP* iv. 1131–9. The import of the republication is detected by Dzelzainis, 'Milton and the Protectorate'.
34. I am grateful to Nicholas von Maltzahn for pointing this out to me.

of *Oceana* to a digest, and voiced his own anti-protectoral sympathies, in his tract *The Art of Lawgiving*, where the veil is removed.

Harrington's principal subject in those works is politics. Milton's, in February 1659, is religion. In *A Treatise of Civil Power*, the tract he now submits to parliament, he resumes the theme of the sonnets of 1652, the freeing of God's spirit from worldly power. But the work has a political import too. Here the writing of Milton, the employee of the protectorate, does, unlike that of Harrington, remain oblique. Late in January of the previous year, at the start of the second session of the parliament that had passed the Humble Petition and Advice, a petition was signed by soldiers and London citizens asking 'that together with the constant succession of frequent parliaments duly chosen, the supreme power and trust, which the people (the original of all just power)' commit to their representatives, 'may be so clearly declared and secured against all attempts to the contrary, that no question may henceforth arise concerning the same'. The petitioners took advantage of the decision of the government, which had forcibly excluded the commonwealthmen from the Commons in 1654 and 1656, to allow them back in January 1658, when, after the six-month adjournment that followed the enactment of the Humble Petition and Advice, the second session of the parliament of 1656 began. Here was a moment of fresh hope for the good old cause. It was the commonwealthmen in the Rump who, in 1649, had persuaded the Commons to declare themselves to be the supreme authority and the people to be 'the original of all just power', and it was they who, by their assertion of that principle, wrecked the brief session of early 1658. The petition was revived during Richard's parliament, when again the commonwealthmen were allowed to sit (though the government had done its best to outmanœuvre them at the polls, and, among its successes, had secured the election of Andrew Marvell at Hull).[35] The petition was a massive demonstration of anti-protectoral opinion. According to observers who had no motive for exaggerating the extent of its circulation, it attracted somewhere between 15,000 and 40,000 signatures. On 15 February 1659 it was presented to parliament by three prominent Baptists, wealthy London citizens, two of whom had been supporters of the protectorate in its earlier days.

It was on the following day that Milton registered *A Treatise of Civil Power* for publication. He dedicated the work 'To the Parliament of the

35. *AMC* 56.

Commonwealth of England', which the opening words of his dedication called 'the 'supreme council'.[36] That phrasing was, in itself, capable of more or less innocent construction. When, in 1654, Milton published his second 'defence of the English people', or when, in 1658, he republished the first, he could have asked, of anyone who detected an element of protest in his wording, what motive there might be for taking exception to such language. So, now, he could have pointed out that one of the meanings of the word 'commonwealth' was uncontroversial, and that parliaments had often been uncontroversially described, if not as the 'supreme council', then at least as 'the great council of the realm'. Yet under the protectorate the phrase 'supreme council' had become a coded term to allude to the principle of parliamentary sovereignty which the regime had violated. Nedham had used it thus in *The Excellencie of a Free State*, and John Streater had taunted Cromwell with references to the 'supreme assemblies' of parliament in his *Observations* two years earlier.[37] After Richard Cromwell's succession there was reportedly a plan by commonwealthmen to occupy the chamber of the House of Commons and 'preten[d] themselves to be the supreme council of the nation'.[38] In the parliament summoned by Richard it was the commonwealthmen's strategy, which they ably executed, to imply that the moral authority of the Commons, in which they were in fact a minority, lay with them as the champions of the people's sovereignty. They would

36. The pertinence of the petition to Milton's tract is discerned by Austin Woolrych in his magisterial introduction to *CP* vii (pp. 20–1, 46–7); but I think that he underestimates the pointedness of Milton's dedication.
37. *Perfect and Impartial Intelligence*, 26 May 1654, 16. In *Defensio*, Milton described the sovereign parliament of the Commonwealth as at once the 'supreme council' of the nation and its 'supreme senate' (*CW* vii. 459). He deployed the terms at two parallel points in 1659. For in his dedication to the restored Rump of the second of his two tracts in that year on ecclesiastical subjects, which formed a pair, he supplies an opening virtually identical to that of the first, but substitutes, for 'supreme council', 'supreme senate'. It is here that he refers to the protectorate as 'a short but scandalous night of interruption' (*CP* vii. 274). In the Humble Petition and Advice of 1657, by contrast, parliament had deferentially described itself to Cromwell not as the nation's 'great council' but as 'your great council' (S. R. Gardiner, ed., *Constitutional Documents*, 449). Elsewhere the term 'supreme council' had been used by writers wishing to indicate, without explicitly stating, that parliament possessed larger constitutional rights than it was allowed. Nedham deployed it thus in *Mercurius Britanicus* (11 May 1646, 1110); see too Milton's own use of comparable language in the 1640s: *CP* i. 593, 599; ii. 582; iii. 467. Fallon, who sees Milton as an unflinchingly loyal Cromwellian, points out (*Milton in Government*, 183) that Milton's mode of address, to 'the Parliament of the Commonwealth of England', had been used in the constitutional bill of the protectoral parliament of 1654, but omits to notice that the bill was drawn up by critics of the regime who were seeking to establish the principle of parliamentary sovereignty.
38. Bodl., Clarendon MS 59, fo. 354.

soon use that method in coming to the rescue of the imprisoned Robert Overton.

Milton uses it too. In so doing he passes over his customary antagonism to parliamentary elections, the process that brought the parliament into being. As when writing for the Rump, he finds it convenient to equate the parliament with a cause to which he knows its majority to be unsympathetic. For now, in the parliament of 1659, his only hope lay in those members who had sat in that earlier assembly, outnumbered as they now were by Presbyterians and neutrals and neo-royalists. The proper power of parliament, his dedicatory epistle to it intimates, is the authority it held under the Rump, before the protectoral usurpation. He remembers his service under that government, when he heard discussions at 'a council next in authority to your own': that is – he surely means – at the council of state, the executive body appointed by and answerable to the sovereign parliament. Milton's dedication declares that 'many eminent' MPs of 1659 are 'already perfect and resolved in' the principle, which it is the purpose of his tract to advance, of the separation of civil from spiritual power. He must have been thinking mostly or wholly of members who had sat in the Rump, the body which would reclaim parliamentary sovereignty three months after Milton's tract, and at whose council of state he here recalls often hearing men expounding the proper relationship between Church and state.[39] He has no such memory from the regime of Oliver Cromwell, when the commonwealthmen were excluded from parliament. In Milton's dedication the protectorate might as well not exist. Having prepared the text 'against the much expected time' of the parliament's sitting, he looks to the assembly as the only hope, and the only legitimate source, of reform.[40] Not only has the nation had to wait for its supreme council to meet. The 'power' which has been allowed the assembly, and which Milton evidently hopes that it will interpret as an executive power, is to last 'but for a time'.[41]

39. Above, p. 244.

40. *CP* vii. 239–40. '[M]uch expected' is a characteristic ambiguity: does it mean 'much longed for' or – instead or as well – 'long-awaited'? If the latter, we wonder how long the tract, and the later one of 1659 that is its partner, had been in preparation. The similarity of its language (vii. 240, 253; above, p. 244) to the sonnet to Vane in 1652 raises the possibility – no more – that he drafted a document around that time from which the tracts of 1659 were taken. The two tracts, which are linked not only by cross-references but by a distinctive prose (Lewalski, 382–3), have the air of jointly belonging to a larger project. Perhaps, like *Defensio Secunda*, they were the result of cumulative composition.

41. *CP* vii. 239.

Milton wants it to make use of it, so as to dismantle the machinery of ecclesiastical power that the protectorate sustains.

In April that regime, which had been the creation of a military coup, succumbed to one. In May the army that had destroyed the Rump restored it. This was the month that produced *A Publick Plea*, the work which reproduced wording from pamphlets of Nedham and anticipated that of *The Readie and Easie Way to Establish a Free Commonwealth*. In *Defensio Secunda*, Milton had portrayed a conflict between the supreme worth of Cromwell and the temptations awaiting him. By the time of *A Publick Plea*, the outcome is beyond doubt. The pamphlet is written by 'one who hates both treason and traitors'. It rejoices in the overthrow of 'a new tyranny (become hereditary)', and of 'so manifest a slavery against the fundamental law'. It voices outrage on behalf of officers who have been cashiered and imprisoned under the protectorate, a group of whom Robert Overton was the most prominent. It welcomes the return to power of the MPs of the Rump, 'whom God hath so highly honoured as once more to make them chosen instruments, and to put into their hands so great an opportunity to make this nation happy'. They must be careful, it warns them, to allow none into their counsels who have 'shamefully forsaken the good old cause' and have 'acted arbitrarily under the usurped power of a single person'. Instead the tract commends for trust 'such as would not act in the counsels of Oliver' and those – of whom again Overton was the most celebrated – who would not act 'in the army' during the protectorate. For who, asks the pamphlet, that 'truly hates' the 'sin' of the protectorate

> can love or praise the memory of... the author thereof'? Especially considering that whatever he did worthy of praise, he did before the time of his breach of faith to his superiors [the Rump], and while he stood fast and fixed to the good old cause, wherein God prospered him; he never since having done anything from the time of his aspiring to monarchy against his own faith and manifest judgement, but lived to his own sorrow and perpetual disquiet, day and night; nay, which is worse, to the sorrow, astonishment, and scandal of all good men (who little expected such things from him).

Now, in his place, there is at last 'so great an opportunity to make this nation, with the dominions thereof, a happy, free, and flourishing Commonwealth'.[42]

42. *Publick Plea*, 1–3.

The dedication to the restored Rump of Milton's *Considerations touching the Likeliest Means to Remove Hirelings* (the work he had begun to write in or by June) welcomes the return of the parliament in the same spirit. It makes its anti-Cromwellian point less bluntly than *A Publick Plea*, but no less bitterly. It is after the 'short but scandalous night of interruption', the phrase which echoes the title-page of *A Publick Plea*, that power has returned to the Rump 'by a new dawning of God's miraculous providence among us'.[43] From 1649 to 1654 Milton had, at least with one half of his mind, distinguished between kingship and tyranny; he had acknowledged that kingship might be appropriate in some times and some places; he had allowed for the possibility of virtuous kings. By 1659–60 he can see redemption only in the 'supreme council' of the nation. Even 'the fond conceit of something like a Duke of Venice',[44] as a balance to parliamentary authority or as an instrument of executive power, dismayed him. Perhaps it did so the more since the 'conceit', it seems, was favoured by a party eager to reinstall Richard Cromwell.[45] For even in the darkest hour of early 1660 Milton was unwilling to contemplate the return of the Cromwells as a means to thwart the Stuarts. It is true that he could still, in gloomy moments, see some form of single rule, with some different ruler, as the only way out of

43. *CP* vii. 274. 44. Ibid. 374.

45. Ibid. 181–2, 374. Anyone familiar with the political literature of the Interregnum will be taken aback by Fallon's supposition (*Milton in Government*, 191, 202–5) that whenever Milton writes, in 1659–60, against rule by a 'single person', he 'always' has Charles II in mind. The term was standard usage in descriptions, friendly and unfriendly, of the protector; it had grown up because Cromwell did not take the title of king. It is of course true that, as the Restoration approached, the prospect of the Stuarts' return was a more urgent matter than the reproaching of the now defunct regime of the protectorate, and that most of what Milton says about the monarchical principle in the expiring phase of the revolution is concerned to avert that threat. But when Milton does use the term 'single person' of Charles II, it is because Charles embodies the same principle of rule as Cromwell. It is only under a republic that 'no single person, but reason only, sways' (*CP* vii. 427). That point surely explains the statements in Milton's 'A Letter to a Friend' in October 1659 (ibid. 331, 332), which have puzzled commentators, that 'there is a single person working underneath', and that the English risk becoming 'the servants of one or other single person, the secret author and fomentor of all these disturbances'. Milton's observations make sense once we take 'a single person working underneath' to mean, not a particular individual, but 'the principle of rule by a single person, whether Cromwellian or Stuart'. (In the same way, Nedham's *The Excellencie* had used the term 'the interest of monarchy' to lump the Cromwellian and Stuart causes together.) Fallon also reasons (pp. 204–5) that, because Milton refers in *The Readie and Easie Way* to the nation's 'ten or twelve years' prosperous war and contestation with tyranny', he cannot have been dismayed by the protectorate. Yet it is evident from the earlier part of Milton's sentence that the 'ten or twelve years' (*CP* vii. 428) are those that preceded, not 1660, but the end of the civil wars at Worcester in 1651. Fallon restates some of his positions on Milton and Cromwell in his '*A Second Defence*: Milton's Critique of Cromwell', *Milton Studies*, 39 (2000), 167–83.

the protracted crisis of the restored Commonwealth that would prevent a Stuart restoration. But that was a counsel of desperation. With the reaction in Milton's thinking away from single rule, there came another reversal. Under the Commonwealth regime of 1649–53, even when he endorsed parliamentary supremacy, he bestowed his esteem, not on parliament, but on the army that repeatedly invaded it. Now it is parliament, not the army, that Milton congratulates on the nation's deliverance from bondage. In *Considerations touching the Likeliest Means*, the MPs are 'next under God, the authors and best patrons of religious and civil liberty that ever these islands brought forth'. In his 'defences' Milton had lauded the regicide, for which he gave the main credit to the army. His tracts of 1659–60 say next to nothing about the regicide.[46] He praises instead the constitutional revolution which followed it and which entrusted power to a sovereign parliament.[47]

We should not exaggerate the transformation of Milton's attitude to the army. His reverence for it, despite the extravagance with which it was expressed, had not been unquestioning, and he did not lose all faith in it now. There are warning notes in the exhortation to the English people in *Defensio Secunda*, which remind them that 'the fidelity of armies ... in whom you confide is uncertain, unless it be maintained by the authority of justice alone'. In that treatise he urges them towards the attainment of a kind of liberty 'which can neither be gotten, nor taken away, by arms'.[48] There is too his lament in 1652 that too many members of the council of state were soldiers and merchants.[49] Equally, in *The Readie and Easie Way* he knows, or anyway hopes, that there is still a virtuous component in the army, which has not been corrupted by Cromwellian rule.[50] Even so, there is a startling contrast between the welcome given by Milton to the expulsion of the Rump in 1653 and his response to the army's second forcible expulsion of it in October 1659, the event which military opponents of it called, in a document prominently printed by Nedham, a 'second interruption of our renowned parliament'.[51] It was Milton's indignation and despair at the later coup that impelled him to return to explicitly political writing (though of the four political tracts of his that survive from the twilight of the revolution, only the second two – *The Readie and Easie Way to Establish a Free Commonwealth* in its two editions of February and April 1660 and the

46. He alludes to it only, I think, at *CP* vii. 426 (unless also at p. 420). 47. Ibid. 355, 409.
48. *CW* viii. 239–41, 243. 49. Above, p. 192. 50. *CP* vii. 365.
51. *MP*, 5 Jan. 1660, 996.

Brief Notes on a royalist sermon in April 1660 – got into print). He had, he wrote in October 1659, been 'overjoyed' when, upon the overthrow of the protectorate, the army 'had been so far wrought to Christian humility ... as to confess in public their backsliding from the good old cause, and to show the fruits of their repentance in the righteousness of their restoring the old famous parliament, which they had without just authority dissolved' in April 1653. God, he argued, had been pleased by the restoration of the Rump. So 'it now amazes me that' the army has so soon returned to 'backsliding' – the charge of *A Publick Plea* too[52] – in a deed 'most illegal and scandalous, I fear me barbarous or rather scarce to be exampled among any barbarians'.

Milton is horrified to observe that the soldiers have brought themselves to 'subdue the supreme power that set them up ... to the sad dishonour of that army lately so renowned for the civilest and best ordered in the world, and by us here at home for the most conscientious'. 'How grievous will it then be', he protests, 'how infamous to the true religion which we profess, how dishonourable to the name of God, that his fear and the power of his knowledge in an army professing to be his' – an army, he might have added, whose sanctity of worship and life he had himself extolled in *Defensio Secunda* – 'should not work that obedience, that fidelity to their supreme magistrates, that levied them and paid them, which the light of nature, the laws of human society, covenant and contract, yea common shame works in other armies, among the worst of men; which will undoubtedly pull down the heavy judgements of God among us, who cannot but avenge these hypocrisies and violations of truth and holiness.' In his wrath Milton urges the soldiers to 'find out the Achan among them'.[53] Achan was the 'troubler of Israel' whose secret sin had reduced the Israelites to military impotence when they stood before Jericho under Joshua. In 1656 Milton's hero Sir Henry Vane had equated Cromwell's usurpation with Achan's transgression, which he identified with the 'private and selfish interest' that governed the protector's rule.[54]

52. Above, p. 42; cf. *CP* vii. 452, 462.
53. *CP* vii. 324–9. Milton's hope, in that passage, that some warrantable explanation of the coup might yet emerge sits oddly with the surrounding denigration.
54. Blair Worden, 'Oliver Cromwell and the Sin of Achan', in Derek Beales and Geoffrey Best, eds., *History, Society and the Churches* (Cambridge, 1985), 136–9. Austin Woolrych proposes that Achan is John Lambert, the ambitious military leader responsible for the coup of October 1659 (*CP* vii. 120). He may well be, though I suspect that the term has, or also has, a larger resonance: that, like 'single person', it stands for a principle (the principle recognized by Vane in the protectoral regime) rather than, or as well as, a person – a principle which Lambert,

Milton returns to the history of military 'interruption' in *The Readie and Easie Way*, which recalls 'the frequent disturbances, interruptions and dissolutions' that the Long Parliament has suffered,[55] and remembers that 'our liberty and religion' have been 'fought for, gained and many years possessed, except in those unhappy interruptions which God hath removed'.[56] Thus does the coup of October 1659 take its place alongside the scandalous one of April 1653. It is in *The Readie and Easie Way*, too, that the army's treatment of parliament exacts from Milton as wretchedly disenchanted a statement as any in his writings. The abiding goal of his involvement in public life was liberty of conscience. It was, albeit within limits that dismayed Milton, the abiding goal of Cromwell's too. Over the Interregnum there hung the question, which Milton asked in his sonnet of 1652 and again in *Defensio Secunda*, whether Cromwell would set God's truth free. Cromwell's support for freedom of conscience aroused widespread suspicion. It was broadly regarded as the engine by which he had created his following and raised himself to power. By early 1660 Milton was ready to agree. If only 'there were no meddling with Church matters in state counsels', he then wrote, 'ambitious leaders of armies would then have no hypocritical pretences so ready at hand to contest with parliaments, yea to dissolve them and make way to their own tyrannical designs'.[57]

★★

It seems that it was in or close to 1658 that Milton, who had left his great poetic aspirations unfulfilled for two decades, reverted to them and began to write *Paradise Lost*. If he composed it in the sequence of the finished

the architect of the protectorate, indeed represented. Fallon (*Milton in Government*, 191) challenges Woolrych's identification of the 'single person' wth Lambert on the ground that Lambert was 'an ardent commonwealthsman' – a description that would have startled contemporary observers of his central role in the extinction of parliamentary sovereignty in 1653.

55. *CP* vii. 430.

56. Ibid. 421. Even if the evidence of *A Publick Plea*, and of the widespread usage of the term 'interruption' to describe the coup of April 1653, did not show that that event is Milton's 'short but scandalous night of interruption', the passages I have here quoted would in themselves be enough to disprove Fallon's claim (*Milton in Government*, 183–5) that the phrase can only refer to events of 1659. It is true that in 1659–60 Milton is more immediately concerned with the current danger from military ambition than with the misconduct of the dead Cromwell; but that threat is a continuation of the earlier one. Fallon is unable to account for the view of the expulsion of April 1653 that was held by Milton in 1659.

57. *CP* vii. 380.

text, then the autobiographical passage at the start of Book VII suggests that he had completed the first half (or some version of it) – the 'half' he has 'sung' (VII. 21) – by late 1660. In 1641 he had set aside prose for poetry. The hopes of his published prose having been betrayed, he returned to verse, this time to fulfil his highest ambitions. Then, in 1659, the faltering of the protectorate introduced a new phase of his prose writing. Did he continue to write *Paradise Lost* during it, or did he once more put verse aside for writing 'of the left hand'? Whatever the answer, the first half of the poem takes on new colouring when we read it beside the prose of the years within which it was apparently written.

Paradise Lost tells of the temptation, not of Cromwell, but of Adam. Yet even in the cosmic strife of Milton's epic, the self-destruction of the Puritan cause obtrudes. It is to be found not only in the explicitly autobiographical account of his imprisonment and suffering in 1660, or in the transparently autobiographical tributes to the angel Abdiel. It is present in the war in heaven, which dominates memories there and in hell no less than, in England, the recollection and legacy of civil war overshadowed what followed it.[58] It is also present, perhaps, in the debate among the fallen angels, that parody, as some have thought, of the parliamentary or clerical debates of the 1640s. It is unmistakably there in the political language of Satan. Applying virtuous principles to vicious ends, and confusing – like the sons of Zebedee in Milton's tracts – the kingdom of Christ with worldly monarchy, Satan exactly reproduces, yet fatally misapplies, the vocabulary which Milton himself used on behalf of expiring liberty in 1660.[59]

Does Satan, the destroyer of earthly bliss, carry Cromwell, the destroyer of the Puritan cause, within him too? If we suppose that great poetry refuses admission to such a degree of historical specificity, then we will flinch at the suggestion of that analogy: of the alignment of a figure from a local period and place with an anti-hero of mythic and archetypal force, whose evil extends across the whole history of time. Yet seventeenth-century readers and writers did not make that supposition. On the contrary, the practices of local allusion indicate that poetry was never taken to perform its improving function more acutely than when it referred to

58. Stella Revard, *The War in Heaven*: Paradise Lost *and the Tradition of Satan's Rebellion* (Ithaca, NY, 1990), 16.
59. Blair Worden, 'Milton's Republicanism and the Tyranny of Heaven', in Gisela Bock, Quentin Skinner, and Maurizio Viroli, eds., *Machiavelli and Republicanism* (Cambridge, 1991), 235–40.

issues of immediate concern to the society it strove to improve.[60] Of course, Cromwell and Satan do not in every way resemble each other, any more than the framework of plot and argument within which Satan moves is in every way akin to the course and the debates of the Puritan Revolution. In any case it is mostly the language of Milton's own prose, not of Cromwell's utterances, that Satan speaks. Yet there are affinities and glances, which two anachronistic modern premisses obscure. The first is the separation of literary expression and political experience, which in Milton's time were intertwined. The second is the distance of things temporal from things eternal. Having removed heaven and hell so far from the world around us, we struggle to recover their looming place in Milton's own environment. In seventeenth-century minds, where the war between Christ and Antichrist was a mirror of quotidian political experience, Satan was an almost corporeal presence. He lurked, as in early verse of Milton and in a wealth of sermons of the period, beneath the House of Commons in the Gunpowder Plot. He directly intervened, as contemporary reports testify, in battles of the civil war.[61] In the protectorate he was everywhere. 'The subtleties of Satan' make their mark in Nedham's analysis of current politics in 1654.[62] A tract of the same year described Satan 'stand[ing] at the very right hand of our Joshua [Cromwell] to resist the work of God'.[63]

Milton moves between two characterizations of Cromwell. There is the flawed hero, the man of 'supreme excellence' and 'worth' and of 'glorious' deeds, whose 'inmost soul' is found wanting and in whose failure of virtue the cause of God is lost. In the second characterization, which has prevailed by 1659, we see only the flaws: the secret ambition, and the hypocrisy (an evil which, in Milton's thinking, 'temptation' has the purpose of unmasking[64]) that conceals it. Milton alternates between the same two characterizations of Satan. Again it is the second that comes to the fore, but the first is essential to Milton's depiction of him, which makes Satan's 'sense

60. A good illustration of that outlook is provided by John Dryden's practice of working contemporary political allusions into his translations of works of other periods and languages. It can be studied in the exemplary annotation of vol. v of Paul Hammond and David Hopkins, eds., *The Poems of John Dryden*, 5 vols. (Harlow, 1995–2005). I have explored the same outlook with respect to the sixteenth century in my *Sound of Virtue*.

61. Revard, *War in Heaven*, 88 ff.

62. Nedham, *True State*, 3; cf. above, p. 253.

63. *Quaking Principles Dashed in Pieces* (165[4]), 2. Cf. the representation of Satan in *Discovery of Some Plots of Lucifer* (on which see above, p. 307, n. 65), 38–9. Nedham's *Mercurius Pragmaticus* (20 June 1648, 6) had called Cromwell 'the great Lucifer'.

64. *CW* xv. 87.

of injured merit' intelligible, even sympathetic.[65] In *Defensio Secunda* Cromwell – or the virtuous side of him – allows himself, on behalf of a cause that he alone can save, to be 'forced as it were' into the ranks of solitary leaders and to 'take upon [himself] the heaviest burden'. Satan's subordinate angels 'failed' not 'to express how much they praised, | That for the general safety he despised | His own; for neither do the spirits damned | Lose all their virtue' (II. 480–3). In *Paradise Regained* the arch-fiend, again misapplying Milton's own political vocabulary, tempts Christ with the Aristotelian principle which awards supreme authority to supreme worth, and which *Defensio Secunda* had applied to Cromwell: 'thou who worthiest art shouldst be their king' (III. 226). Among his companions in Hell in *Paradise Lost*, Satan's awareness of his superior merit is joined to the flaw that destroys it: 'till at last | Satan, whom now transcendent glory raised | Above his fellows, with monarchal pride | Conscious of highest worth ...' (II. 426–9).[66]

With Satan's pride come the two qualities that were most frequently associated with Cromwell by his enemies and by those who felt betrayed by him. The first is ambition. The second is the hypocrisy of 'the first | That practised falsehood under saintly show' (IV. 122); of 'the apostate' (V. 852), that favourite epithet of Cromwell's antagonists; of 'the false dissembler', who provokes the thought, with which Milton might have explained to himself the error of his own hopes of Cromwell, that 'neither man nor angel can discern | Hypocrisy, the only evil that walks | Invisible, except to God alone' (II. 681–4). Milton, who knew what 'hypocritical leaders of armies' had done to God's cause, saw the consequences of Cromwell's plausibility, the gift of a man who, as his enemies perceived him, shared what we learn from *Paradise Regained* to be Satan's 'craft' of 'mixing somewhat true to vent more lies' (I. 432–3). In the cosmic setting of *Paradise Lost* there is observable not only the fall of the Puritan Revolution but the settling of scores. In *Defensio Secunda* Milton, following Nedham's warning that tyrants rise to power 'by pretending themselves great patrons of liberty', had feared lest Cromwell, the ostensible 'patron of liberty', would 'violate' it and so prove 'destructive ... to the very cause of all virtue and piety'. In *Paradise Lost* Gabriel challenges Satan, the 'sly hypocrite, who wouldst seem | Patron of liberty'. Satan's misdeeds, as Gabriel recounts them, have been Cromwell's. Satan has imposed military 'discipline', the feat for which

65. Revard, *War in Heaven*, 210–11.

66. On Satan and the Aristotelian principle see also Abdiel's rebuke to him in *Paradise Lost* VI. 174–80.

Milton had earlier praised Cromwell's forces, but has abused it to his own ends. 'Was this', Gabriel asks Satan, 'Your military obedience, to dissolve | Allegiance to the acknowledged power supreme' (IV. 954–7)? In April 1653 Cromwell expelled what in 1659 Milton would call the 'supreme council' and 'supreme senate'. The coup bore out Marvell's insinuation, in 'An Horatian Ode', that Cromwell would not continue to 'obey' the parliament of which his army was the servant. In October 1659 the Cromwellian army, to Milton's fury, threw off 'that obedience, that fidelity to their supreme magistrates', which it owed.[67]

In Milton's mind Cromwell had corrupted the army, which had allowed itself to be corrupted by him. It had become, like the 'Army of fiends' under Satan, the 'fit body' of a 'fit head' (IV. 953). When Milton urged the soldiers to 'find out the Achan among them', he accused their leaders of 'secret ambition', and then amended 'secret' to 'close'. In *Paradise Lost* the reason why 'the spirits damned' lose not 'all their virtue' is 'lest bad men should boast | Their specious deeds on earth, which glory excites, | Or close ambition varnished o'er with zeal'. Satan 'excused his devilish deeds' by appealing to 'Necessity, | the Tyrant's plea' (IV. 393–4). There was nothing peculiar to Milton's time in that tendency of rulers. Yet we have seen how 'necessity' had a high prominence in vindications of Cromwell's coups and of his rule, and how protests against those claims had animated the opponents of his rise.[68]

★★

Milton and Nedham were as close as ever in the period between Oliver Cromwell's death and the Restoration. Despite his role as propagandist for the protectorate, Nedham was prepared to advertise Milton's criticisms of it. He drew attention, with a flourish, to the republication of *Defensio* in October 1658. Having occasionally suspended, under the Rump, his normal Erastian posture in order to aid Milton's religious radicalism, he did so again in 1659, when he advertised *A Treatise of Civil Power* in February and then, under the restored Rump, *Considerations touching the Likeliest Means*.[69] In February 1660 *Politicus*, during Nedham's last weeks at its desk, bravely advertised the first edition of the most daring of all Milton's writings, *The Readie and Easie Way*, the work that reproduced material from

67. *CP* vii. 327. 68. Above, Ch. 13.

69. *MP*, 25 Nov. 1658, 29; 17 Feb. 1659, 237; 8 Sept. 1659, 713; 20 Oct. 1659, 809.

A Publick Plea. *Politicus* also, in an unusual step for a newsbook, supplied a list of corrections to the misprints of the work, those 'many faults' which, as Milton was dismayed to notice in the second edition, had 'escaped' in the 'haste' of publication.[70] If Nedham promoted Milton's writings, Milton, in the last months of the revolution, freshly adopted a significant component of Nedham's programme. In the early 1650s Milton's sentiments had concurred with Nedham's pleas for the supremacy, both in central and in local government, of the 'well-affected', of the Commonwealth's 'party of its own throughout the nation'. But only now did he make constitutional proposals that would restrict power, not only at Westminster but in local militias and in newly created local councils, to 'the well-affected people', to the 'faithfullest adherents in every county', to the 'rightly qualified'.[71] His proposals for regional assemblies and for a measure of self-government, which are among the most distinctive elements of his programme in the last months of the revolution, have other goals too, among them the re-animation of local communities and their protection from arbitrary power at the centre, but they are also means to the perpetuation of the good old cause in the provinces as well as Westminster.

Milton and Nedham stood together until the last breath of the Puritan Revolution, which helps to explain why a number of tracts linked their names[72] and why their enemies called for them to die by the same rope. Just how far they collaborated in that time it is hard to be sure. Between the two editions of *The Readie and Easie Way* there appeared what Milton's royalist scourge Roger L'Estrange termed 'a bold, sharp pamphlet called *Plain English*', a work that by early April, despite the 'utmost care' of the government and the authorities in London to suppress it, was 'grown too public'.[73] 'Betwixt' Milton and 'his brother Rabshakeh' Nedham, taunted L'Estrange, 'I think a man may venture to divide the glory of it'.[74] L'Estrange addresses 'Milton, Nedham, either or both of you'.[75] He may merely have been guessing. There is nothing in the pamphlet that demands to be attributed to either writer, though some touches do recall Nedham's

70. *MP*, 8 Mar. 1660, 1151; *CP* vii. 409.
71. *CP* vii. 191, 331, 338, 435 (cf. p. 275).
72. Ibid. 198.
73. *Treason Arraigned, in Answer to Plain English* (1659), preface.
74. Ibid. 2–3: quoted by Parker, 561, and by Nicholas von Maltzahn, 'From Pillar to Post: Milton and the Attack on Republican Humanism at the Restoration', in Gentles *et al.*, eds., *Soldiers, Writers and Statesmen*, 282. Von Maltzahn, I should add, emphasizes the differences between the two writers and is sceptical of L'Estrange's attribution to Milton. For Nedham as Rabshakeh see also *True Catalogue*, 76.
75. *Treason Arraigned*, 5.

known writings. There are also two moments that recall Milton's. The pamphlet hopes that Monck will 'break forth, and more visibly appear (through all the clouds of fear and jealousy)', a thought that recalls the sonnet to Cromwell, where the hero emerges from 'a cloud ... of detractions rude'. Secondly, we learn that Pride's Purge 'was a transcendent act', one of 'supreme necessity', not to be measured by 'ordinary rules'. But for it, 'the whole cause and its defenders must inevitably have sunk together'.[76] Just so had Milton, and Nedham, vindicated that coup in the time of the Commonwealth.

Whether or not Nedham or Milton, or both of them, wrote *Plain English*, both men took great risks in the spring of 1660. No two tracts of that period are more defiant, or insult the Stuart cause more boldly, than the two editions of *The Readie and Easie Way* and Nedham's pamphlet *Newes from Brussels*, which appeared around 10 March, two days after Nedham had advertised the first edition of Milton's tract and published the corrections to its text, and around twelve days before the appearance of *Plain English*. Nedham prophesied the exacting of savage revenge by the royalists. On learning of his pamphlet the council of state reportedly offered a reward of £20 for his arrest. In the same month, in the last issues of *Politicus* that he was able to edit, he endorsed the defiant republicanism of Milton's friend and hero Robert Overton. Four months earlier – in the issue of the newsbook that carried its eulogy of John Bradshaw – *Politicus* had publicized Overton's resolve to 'be firm against any temptations of the adverse party'.[77] Now Nedham drew attention to Overton's mistrust of, and opposition to, his old adversary Monck, and to his commitment to his 'country's rights against any arbitrary or kingly innovation'.[78]

Amid the dying embers of the good old cause, the collaboration of Nedham and Milton seems to have found one last, eloquent moment. In April, in the second edition of *The Readie and Easie Way*, Milton argued for the perpetuation of the Rump as a 'standing senate'. To prove his point he turned to historical example. 'It will be objected', he observes, that 'in those places where they had perpetual senates, they had also popular remedies against their growing too imperious.' Critics, he anticipates, will point out the existence of the popular 'senate' of Athens, the ephors of Sparta, the tribunes of Rome. He has two points in reply. First, in those states, and also

76. *Plain English* (1660), 4–5, 8. 77. *MP*, 3 Nov. 1659, 844.
78. *Publick Intelligencer*, 30 Jan. 1660, 1308–9; 12 Mar. 1660, 1157.

among the ancient Hebrews and in modern Venice and the Netherlands, the machinery of popular participation was countered by the power of assemblies whose members were chosen for life. Secondly, the 'remedies' of popular election either 'little availed the people' or led to 'a licentious and unbridled democracy'. Milton also addresses 'the main reason urged' for the entrusting of the people's liberty to 'popular assemblies': 'great men will be still endeavouring to enlarge their power, but the common sort will be contented to maintain their own liberty'. On the contrary, claims Milton, Roman history proves how 'immoderate and ambitious to amplify their power' are 'popularities'. If there has to be a popular assembly, he adds, the 'balance' between it and the senate 'must be exactly so set, as to preserve and keep up due authority on either side'.[79] This last point, which fits uncomfortably with the material immediately preceding it, has the air of a hasty insertion.

In his use of his classical examples, Milton has James Harrington in his sights. Classical models of republican rule, which Nedham had introduced to political debate in the early 1650s, were being widely discussed, mainly through Harrington's influence, by 1659–60, when the successive failure of other remedies had driven men back on them. Behind Milton's words, however, there seems to lie not only the immediate controversy which it addresses but the work that had brought classical history to English republicanism in 1651–2, *Mercurius Politicus*. There Nedham had made use of the same historical examples to make, not the case which Milton advances now, but exactly the opposite one, the one to which Milton objects. The desirability of elections had always divided Milton from Nedham. Yet, less than three weeks before the composition of *The Readie and Easie Way*, Nedham printed a petition that recognized, on grounds similar to those of Milton's tract, the hazard to the good old cause that any elections would bring, at least if they were not narrowly confined to supporters of the good old cause.[80] Did Nedham, so practised in the exact reversal of his own arguments and in the turning of historical examples from one polemical case to its opposite, now come to Milton's aid? The relevant words of *The Readie and Easie Way* are unlikely to have been written by Nedham alone. Nedham, when turning earlier material to an opposite end, usually retained much of the original wording, but the wording of the passage of *The Readie*

79. *CP* vii. 436–40 (cf. ibid. ii. 315). The first point also appears, in slightly different form, in the first edition: ibid. vii. 374–5, 436 n.

80. *MP*, 30 Jan. 1660, 1051.

and Easie Way is not (except incidentally) that of *Politicus*. Yet both in the manner in which the examples of classical history are bunched, and in the choice of the particular examples selected, the passage is more characteristic of Nedham than of Milton.[81] So is the alignment of the classical examples with those of modern Venice and the Netherlands, countries in whose provisions for the 'balance' of constitutional power Milton did not show much interest elsewhere.

Politicus had been as hostile to oligarchy as *The Readie and Easie Way* is friendly to it. A number of its editorials, which attacked the 'grandee government' of the Rump that Milton now sought to perpetuate, had warned against 'standing' powers. In March 1652 *Politicus* insisted that in Athens, in Sparta, and in Rome a 'standing senate' or 'standing power' or 'standing council' had been the enemy to liberty, except where it was subordinate to the democratic component of the constitution.[82] *The Readie and Easie Way* remarks that the 'standing senate' of the Netherlands has been 'the main prop of their liberty': Nedham, arguing the opposite case in his comments of March 1652, maintains that in that country the 'supreme assemblies of the people frequent by election ... preserve[e] their liberties'.[83] Where Milton attacks the 'immoderate' tendencies of 'tribunes' and 'popular assemblies', Nedham, in an editorial of October 1651, appealed to the example of Rome, together with those of Venice and the Netherlands, in arguing for the benefits of 'tribunes' and 'assemblies of the people'. Rome 'ever thrived best, when the people had most power and used most moderation'. Whereas *The Readie and Easie Way* portrays the people's achievement in extracting constitutional powers from the senate as the source of Rome's tyranny, the same editorial presents it as the source of its liberty. So whereas Milton attributes the collapse of the republic to 'popularities', the editorial ascribes it to the declension of 'the popular interest'. *Politicus* claims for the Roman system the balance of powers that Milton says is hard to achieve: Rome thrived through its 'equal mixture of both interests, patrician and popular'.[84]

81. Milton's list of non-monarchical governments in *CW* vii. 291 is perhaps the nearest that his own writings elsewhere come to Nedham's in this respect; but Nedham, had he written that passage, would have given supporting illustration, of the kind to be found in the passage of *The Readie and Easie Way* that concerns us here.
82. *MP*, 11 Mar. 1652, 1460–1; 18 Mar. 1652, 1474–5. (It was in the same month that, in another editorial, the newsbook used material from Milton's *Defensio*.)
83. *MP*, 25 Mar. 1652, 1475–6; *CP* vii. 436–7.
84. *MP*, 9 Oct. 1651, 1110–11. Compare, too, the point about 'secrets of state' in the same passage with *CP* vii. 437.

Again, Milton contradicts a persistent theme, and favoured language, of *Politicus* in answering the fear 'that long continuance of power may corrupt sincerest men'.[85] It looks as if Milton was employing material from the newsbook that had been turned upside down by either or both of the two writers.

Other touches in *The Readie and Easie Way* bring *Politicus* to mind, and suggest Nedham's influence not only on the second edition but also on the first. The reference, in the first edition, to the boast that the English republic would become 'another Rome in the West' is closer to Nedham's editorials than to the main tenor of Milton's tract. So is a moment, again in the first edition, when the pamphlet unexpectedly harks back to the mood of international republicanism which he and Nedham had promoted in 1650–1, but which had subsequently disappeared from their writings. Milton remembers that the overthrow of the English monarchy and the establishment of a 'free commonwealth' had achieved 'the admiration and terror of our neighbours, and the stirring up of France itself, especially in Paris and Bordeaux, to our imitation'.[86] The passage takes us back to the support of *Politicus* for the Frondes and other Continental challenges to monarchy, and especially for the 'brave Bordelois' and 'French Roundheads'.[87] It was then that Nedham had urged the people of Europe to make themselves 'happy forever hereafter' by seizing their present opportunities for deliverance, and then too that he had congratulated the parliament on 'lay[ing] hold on a season of liberty after that the nation had groaned for almost 600 years under misery and slavery'. Then, too, Nedham had written of the French that 'now is the time they must win their liberty or never'.[88] It is in the same spirit that *The Readie and Easie* Way, echoing *A Publick Plea*, tells the English that 'Now is the opportunity, now the very season wherein we may establish a free Commonwealth and establish it forever in the land'.[89] Then there are Milton's statements that among the benefits of 'a free commonwealth' is its capacity to promote 'proportioned equality' and to enable the 'advancements of every person according to his merit'.[90] 'Free states', *Politicus* had observed, foster 'a due proportion, equability or harmony of condition among all the members', and ensure

85. *CP* vii. 434, 461. 86. Ibid. 355–6 (cf. *CW* vii. 177–9; viii. 87).
87. Above, p. 67. 88. Above, p. 69; cf. pp. 284–5; *MP*, 5 June 1651, 832.
89. *CP* vii. 430; above, p. 399 (cf. pp. 69, 129). 90. Ibid. 359, 383.

that public offices are held 'by men of merit, without distinction' and 'purely upon the account of merit' – for in them 'the door of dignity stands open to all (without exception) that ascend thither by the steps of worth and virtue'.[91]

At some point in the spring of 1660 Nedham may have slipped over to Holland, a country which had so long interested him and where he had many possible sources of contact, to save himself. If so he was soon back. On the king's return, according to Anthony Wood, he 'skulked until such time as he could get his pardon'. Whether his 'skulking' involved contact with Milton, to whose own self-concealment in the same period we shall soon come, we cannot say, for from the Restoration there is nothing to show the two writers in touch with each other – even though, as we shall see, Milton would cling to values that he had shared with Nedham.[92] It is not inconceivable that they preserved contact, but outwardly, at least, the return of the monarchy divided them. The restored regime approached Nedham and (apparently) Milton in the hope that they would write for it.[93] It was eminently worth its while to approach Nedham, pointless of it to approach Milton. Within the anti-Stuart and anti-Presbyterian camps, the two writers could jointly cross boundaries of allegiance. Outside them their paths could only diverge. There is neither indication nor likelihood that during the protectorate Milton had ever contemplated, as Nedham and

91. *MP*, 1 Jan. 1652, 1303–6; 19 Feb. 1652, 413; 17 June 1652, 1659. Further suggestive parallels between *The Readie and Easie Way* and Nedham's writings may be observed. Milton's statement that kingship may occasionally produce a good ruler, but that 'this rarely happens in a monarchy not elective' (*CP* vii. 377), recalls Nedham's point in *The Case of the Commonwealth* (pp. 117–18) that 'hereditary monarchies' occasionally yield 'some respite ... by the virtue and valour of the prince, yet this is very rare'. In *The Readie and Easie Way*, too, and in the brief tract that followed the publication of the second edition, Milton used an argument which Nedham had employed in 1650 but of which hitherto Milton had been wary (*CP* vii. 367, though cf. iv. 917): that the occupants of power are entitled, by the conquest that has brought them there, to exclude their enemies from it (*CP* vii. 455, 481, 483; *Case*, ch. 4) – though characteristically Milton sought to merge, as Nedham did not, the claims of conquest with those of virtue. The relations of Milton and Nedham in 1660 are also discussed in Joad Raymond, 'The Cracking of the Republican Spokes', *Prose Studies*, 19 (1996), 255–74.

92. Below, Ch. 16.

93. Nedham: NA, SP25/114, fo. 155; Milton: Darbishire, 32. It must be possible that Nedham had at least a hand in the document 'Concerning the Forraigne Affaires in the Protector's Time' (Scott, *Somers Tracts*, vi. 329–36) which Thurloe submitted to the restored monarchy. The cool presentation of diplomacy in terms of national interest is characteristic of him; and compare the language about the control of the Sound in a letter from Leiden (*MP*, 4 Dec. 1651, 1251) with Scott, *Somers Tracts*, vi. 331 ('carried the keys of the continent at his girdle'). (Compare too *MP*, 28 Sept. 1654, 3794, with Scott, *Somers Tracts*, vi. 333: 'the growing greatness of the Dutch'.)

Overton seem to have done, an alliance of commonwealthmen and royalists to topple Cromwell. Milton's political course had its inconsistencies, but vacillation over the acceptability of Stuart rule, the area of the most spectacular of all Nedham's inconsistencies, was not among them.

**

In his last phase of Roundhead pamphleteering, the need to forestall a Stuart restoration increasingly overrode all other considerations in Milton's mind. Political realism was not his *forte*. Never is he less realistic than in *The Readie and Easie Way*, where he imagines that the return of the monarchy can be avoided by the entrenchment of a hated oligarchy – a view the more surprising in light of his perception in the same period that 'no government' which lacked public 'consent' was likely to endure.[94] Yet, as the good old cause disintegrated, his thinking acquired, if not realism, then at least a readiness to acknowledge the limitations, and the necessary compromises, which reality imposes. Hitherto he had been content to portray virtuous actions as the outward expression of the transcendent virtue of the actors. The glorious deliverance of Pride's Purge and the regicide had, by the very act of breaking the ordinary rules of political conduct, risen above them. Now, in his disenchantment with the army, he viewed those events with a more sober eye. Among the instruments of deliverance, there had, he now admitted, been 'bad intentions in things otherwise well done'.[95] 'Some' men had had 'covetous and ambitious ends.'[96] Those failings, he explains, are not grounds for disowning the actions. After all, if 'a just and noble cause' ought to be abandoned merely because of 'the mixture of bad men who have ill managed and abused it',[97] what would have become of the Reformation, that beneficial outcome (or anyway beneficial up to a point) of royal vice? By 1659, Milton's eulogies, those deliberate departures from realism, have become less frequent and less extravagant. Before that time, it is true, his most gigantic praise had been confined to his works of propaganda. Yet before he wrote them, in his pamphlets before and during the first civil war, his commendations of parliament had soared to a higher level than, for the most part, he was ready to reach now. The virtues even of the Rump, a body newly applauded by him as 'the authors and best patrons of religious and civil liberty that ever these islands brought forth', are only relative. It is 'the famous parliament,

94. *CP* vii. 336. 95. Ibid. 414. 96. Ibid. 422; cf. p. 458. 97. Ibid. 422.

though not the blameless, since none well-affected but will confess, they have deserved much more of these nations than they have undeserved'.[98]

The Milton of the fragmenting revolution may lack a grasp of the practical, but he seeks to adjust to events as the dread prospect of the restored monarchy advances. Though he had made political calculations before, he had presented them never in a practical light, only as a choice between vice and virtue. Here too he had changed – not from any revision of his principles, or any diminution of his sense of his own integrity, but from alarm and from the sense of tactical necessity that it had induced. Even in his indignation following the second dissolution of the Rump, he was ready to concede that 'the army now have the power' and to frame his political solutions, which allowed the officers their 'places during life',[99] within that restraint. With the absolutes of eulogy Milton had dropped the absolutes of reform. The change came only in the course of 1659. In February he insisted, as confidently as in 1641–2, on uncompromising reformation of the Church as the indispensable prelude to security in the state. It was then that he asserted that until 'religion' was 'set free from the monopoly of hirelings', and until those in power grasped the distinction between civil and religious power – even, perhaps, until the occupancy of power were restricted to men who accepted that principle – 'I dare affirm that no model whatsoever of a commonwealth will prove successful or undisturbed'. Instead 'nothing but troubles, persecutions, commotions can be expected'.[100] Yet from October 1659, when he re-entered the fray of political writing, his position was modified. The political benefits of liberty of conscience are now relative. It would reduce (rather than eliminate) faction, would remove 'much hindrance and disturbance in public affairs', and would produce 'much peace and tranquillity'.[101] Whereas in 1641 Milton brought in political arguments to win support for his religious programme, in the desperation of *The Readie and Easie Way* he almost seems to appeal to the friends of liberty of conscience so as to win support for his present political programme – the programme on which he himself knows religious freedom to depend.[102] As an essential qualification for office, commitment to religious liberty comes to be first partnered, then replaced, by a political principle, the renunciation of rule by a single person.[103] Even on that

98. Ibid. 324–5 (though see also p. 420). 99. Ibid. 330.
100. Ibid. 240, 275; above, p. 160. 101. Ibid. 380, 381; cf. p. 338. 102. Ibid. 382.
103. Ibid. 330–1, 337, 368. See too p. 444; Corns, *Uncloistered Virtue,* 281.

subject pragmatism creeps in. Through the choice of a Roundhead king, as he momentarily suggests as the good old cause expires, for 'the space of an age or two we may chance to live happily enough, or tolerably'.[104]

How far, in viewing that restricted horizon, Milton has retreated from his apocalyptic expectations of 1641! In 1649 the expectations had been briefly revived, in language that anticipated the millenarian component of Marvell's 'The First Anniversary' five years later.[105] During the Restoration, in Marvell's eyes, the normal timetable of humanity was restored: 'the world will not go the faster for our driving'.[106] *Paradise Lost* has the angel Michael instruct Adam in a comparable perspective: 'so shall the world go on, | To good malignant, to bad men benign, | Under her own weight groaning' (XII. 537–9). It will end only with a day of judgement which nothing in Milton's writings since the 1640s has indicated to be near at hand, and which, in his wording in *The Readie and Easie Way*, sounds a long way off.[107] Like almost everyone else who had been caught up in the millenarian hopes of the revolution, Milton had to adapt to an altered conception of the divine timetable, which God, it transpired, hides from his over-inquisitive followers. The civil wars proved to have been, not the climactic episode of providentially ordained history, but merely one event in its long march.

In 1648 the swelling of public feeling, and the betrayal of the cause by a parliamentary majority, had led towards the restoration of the monarchy and the extinction of liberty. Then had come the miraculous deliverance of 1648–9. From the winter of 1659–60 the same tide of public opinion and parliamentary decision making surged again, sweeping Milton's countrymen to what now, as in writing earlier of the crisis of 1648, he called the 'utter ruin'[108] of a return to the Stuart monarchy. Then he had witnessed the 'rage and torrent' of royalist feeling: now he saw its 'insolence and rage'.[109] In December 1659 he expected a return to 'civil war',[110] but in the following months it became clear that the king could return without it. The 'low dejection and debasement of mind' that he had observed in his countrymen in the late 1640s now found their counterpart in their 'strange degenerate corruption'. In the wake of the regicide Milton had expected his nation to export its new-won liberty to the Continent: now it seemed that the revolution would 'have left no memorial ... but in the common laughter of Europe'.[111] Despairingly, Milton watches his countrymen 'basely and

104. *CP* vii. 482. 105. Above, pp. 201–2. 106. *PWAM* i. 192.
107. *CP* vii. 366, 374. 108. *CW* vii. 511; *CP* vii. 339. 109. *CP* iii. 348; vii. 463.
110. Ibid. vii. 336. 111. Ibid. 357.

besottedly ... run their necks again into the yoke which they have broken', 'prostrate all the fruits of their victory for nothing at the feet of the vanquished', 'creep back so poorly as it seems the multitude would to their once abjured and detested thraldom of kingship', and, 'of our own foolish accord', run 'headlong again with full stream wilfully and obstinately into the same bondage'.[112] As elsewhere, ethical corruption is aligned in Milton's mind with the want of civil prudence in a nation so courageous in war and so unwise in peace.[113] Now he casts around for a new deliverer or new form of deliverance. This time there is none. Milton is left to speak 'the last words', or almost the last by him, of 'our expiring liberty'.[114]

Yet if there was every cause for bleakness, there was none for the sin of despairing of God's providence. Perhaps it was even needless to despair of men. 'God hath yet his remnant,' declared *The Readie and Easie Way*.[115] In 1648–9 the virtuous minority, God's 'sole remainder' as he had then called them,[116] had been summoned to the premeditated heroism of action. After the return of Charles II the task of the 'remnant' lies in preservation and survival, amid events beyond their control or prediction. They are called, not to revolution, but to 'patience', that recurrent theme of Milton's late poems: to 'the saintly patience' which sustains, in God's service, the bearing of the 'wrongs' that are visited on them.[117] We shall next see how, in *Samson Agonistes*, Milton offers, out of a seemingly unanswerable image of despair, a counsel of hope to those who are ready, like Milton himself, to 'stand and wait'.[118] Patience should not be mistaken for resignation.[119] The early 1660s, the time which the poem mirrors, was the saints' darkest time. Yet in the years thereafter, when the congenital insecurity of mid- and later seventeenth-century politics resurfaced, the 'remnant' might find new challenges, even new opportunities. In the final chapter we shall move beyond *Samson Agonistes* to find how, in his prose as well as in his verse of the Restoration, the memory of the Puritan Revolution lived in Milton's mind and shaped his vision of the present.

112. Ibid. 356–63. 113. Ibid. 363. 114. Ibid. 463. 115. Ibid. 363.
116. Ibid. 348. 117. *Paradise Regained* III. 92–3. 118. Sonnet XVI.
119. The point is made by Laura Knoppers, *Historicizing Milton: Spectacle, Power, and Poetry in Restoration England* (Athens, Ga., 1994), 155 ff.

15

Milton and *Samson Agonistes*

Until now we have been dealing almost entirely with occasional literature: with writings which, whether in verse or prose, were explicitly concerned with current political events. Now, in *Samson Agonistes*, we move to one which was not. We have to decide, not how the political background shaped the text, but whether it shaped it at all. This is contentious territory, for on no poem have the explanatory claims of context provoked wider disagreement. From Thomas Newton and William Hayley in the eighteenth century, to William Godwin and David Masson in the nineteenth, and to Christopher Hill and others in recent times, a succession of commentators has supposed that *Samson Agonistes* incorporates events and experiences of the Restoration.[1] Influential modern commentators have taken indignant exception to that view. They have maintained that the poem is healthily free of any 'personal' or 'political allusions'; that 'any attempt ... to make political allegory the heart of this poem is indefensible'; that the 'echoes' of Restoration politics which have been detected in it 'are merely the contemporary reverberation of a universal paradigm recurring throughout history'.[2] Over the last third of a century or so, such views have become much less common.[3] Yet the aspiration which they have represented – the elevation of literature above

1. Parker, 905; William Hayley (or Hailey), *The Life of John Milton* (1799), 190–5; William Godwin, *Lives of Edward and John Philips* (1815), 84–5; Masson, vi. 670–8; Christopher Hill, *Milton and the English Revolution* (London, 1977), 428–48, 481–6, and *idem*, *The Experience of Defeat: Milton and Some Contemporaries* (London, 1984), 310–19.
2. Parker, 313–22, 903–17; E. M. Krouse, *Milton's Samson and the Christian Tradition* (Princeton, 1949), 93; Barbara Lewalski, '*Samson Agonistes* and the "Tragedy" of the Apocalypse', *Publications of the Modern Language Association*, 85 (1970), 1061. Lewalski has substantially modified her position in her admirable *Life of John Milton*, 525–36.
3. There has been a profusion of publication on the poem in recent years. See Mark R. Kelley, and Joseph Wittreich, eds., *Altering Eyes: New Perspectives on 'Samson Agonistes'* (Newark, Del., 2002).

history, and of poetic inspiration above the banality of fact – has a legacy not easily disburdened. The other-worldliness which the rise of academic criticism brought to literature still inhibits, albeit at a less conscious level, the re-creation of the relationship of writers to politics.

Samson Agonistes, the nearest thing to a Greek tragedy in the English language, will always speak beyond the context that produced it. Being a triumph of imagination, it mirrors a wider range of experience than Milton's own, which is why the stature of the poem has been evident to countless readers ignorant of or indifferent to its background. Yet anti-historical critics have imposed artificial choices on their readers. No one in the seventeenth century would have been impressed by the modern argument that because *Samson Agonistes* conforms to literary types or traditions – to the characteristics of Sophoclean tragedy or biblical typology – it cannot have been animated by the poet's personal and political experience. *Samson Agonistes*, however many other things it may also be, is about Restoration England, which is as forcefully present in it as Puritan England is in Milton's political prose. Samson's tragedy is that of Milton's nation, which proved unequal to its trial of virtue; of the cause of liberty that was betrayed by its deliverers; and of Milton himself, who devoted the central two decades of his life to the revolution and saw the most exalted hopes crash to self-inflicted defeat. The poem is not a *pièce à clef.* Its analogies are not sustained or protracted. Yet analogies there are, at every turn. They are essential to the content of the poem and to its feeling.

We cannot say when *Samson Agonistes*, which was registered for publication in September 1670 and was published no later than the following May, was composed. Like other works of Milton, it may have been written and revised over time. Perhaps it was at least mostly written in or soon after 1662. For it is the experience of the time from the return of monarchy in 1660 to the final trials of Charles I's judges in 1662 that pervades the poem.[4] To demonstrate its presence I shall set poetry beside prose. I shall place

4. Some critics have detected allusions to the Anglo–Dutch war of 1665–6. References to other events and issues later than 1662 are proposed by Janel Mueller, 'The Figure and the Ground: Samson as a Hero of London Nonconformity, 1662–1667', in Parry and Raymond, eds., *Milton and the Terms of Liberty*, 137–162; and a date after 1666 is implicitly suggested by Knoppers, *Historicizing Milton*, ch. 6. Stimulating as those arguments are, they do not seem to me to make claims on the dating of the poem of the kind that point to 1660–2. The poem is also related to the world of Restoration Nonconformity by Sharon Achinstein, *Literature and Dissent in Milton's England* (Cambridge, 2003), 118 ff. See too John Coffey, 'Pacifist, Quietist, or Patient Militant? John Milton and the Restoration', *Milton Studies*, 42 (2002), 149–74.

Milton's writing, not, this time, together with that of Nedham, whose discernible place in his life ended in 1660, but alongside the compositions of three politicians who recorded their responses to the Restoration and its aftermath. Milton did not always agree with them – or with anyone – in either his political or his religious convictions. Even so, the common ground of belief and experience between him and them was broad and firm. It was never more so than amid the pain and loss of the Restoration.

The three politicians are Edmund Ludlow (or Ludlowe), Algernon Sidney (or Sydney), and Sir Henry Vane. All three were commonwealthmen. All had been prominent in the government of Britain under the Commonwealth of 1649–53. All had broken with Cromwell upon what they called his 'usurpation' of 1653. All were bitter opponents of the protectorate. To Ludlow, Cromwell's elevation was the moment when God's purpose in the revolution was betrayed. Sidney, with many before him, compared the protector to Julius Caesar and judged him 'a tyrant, and a violent one'.[5] Vane was imprisoned for his opposition to the protectorate in 1656. All three proclaimed allegiance to that 'good old cause' whose 'language' Milton 'speak[s]' in *The Readie and Easie Way*.[6] The language spreads across the writings of the three men, and permeates *Samson Agonistes*. There are consequently resemblances not only of thought and emotion between the poem and the prose, but, time and again, of wording.

When the three writers sought to explain England's apostasy at the Restoration, they turned to the biblical illustration which Milton, in *The Readie and Easie Way*, likewise selected: the nation chose 'a captain back to Egypt'.[7] For the deployment of biblical analogies, far from being evidence of the political detachment, or the timelessness of perspective, which have been admiringly located in the poem, pervaded the political language and calculations of the civil war Puritans. To them Israelite history, which they knew so well, was a world not of remote and alien antiquity but of the here and now. In it they found the figurative models, the 'parallels', through which they made sense of the convulsions of their own time. 'Our case', remarked the commonwealthman Henry Stubbe in 1659, 'hath been

5. Algernon Sidney, 'Court Maxims, Refuted and Refelled', Warwickshire Record Office MS, p. 70. Sidney's text has been edited by Hans Blom and E. Haitsma Mulier as *Court Maxims* (Cambridge, 1996), where the page numbers of the manuscript are conveniently provided in the margins of the printed text.
6. *CP* vii. 387, 462.
7. *Ibid.* 463 (cf. p. 325); Ludlow, *Voyce*, 115, 150; Sidney, 'Court Maxims', p. 203; *The Tryal of Sir Henry Vane, Kt.* (1662), 117.

parallel' to that of the Israelites, 'and we may herein read the grounds of our confidence that through a resemblance of events the same providence operateth now in us which did of old, and we expect the same issue.'[8] Or, as Milton's Chorus has it, 'God hath wrought things as incredible | For his people of old; what hinders now?' (1532–3).[9] Any Puritan reader of a poem about Samson – with whom Milton had earlier compared first Charles I and then the nation which opposed him[10] – would have read it with an eye to the present.

The first of our commonwealthmen, Edmund Ludlow, who had signed the king's death-warrant in 1649, fled to Switzerland on the return of the Stuart monarchy in 1660. There he composed an enormous autobiography, 'A Voyce from the Watch Tower'. In it he strove to confront the calamity of the Restoration and to explain it, as he sought to explain everything, in terms of God's providence.[11] To him the Puritan Revolution had seemed a decisive stage in the divine scheme of history. He expected God's chosen people, his 'saints', to purge and purify Church and state, and perhaps to prepare the way for the Second Coming. In 1660 those hopes lay in ruins, 'all things running counter to what the providences of the Lord had led [the godly] to for twenty years past'. Now God was pleased 'to make them the tail, who before were the head', and his people were forced to 'bow down that their enemies may go over them'.[12] No less than Samson's 'restless thoughts' do Ludlow's meditations 'present | Times past, what once I was, and what am now' (19–22). No less than Samson in his 'miserable change' (340), his 'change beyond report, thought, or belief' (117), is Ludlow's cause 'the glory late of Israel, now the grief' (179). He discovers what Milton's Chorus, in addressing God, tells of his way with 'such as [he] hast solemnly elected':

thou oft
Amidst their height of noon,
Changest thy countenance, and thy hand with no regard

8. Henry Stubbe, *Malice Rebuked* (1659), 4; Blair Worden, 'Providence and Politics in Cromwellian England', *Past and Present*, 109 (1985), 89.

9. John Barkstead, one of the regicides executed in 1662, compared the suffering saints of the Restoration with the Nazarites (whom Samson represented): *The Speeches, Discourses and Prayers of Col. John Barkstead, Col. John Okey, and Mr. Miles Corbet* (1662), octavo edn., 27.

10. Above, pp. 163, 173.

11. Blair Worden, 'Whig History and Puritan Politics: The *Memoirs of Edmund Ludlow* Revisited', *Historical Research*, 75 (2002), 209–37; *idem*, *Roundhead Reputations*, chs. 1–4.

12. Ludlow, *Voyce*, 123.

Of highest favours past
From thee on them, or them to thee of service.

God 'throw'st them lower than [he] didst exalt them high' (678–89). Like Samson, who is 'by himself given over' (121), Ludlow knows that the defeat of God's cause owes nothing to its enemies – to the Philistines in Samson's time, to the Cavaliers in Ludlow's – and everything to the sin which God punishes in his servants.[13] Like Samson, Ludlow has to absorb the lesson of divine humiliation. And like Samson, he has to learn how to keep faith with – in Ludlow's words – God's 'seemingly dead and buried cause'.[14]

Ludlow, a hard-line Calvinist, shared none of Milton's classical and humanist values. He was horrified to watch the spread of the blasphemous notions that 'we are to take the holy Scriptures as those of Titus Livius or Polybius', and that 'reason ought to be the judge of the Scripture'.[15] Our second figure, Algernon Sidney, another exile of the Restoration, was in that as in other respects closer in mind to Milton.[16] He saw both reason and classical history as friends to religion, even though – perhaps with the aim of winning Nonconformists to his insurrectionary plans – he sometimes spoke the enclosed, self-conscious language of the godly which was Ludlow's standard form of expression, and which Milton eschewed. In the mid–1660s Sidney attacked the restored monarchy in his treatise 'Court Maxims, Refuted and Refelled' (though he did not get it into print). He acknowledged the Restoration to have been an act of voluntary national consent, and, with Milton, found in it an illustration of men's weakness for self-inflicted slavery. The Chorus of *Samson Agonistes* regrets that 'nations grown corrupt' prefer 'bondage with ease' to 'strenuous liberty' (268–71): Sidney lamented that in 1660 a previously 'free and gallant nation' could not 'be contented until we return again ... into bondage'.[17] For Sidney, for Milton, and for Ludlow too, the spectacle of self-betrayal brought agony of spirit. Ludlow tells how the sweeping tide of royalist emotion in 1660 caused 'my heart to ache'; Sidney tells how it generated 'the anguish of my spirit';[18] Samson, as he contemplates the consequences of his own self-betrayal, endures 'anguish of the mind' (458), 'The anguish of my soul' (600).

13. Ibid. 149, 200. 14. Ludlow, 'Voyce', p. 1111.
15. Ibid. pp. 1225, 1238.
16. For their common perspectives see my 'Republicanism and the Restoration', in Wootton, ed., *Republicanism, Liberty, and Commercial Society*, 153.
17. Sidney, 'Court Maxims', pp. 54, 203.
18. Ludlow, *Voyce*, 123; Sidney, 'Court Maxims', p. 203.

Our third figure is Sir Henry Vane, who had been a dominant figure in the Long Parliament and whom we have met as the champion of unlimited liberty of conscience praised in Milton's sonnet of 1652. Vane, who commanded a heroic stature among his followers, was revered by Milton, by Ludlow, and by Sidney, who was his adoring memorialist.[19] Vane's opaque political ideas and religious beliefs are now barely intelligible. Yet they, like his political leadership, attracted a loving following at the time, which his death enhanced. To Ludlow he was 'this choice martyr of Christ'.[20] 'The nation', remembered Sidney, 'had not another man equal to' Vane 'in virtue, prudence, courage, industry, reputation and godliness.'[21] Milton's and Sidney's language is Vane's too. To Vane as to Milton, 'bondage' is the partner of 'corruption', for in Vane's mind 'no nation is truly free that is in bondage to corruption'.[22] After Vane's death a number of writings by and about him were rushed out. Among them was the biography by his chaplain George Sykes in which Milton's sonnet to Vane was (anonymously) first published; if Milton sanctioned the poem's appearance, it was a very brave step. Sykes's biography repeats Ludlow's and Sidney's diagnosis of the Restoration: the English, in 'bondage' to their lusts, had irrationally yielded to slavery under the basest of rulers.[23]

Sykes is alert to the contemporary pertinence of the Samson story. His opening page refers to it. In a later passage he writes that Vane 'has more advantaged a good CAUSE and condemned a bad one, done his honest countrymen more service and his enemies more disservice, by his death (as Samson served the Philistines) than before in all his life, though that also were very considerable'.[24] The resemblances between Vane's person and words and those of Milton's Samson are so close as to suggest that Milton knew the writings by and about Vane which were published in 1662, and that they made an imprint on *Samson Agonistes*. Samson is destined to be Israel's 'deliverer':[25] Vane, in Sykes's words, is 'this English Joseph and

19. Sidney's tribute to Vane is printed in Violet Rowe, *Sir Henry Vane the Younger* (London, 1970), Appendix.
20. Ludlow, *Voyce*, 313.
21. Sidney, 'Court Maxims', p. 188.
22. Vane (attrib.), *A Needful Corrective or Balance in Popular Government* (1659), 7. (This pamphlet, though probably written by Vane, may alternatively have been composed by a different author with Vane's 'advice or approbation': Austin Woolrych, 'The Good Old Cause and the Fall of the Protectorate', *Cambridge Historical Journal*, 13 (1957), 153.)
23. George Sykes, *The Life and Death of Sir Henry Vane, Kt.* (1662), 23.
24. Ibid. 119.
25. ll. 38–9, 274, 1214, 1270.

deliverer'.[26] Samson is 'single' in God's service (344, 1111): Vane maintains that God did 'single me out to the defence and justification of his cause', and declares himself willing 'to stand single in the witness I am to give to this glorious cause'.[27] The Philistines 'put out' Samson's 'eyes' (33, 1103, 1160): Vane's chaplain protests at the government's determination 'to put out the eyes of all the good people of England'.[28] Samson, despairing at his impotence and his affliction, thinks his 'race of glory run' (597): Vane, his 'race of action being run' after his fall from power, subsequently endured his 'suffering scene'.[29] Only 'secret refreshings' of the spirit (665) can 'repair' Samson's 'strength': for Vane, 'secret dew' nourishes the godly soul under the persecution of the Restoration.[30] Where Samson's sin has broken his military prowess, in Vane's mind 'our sins have been the cause that our counsels, our forces, our wit, our conquests, and ourselves have been destructive to ourselves'.[31]

Shortly before his imprisonment in October 1660, the month of the first executions among Charles I's judges, Vane delivered a sermon to his family. It focused on another Old Testament figure whose experience had exposed the failings of the Israelites: Baruch, that 'choice and dear servant of the Lord that on proof and trial had showed himself very courageous and bold in the service of God'. Milton's Samson experiences 'humours black' and 'black mortification' (600, 622): Vane's sermon recalls the 'black and dismal prospect' that confronted Baruch, and fears 'that the like ... may be brought to pass in our days'. Milton's Samson, once so privileged in his closeness to God, is tormented by 'restless thoughts' (19): Vane's Baruch, 'after all the experience he had had of God ... could find no rest at all in any way ... no visible support or help'.[32] Yet Vane, like Samson, would find a renewed purpose in martyrdom. Preparing for his execution, he was 'certain' that 'this cause shall have its resurrection in my death'.[33] Milton's Chorus assures us at the end that God's benevolent providence, which has

26. Sykes, *Life and Death*, 121.

27. *The Substance of what Sir Henry Vane Intended to have Spoken on the Scaffold on Tower Hill* (1662), 3; *Tryal of Sir Henry Vane*, 62.

28. Sykes, *Life and Death*, 138, 142.

29. Ibid., 105.

30. Sir Henry Vane, *Two Treatises* (1662), 2.

31. *Tryal of Sir Henry Vane*, 120.

32. Victoria and Albert Museum, Forster MS 48 D. 41 (Vane's sermons), pp. 1–3.

33. Vane, *Two Treatises*, 79–80. Vane knew that the execution would occur 'as upon a public theatre', and saw his death as belonging to the 'last act' or 'spectacle' of a divine scheme of history: *Tryal of Sir Henry Vane*, 89; *Substance of what Sir Henry Vane Intended*, 1; Vane, *Two Treatises*, 54–5. Jose, *Ideas of the Restoration in English Literature*, ch. 8, emphasizes the physical resemblances between the Philistine temple and the Restoration playhouse.

seemed so remote or improbable, has become evident 'in the close' (1748): Sykes's biography, in its conclusion, assures the persecuted saints that God 'will send deliverance in the close'.[34]

England's 'condition' at the Restoration, explained Vane, 'held much resemblance with that of the Old Testament Jews' when they provoked God by establishing monarchy, 'and we deserve as well to be rejected as they were'.[35] Sidney drew the same parallel – though he was glad to recall that, even in the Israelites' self-inflicted adversity, God 'kept a lamp burning still in the house of David'.[36] The Puritan imagination was especially struck by Old Testament episodes, of which the Samson story is but one, that centred on divine punishment. In 1656 Vane blamed the recent humiliation of Cromwell's hitherto victorious forces in Spanish territory in the Caribbean on the hypocrisy and ambition behind the founding of the protectorate. It was then that Vane compared Cromwell's misdeeds to the sin of Achan, whose act of embezzlement had rendered Joshua's previously invincible forces as helpless as Dalila's wiles made Samson, and had exposed them to devastating defeat.[37] We saw that in 1659 Milton – who had contemplated writing a tragedy about Achan – portrayed the Cromwellians among the officers of the new model army as 'the Achan among them.'

★★

The Old Testament God was a God of battle and of honour. Samson is wretched to think of the 'honour' that his impotence has given to Dagon, the deity of the Philistines, and of the 'dishonour' it has brought upon God (449–52). The condemned regicides, who knew as well as Samson that 'death to life is crown or shame' (1579), were as anxious as he to 'honour' and not 'dishonour' God by the manner of their deaths.[38] They and their fellow saints of the Restoration were as conscious as Samson, too, of having already brought 'dishonour' on God by failure in his service.[39] For in the civil wars as in the Samson story, the outcome of battles determined 'whose

34. Sykes, *Life and Death*, 143.
35. *Tryal of Sir Henry Vane*, 119–20.
36. Sidney, 'Court Maxims', pp. 36, 200.
37. Above, p. 342; Worden, 'Oliver Cromwell and the Sin of Achan', 136–9; cf. Ludlow, *Voyce*, 200.
38. H. G. Tibbutt, 'Colonel John Okey 1606–1682', *Bedfordshire Historical Record Society*, 35 (1955), 145, 150.
39. e.g. *Speeches, Discourses and Prayers*, 84.

God is God' (1176), 'whose God is strongest, thine or mine' (1155). In Milton's poem

> all the contest is now
> 'Twixt God and Dagon; Dagon hath presumed,
> Me overthrown, to enter lists with God,
> His deity comparing, and preferring
> Before the God of Abraham.
>
> (461–5)

Cavaliers and Roundheads had always 'appealed' to God to declare for their cause in battle. The Roundhead victory at Cheriton in 1644, a Puritan preacher told parliament, 'was a victory after a mutual appeal to God': 'the enemy's word was, *God is for us*. Our word was, *God is with us*.' So 'the Lord seemed to decide the great doubt, and to resolve the question which side was right, whose cause was his.'[40] In 1649 the new Commonwealth declared that 'the great God of battle', by 'a continued series of providences and wonders', had 'determined very much in favour of the parliament'.[41] Yet in 1660 the Puritans were subjected to royalist mockery as Samson is taunted by the Philistines' champion Harapha. 'The court of heaven', crowed the royalist clergyman Gilbert Ironside in that year, 'hath been solicited this many years *pro* and *con* ... and now let the world judge whose prayers have been heard.'[42] God's verdict on parliament's behalf, Vane conceded, had been 'made void' by the sins of his people.[43]

Milton's entry into political polemic in 1649 had coincided with his realization that religious and civil idolatry are inseparable. The Restoration gave hideous illustration to his conviction. Of all the causes for Puritan self-reproach, there was none so crushing as the return of the rites of the Church. As Manoa, Samson's father, tells the son,

> So Dagon shall be magnified, and God,
> Besides whom is no god, compared with idols,
> Disglorified, blasphemed, and had in scorn ...
> Which to have come to pass by means of thee,
> Samson, of all thy sufferings think the heaviest,
> Of all reproach the most with shame that ever
> Could have befall'n thee and thy father's house.

40. Obadiah Sedgwick, *A Thanksgiving Sermon* (1644), 81.
41. *The Parliamentary or Constitutional History of England*, 21 vols. (1751–62), xix. 68, 177.
42. Gilbert Ironside, *A Sermon Preached at Dorchester* (1660), 13.
43. *Tryal of Sir Henry Vane*, 119.

Samson acknowledges the truth that Manoa has spoken: 'I do acknowledge and confess' that 'I this pomp have brought | To Dagon, and advanced his praises high | Among the heathen round' (440–51). In 1660 the orgy of public idolatry (as Puritans saw it) swept up politics no less than religion. By restoring monarchy, lamented Algernon Sidney, 'we set up an idol, and dance about it'; Ludlow was horrified to observe the nation's 'great zeal to the idol that was set up' in 1660; Vane's chaplain lamented that England's 'most successfully acquired liberty' was being 'swallowed up again into downright heathenish idolatry'.[44] The theme of idolatry runs through Milton's poem.[45] The Philistines, an 'idolatrous rout amidst their wine' (443), are 'Drunk with idolatry, drunk with wine' (1670). So are the English in 1660. Milton, who in April of that year noted the place of 'tigers of Bacchus' in resurgent royalism,[46] discloses in *Paradise Lost* that, while 'with dangers compassed round', he heard 'the barbarous dissonance | Of Bacchus and his revellers' (VII. 27–33); Sidney noticed that at the Restoration 'the rites of Bacchus' were being 'publicly celebrated' by 'wicked idolaters';[47] Ludlow, like Milton hiding in London to avoid arrest, contrived to be 'an eye and ear witness' of the drunken revelry of the king's return, when

> the debauched party through London manifested great joy that now they were in a way of enjoying their lusts without control. And I observed a vintner, who set out a hogshead of wine, making those drink the king's health who passed by, which they did upon their knees till they lost the use of their legs.[48]

Ludlow's movements in London in the spring and summer of 1660 are vividly recorded in his autobiography. For five months he moved back and forth from safe-house to safe-house, bolting doors, checking escape routes, venturing out only at night, hoping for a moonless sky, hiding in alleys or behind boards when potential enemies passed by.[49] Other regicides who sought to conceal themselves were less fortunate, and went to their deaths; but the sergeant-at-arms had to inform the House of Commons that Ludlow was 'not to be found' – just as the official proclamation against Milton admitted that, by 'obscuring himself', he had thwarted the

44. Sidney, 'Court Maxims', p. 203; Ludlow, *Voyce*, 170 (see also pp. 122, 204, and Ludlow, 'Voyce', pp. 1131, 1150, 1154); Sykes, *Life and Death*, 130.

45. ll. 13, 441, 453, 456, 1297, 1364, 1378.

46. *CP* vii. 452–3.

47. Sidney, 'Court Maxims', p. 194.

48. Ludlow, *Voyce*, 118, 158.

49. Ibid. 114, 119, 150–1, 158, 169, 178, 182–3, 188–90.

government's intentions to try him for treason.[50] Through a network of faithful friends and kinswomen, Ludlow was able to keep in touch with other regicides nearby.[51] While the parliament (or Convention), a body now captured for ardent royalism, debated the Act of Oblivion and decided which offenders to punish, he and his associates confronted urgent decisions. Should they give themselves up, and rely on the spirit of clemency which Charles II had promised in the declaration issued at Breda in Holland just before his return? Or should they stay in hiding until the government's real intentions towards the regicides became clear?

Like Ludlow, Milton concealed himself in London for several months. He went into hiding in May, the month of the king's return. The Commons ordered his arrest in mid-June. Only at the end of August did the passage of the Act of Oblivion exempt him from punishment. His *Eikonoklastes* and *Defensio* had been publicly burned two days earlier. When *Defensio* had been burned in France during the rule of the English Commonwealth, he had exulted in that impotent reaction.[52] Now, in the summer of 1660, his plight – 'In darkness, and with dangers compassed round', as *Paradise Lost* discloses (VII. 27) – was desperate: as desperate in its way as Samson's, who tells the Chorus 'How many evils have enclosed me round' (194).[53] When he emerged from hiding in September he moved to Holborn, where Ludlow had hidden that summer,[54] and where the godly network would have been ready to shelter him or help him flee if the threat to his life were renewed.[55] None the less Ludlow's account testifies that the hunted regicides had lonely moments – as, *Paradise Lost* indicates (VII. 27–8), did Milton.

Despite the Act of Oblivion, Milton was arrested at some point in or after October. Only with his release in mid-December did his ordeal of seven months end. His survival, like that of other advocates of the execution of Charles I, depended on the mercy of parliament. In 1660 we can watch Ludlow seeking that mercy and calculating his chances. Thanks to the memoirs of Lucy Hutchinson we can also watch her husband, the regicide Colonel John Hutchinson, who 'lay very private in the town' until the

50. Ludlow, *Voyce*, 186; Parker, 573.
51. Ludlow, *Voyce*, 150, 176, 178.
52. Above, pp. 272–3.
53. Like Samson (l. 8), Ludlow suffered from a want of 'air' in his confinement (*Voyce*, 183). W.R. Parker's vividly imagined account of Milton's experience in hiding (pp. 567 ff.) will ring true to any reader of Ludlow's autobiography.
54. Ludlow, *Voyce*, 114, 150, 158, 188–9.
55. For that network see also *Speeches, Discourses and Prayers*, 23.

Act of Oblivion was passed,[56] confronting the same quandary. Intermediaries for both Ludlow and Hutchinson lobbied members of both houses, just as intercessors did on behalf of Milton, among them Andrew Marvell, who 'made a considerable party for him' and who was one of the 'many good friends to intercede for him'.[57]

Such exertions help us to understand the considerable presence in Milton's poem of a theme that owes nothing to biblical or literary tradition: the efforts of Manoa to secure Samson's release through the payment of a ransom. Just as Manoa, by 'solicitation', has 'attempted one by one the lords' (488, 1457), so Ludlow records that 'my father Oldsworth' – his father-in-law – approached 'the Lords' and 'solicited many of them' to get Ludlow spared.[58] Mrs Hutchinson, in striving to save her husband, 'made it her business to solicit all her friends for his safety', and persuaded an ally in the Commons to 'solicit all his friends' too.[59] Three figures who appear to have aided Milton's bid for clemency – Lady Ranelagh, the secretary of state Sir William Morice, and the MP Arthur Annesley – also tried to help Ludlow.[60] They met mixed responses. In Ludlow's and Lucy Hutchinson's accounts, some MPs responded to pleas for leniency with bitter vindictiveness, others with personal or financial opportunism, others still with heart-warming magnanimity.[61] The stories told by those authors resemble Manoa's as he solicits on his son's behalf:

> Some much averse I found and wondrous harsh,
> Contemptuous, proud, set on revenge and spite;
> That part most reverenced Dagon and his priests,
> Others more moderate seeming, but their aim
> Private reward, for which both gold and state
> They easily would set to sale, a third
> More generous far and civil, who confessed
> They had enough revenged, having reduced
> Their foe to misery beneath their fears.
>
> (1461–9)

If the potential friends of the regicides responded variously to solicitation, the regicides and their friends differed among themselves. Having pledged their lives to the godly cause, they could hope to save them only by disowning it, or at least by accommodation with the political and religious

56. Hutchinson, *Memoirs*, 231. 57. Darbishire, 74, 177. 58. Ludlow, *Voyce*, 165.
59. Hutchinson, *Memoirs*, 229, 232. 60. Parker, 571–2; Ludlow, *Voyce*, 119, 165, 166.
61. Ludlow, *Voyce*, 125, 165–6, 180; Hutchinson, *Memoirs*, 230–3.

forces they had reviled. It was a humbling prospect. Yet might not God wish his servants to survive, as Samson does, so as to help preserve the divine cause and to remain instruments of it? Milton, after his arrest, sued successfully for pardon, an act of submission that cost him heavy gaolers' fees (against which Marvell protested in parliament), and, we can only suppose, some abasement of spirit.[62] Manoa's exertions on his son's behalf confront Samson with a parallel dilemma. Samson longs only to die, and meanwhile to 'expatiate, if possible, my crime' through servitude and imprisonment.[63] Manoa retorts that 'self-preservation bids' his son to use the 'means' that might bring him release and safety (505–16). The sceptical Samson asks how, once released, he could be 'useful' and 'serve | My nation' (564–5). Manoa by contrast is sure that it is God's 'purpose' to 'use' Samson 'further yet in some great service' (1498–9).

The argument between Samson and Manoa corresponds to a debate among the commonwealthmen. In 1662, Vane, like Samson declaring a longing for death, 'might have had an opportunity of escaping', or have avoided his execution 'by policy', but he felt 'unable to decline that which was come upon him'. 'Friends' urged him 'to make some submission to the king'. But when some of them spoke of 'giving some thousands of pounds for his life', he replied that 'If a thousand farthings would gain it, he would not do it.'[64] The regicide Thomas Harrison, before his execution in 1660, was said to have been equally firm. He took no steps to avoid arrest, being so certain 'of his duty to seal the truth' of the 'cause which the Lord had honoured him to be an instrument in' that 'he was not free to withdraw himself out of his house for the saving of his life, as apprehending his doing so would be a turning of his back upon the cause of God'.[65] But if Vane and Harrison take Samson's line, Ludlow follows Manoa's. Ludlow believed it his duty to use all possible 'means' for his 'preservation', so that he might remain useful 'for the serving of his generation'.[66] Colonel Hutchinson, having initially resolved to give himself up, was persuaded by his wife that

62. Parker, 576. The payment of fees or sweeteners was a necessity for other regicides too: Ludlow, *Voyce*, 164, 174–5; Hutchinson, *Memoirs*, 232. Hints that regicides might be able to save their lives by bribes (*Speeches, Discourses and Prayers*, 21; *Tryal of Sir Henry Vane*, 81; R. H. C. Catterall, 'Sir George Downing and the Regicides', *American Historical Review*, 17 (1912), 268–9, 282) perhaps correspond to the offer of 'magnanimity' by some Philistine lords 'if some convenient ransom were proposed' (ll. 1470–1).

63. l. 490; and see l. 1263.

64. *Tryal of Sir Henry Vane*, 77, 81.

65. Ludlow, *Voyce*, 126; cf. *CW* xvi. 317.

66. Ludlow, *Voyce*, 108, 169, 182, 302, 305, 312.

God had 'singled him out for preservation'. Thereafter he 'would often say the Lord had not thus eminently preserved him for nothing, but that he was yet kept for some eminent service' in God's cause.[67] Milton himself was lastingly preoccupied by the yearning, as he put it in 1666, to be not 'useless', to perform 'whatever duty remains for me to carry out in this life'.[68] Even during his cause's hour of prosperity – at the point, apparently somewhere between 1651 and 1655, when he wrote the sonnet 'When I consider how my light is spent'[69] – 'That one talent which is death to hide' had been 'lodged with me useless'. What then of the Restoration? He may have been an Abdiel in resisting it, but unlike Abdiel he had been on the losing side. The prose for which, for nearly two decades, he suspended his poetic ambitions had been written for a cause which proved to have been flawed at its heart and which was now ignominiously ruined and abased. Did he resolve to preserve himself, in 1660, for the 'great service' of his writing, so that he might even now be 'useful' and 'serve | My nation'?[70]

★★

In October 1660 sleds carrying condemned regicides to execution passed close to Milton's house in Holborn. Two years later Vane and three other victims were likewise carried to execution, Vane, in a pointed gesture, on the anniversary of the decisive battle of the civil war at Naseby. To the commonwealthmen and the 'saints', those deaths were judicial murders, which mocked elementary principles and procedures of justice. Sidney, indignant at the conduct of the 'tribunals', found a parallel in the Old Testament murder of Naboth, and remarked that 'the men of Belial, false witnesses and corrupt judges', had been 'the pillar upon which' the 'monarchy' of that time had 'stood'. But Sidney did not despair, for he remembered that the 'pillars' had fallen when 'God raised up an avenger' to overthrow Naboth's persecutors.[71]

There were other atrocities (as the saints saw them) to endure. In January 1661 – on the twelfth anniversary of the regicide, and ten years after

67. Hutchinson, *Memoirs*, 229, 234. 68. French, iv. 425. 69. *MC* 160.

70. Samson dreads to be, in useless idleness, 'to visitants a gaze', even unto 'a contemptible old age obscure' (ll. 567, 572). Was there perhaps a similar fear in the Milton of the Restoration when, as John Aubrey tells us, he was 'visited much, more than he did desire', and when Samuel Parker 'incessantly' visited him (Darbishire, 6)?

71. Sidney, 'Court Maxims', pp. 37, 137, 194.

Milton's radical allies had got the Commonwealth to commemorate the second anniversary – the corpses of regicides who had already been buried, among them Milton's friend and hero John Bradshaw, were ripped up and exposed to public contempt on poles at Tyburn. Other commonwealthmen, who were spared in 1660, were soon afterwards imprisoned on suspicion of conspiracy, among them another friend and hero of Milton, Robert Overton, who as Ludlow records was 'barbarously treated'.[72] The prisoners experienced miserable conditions in their dungeons, where some died (among them Colonel Hutchinson, who had been arrested after his pardon) and others were broken in body or mind. God's chosen were afflicted in Restoration England as in *Samson Agonistes*, where the Lord

> Oft leav'st them to the hostile sword
> Of heathen and profane, their carcases
> To dogs and fowls a prey, or else captived:
> Or to the unjust tribunals, under change of times, ...
> . . . .
> If these they scape, perhaps in poverty
> With sickness and disease thou bow'st them down.
> (692–8)

Ludlow repeatedly describes the saints of the Restoration as 'prey' and their persecutors as 'birds' or 'beasts of prey'.[73] The three regicides who were executed in April 1662 proclaimed that their cause would survive 'when the fowls have eaten of our dead bodies'.[74]

Among the afflictions visited on the elect, notes the Chorus, is the 'condemnation of the ungrateful multitude' (696). Samson is 'sung and proverbed for a fool | In every street' (203–4). On the king's return, says Lucy Hutchinson, 'every ballad singer sang up and down the streets ribald rhymes made in reproach of the late Commonwealth and all those worthies that therein endeavoured the people's freedom and happiness'.[75] When the Cromwellian John Desborough was brought into captivity, he was jeered by boys who lined the streets chanting 'Fanatic! Fanatic!'[76] Samson suspects that his enemies, whose 'daily practice is to insult me more', 'come to stare' at his 'affliction' and 'to insult' (112–14). In 1660, Lucy Hutchinson tells us,

72. Ludlow, 'Voyce', p. 962.
73. Ludlow, *Voyce*, 124, 151, 195; Ludlow, 'Voyce', pp. 1052, 1063, 1082, 1192, 1197.
74. *Speeches, Discourses and Prayers*, 41.
75. Hutchinson, *Memoirs*, 227.
76. Richard L. Greaves, *Deliver us from Evil: The Radical Underground in Britain, 1660–1663* (New York, 1986), 30.

Colonel George Monck, who had been the architect of the Restoration, came gloatingly with his wife to Lambeth House, where the regicides were being held, and 'caused them to be brought down, only to stare at them; which was such a barbarism for that man who had betrayed so many poor men to death and misery ... to glut his bloody eyes with beholding them in their bondage, as no story can parallel the inhumanity'.[77] Samson has to endure his 'foes' derision' (366). Soon after 1660 there would become fashionable not only 'the jeering of godliness and good men, but the histrionical acting of the zeal and affection' of Puritan ministers 'by way of mockery and derision upon stageplays'. The regicides who were condemned in April 1662, fearing to 'die like fools', had to suffer at their executions the taunts of a lord and a courtier 'by way of derision'.[78] Milton was derided too. Pamphlets rejoiced in the overthrow of a writer whose boasts of Puritan triumph, and whose violent and contemptuous diatribes against defeated royalism, had been noised across Europe. His blindness was described as a punishment for writing his vindications of the regicide.[79] The imputation was not new to him, but only now did he encounter it in defeat and degradation. The enemies of the blind Samson say 'How well | Are come upon him his deserts' (204–5).

The regicides whose fates were mocked 'by way of derision' – John Barkstead, Miles Corbet, and John Okey – had fled to the Continent in 1660. They owed their deaths to the subtle and ruthless coup of George Downing, Okey's former chaplain. Downing, who had been Cromwell's agent in Holland in the 1650s and was Charles II's in the 1660s, lured the exiles to Delft, kidnapped them, and sent them back to England.[80] By cunning and bullying he secured the complicity of the Dutch government, which had traditionally sheltered political exiles but which in 1652–4 had fought a bitter war with Puritan England. The saints in England would never forgive the Dutch for the coup. The arguments used by Downing to the Dutch were those addressed to Dalila, Samson's betrayer, by the Philistines, who, she reports,

> came in person,
> Solicited, committed, threatened, urged,
> Adjured by all the bonds of civil duty
> And of religion, pressed how just it was,

77. Hutchinson, *Memoirs*, 232.
78. *Speeches, Discourses and Prayers*, 6, 10, 24.
79. Parker, 568–9, 571.
80. Catterall, 'Sir George Downing'.

How honourable, how glorious to entrap
A common enemy, who had destroyed
Such numbers of our nation.

(851–7)

Samson tells Dalila that 'If aught against my life | Thy country sought of thee, it sought unjustly, | Against the law of nature, law of nations' (888–90): Ludlow records that the regicides were seized in Holland contrary to all 'laws ... of nature or nations'.[81]

Ludlow writes of the 'lust and rage' with which the Cavaliers pursued their 'prey' among the saints and regicides; Vane tells of the 'rage and indignation of the world and the powers of it' against the victims of the restored regime's victims; Sidney, with violent indignation, speaks of the 'lust and rage' of Charles II against men 'who had been the most worthy and successful instruments in our deliverance'.[82] If, in *The Readie and Easie Way*, Milton had noticed 'how open and unbounded' was 'the insolence and rage' of the royalists, in *Samson Agonistes* the Chorus tells how 'violent men' who 'support | Tyrannic power' are 'raging to pursue | The righteous and all such as honour truth' (1273–6). Happily, God will avenge his people in England as he did in Israel. Samson's triumph brings down Dagon's temple 'Upon the heads' of the Philistines (1589, 1652): Vane's chaplain predicts that the 'mischief' of the royalists 'shall return upon their own heads', Ludlow that God 'will certainly ... bring down vengeance upon their heads'.[83] Ludlow and Vane subscribed to a commonplace among the martyrs of the 1660s, that 'the blood of the saints ... cries out for vengeance'. God, claimed Vane, 'hath the weapons of vengeance in readiness'.[84] Those weapons would be deployed, the saints knew, when the royalists, by glorying in their wickedness and in blood, had 'filled up the measure of their iniquity'.[85] Sidney says that the royalists are 'ripening themselves for destruction'; Ludlow that God's anger will culminate in the 'destruction of his enemies';[86] Milton's Semichorus, that the Philistines 'Unweetingly importuned | Their own destruction' (1680–1). Like the Philistines, the royalists are so foolish as to 'resist' God's 'uncontrollable intent' (1753–4).

81. Ludlow, *Voyce*, 297–8. Here as elsewhere Ludlow reproduces words from the martyrological literature published in England during 1660–2 and sent to him in exile.
82. Ibid. 150; Vane, *Two Treatises*, 2; Sidney, 'Court Maxims', p. 203.
83. Sykes, *Life and Death*, 138; Ludlow, *Voyce*, 208; cf. Ps. 7: 16.
84. Vane, *Two Treatises*, 2.
85. Ludlow, 'Voyce', pp. 1079, 1136; Sidney, 'Court Maxims', pp. 78, 195, 200.
86. Sidney, 'Court Maxims', p. 78; Ludlow, *Voyce*, 127.

For the saints knew that God, who for his own purposes may sometimes prosper the wicked, does so only for a season. Samson is confident that Dagon will be humiliated 'ere long' (468), an assertion which Manoa welcomes as a 'prophecy', 'for God, | Nothing more certain, will not long defer | To vindicate the glory of his name' (473–5). Thus too is Vane's chaplain sure that God will overthrow the Cavaliers 'ere long'; thus does Sidney proclaim that God 'will not long delay his appointed vengeance'; thus does Ludlow await the approaching hour when God will act 'for the vindicating of his honour.'[87] In that expectation Ludlow records the 'continued prodigies'[88] – divine portents – that the saints eagerly detected in the 1660s and interpreted as evidence of God's wrath upon their enemies. He is particularly struck by a prodigy which ruined the dinner held in Westminster Hall on the evening of the restored king's coronation, that 'superstitious ceremony', as Ludlow calls it, of 'anointing their idol'.[89] Ludlow was always repelled by the 'feasting and carousing' of Charles II's court.[90] In *Samson Agonistes* the Philistines, on the day of their destruction, 'their hearts' filled 'with mirth, high cheer, and wine', 'turned' to their 'sports' (1613–14). Amid the cavortings of Charles's dinner the courtiers, as Ludlow informs us, indulge a taste for entertainment by 'riders': 'riders' perform for Milton's Philistines too (1324). The courtiers have their own Harapha. 'The champion Mr. Dimmock', Ludlow reports, 'armed *de cap à pied*, enters on horseback, challenging to fight with any person who should deny Charles Stuart to be lawful king of England.' The sequel also supplies its parallels to Milton's poem. For in Restoration England as in Gaza, God finds ways to make his purposes apparent, at least to those willing to comprehend them. In *Samson Agonistes* the 'deliverance' of the Israelites is accomplished when the roof falls on the Philistines' head 'with burst of thunder' (1651). Charles's dinner, records Ludlow,

> was not half ended, before the mock king was enforced to rise and run away to Whitehall, by reason of the unheard-of thunder, lightning, and rain; which though his own flatterers profanely applied to the greatening of their solemnity, as if heaven itself expressed its joy thereat by the discharge of their cannon, yet others, more understanding in the dispensations of the

87. Sykes, *Life and Death*, 109; Sidney, 'Court Maxims', p. 195; Ludlow, *Voyce*, 115.
88. Ludlow, *Voyce*, 10, 294.
89. The episode is related in *Voyce*, 286–7; see also p. 294 and Ludlow, 'Voyce', pp. 1237, 1260–1, 1387.
90. Ludlow, 'Voyce', p. 1271.

> Lord, supposed it rather a testimony from heaven against the wickedness of those that would not only that he should rule over them, but were willing to make them a captain to lead them into Egyptian bondage; from which the Lord by his providence plainly spake his desire to have delivered them.[91]

★★

Samson's 'dreadful' and 'dearly-bought revenge' (1591, 1660)[92] appeases God's 'wrath' towards the Philistines (1683) and his 'ire' towards Samson (520). Yet God's followers could not hope to reach the 'understanding' of God's 'dispensations' which Ludlow urges merely by examining his punishment of his enemies. They need to grasp the benevolence of his intentions towards his afflicted ones. That benevolence can be hard to trust in, as Samson finds. In *Paradise Lost* Milton sought to 'assert eternal providence, | And justify the ways of God to men'. There he wanted to refute the Calvinist dogma which turns the Fall into an act of divine tyranny, and to demonstrate the justice and wonder of God's scheme of salvation. In *Samson Agonistes*, too, Milton insists that 'Just are the ways of God, | And justifiable to men' (293–4). This time he seeks to demonstrate the benevolence of providence amid the sufferings of his servants in Restoration England.

Milton addresses those 'who doubt his ways not just' (300). Samson doubts, or is on the edge of doubting. He struggles not to 'call in doubt | Divine prediction' (43–4), or to 'quarrel with the will | Of highest dispensation, which herein | Haply had ends above my reach to know' (60–2). Yet the 'hornets' of Samson's 'restless thoughts' 'rush upon' him (19–21). 'Why' and 'wherefore', he asks, did God select him for 'great exploits', for the deliverance of his nation, only to cast him into deepest humiliation and despair (23, 30–2, 85)? Samson's 'sense of heaven's desertion' (632) leaves him outside 'the list of them that hope' (647). It is, in Puritan terms, a terrible statement. To despair of God's providence is to betray the faith which alone can save us. 'To murmur against God's verdict, and resist his doom', Vane reminded himself as he surveyed the cataclysm of the Restoration, 'is to become adversaries to God, and to betray our country.'[93] Yet in one respect, at least, Samson has grasped more than his

91. Ludlow, *Voyce*, 286–7; cf. p. 194, and Ludlow, 'Voyce', pp. 1237, 1260–1, 1387.
92. Cf. l. 1702.
93. *Tryal of Sir Henry Vane*, 119; cf. Worden, 'Providence and Politics', 79.

advisers. The Chorus, and Manoa, think that Samson's punishment exceeds the crime (368–72, 691), but Samson warns his father to 'Appoint not heavenly disposition', for 'Nothing of all these evils hath befallen me | But justly; I myself have brought them on, | Sole author I, sole cause' (372–5).[94] In the disintegration of the Puritan cause, as the saints accepted, 'the Lord had blasted them and spat in their faces'.[95] The defeated godly, Vane among them, recognized that God had punished them 'justly'.[96] Samson traces his trespass, and his subsequent failure to deliver his people, to his 'impotence of mind, in body strong' (52). He has failed because he lacks 'wisdom' or 'virtue' proportionate to his 'strength' (54, 173), the charge that Milton levelled against the English people in explaining their inability to seize the opportunities for liberty which the heroic victories of the civil war had given them.[97] Ludlow concurred: God 'put a prize into our hands, which had we wisdom we might have made a wonderful improvement of'.[98]

England's saints, like the 'saints' of *Samson Agonistes* (1288), will be 'delivered'. The verb runs through the saintly literature of the Restoration as through Milton's poem. It had run through Milton's prose too. Milton had seen the Cromwellian army, the nation's 'deliverer' of 1648–9, betray itself and its cause. Earlier he had hymned its 'matchless deeds' in warfare and politics; he had looked to it to subdue the 'European kings'; and he had identified it, and its followers, with the people of England. In 1660 the army, caught up in, and largely responsible for, the nation's self-desertion, collapsed without a fight. Samson is 'himself an army' (346), 'matchless in might' (178), 'whose locks, | That of a nation armed the strength contained' (1493–4), and 'whose strength, while virtue was her mate, | Might have subdued the earth' (173–4). His hair, when grown again, is 'Garrisoned round about him like a camp | Of faithful soldiery' (1496–7). Yet he has been vanquished, not by the sword, but 'with a peal of words' (235).

Before deliverance can come, the saints of the Restoration must come to terms with their past and with their failures and, like Samson, 'Repent the sin' (504).[99] Milton had long questioned the 'fitness' of the English people for godly reformation, and had long judged them 'fitter to be led back into

94. Cf. l. 1171.
95. C. H. Firth, ed., *The Clarke Papers*, 4 vols. (Camden Society, 1893–1901), iv. 220.
96. *Tryal of Sir Henry Vane*, 120; *Speeches, Discourses and Prayers*, 68, 84.
97. Below, pp. 395–6.
98. Ludlow, *Voyce*, 307; cf. p. 248.
99. *Tryal of Sir Henry Vane*, 119–20; *Speeches, Prayers and Discourses*, p. 68.

their own servitude'.[100] Ludlow, too, judged that the nation 'seemed not to be fitted for that glorious work'.[101] Yet he, unlike Samson, is 'in the list of them that hope' (647). For, he writes, 'when God hath humbled a people and fitted them for himself', when he has 'purified' them in 'the furnace of affliction', 'making them willing to be abused for him, he will certainly lift them up and bring them to honour'.[102] Samson, lifted up, at the last restores 'honour' to Israel (1715). Ludlow knows what Milton's Chorus learns: 'Oft he seems to hide his face, | But unexpectedly returns' (1749–50). Like Milton, Ludlow finds, in the suffering of the saints from 1660, a regenerative purpose.

To prepare themselves, God's people will need one virtue above all: patience. Samson's blindness, thinks the Chorus, is likely to 'number' him with 'those | Whom patience finally must crown' (1295–6). For patience is

> more oft the exercise
> Of saints, the trial of their fortitude,
> Making them each his own deliverer,
> And victor over all
> That tyranny or fortune can inflict...
>
> (1287–91)

Ludlow repeatedly tells his kindred spirits that 'this is the day of the patience of the Lord and his saints'.[103] Vane's advice to God's people recalls the experience of Milton's Samson: they must be 'patiently waiting till God's time come wherein he will open the prison doors, either by death, or some other way'.[104] The duty of the saints to 'wait upon God', in a 'waiting posture', was well known to Puritans. To attune oneself, and submit one's faith, to God's timetable was an essential step in the believer's submission to his sovereignty. But it is in God's time, not man's, that the faithful must learn to act, as Samson does.[105] Ludlow, wondering how the saints could or should seek to bring down the restored regime, for his part asks the Lord to 'give us wisdom to know when to go forward and when to stand still'. Ludlow himself recommends a middle course, so that 'by making haste we may not strengthen the hand of the enemy, nor by standing still neglect the opportunity he puts into our hands, but that, being on our watch tower,

100. *CP* iii. 581; above, Ch. 10. 101. Ludlow, *Voyce*, 149.
102. Ibid. 11, 115; Ludlow, 'Voyce', p. 1082.
103. Ludlow, *Voyce*, 11–12; Ludlow, 'Voyce', p. 1019; see also *CP* xvii. 65–7.
104. Vane, *Two Treatises*, 98. 105. Worden, 'Providence and Politics', 64–6.

and living by faith, we may see our duty so plainly, that when the Lord's time is come we may' – like Samson at the last – 'up and be doing'.[106]

At some times the saints and commonwealthmen thought that the hour of 'deliverance' was 'very near', that it would come 'in a very little time', in 'but a little moment'. At others they acknowledged that it 'was not yet come', that God 'seems to permit the scales to continue', that 'the Lord's people seem as yet unworthy' of deliverance, and that consequently 'there is more of the bitter cup' of divine punishment left 'behind for his people to drink of'.[107] Yet was such speculation about the divine timetable legitimate? One 'sin' of the godly during the civil wars had been to presume too much upon providence, to pry into its secrets, into 'ends' which, in the poem, belong to the 'unsearchable dispose | Of highest wisdom' (1745–6), and which it may be 'above' Samson's 'reach to know' (62). The dénouement of *Samson Agonistes* confounds every human calculation that has been made in the poem, and exposes man's 'ever-failing trust | In mortal strength' (348–9). The retribution that awaited the godly if they trusted to an 'arm of flesh', to man's means rather than God's, was a perpetual theme of Roundhead writing and preaching. To demonstrate his sovereignty, and to contrast his might with the helplessness of unaided humanity, the Puritan God liked to confound the odds of battle, so as to bring improbable victory or defeat out of its opposite. Thus during the Battle of Dunbar in 1650, when defeat stared Cromwell's army in the face, God did what he does in Milton's poem: he 'stepped out of heaven to raise those who were even as dead, and to judge his adversaries'.[108] Ludlow, writing about the fate of the regicides in England, remarked on the Lord's tendency 'to show his prerogative, and that he can when he pleaseth work by unlikely, yea contrary means'.[109] One method by which God emphasized his sovereignty, in Puritan minds as in *Samson Agonistes*, is by the suddenness and unexpectedness of his mercies, which mocked the plans and predictions of men. Cromwell remarked that God's dispensations are best 'when they have not been forecast, but sudden providences'.[110] After the Restoration Vane thought that the 'revival' of God's seemingly sunken cause would be 'sudden'.[111]

106. Ludlow, *Voyce*, 309–10.

107. e.g. ibid. 11; Ludlow, 'Voyce', pp. 1139, 1260. Samson 'bitterly hast... paid, and still art paying' (l. 432).

108. Worden, 'Providence and Politics', 68–9.

109. Ludlow, *Voyce*, 295.

110. Abbott, ed., *Writings and Speeches*, iii. 591.

111. *Substance of what Sir Henry Vane Intended*, 5–6. Other parallels between the attributes of God's sovereignty in the poem and those portrayed by Puritans are described in my 'Milton,

Yet if God's people were not to trust to human means, they knew that, in the service of God's ends, they were duty-bound to make use of them. If God punishes human presumption, he can equally be provoked by human inaction or inertia in his cause.[112] What, then, would the godly of the Restoration contribute to their deliverance? There were those, Algernon Sidney among them, who argued for the right of armed resistance to tyranny, a principle which Milton had espoused in *The Tenure of Kings and Magistrates*. On the same side was the Puritan minister Nicholas Lockyer, who – alluding to the Samson story – claimed that 'there wants but the jawbone of an ass' to overthrow the Restoration monarchy.[113] Yet the main thrust of saintly literature after 1660 warns God's chosen not to 'resist' or use unlawful 'means' of conspiracy or rebellion.[114] Vane, and Ludlow in his more resigned moods, believe what Samson in his despair has concluded: that his own role as divine instrument is passed; that 'the strife | With me hath end'; that God will now fight Dagon not through human intermediaries but directly (460–7). Vane decides that God has resolved 'to take the business into his own hands, and to put forth the power of his wrath by heavenly instruments, forasmuch as earthly ones' – those of the Puritan Revolution – 'have proved ineffectual'. So we must 'depend upon God for the avenging of his people, even when all human ability to perform it is vanished'. Vane tells the saints that, having failed in the world, they should be 'retiring into the life of your head and root, the life that is hid with Christ in God'.[115] For Ludlow, too, 'the weapons which the Lord hath appointed for the destruction of Antichrist' are now 'not carnal but spiritual'.[116] It was a perspective that infuriated Algernon Sidney, who, because of it, was unable to persuade Ludlow to lead a conspiracy to overthrow the restored monarchy.

Samson is proved wrong. God turns to his chosen instrument once more, for the act that will give meaning to his life. Samson does not act on the basis of human argument, or calculation, about the right or the wisdom of resistance (though traces of Milton's earlier commitment to

Samson Agonistes, and the Restoration', in Gerald MacLean, ed., *Culture and Society in the Stuart Restoration* (Cambridge, 1995), 129–30.

112. Worden, 'Providence and Politics', 70–1.
113. Ludlow, 'Voyce', p. 1079 (cf. *CP* i. 859).
114. e.g. Ludlow, *Voyce*, 79; Ludlow, 'Voyce', pp. 1049, 1211; Sykes, *Life and Death*, 117; Vane, *Two Treatises*, 3, 92; Tibbutt, 'Colonel John Okey', 160–1.
115. Vane, *Two Treatises*, 2–3; and see Sykes, *Life and Death*, 121–2.
116. Ludlow, 'Voyce', p. 1248.

that principle can be found in the poem).[117] His deeds are prompted by the 'intimate impulse' which signals that 'what I motioned was of God' (222–3); by 'Divine impulsion prompting' (422); by the 'rousing motions in me' (1382) through which he is 'persuaded inwardly that this was from God' ('Argument', [72–3]). For Ludlow, divine promptings superseded or suspended other laws of political conduct. Though he questioned the decision of his fellow regicide Thomas Harrison to give himself up as a sacrifice in 1660, he suspended judgement on the ground that Harrison had been moved 'by a more than ordinary impulse of spirit'.[118] Ludlow's opposition to violence that was committed contrary to law could be undermined by the same principle. During his exile he was torn on hearing that a Frenchman, without premeditation, had run his sword through a 'Romish priest' in Paris while the priest was celebrating Mass. On the one hand Ludlow was troubled by the illegality of the act and, by ordinary standards, its sinfulness. On the other he was impressed by the assassin's testimony that he had acted as 'moved in his spirit' to 'bear that witness against the idolatry'. Even under the terrors of execution, noticed Ludlow, the murderer 'continued fixed in his testimony, rejoicing that the Lord had honoured him to die as a martyr for his cause'. So 'I dare not judge the person, not knowing the extraordinary call he had' from heaven.[119]

★★

In *Defensio Secunda* Milton compared his life's destiny to that of the blind heroes of antiquity.[120] In *Paradise Lost* he aligned himself with 'Blind Thamyris, and blind Maeonides, | And Tiresias and Phineus prophets old' (III. 35–6). If Samson stands for God's people in Israel and England, there must also be, in the blind hero, something of the blind poet. Milton's 'light is spent': in Samson's 'total eclipse', 'Light the prime work of God', which 'so necessary is to life, | And almost life itself', 'is extinct' (70, 81, 90–1). Perhaps the parallel goes further. Milton, like Samson, knew himself 'Designed for great exploits' (32). He, like Samson, 'grew up' 'Abstemious' (637) in preparation for 'The work to which I was divinely called' (226). In 1642 he acknowledged, as Samson does, a divine impulse – an 'inward

117. Worden, 'Milton, *Samson Agonistes* and the Restoration', 131–4.
118. Ludlow, *Voyce*, 126.
119. Ludlow, 'Voyce', pp. 1248–9.
120. *CW* viii. 65.

prompting'[121] – to serve God and country. Yet in 1660 God's servants were humbled. We could not imagine Milton castigating himself for the failings and failures of his fellow subscribers to the good old cause. But may it not have struck him that in his own support for the great apostate Oliver Cromwell he, like Samson, had been 'ensnared' (365)? May not his service of the protectorate, that 'scandalous night of interruption', have come at some level of his mind to seem what Samson's 'former servitude', when he 'saw not how degenerately I served', had been: 'ignoble, | Unmanly, ignominious, infamous, | True slavery' (416–19)?

Even if we reject that interpretation – and even if the inconsistencies of his political career were as hidden from him as they are from the surface of his prose – there is another question. Did Milton, amid the collapse of the cause to which he had devoted the central decades of his adulthood, become, as Samson does, 'As one past hope' (120)? Can he, amid the peril and the mockery to which he was now subjected, have been immune to the feelings that hit the saints and commonwealthmen around him: to what for Samson is a 'sense of heaven's desertion'; to the fear that God's servants have now been 'cast ... off as never known' by a deity who

to those cruel enemies,
Whom I by his appointment had provoked,
Left me all helpless with the irreparable loss
Of sight, reserved alike to be repeated
The subject of their cruelty, or scorn?

(641–6)

When Milton had considered how his light was spent, he was tempted to 'murmur' against providence. 'Patience' had quelled that incipient protest – but for how long? In the sonnet 'To Mr Cyriack Skinner upon his Blindness', perhaps written in late 1655,[122] he reflected again on the providence that had afflicted him. In that poem he could 'argue not | Against heaven's hand or will', because his 'conscience' assured him that he had become blind through writing 'in liberty's defence, my noble task'. Yet in 1660 that writing was derided and burned. 'All is best', concludes the Chorus, 'though we oft doubt, | What the unsearchable dispose | Of highest wisdom brings about' (1745–8). What might Milton have been through before he could give voice to that conviction?

121. *CP* i. 810. 122. *MC* 162.

Samson's wait to serve God has its correspondence in Milton's literary life. In the poet's 'late spring no bud or blossom showeth', and 'inward ripeness doth much less appear'.[123] And yet, 'Beginning late',[124] he writes *Paradise Lost* and justifies the ways of God to men. If he really composes its central section amid the national catastrophe and personal danger and affliction of 1660, then the achievement, like Samson's, is one to defy human calculation. Samson's locks have grown again. Like his hero, Milton proves not to be 'useless':

And which is best and happiest yet, all this
With God not parted from him, as was feared,
But favouring and assisting to the end.

(1718–20)

123. Sonnet VII. 124. *Paradise Lost* IX. 26.

16

Milton and the Fall of England

Milton died, aged almost 66, in 1674, four years before Marvell and Nedham. His concern with public life, and his will to influence it, persisted to the end, even though only once after the Restoration did he comment explicitly on current events. This was in his tract *Of True Religion*, written in the spring of 1673. It brought him into alliance of a sort with Marvell, whose first prose work, *The Rehearsal Transpros'd*, had provoked a storm on its publication in the previous autumn. Both tracts were prompted by Charles II's assertion of a prerogative power to dispense Puritans and Catholics alike from the statutes that proscribed them. Marvell's work argued for the toleration of Puritans, Milton's against the toleration of Catholics. Milton does defend the persecuted Puritans, but prudently hides his commitment to the principle, which after 1660 was the most extreme of positions, of the separation of Church from state (or tries to hide it, for the tract encountered sceptical scrutiny on that front).[1] There is a basic difference in the approaches of Marvell and Milton to religious liberty. Marvell, whose hatred of 'persecuting men for their consciences'[2] arose from respect for human decency, was ready to accept boundaries to religious liberty in decency's cause. Milton knew religious liberty to be the prerequisite of God's truth and could brook no limits to it. The distinction was largely concealed in their publications of 1672–3.

Their political pasts were concealed too. Milton's tract, which is aimed to persuade unrevolutionary opinion of the dangers of popery, understandably says nothing of the civil wars. Marvell's recalls them. He regrets, not the parliamentarians' cause, but their readiness to go to war for it: 'upon

1. *CP* viii. 413; Martin Dzelzainis, 'Milton's *Of True Religion* and the Earl of Castlemaine', *The Seventeenth Century*, 7 (1992), 53–69.
2. *PWAM* i. 60.

considering all, I think the cause was too good to have been fought for. Men ought to have trusted God; they ought to have trusted the king with that whole matter.'[3] It is a qualified disavowal, perhaps cleverly so. The Roundheads, it appears, did not sin when they took arms against their king in 1642. They merely made what, on balance, he now judges to have been a mistake. If so, it was surely an intelligible one, for no king has inspired less 'trust', even among his own followers, than Charles I. Marvell's argument contrives to dissociate the principle of liberty of conscience – and, in a subtle passage of autobiographical whitewashing, his own spokesmanship for it[4] – from the memory of rebellion. He, of course, had been no rebel. He had played no part in the politics of the 1640s, save as a young writer in the royalist cause near their end. Milton, the champion of regicide whose life had been in hazard in 1660, bore a blackened past. He had never lacked courage in the promulgation of contentious opinions, as his role in facilitating the printing of *The Racovian Catechism* and his publication of *The Readie and Easie Way* remind us. But courage, in his as in most seventeenth-century minds, required to be guided by prudence.

If Milton had to tread carefully on religious subjects, he needed likewise to be wary of making explicit observations on political ones. Under Cromwell, however, he had learned the uses of oblique political commentary. He had commented obliquely again – albeit in a work that transcended that impulse – in *Samson Agonistes*. He did so for the last time in the final months of his life. He then published, anonymously, a translation, which makes austere reading, of an official Latin declaration announcing the election of a new King of Poland, Jan Sobieski. It was published as *A Declaration, or Letters Patent of the Election of this Present King of Poland John the Third.* Conceivably he did the translation for the sake of a fee. Yet even if he did, his choice of that particular work – or the selection of him for it – should rouse our curiosity, as should the fact that his responsibility for it became known. The sole intelligible explanation of the publication is as a response to the emergence in 1673 of decisive evidence of the conversion of the heir to the throne, James Duke of York, to Catholicism, and to his marriage in the same year to the Catholic Mary of Modena, an alliance that promised a further succession of Catholic heirs.[5] The printing of the translation can

3. Ibid. 192. 4. Ibid. 288.

5. Von Maltzahn, 'Whig Milton', 231; Martin Dzelzainis, 'Milton's *A Declaration, or Lellers Patent* (1674) and the Problem of the Succession', forthcoming.

only have been intended to promote the discussion of elective as opposed to hereditary monarchy. That was, within the context of Restoration politics, a radical initiative, particularly from a man with Milton's past. A few years later the elective principle would be taken up by the more extreme Whigs of the exclusion crisis. In 1660, in his despair at the prospect of the Stuarts' return, Milton had swallowed his revulsion against single rule and had suggested the election of a single ruler from within the Roundhead cause. Now, in what may have been the last thing he wrote, he reverted to that principle to help withstand James's succession. His point was conveyed under a cover as ingeniously protective as the one which, if its purpose has been interpreted aright, had shielded *The Cabinet-Council* fifteen years earlier.[6]

A high proportion of Milton's writings were published in his late years. It is usual, and perhaps right, to think of their preparation for the press as the gathering of his literary legacy. Yet if he had an eye to posterity, he wrote to instruct his own time too. His late publications are a formidable accumulation, in verse and prose, of material for the guidance and education of the nation. *Paradise Lost* appeared in 1667, *Paradise Regained* and *Samson Agonistes* in a single volume in 1670 or 1671. A new edition of his shorter poems appeared in 1673. It contained, as an appendix, a reprint of his tract of 1644 *Of Education*, that blueprint for the ethical reconstruction of England. Here we shall concentrate on another late publication. This is his *History of Britain, That Part especially now called England... Collected out of the Ancientest and Best Authors thereof*, which was in print by the end of 1670. In December, when the *History* and the volume containing *Paradise Regained* and *Samson Agonistes* were announced or pre-announced together, one reader wrote that 'Milton is abroad again, in prose and in verse'. It was the same reader who, after reading the *History*, remarked that 'we needed all... his sharp checks and sour instructions. For we must be a lost people if we are not speedily reclaimed.'[7] Much has been speculated – though nothing can be known – about the motives and circumstances that brought *Paradise Regained* and *Samson Agonistes* into print together. Less has been said about the appearance of the *History*.

6. Above, pp. 323–5. Oblique methods of political commentary by the post-Restoration Milton are also detected by Wyman H. Herendeen, 'Milton's *Accedence Commenc'd Grammar* and the Deconstruction of Grammatical Tyranny', in P. G. Stanwood, ed., *Of Poetry and Politics: New Essays on Milton and his World* (Binghampton, NY, 1995), 295–312.

7. Above, p. 8.

The book was ambitiously conceived. It was meant to proceed, 'in one unbroken thread', from remote antiquity 'to our own times'.[8] The absence of a general history of the nation was widely felt. In the event Milton only reached 1066, in a book of about 80,000 words. What he did write was largely derivative. Though he disparaged the medieval chronicles that were his main sources, he was essentially dependent on them for his narrative. According to Anthony Wood, the *History*, 'when it first came abroad, had only the reputation of the putting of our old authors together in a connexed story'.[9] Yet if the book did not meet the scholarly requirements of the antiquary Wood, its teaching found a large enough audience. There were fresh editions in 1677 and 1695 before the work was included in the collected edition of Milton's works in 1698.[10]

Milton had worked on the *History* at least since the late 1640s. To give dates to the process of its composition is only partially possible, and what we can learn is to be discovered only by a complex process of assessment which will be best set out separately (in Appendix C). Some inferences are, I hope, uncontroversial. By 1649 he had written the heart of the narrative up to a stage near the end of Book IV, the point at which Bede's *Ecclesiastical History* gives out as a source. He resumed work in the mid- or later 1650s, and perhaps continued to write at intervals during the composition of his great late poems. At some point, perhaps shortly before publication, he finished the book. This is where our difficulties begin. Until that point he seems to have written the *History* as a 'private study', without thought of publication or anyway of immediate publication. To my mind the evidence suggests that the work now acquired, through the introduction of passages of didactic commentary, its purpose, or a more immediate purpose, of public instruction. It was, I think, also at this time that Milton wrote the 'Digression' from the *History*, the passage of the work that is of most direct interest to students of his political thinking, for it contains what have been aptly called his 'frankest reflections' on the civil wars.[11] But the dating of the 'Digression', and of the openly didactic passages of the main text of the *History*, is controversial and inevitably unsure ground. Even if the evidence

8. *CW* viii. 137. 9. Darbishire, 46.

10. It was also considered useful enough to be included in John Hughes's composite *A Complete History of England* in 1706.

11. Austin Woolrych, 'The Date of the Digression in Milton's *History of Britain*', in Richard Ollard and Pamela Tudor-Craig, eds., *For Veronica Wedgwood These: Studies in Seventeenth-Century History* (London, 1986), 217.

permitted certainty about the dating, we could not be confident that either the 'Digression' or those passages of the main text did not replace an earlier version on which it might have drawn. What we can say is that, shortly before its publication, Milton worked on the *History* with its prospective audience in mind, and that what he published or intended to publish in 1670 was the text from which, a decade after the Restoration, he wanted the nation to learn.[12]

★★

Why did he keep returning to the *History*? Not for literary pleasure. It 'is a penance to think', he reflects at one point, 'what labour is to be endured' if his task is to be completed, and what 'unpleasing labour' lies ahead in the 'turning over' of those 'volumes of rubbish', the barren or credulous or self-serving compilations of monks. Yet 'this travail, rather than not know at once what may be known of our ancient story, sifted from fables and impertinences, I voluntarily undergo' (230). The extent of his self-affliction measures the importance of the project to him. Only if we think of his prose as a diversion from his poetry does his immersion in history perplex us. He thought of himself, and represented himself, at least as much as a man of learning as a poet. Contemporaries described him in the same terms. Serious poets were expected to be learned and to be versatile in their learning. Often they were historians. In moving between poetry and history, Milton followed where Thomas More and Walter Ralegh and Samuel Daniel and countless more had been before him. To him as to them, history and poetry were alternative and complementary methods of instruction.[13]

Over the course of the seventeenth century the differences between the two genres were increasingly recognized. In the 1640s Milton came to

12. Gary D. Hamilton, 'The *History of Britain* and its Restoration Audience', in Loewenstein and Turner, eds., *Politics, Poetics, and Hermeneutics*, 241–55, senses that the work was revised in Milton's later life. David Norbrook, 'Republican Occasions in *Paradise Regained* and *Samson Agonistes*', *Milton Studies*, 42 (2002), 123–4, and *idem, Writing the English Republic*, 438–9, also draws attention to the Restoration context of the publication. In an essay of 1991, 'Milton's Republicanism and the Tyranny of Heaven', I took a different, and I now think mistaken, view of Milton's thinking in his later years (though I am a little surprised to learn from Norbrook's *Writing the English Republic*, 433, that the article embodies the mentality of 'the Cold War period'). But the question I tried to answer, why it is that Satan's political language so exactly and persistently rehearses Milton's own, persists. Christ's rejection of classical political virtue (or anyway of aspects of it) in *Paradise Regained* also remains a problem.

13. Blair Worden, 'Historians and Poets', in Kewes, ed., *Uses of History*, 71–93.

recognize them himself. When, in his youth, he had aspired to write of 'kings and queens and heroes old', he did not worry whether his poetic tales would be factually true.[14] Subsequently he developed doubts about the legitimacy of a historical epic based on legend. Yet it was only in working on the *History* in the late or later 1640s that he acquired what has been called a 'critical animus' against historical invention,[15] and a determination to sift truth from fable, from deeds 'more renowned in songs and romances than in true stories' (156). Now he saw, in the legends of the Trojan foundation of Britain and of Arthurian chivalry, abettors of 'the fond zeal of praising... nations above truth' (134). In the years following the execution of the king, it is true, he would find fresh opportunities to exercise his powers of praise and idealization. In the eloquence of his 'defences' of 1651–5 his prose regained its poetic aspirations and character.[16] What persisted was his separation of truth from heroic or chivalric legend. He would discover the fullness of his poetic powers only when he had found, in the subject of *Paradise Lost*, the scope for a new kind of 'heroic song', which treated not of martial exploits 'hitherto... | Heroic deemed', not of the 'battles feigned' and chivalric furniture of 'fabled knights' or of 'the wrath/Of stern Achilles', but of 'the better fortitude | Of patience and heroic martyrdom'.[17] The writing of the *History of Britain* has an essential place in that transition.

For Milton as for Nedham, history teaches by examples. Nedham's editorials illustrate general principles by a range of historical illustration. 'Shall we never grow old enough', asks Milton in 1660 as he watches the nation fatally ignoring the lessons of history, 'to be wise to make seasonable use of gravest authorities, experiences, examples?'[18] He published the *History* for 'the good of the British nation' and to 'instruct and benefit' his readers (4). In 1642 he had looked to other literary forms for national instruction: to poetry, whose task is 'to imbreed and cherish in a great people the seeds of virtue and public civility'; to drama, which is to be 'doctrinal and exemplary to a nation'; and to public performances of oratory, for 'instructing and bettering the nation'. It was a poet's task, he then explained, both 'to sing... the deeds and triumphs of just and pious nations doing valiantly through faith against enemies of Christ', and to 'deplore' their 'general relapses'.[19] At that stage he saw poetry and history as allied forms, which

14. Von Maltzahn, *Milton's 'History of Britain'*, 60–1. 15. Ibid. 106.
16. *CP* iv. 687 n., 747 n.; Lewalski, 307–8. 17. *Paradise Lost* IX. 13–41.
18. *CP* vii. 448. 19. Ibid. i. 814–19.

had the overlapping literary methods that they shared too with oratory, with eloquence, with rhetoric.[20] 'History, skilfully related', observed the early Milton, 'now calms and soothes the restless and troubled mind, now fills it with delight';[21] poetry properly works to 'allay the perturbations of the mind', and 'teaches over the whole book of sanctity and virtue', with 'such delight';[22] eloquence instils virtue through 'true and constant delight'.[23] By the late 1640s, however, he had prised history apart from poetry and from eloquence. Previously he had viewed 'grave orators and historians' together, and had proposed an educational course of 'choice histories, heroic poems ... with all the most famous political orations'.[24] Yet by 1657 he was ready to observe that 'the functions of rhetorician and historian are different', and to call for the writing of history in 'plain and temperate' rather than 'ornate language; I ask for a historian, not an orator'.[25]

His growing alertness to the differences between history and other forms of literary persuasion did not demote its stature in his mind. The climax of the revolution in 1648–9 found him immersed in history, while his gifts of verse, and even perhaps his taste for it, were almost in abeyance.[26] Of course, they would amply return. We could hardly imagine two more contrasting methods of literary instruction than the poetry and the history that he published in 1667–71. In *Paradise Lost*, to reach 'the height of this great argument', 'my adventurous song | ... with no middle flight intends to soar | Above the Aonian mount' (I. 13–24). The *History* is no song. There is no difficulty in agreeing with Edward Phillips, when he sets the writing of *Paradise Lost* beside the composition of the *History*, that the 'height' of Milton's 'noble fancy and invention' was 'mainly employed' in the epic.[27] It seems unlikely that Milton the historian was visited 'nightly' by his muse, as the writer of *Paradise Lost* was, in his 'slumbe[r]' (IX. 22–3). Milton's model for the *History* is Sallust, whose theme of corruption, and whose economy of style, he imitates. But whereas Sallust's interpretative drive brings tension to every sentence of his story, Milton's sentences rarely acquire life except when he stands back from his narrative to remark on its lessons. Yet he persists, over the decades, in his joyless task. The autobiographical passage of *Defensio Secunda* speaks proudly of the *History*. We have no warrant to suppose that he was less conscious of the instructive

20. Ibid. 243–4, 899; cf. pp. 240, 268, 288–9. 21. Ibid. 244.
22. Ibid. 816–17; cf. *Samson Agonistes*, prologue, ll. 4–15. 23. *CP* i. 746.
24. Ibid. 889; ii. 400–1. 25. Ibid. vii. 501, 506. 26. Above, p. 50.
27. Darbishire, 72.

import of the *History* than of *Paradise Lost*; or that when, 'imploring divine assistance, that it may redound to [God's] glory, ... I now begin' the *History*, he is less in earnest than in embarking on the epic.

Like the hero of *Samson Agonistes*, to whom his 'country is a name so dear',[28] Milton asks how he can 'serve | My nation'. If the writing of that poem is itself one answer, the publication of the *History* is another. The *History* is a study of the national character. We may be surprised by the hold of his 'country' or 'nation' on Milton's mind and loyalties. He was, after all, the most cosmopolitan of figures, a man of commanding international connections and outlook. He could weary of England's northern and Gothic traits, which impeded the wit and eloquence that had flourished in the lands of classical antiquity. He wished his compatriots to look abroad for political instruction, and bemoaned their insularity when they did not. He heaped disapproval on their ethical and religious shortcomings. His ecclesiastrical principles seem to have had nothing to do with nationhood. Insisting that the Church 'is universal' and 'not tied to nation',[29] he spoke for an ideal of spiritual purity that knew no territorial frontiers. His political outlook was international too. In the 1650s he saw his writings as a means to restore liberty, not merely to England, but 'to every nation'.[30] Amid the degeneracy of the Restoration, he consoled himself with the reflection that a man's '*patria* is wherever it is well with him'.[31] Besides, his ever-larger awareness of the contrast between the virtuous few and the degenerate many seems hard to reconcile with his hopes for corporate or communal well-being of any kind. Yet his love of and concern for 'my country' are ubiquitously expressed, even when his assessments of his native land are at their most pessimistic. With respect to his own writings he remarks that 'there ought no regard be sooner than to God's glory by the honour and instruction of my country'.[32] Alongside obligation lies a proper pride, for 'who considers not the honourable achievements of his country as his own?'[33] For all his criticisms of his countrymen, he takes exception to the 'undervaluing and vilifying of the whole nation' by others.[34] He comes to England's defence when the ignorance or degeneracy of earlier historians has belittled it: when its 'noble achievements' have been 'made small', or when its 'honour' has been affronted by the passing over of a military triumph of that 'great and warlike nation'.[35]

28. l. 895. 29. *CP* vii. 292. 30. *CW* viii. 15. 31. *CP* viii. 4.
32. Ibid. i. 810. 33. *CW* viii. 7. 34. *CP* ii. 535. 35. Ibid. i. 616, 812; v. 267.

Since the Reformation, the celebration of England's past, often a mythological past, had been a powerful current of political and intellectual development. Milton, instead, means in the *History* to help his nation, through the historical education he offers it, to face truths about itself, 'rather than [be] puffed up with vulgar flatteries and encomiums, for want of self-knowledge'. He aims 'to raise a knowledge of ourselves both great and weighty, by judging hence what kind of men the Britons generally are' (130). On his Aristotelian principle, which envisages the state as an extension of its citizens, he thought of a nation as an individual writ large. A virtuous man, he maintained, must be 'a true knower of himself', and 'if it be a high point of wisdom in every private man, much more is it in a nation to know itself'.[36] It is on the same premiss that the virtuous man is a 'commander first over himself' while a virtuous people are 'masters of [them]selves'.[37] A nation has not merely its own characteristics but its own spirit and will, which are the sum of those of its citizens. During his massive early reading of history, he asked himself 'what each state did by its own effort'.[38] The struggle of fallen man, who is likewise cast upon the resources of his own efforts, thus has its national counterpart. God grants to individuals (as he did to Adam) freedom of will and of 'choosing', and subjects them to 'trials' of their 'virtue'.[39] So does he deal with nations, which, like persons, are 'masters of their own choice'.[40] The individual who fails the trial of virtue becomes enslaved to sin. The nation which fails it 'grow[s] corrupt' and prefers 'bondage with ease' to 'strenuous liberty'.[41] Sometimes, as Adam and Eve are foretold,

> nations will decline so low
> From virtue, which is reason, that no wrong
> But justice, and some fatal curse annexed
> Deprives them of their outward liberty,
> Their inward lost ....[42]

Milton's England had declined so low as to betray the God-given opportunity of the revolution. The *History* seeks the causes of its degeneracy.

It does so above all in the 'Digression'. The 'Digression' is an exercise in comparative history. In the 1640s, it explains, God 'had drawn so near a parallel' between the state of the Britons upon the removal of the Romans 'and ours in the late commotions' (441). The same point is made at the start

36. Ibid. i. 753; v. 130. 37. Above, p. 320. 38. *CP* i. 327. 39. Ibid. ii. 514.
40. Ibid. v. 441. 41. *Samson Agonistes* ll. 268–71. 42. *Paradise Lost* XII. 97–101.

of the third book of the *History*, in a passage which the 'Digression' echoes and which calls to be read alongside it. The first book covered remote and legendary history, the second the Roman occupation. It is in Book III, which traces the collapse of the British state in the aftermath of the Roman occupation, that Milton departs most radically from conventional thinking. In his principal source, the *De excidio et conquestu Britanniae* ('On the ruin and conquest of Britain') of Gildas, the writer of the late fifth or early sixth century, he found a medieval history to his liking: an attack on national degeneracy to match and to spur his denunciations of his own fractured time. The opening of Book III of Milton's *History* invites its readers to instruct themselves by 'comparing seriously ... that confused anarchy with this interreign ... two such remarkable turns of state producing like events among us' (129–30).

At those two great crises of their history, the first after a release from external dominion, the second after one from internal tyranny, the natives had the kinds of 'opportunity' for the establishment of liberty on whose decisive importance for posterity Marchamont Nedham had insisted in addressing English and Continental audiences in the early 1650s. The Britons had 'such a smooth occasion given them to free themselves as after ages have not afforded' (441). 'At first', explains Milton in the passage of Book III that echoes the 'Digression', they were 'greedy of change and to be thought the leading nation to freedom from the empire'. They 'seemed ... to bestir themselves with a show of diligence ... some secretly aspiring to rule, others adoring the name', but not the substance, 'of liberty'. But having 'enterprize[d] rashly and come off miserably in great undertakings', they soon found 'what it was to govern well themselves, and what was wanting within them': 'not stomach or the love of license, but the wisdom, the virtue, the labour, to use and maintain true liberty'. Thus 'they soon remitted their heat, and shrunk more wretchedly under the burden of their own liberty than before under a foreign yoke' (130–1). Thus, too, as the 'Digression' recalls, did they let the 'smooth occasion ... pass through them as a cordial medicine through a dying man without the least effect of sense or natural vigour. And to no less purpose if not more usefully to us it may withal be enquired' why 'they who had the chief management' of affairs in the 1640s, and who acquired, 'though not so easily', an equivalent opportunity, 'were not found able after so many years doing and undoing to hit so much as into any good and laudable way that might show us hopes of a just and well-amended common-wealth to come' (441). In both periods the natives had valour and military accomplishment on their side. Yet in both cases they were unequal to the challenge of peace. They were failed by 'the ill husbanding of those fair opportunities which might seem to have put liberty, so long desired, ... into their hands'. In both cases the causes of downfall were 'vices' of 'ruler, priest and people ... which as they brought those ancient natives to misery and ruin by liberty, which rightly used might have made them happy, so brought they these of late after many labours, much bloodshed and vast expense to ridiculous frustration' (443).

The 'Digression' recalls the blighting of the hopes of 1640. At the beginning of the parliament the people looked to their elected representatives with 'courage and expectation'. 'Some indeed' of the MPs were 'men of wisdom and integrity', but 'the greatest part' were governed by wealth or ambition. Once the 'superficial zeal and popular fumes that acted their new magistracy were cooled and spent', professions of public spirit gave way to private interest, injustice, corruption, and fraud, so that 'spite and favour governed all'. Shopkeepers, and others 'without merit', and men of 'hypocritical zeal', were placed in positions of high authority and 'fell to huckster the common-wealth' (443–5). There follows a diatribe against the practices of peculation that thrived on the exorbitant levels of taxation for which the war gave opportunity. Then Milton turns, in terms familiar from his other writings, to the Presbyterian clergy and to the consequences of their greed and worldliness and bigotry for the cause of reformation. He concludes that the leaders both in the state and in the Church, having initially been hailed – by no one more boldly, we may remember, than Milton himself – as 'deliverers', and having 'had a people wholly at their devotion', 'unfitted' not only themselves but also 'the people', who 'were now grown worse and more disordinate to receive or digest any liberty at all' (449).

In its despairing eloquence, and in the urgency of its lament and of its warning, the 'Digression' is closer to *The Readie and Easie Way* than to any of Milton's other prose works. If anything its despair goes deeper. In 1659–60 he turned both on those old enemies of the 'good old cause', the royalists and the Presbyterians, and on its betrayers in the 1650s, the Cromwellians. Yet in the 'Digression', at least in the form in which it was prepared for publication, the cause was lost long before the king had been killed or before the republic, and then Cromwell, had replaced him. It was doomed within the hearts of the leaders of state and Church and of the people whom they 'unfitted'. The anxiety which Milton had apparently felt even in the early 1640s, lest the nation might not be 'fit to be free', had been borne out. Then he had recalled the nobly intentioned, but mistaken, slaying of Julius Caesar.[43] It is in the 'Digression' that, having in the interim exulted in the regicide as England's equivalent of that feat, he returned in a melancholy vein to the Roman example: 'stories teach us that liberty sought out of season in a corrupt and degenerate age brought Rome itself into further slavery' (449). Marvell said that in 1642 the cause was too good to have been fought for. The 'Digression' says that the men were not good enough to fight for it.

★★

The ethical failings of the English had long preoccupied Milton. Yet in the 'Digression' they do not by themselves account for the failure of his countrymen, past and present, to sustain liberty. It is not only their taste for superstition and idolatry that has disabled them, not only their subjection to a corrupt and worldly clergy, not only their wantonness and addiction to vice, but their distance from the civic prudence which flourished in pagan lands, and which is no less essential to the attainment of virtue and liberty in Christian ones. His plea for political cosmopolitanism takes us back almost twenty years from the publication of the *History*, to the editorials of *Mercurius Politicus* in 1651–2, when Milton and Marchamont Nedham worked so closely together, and when the newsbook pressed the English to emulate ancient Rome and other Mediterranean republics both of classical antiquity and of the early Renaissance. The 'Digression' contains Milton's observation on the contrast between the failures of his compatriots and the exploits of 'other nations both ancient and modern', which 'with extreme hazard and danger have strove for liberty as a thing invaluable, and by the purchase thereof have so ennobled their spirits as from obscure and small to grow eminent and glorious commonwealths' (441). Perhaps the fault of the English lies in their country's cold climate, which militates against civil prudence:

> For Britain (to speak a truth not oft spoken) as it is a land fruitful enough of men stout and courageous in war, so is it naturally enough not over-fertile of men able to govern justly and prudently in peace; trusting only on their mother-wit, as most men do, and consider not that civility, prudence, love of

43. Above, pp. 233–4.

> the public more than of money and vain honour are to this soil in a manner outlandish. For the sun, which we want, ripens wits as well as fruits.... (451)

The nation's leaders lack 'the happy skill to know what is grievance and unjust to a people, and how to remove it wisely', and 'to know these exquisite proportions, the heroic wisdom which is required' (449–51).

That is not a concern which we customarily associate with the late Milton, who takes the subjects of his greatest poems not from classical history but from the Bible. Yet everything he had learned from pagan thought and literature was invested in those poems. In his late years as before them, he sees the virtuous man as citizen as well as saint. The claims of the spirit still merge with those of civic life and with the classical teaching that defined and inspired it. Cyriack Skinner observed that *Paradise Lost* and *Paradise Regained* 'taught all virtue'.[44] The *History* teaches the virtue of civic life. The tests which it imposes on the English, of 'justice and civility', 'industry and virtue', 'prudence [and] love of the public', are civic tests, the ones that have been passed by the 'other nations ancient and modern' which 'strove for liberty as a thing invaluable'. Alas, among his own countrymen civic virtue has fallen, as its spiritual partner succumbed in Eden. The parallel produces an echo of the epic in the *History*. For if, in *Paradise Lost*, nations sometimes 'decline so low | From virtue', the *History* reveals that, 'when the esteem of science and liberal studies waxes low in the commonwealth', 'all civil virtue and worthy action is grown to as low a decline' (40).

In Eden the fate of mankind rests on the choice, made by free agents, between spiritual liberty and slavery. The opening of the 'Digression' places a parallel alternative at the centre of public life: 'the gaining or losing of liberty is the greatest change to better or worse that may befall a nation under civil government' (441). Milton's perorations to the English people in *Defensio* and *Defensio Secunda* had said the same. His countrymen, as they confront the 'fair opportunities' and 'smooth occasion[s]' for liberty before them, have the freedom of will and choice that was Adam's too.[45] When, in the concluding lines of *Paradise Lost*, Adam and Eve descend from Eden, 'The world was all before them, where to choose'. In the 1640s, as we learn from the *History*, the English, being 'masters of their own choice',

44. Darbishire, 29.
45. This is true, it seems, despite his suggestion that they have been disqualified from civic prudence by their northern climate.

attained to 'a condition which had set before them civil government in all her forms' (441). In civic matters they, like Adam in spiritual ones, are 'sufficient to have stood, though free to fall' (III. 99). Like Adam, too, they have discovered the strenuousness of freedom. When the departure of the Romans 'left them to the sway of their own counsels', they 'felt by proof the weight of what it is to govern well themselves' (129–31).

The 'Digression' is an indictment of past moments. Yet in a mind whose didactic impulses were as strong as in Milton's, the failings of other times could not be a matter merely for regret. They offered lessons, as in his thinking history always did, to the present and the future. When Milton writes about the Fall, it is not only to explain our inherited predicament but to tell us how to live now. England's history has the same pertinence. It will tell 'them who can judiciously read ... what kind of men the Britons generally are' (129–30), and equip them to make use of that self-knowledge. On the Romans' departure, alas, the natives 'shrunk ... under the burden of their own liberty' (131). Milton's contemporaries likewise had not chosen aright. In 1660 they 'ch[o]se a captain back to Egypt'. In the Restoration they lived, as did Adam and Eve in their tragedy, with the consequences of their fall. Yet in religion there is a way back, or half-way back. It is to be discovered through the exercise of reason, which 'also is choice',[46] and virtue. Is there a way back in civic life, too, through the deployment of the same qualities? Perhaps divine providence, whose inscrutability *Samson Agonistes* has explained, will not tell us. This much, however, can be gleaned. If a way can be found it will be only on the condition that the English, before 'the attempt of any great enterprise' (451), equip themselves with the civic prudence in which, at the two great crises and opportunities of their history, they have been found wanting, and which alone can prepare them to form a 'well-amended commonwealth'.

At the end of his life Milton invited the nation, by oblique commentary, to seek constitutional change, in order to thwart the succession of James Duke of York. If it did so, a 'great enterprise' would indeed await it. So might it at any time amid the instability that became a persistent feature of Restoration politics from the late 1660s. *Samson Agonistes* counselled patience to the friends of truth and virtue, but it also enjoined them to preparedness. Who knew when the English might again have 'civil government set before them in all her forms', or find new 'hopes' of a 'well-amended

46. *Paradise Lost* III. 108.

commonwealth to come'? In the winter of 1659–60 James Harrington had predicted that, if the king returned, only seven years would elapse before the leaders in parliament would 'all turn commonwealthsmen'.[47] He was wrong. Yet by 1667, the year of the fall of Clarendon and of the Dutch invasion of the Medway, and the year in which, as Pepys tells us, the public nostalgically recalled the rule of Cromwell, the regime seemed in serious trouble. In 1668 the commonwealthman Slingsby Bethel judged the moment ripe to publish (illicitly) his tract *The World's Mistake in Oliver Cromwel*, which invited its readers to rejoice in the memory not of the protector, the misguided enthusiasm for whose memory he was alarmed to notice, but of the Rump, which Cromwell had expelled. In 1669, the year before the appearance of Milton's *History*, Marvell passed on to his constituents a report that 'commonwealthsmen', Henry Neville apparently among them, had 'flocked about the town' and were propounding 'new models of government'.[48] The 'Digression' was prepared for publication, in old age, from an ethical position that is far removed, as Milton's always was, from Marchamont Nedham's, and – the Restoration having divided the two men – from a political position equally afar. Yet it urges on Milton's compatriots and their posterity a lesson that again takes us back to the early 1650s, and to the conviction voiced by *Mercurius Politicus* that the English must look beyond their own traditions of constitutional thought and practice. 'As wine and oil are imported to us from abroad', exhorts Milton, 'so must ripe understanding and many civil virtues be imported into our minds from foreign writings and examples of best ages. We shall else miscarry still' (451).

47. Aubrey, *Brief Lives*, i. 291. 48. Margoliouth, ii. 91–2, 93.

Appendix A: Marvell and the Embassy of 1651

In Chapter 5 we puzzled over some difficulties of Marvell's poem of 1651 'In Legationem Domini Oliveri St John ad Provincias Foederatas'. There are others. How was it that Marvell, a man unknown in early 1651 save among fellow poets and among employers of tutors, came to address lines of verse – if we are right to assume that he did address them to him – to so grand a figure as Oliver St John: a poem, moreover, that advises the ambassador, firmly and candidly, to know and use his own strength and to adopt a contentious policy?[1] In 1654, when he was no better known, Marvell would compose a poem for the embassy to Queen Christina of Sweden led by Bulstrode Whilelocke, who in presenting the poem to her described its author as a 'friend' of his.[2] Yet Marvell did not presume to address it to the ambassador himself. He addressed it to Dr Nathaniel Ingelo, a friend of Marvell at Eton when Marvell was supervising Cromwell's ward William Dutton. Here two hypotheses about the composition of the poem on the earlier embassy will be advanced. They are only hypotheses. Neither has documentary evidence to support it; neither need be right; and both have arguments against them. The argument for them is that, if they are correct, they make the writing and the content of the poem more intelligible. Either hypothesis can be accepted, or rejected, without the other, but they strengthen each other and work better together than apart.

The first is that by early 1651 Marvell's search for employment in diplomacy, to which Milton's letter to Bradshaw attests two years later, not only had begun but had borne its first fruit. Marvell, that is, had a place on the embassy, in St John's entourage. The legation was an imposing one. A large party accompanied it, with the encouragement of parliament, which wanted to demonstrate both its domestic and its international standing by the size and stateliness of the mission's

1. Marvell became a friend of St John's brother-in-law John Oxenbridge, but only, as far as we know, after Marvell's move to Eton, where Oxenbridge was a Fellow, in 1653. Oxenbridge had been military chaplain to Robert Overton in Hull: *AMC* 39.
2. Above, p. 133.

following, and which expressed its appreciation, after the return of the embassy, to 'divers' men who had accompanied it and who now attended the Commons to receive its thanks.[3] There were 246 people in the solemn procession of entry on the embassy's arrival at The Hague.[4] Some of them belonged to aristocratic or gentle families, but most cannot have done. In general the party does not sound a particularly Puritan or republican one. Nedham's *Politicus* reported on the gallantry of the retinue and on the scrapes into which a number of its members, 'young sparks' among them, got themselves as they travelled 'to see the fashions'[5] or quarrelled with Dutchmen and exiled English royalists.[6] For an aspiring diplomat there would have been more earnest business to attend to. If Marvell was in St John's entourage, he would have perhaps worked under the supervision of St John's client, and secretary on the mission, John Thurloe, in whose office at Whitehall, when Thurloe was secretary of state, Marvell would at last gain a post in 1657.

Dutch politics and society, a subject of enduring interest to Marchamont Nedham, were significant in Marvell's life too. 'Upon Appleton House', probably written in the second half of 1651 or in 1652, appears to draw on Dutch sources, especially the verse of the Dutch poet-statesman Constantine Huygens[7] – whose son Lodewick came to England in a party of young gentleman which accompanied a Dutch embassy in December 1651. Eleven years later, in May 1662, Marvell was reported to be 'safe at The Hague' at the house of Sir George Downing, who had been England's ambassador in Holland during the protectorate.[8] What was Marvell doing there? And was he 'safe' merely after a journey, or from something else? Two months previously Downing had tricked the Dutch government into handing over three refugee regicides, whom he shipped back to England for execution. Was Marvell involved in that episode (we could only guess in what capacity or on whose behalf)? Downing was the brother-in-law of the Earl of Carlisle, whose own embassy Marvell joined, as his secretary, the following year. During the mission, Downing wrote from The Hague that Carlisle 'hath no language and so must wholly trust his secretary, and act by him'.[9] Marvell's knowledge of the Dutch language would have helped the embassy of 1651. Thurloe had poor languages,[10] and St John himself was

3. *Journal of the House of Commons*, 28 Jan. 1651, 2 July 1651.
4. S. R. Gardiner, *History of the Commonwealth and Protectorate*, i. 323. Cf. *MP*, 20 Feb. 161, 604; 10 Apr. 1651, 714.
5. *MP*, 17 Apr. 1651, 726.
6. Ibid. 10 Apr. 1651, 713, 714, 716–17; 24 Apr. 1651, 749; 15 May 1651, 793; etc.
7. Smith's commentary on the poem brings out this feature.
8. *AMC* 73.
9. Ibid. 81.
10. Lodewijck Huygens, *The English Journal 1651–1652*, ed. A. G. H. Bachrach and R. G. Collmer (Leiden, 1982), 50.

appointed to the embassy even though he was 'not much read in foreign affairs or languages'.[11]

That hypothesis would have two immediate advantages. In the first place it would position Marvell in proximity to St John, and might thus account for the poet's apparent presumption in addressing him as he does. Secondly it might begin to explain why the poem speaks to him as the man 'to whom alone the republic was willing to be entrusted' ('tu, cui soli voluit respublica credi'). There were two ambassadors, not one. They had separate entourages or households, and we may assume from the poem that, if Marvell did travel with the embassy, he belonged to St John's.[12] Strickland was no lightweight. He was elected to the council of state in 1651, and would be one of Cromwell's closest advisers during the protectorate. His appointment to the joint embassy was uncontentious, as St John's was not (though the grounds of the objection to St John, which won little support, are unknown).[13] It is true that, as Whitelocke said, St John 'was looked upon as the principal man'. According to Clarendon, indeed, St John 'had the whole trust of the embassy'.[14] Even so, Marvell's assertion is impertinent to Strickland.[15] Would he have risked it without the expectation that St John would approve of it?

The second hypothesis is that the poem was written not, as seems always to have been assumed, between the appointment of the embassy in January and its departure in mid-March, but during the ensuing months, at some point before the return of the mission in mid-June. That would not prove that Marvell was on the embassy. He could have sent the poem over to Holland, as, in connection with Whitelocke's embassy, he would send poems to Sweden. But if he had no connection with the embassy to Holland, that would have been a strange move, and one surely unlikely to win St John's attention. If the poem was indeed composed when the legation was in Holland, it is easier to think of Marvell's lines being written inside the embassy, in Holland, than outside it, in England. Two other considerations favour the hypothesis. First, the statement that the embassy has been entrusted to St John alone, while remaining a surprise, would be a smaller one. The statements by Whitelocke and Clarendon that the embassy was essentially only St John's were written in retrospect. It was during the embassy, not before it, that his dominance

11. BL Add. MS 37345, fo. 122^{v}. A correspondent of *Politicus* on the mission described an episode in which one of its members, apparently in St John's entourage, proved useful because 'he could speak Dutch': *MP*, 10 Apr. 1651, 717.
12. That is evident from the reports from the mission published in *Politicus*.
13. *Journal of the House of Commons*, 23 Jan. 1651.
14. Pincus, *Protestantism and Patriotism*, 24–5.
15. The impertinence is the more surprising if, as has been considered possible (Smith, 178), Marvell's poem 'To his Worthy Friend Doctor Witty' alludes to Strickland's sister-in-law, to whom the book in which the poem appeared was dedicated; see too *AMC* 36, 56.

became clear. Nedham's *Politicus*, having initially given full attention to the roles of both the English ambassadors, gradually reduced its coverage of Strickland, who became merely 'the other gentleman', to be mentioned parenthetically.[16] In the newsbook's reports from Holland, as in Marvell's poem, it is St John who counts.[17]

Secondly there is the profound change in St John's attitude to the Dutch during the negotiations. If Marvell wrote after that change, then the puzzle of the boldness and contentiousness of his advice disappears. St John went to Holland to secure Dutch friendship. His was not at all the mood of Popilius, the Roman envoy who refused the hand of friendship from King Antiochus, and whose example Marvell urges on him. But by April St John's mood would sharply alter. The embassy received ignominious affronts from the royalist exiles at The Hague, whom the Dutch authorities were unable or unwilling to control, and its proposals, though superficially welcomed, were held at bay while the Dutch waited to see the outcome of Cromwell's campaign in Scotland. The English bitterly accused the Dutch of negotiating in bad faith and of stringing the English mission along in a treaty they never intended to complete. As Nedham would put it in 1652, 'they had war in their hearts from the very beginning' of the negotiations.[18] In that new context the negotiations deserved Marvell's adjective 'fallax' – if indeed it was aimed at the discussions; and if the adjective applies to St John himself, then in the ambassador's own eyes he might merely have been playing the Dutch at their own game. At all events he was furious at the conduct of the Dutch negotiators. After his return to England he steered through the Commons the Navigation Act of October 1651, that frontal and provocative challenge to the Dutch maritime and commercial supremacy over England which played a large part in the drift to war in 1652. It was almost as ambitious and epochal a measure as the union of the two republics would have been. Would Marvell, a man habitually prudent in his search for patrons, have written in such militant terms about the embassy, and have recommended so militant a stance to St John, before the ambassador's mood had taken on a militancy of its own? St John's mind is never easy to fathom, but it is likely enough that, from the time of the breakdown of the talks, he saw union as a goal to be reached not by amicable negotiation but by the imposition on the Dutch of the choice between new alliances and new wars with which Marvell's poem confronts them. The head of the Commonwealth's intelligence service, Thomas Scot, through whose hands

16. *MP*, 20 Feb. 1651, 604; 10 Apr. 1651, 717.
17. Who wrote those reports (which are not from a single hand)? If Marvell was on the mission, there must be a chance, given what we have found of his closeness to Nedham, that he was responsible for some of them.
18. Selden, *Of the Dominion of the Seas*, ep. ded.

the foreign correspondence that appeared in *Politicus* reached Nedham, would complain in later years that Cromwell's expulsion of the Rump in 1653 had thwarted that regime's hope of achieving, by the war with the Dutch, the union which the embassy had failed to achieve through peaceful means: 'We might have brought them to a oneness with us.... We never bid fairer for being masters of the whole world.'[19] It was the prospect to which St John's change of heart in 1651 had led.

This does not mean that St John and Marvell were of a single mind. There were two arguments for the union of the two countries. The first was pragmatic. The Orange–Stuart–Bourbon axis would be thwarted; the threat of invasion would be much reduced; the new regime would be made much stronger and more secure. The second accepted that reasoning, but went beyond it from pragmatism to ideology: to the international republicanism which Nedham articulated in *Politicus* and which, at some level, is present in Marvell's poem. St John would not have countenanced international republicanism. Like his fellow envoy Strickland, with whom he could at least have agreed in this, he had accepted the existence of the Commonwealth but had no enthusiasm for kingless rule. St John did see the diplomatic point of emphasizing the common interests of the two republics. He reminded the States-General of the Netherlands that neither state 'depended upon the uncertainties of the life, allegiance, change of affections, and private interest of one person'.[20] Yet for his own part he regretted the abolition of the English monarchy, and in late 1651 he argued for a return to some form of kingship.[21] But if St John and Marvell held different premisses, the practical goal, the overcoming of the Dutch by the exertion of English might, was – once the negotiations had failed – the same. It was only from that time, however, that we can readily imagine Marvell expecting St John to warm to the argument of the poem. Strickland, for his part, would never have warmed to it. Amity with the Dutch was to him a cardinal principle of foreign policy. He would not have approved of the threat

19. Rutt, ed., *Diary of Thomas Burton*, iii. 111–12.
20. Pincus, *Protestantism and Patriotism*, p. 18.
21. Abbott, ed., *Writings and Speeches*, ii. 5–6. The moderation of St John's religious views also separates the ambassador from Nedham's portrait of Ango–Dutch relations (Nickolls, 25, 48). The embassy was accompanied by leading divines who, though Independents themselves, opposed separatism and favoured accommodation with Presbyterians, Nedham's *bête noire*. In the negotiations St John stressed the common religious ground between Dutch and English Protestantism (Pincus, *Patriotism and Protestantism*, 26). That, like his emphasis on the common interest of the republics, was an obvious diplomatic tactic. Yet it distinguished his outlook from that of the English religious radicals, with whom, on the subject of the Dutch (though normally not in other matters), Nedham was at one. While my account of St John's position differs from that proposed by Professor Pincus, his important book, which restores the link between foreign policy and ideology in seventeenth-century thinking, is essential to an understanding of the embassy.

to them made in Marvell's poem or of the English belligerence that followed the embassy. If the poem was written after the negotiations had turned acrimonious, then its exclusion of Strickland, whose conciliatory policy had failed, signals not merely the slimness of his influence on the course of the embassy but the parting of the ways between the two ambassadors.[22]

22. To the hypotheses I have advanced there are three foreseeable objections, though none of them seems to me insuperable. The first lies within the poem itself, which can be read as looking ahead to the embassy. Donno (in Andrew Marvell, The *Complete Poems*) implies that the subjunctive in line 6 has that implication, while the parallel with Antiochus in the last line can be read in the same way. But the lines do not seem to me to demand that interpretation. Secondly, there is the view that Marvell was already at Appleton House by the time of the embassy. I question this view above, p. 216. It is conceivable, however, that Marvell established his connection with the Fairfaxes through the embassy; or that he secured a place on it through them. (*Mercurius Politicus* (10 Apr. 1651, 709; cf. p. 717) makes a point of the fact that one of the gentlemen who accompanied the embassy, a Fairfax, was a cousin of the general.) Thirdly, why does Milton's letter of recommendation to Bradshaw in February 1653, which emphasizes Marvell's travels and linguistic accomplishments as qualifications for activity in diplomacy, not mention the embassy? The letter has the air of being written for the eyes not only of Bradshaw but of other, maybe less sympathetic readers, in whose eyes, perhaps, Milton does not wish to appear to be doing a close friend a favour. Bradshaw, a man less powerful than he had been in the earlier period of the Commonwealth, would not have had the post that Milton asks for Marvell in his gift; and the information which the letter gives Bradshaw is perhaps unlikely to have been altogether new to that friend of Milton. If Milton indeed wrote for more than one pair of eyes, he might have had either one or both of two reasons for reticence. First, the mission could have involved Marvell in intelligence work, and Milton would have known the need to protect the identities of the government's agents (cf. *CP* iv. 716 n.). Secondly, the wait before Marvell's employment in Thurloe's office may suggest that, if he was on the embassy, he did not distinguish himself on it (or else, perhaps, that his conduct raised doubts about his allegiance to it). He hardly shone on Carlisle's mission in the 1660s, or indeed in any branch of public activity outside his writing.

Appendix B: Milton and Cromwell's Advisers

Here we shall look more fully at a passage of *Defensio Secunda* (229–35) which was briefly discussed in Chapter 12 (pp. 286–7), and explain the reasoning behind the conclusions about it that were advanced there. It names the men whom Cromwell should choose as his advisers. They are the soldiers Charles Fleetwood, John Lambert, John Desborough, Edmund Whalley, and Robert Overton, who were the 'first ... companions' of Cromwell's 'labours' and 'dangers'; and the civilians, 'distinguished for the robe and arts of peace', Bulstrode Whitelocke, Sir Gilbert Pickering, Walter Strickland, William Sydenham, Viscount Lisle, Edward Montagu, and Henry Lawrence, men 'who are known to me either by friendship or reputation'. The passage poses an immediate problem. In the cases both of the soldiers and of the civilians Milton says, paradoxically, that Cromwell ought to name the men concerned and also that he has done so. Cromwell's best hope of meeting the challenges before him would be 'by associating, as you do, among the first in your counsels' his old military comrades. As for the civilians, Cromwell has nominated them 'for your counsellors' ('consiliaros tibi advocasti'), and at the same time 'doubtless might properly commit the care of our liberty' to them; 'indeed it is not easy to say to whom it could more safely be committed or confided'.[1] From what we have seen of the composition of *Defensio Secunda*, the contradiction seems likely to be the result of rewriting, perhaps at speed. We can only guess when, and precisely why, such revision might have occurred, but the probability of it conforms to a pattern of accretion and adjustment that we find generally characterizing the advice of *Defensio Secunda* to Cromwell.

It is customarily supposed that the passage tells Cromwell who should sit on the council of the protectorate. If so, it must have been written in the frantic days following the dissolution of Barebone's on 12 December 1653 (which would not have been a demanding feat for a writer who, in three days of February 1660, would fundamentally revise a text he had written previously and publish it as

1. The problem is not one of translation. The passage, which I have quoted in one of the two standard modern translations, presents the same difficulty in the other (*CP* iv. 676, 678).

The Readie and Easie Way[2]). The initial membership of the protectoral council was laid down in the Instrument of Government, the constitution by which Cromwell assumed his new office on the 16th. Three of the five soldiers Milton names (Fleetwood, Lambert, and Desborough), and all but one of the seven civilians, were indeed appointed. It is, as we shall find, likely that Milton did work on the passage at some point after the end of Barebone's, when he also revised other material in the light of Cromwell's elevation. But the passage was not first written then. For Cromwell is urged to appoint – and is simultaneously commended for having appointed – not only the civilians whom Milton names but many other 'men and chosen citizens': 'numberless other citizens, distinguished for their rare merits, some for their former senatorial exertions, others for their military services'. Milton cannot be referring to the protectoral council, which the Instrument required to be a small body. The only context that makes his words comprehensible is the calling of Barebone's Parliament in the weeks after the expulsion of the Rump.[3] With one exception (to which we shall come), the civilians he lists were summoned to that assembly. In other words, the passage, at least in its initial form, belongs, like the account of the evils of parliamentary elections, to the aftermath of the expulsion of the Rump. The same civilians would, with the same exception, form the core of the Cromwellian party in Barebone's. They were then appointed, again with the same exception, to the protectoral council in December, which is why, at first glance, the list may look as if it was drawn up about or after that time.

Two days after the Rump's demise on 20 April 1653, the army put out a declaration, probably penned by Marchamont Nedham, which announced its 'clear intentions and real purposes of heart to call to the government persons of approved fidelity and honesty'. For 'good men will hope that if persons so qualified be chosen, the fruits of a just and righteous reformation, so long prayed and wished for, will, by the blessing of God, be in due time obtained, to the refreshing of all those good hearts who have been panting after those things'.[4] Perhaps Milton's passage was originally written in response to that statement or as a development of it, and was then expanded a little later to include the suggestion about 'numberless citizens'. For in the immediate wake of the dissolution of the Rump it was uncertain what kind, and what size, of nominated body would

2. Robert Ayres's argument that the entire pamphlet was probably written on those days (*CP* vii. 343–5) is incompatible with ibid. 353. Perhaps the echoes of *Politicus* of 1651–2 in the tract intimate that Milton drew on material he had drafted much earlier.

3. Although serving officers were not permitted to sit in Barebone's, many men with 'military service' in the civil wars behind them sat in it.

4. S. R. Gardiner, ed., *Constitutional Documents*, 402. For Nedham's likely authorship see above, pp. 305–6. That passage of the declaration was omitted from the version published in *Mercurius Politicus* on 28 April 1653 (pp. 2386–91), an indication of the uncertainty of the new rulers' constitutional intentions at that time. The politics of the period following the dissolution of the Rump, as of the year 1653 as a whole, are authoritatively described in Woolrych, *Commonwealth to Protectorate*.

replace it. But the decision to call some such assembly as Barebone's seems to have been taken by late April. There followed an extensive process of selection, which culminated with the sending out of writs of summons on 6 June. Maybe Milton adapted or re-adapted the passage when the choice of the members was complete, to acknowledge that Cromwell, whom Milton has advised to call the civilian nominees to his aid, has indeed done so. In the selection of civilians to aid the army just after the dissolution of the Rump, Cromwell pleased himself. The members of Barebone's, it is true, were chosen not by him alone but by a council of army officers. Yet his was the leading voice, as it would be in the choice of the councillors named in the Instrument of Government.

Milton adds the seven civilians whom he names, and the numberless 'accomplished men and citizens' whom he does not, to the army officers whom he also commends to Cromwell. But the army men could not be appointed to Barebone's, from which serving officers were excluded. Milton could, it is true, have recommended the military names immediately after the dissolution of the Rump. For it was only towards the end of May 1653 that the decision to exclude army officers from Barebone's was taken. At that time at least two of the officers in Milton's list, Lambert and Whalley, had been expected to be chosen.[5] Yet there is a likelier scenario. It is that, in counselling Cromwell about the choice of advisers in the published text of *Defensio Secunda*, Milton has stitched together two passages, the first concerning the soldiers, the second the civilians, which had originally been written at different times and with different purposes. The account of the soldiers is notably the fuller of the two, and is joined, as the other is not, by a passage of panegyric. To Milton, after all, soldiers were the real heroes of the revolution. Yet his admiration for them only partly explains the contrast. Milton does not say of the soldiers, as he does of the civilians, that they have been 'nominated' or 'summoned'. He states only that they should be associated in, or admitted to, Cromwell's 'counsels' ('consiliorum'). There is here a semantic problem familiar to historians of the period, whose denizens did not consistently differentiate between 'council' and 'counsel', or between 'councillors' and 'counsellors'. In any case the Latin word used by Milton does not allow for the distinction. But whereas the passage about the civilians refers to official appointments, there is no reason to assume that the one about the soldiers does so, or that Milton has in mind anything more than informal consultations with friends and allies. His remarks about the officers, which are accompanied with the warning lest we 'suffer ourselves to think that there are any who can preserve' liberty 'with greater diligence', are likeliest to belong to the later Rump period, when Cromwell was blamed for choosing 'new friends'.

The probability is supported by the only point in the eulogy of the army officers that contains an element (admittedly a brief one) of narrative, the tribute to Robert Overton, which takes the story only up to his establishment of a garrison in the Orkneys in February 1652. Perhaps the tributes to the soldiers are, or are part of,

5. Firth, ed., *Clarke Papers*, iii. 7.

the 'eulogy of those most saintly men and lovers of the truth' which Milton tells us in *Defensio* that he has decided 'not now to begin'.[6] If the passage was written under the Rump, Milton found in it an opportunity to warn Cromwell against distancing himself from the officers while simultaneously naming and congratulating his own heroes. On the same assumption, the information that Cromwell, who ought to give the soldiers primacy in his counsels, in fact does so, could have been interpolated made after the fall of that body, when the officers took control of the nation. The contrast none the less persists between the list of civilians, which tells Cromwell more or less what he would like to hear, and that of the soldiers, which has a monitory intent. The monition lies partly in the implied complaint that Cromwell has failed to stick to his true friends, and partly in the nomination of Milton's friend Robert Overton, whose difficulties with Cromwell we saw in Chapter 14.

In the list of civilians, one name protrudes: that of Bulstrode Whitelocke, one of the Commonwealth's Commissioners of the Great Seal. But for his presence, we could simply conclude that the whole passage about Cromwell's advisers had been written, in the form in which we have it, by the time Barebone's met. Unlike the other six civilians, Whitelocke was not a member of Barebone's, or in Cromwell's inner counsels in 1653, or a member of the protectoral council. His name appears at the head of the list of civilians. Given the differences between him and the other civilians, his name seems likely to have been an addition to a list already drawn up. But if so, when was it added? The answer is most unlikely to be the spring of 1653. Lawyers were in bad odour among the military rulers at the time of the Rump's expulsion, and a week after the coup army sources were asserting that in the assembly which was to replace the Rump 'no professed lawyer is to be of the number'.[7] In any case Whitelocke opposed the dissolution of the Rump and was far removed from Cromwell's favour in the months after it. Later in the year, however, his stock improved. It was Cromwell who, in the early autumn, fixed Whitelocke's appointment as ambassador to Sweden, on the mission that preoccupied Marvell and Nedham. He was there during the early stages of the protectorate. He longed for an invitation to join the council.[8] He had nothing of Milton's political radicalism; indeed in the Rump period he was a thorn in the radicals' flesh; but he was a consistent and resolute advocate of

6. *CW* vii. 179 (cf. viii. 119). And is it a coincidence that Hermann Mylius, the envoy from the principality of Oldenburg who saw so much of Milton during his stay in London in 1651–2, describes the new model army in September 1651 in terms so close to those of *Defensio Secunda* (179) on the same subject? 'Never has there been seen', writes Mylius (in a Latinized German), 'an army more modest and more scrupulously religious in external form of worship, which submits so willingly and obediently to such strict discipline. Depravity, blasphemy, swearing, profanation of the Sabbath or any wantonness, in word or deed, are neither heard nor seen' (Miller, *John Milton and the Oldenburg Safeguard*, 40). That view of the army was, admittedly, widely propagated: BL, Add. MS 37346, fo. 112.
7. Worden, *Rump Parliament*, 357.
8. Bulstrode Whitelocke, *Journal of the Swedish Embassy*, 2 vols. (1855), i. 5, 322; Spalding, ed., *Diary of Bulstrode Whitelocke*, 401–2, 438.

liberty of conscience. He would have earned Milton's approval by defending the anti-trinitarian MP John Fry when parliament turned on him in 1651.[9] He was a friend of Marvell and was also close to Nedham, who corresponded with him during Whitelocke's embassy.[10] He had literary tastes of which Milton must have been aware. The most plausible explanation of his presence in the civilian list is that Milton, having drawn up the names in the spring or early summer of 1653, added Whitelocke's to them at some point after the end of Barebone's, either between 12 and 16 December 1653, when the council was being formed, or during the weeks or months thereafter, when Cromwell was seeking to expand its membership. Milton had had frequent contact with Whitelocke when working for the Commonwealth.[11] If he needed any prompting in proposing him, the idea would have been likely to come from Whitelocke's client Nedham, whose contacts with the embassy in Sweden we saw in Chapter 5.[12]

9. Worden, *Rump Parliament*, 131. 10. Above, pp. 134–6. 11. *MC* 124–34.
12. On Whitelocke and Nedham see also Longleat House, Whitelocke MS XIII, fos. 49–53.

Appendix C: The Composition of Milton's History of Britain

We saw in Chapter 12 how Milton's *Defensio Secunda* can be read afresh if we seek the layers of composition beneath the text. The same is true of the *History of Britain*. But the problems of dating, difficult enough in *Defensio Secunda*, are more taxing still in the *History*. *Defensio Secunda* was written over four years or so at the most. The *History* has passages which it is possible to interpret as products of the 1640s, or of the late 1660s, or of a number of points in between. *Defensio Secunda* provides its student, by its frequent references to current or recent events, with landmarks of navigation. The *History* offers very few such aids.

History was an essential component of Milton's literary self-preparation. In his youth he studied it intensively and systematically. He began with the early history of the Christian Church, with the Greeks and Italians, and with the history of early medieval Europe. It looks from his surviving commonplace-book as if he turned to English history on his return from Italy, and that he read comprehensively in it from 1639 to 1644.[1] He seems to have written the nine-page historical review of English prelacy that formed an appendix to a leading anti-episcopal tract of March 1641, and he presented himself as a historian in his assault on the bishops in *Of Reformation* two months later.[2] It is not until 1648, however, that we first hear of the projected *History of Britain*. In midsummer Samuel Hartlib learned from a friend who knew (or would soon know) Milton, Theodore Haak, that 'Milton is not only writing a Univ[ersal] History of Engl[and]' – that is, a history from the beginning to the present day – 'but also an Epitome of all [Samuel] Purchas's volumes' (a work now unidentifiable, unless it was some version of Milton's *A Brief History of Moscovia*). The wording possibly implies that this was not the first that Hartlib had heard of the project for a history of England. It has been suggested that Milton embarked on the writing in the mid-1640s, perhaps after the publication of his poems in 1645, perhaps after the conclusion of his divorce tracts, perhaps after the end of the civil war in 1646. Until recently, indeed, the greater part of the *History* was regarded as essentially the product of the years 1645–8.[3] Yet

1. *CP* v. pp. xxiv–xxvii, xxxviii.
2. Lewalski, 126, 128–9.
3. The commentary by French Fogle in *CP* v. pp. xxxvii–xl summarized and added to the discussion.

Milton's autobiographical account in *Defensio Secunda* gives a different picture. After describing the writing of *The Tenure of Kings and Magistrates* in early 1649, Milton writes that 'having dispatched these things' – by which he evidently means not only *The Tenure* but his earlier writings for liberty as well – 'and thinking that for the future I should now have abundance of leisure, I undertook a history of the nation from its remotest origin; intending to bring it down, if I could, in one unbroken thread to our own times. I had already finished four books, when' he received the summons, in mid-March, to serve the council of state.[4] Nicholas von Maltzahn, the leading authority on the *History*, accepts Milton's account. Preferring its testimony to that of Hartlib's note of 1648, he argues that the writing was begun after the execution of the king.

The evidence is finely balanced. We have discovered the perils of taking Milton's autobiographical statements on trust. Between his reference to *The Tenure* and that to the *History*, his narrative is interrupted by a tribute to his immunity to self-advancement, a virtue of which his description of the writing of the *History* is then offered as testimony. He allows us to understand that, rather than seeking preferment on the strength of his defence of the king's trial, he retired to his private studies, in which he was immersed when he received the unexpected and unsolicited call from the council. His account may be distorted by that slant. Yet it seems unlikely to have been wholly invented or imagined.

Two objections have been lodged against it. First, the pessimistic tone of the *History*, and especially of the third book, which takes its inspiration from the wretched assessment of the early Britons by the historian Gildas, seems hard to square with the enthusiasm proclaimed by his published work for the regicide. Book III of the *History* opens with a parallel between the calamitous deficiencies of the Britons when they were presented with the chance of self-government and the conduct of Milton's compatriots during 'the like events among us' (129–31). Scholars have linked the pessimistic mood of that passage to the dismal condition of England in the years 1646–8, and especially to the gloom of Milton's translations from the Psalms in April 1648 and of his sonnet to Fairfax in the summer. Can he have remained so melancholy, it has been asked, after Pride's Purge and the regicide? We have seen that those events brought him back into the political fray and transformed his attitude to it. That question-mark against Milton's account, however, is smaller than it looks, for two reasons. First, although he delighted in and hailed the coup of 1648–9, and although the survival of the new regime was of the most fundamental importance to him, he never wrote anything to suggest that he had confidence in the parliament whose rule replaced the king, or in the nation at large which it ruled. The regicide proved to him that England contained a party of virtue, but not that the nation was virtuous or that it was equal to the challenge before it. His vindications of the coup of 1648–9 – *The Tenure of Kings and Magistrates*, *Eikonoklastes*, the two 'defences' – combine exultation at its

4. *CW* viii. 139.

achievement with doubt or even dismay about the country's prospects for virtue and liberty. Sometimes the exultation itself is at odds with his private thoughts. 'I cannot but congratulate myself', he told his European audience in *Defensio* in 1651, 'upon our ancestors, who founded this state with no less prudence and liberty than did the most excellent of the ancient Greeks and Romans.' The statement belies everything Milton wrote privately, and even what he later came to acknowledge publicly, about the dearth of civic and constitutional 'prudence' among his countrymen.[5] In the late 1640s, as for long afterwards, the *History* appears to have been a 'private study', written without an eye to immediate publication. Secondly, we shall find reason to think that the opening of Book III was a later addition to Milton's text, written well after 1649. Though the rest of Book III, which is indeed likely to have been composed by that year, shares the baleful view of Milton's compatriots offered by Gildas, it does not explicitly apply the analysis, as the opening passage of the book does, to current events.

The other question has been whether, in those few weeks between the completion of *The Tenure* and his employment by the council, he could have written so much. Here a new complication arises, for we cannot be certain what, when he wrote *Defensio Secunda*, the 'four books' consisted of. This, after all, was the author who would convert the ten books of *Paradise Lost* into twelve. He could have done something similar to the *History* between the writing of *Defensio Secunda* and the publication of the *History* in 1670. Besides, he cannot have written the last part of the published fourth book before 1652, for it uses a source (Simeon of Durham) that became available only in that year. Yet in the evidence of that dependence there lies a reassuring clue. Milton's debt to his new source begins just after a passage – the one in which he complains of the 'penance' of the writing of the work – that looks like a fresh start to the writing. From that juxtaposition we can infer the likelihood that in or by 1649 he had written a narrative that approached, but did not quite reach, the end of the published Book IV. With significant but brief exceptions to which we shall come, that portion of the *History* reads like a text undisturbed by subsequent amendment. If so, then Milton's account requires him to have written around 50,000 words in those weeks. That rate of composition – somewhere between 1,200 and 1,800 words a day, depending when *The Tenure* was completed – would have been well within his usual grasp, at least if we assume that the reading for the work had been done and the materials for the writing been ordered.[6]

So neither the tone of the first four books nor the question of speed disproves Milton's account. Even so, doubts persist. It is possible that Hartlib misunderstood or over-interpreted what Haak told him in 1648. It seems likelier, however, that the writing was under way by then. Milton's nephew and early biographer Edward

5. Ibid. vii. 451; and see von Maltzahn, *Milton's 'History of Britain'*, 211–13. Von Maltzahn has rightly stressed the pessimistic component of Milton's thinking in 1649.
6. Von Maltzahn, *Milton's 'History of Britain'*, 24–8.

Phillips, who supplies almost the only useful evidence about the composition of the work other than that provided by Hartlib and by *Defensio Secunda*, tells us that between August 1647, when the new model army first marched into London, and the writing of *The Tenure* Milton 'lived a private and quiet life, still prosecuting his studies and curious search into knowledge, the grand affair perpetually of his life'; and that after he completed *The Tenure* 'his thoughts were bent upon retiring again to his own private studies, and [upon] falling upon such subjects as his proper genius prompted him to write of, among which was the *History of our own Nation from the Beginning to the Norman Conquest*, wherein he had made some progress'.[7] Neither a grasp nor the communication of chronology was a strong point in Phillips. He has that instinct for purposeless ambiguity about dates and events of which his uncle was himself not free. But he perhaps seems likelier to mean that the progress 'had' been 'made' before 1649 than during it. Either way, his wording does not lead us to suppose that Milton's 'private studies' of 1649 took a different form from those of 1647–8, or that in the weeks after *The Tenure* he gave the *History* the undivided attention which, to support von Maltzahn's interpretation, it would surely have needed. On balance it seems probable that Milton had begun to write the *History* by 1648, but that he took it up again in the weeks after the regicide. Short of new evidence, however, the question will remain one for individual judgement.

In Phillips's narrative the next stage of composition came in the 1650s. After the publication of *Pro Se Defensio* in August 1655, we learn, the defeated More 'quitted the field'. Milton, 'now quiet from state-adversaries and public contests', 'had leisure again for his own studies and private designs; which were his aforesaid *History of England*, and a new *Thesaurus Linguae Latinae*'. Presumably he now finished Book IV and embarked on the last two books, the first of which describes the Danish invasion, while the second completes the story to the Battle of Hastings. We have to guess quite when this new phase began. How long did Milton wait before concluding that More would not reply to *Pro Se Defensio*? It is here that Phillips proceeds: 'But the height of his noble fancy and invention began now to be seriously and mainly employed in a subject worthy of such a muse', *Paradise Lost*.[8] If John Aubrey, who in this was guided by Phillips, was right to say that Milton began *Paradise Lost* 'about two years before the king came in',[9] then we may be tempted to deduce that he must have resumed the *History* and the *Thesaurus* before he embarked on the epic. Yet Phillips's own words are at least as much open to the inference that Milton resumed the prose works at the time that he began the poem. For Phillips does not say that Milton set them aside once he started to write *Paradise Lost*. He tells us, indeed, that Milton 'went on with' the *Thesaurus* 'at times, even very near to his dying day'. Perhaps he 'went on with' the *History* 'at times' too, maybe in those summer months when, according to Phillips, the muse of poetry did not visit him.[10] Perhaps he still hoped to bring the *History* down to the present day, and studied to that end.

7. Darbishire, 68–9. 8. Ibid. 72. 9. Ibid. 13. 10. Ibid. 72, 73.

Finally, Phillips informs us that after his move 'to a house in the Artillery-walk leading to Bunhill Fields', which may have occurred as early as 1663 or as late as 1670, Milton 'finished and published his *History of our Nation to the Conquest*, all complete so far as he went'.[11] Cyriack Skinner's biography, too, says that the *History* was 'finished after the Restoration'.[12]

★★

To the enquirer into Milton's relations with the events of his time, the part of his *History* of keenest interest is the 'Digression'. Here the problems of dating multiply. In terms of Milton's political biography they also become more pressing.

The 'Digression', which was not included in the published *History*, survives in two forms, one in manuscript, one in print. They mostly but not entirely concur. (They are conveniently printed on facing pages in the Yale edition of Milton's prose.) The manuscript, now at Harvard, is a copy made at some time after the publication of the *History*. The printed version was a brilliant propaganda coup by the Tory licenser of the press, Roger L'Estrange.[13] During the exclusion crisis of 1679–81, when Whig plans to bar James Duke of York from the succession, or else to revise the constitution in parliament's favour, roused fears of a return to the chaos of the 1640s, the lessons of the earlier conflict were widely touted. L'Estrange found in the words of the 'Digression' an eloquent condemnation of the parliament in whose most revolutionary deeds Milton had rejoiced, and of its allies among the Presbyterian clergy. Coming from that hand, it was a portrait more damning than any that a Tory could have drawn. So in 1681 L'Estrange recruited the dead Milton to the royalist and Anglican ideals against which his career had been fought. He turned it, indeed, to the very purpose, the succession of James Duke of York to the throne, which Milton's translation of the Polish declaration at the end of his life had been intended to impede. L'Estrange printed the 'Digression' as *Mr John Miltons Character of the Long Parliament and Assembly of Divines*, and on the title-page declared the work to be 'very seasonable for these times'.[14] In both the manuscript and the printed version we are told that the 'Digression' would have been incorporated into Book III of the published *History*, the part of the work which is based on Gildas's condemnation of the early Britons, and to which indeed the 'Digression' is, in both spirit and subject-matter, most nearly allied.

The largest difference between the two versions is at their outsets, where the first 400 words or so of the manuscript have no equivalent in the text published by L'Estrange. The opening of the manuscript, which we can call the preamble, proclaims Milton's intent of drawing his comparison between past and present. It

11. Ibid. 73. Phillips mentions the omission from the printed text of anticlerical passages which were removed by the licenser.

12. Ibid. 29.

13. Von Maltzahn, *Milton's 'History of Britain'*, ch. 1.

14. *CP* v. 439.

is here that he announces 'so near a parallel' between the state of the Britons upon the removal of the Romans 'and ours in the late commotions'. The parallel did not interest L'Estrange, who was solely preoccupied with Milton's description of the 1640s. The obvious explanation of the contrast between the two beginnings is that L'Estrange pruned the start of Milton's text so as to create a self-sufficient document which would take the reader straight to L'Estrange's polemical point. L'Estrange's text starts with the failings of 'those who swayed most in the late troubles'.[15] From that point – the one at which the two versions join – Milton traces the shortcomings of the leaders of the Long Parliament, of the Presbyterian clergy, and of the people whose lay and spiritual guides had 'unfitted' them, and inveighs against the corrupt practices of the parliament and its administrators. Thence the 'Digression' proceeds to its generalizations about the hazard of seeking liberty 'in a corrupt and degenerate age' and about the incapacity of the Britons to sustain the conditions of public virtue. In conclusion Milton returns briefly to the deficiencies of the politicians and clergy of the 1640s, and concludes that 'from the confluence of all these errors, mischiefs and demeanours' there could only be expected 'what befell those ancient inhabitants whom they so much resembled, confusion in the end' (451).

The 'Digression' may not all have been written at once. Though its main narrative of the 1640s, which comprises most of the document, has material on either side of it that compares the English of the 1640s with the early Britons, that narrative itself does not mention the parallel. It concerns itself only with Milton's own time (which is why it suited L'Estrange's purpose so well). It, or something from which it was taken, could originally have been drawn up separately from the rest of the 'Digression'. In the Harvard manuscript there is a break around the point where the preamble ends and the narrative begins, a sign, perhaps, that stitching has occurred.[16] The narrative could even – though this is speculation – have been composed for a separate purpose. Could it be that Milton, who in December 1659 disdained the suggestion that he should write a history of the civil wars,[17] thought differently in another phase of his life, and drew up an account from which the narrative is taken? However that may be, there is a second sudden change of direction in the 'Digression'. The observations on the challenges of liberty in a corrupt age, and on the incapacity of the Britons to sustain the virtue that liberty requires, have the appearance of a digression within the

15. L'Estrange does print the last third or so of the preamble, but by omitting the rest he deprives it of its preliminary character.
16. If so the preamble must have replaced an earlier one, for no text would have begun at the exact point of the break in the manuscript (which is followed by the words 'The rest, and to be sure ...', 443). It is presumably in order to secure continuity with the later portion that the scribe – or an earlier one whom he follows – has carried on for one sentence beyond the opening sentence of the narrative, which may itself have needed adjustment to accommodate the new preamble. I am grateful to Martin Dzelzainis for information about the manuscript, though he bears no responsibility for my inference from it.
17. *CP* vii. 515.

'Digression', or what we can call a sub-digression. In theme the observations look back to statements in the preamble, the part of the document from which they would more easily follow. They are themselves followed by words – 'Hence did their victories prove as fruitless' (451) – which in turn would follow more easily from those that immediately precede the sub-digression.[18] After 'hence did their victories ...' there are only a few more lines. They are of uncertain direction; they repeat points made in the bulk of the narrative; and they look like the outcome of an uncomfortable effort to join the story of the 1640s to the parallel with the ancient Britons.

Previous commentators have assumed that the 'Digression' was the product of a single moment. Until recently it was thought that it was composed, with most of the rest of the *History*, before 1649. That view has been rejected by both of the combatants in a distinguished recent debate, which has breathed fresh life into perceptions of the 'Digression' and given it a new and apt prominence in discussions of Milton's political thinking. Nicholas von Maltzahn, who places the writing of most of the first four books of the *History* in 1649, puts the 'Digression' there too. The late Austin Woolrych maintained that it was added in 1660, in the weeks or months before the Restoration.[19] In both cases much of the apparent force of the argument lies in the close resemblances between the 'Digression' and other writings of Milton in the same year. Von Maltzahn is especially impressed by the similarities with *The Tenure of Kings and Magistrates* in 1649. Woolrych was struck by the likenesses to *The Readie and Easie Way* in 1660. The parallels, in both cases, are indeed close. Yet they may merely reflect Milton's readiness to repeat himself over time on subjects on which his thoughts remained the same. For beside the changes in his thinking, there are long and strong continuities both of opinion and of language. Von Maltzahn and Woolrych cannot both be right; and if both cannot be, neither need be.

There is, in their interpretations, an essential difficulty. The 'Digression' refers to 'the late commotions' (441) and describes the faults of 'those who swayed most in the late troubles' (443). It argues that, during those troubles, liberty 'was sought out of season' (449), and that the victories of the parliamentarians proved, 'after so many years doing and undoing' (441), 'as fruitless as their losses dangerous', with the result that they 'sunk as those unfortunate Britons before them' (451). Milton surely wrote all those words, and others in the Digression like them, when 'the late commotions' and 'troubles' were over. Yet von Maltzahn and Woolrych both

18. I take the sub-digression to begin either at 'For stories teach us ...' or at the next sentence, 'For liberty hath ...' (449). Here as elsewhere in the document, it could be that the presence of the word 'For' at the beginning of a sentence is a consequence of editorial adjustment by Milton.

19. The initial positions were set out in Woolrych, 'Date of the Digression'; von Maltzahn, *Milton's 'History of Britain'*, ch. 2. Battle was joined in *Historical Journal*, 36 (1993): Woolrych, 'Dating Milton's *History of Britain*' (929–43); von Maltzahn, 'Dating the Digression in Milton's *History of Britain*' (945–56).

place them in the thick of them, von Maltzahn in the aftermath of the regicide, Woolrych in the anarchy that preceded the Restoration.[20] Milton's phrases do not in themselves prove that the 'Digression' was written after the Restoration. As early as November 1652 Marchamont Nedham referred to the civil wars as 'the late commotions'.[21] Admittedly he was writing for a government which, after the defeat of the Scots the previous year, was eager to present the wars as a thing of the past. Yet it was probably around the same time, but without that purpose of persuasion at the front of his mind, that Milton himself, in the autobiographical passage of *Defensio Secunda* that describes the writing of the *History*, used the phrase 'this civil broil' ('hoc civili tumultu') in the past tense.[22] There is no reason in principle why he could not have written of the 'late commotions' and 'troubles' when he returned to the writing of the *History* in the 1650s. He then had a chance, if he wanted one, to amend or expand material he had written by 1649. If he did compose the 'Digression' in the 1650s, then he must have seen, in Cromwell's rule, evidence not only that the 'troubles' were past but of the profound and final loss of liberty that the text laments.

He may indeed have had that thought. Yet a date of composition after 1660 is likelier than one before it. At the least, there is conclusive evidence that he worked on the text of the 'Digression' when he prepared the *History* for publication in the Restoration. But before we meet it we must return to L'Estrange. Though the 'Disgression' was not included in the published text, L'Estrange tells us that Milton 'designed' it 'to be printed', while the headnote to the 'Digression', which identifies the point in the published text where the 'Digression' is 'to come in', implies as much.[23] Perhaps the acquisition of the text by the licenser L'Estrange itself suggests that it had been in a printer's hands.[24] The decision to publish the 'Digression' (whenever it was written) was courageous. Admittedly it could not, unless on a very strained reading, have been judged treasonable. It says nothing about Charles I, nothing about the regicide, nothing to incite resistance to the prevailing power. Yet anyone wanting evidence that Milton retained anti-monarchical principles would have found it in the 'Digression'. Only his characteristic vagueness on constitutional matters could have protected him if

20. Woolrych originally suggested that the 'Digression' was written later in 1660, after the king's return, but came to recognize difficulties in that view. The conclusiveness of the judgement of the 'Digression' on the failure of the revolution registers pessimism of an order different from the general tone of the *History*, and seems incompatible with von Maltzahn's argument that the 'Digression' was written in 1649. Yet any view of the dating of the 'Digression' will have its problems. I have changed my own more than once.

21. Selden, *Of the Dominion of the Seas*, 482.

22. *CW* viii. 137.

23. *CP* v. 440, 441. Perhaps the scribe's direction was intended for a fresh edition which would have included the 'Digression': either for one which for some reason did not appear, or for one of the editions produced later in the century (in which case the 'Digression' must have been omitted for a second time). Or does the direction even signify a last-minute attempt to include the Digression in the first edition after all?

24. Von Maltzahn, *Milton's 'History of Britain'*, 24–7.

he had been charged, on the basis of that document, with publicly regretting the Roundheads' failure to establish a true and lasting government. In intending to publish the 'Digression', Milton evidently planned to test once more the limits of publishable expression. Once more he deployed oblique methods of commentary, of which historical writing was society's most frequent instrument.[25]

L'Estrange explains that, 'out of tenderness to a party', the 'Digression' 'was struck out' of the *History* 'for some harshness'.[26] The 'party' would have been the Presbyterians – the religious Presbyterians certainly, the political ones perhaps. L'Estrange's use of the passive leaves open the question whether Milton himself agreed to the excision, or whether it was taken on his behalf; but L'Estrange plainly means that the decision to withdraw the 'Digression' was taken from within Milton's circle, not by the licenser.[27] 'Tenderness' to the Presbyterians was not a plentiful commodity in Milton's mind. After the Restoration the Puritan groups which had fallen out in the civil wars needed to make common cause against Anglican repression. The depth and endurance of Milton's detestation of Presbyterianism are manifest in his inclusion, in the volume of verse he published in 1673, of the poem to which he gave the title 'On the New Forcers of Conscience under the Long Parliament': a new title, for the Long Parliament had not been known as 'the Long Parliament' at the time. His feelings are still more evident in his willingness to publish the 'Digression', a document which, in 1670 scarcely less than in 1681, would have stoked old quarrels within the Roundhead camp and exposed mainstream Puritanism to mockery. However, the Harvard manuscript contains a passage which appears to show that Milton, at a time when he still expected the 'Digression' to be published, did think, with its publication in mind, of modifying his assault on Presbyterianism, albeit only slightly. The passage, at which he seems to have made a series of attempts, was scored out and is hard to read. But he evidently wrote that while 'the more active' of the Presbyterian clergy were guilty of the evils he describes, 'all were not such', as 'many yet living can witness' (466–7). Perhaps he had in mind, not the existence of a virtuous party among the Presbyterians of the 1640s (though he had conceded the existence of one in 1649: *CP* iii. 238), but the steadfast clerical resistance to the evils of Laudianism in the 1630s. At all events only after the Restoration, even some years after it, would the passage of time have made the words 'many yet living' apposite. Milton himself, whose *History* appeared around the time of his

25. Nicholas von Maltzahn, 'The Royal Society and the Provenance of Milton's *History of Britain* (1670)', *Milton Quarterly*, 32 (1998), 90–5, suggests that the publisher of the book, Richard Allestry, may have been chosen for the eminent respectability of his credentials, which might have allayed a licenser's concern. Perhaps, too, Milton hoped, in the period following the fall of the Earl of Clarendon in 1667 and the consequent broadening of Charles II's regime, that the press might have become freer.

26. *CP* v. 440.

27. We cannot be sure that L'Estrange was being candid, and that there was no other cause of the withdrawal of the 'Digression'. In 1681 he saw the propaganda value of the 'Digression' for his own cause, but a licenser of 1670 might have responded to it differently.

sixty-second birthday, had already been in his twenties when the personal rule of Charles I began in 1629.[28] As a survivor from that period after 1660, he was in a minority but was hardly a rarity.

Of course, the words 'as many yet living can witness' could have been written in a late attempt to correct a text which had otherwise been written much earlier. Yet they conform to the retrospective tenor of the 'Digression', which is as evident in the narrative (where the excised passage lay) as we have seen it to be in the preamble and the sub-digression. The narrative reads most naturally if we take it to be the work of an old man writing at a time when, for the majority of his potential readers, the events of the 1640s were at most a blur. 'A certain number of divines were called' to the Westminster Assembly (447); 'a parliament being called...' (443: not 'the parliament', as we might expect him to have written if the Long Parliament had still been sitting)[29] – this seems language written from a remote distance, too remote to have been produced during the revolution. Indeed the later the date for the composition of the 'Digression' that we propose, the likelier it may be to be correct. For only as the Restoration itself receded into memory would those events of the 1640s – like the defiance by virtuous Presbyterians in the 1630s – have belonged to a past as distant as the 'Digression' indicates them to be.

Hitherto one aspect of the document has seemed puzzling. Why does it refer only to events before 1649? Why, if Milton wrote it at any time between the regicide and the Restoration, does he not mention the execution of the king, which so delighted him? Why does he not attempt to square what, at least from 1649 to 1654, he was ready to hail as that true 'deliverance' with his judgement in the 'Digression' on the false 'deliverers' of 1640–2? And if he wrote it after 1649, but before the Restoration, why did he not refer to events subsequent to the regicide? If, on the other hand, he composed it, with the aim of publication, after 1660, the difficulty disappears. The document itself is brave enough in its regret at the missed opportunities of the 1640s. But after 1660 the regicide itself was mentionable in print only by those who were ready to vilify it, while the events

28. In the same passage, which evidently gave Milton trouble, the vices of the Presbyterians are themselves described slightly differently in the two versions of the 'Digression' (448–9). There is perhaps another moment when we can glimpse Milton revising the 'Digression' with an eye to its Restoration audience. The copy printed by L'Estrange voices, albeit in a fleeting and subdued form, the religious radicalism familiar from the Milton of the 1650s. It expresses his belief in the efficacy of 'spiritual weapons... to pull down all thoughts and imaginations that exalt themselves against God', and insists that 'civil laws have no cognizance' of the punishment of 'church-delinquencies'. The corresponding passage of the Harvard manuscript confines itself to the complaint, safely compatible with Erastianism, that the Presbyterian clergy aimed at a 'spiritual tyranny' which would advance their authority 'above the magistrate' (446–7). The manuscript version is akin to the prudent concealment in *Of True Religion* of Milton's views on the relations of Church and state. Should we infer that the manuscript version of the 'Digression' is the later of the two?

29. Cf. *CP* vii. 355.

of the 1650s would have been the most treacherous of terrain for a writer with Milton's past.

**

If the 'Digression' is a late work, other passages of the *History* may be late too. This becomes apparent when we try to recover the relationship of the 'Digression' to the main text of the *History*. The Harvard copyist, whom modern authorities have followed here, specifies a point in Book III, between a quarter and a third of the way through it, at which the 'Digression' was to have been inserted (144). L'Estrange, on the other hand, tells us that it was to have been placed 'very near' the 'beginning' of Book III. Neither at the point specified by the copyist, nor at any other point of the *History*, would the 'Digression' have fitted seamlessly. Its insertion at any point of it would have made a bulge. The 'Digression' bulges accordingly in the first published version of the *History* to include the 'Digression', that produced by Thomas Birch, from the text printed by L'Estrange, in Birch's edition of Milton's works in 1738.[30]

Yet Birch chose a point of insertion (130) which, if we inspect it, can take us into the process of Milton's decision making. Birch placed the 'Digression' after the first sentence (a long one) of Book III. Perhaps he had somehow acquired a knowledge of Milton's intentions that would die with Birch himself. Or perhaps he merely followed L'Estrange's lead and guessed how 'near' to the beginning the 'Digression' should lie. Either way, his chosen point is instructive. Edward Phillips, who links the writing of the *History* to the composition of Milton's *Thesaurus Linguae Latinae*, writes of the second work that, though he 'went on with it … even very near to his dying day', 'the papers after his death were so discomposed and deficient, that it could not be made fit for the press'.[31] The *History* escaped that fate, but its text, too, was evidently in less than perfect order. At Birch's point of insertion we can glimpse a scribe or scribes struggling to observe the blind author's directions.

To grasp the scribal difficulty we must trace it to its evident source, which lies in the resemblances between the opening of Book III and the 'Digression' – especially the preamble to the 'Digression', and the sub-digression which appears to be the preamble's partner. Indeed the start of Book III (129–31) says, often in more or less the same language though more succinctly, almost exactly what the 'Digression'

30. A reference in the 'Digression' (443) to 'causes' of the British degeneracy 'belonging both to ruler, priest and people', which 'above' have been 'related', may seem to support the copyist's placing, since those failings are described in a passage in Book III (140) that comes earlier than the point identified by the copyist but later than the one identified by Birch. Yet the failings are more fully set out in a passage of Book III (174–5) which comes well after both of the suggested points of insertion. Can we be sure that Milton had decided – or anyway, finally decided – where the 'Digression' should go?

31. Darbishire, 72.

says. As in the 'Digression', Milton draws a parallel between what both texts call the 'condition' of the nation after the departure of the Britons and what he now terms 'the late civil broils'. The 'Digression' asks 'what disposition to justice and civility' there is among Milton's countrymen (441); it relates their want of 'industry and virtue', of 'civility, prudence, love of the public', and of 'heroic wisdom'; it warns of their disadvantages 'in the attempt of any great enterprise' (451); it declares that they have been 'unfitted' to 'digest any liberty at all' (449). The opening of Book III enquires 'what kinds of men the Britons generally are in matters of so high enterprise, how by nature, industry or custom fitted to attempt' them; it regrets their want of 'the wisdom, the virtue, the labour to use and maintain true liberty'; it laments their tendency 'to enterprise rashly and come off miserably in great undertakings'. If in the 'Digression' the initial 'zeal and popular fumes' of the Roundhead leaders 'were cooled and spent' (443), so that the people 'after a false heat became more cold and obdurate than before' (449), in Book III the early Britons, 'though at first greedy of change', 'soon remitted their heat'. When, in the 'Digression', the nation's mask of public spirit slips, 'the love of rule' is seen to prevail (445): in Book III 'some' are found 'secretly aspiring to rule'. In the 'Digression' the English of the 1640s, having failed the challenge of liberty, 'sunk as those unfortunate Britons before them' (451): in Book III the Britons 'shrunk ... under the burden of their own liberty'.

Yet to the flow of the opening of Book III there is an interruption. The point at which Birch inserted the 'Digression' is followed by two sentences (also long ones) which, in the text of 1670 that he used, are evidently printed in the wrong order. The sentence that appears immediately after Birch's point of insertion expresses a view which the preamble to the 'Digression' contradicts; and it must have been written at a different time from it. Following Gildas, it states that the succession of invasions which followed the removal of the Romans is to be explained by the natives' lack of military prowess. The land 'was in a manner emptied of all her youth, consumed in wars abroad, or not caring to return home', while those who stayed had become 'through long subjection servile in mind, slothful of body, and with the use of arms unacquainted'. Yet in the preamble to the 'Digression' (which in other respects the opening of Book III so resembles) Milton turns against Gildas's explanation. For though 'it is alleged that their youth and chief strength was carried over sea to serve the [Roman] empire', the Britons, having been trained by the Romans, 'could not be so ignorant of war'. It is 'in no way credible' that 'they were so timorous and without heart as Gildas reports them'. The 'few' who, in the misplaced sentence of Book III, 'had the courage', but are impotent, stand in contrast to the British soldiers described in the same preamble, who, though 'few', 'in the greatest weakness t[ook] courage' and repulsed the Scots (always an occasion of satisfaction to Milton) and the Picts. The 'Digression' refutes the military explanation in order to shift the blame, in both periods, to the ethical failings of his countrymen, who 'to speak a truth not oft spoken' are 'valiant indeed and prosperous to win a field, but to know the end and reason of winning unjudicious and unwise, in good and bad success alas unteachable' (451).

Once we transpose the two sentences that follow Birch's point of insertion, things fall into place. The sentence that ought to come first after that point, but instead comes second, would in its rightful place belong to, and conclude, the general observations about the British character with which Book III begins. The sentence which precedes that one in print, but which ought to succeed it, would in its rightful place begin the narrative of Book III, which follows the observations. The obvious inference is that the opening of Book III has been added, in a flawed process, to the narrative that follows it – just as the opening of the 'Digression' is a preamble to the narrative of the 1640s. The preamble to Book III frames what follows and tells readers how to interpret it. 'This third book', declare its opening words, 'having to tell of accidents as various and exemplary as the intermission or change of government hath anywhere set forth, may deserve attention more than common, and repay it with the like benefit to those who can judiciously read: considering that the late civil broils had cast us into a condition not much unlike to what the Britons then were in.'

When, then, was the beginning of Book III written? Here a puzzle leaps from the page. The text, having referred to 'the late civil broils', enjoins us in the same sentence to 'compar[e] seriously' the 'times' after the Romans' departure 'with these later [ones], and that confused anarchy with this interreign'. We have all supposed 'this interreign' to refer to some time or period during the Puritan Revolution. There was, after all, an 'interreign' from 1649 to 1660, and perhaps in the years before 1649 too. The apparent contradiction could be the result of amendment, written after the 'civil broils', of a passage written during them. We shall find another point in the *History* where a similar oddness of wording seems to be the result of such revision. But in this instance a likelier explanation is a simpler one. It is discernible when we reunite the words to their companions: 'considering especially that the late civil broils had cast us into a condition not much unlike to what the Britons then were in, when the imperial jurisdiction departing hence left them to the sway of their own counsels; which times by comparing seriously with these later, and that confused anarchy with this interreign, we may ... raise a knowledge of ourselves'. By 'this interreign' Milton does not, I suggest, mean 'the present interreign'. Rather the 'this' of 'this interreign' is opposed to the 'that' of 'that anarchy'. When we also relate the words 'these later' back to 'the late civil broils', we see that the passage has a consistency which makes the suggestion of revision unnecessary if not implausible. Once more, the opening of Book III has its suggestive parallel in the preamble to the 'Digression', where, in the analogy with 'the late troubles', 'those ancient natives' are compared to 'these of late' and 'these lately' (443).

Why do the two texts resemble each other so closely? Did the beginning of Book III originally have some other life? Was it an alternative version, or part of an alternative version, of the 'Digression'? Was it perhaps added to the beginning of

Book III after the decision to omit the 'Digression' had been taken? Beside those possibilities many others could be entertained. Whatever explanation we might favour, it must be likely that the preamble to Book III was written – at least in the form in which we have it – around the same time as the 'Digression'.[32]

If we accept that conclusion, others may follow from it, though they are not ones that could be defended dogmatically. Of the six books of the printed *History*, at least three begin, and at least four end, with a passage of reflection which differs, in that quality, from most (though by no means all) of the rest of the History. Were those passages added around the same time as the beginning of Book III, which they resemble in character? The cheerless opening three paragraphs of the *History* (which end 'I now begin') have a prefatory air akin to that of the start of Book III. Milton introduces Book III by announcing the 'benefit' that it will bring 'to them who can judiciously read': the opening of Book I states his aim to 'best instruct and benefit them that read'. The first and second books end with passages that stand back from the preceding narrative, as, arguably, does Book IV. The opening (which concludes 'I shall assay') of Book II starts with generalizations about the writing of history that complement observations in the opening section of Book I. The end of Book III summarizes the book's content and reflects on 'the many miseries and desolations brought by a divine hand on a perverse generation', a statement that echoes not only the opening of the same book but also perhaps the judgement passed by Milton at the beginning of Book I on 'perverse ... persons and their actions'.[33]

The pattern continues in Books V and VI. In Book V the narrative takes on a new form of organization, which divides the material into the reigns of the successive kings. But the account of the first reign – Egbert's – is preceded by a preamble which describes the nation's sins, and its divine punishment, in a manner which we recognize from Milton's earlier generalizations and from the 'Digression'. The preamble carries, oddly if it was written at the same time as the narrative that follows it, words which half-repeat but also half-question the opening sentence (again on the subject of 'laying down of arms') of the section on Egbert.[34] Remarks at the opening of the sixth and last book possibly suggest a retrospective shaping. The same book, which otherwise almost entirely avoids division into paragraphs (except at the beginning of each reign), ends with a brief paragraph that again brings us back to the present: 'If these were the causes of such misery and thraldom

32. It should also be said that the opening of Book III, while it invites that comparison, does not state, as the 'Digression' does, that the revolutionary endeavours of the 1640s were doomed (though that inference can be drawn from it).

33. If this hypothesis is correct, we can envisage the first three books having the following beginnings (or ones like them). Book I: 'That the whole earth was inhabited before the flood' (4); Book II: 'Julius Caesar (of whom, and of the Roman free state, more than what appertains is not here to be discoursed of' (41); Book III: 'The Britons thus as we have heard being left without protection' (130: perhaps 'as we have heard' is an interpolation made to adjust the text to the insertion of the preamble).

34. The same theme figures at what is likely to have been the original ending of Book IV (229).

to those our ancestors, with what better close can be concluded than here in fit season to remember this age in the midst of her security, to fear from like vices without amendment the revolution of like calamities.'

If we set aside all those passages of generalization and reflection (as well as the 'Digression') from the *History*, we are left with a flatter text, one short on reflection and differentiation (and perhaps closer than the published text to Milton's colourless *A Brief History of Moscovia*). The simplest and most convenient explanation of the transitional moments that we have identified would be that the reflective passages were all introduced when Milton 'finished' the book for publication. So they may have been. Yet in these matters straightforwardness is an elusive commodity.

For the subject-matter of the reflective material is essentially of two kinds. There are passages on the depravity of the Britons, and others on the problems which the deficiencies of the evidence pose to the historian. Since Milton argues that bad societies produce bad sources, the two themes interweave. Yet at the beginnings and ends of the first two books it is his relationship with his evidence that predominates. He returns to the subject, in a very similar vein, at the point, towards the end of Book IV, at which – so all the signs suggest – he resumed the writing of the *History* in the 1650s. Perhaps at that stage – indeed, perhaps until some much later one – he meant to begin a new book of the *History* at that point and with that theme. That would explain his statement in *Defensio Secunda* that he had 'finished four books' by 1649, and it would explain why that passage in Book IV contains a series of general reflections of a kind we normally meet only at the beginnings and ends of the books.

That passage is again the one where he complains of the 'penance' before him, and of the 'volumes of rubbish' he must confront. He writes it as if he has yet to compose the material to which the reader is about to come. He does the same thing in each of his other passages of historiographical reflection. The one at the beginning of the first book ends at the point where, 'imploring divine assistance', 'I now begin'. That which opens Book II tells of the 'diligence' with which, 'since I must through it', 'I shall assay'. That in Book IV, having described the labour 'that I voluntarily undergo', concludes 'but to my task as it now befalls'. Do we take him literally, and suppose that blank pages awaited him when he wrote? Or did he compose all those preliminary passages after the writing of the narrative, and try to create the impression of a seamless whole, written at a single time? Would we accept the appeal to the 'heavenly muse' at the start of *Paradise Lost* as evidence that he has yet to start the rest of the work?

If we do take him literally, then we must suppose the historiographical reflections to have belonged (even if not necessarily in their final forms) to the original writing. Certainly there is a contrast between them and those reflective passages which do not comment on the sources and which instead confine themselves to the evils of the Britons. Those latter sections do not have the anticipatory element of the historiographical commentaries. Were it not that the two categories overlap, we might decide that they belong to two stages of composition, the historiographical passages to the initial writing, the others to a later time. But they do overlap, especially in the openings of the first two books and in the passage towards the end of Book IV. Consequently, there are sentences that bear close similarities, first to restrospective material that we find both in the opening of Book III and in the 'Digression', and secondly to the statements about Milton's sources that we find elsewhere. When, then, were the overlapping passages written? If the historiographical passages were composed before the stretches of narrative that follow them, then the likely answer is that he rewrote them, and inserted material about the failings of the Britons, at the time when he readied the book for publication and wrote the 'Digression'. Alternatively, we can regard the anticipatory element as artistic licence, and think of all the reflective material as the product of late writing.

One last problem about the composition of the *History* must be addressed. For if Milton revised it for publication, he need not have confined himself to the beginnings and ends of books (or to the historiographical thoughts in Book IV). While the main narrative of the *History* has an evenness of composition and tone that resists suggestions of significant revision, there are unexpected moments of generalization, even of epigram.[35] Were they part of the original writing, or were they introduced later to shape and ginger it? We cannot say. But there is what seems to be one tell-tale sign of revision. Outside the 'Digression' and the start of Book III, the *History* contains only one explicit reference to events of Milton's own time. In it he aims a side-swipe at 'the presbyters of our age'. In the 'Digression' the Westminster Assembly is a thing of the past. But in Book II 'the presbyters of our age... like well to sit in Assembly on the public stipend, but liked not the poverty that caused' their counterparts in early Britain 'to do so' (116). Why that shift of tense, from 'like' to 'liked'? Is not the probable explanation that the sentence, first written while the Assembly was sitting in the 1640s, was rewritten (incompletely) later?

★★

From those complexities an intelligible pattern emerges, all of it probable, some of it as near to certainty as we could hope. By March 1649 Milton had written the basic narrative of the first two-thirds or so of the *History*. He returned to that narrative in the mid- or later 1650s, though we cannot tell whether he had finished it by the Restoration. Equally we cannot tell whether the narrative, at the stages when he composed it, was accompanied by observations on the problems of evidence by which Milton was confronted. But, with the single exception that we have just glimpsed, he did not yet draw his explicit parallels with the present; or, if he did, they then took forms which have not come down to us and which were replaced by passages of generalization written when, late in his life, he prepared the book

35. One of Milton's statements about historical writing (134) lies in the body of the narrative.

for publication. The 'Digression', though it may have drawn on earlier texts (one of them conceivably a history of the civil wars), was written during that late time. Whether or not those inferences are accepted, the difficulties in reaching conclusions on this subject are themselves cause for reflection, arising as they do from the persistence of distinctive values and language even in a writer in whom the convulsions of his time induced profound alterations of perspective.

List of Works Cited

MANUSCRIPTS

Beinecke Library, Yale University
Joseph Spence papers, MS4, box 4, folder 107 (poems of Henry Neville)

Berkshire Record Office
MS D/EN/F8/1 (Henry Neville papers)

Bodleian Library
Carte MSS
Clarendon MSS
Nalson MSS
Rawlinson MSS
MS Eng. hist. c. 487: Edmund Ludlow, 'A Voyce from the Watch Tower'

British Library
Additional MS 37345–6 (Annals of Bulstrode Whitelocke)
Additional MSS 28001–13 (Oxinden papers)
Loan 331 (microfilm): Northumberland MS 552 (Fitzjames letter book)

Canterbury Cathedral Library
Elham Pamphlets (MS annotations by Henry Oxinden)

Folger Library, Washington
MS 4018
MS V. a. 300

Harvard University (Houghton Library)
MS Eng. 901: The 'Digression' from *Milton's History of Britain*

Longleat House
Whitelocke MSS

National Archives (formerly Public Record Office)
SP 25, 46 (council records)

Society of Antiquaries
SAL/MS/138 (letters relating to Oliver Cromwell)

Victoria and Albert Museum
Forster MS 48 D. 41 (Vane's sermons)

Warwickshire Record Office
Algernon Sidney, 'Court Maxims, Refuted and Refelled'

PRINTED SOURCES

1. Pamphlets by or partly by Marchamont Nedham

Most of the attributions below are uncontroversial; some have been explained in the course of this book. *A Cat May Look upon a King* has been attributed both to Nedham (*Manuscripts of the Harleian Collection*, 4 vols. (1812–18), i. 609) and to Sir Anthony Weldon. I suspect that either Weldon or another author shared the writing with Nedham, whose characteristics are present in many passages but not in all. Nedham's authorship of *A True State of the Case of the Commonwealth* has occasionally, but to my mind not persuasively, been contested. Of *Vox Plebis*, a work which contains sharp contrasts of literary manner, Nedham is likely to have written only a portion or portions. He may have had a hand in *Plain English* (below); and see below under 'Selden'. Nedham's newsbooks are listed under '2'.

An Answer to Nine Arguments (1645).
The Antiquity of England's Superiority over Scotland (1652).
The Case of the Commonwealth of England, Stated (1650), ed. Philip A. Knachel (Charlottesville, Va., 1969).
The Case of the Kingdom Stated (1647).
The Case Stated between England and the United Provinces (1652).
A Cat May Look upon a King (1652).
Certain Considerations Tendered in all Humility to an Honourable Member of the Council of State (1649).
Christianissimus Christianandus (1678).
Digitus Dei (1649).
A Discourse concerning Schools (1663).
The Excellencie of a Free State, or The Right Constitution of a Commonwealth (1767 edn.).
The Great Accuser Cast Down (1657).
Honesty's Best Policy (1678).
Independencie no Schisme (1646).
Interest Will not Lie (1659).
The Lawyer of Lincolnes Inne Reformed (1647).
The Levellers Levell'd (1647).
A Pacquet of Advices (1676: Bodl. Ashm. 1008).
A Parallel of Governments (1648).
A Plea for the King and Kingdom (1648).

The True Character of a Rigid Presbyter (1661).
A True State of the Case of the Commonwealth (1654).
Vox Plebis, or The People's Outcry against Oppression, Injustice and Tyranny (1646).

2. Newsbooks and Related Anonymous Sources

The fullest account of the authorship of newsbooks is Joseph Frank's *The Beginnings of the English Newspaper*. Individual issues are listed in G. K. Fortescue, ed., *Catalogue of the Pamphlets … Collected by George Thomason*, 2 vols. (London, 1908), ii.

Anti-Aulicus.
A Briefe Relation.
Britanicus Vapulans.
The Man in the Moon.
Mercurius Anti-Britanicus, or, The Second Part of the King's Cabinet Vindicated (1645).
Mercurius Aquaticus his Answer to Britanicus ([1643]).
Mercurius Aquaticus, or, The Water-Poets Answer (1643).
Mercurius Bellicus.
Mercurius Britanicus.
Mercurius Britanicus his Apologie (1645).
Mercurius Britanicus his Welcome to Hell (1646).
Mercurius Elencticus.
Mercurius Politicus.
Mecurius Pragmaticus.
Mercurius Pragmaticus (for King Charles II).
Observations, Historical, Political and Philosophical, upon Aristotle's First Book of Politics.
The Observator.
Perfect and Impartial Intelligence.
A Perfect Diurnall.
A Politick Commentary on the Life of Caius Julius Caesar, written by Caius Suetonius Tranquilius.
The Publick Intelligencer.
The Recantation of Mercurius Aulicus (1644).
The Royall Diurnall.
Severall Proceedings in Parliament.
Severall Proceedings of State Affairs in Parliament.
The Spie.

3. Other Primary Printed Sources (including modern editions, calendars and indexes)

Abbott, W. C., ed., *Writings and Speeches of Oliver Cromwell*, 4 vols. (Cambridge, Mass., 1937–47).
Aristippus, or Monsieur de Balsac's Masterpiece: Being a Discourse concerning the Court (1659).
Aubrey, John, *Brief Lives*, ed. Andrew Clark, 2 vols. (Oxford, 1898).
Balsac *see Aristippus.*
Beal, Peter, *Index of English Literary Manuscripts*, 2 vols. (London and New York, 1987–93).
Beaumont, Francis *see* Glover and Waller.

Bethel, Slingsby, *The World's Mistake in Oliver Cromwel* (1668).
Birch, Thomas, ed., *A Collection of the State Papers of John Thurloe*, 7 vols. (1742).
Blackleach, John, *Endeavours Aiming at the Glory of God* (1650).
Burton, Thomas *see* Rutt.
Calendar of State Papers Domestic.
Calendar of State Papers Venetian.
The Cause of God (1659).
Chaloner, Thomas, *A True and Exact Relation of the Strange Finding out of Moses his Tombe* (1657).
Clarendon *see* Hyde; Ogle. *et al.*
Clarke see Firth.
Cleveland, John, *The Character of Mercurius Politicus* (1650).
—— *The Second Character of Mercurius Politicus* (1650).
'Concerning the Forraigne Affaires in the Protector's Time', in Scott, *Somers Tracts*, vi. 329–36.
Considerations upon the Late Transactions and Proceedings of the Army (1659).
Cook, John, *King Charls his Case* (1649).
Cornubiensis, Johannes [pseud.], *The Grand Catastrophe* (1654).
Cowley, Abraham, *A Discourse by Way of Vision, concerning ... Oliver Cromwell* (1659).
Darbishire, Helen, ed., *The Early Lives of Milton* (London, 1932).
A Declaration of the Army concerning the Apprehending of Major Gen. Overton (1655).
A Declaration of the Parlement of England, upon the Marching of the Armie into Scotland (1650).
A Discovery of some Plots of Lucifer (1656).
Donno, Elizabeth Story, ed., *Andrew Marvell: The Critical Heritage* (London, 1978).
—— *see* Marvell.
Dryden *see* Hammond and Hopkins.
Eliot, John, *The Christian Commonwealth* (1659).
Evelyn, John ['N.P.'], *A Reply to that Malicious Letter* (1660).
Firth, C. H., ed., *The Clarke Papers*, 4 vols. (Camden Society, 1893–1901)
—— ed., *Memoirs of Edmund Ludlow*, 2 vols. (Oxford, 1894).
French, J. Milton, *The Life Records of John Milton*, 5 vols. (New Brunswick, NJ 1949–58).
Gardiner, Dorothy, ed., *The Oxinden and Peyton Letters 1642–1670* (London, 1937).
Gardiner, S. R., ed., *Constitutional Documents of the Puritan Revolution 1625–1660* (Oxford, repr. 1958).
—— ed., *Letters and Papers Illustrating the Relations between Charles the Second and Scotland* (Scottish History Society, xvii (1894)).
Glover, Arnold, and Waller, A. R., eds., *The Works of Francis Beaumont and John Fletcher*, 10 vols. (Cambridge, 1905–12).
Goodwin, John, *Peace Protected, and Discontent Disarmed* (1654).
Hall, John, *Confusion Confounded* (1654).
—— *A Gagg to Love's Advocate* (1651).

____'The Grounds and Reasons of Monarchy', in Toland, *Oceana of James Harrington.*
____*An Humble Motion to the Parliament concerning the Advancement of Learning* (London, 1649).
____*A Letter Written to a Gentleman in the Country* (1653).
____*A Serious Epistle to Mr William Prynne* (1649).
____*A True Relation of the ... Proceedings ... at Amboyna* (1651).
Haller, William, and Davies, Godfrey, eds., *The Leveller Tracts 1647–1653* (New York, 1944).
Hammond, Paul, and Hopkins, David, eds., *The Poems of John Dryden*, 5 vols. (Harlow, 1995–2005).
Harrington, James *see* Pocock; Toland.
Herford, C. H., and Simpson, P. and E., eds, *Ben Jonson*, 11 vols. (Oxford, 1925–52).
Heylyn, Peter, *The Historical and Miscellaneous Tracts* (1681).
Historical Manuscripts Commission Reports: *De Lisle and Dudley*, vi.
Historical Manuscripts Commission Reports, xiii, *Appendix 1: Portland.*
Hughes, John, ed., *A Composite History of England* (1706).
Hutchinson, Lucy, *Memoirs of the Life of Colonel Hutchinson*, ed. N. H. Keeble (London, 2000 edn.).
Huygens, Lodewijck, *The English Journal 1651–1652*, ed. A. G. H. Bachrach and R. G. Collmer (Leiden, 1982).
Hyde, Edward, Earl of Clarendon, *History of the Rebellion*, ed. W. D. Macray, 6 vols. (Oxford, repr. 1958).
Ironside, Gilbert, *A Sermon Preached at Dorchester* (1660).
Jonson *see* Herford and Simpson.
Journal of the House of Commons.
A Letter of Addresses to the Protector occasioned by Mr. Needhams reply to Mr. Goodwins Book (n.d. [1657]).
A Letter from a True and Lawfull Member of Parliament (1656).
The Life and Reign of King Charls. Or, The Pseudo-Martyr Discovered (1651).
Ludlow, Edmund, *A Voyce from the Watch Tower 1660–1662*, ed. Blair Worden (Camden Society, 1978).
____*see* Firth.
Margoliouth, H. M., ed., *The Poems and Letters of Andrew Marvell*, revised by Pierre Legouis with E. E. Duncan-Jones, 2 vols. (Oxford, 1971).
Marvell, Andrew, *The Complete Poems*, ed. Elizabeth Story Donno (Harmondsworth, 1972).
____*see* Margoliouth; McQueen and Rockwell; A. Patterson *et al.*; Smith.
May, Thomas (attrib.), *The Changeable Covenant* (1650).
McQueen, William A., and Rockwell, Kiffin A., eds., *The Latin Poetry of Andrew Marvell* (Chapel Hill, NC 1964).
Milton, John, *Political Writings*, ed. Martin Dzelzainis (Cambridge, 1991).

Milton, John, *see* F. A. Patterson; Wolfe *et al.*

More Hearts and Hands appearing for the Work (1653).

Neville, Henry (attrib.), *Newes from the New Exchange, or The Commonwealth of Ladies* (1650).

Nickolls, J., ed., *Original Letters and Papers of State ... addressed to Oliver Cromwell* (1743).

Ogle, O., *et al.*, eds., *Calendar of Clarendon State Papers*, 5 vols. (Oxford, 1869–1970).

An Oration of Agrippa to Octavius Caesar Augustus against Monarchy (1659).

Oxinden, Henry, *Charles Triumphant* (1660).

—— *see* D. Gardiner.

The Parliamentary or Constitutional History of England, 21 vols. (1751–62).

Patterson, Annabel, *et al.*, eds., *Prose Works of Andrew Marvell*, 2 vols. (New Haven, 2003).

Patterson, F. A., ed., *The Works of John Milton*, 18 vols. (New York, 1931–8).

Phillips, John, *Joannis Philippi Angli Responsio* (1652).

—— *The Religion of the Hypocritical Presbyterians in Meter* (1661).

—— *A Satyr against Hypocrites* (1655).

—— *Sportive Wit* (1656).

Plain English (1660).

Pocock, J. G. A., ed., *The Political Works of James Harrington* (Cambridge, 1977).

Price, John, *Tyrants and Protectors set forth in their Colours* (1654).

The Protector (so called) in part Unvailed (1655).

Prynne, William, *King Richard the Third Revived* (London, 1659).

Quaking Principles Dashed in Pieces (165[4]).

The Racovian Catechism (1652).

Richardson, Samuel, *Plain Dealing* (1656).

Rutt, J. T., ed., *Diary of Thomas Burton*, 4 vols. (1828).

The Sad Suffering Case of Major-General Robert Overton (1659) (by 'J. R'.).

Scott, Walter, ed., *Somers Tracts*, 13 vols. (1809–15).

Sedgwick, Obadiah, *A Thanksgiving Sermon* (1644).

Selden, John, *Of the Dominion of the Seas*, ed. and trans. Marchamont Nedham (1652).

Sidney, Algernon, *Court Maxims*, ed. Hans Blom and E. Haitsma Mulier (Cambridge, 1996).

Smith, Nigel, ed., *The Poems of Andrew Marvell* (London, 2003).

Somers *see* Scott.

Spalding, Ruth, ed., *The Diary of Bulstrode Whitelocke* (Oxford, 1990).

The Speeches, Discourses and Prayers of Col. John Barkstead, Col. John Okey, and Mr. Miles Corbet, octavo edn. (1662).

Streater, John, *The Continuation of this Session of Parliament Justified* (1659).

—— *Government Described* (1659).

—— *Secret Reasons of State* (1659).

—— *A Shield against the Parthian Dart* (1659).

——— *see*, under 2 above: *Observations*; *Perfect and Impartial Intelligence*; *A Politick Commentary*.

Strena Vavasoriensis (1654).

Stubbe, Henry, *Malice Rebuked* (1659).

The Substance of what Sir Henry Vane Intended to have Spoken on the Scaffold on Tower Hill (1662).

Sykes, George, *The Life and Death of Sir Henry Vane, Kt.* (1662).

Thurloe *see* Birch.

Toland, John, ed., *The Oceana of James Harrington and his Other Works* (London, 1700).

Traytors Deciphered (1650).

Treason Arraigned, in Answer to Plain English (1659).

A True Catalogue, or, an Account of the Several Places ... where ... Richard Cromwell was Proclaimed (1659).

The Tryal of Sir Henry Vane, Kt. (1662).

Vane, Sir Henry, *A Healing Question Propounded* (1656).

——— (attrib.), *A Needful Corrective or Balance in Popular Government* (1659).

——— *The Retired Mans Meditations* (1655).

——— *Two Treatises* (1662).

——— *see Substance*.

Whitelocke, Bulstrode, *Journal of the Swedish Embassy*, 2 vols. (1855).

——— *Memorials of the English Affairs*, 4 vols. (1853).

——— *see* Spalding.

Wildman, John, *The Lawes Subversion* (1648).

Wither, George, *Westrow Revived* (1654).

Wolfe, D. M., *et al.*, eds, *Complete Prose Works of John Milton*, 8 vols. (New Haven and London, 1953–82).

Wood, Anthony, *Athenae Oxonienses*, 4 vols. (1813–20).

4. Secondary Sources

Achinstein, Sharon, *Literature and Dissent in Milton's England* (Cambridge, 2003).

Armitage, David, 'John Milton: Poet against Empire', in Armitage, *et al.*, eds., *Milton and Republicanism*, 206–25.

——— 'The Cromwellian Protectorate and the Languages of Empire', *Historical Journal*, 35 (1992), 531–55.

——— Himy, Armand, and Skinner, Quentin, eds., *Milton and Republicanism* (Cambridge, 1995).

Atherton, Ian, and Como, David, 'The Burning of Edward Wightman: Puritanism, Prelacy and the Politics of Heresy in Early Modern England', *English Historical Review*, 120 (2005), 1215–50.

Beller, Elmer A., 'Milton and *Mercurius Politicus*', *Huntington Library Quarterly*, 5 (1942), 479–87.

Bock, F. E., *Isaac Vossius and his Circle* (Groningen, 2000).

Campbell, Gordon, *A Milton Chronology* (Basingstoke, 1997).

Catterall, R. H. C., 'Sir George Downing and the Regicides', *American Historical Review*, 17 (1912), 268–89.

Collins, Jeffrey R. *The Allegiance of Thomas Hobbes* (Oxford, 2005).

—— 'The Church Settlement of Oliver Cromwell', *History*, 87 (2000), 18–40.

Corns, Thomas N., 'Milton and the Characteristics of a Free Commonwealth', in Armitage *et al.*, eds., *Milton and Republicanism*, 25–42.

—— 'Milton before *Lycidas*', in Parry and Raymond, eds., *Milton and the Terms of Liberty*, 23–36.

—— 'Milton's *Observations upon the Articles of Peace*: Ireland under English Eyes', in Loewenstein and Turner, eds., *Politics, Poets, and Hermeneutics*, 123–34.

—— *Uncloistered Virtue: English Political Literature 1640–1660* (Oxford, 1992).

Coward, Barry, *The Cromwellian Protectorate* (Manchester, 2002).

Creaser, John, 'Prosody and Liberty in Milton and Marvell', in Parry and Raymond, eds., *Milton and the Terms of Liberty*, 37–55.

Dawson, George, *Biographical Lectures* (1888).

De Luna, Barbara, *Jonson's Romish Plot: 'Catiline' and its Historical Context* (Oxford, 1967).

Dobranski, Stephen B., 'Licensing Milton's Heresy', in Dobranski and Rumrich, eds., *Milton and Heresy*, 139–58.

—— and Rumrich, John P., eds., *Milton and Heresy* (Cambridge, 1998).

—— *Milton, Authorship and the Book Trade* (Cambridge, 1999).

Duncan-Jones, E. E., 'The Erect Sword in Marvell's Horatian Ode', *Etudes Anglaises*, 15 (1962), 172–4.

Dzelzainis, Martin, 'Andrew Marvell and the Restoration Literary Underground: Printing the Painter Poems' (forthcoming).

—— 'History and Ideology: Milton, the Levellers, and the Council of State in 1649', in Kewes, ed., *Uses of History*, 269–87.

—— 'Juvenal, Charles X Gustavus and Milton's Letter to Richard Jones', *The Seventeenth Century*, 9 (1994), 25–35.

—— 'Milton and the Protectorate in 1658', in Armitage *et al.*, eds., *Milton and Republicanism*, 181–205.

—— 'Milton's *A Declaration, Or Letters Patents* (1674) and the Problems of the Succession', forthcoming.

—— 'Milton's Classical Republicanism', in Armitage, *et al.*, eds., *Milton and Republicanism*, 3–24.

—— 'Milton's *Of True Religion* and the Earl of Castlemaine', *The Seventeenth Century*, 7 (1992), 53–69.

—— 'Milton and Antitinitarianism', in Achinstein and Sauer, eds, *Milton and Toleration* (Oxford, 2007)

Everett, Barbara, 'The Shooting of the Bears', in R. L. Brett, ed., *Andrew Marvell: Essays on the Tercentenary of his Death* (Hull and Oxford, 1979), 62–103.

Fallon, Robert Thomas, *Milton in Government* (University Park, Pa., 1993).

____ '*A Second Defence*: Milton's Critique of Cromwell', *Milton Studies*, 39 (2000), 167–83.

Firth, C. H., and Davies, Godfrey, *A Regimental History of Cromwell's Army*, 2 vols. (Oxford, 1940).

Fixler, Michael, *Milton and the Kingdoms of God* (London, 1964).

Frank, Joseph, *The Beginnings of the English Newspaper 1620–1660* (Cambridge, Mass., 1961).

____ *Cromwell's Press Agent: A Critical Biography of Marchamont Nedham* (Lanham, Md., 1980).

French, J. Milton, 'Milton, Needham, and *Mercurius Politicus*', *Studies in Philology*, 33 (1936), 236–52.

Gardiner, S. R., *History of the Commonwealth and Protectorate*, 4 vols. (New York, 1965 edn.).

Gentles, Ian, Morrill, John, and Worden, Blair, eds., *Soldiers, Writers and Statesmen* (Cambridge, 1998).

Geyl, Pieter, *Orange and Stuart 1641–72* (London, 1939).

Godwin, William, *Lives of Edward and John Philips* (1815).

Greaves, Richard L., *Deliver us from Evil: The Radical Underground in Britain, 1660–1663* (New York, 1986).

Haan, Estelle, *Andrew Marvell's Latin Poetry: From Text to Context* (Brussels, 2003).

Hale, John K., 'Milton's Rationale of Insulting', in Dobranski and Rumrich, eds., *Milton and Heresy*, 159–75.

Hamilton, Gary D., 'The *History of Britain* and its Restoration Audience', in Loewenstein and Turner, eds., *Politics, Poetics, and Hermeneutics*, 241–55.

Hammond, Paul, 'The Date of Marvell's "The Mower against Gardens" ', *Notes and Queries*, 53 (2006), 178–81.

____ *The Making of Restoration Poetry* (Woodbridge, Suffolk, 2006).

Hayley (or Hailey), William, *The Life of John Milton* (1799).

Herendeen, Wyman H., 'Milton's *Accedence Commenc'd Grammar* and the Deconstruction of Grammatical Tyranny', in P. G. Stanwood, ed., *Of Poetry and Politics: New Essays on Milton and his World* (Binghampton, NY, 1995), 295–312.

Hill, Christopher, *The Experience of Defeat: Milton and Some Contemporaries* (London, 1984).

____ *Milton and the English Revolution* (London, 1977).

____ 'Society and Andrew Marvell', in Hill, *Puritanism and Revolution* (London, 1986 edn.), 324–50.

Hingley, Sheila, 'The Oxindens, Warlys and Elham Public Library' (University of Kent Ph.D. thesis, 2004).

Hirst, Derek, ' "That Sober Liberty": Marvell's Cromwell in 1654', in John M. Wallace, ed., *The Golden and the Brazen World: Papers in Literature and History, 1650–1800* (Berkeley and Los Angeles, 1985), 17–53.

____ and Zwicker, Steven N., 'High Summer at Nun Appleton, 1651: Andrew Marvell and the Lord Fairfax's Occasions', *Historical Journal*, 36 (1993), 247–69.

Holberton, Edward, 'The Textual Transmission of Marvell's "A Letter to Doctor Ingelo": The Longleat Manuscript', *English Manuscript Studies*, 12 (2005), 233–53.

Honeygorsky, Stephen, 'Licence Reconsidered: Ecclesial Nuances', *Milton Quarterly*, 25 (1991), 59–66

Jose, Nicholas, *Ideas of Restoration in English Literature 1660–1671* (Basingstoke, 1984).

Kajanto, Iiro, *Christina Heroina: Mythological and Historical Exemplification in the Latin Panegyrics on Christina Queen of Sweden* (Helsinki, 1993).

Kelley, Mary R., and Wittreich, Joseph, *Altering Eyes: New Perspectives on 'Samson Agonistes'* (Newark, Del., 2002).

Kewes, Paulina, ed., *The Uses of History in Early Modern England* (*Huntington Library Quarterly* special issue, 2005; republished as a book with the same title, San Marino, 2006).

Knoppers, Laura, *Constructing Cromwell: Ceremony, Portrait, and Print 1645–1661* (Cambridge, 2000).

—— *Historicizing Milton: Spectacle, Power, and Poetry in Restoration England* (Athens, Ga., 1994).

Krouse, E. M., *Milton's Samson and the Christian Tradition* (Princeton, 1949).

Legouis, Pierre, *André Marvell. Poète, Puritain, Patriote* (New York, 1965 edn.).

—— *Andrew Marvell. Poet, Puritan, Patriot* (Oxford, 1968 edn.).

Leonard, John, 'Revolt as Backsliding in Milton's Sonnet XII', *Notes and Queries*, 241 (1996), 269–73

Lewalski, Barbara, *The Life of John Milton: A Critical Biography* (Oxford, 2000).

—— '*Samson Agonistes* and the "Tragedy" of the Apocalypse', *Publications of the Modern Language Association*, 85 (1970), 1050–62.

Lieb, Michael, *Theological Milton* (Pittsburgh, Penn., 2006).

Little, Patrick, ed., *The Cromwellian Protectorate* (Woodbridge, Suffolk, 2007).

Loewenstein, David, *Milton and the Drama of History* (Cambridge, 1990).

—— 'Treason against God and State', in Dobranski and Rumrich, eds., *Milton and Heresy*, 176–98.

—— and Turner, James Grantham, eds., *Politics, Poetics, and Hermeneutics in Milton's Prose* (Cambridge, 1990).

Loxley, James, 'Marvell, Villiers, and Royalist Verse', *Notes and Queries*, 239 (1994), 170–2.

—— ' "Prepar'd at last to Stricke in with the Tyde"? Andrew Marvell and Royalist Verse', *The Seventeenth Century*, 10 (1995), 39–62.

—— *Royalism and Poetry in the English Civil Wars* (Basingstoke, 1997).

Macadam, Joyce, ' "Mercurius Britanicus": Journalism and Politics in the English Civil War' (Sussex University D. Phil. thesis, 2005).

Macaulay, Thomas Babington, *Literary and Historical Essays* (Oxford, 1913 edn.).

McCabe, Richard A., *Joseph Hall: A Study in Satire and Meditation* (Oxford, 1982).

McDowell, Nicholas, 'Family Politics; or, How John Phillips Read his Uncle's Satirical Sonnets', *Milton Quarterly*, forthcoming.

____'Urquhart's Rabelais: Translation, Patronage, and Cultural Politics', *English Literary Renaissance*, 35 (2005), 273–303.

McLachlan, H. J., *Socinianism in Seventeenth-Century England* (Oxford, 1951).

McNeill, W., 'Milton and Salmasius, 1649', *English Historical Review*, 80 (1965), 107–8.

McRae, Andrew, *Literature, Satire and the Early Stuart State* (Cambridge, 2004).

Maltzahn, Nicholas von, *An Andrew Marvell Chronology* (Basingstoke, 2005).

____'Blank Verse and the Nation: Milton and his Imitators', in Paul Stevens and David Loewenstein, eds., *Early Modern Nationalism and Milton's England* (Toronto, forthcoming).

____'Dating the Digression in Milton's *History of Britain*', *Historical Journal*, 36 (1993), 945–56.

____'The First Reception of *Paradise Lost* (1667)', *Review of English Studies*, 47 (1996), 479–99.

____'From Pillar to Post: Milton and the Attack on Republican Humanism at the Restoration', in Gentles *et al.*, eds., *Soldiers, Writers and Statesmen*, 265–85.

____'Laureate, Republican, Calvinist: An Early Response to Milton and *Paradise Lost*', *Milton Studies*, 29 (1992), 181–98.

____*Milton's 'History of Britain': Republican Historiography in the English Revolution* (Oxford, 1991).

____'The Royal Society and the Provenance of Milton's *History of Britain* (1670)', *Milton Quarterly*, 32 (1998), 90–5.

____'The Whig Milton 1667–1700', in Armitage, *et al.*, eds., *Milton and Republicanism*, 229–53.

Masson, David, *Life of John Milton*, 7 vols. (1859–94).

Matthews, Nancy L., *Cromwell's Law Reformer* (Cambridge, 1984).

Mazzeo, J. A., *Renaissance and Seventeenth-Century Studies* (New York, 1964).

Miller, Leo, *John Milton and the Oldenburg Safeguard* (New York, 1985).

____'Milton's *Defensio* Ordered Wholesale for the State of Holland', *Notes and Queries*, 231 (1986), 33.

Mohamed, Feisal G., 'Confronting Religious Violence: Milton's *Samson Agonistes*', *Publications of the Modern Language Association*, 120 (2005), 327–40.

Montgomery, James A., *A Critical and Exegetical Commentary on the Books of Kings* (Edinburgh, 1951).

Mortimer, Sarah, 'The Challenge of Socinianism in mid-Seventeenth Century England' (Oxford University D.Phil. thesis, 2007).

Mueller, Janel, 'The Figure and the Ground: Samson as a Hero of London Nonconformity, 1662–1667', in Parry and Raymond, eds., *Milton and the Terms of Liberty*, 137–62.

Norbrook, David, '"The blushinge tribute of a borrowed muse": Robert Overton and the Overturning of the Poetic Canon', *English Manuscript Studies*, 4 (1993), 220–66.

—— 'Republican Occasions in *Paradise Regained* and *Samson Agonistes*', *Milton Studies*, 42 (2002), 122–48.

—— *Writing the English Republic: Poetry, Rhetoric and Politics 1627–1660* (Cambridge, 1999).

Parker, William Riley, *Milton: A Biography*, 2 vols., continuous pagination, revised by Gordon Campbell (Oxford, 1996).

Parry, Graham, and Raymond, Joad, eds., *Milton and the Terms of Liberty* (Cambridge, 2002).

Peacey, Jason, '"The Counterfeit Silly Curr": Money, Politics and the Forging of Royalist Newspapers in the English Civil War', *Huntington Library Quarterly*, 67 (2004), 27–57.

—— 'The Management of Civil War Newspapers', *The Seventeenth Century*, 21 (2006), 99–127.

—— 'Marchamont Nedham and the Lawrans Letters', *Bodleian Library Record*, 17 (2000), 24–35.

—— *Politicians and Pamphleteers: Propaganda during the English Civil Wars and Interregnum* (London, 2004).

—— 'The Struggle for *Mercurius Britanicus*: Factional Politics and the Parliamentarian Press', *Huntington Library Quarterly*, 68 (2005), 517–43.

Pennington, Donald, and Thomas, Keith, eds., *Puritans and Revolutionaries* (Oxford, 1978).

Pincus, Steven A., *Protestantism and Patriotism: Ideologies and the Making of English Foreign Policy, 1650–1668* (Cambridge, 1996).

Pocock, J. G. A., *The Machiavellian Moment* (Princeton, 1975).

—— 'Thomas May and the Narrative of Civil War', in Derek Hirst and Richard Strier, eds., *Writing and Political Engagement in Seventeenth-Century England* (Cambridge, 1999), 112–44.

Polizotto, Carolyn, 'The Campaign against the Humble Proposals of 1652', *Journal of Ecclesiastical History*, 38 (1987), 569–81.

Prichard, Allan, 'Marvell's "The Garden"', *Studies in English Literature*, 23 (1980), 371–88.

Raylor, Timothy, *Cavaliers, Clubs, and Literary Culture: Sir John Mennes, James Smith, and the Order of the Fancy* (Newark, NJ, 1977).

—— 'Reading Machiavelli, Writing Cromwell: Edmund Waller's Copy of *The Prince* and his Draft Verses towards *A Panegyrick on my Lord Protector*', *Turnbull Library Review*, 35 (2002), 9–32.

—— 'Waller's Machiavellian Cromwell: The Imperial Argument of *A Panegyrick to my Lord Protector*', *Review of English Studies*, 56 (2005), 386–411.

Raymond, Joad, 'The Cracking of the Republican Spokes', *Prose Studies*, 19 (1996), 255–74.

—— *The Invention of the Newspaper: English Newsbooks 1641–1649* (Oxford, 1996).

—— *Making the News: An Anthology of the Newsbooks of Revolutionary England 1641–1660* (Moreton-in-Marsh, Oxfordshire, 1993).

Reece, H. M., 'The Military Presence in England, 1649 – 1660' (Oxford University D. Phil. thesis, 1981).

Reedy, Gerard, ' "An Horatian Ode" and "Tom May's Death" ', *Studies in English Literature*, 20 (1980), 137–51.

Revard, Stella, *The War in Heaven: Paradise Lost and the Tradition of Satan's Rebellion* (Ithaca, NY, 1990).

Rowe, Violet, *Sir Henry Vane the Younger* (London, 1970).

Rumrich, John P., 'Milton's Arianism: Why it Matters', in Dobranski and Rumrich, eds., *Milton and Heresy*, 75–92.

Sellin, Paul R., *Daniel Heinsius and Stuart England* (Leiden, 1968).

Sherwood, Roy, *The Court of Oliver Cromwell* (Stroud, 1989).

—— *Oliver Cromwell: King in all but Name* (Stroud, 1997).

Skinner, Quentin, 'Conquest and Consent: Thomas Hobbes and the Engagement Controversy', in G. E. Aylmer, ed., *The Interregnum: The Quest for Settlement, 1646–1660* (Basingstoke, 1972), 99–120.

—— 'John Milton and the Politics of Slavery', in Parry and Raymond, eds., *Milton and the Terms of Liberty*, 1–22.

Smith, David L., 'Oliver Cromwell, the First Protectorate Parliament and Religious Reform', *Parliamentary History*, 19 (2000), 38–48.

Smith, Nigel, *Literature and Revolution in England 1640–1660* (New Haven and London, 1994).

—— 'Popular Republicanism in the 1650s: John Streater's "Heroic Mechanics" ', in Armitage, *et al.*, eds., *Milton and Republicanism*, 137–55.

Spalding, Ruth, *Contemporaries of Bulstrode Whitelocke* (Oxford, 1990).

Stevens, Paul, 'Milton's "Renunciation" of Cromwell: The Problem of Raleigh's *Cabinet-Council*', *Modern Philology*, 98 (2001), 363–92.

Taft, Barbara, ' "They that pursew perfection on earth": The Political Progress of Robert Overton', in Gentles, *et al.*, eds., *Soldiers, Writers and Statesmen*, 286–303.

Thomas, Keith, 'The Puritans and Adultery', in Pennington and Thomas, eds., *Puritans and Revolutionaries*, 257–82.

Thomas, Peter W., *Sir John Berkenhead 1617–1679: A Royalist Career in Politics and Polemics* (Oxford, 1969).

Tibbutt, H. G., 'Colonel John Okey 1606–1682', *Bedfordshire Historical Record Society*, 35 (1955).

Trevor-Roper, Hugh, *Catholics, Anglicans and Puritans in Seventeenth-Century England* (London, 1987).

—— *Europe's Physician: The Various Life of Sir Theodore de Mayerne* (London and New Haven, 2006).

—— *Religion, The Reformation and Social Change* (Basingstoke, 1967).

Underdown, David, '"Honest" Radicals in the Counties', in Pennington and Thomas, eds., *Puritans and Revolutionaries*, 186–205.

——*Pride's Purge* (Oxford, 1971).

Vickers, Brian, 'Machiavelli and Marvell's *Horatian Ode*', *Notes and Queries*, 36 (1989), 32–8.

Von Maltzahn *see* Maltzahn.

Wallace, John M., *Destiny his Choice: The Loyalism of Andrew Marvell* (Cambridge, 1968).

Wilcher, Robert, *The Writing of Royalism 1628–1660* (Cambridge, 2001).

Williams, C. M., 'The Political Career of Henry Marten' (Oxford University D. Phil. thesis, 1954).

Winn, James, *John Dryden and His World* (New Haven and London, 1987).

Woolrych, Austin, *Commonwealth to Protectorate* (Oxford, 1982).

——'The Date of the Digression in Milton's *History of Britain*', in Richard Ollard and Pamela Tudor-Craig, eds., *For Veronica Wedgwood These: Studies in Seventeenth-Century History* (London, 1986), 217–46.

——'Dating Milton's *History of Britain*', *Historical Journal*, 36 (1993), 929–43.

——'The Good Old Cause and the Fall of the Protectorate', *Cambridge Historical Journal*, 13 (1957), 133–61.

Wootton, David, ed., *Republicanism, Liberty, and Commercial Society 1649–1776* (Stanford, Calif., 1994).

Worden, Blair, 'Ben Jonson among the Historians', in Kevin Sharpe and Peter Lake, eds., *Culture and Politics in Early Stuart England* (Basingstoke, 1994), 67–89.

——'Cromwellian Oxford', in Nicholas Tyacke, ed., *The History of the University of Oxford*, iv: *Seventeenth-Century Oxford* (Oxford, 1997), 733–72.

——'Friend to Sir Philip Sidney', *London Review of Books*, 3 July 1986.

——'Harrington's "Oceana": Origins and Aftermath', in Wootton, ed., *Republicanism, Liberty, and Commercial Society*, 110–38.

——'Historians and Poets', in Kewes, ed., *Uses of History*, 71–93.

——'John Milton and Oliver Cromwell', in Gentles, *et al.*, eds., *Soldiers, Writers and Statesmen*, 243–64.

——'Marchamont Nedham and the Beginnings of English Republicanism', in Wootton, ed., *Republicanism, Liberty, and Commercial Society*, 45–81.

——'Milton, *Samson Agonistes*, and the Restoration', in Gerald MacLean, ed., *Culture and Society in the Stuart Restoration* (Cambridge, 1995), 111–36.

——'Milton's Republicanism and the Tyranny of Heaven', in Gisela Bock, Quentin Skinner, and Maurizio Viroli, eds., *Machiavelli and Republicanism* (Cambridge, 1991), 225–45.

——'Oliver Cromwell and the Council', in Little, ed., *Cromwellian Protectorate*, 82–104.

——'Oliver Cromwell and the Sin of Achan', in Derek Beales and Geoffrey Best, eds., *History, Society and the Churches* (Cambridge, 1985), 125–45.

——'The Politics of Marvell's Horatian Ode', *Historical Journal*, 27 (1984), 525–47.

——'Providence and Politics in Cromwellian England', *Past and Present*, 109 (1985), 55–99.

——'Republicanism and the Restoration', in Wootton, ed., *Republicanism, Liberty, and Commercial Society*, 139–93.

——'Republicanism, Regicide and Republic: The English Experience', in Martin van Gelderen and Quentin Skinner, eds., *Republicanism: A Shared European Heritage*, 2 vols. (Cambridge, 2002), i. 307–27.

——*Roundhead Reputations: The English Civil Wars and the Passions of Posterity* (London, 2001).

——*The Rump Parliament 1648–1653* (Cambridge, 1977 edn.).

——*The Sound of Virtue: Philip Sidney's 'Arcadia' and Elizabethan Politicus* (London and New Haven, 1996).

——'Toleration and the Cromwellian Protectorate', *Studies in Church History*, 21 (1984), 199–233.

——'Whig History and Puritan Politics: The *Memoirs of Edmund Ludlow* Revisited', *Historical Research*, 75 (2002), 209–37.

——'"Wit in a Roundhead": The Dilemma of Marchamont Nedham', in Susan D. Amussen and Mark A. Kishlansky, eds., *Political Culture and Cultural Politics in Early Modern England* (Manchester, 1995), 301–37.

Index

Abbreviations
OC = Cromwell, Oliver AM = Marvell JM = Milton MN = Nedham